Teaching Young Children Using Themes

Marjorie J. Kostelnik, Editor

Donna Howe

Kit Payne

Barbara Rohde

Grace Spalding

Laura Stein

Duane Whitbeck

Michigan State University

Illustrated by
Barbara Rohde

GoodYearBooks
An Imprint of ScottForesman
A Division of HarperCollinsPublishers

Cover art by Anna Doherty, Kirk Reimer, Kyle Reimer, Jason Siok, Jeffery Siok, and Jenna Siok.
Cover photograph by Tom Lindfors©.

Good Year Books
are available for preschool through grade 6 for every basic curriculum subject plus many enrichment areas. For more Good Year Books, contact your local bookseller or educational dealer. For a complete catalog with information about other Good Year Books, please write:

Good Year Books
Scott, Foresman and Company
1900 East Lake Avenue
Glenview, IL 60025

Library of Congress Cataloging-in-Publication Data
Teaching young children using themes / Marjorie J. Kostelnik, editor ;
  Donna Howe . . . [et al.] ; illustrated by Barbara Rohde.
        p.   cm.
  Includes bibliographical references and index.
  ISBN 0–673–46057–6
  1. Education, Preschool—Activity programs.   2. Education,
Preschool—Curricula.   3. Creative activities and seat work.
  4. Preschool teaching.   I. Kostelnik, Marjorie J.   II. Howe,
Donna.
  LB1140.35.C74T43   1991
  372.13—dc20   91–6499
                                                            CIP

ISBN 0-673-46057-6

   3 4 5 6 7 8 9 - MAL - 99 98 97 96 95 94 93 92 91

Preface

- What is theme teaching?
- What kinds of themes are most appropriate for preschoolers?
- How can theme teaching be used with kindergarten and first-grade students?
- Is there more than one way to carry out a given theme?
- How long should each theme last?

Teaching Young Children Using Themes was written to answer teacher questions such as these. Created as a practical resource, this book offers a broad array of background information and activity ideas practitioners can use to create their own thematic units. Our purpose was not to prescribe one particular set of activities to represent each theme, but rather to give teachers the means to pick and choose the approach and specific activities best suited to the needs and interests of the children in their own classes.

Additionally, we hoped to provide teachers with a tool for creating wholistic, integrated early education programs for young children. By wholistic, we mean a composite of activities to address all facets of child development—aesthetic, cognitive, social, emotional, language, and physical. By integrated, we mean an approach in which content overlaps and is interwoven across learning activity centers (such as a story corner, housekeeping area, manipulative table, and so forth) or throughout subject matter (math, science, social studies, etc.). Both of these attributes, wholism and integration, combine to enhance children's learning and to make their early school experiences more meaningful.

Audience

Teachers in training, as well as those already employed in the field, will find a wealth of valuable information in *Teaching Young Children Using Themes*. The more than one thousand theme-related activities in this volume have been implemented successfully by nursery school, day-care, Head Start, Chapter I, Pre-primary Special Education, kindergarten, and first-grade teachers. The ideal reader is one seeking guidance and ready ideas for theme-teaching, who, at the same time, desires to put his or her personal stamp on the final unit created.

Each lesson was developed with four- and five-year-old children in mind. However, we have provided suggestions within each unit for ways teachers might simplify or extend the activities to broaden the age span covered.

Background

This book was written for teachers by teachers. The authors and editor have had many years of experience in a broad array of early childhood settings. Currently, all of us are still actively engaged in the education of young children. We carry out the theme teaching methods described here in the Child Development Laboratories, administered by the Department of Family and Child Ecology at Michigan State University. Consequently, the ideas for particular themes and activities originated with the children and families in our own classrooms. These youngsters are diverse in age, socioeconomic, ethnic, and developmental characteristics, as well as in the languages they speak.

Not only did we have the advantage of seeing how children reacted to prototype activities, but we had the additional benefit of observing first-hand how well students-in-training and parent volunteers could follow our written directions. These pilot efforts led to many revisions, adaptations, and eliminations. New activities as well as novel thematic approaches also came about as a result of child, student, and parent input.

Yet, to be truly perfected, we believed the units must prove successful in settings outside our own. Thus, over a three-year-period, each and every activity was field tested by early childhood practitioners eager to offer insight into their educational value, practicality, and the extent to which children and teachers enjoyed trying them. Teachers used and critiqued all of the units in large classes and small, in urban, rural, and suburban settings, in full-day and half-day programs, and with children ranging in age from two to eight years. The classroom structures and routines represented within this group were also quite varied. In accordance with all the suggestions we received, *Teaching Young Children Using Themes* took its final form.

Content

Out of the many thematic units we originally envisioned, we settled on twenty-four. Several criteria were used in the selection of these. Most important was relevance to children. Thus many of the themes center on the everyday phenomena that dominate children's lives: families, homes, clothing, vehicles, birds, and stores. Others deal with issues critical to children's development in the early years, such as friendship and self-awareness. The remainder are themes about which children often expressed curiosity, such as the sky ("Where does the rainbow come from?") or dinosaurs ("What happened to all the dinosaurs?").

Secondly, we made sure to include some of the traditional themes teachers use year after year (dental health, pets, plants) as well as some less common ones (measuring, writers, music makers).

A third criterion was how well the content of the unit lent itself to the creation of related hands-on activities. We included only those with content children could experience through the direct manipulation of objects. Once this standard was satisfied, we also considered the degree to which potential activities represented varying instructional modes. For example, topics that prompted many craft ideas, but which were not well suited to pretend play, games, or problem-solving activities, were rejected as too limited. Instead, we chose themes conducive to many different activity types.

General availability of props and other support materials was a final consideration. Teachers indicated that materials available in one part of the country were not always obtainable elsewhere. Hence, none of the themes rely on teacher access to scarce resource items.

Viewed as a whole, we found the twenty-four themes could be divided among four content areas: social studies, science, language arts, and mathematics. Since many teachers are already familiar with such designations, we organized the units under these headings for ease of reader reference.

Part I, "Social Studies Concepts," includes units in which children have opportunities to learn more about themselves and the people-oriented world around them. In Part II, "Science Concepts," you will find themes whose main emphasis is on enabling children to explore biological or physical objects and events. The child as an active communicator provides the focus for Part III, "Language Arts Concepts." Part IV, "Mathematical Concepts," offers themes within which children investigate the properties and relations of quantity and magnitude within familiar contexts such as home and community.

Sections I and II contain the greatest number of themes. It has been our experience that such topics are of particular relevance to young children, and our reviewers, representing preschool through the primary grades, concurred. Consequently, it is the concepts associated with social studies and science that we have chosen to highlight. However, in keeping with the growing emphasis on integrating language arts and mathematical content and processes throughout the school curriculum, we created the units in Parts III and IV to illustrate how this might be accomplished. In every case, although social studies, science, language arts, or mathematics concepts are accentuated in relation to a given unit, all curriculum areas are addressed within each theme.

Acknowledgements

We would like to thank the following persons for their contributions to our work:

Mariella Aikman, Carol Baynes, and Janet Ronk provided valuable insights and background material to our initial efforts to commit our ideas to paper.

Sue Grossman, Helen Hagens, Kristi Hannon, Kim Michaud, Kit Payne, Deb Sharpe, Jean Sukis-Allison, and Fran Wilson provided able research assistance and sparked many activity ideas.

Anne Soderman and Alice Whiren expanded our understanding of the integrated curriculum, offering helpful suggestions regarding domain-related content and processes.

Judith Anderson, Bob Berghage, John Biernbaum, Sheila Fitzgerald, David Kostelnik, Vicki Schram, Daniel Sadler, Robert Stein, and Alice Whiren reviewed specific TFPs for accuracy, relevance, and completeness.

Verna Hildebrand gave numerous suggestions during the early phases of writing.

Cathleen Gardner and Marilyn Waters provided invaluable assistance throughout the life of the project.

Children and teachers in the following centers and schools piloted these materials in their various stages. To them we offer particular appreciation.

Battle Creek Public Schools

Carman-Ainsworth Public Schools

Capital Area Community Services Head Start

Haslett Public Schools

Hong Kong International School

Laboratory Preschool

Lennawee Intermediate School District

Perry Child Development Center

Robert Byrd Elementary School

Shiawassee County Pre-primary Special Education Program

Spartan Nursery School

Sullivans School

Traverse City Head Start Program

Traverse City Public Schools

Waverly Early Childhood Program

Finally, over the years we have worked with many students whose enthusiasm and excitement have invigorated us. Simultaneously, we have been privileged to know hundreds of children throughout their formative years, and their families. From them we have gained the insight and motivation to pursue this project. We dedicate this book to them.

TABLE OF CONTENTS

Introduction

•

As the children create their own leaf rubbings, they note differences in the size, shape, and edges of the leaves.

The children and their teacher prepare, then eat, a salad using vegetables that represent the roots, buds, leaves, fruits, and stems of different plants.

The children mark off a square-foot area outside and count all the dandelions within it. Several youngsters come up with one grand total; a few announce two numbers—one for the buds, a second for the "full" blooms.

In a make-believe florist shop, some children create varied arrangements of plastic flowers in vases and bowls; others pretend to be customers buying their wares.

The teacher reads a storybook about plants, then guides the children in recalling the sequence of events leading to its conclusion. Later, children are given props to act out the events as they remember them.

A lively discussion ensues when the teacher asks the children whether or not a cactus that he has brought to class is a plant and then asks the reasons for their ideas.

•

These activities are typical of any early childhood classroom from preschool through the lower elementary grades. All of them involve hands-on experiences for children and provide youngsters with information or insights about plants. They also give children opportunities to develop further such skills as fine motor control, observing, comparing, inferring, remembering, counting, role-playing, and expressing ideas.

In one classroom these activities might be scattered throughout the year; in another, they might be presented within the framework of a multiweek theme, unit, or project focusing on plants. With either approach, children would benefit from the activities and would probably increase their knowledge of plant life. However, youngsters whose teachers choose to carry out several plant-related activities simultaneously over a short time span have the added advantage of being able to make links among those activities that are harder for children to forge when the lessons are more dispersed. It is the creation of such links that constitutes the essence of thematic teaching.

CHARACTERISTICS OF THEME TEACHING

Using themes to organize instruction for young children has been popular since Dewey first proposed that curriculum be related to real-life experiences. In developing a theme, teachers select topics they believe to be relevant and of interest to children, then build an array of lessons around that central idea. Such activities usually cut across the curriculum and take place either simultaneously or within a relatively condensed period of time. Relating activities through a common theme facilitates children's generalization of knowledge and skills from one experience to another (Eliason and Jenkins, 1986; Machado and Meyer, 1984; Kostelnik, Palmer, and Hannon, 1987).

Early childhood educators who use theme planning well incorporate into their teaching the principles of developmentally appropriate practice as defined by the National Association for the Education of Young Children. Such principles of practice form the foundation

upon which themes can be developed and implemented (Bredekamp, 1988). Among these principles are:

- Providing hands-on experience with real objects for children to examine and manipulate
- Creating activities in which children use all of their senses
- Building activities around children's current interests
- Helping children develop new knowledge and skills based on what they already know and can do
- Providing activities and routines that address all aspects of development—cognitive, social, emotional, and physical
- Accommodating children's needs for movement and physical activity, social interaction, independence, and positive self-esteem
- Providing opportunities to use play to translate experience into understanding
- Respecting the individual differences, cultural backgrounds, and home experiences that children bring with them to the classroom
- Finding ways to involve members of the children's families

Added to these optimal instructional strategies, theme teaching helps children develop an overall sense of direction and consolidation in their learning (Hendrick, 1986). Through theme-based programs, children build relationships among fragments of information to form increasingly abstract and complex concepts (Osborn and Osborn, 1983; Bredekamp, in press).

USING THEMES TO PROMOTE CHILDREN'S CONCEPT DEVELOPMENT

Concepts are the fundamental ideas that children form about objects and events in the world. They are the cognitive categories that allow people to group together perceptually distinct information, events, or items (Wellman, 1988). As such, concepts serve as the building blocks of knowing, thinking, and reasoning.

Children form concepts deductively through firsthand experiences (Lawton, 1987). When they act upon objects or interact with others, children extract relevant bits of meaning from each encounter. The mind stores these smatterings of data, to combine with previously acquired knowledge and perceptions, to clarify or modify current understandings, and to use later in assimilating new ideas (Hunt, 1961). By mentally cataloging a growing number of experiences and making finer distinctions as well as more abstract connections among them, children build, adjust, and expand their concepts over time (Kostelnik et al., 1988).

Because young children are continually searching for meaningful relationships in their environment, the early childhood years are ones of rapid concept development (Eliason and Jenkins, 1986). There is increasing support for aiding children in making such connections through an integrated school curriculum that provides conceptual organizers, such as themes, units, or projects (Bredekamp, in press; Katz and Chard, 1989).

Because children integrate learning from many different curriculum areas simultaneously, thematic studies promote the acquisition and development of concepts rather than of quantities of unrelated facts (Cummings, 1989). As they participate in reading, math, science, and social studies activities permeated by a common idea, children break the boundaries of traditional subject matter to form holistic, comprehensive constructs (Hendrick, 1986). Themes also enable teachers to structure the presentation of concepts more coherently, making it simpler for children to take in new information and combine it with what they already know (Eliason and Jenkins, 1986). As youngsters become involved in the topic and demonstrate to what extent they understand it, teachers can more readily identify what children already know, what their erroneous ideas are, and what further information would benefit them. Such assessments are accomplished most easily when the adult has one concept on which to focus. Attempting to address children's concept development at random or on a child-by-child basis without the benefit of a unifying framework within which to make judgments is difficult.

USING THEMES TO INTEGRATE CONTENT AND PROCESS LEARNING

Not only does theme teaching enhance children's concept development, it also provides a means for integrating content learning and process learning in ways that are meaningful to them. Content learning uses such mental abilities as attending, listening, observing, remembering, and recalling (Hendrick, 1986). It consists of the social-conventional knowledge around which the theme is designed. Thus, a group of kindergartners studying honeybees might engage in a variety of experiences to find out that:

- A honeybee is a kind of insect with a shiny, brown, hairy body.
- The three parts of the bee's body are the head, the thorax, and the abdomen.
- The head of a bee has a mouth, antennae, and several eyes.
- Honeybees live together in groups called colonies.
- Honeybees build complex nests called hives in which the colony lives.
- Honeybees gather pollen and nectar from flowers.
- Honeybees suck up the nectar by inserting their long tongues into the flower.
- Honeybees pack pollen into small pockets on their hind legs for carrying.
- Honeybees combine the pollen and nectar to make honey or beeswax.
- There are three types of honeybees: queen and worker bees that are female and drones that are male.
- There is only one queen bee per hive; there are hundreds of worker and drone bees per hive.

Simple exposure to such content does not teach in and of itself. It is only when children become involved in and talk about and reflect on their experiences that they learn from them (Elkind, 1988). Children might gain access to data about honeybees through hands-on activities, such as tasting honey, examining a real beehive, or watching bees gather nectar and pollen outdoors. In addition, teachers might provide children with wings and antennae to use in acting like bees in a colony, or work with them to construct a replica of a beehive, or invite children to suck syrup through a short straw to simulate the tongue of the bee in the flower. Examining a model of a bee as well as exchanging ideas about why bees live in colonies are other ways children could explore honeybee content.

Process learning, on the other hand, comprises the cognitive, social, emotional, and physical elements that form the basis for all experience within the early childhood classroom. Because it encompasses the "whole child," the processes involved range from mental abilities such as grouping, differentiating, inferring, and concluding, to such physical skills as developing strength or endurance, to the social skills of learning how to delay gratification or how to initiate an interaction. Children's participation in activities enhance these learnings, too. Indeed, the same activities cited earlier could provide the means for increased competence and understanding in any of these realms. However, at this level the content included in each activity is simply the medium through which to teach other more process-oriented skills (Hendrick, 1988). Children engaged in acting out the roles of bees in a hive not only gain factual insight into "bee life," but can also practice offering ideas ("You be the drone—I'll be the queen"), reaching compromises ("OK—I'm queen first, then you"), creating symbols (the children make a "hive" by draping a sheet over a card table), drawing conclusions ("If we have two queens, we'll need two hives"), and so forth. In all of these examples, the subject matter provides a background against which to address other long-range learning goals.

ADDITIONAL BENEFITS TO CHILDREN

Besides integrating concepts and unifying content and process, theme teaching provides other benefits for children. For instance, children have opportunities to encounter a central pool of information by many different routes. Regardless of whether they prefer very structured or less structured activities, large groups or small, or active or passive modes of interac-

tion, children can gain access to the topic in ways that best suit their individual styles of learning. If one activity is unappealing, does not match their learning style, or is not developmentally appropriate for them, they can learn about the theme in other ways. This would not be the case were the information presented only once or in only one mode.

A thematic curriculum also allows children to immerse themselves in a particular area of study. As youngsters become interested in a topic, they often want to know "all" about it. Exploring the concept represented within the theme satisfies this desire and therefore promotes children's tendency to become involved and mentally absorbed in pursuing an idea (Katz and Chard, 1989). However, while a typical unit is made up of many theme-related activities, not every experience offered to children in school has to focus on the theme. Thus children who are less interested in the topic can either concentrate on the processes within each activity independent of thematic content or can become involved in other non-theme-related activities.

Additionally, the collective involvement of studying a particular topic promotes group cohesiveness. Children who have experiences and knowledge in common develop a foundation of mutual interests that leads to positive peer relations. As children discover classmates whose interests match their own, their social circles widen. Patterns of interaction vary over time and provide a natural context for cooperative learning among peers. Perceptions broaden, too, as children assume novice or expert roles with each topic.

Finally, thematic teaching can accommodate children's changing interests throughout the year by highlighting the topics that are important to them at a given moment. Furthermore, themes developed in response to a particular child or group of children may spark the curiosity of other youngsters in the class.

ADVANTAGES FOR TEACHERS

Children are not the only ones to benefit from the thematic approach to instruction. The advantages to teachers are also numerous.

Theme planning prompts practitioners to establish a focus around which to develop their teaching unit. Such an emphasis helps them organize their thinking and planning. This in turn enables teachers to choose activities to support their aims. Thus teachers become more purposeful in their instruction by developing learning experiences based on how well they uphold the educational goals of the unit rather than simply on how convenient or clever they seem. As a result, theme teaching is not only purposeful but substantive as well.

Teachers who use theme planning appropriately research particular topics to generate a pool of data on which to base their plans. This increases the accuracy of the information they provide children, allows them to consider in advance how to handle sensitive issues inherent in the topic, and stimulates them to think of original activity ideas.

Theme planning also enables teachers to present a topic with sufficient breadth and depth to give all children a chance to learn something about it. Breadth and depth are achieved by using many theme-related activities and by creating links among some of them. In this way, teachers can devise sequences of plans that increase children's understanding of the concept represented by the theme.

Theme teaching keeps the early childhood curriculum varied and interesting. Both teachers and children experience a sense of freshness with each new unit. As subjects for study change, so do props, activities, and classroom decorations, thereby enlivening the teaching environment. Not only do new units spawn new activities, but they also afford the same or similar activities a novel emphasis as they relate to each different theme.

A theme approach often stimulates practitioners to seek out resources in advance. They can also take advantage of unexpected finds to augment favorite or upcoming themes.

Theme planning can be implemented within a variety of classroom structures and across age groups by teachers and children whose interests and needs vary. Moreover, once teachers learn the basic guidelines for planning and implementing thematic programs, they can move from relying on themes that others have developed to creating their own. Thus, theme planning is universally adaptable.

Finally, parents informed of upcoming themes can contribute their knowledge, expertise, and resources to their children's educational experience. They can often envision more easily how they might participate in their child's schooling in relation to a specified topic than to the more generalized instruction that takes place each day. Consequently, the teacher's plans may be supplemented in ways that go beyond the traditional donations of egg cartons and toilet paper rolls. Such parental involvement promotes constructive home-school relationships and helps parents feel more a part of their children's education.

CRITICISMS AIMED AT THEME TEACHING

In light of all these advantages, one might assume that theme teaching is wholly beneficial and that its implementation is sure to yield positive results. Unfortunately, the notion of teaching using themes has sometimes been misapplied and has drawn criticism (Goetz, 1985; Hendrick, 1986). Some teachers violate the tenets of developmentally appropriate practice by equating a theme with a chapter in a textbook, complete with a test at the end. Some assume that theme teaching involves little more than coordinating one's ditto sheets with a common idea.

Misguided attempts at dealing with content are a second source of inappropriate theme use. Some teachers become extremely fact oriented, rigidly adhering to a topic and thereby ignoring spontaneity and children's interests beyond the theme. They so value content over process that the integrated, child-centered nature of appropriate theme teaching is negated. Still other practitioners of the opposite extreme offer superficial attention to content. They may do this in one of two ways: either by creating a theme with no real data to support it, or by assuming that a few decorations and craft projects constitute theme teaching. Teachers in both cases pay minimal attention to conveying accurate, meaningful information to children. As a result, youngsters may miss valuable content that would be relevant to them, or worse, obtain inaccurate facts from teachers whose general store of knowledge is inadequate to support the topic.

Another problem occurs when teachers select themes that fail to promote children's concept development. When topics are too narrow or when the links between the topic and the activities are contrived, the theme lacks the depth and substance necessary to stimulate children's thinking. This is exemplified, for instance, by weekly plans centered around the letter R. As children paint with red at the easel, string rigatoni, and circle the R sounds on a worksheet, the teacher may confidently believe that youngsters are learning about R. In reality, the children may be focusing on the subject of their paintings, assume they're stringing pasta or noodles, and misunderstand the R sound pictures. Since R is not a concept and does not directly relate to children's real-life experiences, this is a poor attempt at theme teaching.

Finally, some teachers assume that they are using a thematic approach correctly when they relate several activities to a central prop, such as an umbrella (Cummings, 1989). Children may sing about umbrellas, hear a story about umbrellas, twirl like spinning umbrellas, and decorate paper parasols. Yet, they can extract little relevant social-conventional knowledge from these experiences, and the actual learning processes involved are perfunctory. Although the activities may keep children busy or entertained, they fail to engage their minds in the challenge of real learning. Since this type of theme planning addresses neither content nor process learning, its educational value is limited.

PRINCIPLES THAT ENSURE EFFECTIVE THEME TEACHING

True theme teaching is much more complex and comprehensive than any of these less developed approaches (Cummings, 1989). It is most effective when teachers incorporate the following principles into the planning and implementation of their themes (Goetz, 1985; Dearden, 1984; Katz and Chard, 1989).

1. Themes should relate directly to children's real-life experiences and should build on what they know.
2. Each theme should represent a concept for children to discover more about. An emphasis on helping children build theme-related concepts rather than on expecting them to memorize isolated bits of information is essential.
3. Every theme should be supported by a body of content that has been adequately researched.
4. All themes should integrate content learning with process learning.
5. Theme-related information should be conveyed to children through hands-on activities and discussion.
6. Theme-related activities should represent a variety of curricular foci and modes of involving children.
7. The same content should be offered more than once and incorporated into different kinds of activities.
8. The theme should allow for integration of several subject areas in the program.
9. Each theme should be expandable or revisable according to children's demonstrated interests and understandings.

We wrote *Teaching Young Children Using Themes* with these principles in mind. Our aim was to eliminate the shortcomings so often associated with theme teaching while preserving and enhancing its benefits.

STRUCTURAL FOUNDATIONS

Each of the twenty-four themes that follows represents a concept around which a unit is planned. Potential content learning associated with that concept is embodied in a collection of related terms, facts, and principles (hereafter referred to as TFPs). The TFPs contribute to children's social-conventional knowledge regarding the theme and give it substance. *Terms* are the vocabulary children should know to describe objects and events linked to the theme. Something known to exist or to have happened is a *fact*. *Principles* involve combinations of facts and the relationships among them.

All of the themes include process learning addressed through eight curricular domains: aesthetic learning; affective learning; cognitive learning; language learning; physical learning;

social learning; construction play; and pretend play. The first six domains encompass learning processes related to major facets of child development; the latter two are the means by which these facets are integrated. Together, the entire array incorporates learning processes essential to the "whole child." These processes are summarized in Table 1. Appendix A offers a more detailed listing of the goals addressed within each of the eight domains.

These learning processes encompass knowledge, concepts, and skills related to the development of:

Aesthetics	• self-expression through the visual and performing arts • aesthetic appreciation
Affective skills	• self-awareness • decision making • independence • instrumental know-how • appreciation of own cultural identity and heritage • self-confidence • positive self-esteem
Cognition	• critical and creative thinking • organizing, analyzing, generating, integrating, and evaluating skills • scientific understanding • mathematical understanding
Language	• effective communication through listening, speaking, writing, and reading
Physical skills	• competence in use of large and small muscles • physical fitness • care and respect for the body • appreciation and enjoyment of human movement
Social skills	• internal behavior controls • successful patterns of interaction • cooperative attitudes and actions • helpful attitudes and actions • responsible attitudes and actions • appreciation and respect for individual and cultural similarities and differences • respect for the environment
Construction skills	• concrete representation through modeling, drawing, and building
Pretend Play skills	• active representation through imitating, role-playing, and dramatizing

Table 1 *Learning Processes Essential to "Whole Child" Teaching*

RATIONALE FOR DEVELOPMENTAL DOMAINS

Practitioners more accustomed to the traditional subject matter designations of art, math, science, reading, social studies, and the like may question these development-oriented categories. They may wonder whether the processes included will fit their needs and to what degree they will be able to make use of the materials in this book. While it is true that standard curriculum divisions are comfortable because they are familiar, they are not comprehensive enough to suit our purposes. Our aim is to provide children with process-learning experiences related to all aspects of their being. The ultimate goal is to foster children's competence to deal with life, both now and in the future.

We view subject matter as derivative of development—thus art and music are part of aesthetics, and the affective domain stresses process learning related to self-awareness, the development of independence, and positive feelings of self-esteem. Science and math are components of cognition but do not constitute all of it. This domain has been broadened to include problem solving, critical thinking, and perception processes. Reading processes are found within the language domain as are those related to listening, speaking, and writing. The physical domain addresses gross and fine motor processes, health, and body image. The social domain incorporates social studies processes along with concepts fundamental to children's social skills and socialization.

The curricular domains of construction and pretend play are afforded categories of their own because of the critical role they perform in children's learning and development. When children create models or pictures that represent their internal vision of an object or event, they are involved in construction play. Hence construction constitutes the concrete way that children symbolize the world. Subsequently, it is a highly cognitive process. Yet for youngsters to build the models or pictures that originate in their minds out of real materials, they must draw on other abilities as well: creativity; imagination; aesthetic appreciation; fine

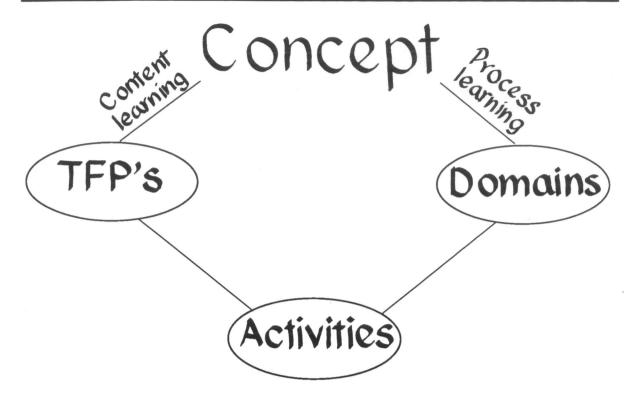

FIGURE 1 *The Relationship Between Concepts as Represented by a Theme and Related Activities*

motor, gross motor, and perceptual skills; planning strategies; language; and social interaction techniques. Thus, as children construct something out of paper and paste, clay, or blocks, they coordinate all aspects of the self. It is this synthesizing that makes construction important to young children.

As children engage in pretend play they have chances to talk, listen, interact socially, express emotions, explore attitudes, manipulate objects, practice creative thinking, experiment with problem solving, use their imaginations, and assimilate a variety of role behaviors. Moreover, pretending is one of the purest forms of symbolic thought available to young children. It permits them to symbolize objects and events using words, actions, situations, and materials. In pretend play, children draw on all aspects of the self to create their own interpretations of the world.

The content (expressed within the TFPs) and the processes (represented by the eight curricular domains) come together within the hands-on activities suggested for each unit. These activities form the basis for instruction and offer children the applied means to build, expand, and adjust their understanding of the concept represented by the theme. This relationship between concepts, content, processes, and activities is pictured in Figure 1.

FORMAT

The format of all the units is the same and consists of the following components:

1. *Chapter Title.* The title of the chapter identifies the concept around which the unit is planned.
2. *Rationale.* The purpose of the rationale is to give readers the background information they will need to carry out the theme more effectively. It serves as an introduction to the unit and begins with an explanation of the significance of the theme to young children. Next comes a shorter discussion of how and why certain approaches within the unit were taken. Suggestions for how the unit could be adapted to suit the needs of varying groups of children are also provided.
3. *Terms, Facts, and Principles.* The central core of every theme is the list of terms,

facts, and principles that accompany it. Thirty-five to more than a hundred TFPs are listed for each unit. Teachers will select only a few to focus on directly, using the others as background information or as a resource in responding to children's interest or queries regarding the topic.

Individual TFPs are categorized as simple or advanced. Simple TFPs are fundamental to children's understanding of the theme and form the foundation upon which the advanced TFPs build. They consist of beginning definitions or facts that can be directly observed or experienced. Principles, because they involve deduction, are more abstract, and so are seldom identified at this level. Advanced TFPs consist of more elaborate vocabulary, more complicated facts, and introductory principles. Often, they represent information that youngsters learn about indirectly through simulated experiences. Because of the complexity of advanced TFPs, children generally need more opportunities and time to grasp them than they do to understand simple TFPs. In assigning information to these two levels we moved from the tangible to the abstract, from the known to the unknown, from exploration to acquisition of skills and knowledge.

These designations enable the teacher to identify which category of TFPs to emphasize when working with a particular group of children. Simple TFPs are designed for use with preschoolers and older children who have had little experience with the theme. Advanced TFPs are more suitable for preschool children who know the theme well, or for children of elementary-school age. Advanced TFPs are designated with an asterisk in the list at the front of each unit. This stratification makes it possible for teachers to choose the subset of TFPs that best corresponds to the needs of the children in their class. Depending on the topic, the subset may be composed of TFPs representing one or both levels of difficulty.

4. *Activity Ideas.* A collection of forty to sixty activity ideas has been developed for each theme. These provide the applied means for implementing the TFPs and process learning goals and presenting them

to children. Activities have been developed for all of the curricular domains described earlier. Although we do not intend one facet of development to be isolated from another, we have found that purposeful planning for particular domains results in a more comprehensive approach to teaching for practitioners and a more cohesive learning experience for children.

Most activity ideas are described in a few sentences. However, some require more elaborate directions using the format depicted in Figure 2. Within each domain, these longer versions follow the shorter ones and are identified in the index by an asterisk.

Unit:
The name of the theme to which the activity pertains.

Domain:
The process-learning component of the curriculum into which the activity has been categorized.

Activity Name:
The title of the activity.

General Purpose:
A broad goal statement describing what children learn through the activity.

Terms, Facts, and Principles:
Numerical identification of specific TFPs within the unit to which the activity relates.

Materials:
A listing of all necessary props.

Procedure:
A step-by-step description of how the adult is to carry out the activity. The procedure includes descriptions of what instructors are to do, as well as suggestions for what they might say, in a classroom of four- or five-year-olds.

Hints for Success:
Suggestions for how adults should structure the activity to meet the needs of children of differing ages and abilities.

How to Simplify this Activity:
Ideas for making the activity more suitable for three-year-olds or other inexperienced children.

How to Extend this Activity:
Suggestions for ways to increase the complexity of the activity, making it more appropriate for kindergarten children and first- or second-graders.

Figure 2 *Activity Plan Format*

The activity ideas for each theme include lessons that can be used with large groups, small groups, or individual children, as well as those that rely on direct instruction and others that focus on self-discovery. Together they represent an array of instructional modes—firsthand experiences, simulations, demonstrations, discussions, group projects, and indirect teaching of the theme through theme-related props. All of the activities have been extensively field-tested by children and practitioners in a wide variety of early childhood settings—preschools, family day-care homes, child-care centers, Head Start programs, kindergartens, and first- and second-grade classrooms.

Some activities that involve certain universal processes such as grouping, comparing, ordering, or counting materials; creating patterns with objects; tracing; lacing; or developing experience stories are applicable and useful for all themes. However, in the interest of saving space we have not offered duplicate descriptions within every unit. Instead we have written comprehensive plans for carrying out each of these and have inserted them in particular units. We assume readers will use these to model similar experiences related to the other themes. When activities are repeated from one unit to another, either the focus or method of presentation have been changed enough to warrant separate treatment.

5. *Teacher Resources.* At the end of every unit readers will find a list of resource materials. These include suggested field trips, ideas for potential visitors, children's books related to the topic, and reference books adults might use to increase their own knowledge of the theme. At the time this volume went to press, all of the books for each theme were still in print or were readily available at public libraries.

PROCEDURES FOR USING THIS BOOK

1. Choose a theme. At first, select ones that are familiar to you. Gradually branch out into areas about which you know less.
2. The number of TFPs in each unit varies from thirty-five to over a hundred. Do not attempt to cover them all in a single week.

Select a subgroup of TFPs; ten to fifteen are recommended. Use the others as background information or as a guide in responding to children's queries regarding the topic.

Make your selections with the following ideas in mind:

First, decide whether a general survey of the theme or a more in-depth study of a particular subtopic is best suited to your class. If the former is true, choose a few TFPs from each of the subcategories identified for the theme; if the latter is your choice, focus primarily on one sub-category.

For example, "The Sky" is divided into General Information, The Sun, Clouds and Rainbows, The Planets, The Moon, and The Stars. Some teachers may decide to concentrate on one of these, such as planning a unit on The Planets. Others may select TFPs regarding The Planets, The Moon, and The Stars, thereby giving children a broad overview of the Night-time Sky.

Second, make sure the TFPs are relevant and age appropriate for the children in your group. Select simple TFPs for use with children three to five years of age and older children who have had little experience with the theme. For children who are six or seven, or who are more familiar with the content, use a core of simple TFPs, adding a few advanced ones as well.

3. Go through the activity suggestions and select those that seem to support the TFPs you've chosen. Be sure to pick at least one from each process-learning domain. Also, make certain that activities represent varying modes of presentation such as firsthand experiences, demonstrations, investigations, and discussions.

4. Incorporate the activities into a weekly plan. Disperse the theme-related activities over the week. Decide whether each of these will be presented once or several times. Plan additional non-theme-related activities to fill in the rest of the instructional time.

5. Consider classroom management issues such as availability of materials, number of adults available, and special events. Make adjustments in your plan if necessary. For instance, if you have scheduled

finger painting and washing baby dolls for the same day and time but have only three smocks in your room, move one of these activities to another time in the day or another day altogether so you will have enough smocks for children at both areas.

6. Gather your materials. Create any props you will need. Make an effort to use some of the same props for more than one activity as a way to minimize preparation time.

7. Create a thematic atmosphere. Post theme-associated pictures at children's eye level. Choose records, books, finger plays, and songs related to the topic.

8. Carry out your plan. Take advantage of spontaneous events that may further children's understanding of the concept they are exploring.

9. Assess children's understanding and interest in the theme through observations. Make note (either mentally and/or through brief written anecdotes) of times when children talk about the theme, when they exhibit theme-related behaviors and knowledge in their play, and when parents mention incidents illustrating children's awareness of and reactions to the topic. If a free-choice or learning-center period is part of your day, keep track of the activities children choose and the amount of time they spend at them. Use a participation chart for maintaining this type of record; see the sample in Appendix B.

10. Evaluate your implementation of the theme. Write down the changes you made in the weekly plan and what you might do differently were you to repeat the plan in the future.

11. Consider extending the theme if children's interest is high. As children demonstrate an understanding and interest in the subject matter, introduce additional TFPs in subsequent weeks. In this way, two-, three-, and four-week units can be sequentially designed.

CREATING YOUR OWN THEMES

1. Select a general idea that meets the following criteria:
   a. It is a topic in which children are interested.

   b. Potential TFPs involve information that children can learn through hands-on activities.
   c. The idea is broad enough to merit children's attention for at least a week.

2. Generate a master list of TFPs that is accurate and represents varying degrees of complexity. Begin by writing down every item that seems relevant to the theme. Use resource books and resource persons to expand your knowledge.

3. As the list grows, determine whether natural subtopics begin to emerge. If they do, group the TFPs accordingly.

4. Decide whether a general survey or a more in-depth study of a subgroup is best suited to your class. If the former is more appropriate, choose a few TFPs from each of the subcategories; if the latter is your choice, focus primarily on one subgroup.

5. Generate activity ideas based on the TFPs you have picked.

6. Assign each activity to one of the eight curricular domains described in this book. Use the theme planning worksheet provided in Appendix C as a tool for planning.

7. Proceed with items three through eleven as described in the previous section.

PITFALLS TO AVOID

Teachers can be assured that their theme teaching conforms to developmentally appropriate practice by not succumbing to the following pitfalls.

1. *Teaching off the top of your head.* Adults sometimes assume that because they are more experienced than children, their store of general knowledge will be adequate to support the theme. This often leads to superficial treatment of the subject, too narrow an interpretation, or the teaching of inaccurate information.

   How to avoid this pitfall. Read the TFPs for each unit carefully to insure your understanding of the topic.

2. *Selecting activities prior to reviewing the TFPs.* As soon as you settle on a topic, it is natural to envision activities that might fit into a teaching unit on that subject. However, creating an entire unit this way neglects the essential step of linking activities

to the specific bits of information you will be teaching. The result may be an array of activities that lacks substance and cohesion.

How to avoid this pitfall. Make sure to consult the master list of TFPs that serves as the basis for each unit. Even if certain activities seem immediately attractive, be sure to determine to which TFPs they relate. Check your plan to evaluate how well the activities you have chosen support the concept you are trying to get across.

3. *Scheduling a whole year of themes prior to the beginning of school.* This strategy, while convenient for the teacher, fails to take into account children's changing needs and interests. It violates the basic principle of good theme planning—selecting themes based on children's desire and need to know about certain topics. Schedules of themes that look the same year after year ignore the individuality of each group and often lead to lackluster teaching or reliance on outdated topics or props.

How to avoid this pitfall. Consider in advance what your first few themes will be. Select subsequent themes after you begin to know the children's interests and needs.

4. *Teaching familiar themes only.* Adults who teach only what they already know may overlook or fail to address topics children would benefit from learning more about. They also do nothing to expand their own knowledge base.

How to avoid this pitfall. Once you have tried some units that cover familiar territory, begin to branch out by choosing topics with which you are less conversant. Some teachers report that it helps to try new themes in conjunction with a colleague as a way to gain support and to share resources.

5. *Making every activity relate to the theme.* In the teacher's enthusiasm for a particular theme he or she may plan a unit in which every activity is in some way theme related. This is problematic for several reasons. First, adults must realize that not all children will share their interest in the topic. If confronted with the same subject matter at every turn, youngsters may have

access to few activities that genuinely excite their curiosity. Subsequently, they may develop an entirely negative perception of that topic. Even children who find the theme attractive may perceive the classroom as so saturated that the subject matter loses its appeal. Furthermore, many teachers work so hard at making everything theme-related that they lose their own enthusiasm. Finally, the link between activities and the theme may become contrived rather than obvious and real.

How to avoid this pitfall. Intersperse several non-theme-related activities throughout your weekly plan. Children's favorite activities are appropriate, as are teacher-initiated activities that support goals other than those generated by the theme.

6. *Presenting too many terms, facts, and principles in a given week.* Sometimes the TFPs for a theme may seem so interesting that teachers are tempted to try to convey all of them to children in a short time. The result is overwhelming, however, and children take little away from the theme that is meaningful to them.

How to avoid this pitfall. Concentrate on a subset of TFPs. The exact number you select will be determined by the nature of the theme. Themes that deal with concrete entities, like insects, may successfully encompass more TFPs than abstract topics, such as personal safety. We have found that a selection of ten to fifteen TFPs works best. If you wish to use a larger subset of TFPs for a certain theme, allow more than one week for study.

7. *Quizzing children on the terms, facts, and principles.* Teachers may assume that rote recitation of the TFPs by youngsters is a sign of successful teaching. This is an inappropriate expectation because it violates the conceptual nature of theme planning.

How to avoid this pitfall. Observe children for demonstrations of their understanding of the theme. Watch their interactions and listen to their conversations to gain knowledge about what they have learned. Conduct discussions to give children opportunities to express their own interpretation of each concept.

8. *Expecting each child to show evidence of having learned all of the terms, facts, and principles offered during the week.* Teachers are sometimes disappointed when children ignore or do not seem to know some TFPs covered in a particular unit. They assume that their teaching was ineffective or that children were not interested in the topic. While these considerations are worth exploring, they are not always the explanation. It is normal for youngsters to learn some TFPs and not others. The point of each unit is that children add to the concepts they have already formed. This does not mean that they learn everything there is to know about the concept at once.

How to avoid this pitfall. Remember to judge effectiveness by the relative, rather than the absolute, increase in children's knowledge. Expect each child to demonstrate varying degrees of understanding. Youngsters already familiar with the topic and those extremely interested in it will exhibit greater depth of knowledge than children for whom the topic is new or less appealing. Extend themes that seem more difficult for children to grasp or repeat them at another time.

SUMMARY

A program planned around a theme that is important for children to understand is valuable for both children and teachers. This approach helps children make links among diverse bits of information so that they derive greater meaning from what they are experiencing. Additionally, teaching in this manner helps to integrate content learning (represented by the TFPs) and process learning (represented by the curricular domains). Furthermore, theme teaching offers flexibility for the planner as well as the learner. Building on children's interests evolves naturally and comfortably out of this approach. Theme teaching also helps

teachers organize information and helps students process it.

Developing quality units that truly teach is a goal for every educator. This can be achieved by following the guidelines set forth in this book. Because the units have been checked for accuracy and field-tested in a variety of educational settings, teachers can be assured that they are feasible. In addition, the range of activities follows the teaching principles of developmentally appropriate practice for young children and so are beneficial for them. Using the structure and content presented here will enhance both teaching and learning in the classroom for years to come.

RESOURCES

Bredekamp, S. "Developmentally Appropriate Practice in Early Childhood Programs Serving Children from Birth Through Age 8." Washington, DC: National Association for the Education of Young Children, 1988.

Bredekamp, S. "Guidelines for Appropriate Curriculum Content and Assessment in Programs Serving Children 3 Through 8 Years of Age." A Position Statement of the National Association of Early Childhood Specialists in State Departments of Education. Washington, DC: National Association for the Education of Young Children, in press.

Cummings, C. *Translating Guidelines into Practice.* Saginaw, MI: Mid-Michigan Association for the Education of Young Children, 1989.

Dearden, R. F. *Theory and Practice in Education.* London: Routledge and Kegan Paul, 1984.

Eliason, C. F., and L. T. Jenkins. *A Practical Guide to Early Childhood Curriculum.* Columbus, OH: Merrill Publishing Company, 1986.

Elkind, D. "The Miseducation of Young Children." *The Education Digest* 54(October 1988):11–14.

Goetz, E. M. "In Defense of Curriculum Themes." *Day Care and Early Education* 13 (Fall 1985): 12–13.

Hendrick, J. *Total Learning: Curriculum for the Young Child.* Columbus, OH: Merrill Publishing Company, 1986.

Hunt, J. M. *Intelligence and Experience.* New York: The Ronald Press Company, 1961.

Katz, L., and S. Chard. *Engaging Children's Minds: The Project Approach.* Norwood, NJ: Ablex Publishing, 1989.

Kostelnik, M. J., L. C. Stein, A. P. Whiren, and A. K. Soderman. *Guiding Children's Social Development.* Cincinnati: Southwestern Publishing, 1988.

Kostelnik, M. J., S. Palmer, and K. Hannon. "Theme Planning in Early Childhood." Paper presented at the National Association for the Education of Young Children Conference in Chicago, November 1987.

Lawton, J. T. "The Ausubelian Preschool Classroom." In *Approaches to Early Childhood Education,* edited by J. L. Roopnarine and J. E. Johnson. Columbus, OH: Merrill Publishing Company, 1987.

Machado, J. M., and H. C. Meyer. *Early Childhood Practicum Guide.* Albany, NY: Delmar Publishers, 1984.

Osborn, J. D., and D. K. Osborn. *Cognition in Early Childhood.* Athens, GA: Education Associates, 1983.

Welman, H. M. "First Steps in the Child's Theorizing about the Mind." In *Developing Theories of Mind,* edited by J. Astington, P. L. Harris, and D. R. Olson. New York: Cambridge University Press, 1988.

Part I

Social Studies Concepts

Chapter 1

Self-Awareness

•

Who Am I?

What Am I Like?

What Can I Do?

What Makes Me Special?

•

iguring out the answers to these questions is a major developmental task for young children. As youngsters interact with other people and explore the world around them, they continually acquire bits of information that contribute to greater self-awareness. It is in this way that children gradually construct the concepts of "me" and "not me," thereby defining their notion of self.

In the early preschool years, children think of themselves in purely physical terms—whether they are a boy or a girl, what they look like, what they own, and where they live ("I am a girl," "I have brown shoes," "I live in an apartment"). Later this focus expands somewhat to encompass comparisons with other people ("I'm bigger than he is," "I have more blocks than she does"). By the time they are five or six, children also include their activities as a part of self-concept ("I like to ride bikes," "I can run fast"). These physical actions continue to be an important aspect of self-awareness for several years, although the manner in which children think about them changes over time. Kindergartners say, "I jump high," third-graders proclaim, "I can jump higher than you can." Just as with physical attributes, children begin by thinking about what they themselves can do, and then later make comparisons between their own capabilities and those of the people around them (Kostelnik et al., 1988).

Only in the final elementary years do children consider internal psychological traits as parts of who they are. "I am shy," "I am a happy person," "I am a hard worker" are now the kinds of descriptors they think of when defining "who am I?"

While this increasingly sophisticated sense of self is evolving, children are also making positive and negative judgments about their self-worth. They gather this information primarily through interactions with the significant people in their lives—family members, teachers, and other children. These people serve as the mirror in which children see themselves and evaluate what they see. If the reflection is good, children will make a positive evaluation of the self; if it is negative, children's judgments will be as well (Kostelnik et al., 1988). While it is possible for children to avoid some negative self-appraisals, our aim as early childhood educators is to maximize children's feelings of positive self-esteem.

PURPOSE

The general thrust of this theme is to enhance children's self-concept and self-esteem while at the same time addressing all areas of the curriculum. Although all of the units in this book are intended to be consistent with these aims, we believe that a theme devoted entirely to self-awareness and positive self-appraisal will provide an effective means for teachers to emphasize these processes.

The TFPs in this unit are stated in the first person, that is, from the child's own point of view rather than the teacher's. We adopted this approach to encourage children to internalize the content, applying what they learn to their own sense of self as they participate in the activities included here.

IMPLEMENTATION

In structuring this unit, we have taken into account the sequence through which children proceed to greater self-awareness. Since very young children tend to see themselves in terms of physical attributes, teachers working with toddlers and three- and four-year-olds should choose activities that focus on this aspect of self-concept (appearance, clothes, possessions). Awareness of less obvious characteristics (preferences and abilities) can be developed more easily at a later time.

On the other hand, because five- and six-year-olds have a greater ability to recognize the less physical characteristics that they possess, their teachers could focus on the more complex TFPs indicated in the unit. These will give children practice with more subtle notions of self-awareness and greater opportunities to compare themselves to others.

The Self-Awareness theme may be carried out in a variety of ways: a) as a one-time unit early in the year, b) as a theme that is used at various times throughout the year, or c) separated into individual activities that could be used within other units, whenever a stronger emphasis on the self is desired.

Teachers also will find that the unit can be logically extended in a variety of directions. Self-Awareness could be followed by a unit devoted to greater understanding of the near environment, such as The Neighborhood or

My School. Alternatively, teachers may wish to explore Books as a follow-up unit, focusing on autobiographies of other people. For some teachers, the Self-Awareness unit may be used as a concrete way for children to consider their immediate past and present, followed by a contrasting look at the future through themes such as When I Grow Up or Occupations.

TERMS, FACTS, AND PRINCIPLES

1. I am distinct from every other person.
2. No person in the world is exactly like me.
3. I have a name.
*4. I share part of my full name with my family.
5. I have a birthday that tells the day I was born.
*6. I am an age that is determined by the number of years since I was born.
*7. I am more like some people than other people.
8. I am special.
*9. I have a unique history.
10. Words can be used to describe how I look.
*11. Words can be used to describe my emotional state.
*12. I have thoughts and feelings that can be communicated to others.
13. I am either a boy or a girl; male or female.
14. I have skills.
15. I have preferences.
16. I have knowledge.
17. I can make choices.
18. I can learn new things.
19. I have relationships with other people.
20. I am a member of a family.
*21. I am a member of other groups; for example: my neighborhood, my class, this school, my small group, my church, etc.
*22. I am a member of a cultural and racial group with my own cultural and racial heritage.
23. I have possessions.
24. I have places in which to keep possessions at school and at home.

*25. In some ways I change from day to day: my body grows, I wear different clothes, I learn, I have different emotions, I find new ways to think about things. In some ways I will always stay the same: I am the same person, I have the same body and mind.
*26. I am like other people in some ways; I am unique in some ways.
*27. There are some things about me that others can learn by listening and looking at me; there are other things that can only be learned if I tell other people about me.
*28. I can do some things better than others; I can do some things less well than others.
*29. I can teach things to other people; I can be taught things by other people.
*30. Some things I would like others to know about me; I prefer to keep some things to myself.
*31. I have an imagination with which to create ideas and solutions to problems.
32. I am valued by others.
33. I like myself.
*34. There are many things about myself I like; there are some things about myself I want to change.
*35. My ideas and thoughts are valued by others.

ACTIVITY IDEAS

Aesthetics

1. *I See Me.* Set up mirrors around the room and encourage children to look at themselves and enjoy their own reflections.
2. *Self-Portraits.* Show children two or three works of art in which the artist drew a self-portrait. Norman Rockwell's painting of himself looking in a mirror while painting his own portrait is a good one to include. Talk with the children about what the artists wanted people to know about themselves based on the pictures they made. Explain to the children that they, too, will have a chance to make pictures of themselves. Invite them to look in a mirror, describe what they see, and draw a self-portrait using crayons, paints, or markers.

*3. *Choosing Favorites.*

General Purpose: For children to derive pleasure from nature and diverse art forms; to state preferences.

TFPs: 7, 8, 12, 15, 19, 21, 29, 31, 34, 35.

Materials: None

Procedure:

a. Introduce the activity by discussing people's preferences. Every person has favorite foods, colors, books, toys, etc. Some personal favorites are the same as one's friends; some are different from one's friends. Sometimes our favorites change. Ask children to give examples of "favorites."

b. Explain that a new special job in your classroom will involve children taking turns sharing their favorite song or story with their friends.

c. Describe a procedure for carrying out this plan. If you already have a job chart, consider adding "song/story-chooser" to the chart. Otherwise, see the plan in this unit for creating one.

d. Early in the day, remind the child who will choose that day's song or story so that he or she can determine a preference. Encourage children to select a different song or story than someone else chose on the preceding day.

Hints for Success:

• Encourage children to teach their classmates new songs/stories if they wish. Accept impromptu, self-written songs/stories or out-of-season songs/stories with enthusiasm and support for the child's display of creativity.

• Make a list of song/story titles to refer to when making suggestions.

How to Simplify this Activity:

• Children who are just beginning to participate in song/story choosing may need several days of prompting before beginning to take initiative.

How to Extend this Activity:

• Keep track of the songs/stories children chose by making a chart. Have children "vote" for their favorite, or tally how many children like a particular one best, how many don't.

Affective

1. *Name Chant.* Play a chanting game with children using clapping or finger-snapping. Clap or snap in rhythm with the words. Say the words: "Names go up, names go down. Tell us how your name sounds." At the end of this phrase, have one child say his or her name; repeat the name while clapping the syllables (*Mar y, Jo se, An na, Ma ri a*). Continue the entire chant with another name.

2. *All About Me Book.* Assist the children in describing themselves on paper and then binding the pages together in a book. Pages that could be included may contain: "This is me," a self-portrait; "Here is my hand," a hand-tracing; "Some things that I can do," a dictated list of skills; "My favorite foods" or "My favorite animals," magazine picture cutouts. Preface each page with the words "I am special."

3. *Sing Us Your Name.* Sing the two-note phrase Do Do La Do to individual children using the words "Sing Us Your Name." Ask each child to respond with "My name is *Peter*" using the same two-note phrase and filling in his or her name. Expect that the inexperienced child may progress through stages with this activity, starting by whispering the name, then whispering the phrase "My name is *Peter*," later saying "My name is *Peter*," then singing "My name is *Peter*" (not matching the same pitches), and finally singing the phrase using the correct notes. Invite the group to respond with "His name is Peter."

4. *Identifying Preferences.* Provide opportunities for children to express a preference for one object among several. Organize a choosing table displaying variations of one type of item each day. From this array children could select their favorite food, texture, smell, or color. Record the results and compare them. Keep a group chart over time, adding preferences as children make them known. Eventually, use the chart to point out similar preferences among children, encouraging children to suggest additional categories of choices over an extended period of time, perhaps over a month. Later use this information to form small interest groups, helping children learn more about a par-

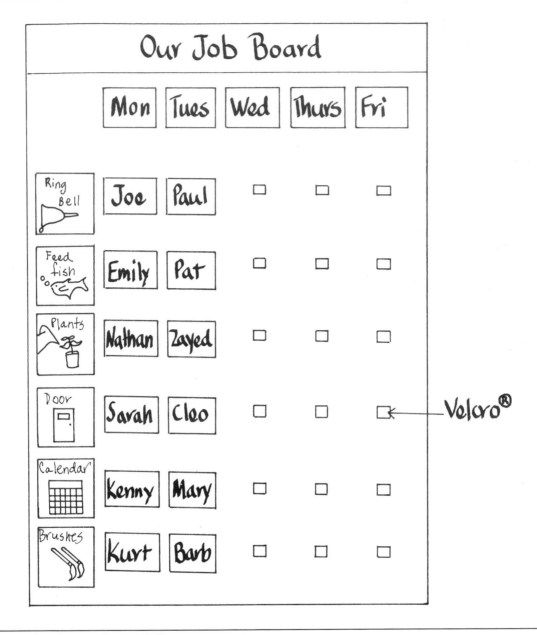

Figure 1.1 *A Sample Class Job Chart*

ticular topic of interest they have in common.

5. *Making a Class Job Chart.* Think of several "jobs" around the classroom that children could learn to do themselves, such as watering the plants, feeding the pet, ringing a bell to signal clean-up time, holding the door open for others, etc. Make a chart listing these jobs. (Figure 1.1) Add a picture symbol to illustrate each one. Make name labels for each child in the room and rotate the children's names daily so each child gets one job each week. Help children learn the jobs so that they can become more independent in carrying them out over time.

6. *Painting at the Easel by Myself.* Provide a painting area with an easel. Spread newspapers on the floor under the easel and provide several paint aprons, different sized brushes, a variety of tempera paint colors in nonspill containers, and large sheets of newsprint. Consider ways to make painting at the easel as independent as possible, such as having the paper available nearby, putting the brushes and

Figure 1.2 *The Sequence of Easel Painting*

paints on a tray at child-height, providing a sponge for wiping up spills, and arranging a drying rack for wet paintings that is accessible to children. During a large group time, demonstrate the step-by-step process of how to paint by yourself. (Figure 1.2) Include putting on an apron, attaching paper to the easel, choosing paint colors, writing your name on the finished work (or asking the teacher to do this), hanging up paintings to dry, wiping up spills, washing hands, and hanging up the apron. Repeat this demonstration a second day, having the children "talk" you through it. Also, make a few "mistakes" so children can correct you. To help children remember the steps demonstrated, make a series of pictures that illustrates this process and hang them near the easel.

Additional easel activities:

- Vary the paper provided for painting at the easel; occasionally offer large construction paper, large finger paint paper (shiny side up), large- or medium-sized manila, large sheets of textured wallpaper, aluminum foil, or computer paper.

- Vary the size and shape of the paper. As an incentive to creativity, cut long rectangles—suggest they paint something tall; cut circles—suggest children paint something round; or cut triangles.

- Cut one or two holes randomly in the painting paper. Children could paint around the holes or fill them in to paint on a second paper fastened underneath.

- Offer a variety of media to be used at the easel: crayons, chalk, watercolors, markers, pencils, or fingerpaints.

- Offer a variety of implements with which to paint at the easel: small sponges, cotton swabs, feathers, sticks, brayers, or tiny model cars.

7. *I Can Relax!* The purpose of this activity is to heighten children's awareness of bodily tension and relaxation. Their ability to recognize these different feelings is a first step in children's positive stress management. Have on hand a stiff, unflexible toy figure as well as a floppy cloth one. Also collect a few records—some marches and some languid tunes.

   Talk with the children about how people's bodies are hinged together. Have them identify the places where there are hinges (in the neck, shoulders, elbows, wrists, fingers, waist, knees, ankles, toes, etc.). Show the group the stiff toy figure and say: "Some toys are stiff. They like to lock up all of their hinges. Let's do that." Direct children to lock up one hinge at a time and, when all are locked, to march to music as stiff toys.

   To provide the contrast between the tense, "locked-up" feeling and the feeling of relaxation, tell the children to change from stiff toys into cloth dolls. Show the cloth figures and discuss how limp and floppy the dolls are. Ask the children to sit down for the exercise, showing you first how a stiff toy might sit. Then have them sequentially unlock each hinge, shaking it out and allowing it to go limp until they are completely relaxed. Playing relaxing music during this latter experience will enhance their holistic differentiation between tension and relaxation.

   Following the two experiences, contrast with the children the way that people sometimes feel when they are angry or upset and the way they feel when they are happy and relaxed, connecting the former feeling with the stiff, locked-up figure and the latter feeling with the cloth dolls.

8. *A Special Self-Award.* Discuss the ideas of valuing yourself and liking things that you do well. Explain that awards are sometimes given to people to show what special things they do well. Ask the children to think of something they like about themselves and to design a special award for themselves. For children who have difficulty thinking of something, ask others in the group to help them by suggesting the things they do well. Provide a variety of precut shapes in colored and gold and silver paper, ribbons, glue, and labels that say "I'm Special Because I _____ ." (Figure 1.3)

   Invite children to put the materials together any way they wish and help them fill in the blank for their special award. Hang the awards on the children's cubbies or suggest they wear them.

9. *Pick-a-Print.* This activity gives children an opportunity to identify a unique characteristic of themselves—their fingerprints.

Figure 1.3 *A Special Self-Award*

Cut enough unlined index cards in half for each child to have two halves. Prepare a number of wet and dry paper towels (for clean-up) and set out a few ink pads and magnifying glasses. Invite children to examine the tips of their fingers with their naked eyes as well as with the magnifiers. Point out the "swirls" that create the designs. Ask them to examine a neighbor's fingertip, comparing the patterns as best they can. Have each child make a thumb (or finger) print on one of their cards. Label these with the child's name. Encourage them to look at their own print (with and without the magnifying glass) and to compare it with their neighbor's. Point out the similarities and differences. Ask children to describe what they see. Next, have each child make a second print with the same finger on another card. This time, write the child's name on the back. Put all of these cards, face up, on the table and have each child choose the print that matches the one they have. Ask children to see if they've picked their own fingerprint.

An extension of this game would be to give children random cards (not necessarily their own) and have them select the match from the pile.

*10. ***When I was a Baby.***

General Purpose: To help children learn about themselves.

TFPs: 1–3, 5, 8–10, 13, 25–27.

Materials: Baby books, photographs, written anecdotes or other information supplied by the parents of each child in the class.

Procedure:

a. Invite children in small groups to join you in looking at their baby books. Explain why people keep photographs of babies, "Some of you brought things from home that show what you were like when you were a baby. Pictures help us see how you've changed and help your family remember when you were littler. A baby book is a book in which parents write things about their babies to help them remember."

b. Select some of the information from each baby book or photograph and describe it in ways that the children can understand: "When you were born, you were nineteen inches long" (show with hands). Encourage children to join in by asking questions that elicit comparison between then and now, such as, "Your baby book says you liked bananas when you were little. What do you like to eat now?"

c. Use a mirror or current photo of the child to help draw attention to changes that have taken place in the child's appearance, activities, and abilities.

d. Make sure everyone's hands are clean before handling pictures.

Hints for Success:

• Give parents the option of providing a baby book or written information about their child. Make a short questionnaire for parents asking for specific information and anecdotes about their child as an infant.

Dear Parents:

Soon we will be focusing on your child's Self-Awareness. We need some *pictures and information* about your child as a baby. Please fill out this form and use this bag to send in one or two baby pictures of your child or your child's "baby book" if you have one. We will be sure to keep things clean and safe and will return them by the end of next week.

My Child As An Infant

My child, _____ , was _____ inches long at birth and weighed _____ pounds. My child liked to eat _____ when he/she was a baby. He/she didn't like _____ . His/her first word was _____ . His/her hair was _____ . (Please share any other information that would tell us about your child as a baby such as habits, sleeping patterns, favorite toys, etc.)

_____

How to Simplify this Activity:

- Work with one child at a time. Hold the book and turn the pages while children look at them. Focus discussion on observable, physical characteristics.

How to Extend this Activity:

- Compare information about the children as infants to help them discover characteristics common to all babies.

*11. *Autobiographies.*

General Purpose: For children to identify the characteristics and qualities that make each of them unique.

TFPs: 1, 2, 3, 8–14, 25, 27–34.

Materials: Hand or full-length mirror, tape recorder or pencil and paper, Polaroid camera and film. Optional: past photos of the child.

Procedure:

a. Select a quiet area of the room. Have materials close by. Introduce the activity by explaining that everyone is the star of his or her own life and no one knows a person's life story as well as he or she does.

b. Direct one child at a time to begin by looking in the mirror and telling about the person he or she sees there. Prompt children by pointing out physical characteristics: "You may want to tell about your hair or eyes." "What is the thing you like best about the person you see?" "Tell me about the clothes you are wearing today." "What do you like to play at home?" Record the child's words on audio tape or on paper.

c. Encourage children to tell about when they were a baby. Mention toys, clothes, furniture that the child may have used in the past.

d. Encourage other children to ask questions of the storyteller. For example, explain that "Jamie is telling her autobiography. This is the story of important things that make her special or that happened in her life. You can help by asking Jamie some questions about her family or herself."

e. Invite children to illustrate their stories with drawings or photographs.

Hints for Success:

- Take an instant picture of the child if a mirror is unavailable, or ask parents to send in a current picture of their child.

- Ask parents to provide you with some information about meaningful past events in the child's life, such as the child's favorite toy, a visit to grandma's, foods, the child's likes, and so forth. Begin a story about the child using this information, and ask the child to add something you didn't mention.

- Use paper and pencil rather than a tape recorder unless children have had previous opportunities to operate and experiment with the recorder.

How to Simplify this Activity:

- Focus on the child's physical characteristics and favorite possessions. Some children may need more structure to help them think of things to say. Provide a fill-in-the-blank story, asking children to finish incomplete sentences such as: My name is _____ . I am _____ years old. I like to play _____ . Some of my friends are _____ and _____ . When I was a baby I _____ .

How to Extend this Activity:

- Put all the finished autobiographies together into a class volume. Reread the stories at various times during the year. Allow children to update their stories if they choose. Read one child's autobiography to other children and ask them to guess who the story is about.

Cognition

1. *Just Like Me.* Cut out pictures of people from magazines or catalogues. Ask children to group them in various ways, according to characteristics that are similar to or different from their own.

2. *That's Me!* Explain that in this game children will listen carefully and then follow directions. First, state a characteristic that describes more than one child; then tell children to carry out an action if they share that characteristic. For example, "Jump up if you are a girl. Wave if you are a boy. Stand up if you have two legs." Make the characteristics obvious at first, then more subtle as children get good at the game. Subtle characteristics may include wearing a ring, having freckles, brushed teeth today, having a zipper, ability to swim, or liking to sing.

3. *I'm Changing.* Assist children in developing a chart or graph of personal characteristics that change over time. Sample characteristics include height, weight, how far the child can long jump, what letters a child knows, or names of friends a child knows. Keep the graph going for several weeks or months, referring back to it occasionally and adding new information.

4. *Today/Tomorrow.* Invite a willing child to stand in front of the group. Point to physical characteristics such as eyes, hair, skin color, or clothes and ask the children to tell whether each thing will change or stay the same in the future. Write a list of attributes children think will remain stable and make another list of things they predict will be different. Repeat the activity with the same child a second day. Refer to the list you made to help children evaluate their predictions. As a variation on this activity, take a Polaroid picture of the child two days in a row. Display them together and ask children to notice things about themselves that are the same and things that are different.

5. *Children Everywhere.* Hang pictures of children from around the world or provide picture books showing other cultures. Talk with the children, encouraging them to notice similarities and differences between the children pictured and themselves.

6. *Letters and Names.* Make alphabet cards with letters large enough to be seen by the group. Holding up one letter at a time, chant or sing (to the tune of "Mary Had a Little Lamb"), "If your name begins with A, Stand up please, Stand up please. If your name begins with A, sit back down." Use this as a game for large-group time. Later, modify the song to direct children to move in different ways.

7. *Comparing Baby and Child Heights.* Ask parents to give you information regarding the length of their child at birth. For each child, demonstrate this baby height using a yardstick to mark it on a long piece of paper attached to the wall. Then, having the child stand next to the line, mark how tall they are now. Compare the two marks pointing out how much they've grown.

*8. *Name That Face.*

General Purpose: To attach meanings to symbols in the environment, to explore the implications of individual similarities and differences.

TFPs: 1–3, 10, 11, 12, 18, 21, 24–26, 27–28, 32, 33, 34.

Materials: Name tags for each child, safety pins, photos of each child.

Procedure:

a. Arrange a display of name tags, with a matching photo of each child above their tag. Explain to the children that every person in the room has a name. Names can be written. The letters in people's names look a certain way and people can practice remembering what their name looks like.

b. Ask each child to find his or her own name tag, using the picture as a clue.

c. Another day, still using the pictures as clues, challenge each child to find someone else's name tag and take it to him or her. Read the name aloud to the child.

d. As children get more experienced with this task, remove the pictures, asking them to find their own tag by remembering how their name looks.

e. Finally, after much practice, ask children to find a friend's tag without using a picture clue, and take it to him or her.

Hints for Success:

• Ask parents to donate a recent picture or take one of each child. If the cost of this is prohibitive, take a group picture, have it enlarged, and cut out individual faces.

• If more than one child has the same first name, make the tags look different by adding the last initial, such as Sue B. and Sue L.

How to Simplify this Activity:

• Place a few tags with their matching pictures in small groups, keeping the pictures and tags in the same position each day.

How to Extend this Activity:

• Change the position of the name tags and pictures each day. Increase the number of name tags and pictures the children must sort through until the whole class is displayed together.

*9. *Making A Group Graph.*

General Purpose: For children to approach information, problems, objects, and events in ways original to them.

TFPs: 1, 2, 15, 17.

Materials: A collection of objects, a large plastic tablecloth or shower curtain with a six-by-eight-box grid drawn on it (squares on the grid should be large enough for a child to stand in), paper labels or wipe-off markers.

Procedure:

a. Prior to graphing, give children many chances to explore the characteristics of objects. Provide lots of collections of objects (keys, stuffed animals, shells, buttons, marbles, and so forth), for children to examine and sort.

b. After children have had numerous opportunities to carry out step A above, decide on the objects to graph. Start

with actual objects that are easy to handle. For example, using the shoes on the children's feet may be fun and will add to their understanding of themselves compared to others.

c. Lay the plastic tablecloth or shower curtain on the floor saying, "Today we are going to use this plastic cloth to tell us something about our shoes." Have everyone take off one shoe and place the shoes all together where they can be seen by all the children.

d. Ask everyone to look carefully at the shoes and tell you something they notice about them. Children may point out that some are red, some brown, and others are white. Respond by saying, "You're noticing your shoes are different colors. Let's make a graph about the colors of the shoes in our class."

e. Start the graph by indicating colors along the top of the grid. (Figure 1.4) Write the words red, brown, and white or use symbols (colored paper squares) to indicate the categories along the top edge. Then place a shoe in a square on the graph under the correct color. Ask children to take turns doing the same with their shoes, until everyone's shoe is on a separate square on the graph under the correct color.

f. Ask children to look at the graph saying, "What does the graph tell us about the shoes in our class?" Point out that by counting the shoes in a column, the graph tells them how many people wore brown shoes today, how many wore white ones, etc. By comparing the length of the columns, children can tell which colors occur the most, the least, and not at all among their shoes.

g. If children are interested, repeat the activity using a different characteristic and the same objects, such as different kinds of shoe fasteners (tie, Velcro, buckles, or slip-ons) or number of colors on the shoe (all one color, two colors, three colors).

Note: For this unit, it is appropriate to choose children in the class to be the "objects." Classify children according to gender, hair color, color of eyes, number of people in

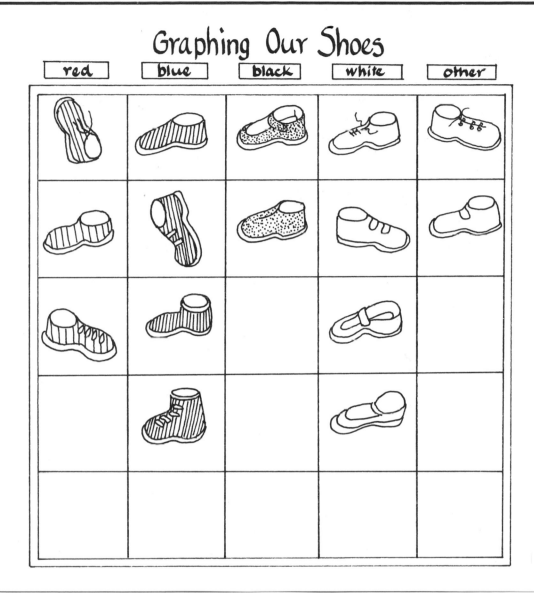

Figure 1.4 *A Group Graph of the Children's Shoes*

their families, or preferences. Choose one characteristic upon which to focus for each graph.

How to Simplify this Activity:
- Choose objects with obvious differences (a group of dogs, cats, and birds or a group of red, blue, and green circles).

How to Extend this Activity:
- After the children experience considerable graphing of real objects, increase the complexity and level of abstract thinking required by making the graph on the floor and then demonstrating it

on a large chart using symbols for the objects. Show children how the graphs correspond and show the same things about the objects. Older groups, or children with much experience, may be ready to graph groups of objects according to two criteria at the same time, such as apples graphed by color and size.

Construction
1. ***Things I Like.*** Suggest that children make a collage picturing favorite foods, cars, toys, or animals. Provide a collection of magazine pictures for children to look

through, tear out, or cut out and mount on background paper. Write the child's name and the words "This is what I like" on the top of the collage.

2. ***This is Me.*** Provide children with paste, a large piece of background paper, and a collection of precut eyes, noses, hair, ears, mouths, cheeks, head shapes, eyebrows, glasses, and so forth that have been drawn or cut from magazine pictures in a variety of shapes and colors. Display the materials, encouraging children to label each body part as they look them over. Suggest that each child choose facial features that could be used to make a picture of himself or herself. Ask the children to arrange their pieces into a face and then paste them down on the background.

Language

1. ***Experience Stories—What I'm Learning.*** Take dictation from individual children about something they have already learned to do well, something they are learning now, and something they hope to learn.
2. ***It's a Small World.*** Read factual stories to the class about other children. Encourage them to think about whether the children portrayed are like or unlike themselves. Record the group's ideas. Repeat this activity using stories in which the setting is similar to those of the children in your group and again using stories with different settings.
3. ***Mirror, Mirror . . .*** Have children view themselves, one at a time, in a full-length mirror. Ask each child to describe "me." Write down the child's words exactly. Read the description back to the child to make sure it's complete. Later, read an individual description to the class without telling whose it is and ask them to guess the child's identity.
4. ***Sounds Like Me/Looks Like Me.*** Have one child describe his or her physical features (I am tall, have a round face, have black hair, and so forth). At the same time, have an adult sit with back turned to the child and secretly draw what the child says. Then give the drawing to the child,

pointing out the features described. Encourage children to practice describing themselves in greater detail.

5. ***The Letters in My Name.*** Give each child an envelope containing the letters in his or her first name. Help children arrange them correctly. Initially, provide a card with their names written in the same type of letters for children to use as a model. Later, replace the exact model with a card containing the child's name in a different form, typed or in block letters, printed in a different color (or colors), or using both upper- and lower-case letters. Eventually, eliminate the model altogether. As the children become proficient at spelling their first names, add last names as well. Later, include some letters in the envelopes that do not belong in either their first or last names.

6. ***Making My Initial Pretzel.*** Teach children what the first letter in their name looks like. Provide them with a model and help in making their letter with pretzel dough using the following recipe. Bake the pretzels and eat them. (Figure 1.5)

Ingredients:

½ pkg. dry yeast

½ tsp. salt

¾ tsp. sugar

¾ cup warm water

1 egg (beaten)

Kosher salt

2 cups flour and extra

Utensils:

recipe chart (optional)

aluminum foil

cookie sheets

bowls

mixing spoon

pastry brush

oven

hot pads

Procedure:

1. Arrange ingredients and utensils on or near a large table.

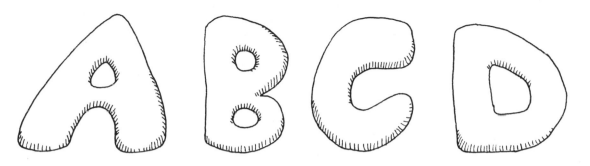

Figure 1.5 *Pretzel Initials*

2. Direct children who will be making pretzels to wash their hands before participating.

3. Read the recipe to the children and work with them to follow the steps listed below to create delicious initial pretzels: Tasks marked with a * are especially suitable for the young cooks.

   a. Preheat oven to 400°.

   *b. Cover a cookie sheet with foil.

   c. Soften yeast in warm water.

   *d. Add salt and sugar. Mix.

   *e. Mix in flour and turn out onto a floured surface.

   *f. Knead dough for 8 minutes, until it looks smooth.

   *g. Cut into 8–10 pieces. Shape each into a long rope. Arrange ropes into letter shapes.

   *h. Place on foil, brush with beaten egg, sprinkle with Kosher salt.

   i. Bake for 15 minutes or until light brown.

   *j. EAT!

7. ***Stand Up Name Story.*** Make up a funny story to tell the children that uses all of their names at least twice. Ask them to listen very carefully as you tell it and to stand up when they hear you say their name the first time. They should sit down when they hear their name a second time. In a variation of this activity, give children a sound to make or a gesture to do (wave, stomp, or turn around) when they hear their name in the story. Sounds and gestures should vary from child to child to add to the fun and to emphasize the importance of listening.

To do this activity another way, print each child's name on a six-by-twelve inch strip of cardboard. Use block letters, both upper and lower case, large enough for children to see when they are seated a few feet away from you. Explain that you will be telling a special story including some or all of the children as characters. When you get to the part that involves them, you will hold up their name for everyone to see. When children recognize their name, they should stand up, turn around, then sit down so the story can continue.

Repeat the story on more than one occasion so all children can be included. Vary the activity by changing the action required for name recognition or by holding up only the first letter of several names, making it possible for more than one child to "act" at a time.

*8. ***Picture Talk.***

General Purpose: For children to expand their ability to use words to represent knowledge, events, ideas, imaginings, and perceptions.

TFPs: 1–3, 7, 9–13, 20, 21, 25, 31, 32, 33.

Materials: One photograph of each child, paper, marker.

Procedure:

a. Display the pictures of the children. Encourage each child to point to the picture of himself or herself and tell something about the picture. Ask questions that help the children consider things about themselves, such as "How old are you?" or "What are you wearing in the picture?"

b. Write the children's words under the picture and read it back to them. Praise children for telling something about themselves.

Hints for Success:

• Accept short sentences.

• For children who are speaking English as a second language or are feeling shy, try asking specific questions like "Are you a boy or a girl?" If the child responds "girl," write the full sentence "I am a girl" under the picture.

How to Simplify this Activity:

• Focus on the concrete aspects of the picture. Point at objects or people in the picture and ask, "What's this?" "Who is this?"

How to Extend this Activity:

• Ask the child to recall the day the photograph was taken and tell a little "story" about that day.

• Record the story.

• Display the picture and the story together where it can be read aloud.

Physical

1. *Rolling Names Game.* Roll a ball to the children sitting in a circle on the floor, saying each child's name as you roll it to him or her. Ask the group to repeat the name each time. Eventually direct the children to roll the ball to someone, calling out the name of the person for whom it is intended.

2. *Pass the Beanbag Name Game.* Play this name game with the whole class or with a small group of children. Sitting in a circle on the floor, demonstrate passing a beanbag to the person on your right while saying your own name. Continue until everyone has had several chances to do this. Then, change the game so the person with the beanbag says the name of the person on their right before passing the beanbag

to him or her. Keep the beanbag moving around the circle; then reverse the flow, saying the person's name on your left as you pass the beanbag.

3. *Who's Coming Out?* Provide a crawling tunnel and assign one person to be at the "out" end, calling "Who's coming out? Oh, it's Hector!" and clapping. Children should crawl through to surprise that person.

4. *Strut Miss Mary.* To the tune of "Mammy's Little Baby Loves Shortnen' Bread," sing or chant the words "Strut Miss Mary, Strut Miss Mary, Strut Miss Mary, all day long. Strut Miss Mary, Strut Miss Mary, Strut Miss Mary all day long." Clap on the off beats. Keep the rhythm moving. Demonstrate and define "strutting" as a special way of walking. Substitute the children's names in the song, using "Miss" for the girls, and "Mister" for the boys. Ask children to practice strutting in different ways; encourage imaginative ways of strutting. Form a circle of children and have them strut around the middle of the circle, one pair at a time, as others sing or chant the song. To vary this activity, form two lines of children facing each other as partners. Everyone sings the song as a child from one side struts down the alley followed by his or her partner from the other side, imitating that strutting movement. When the second child begins, sing or chant the following verse: "Here comes another one just like the other one all day long." Continue with each pair of children, until everyone has had a turn to "strut."

5. *See Me Do Things.* Play this group game with one child in the middle of the circle of players showing something physical he or she can do (jumping, hopping, bowing, waving, spinning, clapping, etc.). Singing the song (or chanting the words), "I can do things, as you can see. Now everybody do this, just like me," the others watch and imitate the movement. Then, choose another child to be in the middle.

Pretend Play

1. *Baby Role-Play.* Encourage children to act out behaviors they displayed as an infant. Provide baby objects large and strong enough for children to use, such as

rattles, bottles, stuffed animals, blankets, full-sized high chairs, and cribs. Children may choose the adult, child, or baby roles.

2. *Dress-up Clothes with Mirror.* Gather a collection of dress-up clothes that appeal to both boys and girls (hats, scarves, vests, skirts, jackets, pants, and shoes), clothing representative of various cultures (kimono, sombrero, and poncho), fancy pieces for both boys and girls (shiny cloth, bright colors, sparkles), and some items that suggest a variety of roles in society (parents, community workers, or service people) that can be used by both males and females, and a full-length mirror. Encourage children to try on the clothes and "become" someone new. To get children started, try on some clothes yourself, talking about who might wear them. Be available to assist with snaps, buttons, and zippers. However, avoid taking over the play.

Social

1. *Match Mate.* Play this as a circle game. Pick one child to be in the center. Teach the children the following song to the tune of "Ring Around the Rosie."

> Match Mate
> Match Mate
> Looking for a Match Mate
> Match Mate
> Match Mate
> You are it

As the children sing and hold hands the "center" child moves about the circle stopping in front of someone on the words "you are it." When the song is over, the other children will guess in what way the two children match. The child who was chosen as the "mate" will then become "it" for the next round.

2. *We All Eat Bread.* Ask parents to send in a sample of the kind of bread their family eats that is typical of their cultural heritage. Ask for information about the bread, such as its name and the countries where it is eaten. Provide a tasting table so that the children can sample the different breads,

or pass them around in a large group, talking about each one.

*3. *Show or Share.*

General Purpose: To give children opportunities to explore the idea of ownership.

TFPs: 1, 12, 17, 19, 20, 22, 23, 25, 26, 28, 29, 34.

Materials: Object a child has brought from home.

Procedure:

a. Each day, ask one child to bring an object from home that interests him or her and that he or she is willing to share with the group.

b. In a large or small group setting, ask the owner to show the object and tell something about it.

c. Encourage the child to describe aspects of the object that are important to him or her, what he or she likes about it. To elicit more responses, ask the owner specific questions about the object, but avoid leading the presentation.

d. Ask the child to make a rule about the way others will be allowed to interact with the object. For example, "Other children can touch it carefully," or "They can only look at it."

e. Help the owner carry out the rule, applying it fairly to everyone.

Hints for Success:

• Send a note home explaining your objectives, the guidelines you want to establish for choosing an object, and information about when their child may bring something to share. Limiting children to *one* object and one designated day can make this activity easy to manage.

• Remind parents that some children may not want to do this activity, and that's all right.

How to Simplify this Activity:

• Have the child place the object on a "Show or Share" tray with a sign that indicates whether the other children should look at it (eyes) or touch it (eyes and hands). Leave the object available during free-choice time, but keep it on the tray.

How to Extend this Activity:

• Ask children to bring specific things each week for "Showing or Sharing." In a weekly newsletter (or a note) tell parents what the "Show or Share Objects" will be for the coming week. Ask for theme-related objects or ask that objects have particular characteristics depending on the week (one week soft objects, another week red objects, another week objects that begin with the letter A, and so forth).

*4. *Cultural Diversity in Cooking.*

General Purpose: To provide opportunities for children to develop an appreciation of their own ethnic backgrounds and cultures as well as those of others.

TFPs: 14, 18, 22, 26, 29e

Materials: One or more recipes from a variety of cultures; ingredients and cooking implements needed for those recipes; a stove, hot plate, or electric skillet.

Procedure:

a. Use one of the following recipes or ask parents to supply simple recipes and instructions for preparing food representative of their culture. (Avoid recipes that are high in sugar or lack nutritional value). Some parents may be willing to come to the classroom to demonstrate the cooking or do it with the children. Gather ingredients and tools for cooking. Arrange a cooking area in the room.

b. Discuss with children what kind of food will be prepared today and what culture it represents.

c. Encourage children to participate actively or watch the food being prepared. Provide aprons and tell children to wash their hands before cooking or preparing the food.

d. Encourage the children to sample the food before leaving for the day.

e. Keep the recipes used in the classroom and make them available to parents.

Individual Pizzas

Ingredients:

Refrigerated biscuit dough rounds (enough for the group)

Grated mozarella cheese

Grated parmesan cheese

Canned pizza sauce

Green pepper slivers

Sliced olives

Sliced mushrooms

Sliced pepperoni

Procedure:

1. Pat dough into a thin, round shape on a piece of foil.
2. Spread with sauce and add the toppings desired.
3. Bake at 375° for 10–15 minutes or until lightly browned.
4. Serve warm.

Quesadillas

Ingredients:

1 corn or flour tortilla for each child

¼ lb. Jack cheese, grated

Procedure:

Preheat greased skillet to 350°.

1. Fill 1 to 2 tortillas with a tablespoon of the cheese.
2. Fold tortillas.
3. Fry quesadilla on both sides until cheese melts.
4. Serve warm.

Capirotada (Mexican Bread Pudding)

Ingredients:

6 to 10 slices dried bread *or* 6 flour tortillas

2 cups brown sugar

2 tsp. cinnamon

2 cups grated cheese

1 cup raisins

½ cup pinons *or* chopped pecans

2 cups water

6 T. butter, oleo, or oil

Procedure:

1. Mix sugar, cinnamon, and water.
2. Spread ⅙ mixture of cheese, raisins, butter, and nuts on tortillas.
3. Stack and repeat until all ingredients are used.
4. Pour syrup over the entire dish.
5. Bake for 20–30 minutes at 350°.
6. Serve warm.

Navajo Fry Bread
Ingredients:

1 cup flour

1 tsp. baking powder

½ tsp. salt

½ cup lukewarm water

Procedure:

1. Mix all ingredients.
2. Roll out dough to ¼–inch thickness.
3. Cut into 2-inch squares.
4. Fry in hot oil until puffy.
5. Turn and brown on other side.
6. Drain on paper towels.
7. Serve warm.

Tsukemons (Japanese Pickles)
Ingredients:

¼ cup salt

½ cup sugar

1 T. white vinegar

3 cups boiling water

1 large stalk Chinese celery or one small head of cabbage

Procedure:

1. Mix the salt, sugar, vinegar, and water together; stir until the salt and sugar have dissolved.
2. Cut the cabbage in half through the heart, then in half again.
3. Soak the cabbage in the solution for 1–1½ days.
4. Remove from the solution, drain, and refrigerate.
5. Cut the cabbage into 1-inch sections and serve with soy sauce.

West African Banana Puffs
Ingredients:

½ cup all-purpose flour

2 T. sugar

1 egg

⅓ cup milk

1 cup very ripe banana, peeled and mashed

Oil (for frying)

Procedure:

1. Combine flour and sugar in a bowl.
2. Add egg and milk.
3. Stir in the bananas.
4. Form the puffs.
5. Deep fry in oil at 375° for 3 minutes to a rich golden brown.
6. Drain on a paper towel.
7. Sprinkle with confectioners' sugar.
8. Enjoy!

TEACHER RESOURCES
Field Trip Ideas

1. Locate a person or establishment that cuts and styles hair for both males and females in the community. Invite them to bring in tools for a demonstration or visit their place of business with the class. Focus on the desire to have a pleasant appearance. Avoid stereotyping either male or female behaviors about hair care.
2. Visit a fitness establishment, pointing out how people weigh themselves and work out to improve their physical appearance and health.
3. Locate a store near your school where children can see themselves from different angles in three-sided mirrors.

Classroom Visitors

1. Have a photographer visit the classroom and take pictures of individuals. Provide combs and brushes for arranging hair at the last minute and be sure to point out positive things about each child as pictures are taken.

Children's Books

Cretan, G. Y. *Me, Myself and I.* New York: William Morrow, 1969.

Erickson, K., and M. Roffer. *I Can Settle Down.* New York: Scholastic, 1985.

Erickson, K., and M. Roffer. *I Can Do Something When There's Nothing to Do.* New York: Scholastic, 1985.

Ets, M. H. *Just Me.* New York: Viking, 1965.

Hallinan, P. K. *I'm Glad to Be Me.* Chicago: Childrens Press, 1977.

Keats, E. J. *Peter's Chair.* New York: Harper and Row, 1967.

McBurney-Green, M. *Is It Hard? Is It Easy?* New York: Addison-Wesley, 1960.

Moore, L., and P. Charlip. *Hooray for Me!* New York: Parents, 1975.

Timmons, C. *The Me Book.* Chicago: Encyclopedia Britannica, 1974.

Weismann, J. *All About Me.* Mt. Rainer, MD: Gryphon House, 1981.

Adult References

Briggs, D. *Your Child's Self-Esteem.* Garden City, NJ: Doubleday, 1975.

Clarke, J. I. *Self-Esteem: A Family Affair.* New York: Winston Press, 1978.

Kendall, F. *Diversity in the Classroom. A Multicultural Approach to the Education of Young Children.* New York: Teacher's College Press, 1983.

Kostelnik, M., L. Stein, A. Whiren, and A. Soderman. *Guiding Children's Social Development.* Cincinnati: South-Western Publishing Company, 1988.

Loo, M. *Meals of Many Lands.* Colorado Springs, CO: Current Publishing Company, 1978.

Zimbardo, P., and S. Radl. *The Shy Child.* Garden City, NJ: Doubleday, 1982.

Chapter 2

Families

•

Where's the whole family?
Where's the whole family?
Here we are! Here we are!

•

veryone is a member of a family. Whether it be large or small, extended, blended, or nuclear, or of traditional or nontraditional configuration, the family unit is fundamental to all human societies. Because children are very interested in learning about things that relate directly to their lives, being part of a family is a natural and logical topic for them to study.

PURPOSE

There are several ways to learn about families. One is to look inward and investigate individual family members: who they are, what their relationships are to one another, and what they do for and with each other. A second approach is to compare families: how they are alike, how they are different, what traditions they share, how their histories are unique. This unit includes activities to support each focus.

IMPLEMENTATION

The Families theme can be implemented in many ways.

Option One: Concentrate on the TFPs related to family life. Focus on family composition and on the roles and interrelationships people have within the family. The study of their immediate family is most relevant for younger children, whereas older children can expand their information to include more distant family members.

Option Two: Extend the family study by emphasizing family traditions for a second week or two. One family tradition with which most children are familiar is the birthday celebration. Although particular customs differ across cultures, the anniversary of a child's arrival in the family is recognized almost universally. Many of the activities center on this all-important day. When planning to carry out this option, teachers should be sensitive to religions that forbid birthday celebrations.

Option Three: Move from a one- or two-week study of human families into an investigation of animal families. Focus on animals that have a family life, such as gorillas, wolves, and most kinds of birds. Compare the role of human parents in teaching their young vital skills with animal parents who, in many cases, must do the same. Examine nurturing behaviors.

TERMS, FACTS, AND PRINCIPLES

General Information

1. A family is a group of two or more people joined by bonds of love and/or kinship.
2. Every person is a member of a family; some people are part of more than one family.
3. Families exist all over the world.
4. Families may differ from one another in size, composition, life-style, rules, traditions, beliefs, and customs.
5. Members of a family are called relatives.
6. Some family members are living.
*7. Some members of your family lived long ago. They are called ancestors.
8. People in a family have special names that identify their relationship within the family. Some of these include: mother, father, husband, wife, child (or offspring), sister, brother, aunt, uncle, grandmother, grandfather, cousin, niece, nephew, parent, stepmother, stepfather, half-sister, half-brother, in-law. A person may have more than one relationship within the family (son and brother).
9. Family members may live in the same or different households.
*10. Families change through birth, death, separation, adoption, marriage, divorce.
*11. Some family relationships can change, such as that of husband and wife.
12. Some family relationships are constant such as parent and child, grandparent and grandchild, and brother and sister.
*13. As people grow older their family roles often expand. For example, children may grow up to have children of their own—they are now parents as well as offspring.
14. Some people have friends that they think of as members of their family.

15. Some people think of pets as family.

16. Some of the people you know are part of your family, some are friends, some are acquaintances.

17. Some of the people you care about and who care about you are part of your family, and some are not family members.

18. Family members are like one another in some ways and different in others.
    a. They may or may not be the same gender or age.
    b. They may have similar or different names.
    c. They may have similar or different physical or personality characteristics.
    d. They may have similar or different interests and preferences.

*19. Sometimes people have certain characteristics that remind others of how another family member looks or behaves.

*20. Family members often develop unique ways of communicating verbally with one another, such as using family nicknames or special words for activities and objects.

21. Family members who do not live together sometimes communicate by letter or telephone, or through others.

*22. Family members often develop special ways of communicating nonverbally with one another that are understandable only to each other.

23. Family members do some things with each other, some things alone, and some things with people outside the family.

24. Family members express a variety of feelings toward each other at different times.

25. Family members sometimes agree and at other times disagree with one another.

26. Family members often teach one another new things.

27. Family members depend upon one another in different ways for different things.

28. Family members can help each other in particular ways by: caring for their own things, cooking meals, earning money to pay for the family's expenses, entertaining each other, enjoying each other, comforting each other when they are unhappy, being cooperative, sharing responsibilities.

29. Families often develop unique ways of doing certain things. Sometimes they do things the same way other families do them.

Family Traditions

30. A tradition is a long-established custom or practice that is repeated over time.

31. Traditions are important to family life.

32. All families have traditions, such as special songs, celebrations, foods, activities, stories, recollections, routines, rules, beliefs, and values.

33. Family celebrations are often governed by tradition.
    a. Particular foods may be prepared.
    b. A particular sequence of events may be followed.
    c. Special clothing may be worn.
    d. Special songs may be sung.
    e. Special stories may be told.
    f. People may have special roles within the celebration.
    g. Special activities may be carried out.
    h. Languages other than English may be spoken.

34. Some family traditions are similar to those in other families and some are unique.

*35. A family's religious and/or cultural heritage influences the traditions it adopts.

36. The same custom may have different importance in different families.

37. Traditions help make certain family events more predictable.

*38. Traditions give families a sense of continuity with past and future generations.

39. Traditions often help family members feel close to one another.

*40. The more often people follow a tradition, the more likely they are to follow it again.

*41. Some traditions have been developed over a number of generations and some are relatively new.

*42. The origins of some traditions have been forgotten while the origins of others are still remembered.

43. Some traditions are very elaborate; others are quite simple.

44. Some traditional practices require a lot of preparation; others can be carried out with no advance planning.

45. Sometimes outsiders are invited to participate in a family tradition and sometimes only the family participates.

46. Some family traditions involve all of the family members and others involve only certain family members.

*47. Different family members derive pleasure from different aspects of the same family traditions.

*48. Traditions often have symbolic meaning.

49. Adult family members often are the ones who tell children about what their family traditions were like in the past.

50. Every family has stories or anecdotes about how certain traditions developed or how certain family members were involved in family traditions.

51. Photographs, home movies, video, or tape recordings are often used to record traditional family events.

*52. Traditions can be changed.
   a. Sometimes families change a tradition to fit their own circumstances.
   b. Sometimes families add new practices to the family's traditions.
   c. Sometimes families stop practicing a custom.

*53. People's familiarity with other people's traditions varies.

54. Many people are interested in sharing their family traditions with others.

55. Many people are interested in learning about the traditions of other families.

ACTIVITY IDEAS

Aesthetics

1. **The Family in the Dell.** This is an adaptation of the traditional singing game "The Farmer in the Dell." Have children form a large circle around one child who portrays the mother or father. Move to the left around the child while singing. Substitute the word "family" for "farmer" in the song. The first child chooses another to accompany him or her into the center and names that child as a family member. After each new member joins the "family," he or she picks the next person. An extension of this game is to have each new member demonstrate a physical action (jumping, spinning, bending, etc.) that the rest of the group imitates. This can be done to the refrain "Hi, ho the derry-o, the family in the dell." Younger children may be more successful if at first they sit in a circle instead of standing up and moving around the circle holding hands. Also, the teacher may choose the children. Older children can make their own choices and should be encouraged to think of more distant family relations (second cousins, mother-in-law, nephew, etc.)

2. **Lullabye and Goodnight.** Make a collection of lullabies that children and their families sing. Record a family member singing each one. If possible, obtain written translations of lullabies in languages other than English. Teach some to the children. Compile all the songs into a booklet that children can illustrate and take home.

3. **Famous Families.** Get reproductions of paintings, photographs, sculptures, or other artistic interpretations of family subjects from the library, a poster store, local artists, or parents. Designate a special place in the classroom for displaying these works. Rotate the display regularly. Discuss the artwork with the children, either individually or as a group, pointing out some ways the artist has portrayed familial relationships or other aspects of family life. Be positive in your discussion. Encourage children to express their interpretation or opinion of the piece in question. As a follow-up activity, have art materials (paints, markers, modeling clay, etc.) available for children to use to portray their own ideas of a family.

4. **Family Fun Book.** After explaining what a joke is (if children don't already know) and giving some examples, ask the children to bring in some jokes that either they or a family member has told. Give the children a time and place to communicate their jokes to the class. Expect that children will vary in their joke-telling abilities and in their notions of what is humorous. Be tolerant of these differences. For older children, follow up by collecting jokes and

descriptions of funny occurrences. Record these in the story corner "Fun Book" that you keep in the classroom. Continue adding to this book throughout the year.

5. *Funny Family Figures.* Cut out pictures of individual people from magazines or other sources. Separate the heads from the bodies of the figures. Present these to children using a tray for heads and a tray for bodies. Tell them to put together people in the funniest way they can think of. Provide glue and construction paper for individual projects or a mural-sized piece of paper for a group effort. More experienced children will benefit from cutting the figures out and apart themselves. Give children opportunities to tell why they think their figures are funny.

Affective

1. *Family Feelings.* Begin this activity with a discussion of emotions. Include both positive and negative emotions as you talk. Explain that people in a family sometimes like the things other family members do, and sometimes they don't. Provide one or more of the following phrases for the children to complete: "I like it when my family . . .," "I don't like it when my family . . .," "Something special about my *family member* is . . .," "It makes me mad when my *family member* . . . ." The child can draw or dictate the remainder of each open-ended sentence. Show acceptance of each child's expression of his or her emotions by acknowledging rather than correcting or trying to talk them out of expressing strong or negative emotions.

2. *Family Festivities.* Ask children to bring in a photograph taken at a family celebration. Display these where children can see them. Encourage children to look at and discuss the pictures. Use open-ended statements, such as "Tell me about this" or "Tell me what the people are doing" to elicit descriptions. Suggest that children talk about why the occasion was special and about their role in the celebration. Older children could find out from classmates about similar celebrations in their families. During these latter discussions focus both on similarities and differences.

Make comments that are specific and non-judgmental. Encourage children to do the same. ("I noticed that you had streamers at your party. Look at Tyrone's picture—he also had streamers.")

3. *Family Heirlooms.* Have children bring in an item that has been handed down from another generation. Set aside a place in the classroom for displaying these. Establish rules for how other children may or may not handle the items. Ask each child to talk about the significance of the item to their family. Record this on a card or paper placed near the object. A child who brings in an heirloom may be designated "curator" for the day. His or her job is to explain the treasure to others. This activity works best when carried out over several days in order to give each child who wishes to a chance to participate.

4. *Family Photos.* Have each child identify family members by name and relationship in photographs or (with older children) drawn pictures. Display these on a bulletin board where all children can see. Encourage children to include pictures of their family in the broadest sense: family pets, distant relatives, honorary members, etc. Suggest that children look for similarities between their families and other people's families. At the end of the unit, put the pictures and stories in an album to keep until the end of the school year. Children will enjoy referring to these pictures again and again.

5. *Visiting Day.* Send a written invitation to parents inviting family members to come to school for a visit during the study of this theme. You can plan for all the visitors to come on one particular day or spread the visits out over the course of the unit. Encourage each child to introduce his or her family member to the group. Discuss the person's relationship to the child and to other family members. Encourage the visitors to participate in classroom activities. Encourage variety (grandparents, aunts, etc.) as well as representation from as many families as possible.

6. *Brothers and Sisters.* Select one or more books about younger and older siblings (*Peter's Chair* by Ezra Jack Keats, *Nobody Asked Me if I Wanted a Baby Sister* by Martha Alexander, *She Come Bringing*

Me that Little Baby Girl by Eloise Greenfield). Invite the children to listen to the story. Introduce the book by saying, "Some of you have brothers and sisters who are older than you. Some of you have younger brothers and sisters. Some of you don't have brothers and sisters. This is a story about a boy who has a new baby sister in his family. After I read the story, we can talk about brothers and sisters." Read the story, using your voice and facial expression to portray the feelings of the characters. Begin a discussion by talking about children's individual experiences: "Kyle, You have a new baby brother. Tell us about being a big brother." "Sometimes the youngest in the family is called the baby, even when he or she isn't a baby anymore. Are any of you called the baby in your family? How does that make you feel? What are some good things about being the baby? Elena is going to have a baby brother or sister soon. What do you think it will be like to be a big sister, Elena?" Relate children's experiences to those in the book as appropriate. Acknowledge and interpret children's feelings during the discussion: "Sometimes you feel lonely when everyone is busy with the baby." Help children figure out ways to cope with negative emotions: "What might help you feel better when your mother is busy?"

Cognition

1. *We are a Family.* Cut out pictures depicting a variety of family compositions (couples without children, single parents with a child or children, grandparents with grandchild, male head-of-household, traditional family). Include white, African-American, Hispanic, and Asian families. Glue each picture on a card for ease of handling. Present these to children with directions for classifying them into groups that are alike in some way.

   If children have difficulty with this task, provide them with pictures of individuals and tell them to form family groups. Provide cards, as described above, or pictures they can glue onto paper.

Other suggestions for sorting activities relevant to the family unit are:

- pictures of family celebrations or other events (such as vacations)
- clothing
- foods their family likes or dislikes.

2. *All Kinds of Families.* Read the book *Families* by Meredith Tax to the children. Later in the day, make the book available to children along with paper, markers, paste, scissors, and magazines featuring both people and animals. Invite each child or a small group of children to select a page or two from the story at random. Ask them to create a family from pictures or drawings that corresponds to the one described on those pages. As more than one child or group completes a "family portrait," talk with the children about all the different forms families may take.

3. *We Like to Eat.* This activity encourages children to sample food that may not be familiar to them and so provides a multi-cultural experience. Request that families send in a recipe or prepare a food item traditional to their family or culture for children to taste in the classroom. They may cook this at home or, depending on your access to a kitchen, prepare the food at school. Encourage the child whose family has shared food or a recipe to tell about his or her perceptions of its traditional significance. Encourage all children to sample the food and to examine and smell it. If children ask questions about the food, refer them to the child whose family shared it.

   Request, especially, that foods from many cultures that include unusual ingredients be shared. Talk about the reasons certain foods are associated with different countries, holidays, religions, or cultures. You may wish to highlight one special food each day, or to plan a "banquet" and serve many new foods. If possible, culminate the study of families and family traditions with a potluck supper, where foods of many cultures are offered and enjoyed.

4. *Far From Home.* Cut out magazine pictures of people and places outside the home, such as a business office, library,

supermarket, school, doctor's office, or other locations where children and/or adults may spend time. Display the materials, inviting children to look at and explore them. Help children label the pieces. Say, "Today we have some places where people in the family might go. What do you think this place is? You know it's a school. How about this one?" and so on. "Here are the people who go to these places. Look and see who they might be in the family. You noticed there is a daddy and a mom. There are also children here." Give children time to see everything. Next, encourage children to put the family members into the places. Say, "Decide where the people will go. Put the family into the places where you think they might go." Ask children to tell why they put certain people in certain places. Say, "Tell me about this, Mary. You put the daddy in the store. Why would he go there? Oh, you know in some families, the daddy shops for the food. What is another place a daddy could go?" Continue with the other family members.

Encourage children who are having trouble or who can't place a family member outside the home to tell some other place he or she thinks that member may go. Ask them to tell why and under what circumstances. "When does grandma go to the market? Why does the baby go to the doctor's office?"

5. *Happy Holiday.* Provide large magazine cutouts or photos of families celebrating various traditions, such as birthdays, Halloween, Hanukkah, Christmas, Thanksgiving, family reunions, Kwanzaa, Fourth of July, or Cinco de Mayo. Add smaller pictures of things associated with these traditions, such as sparklers, flags, Christmas tree, menorah, candles, picnic table with lots of food on it, costume, or a candy bag. Spread the celebration pictures on a table. Invite one or two children to examine them. After a few minutes, bring out the smaller pictures. Hold one up for the children to see.

Ask a child to look again at the large pictures and show you the one with which he or she thinks the small picture belongs. Encourage explanations and acknowledge all ideas. Point out that different families have different traditions, and some differ in the ways they carry out the same tradition.

Direct the child to place the small pictures on the corresponding larger picture. Two children may want to work together, matching the objects to their traditional circumstances. Encourage decision making about where small pictures best belong. Provide several or all of the small pictures at once if the children seem comfortable with the procedure. Challenge children to identify objects that could be associated with more than one of the tradition pictures. Continue encouraging descriptions and explanations as the children work: "Tell me why you've decided the flowers belong here." "Tell me about the way your family celebrates Cinco de Mayo. Does your family observe Cinco de Mayo in a different way? Tell me one way it is different." "Tell me one thing you always do at Hanukkah. Tell me one thing you sometimes do." Comment on the similarities and differences noted in children's descriptions of family traditions.

6. *Family Fundamentals.* Prior to introducing the activity, make a large number of family-member silhouettes using the outlines provided in Figures 2.1a and 2.1b. Provide children with a selection of silhouettes, glue sticks, and long sheets of butcher paper on which to glue their pictographs.

Introduce the activity by explaining that families differ in lots of ways. Some have only two people, some have many; some have brothers and sisters, some don't. Sometimes other people join the household, such as a grandparent, aunt, uncle, or stepbrother. People in the family don't always live in the same house. Some families live with people who are not in their family. And so on. Work with each child to make a pictograph showing who is in his or her family. Encourage children to cut or tear out the silhouettes if they are able, or precut the silhouettes and ask children only to glue them on the paper. *Accept all ideas about whom children want to include.* Take advantage of opportunities to talk about extended families, adoption, and step-families. Some children may want to include pets as family members.

Family Silhouettes

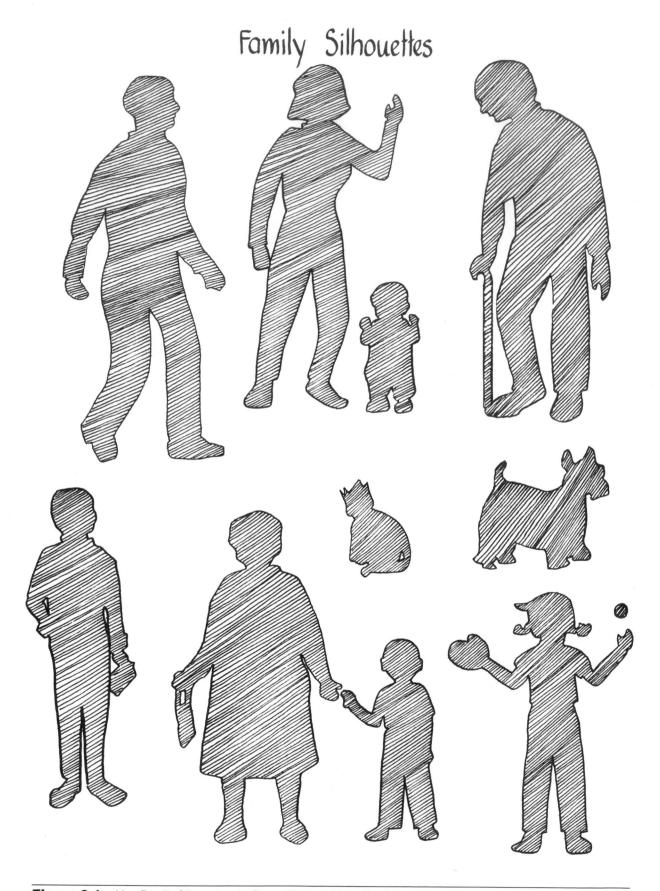

Figure 2.1a *Use Family Silhouettes to Show Who's in Your Family*

Figure 2.1b *More Family Silhouettes*

With younger children, focus on the immediate family. Encourage older children to compare pictographs with their friends, noting the different silhouettes they used. Hang the completed pictographs together as a display so that children can refer back to and discuss them.

Construction

1. *Make-a-Meal.* Cut a variety of food pictures from magazines. Be sure to include ethnic specialties that represent the backgrounds of the children in your group. Talk with children about the traditions celebrated in their families and about the foods they eat. Elicit from them some ethnic favorites that they and their families enjoy on a regular basis. Present the pictures and instruct the children to put together a meal that their family might eat. Children can glue the pictures on paper plates. Older children can select and cut out pictures by themselves. As a follow-up activity, children can compare the food on each other's plates and discuss the similarities and differences they discover. You might use plastic food instead of the food pictures. Children could then arrange and rearrange the food as they wish. As an extension, children can construct a meal based on foods that different family members prefer. Have them identify which family member prefers which food item.

2. *Family Faces.* Precede this project with discussions about the personalities, preferences, and appearances of family members. Provide children with materials to make puppets or masks on a stick, including paper plates with eyes cut out, popsicle sticks or tongue depressors, staples and stapler to fasten sticks on the plates, and markers, glue, felt, yarn, paper, and fabric. Place a child-sized mirror in the area. Suggest that children re-create the face of a family member, beginning with such features as hair, eyes, mouth, mustache or beard, smile, or frown. Older children may wish to look at actual photographs for inspiration. In addition, they may be able to portray other characteristics of disposition or personality. Younger children will be most successful when you point out the features of their own face in the mirror. Expect that children will vary greatly in their ability to reconstruct a face. Be sure to accept all attempts as valid and worthy of encouragement.

*3. *Family Flags.*

General Purpose: To encourage children to clarify concepts of family traditions while creating a tangible, representational product.

TFPs: 30, 31, 32, 33, 35.

Materials: Nation or state flags (or flag pictures); illustrations of "coats of arms"; industrial, agricultural, or craft symbols; recreational symbols; location symbols (beach, mountains, etc.); cloth or paper cut into flag shapes; crayons; stickers; glue.

Procedure:

a. Introduce the activity with a whole-group discussion of symbols that represent occupations, recreational activities, places, values, and ideals (generosity, friendship, etc.). Show the group pictures of emblems that people have designed to represent things they value. Invite children to tell why they think certain items were chosen for emblems. Explain the symbolization of the stars and stripes in the American flag and in any other flags you have.

b. Tell children that they will have a chance to design a flag that represents their families. This can be called a family emblem or a coat of arms. You may want to tell children that long ago, some people wore coats of arms over their armor (special protective clothing) or carried flags made of light fabric and decorated with family or personal symbols. These told others the important traditions and beliefs in their family.

c. Provide the materials at a table. As children join you, explain that they should think of objects or events that have special importance or meaning to their families. Encourage children to begin drawing the things they think of or selecting magazine pictures or stickers that represent them.

d. Point out that each child's flag is a "family emblem" that symbolizes ways their family is special or different from others. Encourage children to explain their symbols to each other or to you.

Hint for Success:
- Some children may be uncertain about how to proceed. Suggest some categories that may remind them of special family values: foods that are always served at celebrations; animals that the family has as pets; favorite places the family visits like the forest or beach. Stick figures representing each family member could be drawn to represent the family, perhaps accompanied by a picture of the family home.

How to Simplify this Activity:
- Ask children to make a collage of family symbols instead of a flag. Invite them to tear pictures from magazines, rather than cut them out.
- Focus on the most concrete aspects of family life, such as activities and physical attributes of family members.

How to Extend this Activity:
- Focus on more abstract concepts, such as family attitudes like loyalty and honesty. Discuss with the children ways of symbolizing these less concrete ideas.
- Implement this activity over a period of time, so that children may add to their family flag as they learn more about their own families.

Language
1. *Letters to Loved Ones.* Introduce this activity by reading to the group a letter you have received or are going to send. Explain the function of mail in communicating with people over long distances. Ask children to bring in the name and address of someone they know who lives elsewhere. Talk to them about things they might like to tell a family member who does not necessarily live at their home (things they did at school, on vacation, their feelings). Elicit a variety of ideas so that children can choose one that interests them. Prompt children's thinking by suggesting a topic or opening line. The letters may be written in either of two ways. The child may dictate a message to an adult and then illustrate it. Or, the child may "write" a letter in his or her own fashion. Do not expect accurate writing and spelling. Rather, encourage children to express themselves in some written form. If this latter approach is chosen, send an explanatory note to the recipient of the letter. Include a request that the "letter" be answered. In either case, actually mail the letters.

2. *Special Names for Special People.* Gather the children in a group. Explain to them that people sometimes call the other people in their families by special names. Ask the children, one at a time, to tell what they call their grandparents, for instance. Make a list, including all the names, even if some are repeated. Talk about how all the names represent the same family relationship, and about how each name represents a special family member.

   With the children, count up and total the number of different names and the number of names that are the same. Make a graph for counting or comparing. Extend the activity by asking the children to draw pictures of their grandparents or to bring in a relevant photo. Label each picture with the child's name and the name they use for their grandparent. Display these pictures on a bulletin board.

3. *Many Happy Returns.* Talk with children about birthdays and the customs surrounding their own birthdays. Tell them that people say "Happy Birthday" to each other in many countries and that they use different languages. If children in your group speak languages other than English at home, find out how to say "Happy Birthday" in those languages. Teach them one or several of the following birthday greetings:

   French—*Bon Anniversaire* (Bon Anna-verse-air)
   German—*Viel Glück Zum Geburtstag* (Feel Glook Zoom Ge-Birds-Tog)
   Spanish—*Feliz Cumpleaños* (Fay-Lease Come-Play-Ah-No)
   Italian—*Felice Compleanno* (Fay-Lee-Chay Come-Play-Ah-No)
   Korean—*Saeng Il Chucka Ham-ni Da*

Mandarin Chinese—*Shung er Kuhy le*
Thai—*Sook-sun/Wun-gird* (said in an even tempo using a "sing-song" tone.)
Japanese—*Otanjobi Omedeto*

4. *Faraway Phoning.* Introduce the activity with a puppet skit or flannel-board story that presents a situation, such as "Bradley's grandparents live far away. Sometimes he wishes he could tell them about a special thing that happens. Think of a way that Bradley could share his ideas." The children may suggest making a phone call. Role-play a call with imaginary telephones, asking children for suggestions about how to proceed and what to say. Encourage them to give a greeting, then a message, and finally a way to close the call. Provide telephones for practicing.

   If children seem reluctant to talk "over the phone," help them by taking one of the roles yourself or by practicing with the child, in advance, some conversational phrases.

5. *The Flannel Family.* Purchase or create figures out of felt or Pellon of people and pets to represent various family configurations on a flannel board, and provide paper and writing tools. Place a different type of family on the felt board every day, telling a story about each family for the first few days. Then write a whole-group story to which all children contribute an idea. Read the story back to the children and post it within their view. Encourage children to "read" the story to each other. To extend the activity, repeat the above procedure, having children dictate individual stories.

6. *My Family Album.* This activity encourages children to use comparative vocabulary when describing their place in their family. Provide paper or booklets for each child. Use headings such as "In my family I am older than my . . .," "I am younger than my . . .," "I am taller than my. . . ." Children can dictate their responses and then illustrate their ideas.

7. *Find That Name.* Discuss the first names of all the children in the group. Point out names that are identical or similar in some way. Have children ask their family to tell them (and write down) names that are

popular within their family. Invite children to share their lists with the group the next day. Post the children's lists and help them find matching names between one family's list and the others.

8. *Remembering Story Events.* Read to the children the book *Aunt Nina and Her Nephews and Nieces* by Franz Brandenburg. Another day, draw on a large piece of easel paper an outline of a house that includes a basement, first and second floors, and an attic. (Figure 2.2) Prior to reading the story a second time, explain to the children that their job will be to listen carefully for what the nephews and nieces find at each level of Aunt Nina's house. Point to the outline, naming each segment of the house, starting in the basement. Read the story all the way through. Do not interrupt your reading to draw children's attention to any particular details.

   When the story is over, ask children where the nieces and nephews began their search for Fluffy, the cat. If they have trouble remembering, show them how to refer back to the story to find out. Starting in the basement and proceeding to the attic, ask the children to recall what was found in each place. Write their ideas on the corresponding part of the outline. Encourage children to provide as much detail as possible. For instance, if they remember that animals were found in the basement, help them remember what kind they were. Periodically refer to the book to clarify details. This activity could be modified by using cut-out pictures or simple line drawings to represent the children's ideas rather than written words. Another variation is to offer children choices of items found at each level and ask them to determine which are correct ("In the basement did the nephews and nieces find toys or live animals?").

9. *Family Journals.* Prepare story kits that include a children's storybook, a simple prop related to something in the story, a pencil, and a notebook or loose-leaf pages. Put the title of the story at the top of the notebook. Send the kits home, rotating them so that within a month or two, every child has had an opportunity to use one. Read the journal entries to the children as

a stimulus to using the kit and to demonstrate that their ideas and words are important enough to be preserved. Include these directions for parents:

Date:

Dear _____ ,

It is _____'s turn to bring home a story kit! Enclosed you will find a book, some pages of a school journal, a special marking pen with which to write on the journal pages, and one or more props for your child to use to reenact parts of the story that you read to him or her. Read the book to your child. Make the prop(s) available for her or him to use as she or he recalls the story. Be an active audience. Praise your child for parts of the story that he or she remembers. Encourage him or her to tell or act out the story for you. Remind him or her of relevant parts of the story line. After several rereadings and reenactments of the story, ask your child to tell about the part of the story kit that he or she liked best. Write the words on journal pages. Include some information about how and where the props were used. Your child might enjoy retelling the story as you write his or her words in the journal. In class, we will all take time to read about your child's "story adventure." We hope you enjoy this activity!

Materials Enclosed: _____

Please Return By: _____

---

10. ***Chants and Games.***
    a. "Aunt Dinah's Gone."
       The following chant is done in a call-response manner. On the line "Well she left like this," the leader strikes a pose that the rest of the group imitates. On the next line, the leader changes poses, and the group follows. All join in on the chorus. On the line "Gonna shake and shimmy," the leader moves according to his or her idea of what that means. Substitute the leader's name for Aunt Dinah, using "Uncle" when appropriate.

       Aunt Dinah's gone. (Say again)
       Well how did she leave? (Say again)
       Well she left like this. (Say again)

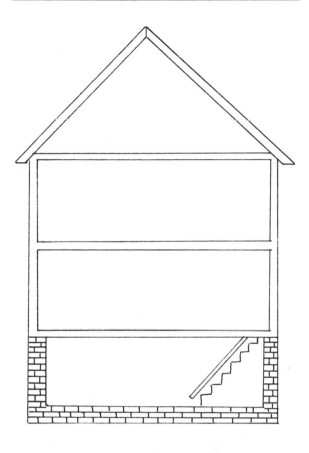

Figure 2.2 *House Outline for Remembering the Story*

Chorus:
She lives in the country
Gonna move to town
Gonna shake and shimmy
Till the sun goes down

b. "Hush Little Baby"
   This lullaby has been sung all over the southern United States. It is equally delightful as a chant if you don't know the tune.

   Hush little baby, don't say a word. (Mama's) (Papa's) going to buy you a mockingbird.

   If that mocking bird don't sing, (Mama's) (Papa's) going to buy you a diamond ring.

   If that diamond ring turns brass, (Mama's) (Papa's) going to buy you a looking glass.

If that looking glass gets broke,
(Mama's) (Papa's) going to buy you a
Billy goat.

If that Billy goat won't pull,
(Mama's) (Papa's) going to buy you a
cart and bull.

If that cart and bull turns over,
(Mama's) (Papa's) going to buy you a
dog named Rover.

If that dog named Rover won't bark,
(Mama's) (Papa's) going to buy you a
horse and cart.

If that horse and cart falls down,
you'll still be the sweetest little baby in
town.

c. "Down Came a Lady"
This chant may be accompanied by a
circle game. One child stands in the
middle with the rest circling around and
chanting:

Down came a lady
Down came a two
Down came old Daniel's wife
And she was dressed in blue

At the word "blue," the child in the
middle points to someone in the circle,
substituting another color word that
corresponds to the chosen child's clothing. That child chooses the next and so
on until all the children are in the center.

*11. *Family Histories.*
General Purpose: To expose children to
family traditions and ways they can be
preserved.

TFPs: 30–34, 48–50.

Materials: A portable tape recorder that
families can borrow, blank tapes, labeling pen.

Procedure:
a. Introduce the activity to families in a
newsletter or on a posted sign. Invite
them to borrow a tape recorder and/or
obtain blank tapes from you, then to
record descriptions of childhood traditions as recalled by grandparents, parents, and/or siblings of the child in your
group. Include a list of suggestions for
the taping. For instance, suggest that
they tell about how a Christmas tree
was obtained, set up, and decorated;
describe customs observed for birthday
celebrations; or tell about special foods
that were prepared for a cultural or religious observation. They could talk
about ways that the observance of Halloween has changed over the years or
describe a trip they took regularly with
their family as a child.

b. Explain to children that they can encourage their own families to help the
class build a "history library" of taped
recollections about old and evolving
family traditions. Explain that children
will take turns sharing their family
recordings with their friends at school.

c. As recordings are returned, set aside a
special sharing time during large-group
time or in a language center in your
room. Invite the child whose family has
contributed the recording to provide
further information about the speakers
or about their perceptions of the described traditions as they are currently
observed in the family.

Hints for Success:
- Plan to carry out this activity over several weeks, so that families do not feel
time pressure and each family will have
an opportunity to participate.

- Remind listeners that everyone has some
unique and special ways of observing
particular traditions with their family.
There are no right or wrong ways to
observe traditions.

How to Simplify this Activity:
- Concentrate on birthday celebrations.

How to Extend this Activity:
- Hold discussions about the recorded
histories.

- Help children identify similarities and
differences in how families carry out
their traditions.

- Keep a record of classroom traditions, such as rules, routines, and special (but regular) classroom practices (every Friday a story is read).

Physical

1. *"Mother/Father May I?"* Traditionally, this game is played outdoors, but may be adapted to an indoor space, such as a hallway or gym. The leader, or "mother/father," stands at one end, while the other players line up beside one another at the other end of the area. (Using a real or imaginary "starting line" helps children know where to begin.) "Mother/father" issues directions to one player at a time. "Greg, you may take (number of steps) (type of steps)." The child responds: "Mother/father may I?" Mother/father responds: "Yes, you may" or "No, you may not. Take _____ steps instead." Upon receiving a positive response, the designated child follows the directions. If the child moves without permission, he or she must return to the starting line. The object of the game is for the players to reach the leader. Older children enjoy an additional part of the game. When close enough, the player tags "mother/father," and they race for the starting line. If "mother/father" tags the player, that person becomes the leader for the next round. With younger children, focus on their physical movements. The teacher should model the leader role for a while until children gain experience. The traditional steps used are as follows:

Baby step—toe to heel
Giant step—as large as possible
Banana splits—slide one foot forward as far as possible
Fire engines—run until "Mother/Father" says "stop"
Umbrella step—place forefinger on top of head and spin around once
Frog leaps—two-footed jump
Bunny steps—one-footed hop

In addition, children may enjoy creating their own steps.

2. *Lost and Found.* This activity focuses on the physical process of cutting. Design simple paths of varying complexities on paper. Draw a simple picture of the child or family at the beginning of the path and the object of the search at the end. Make up stories about these pictures to motivate children to cut along the path. Some possible scenarios include:

- Help the family find its home.
- Show the child the way to grandma's or grandpa's house.
- Help the lost children find their parent(s).
- Bring the family together for a reunion.

Invite children to cut through the middle of the path, beginning at the starting point and cutting to the end. Encourage the children to stay in the center of the path as they cut. Provide multiple sheets of each cut type so children have more than one chance to try the same one.

The examples in Figures 2.3a, 2.3b, and 2.3c range from simple to more complex.

Making the paths narrower or including more turns increases their complexity.

3. *Holiday Hang-ups.* Many fine-motor activities can center around traditional decorations. Introduce the activity by telling children about the different holidays celebrated by people in this country, as well as around the world. Traditional decorations are often associated with these holidays. For example, many celebrations occur during the winter (Christmas, Hanukkah, Kwanzaa, etc.), each of which involves the use of light in some form. Predraw (or have children draw) candle shapes to decorate and cut out. Place these on a holiday mural. A Japanese tradition is the making of origami birds to celebrate peace.

Be alert to racial, ethnic, or religious stereotyping when planning holiday decorations. An example of cultural insensitivity is the "Indian headdress" that many school children make and wear around Thanksgiving. Some Native Americans find this offensive and an inaccurate representation of their culture and history. Better decorations for this time of year might

Lost and Found Pathtracing Level One

Figure 2.3a *Help the Family Find Its Home*

Lost and Found Pathtracing Level Two

Figure 2.3b *Cut the Path from the Family to the Car*

Lost and Found Pathtracing Level Three

Figure 2.3c *Help Each Family Member Find Their Dog*

be fruits and vegetables that represent the harvest bounty in your particular region of the country. Other decorations to make include:

Cherry Blossom Scroll

Scroll paintings hang in many Japanese homes. To make a scroll, take a long, narrow strip of white paper or cloth (approximately eighteen by six inches). Fasten it at the top and bottom to disposable wooden chopsticks or twigs that are slightly longer than the paper is wide. Attach string to the outside corners of the top stick and tie the ends together to form a triangle. (Figure 2.4)

Instruct children to paint a picture of a branch with twigs (they can use paint or ink) by dragging a thin brush tip from top to bottom on the page. Children can then make blossoms out of pieces of pink or white tissue or crêpe paper about one inch in diameter and glue them on the branches. These represent cherry blossoms, a traditional Japanese design.

Paper Flowers

Paper flowers are traditional Mexican decorations. To make simple paper flowers, take two colored facial tissues or two sheets of colored tissue paper (approximately nine inches square). Place the pieces on top of one another and lay them flat on a table. Place your hand in the center of the paper and crumple the pieces by pulling them inward as you make a fist. Fasten at the middle with a pipe cleaner (or paper clip). Spread out the edges.

Pretend Play

1. ***The New Family.*** Precede this activity with a discussion of the ways in which the composition of families change. Provide children with people figures, photographs, or magazine pictures of potential family members. First, instruct the children to compose a family by placing the pictures or figures on trays. Then ask them to change the family in some way by adding or removing family members. Ask children to describe the reasons that they made the changes. Record the changes

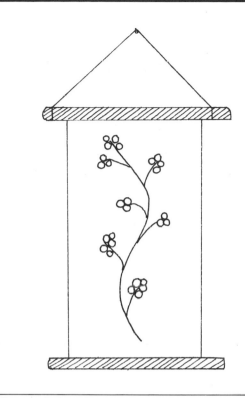

Figure 2.4 *A Simple Cherry Blossom Scroll*

that each child makes in his or her "family" and the reasons given (this family had a new baby; Grandma died; two children went away to live with their aunt).

2. ***Family Events.*** Provide a collection of people figures or dolls, some dollhouse furniture, and other correspondingly sized props. Create rooms using a dollhouse, cardboard boxes, milk crates, or the like. Talk about events in the daily life of a family, such as eating, sleeping, going shopping, watching TV, reading, and so on. Suggest that children pretend to do those activities with the figures. Help children who don't know what to do with the dolls to begin to think about family relationships and events. "You have a woman and a little boy. Tell me who they are. What are they doing together? Which room should they go to now?" Help children relate what they are doing with the materials to real experiences. "You're pretending to eat supper. What will happen at this mealtime?"

3. ***Family Play.*** This activity is a variant of Family Events. Set out an assortment of people and pet figures. Invite children to

explore. As they do, talk to them about the people, their relationships, and the way the children are using them. Some children will use the figures as if they're a family, other children may require assistance, such as "You're playing with the family in the dollhouse. Tell me who that doll is." Encourage children to take various roles while playing. As the play continues, introduce more family members (grandparents). On other days, provide different arrangements of family members. (Leave mother out one day. Children can speculate about where the mother is.) Some days use people figures that represent other cultural or racial backgrounds not yet explored. Set out two houses. Encourage the children to interact as neighbors. Various situations can be introduced using these dollhouses (adoption, family members living in distant locations, step-parenting, etc.).

4. **It's a Party!** Following a discussion of how children in the group celebrate their birthdays, set out simple props for a birthday party. Hats, streamers, party plates, napkins, and wrapped "presents" will enhance the party atmosphere. Children can pretend to be the birthday child or the guests. They can blow out candles, sing songs, open presents, or reenact birthday celebrations of which they have been part.

5. **Playing House.** Here are some ideas for encouraging cross-cultural awareness in the housekeeping area. Use these as supplements or alternatives to the usual house set-up.

Eating: Provide chopsticks instead of cutlery and cushions on the floor and low tables. Remove some kitchen equipment and add a wok, clay baker, steamer, or hot pot. Add plastic food of different types.

Sleeping: Introduce mats, feather beds, hammocks, or futons on the floor instead of beds.

Clothing: Provide clothing that is common among diverse cultural groups, such as scarves, hats, shoes, jackets, and jewelry.

Music: Play recorded music from different countries and sung in different languages in the background. Use current popular music as well as more traditional offerings.

Shopping: Offer cloth or string bags for daily marketing. Show children how to tie squares of cloth around packages to carry them.

6. **Photography Studio.** Explain to children that taking photographs is a way of preserving how family members look at a given time. People also like to record special family events on film. Set up a photography studio using cameras, tables, chairs, a sink, imaginary lights, a stage, backdrops, photo albums of finished pictures, and pictures in frames. Children can pretend to be photographers, subjects to be photographed, or photograph developers and printers. Provide dress-up clothing for the "customers." Children may draw pictures to represent completed photographs.

Social

1. **Helping at Home.** Provide an assortment of pictures or photographs of family members working together at various tasks like gardening, cooking, cleaning. Include pictures of people attempting to do tasks that are too difficult for one person. Introduce the session by telling children the general topic to be covered. Ask children two or three of the following questions. Repeat this activity on other days, using the same or new pictures and asking other questions.

Questions for Helping Skits
- Tell me who needed help.
- Tell me how you knew who needed help.
- Tell me who saw help was needed.
- Tell me how she/he knew help was needed.
- Tell me who tried to help.
- Tell me how the person who needed help let the other know.
- Tell me another way to let someone know help is needed.
- Tell me what _____ did to help.
- Tell me if she/he was helpful.
- Tell me how you know if she/he was helpful.

- Tell me how (the helper) felt when _____ . (Describe corresponding action.)

- Tell me how (the helpee) felt when _____ . (Describe corresponding action.)

- Tell me how you might feel if someone _____ . (Describe corresponding action.)

- Tell me another way _____ could have helped.

- Tell me about a time when you needed help.

- Tell me how you let someone know.

- Were the things people did helpful to you?

- How did you let them know how you felt?

- Tell me some ways to let someone know you appreciate their help.

- Tell me some ways to let someone know that wasn't the kind of help you wanted.

- Tell me some ways to let someone know you don't want any help.

- Now you use the dolls to show us something else that might have happened when _____ .

Observe the following guidelines as children discuss their ideas.

- If a child gives an answer that seems appropriate, paraphrase and then say, "You thought of a way that was helpful."

- If a child gives an answer that seems incorrect, paraphrase and ask, "Tell me why?"

- If a child gives an answer that seems obscure, paraphrase and then say, "You thought of one way to help. Let's think of a way that would be even more helpful."

- If a child gives a reason that is really inappropriate, paraphrase first, then give appropriate information and a reason. Perhaps the child's reason is based solely on his or her own desire rather than taking into account the other child's point of view.

Figure 2.5 *Use This Chart for Considering Family Needs*

- Allow each child an opportunity to talk. This may mean asking a child by name to tell what she or he thinks.

- Do not force a child into participating. ("You may want to talk about it later.")

- Reinforce helping responses, but avoid overreacting either to less appropriate (or more creative!) comments or to those statements that you prefer.

- Don't say, "That's right."

- Do say, "You thought of something" or "That's an idea."

- At the end of the session:
  a) Announce that the session is over.
  b) Compliment children on thinking, working, listening, and helping.
  c) Close with "Maybe you can find a way to help someone today."

2. ***What Can We Do?*** Draw a house on a piece of poster board. Along the left side of the board glue symbols of five basic needs: love (a heart); food (cup or dish); clothing (shirt); shelter (house); help (two clasped hands). (Figure 2.5)

   In a random manner inside the house, glue pictures relating to the above needs. Cover these with construction paper "flaps" so that they can be opened. Add a roof and decorate as desired.

Explain that the symbols represent needs that people have and that these needs are met within the family. Give children turns choosing a "window" flap to open. Discuss how people in their families help them with the needs they have uncovered.

3. *A Family Function.* The focus of this activity is for children to work together toward a common purpose. It will take several days to prepare. Enlist the children's assistance in planning a function for families to be held at school. Children should determine a simple program, such as a sing-a-long. Provide them with materials so that they can decorate (in the case of younger children) or write (for older children) an invitation to the event. A cooking project could be a part of the preparation, or families could provide the treats. The tasks can be divided among the children, or they can all participate in every aspect of the planning.

*4. *Happy Birthday to You!*

General Purpose: To encourage children's voluntary participation in the tradition of making and giving gifts.

TFPs: 33, 36, 39, 44, 45, 54, 55.

Materials: Drawing paper; markers or crayons; newsprint or wrapping paper; tape, stickers, or ribbon.

Procedure:

a. Introduce the activity with a large-group discussion of birthday traditions. Invite children to share descriptions of their favorite birthday activities. Sing birthday songs together.

b. Tell children that they will have a chance to make a "birthday gift" and give it to a classmate at a later large-group gathering.

c. Set up an art table with the materials listed above. Invite the children to join you to make gifts.

d. Encourage children to proceed in any enjoyable way as they create pictures.

e. As children finish pictures, help or direct them to roll them into tubes that the child (or you) tape closed. Cut pieces of wrapping paper or invite children to decorate sheets of newsprint in which to wrap the pictures. Tape or use a sticker to hold the wrap in place. Add ribbon if you wish. Set "gifts" aside,

telling children that they will give and receive them later.

g. Gather the large group later in the day. Allow each child to enjoy presenting a gift to a friend. Avoid assigning gifts to particular children, but make sure that every child gets one. This can be structured by seating the children in two lines of equal number and having each child present to the child directly across from him or her.

h. Sing "Happy Birthday, dear _____ ," using each child's name as each gift is presented.

i. Children may want to open the gifts as they are given or wait until everyone has one and open them all together.

Hints for Success:

• To keep children's attention and to allow each child a turn, sing only the first line of "Happy Birthday."

• Provide a box into which children place their birthday pictures. Store it on a shelf apart from other creations. Label it and decorate it so it is easily identifiable.

How to Simplify this Activity:

• Younger children may not feel comfortable "giving away" something they have created. If this is the case, ask the child to make two pictures, one to give away and one to keep.

How to Extend this Activity:

• Fashion a birthday calendar in the classroom, on which the children's birth dates are listed by the month. At the beginning of the month have the group identify the birthday children and plan ahead a special recognition. Children whose birthdays fall outside the school year may use their "half" birthday date.

TEACHER RESOURCES

Field Trip Ideas

1. Visit a local museum or library to see clothing worn long ago (or ceremonial clothing worn today), implements used by families when they first settled in the area, old toys, or dioramas of early life.

2. Visit a child's house to expose children to other people's life-styles.

Classroom Visitors

1. Invite the children's family members to participate in the classroom. Be sure to introduce them, or have children introduce them, to the rest of the group. Encourage each person to join in the classroom activities. If they are willing, allow time for these special visitors to talk about family traditions, emphasizing their personal recollections as children.
2. Invite members of your own family to visit the classroom. Children are intrigued by the idea that their teacher has a life outside of school.
3. Invite a blended, extended, or adoptive family to talk with children about their family experiences.

Children's Books

Alexander, M. *Nobody Asked Me If I Wanted a Baby Sister*. New York: Dial, 1971.

Baker, B. *My Sister Says*. New York: Macmillan, 1984.

Baumann, H. *Chip Has Many Brothers*. New York: Philomel, 1985.

Blaine, M. *The Terrible Thing That Happened at Our House*. New York: Parents, 1975.

Bond, F. *Poinsettia and Her Family*. New York: Crowell, 1985.

Brandenberg, F. *Aunt Nina and Her Nephews and Nieces*. New York: Greenwillow, 1983.

Bunin, C. *Is That Your Sister?* New York: Pantheon, 1976.

Caines, J. *Daddy*. New York: Harper and Row, 1977.

Child, L. M. *Over the River and Through the Woods*. New York: Coward, McCann and Geoghegan, 1974.

Cooney, B. *Miss Rumphius*. New York: Viking, 1982.

Eisenberg, P. R. *A Mitzvah is Something Special*. New York: Harper and Row, 1978.

Erlich, A. *Zeek Silver Moon*. New York: Dial, 1972.

Flournoy, V. *The Patchwork Quilt*. New York: Dial, 1985.

Gray, G. *Send Wendell*. New York: McGraw-Hill, 1974.

Greenfield, E. *She Come Bringing Me That Little Baby Girl*. New York: Lippincott, 1974.

Henriod, L. *Grandma's Wheelchair*. Niles, IL: Whitman, 1982.

Jackson, L. A. *Grandpa Had A Windmill, Grandma Had A Churn*. New York: Parents, 1977.

Johnson, T., and T. dePaola. *The Quilt Story*. New York: Putnam, 1985.

Keats, E. J. *Peter's Chair*. New York: Harper and Row, 1967.

Levinson, R. *I Go With My Family to Grandma's*. New York: Dutton, 1986.

Mathieu, J. *The Olden Days*. New York: Random House, 1979.

McDermott, G. *Anansi the Spider*. New York: Holt, Rinehart and Winston, 1972.

Musgrove, M. *Ashanti to Zulu*. New York: Dial, 1976.

O'Kelley, M. L. *From the Hills of Georgia*. Boston: Little, Brown, 1983.

Polacco, P. *The Keeping Quilt*. New York: Simon and Schuster, 1988.

Raynor, D. *This is My Father and Me*. Niles, IL: Whitman, 1973.

———. *Grandparents Around the World*. Niles, IL: Whitman, 1977.

Reich, H. *Children and Their Fathers*. New York: Hill and Wang, 1966.

———. *Children and Their Mothers*. New York: Hill and Wang, 1964.

———. *Children of Many Lands*. New York: Hill and Wang, 1984.

Rosenberg, U. *Being Adopted*. New York: Lothrop, Lee and Shepard, 1984.

Ryder, J. *Beach Party*. New York: Frederick Warne, 1982.

Rylant, C. *The Relatives Came*. New York: Bradbury, 1985.

———. *When I Was Young in the Mountains*. New York: Dutton, 1982.

Schwartz, A. *Mrs. Moskowitz and the Sabbath Candles*. Philadelphia: Jewish Publication Society of America, 1983.

Scott, A. H. *On Mother's Lap*. New York: McGraw-Hill, 1972.

Showers, P. *Me and My Family Tree*. New York: Harper and Row, 1978.

Simon, N. *All Kinds of Families*. Niles, IL: Whitman, 1976.

Skorpen, L. M. *Mandy's Grandmother*. New York: Dial, 1975.

Spier, P. *People*. Garden City, NJ: Doubleday, 1980.

Stein, S. B. *That New Baby—An Open Family Book for Parents and Children Together*. New York: Walker and Co., 1984.

Stevenson, J. *When I Was Nine*. New York: Greenwillow, 1986.

Tax, M. *Families*. Boston: Little, Brown, 1981.

Tudor, T. *A Time to Keep*. Chicago: Rand McNally, 1977.

Wilhelm, H. *Let's Be Friends Again*. New York: Crown, 1986.

Yarbrough, C. *Cornrows*. New York: Coward-McCann, 1979.

Zolotow, C. *Timothy, Too!* Boston: Houghton Mifflin, 1986.

Adult References

Crandall, R. *Shaking Your Family Tree*. Dublin, NH: Yankee, 1986.

Dobler, L. G. *National Holidays Around the World*. New York: Fleet, 1968.

Chase, R. *Old Songs and Singing Games*. New York: Dover, 1972.

———. *Singing Games and Playparty Games*. New York: Dover, 1949.

Fletcher, W. *Recording Your Family History*. New York: Dodd, Mead, 1986.

Grunfeld, F. V. *Games of the World*. Zurich: Swiss Committee for UNICEF, 1982.

Jones, B., and B. L. Hawes. *Step It Down*. New York: Harper and Row, 1972.

Krementz, J. *How It Feels When Parents Divorce*. New York: Knopf, 1984.

McCubbin, H., and B. B. Dahl. *Marriage and Family: Individuals and Life Cycles*. New York: Wiley, 1985.

MacFarlan, A., and P. MacFarlan. *Handbook of American Indian Games*. New York: Dover, 1985.

Newell, W. W. *Games and Songs of American Children*. New York: Dover, 1963.

Seeger, R. C. *American Folk Songs for Children*. New York: Doubleday, 1948.

Stoll, E., and M. Stoll. *Pioneer Catalog of Country Living*. Toronto: Personal Library, 1980.

Tudor, B. *Drawn from New England: Tasha Tudor*. New York: Philomel, 1979.

U.S. Committee for Family Traditions. *Joy Through the World*. New York: Bragdon, 1985.

Wernick, R. *The Family*. New York: Time-Life Books, 1974.

Wigginton, E., ed. *The Foxfire Book*. Garden City, NJ: Doubleday, 1972.

Chapter 3

Friends

Children are social beings. From the moment they are born they begin a lifetime of interdependence with others. Although their first interpersonal relationships revolve around home and family, peers soon become an important part of their lives. Babies are attracted to babies. Toddlers revel in one another's company and preschoolers become increasingly interested in having a friend; by first grade, many children report that it is almost intolerable to be without one (Hendrick, 1988). Friends fulfill children's need for companionship, stimulation, feedback, and a sense of belonging. Through interactions with age-mates, children come to understand and value their own traits, attitudes, and behaviors. They learn new skills and refine old ones (Kostelnik, et al., 1988). Moreover, because true friendship is a completely voluntary endeavor, children who have friends receive strong confirmation of their own value and worth. For all of these reasons children want and need friends.

To make friends children must know:

- how to initiate contacts with peers
- how to maintain positive relations over time
- how to resolve conflict constructively

Yet children are not born knowing how to do these things. They learn them by observing others, by practicing, by experimenting, and by experiencing the consequences of their actions. Their individual efforts are met with differing degrees of success. Furthermore, within any one group of children are great variations in involvement in the friendship-making process. Some children are just becoming aware of others; some put great effort into making a friend; still others watch from the sidelines and appear interested but don't know how to get started.

In each case, adults in the classroom are in an ideal position to support children and help to increase their chances for success as they try to establish friendly relations with peers. The Friends theme can help teachers achieve these aims by introducing children to valuable peer-related information and experiences.

PURPOSE

The aim of this unit is to expand children's friendship options within the classroom. The activities will help children to recognize others as prospective friends and encourage them to become more accessible to peers as friendship choices. They will also give children opportunities to become aware of and practice social skills that increase their friendship potential. Thus, this unit describes more than the definition of "friend." It emphasizes instead essential friendship behaviors—how to be a friend, how to make friends, how to get along with friends, and what to do when conflicts arise.

IMPLEMENTATION

We recommend that teachers emphasize the unit's content in two ways: first, by incorporating a selection of the activities suggested here into their daily plans, and second, by taking advantage of naturally occurring opportunities to promote children's friendship skills. When teachers develop some friendship activities in advance, they are assured that essential TPFs are covered and that friendship-related material is being addressed across the curriculum. Conversely, teachers who offer children feedback or model friendship behaviors within the context of spontaneous classroom interactions provide them with information immediately relevant to their developmental needs and interests. A blend of planned experiences and on-the-spot coaching makes the Friends theme most meaningful to young children.

Almost any classroom routine or game can become a "friendship" activity when children are encouraged to work together and their attention is deliberately drawn to the friend-related TFPs that fit the situation. For instance, the easel, the manipulative table, or the "math tubs" could take on a friendship focus if the children were encouraged to invite a friend to work with them or if the teacher periodically identified aloud children's common interest in materials. If children at the sand table or those in pretend play were encouraged to greet classmates who entered the area and to respond to greetings directed at them, these activities would become friendship-focused as well. Even traditionally solitary activities, such as puzzles and journal writing, could emphasize friend-related ideas. For example, children could be given randomly the pieces to two puzzles and asked to help one another sort them out and put them together. Likewise, children could be encouraged to collaborate on journals or to share their completed writings with a friend.

With all of these ideas in mind, the Friends theme could be implemented in any of the following ways.

Option One: Begin the school year with the Friends theme. Focus on helping children discover one another and on creating a sense of cohesiveness within the group. Repeat the theme around Valentine's Day to reinforce social harmony and to introduce more advanced TFPs that the children, now more thoroughly acquainted, would be interested in.

Option Two:
Week One: Focus on the TFPs that define friends and friendship.
Week Two: Concentrate on those TFPs that describe how to make friends.
Week Three: Highlight the TFPs on Being a Friend and Ending a Friendship.

Option Three:
Week One and Two: Focus on initiating and responding to friendly contacts.
Week Three and Four: Focus on negotiating conflicts.

Option Four:
Weeks One and Two: Carry out the unit on Self-Awareness (Chapter 1).
Weeks Three and Four: Focus on the theme of Friends.

Teachers who use this theme may want to extend the ideas into a broader unit on Citizenship emphasizing strategies for cooperation, negotiation, and voting. The theme could tie into a unit on the Post Office focusing on communication between friends. Finally, the theme may serve as a foundation for units on Friends in my Family or Neighborhood Friends.

TERMS, FACTS, AND PRINCIPLES

Friends Defined

1. People who are your friends:
   a. know your name
   b. like you
   c. like to be near you
   d. let you play with them
   e. seek you out
   f. hold your hand, hug you, pat you on the back
   g. say, "I like you"
   h. invite you to play with or use their things
   i. like to talk with you
   *j. care about what happens to you
   k. wait for you
   l. notice when you are absent
   m. miss you when you aren't around
   n. help you do things
   o. let you help them
   *p. try to keep you from being hurt
   *q. share secrets with you
   r. listen to your ideas
   s. pay attention to your feelings
   t. decide with you where to play
   u. decide with you what to do
   *v. help you solve a problem
   *w. like you even after you do things they don't like
   *x. forgive you
   *y. sometimes let you have your way even when it's not their way
   z. comfort you when you are feeling unhappy
   aa. come over to visit
   bb. ask you to visit them.

*2. Some people are friends, some are acquaintances, and some are strangers.

3. Some friends are members of your family; some are outside your family.

*4. Friends may be like you in many ways and different from you in others.

5. Friends may be of any age.

6. Friends may live near each other or far away.

*7. Friends may see each other frequently or only once in a while.

8. Some friends are people; others are animals, toys, or pretend.

*9. Friends may have different ideas about things: sometimes friends agree, sometimes they disagree.

Making Friends

10. People can make friends.

11. Friends can be found in many different places: in the neighborhood, in school, at church, at temple, or other places people go.

12. The way people behave affects their ability to make or keep friends.

*13. There are obvious ways in which people use their body to let others know they want to be friends, including smiling, playing near someone else, and looking directly at the person with whom they are speaking.

*14. There are obvious ways in which people use words to let others know they want to be friends, including offering greetings, offering information, and responding in a positive way to the greetings and questions of others.

*15. When people use less obvious ways to show they want to be friends, it is sometimes hard for others to figure out their message.

16. People feel friendly toward people who:
   a. express an interest in what they are doing
   b. take turns
   c. share
   d. listen to their ideas
   e. let them do some things their way
   *f. have interesting ideas
   *g. think their ideas are interesting
   h. like to do some of the same things
   *i. keep their secrets
   *j. trust them
   *k. stick up for them
   *l. notice the nice things they do
   *m. are thoughtful
   *n. think of ways to solve problems without hurting others.

17. People feel less friendly toward people who:
   a. hurt them
   b. make fun of them
   c. grab their things
   *d. tattle on them
   *e. cheat
   *f. lie to them or about them
   g. always insist on having their own way
   *h. gossip about them.

Being a Friend

18. Being a friend gives people someone with whom to play and work.

19. Being a friend gives people someone to listen to and someone who listens to them.

20. Being a friend gives people someone to comfort and someone who comforts them.

21. Having friends makes people feel good.

22. Having friends gives people someone with whom to share secrets, ideas, and feelings.

23. Having friends gives people opportunities to show they care.

24. Having friends gives people opportunities to help each other.

25. People vary in the number of friends they have; some people have one friend, others have many friends.

*26. People can have more than one friend at a time.

*27. Friends may enjoy doing some things together, some things with other people, and some things by themselves.

28. Friends can remain friends even when they are not together.

29. Friends who are not together sometimes write letters or call each other on the telephone.

*30. The same person can be a friend to more than one person.

*31. People do not always like all of the people with whom their friends are friends.

*32. People experience different feelings about their friends.

33. Sometimes friends hurt each other's feelings.

*34. Sometimes friends can forgive each other and sometimes they cannot.

Ending a Friendship

35. Sometimes friendships end.

*36. There are many different feelings when friendships end.

*37. People have different feelings when friendships end.

*38. It can be sad or confusing when someone no longer wants to be your friend.

*39. After a friendship ends, sometimes the same people become friends again, sometimes they do not.

*40. After a friendship ends, people make new friends.

Figure 3.1 *The Whole Class Contributes to a Hand-Print Mural*

ACTIVITY IDEAS

Aesthetic

1. *Friendly Fingers.* Supply the art area with large finger-paint paper (shiny side up), smocks, several colors of finger paint, and a tub of water for hand-washing. Invite children to finger paint in pairs, on the same paper. As they paint, emphasize that being close to another person is a way of expressing friendship. Put both names on the paper, and when the painting is dry help children decide who will take it home, or how to divide it. Consider expanding this activity by inviting children to work together to make their own finger paint using the following recipe:

   Mix ¼ cup cornstarch with 2 cups cold water. Boil until the mixture thickens. Cool and pour into containers, such as baby food jars. Add food coloring; stir and cover. Makes three jars. After the first use, stir to regain the original consistency.

2. *The More We Get Together.* Teach children the following traditional song. Once they know the words, clap and add hand gestures to indicate "your friends" (point to others) and "my friends" (point to self).

   Finally, suggest that they sing the song standing up in a circle with arms over each other's shoulders, swaying and enjoying the music together.

   The More We Get Together
   (Tune: "Did You Ever See a Lassie?")
   The more we get together,
   Together, together.
   The more we get together,
   The happier we'll be.
   For your friends are my friends,
   And my friends are your friends,
   Oh, the more we get together,
   The happier we'll be.

   To extend this, substitute the word for friend in different languages. For instance, use *ami* (French), *amigo* (Spanish), *freund* (German), or *pang-yo* (Mandarin Chinese).

3. *Friendly Hands.* Help children make a handprint mural showing everyone's hands in the group. Prints may be made using paint, traced with marker or crayon, or traced and cut out and pasted onto the mural surface. Make the mural on large paper or fabric. Label the finished mural and display for all to see. (Figure 3.1)

Figure 3.2 *A Display Focusing on One Classmate Friend*

4. *Art Thou My Friend?* Select several reproductions or photographs of paintings or drawings in which people are shown engaged in activities with others. Ask children to look carefully at each one in turn and tell you whether or not they think the people in the picture are friends and why. Point out that the artist chose to make the people look friendly or not friendly toward one another. Ask the children to try to figure out whether the artist was depicting "friends" or "not friends". Further the discussion by examining how the artist achieved this aim. If they seem to hesitate, use the TFPs to tell children some of the attributes of friends. You might say, "Friends enjoy the same activities" or "Sometimes friends like to dress alike." With older children, focus on unfriendly behavior or demeanor as well. Point out angry facial expressions and talk about friends who disagree or about negative behavior as an obstacle to friendship. Once children are familiar with the paintings, they might enjoy comparing the people and activities. Ask questions such as, "In which picture are the people friendliest? Why do you think so?" Inexpensive reproductions of paintings are available in art books (from museum stores, bookstores, or libraries) or may be purchased through catalogues from picture-framing stores.

Affective

1. *Friend of the Day.* Choose one child to be the "Friend of the Day." Hang that child's photograph in a special place along with one or two self-descriptive statements or statements from others in the group about the child. (Figure 3.2) Encourage the other children to interact with the featured "friend" throughout the day. Later, ask them to identify additional characteristics and preferences of their "friend" based on their contacts during the session. Be sure that over the course of time, every child has an opportunity to be the featured "friend."

2. *See Me Be a Friend.* Discuss what it means to be a friend using the TFPs established for this purpose. Ask the children to think of ways they are a good friend to someone. Make a list of their ideas and entitle it "How to be a Good Friend." Encourage children to practice what they have learned during the day. At the end of the day, allow children time to tell how they behaved as a friend.

3. *Discovering Common Interests.* At group time, ask the children in turn to describe a favorite item, such as a favorite ice cream flavor or a favorite color. Make a chart listing the items across the top and the children's names under their choice. Have the children stand in groups according to their preferences. Point out children who

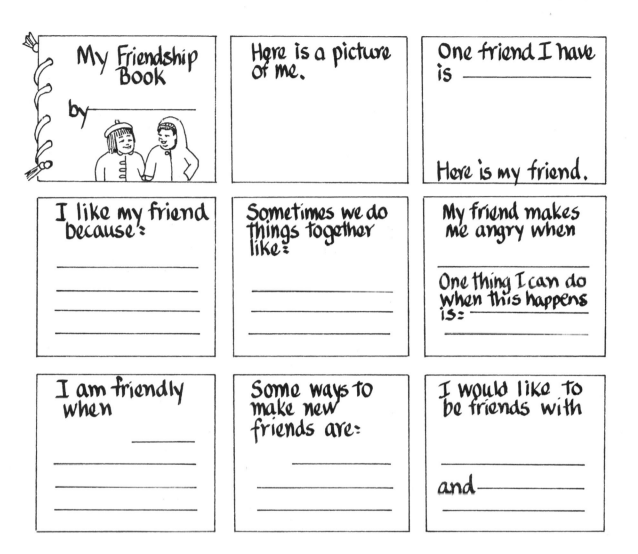

Figure 3.3 *Sample Book Pages*

share the same preference. Discuss the role of these similarities in children's friendship choices. Talk with the children about the way friends like some of the same things and some things that are different. Give the example of hair color and have the children stand together who have brown hair, blond hair, black hair, red hair, and so on. Make other groupings by naming other descriptive categories, such as everyone who is wearing red clothing, everyone who has a little brother, or anyone who has a cat for a pet. When obvious differences are noticed (skin color, language spoken, etc.), acknowledge these and point out more subtle similarities (activities enjoyed, sense of humor, etc.).

Explain that people look "inside" one another as well as "outside" when seeking friends.

4. *My Friendship Book.* Referring to the sample pages that follow (Figure 3.3), create a Friendship Book for each child. Prepare these prior to introducing the activity or show children how to assemble their own. Introduce the activity with a discussion about the friendships people have or are trying to establish. Tell children that today they can make a special book about their own friends. Show the book, turning the pages and reading it aloud. Working with one or two children at a time, read the questions, then ask children to dictate or write their answers.

Cognition

1. *What's a Friend?* Introduce this activity with a puppet play, a large picture of friends doing something together, or a story about friends. Discuss with the children what a friend is and how you know if someone is your friend. Have them generate a list of statements that describe what a friend is to them. When it is complete, read it back to them.

2. *Photo Friends.* Take photographs of each of the children in the class. Hang these at children's eye level and encourage the children to look at them while naming as many classmates as they can. Emphasize that it is easier to be friends with people when you know their names. Over time, ask children to match printed names with the corresponding photos of their friends.

3. *These Are Friends.* To help children consider criteria for being friends, give them a variety of plastic doll-like human figures. After they have had a chance to play with them, ask individuals to arrange the figures into friendship groups. Then ask them to explain why they grouped them as they did.

4. *Different Kinds of Friends.* Show the children pictures of people doing things together that demonstrate various relationships (friends, acquaintances, neighbors, sisters, parents, strangers). Discuss the differences and similarities, helping children guess which relationship describes the people shown. Ask them to think of people in their own lives that fit the different kinds of relationships. Discuss the ways people make friends and point out that strangers can sometimes become friends.

5. *Companionable Counting.* To give children practice in one-to-one correspondence and counting, give each child a collection of two kinds of counters (buttons, chips, counting bears, etc.). Suggest that they make a line of one type of counter and then give each counter a "friend" by placing a counter of the second type next to each one. Have the children count the friends and tell how many they have. Next, rearrange the counters so they are not in pairs, and ask the children whether each counter still has a friend. Realign the counters in their original positions to help children check their predictions.

6. *Who's Missing?* Play a game in which children try to guess who has left a group. Have several children form a group in front of the others. Mention each child's name in the group, then have the class close their eyes and quietly ask one of the children to hide out of sight behind a shelf, under a sheet, or in another room. Then, challenge the class to guess who's missing. Give clues such as hair color, height, sex, or what the child is wearing to make the guessing easier. In a variation, use photographs of all the children. Arrange them on a board and, while the children close their eyes, remove one of the pictures. Then, challenge the group to identify whose picture is gone. To make this simpler, start with a small number of photographs and gradually add more as children seem ready for a greater challenge.

7. *Friendly Patterns.* Provide materials for building a pattern (paper squares of various colors, blocks, cubes, beads, pegs). Suggest that pairs of friends work together to establish and make a continuous pattern. Simple patterns are easiest for less experienced children (red, blue, red, blue, red, blue, for example). More complex ones are more interesting to experienced pattern builders (small pink, large yellow, small green, large red, small pink, large yellow, small green, large red). As an alternative, have one child of the pair make a pattern for his or her partner to copy. Encourage them to alternate roles.

8. *Broken Hearts.* Prior to the children's arrival, make several paper hearts. Cut each one in two in an irregular fashion so that every heart has only one other piece that will fit to make it whole. (Figure 3.4)

   Show children an example of how the heart pieces can be fit together to form a complete heart. Then give each child a portion of a heart, instructing them to find the "friend" whose piece will fit with theirs to make it whole. Simplify the game by making each heart a different color or by carrying out the game with only a few children at a time. This can be a game in itself or a way for children to find partners for a subsequent activity.

Figure 3.4 *Make Broken Heart Puzzles*

9. ***Children's Problem-Solving Books.*** Select one of the following problem-solving books written by Elizabeth Crary and published by Parenting Press, 7750 Thirty-first Avenue NE, Seattle, Washington, 98115: *I Want It* (1982), *I Want to Play* (1982), or *My Name Is Not Dummy* (1983). Introduce the book by explaining that listeners will help determine how the children in the book will solve a friendship problem. When the story comes to a decision point, ask children to decide what the characters will do next. Different endings are possible depending on what choices children make. Turn to the appropriate page and continue reading. When the story for one choice is over, you could stop and put the book aside or try a different set of choices.

10. ***Color Mixing.*** Introduce this activity by explaining that two friends will work together to mix colors. Give each pair of children a four- to five-foot length of clear plastic tubing, one-half to one inch in diameter. Provide a cork to fit into each end. Show both children how to hold on to the tubing. Leaving a cork in one end, ask a child to remove the other cork and invite him or her to fill three-quarters of the tube with water using a hose, a plastic watering can, or a plastic pitcher and funnel. Ask this same child to choose red, yellow, or blue food coloring to add to the water at that end. Once this has been accomplished, cork that end and invite the friend to add a different color to his or her end of the tube. Next, encourage the children to squeeze the tube or rock back and forth so that the colors gradually mix. Ask the friends to describe what they observed and

how they worked together. Let them experiment with color combinations.*

*11. ***Friendship Riddles.***

General Purpose: For children to apply current knowledge to make inferences or predictions.

TFPs: 1, 16.

Materials: Riddles on paper or written on a chalkboard for teacher reference.

Procedure:

a. Demonstrate the idea of a riddle by telling children that they can play a game using words. Explain by saying, "A riddle is like a little story that has a part missing. The game is to figure out what word sounds like it fits the riddle best. Sometimes many different answers can be put into the riddle. The riddle will give you some clues, so listen carefully and you might be able to figure out an answer."

b. Do very simple riddles until the children get the idea that they should fill in the blank with an answer that makes sense to them. At this point, don't worry about rhyming words. Examples:

"If you eat too much, you might get _____ ." Children may say sick, fat, full, and so on; all are acceptable.

"My dog scratches when he has _____ ." Children may say fleas, to go, itches, and so on.

*Adapted from Karen Miller, *The Outside Play and Learning Book*, Mt. Rainier, MD: Gryphon House, 1989.

c. Suggest that the riddle's answer could rhyme with another word in the riddle: "'Meow' said my cat, when she bumped into the _____." Children may say rat, hat, mat, bat, and so on.

d. Read each of the riddles provided here, encouraging children to think of a word that could make sense and that relates to friendly behaviors. Accept answers that don't rhyme as well as those that do. Praise any words that represent friendly behaviors.

Hint for Success:

- Ask children who give answers that seem inappropriate to explain them. For example, when you say the riddle "If you eat too much, you might get _____," the child may answer, "cold." Upon asking why, you could learn that the child was thinking of eating too much ice cream. Pause to discuss each riddle briefly, eliciting children's ideas and discussing friendly behavior alternatives.

How to Simplify this Activity:

- Supply two different words, one that fits the riddle and one that doesn't. Ask children to choose between them.

How to Extend this Activity:

- Suggest that children make up their own friendship riddles; write them down in a Friendship Riddle book or make a Riddle Poster to display.

Riddle 1
Some food is on the table,
a friend is standing back.
You walk right up to her and say:
"Let's go share our (snack)."

Riddle 2
Looking sad and lonely,
Your friend sits on the rug
Since you want to cheer him up,
You offer him a (hug).

Riddle 3
You have two robots in your hand;
You see a watching boy.
Now, you could play alone or say
"I'd like to share this (toy)."

Riddle 4
A girl sits on a two-seat swing
looking sad and blue.
You think "I'd like to be her friend";
You say "I'll swing with (you)!"

Riddle 5
You really wish that doll was yours,
Now help your friends to learn:
Would it be best to grab, or say
"Could I please have a (turn)?"

Riddle 6
Just one more time, think hard and say
the words to answer this:
To show you are a friend you can
give a friend (a kiss).

Construction

1. *Friendship Necklaces.* Point out that friends sometimes make things for each other. Provide cut up drinking straw pieces, paper shapes with holes punched in them, and other materials for stringing necklaces. Suggest that children make a necklace for a friend. Attach a paper tag to the completed necklace telling who made it and for whom it was made. A variation on this activity is to have the children make necklaces for themselves, attaching paper pieces with the name of a friend written on each. (Figure 3.5)

2. *Friends' Place.* Talk with the children about making a special place in the classroom for friends out of large blocks. Assist them in generating ideas and making decisions. Praise cooperative efforts. Ask open-ended questions, such as, "Where's the door? How many friends can fit inside? What do you want to call your place?" Help the children make a sign to hang on the structure telling others about it. Take a picture of the building and those who worked on it. Display the photograph after the structure is put away.

*3. *Modeling Dough Friends.*
General Purpose: For children to represent various objects and events using one medium.

TFPs: All.

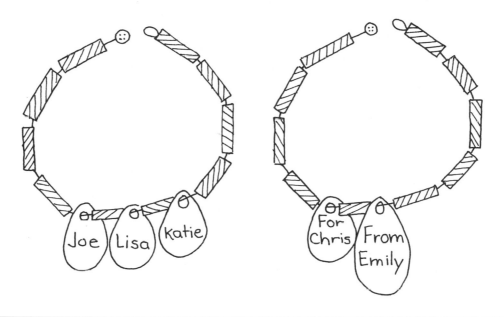

Figure 3.5 *Use Straws and Paper to Create Friendship Necklaces*

Materials: Modeling dough, interchangeable facial features such as eyes, noses, ears, mouths, glasses, etc.

Procedure:

a. Give each child a ball of modeling dough and two eyes. Display other face parts on the table.

b. Flatten a ball of modeling dough slightly and stick in two eyes. With a surprised expression say, "Oh! This creature is looking at me! I think it's trying to tell me something." (Lean close, listening.) "It says, 'Let's be friends'!"

c. Encourage children to ask questions, such as, "Ask her what her name is." Model friendship strategies for the children, using the modeling dough as a puppet: "I see some strangers here I'd like to know. Looks like you're all friends. Maybe you could introduce me to your friends."

d. As children become involved with your creature, suggest that they look over the materials and choose a way to make a friendly creature of their own.

e. As creatures are forming, have yours talk to others, asking names inviting them to play, suggesting friendly interactions. "We could share a snack together!" Pull off a small piece of modeling dough, offering it to another child's "creature."

f. Point out facial features and friendly behaviors that children choose and role-play. "You put a smile on that face! She looks friendly." "You decided to share some dough with a friend. That made her smile!" Encourage children to begin role-playing with each other's dough friends. Sit back and observe as soon as possible, allowing children to imitate and symbolize friendly behaviors on their own.

Hint for Success:

• Look in craft stores for "eyes" and beads that could be used for other features. Alternately, features could be cut out of Styrofoam meat trays or paper.

How to Simplify this Activity:

• Do this activity with only a few children at a time.

How to Extend this Activity:

• Suggest situations that could inspire more involved friendship skills practice. For example, two modeling-dough friends can't figure out how to share something; a third modeling-dough friend wants to join a game that's hard to share; or a modeling-dough friend insists on his own way all the time. Encourage children to act out the scenarios with their modeling dough friends, trying to solve problems that come up.

Language

1. *Friendly Words.* Suggest that children think about being a friend to someone. Start them off by asking what they call their friends. Some possible words could be "pal," "buddy," "friend," or "amigo." Then ask them to suggest friendly things pals say to each other. Write their suggestions on a list called "Friendly Words." Hang it in the classroom and praise the children when you hear them using friendly words during playtime.

2. *Going on a Picnic.* Discuss a picnic or go on one with the children. Point out that a picnic is one activity that friends can enjoy together. Teach the class the following chant, giving examples of words to insert at the appropriate time. Then ask the children to think of other things friends could take on a picnic. Repeat the chant, using their ideas, even if they are really silly. Encourage creative thinking and vocabulary expansion.

Going on a Picnic
Going on a picnic, leaving right away,
If it doesn't rain, we'll stay all day.
[Leader says] Friend, did you bring the
_____ ?
[Group echoes] Yes, we brought the
_____ .
Going on a picnic, here we go!
(Repeat as many times as desired, using different picnic items, such as hot dogs, potato chips, mustard, rolls, radio, football, blanket, and so on.)

3. *Friends' Story.* Ask a small group of children to dictate a group story about some friends and something that happened to them. Start them off with a lead sentence such as "Once upon a time, there were some friends and their names were . . . ." Have children take turns telling a sentence or two of the story. Write down what they

say, using their exact words whenever possible. If a child gets stuck, ask questions such as "And then what happened?" or "Then what did they do?" Write large enough for the children to be able to see the words clearly. Read the story back to them and then to the whole group. Eventually, the "writers" may "read" the story to the entire group after having several opportunities to practice with help from an adult.

4. *World Friends.* Display pictures of children in various cultures and countries around the world. Discuss some of the things children in your class notice about the pictures. Focus on the fact that people all around the world have friends, make friends, and learn to behave in friendly ways. Talk about similarities among cultures, as well as differences. For instance, everyone needs food and shelter, but these may take different forms.

5. *More Than Hello.* Demonstrate different ways people greet friends. Use both verbal and nonverbal greetings, such as saying "Hi" or shaking hands. Ask the children to think of others they use or have seen people use. Discuss the fact that different cultures use different greeting techniques. In some cultures, people hug each other. In others, people bow or kiss each other on the cheek. Have children practice some simple greetings in pairs; then mix the pairs up and repeat the activity.

   Extend children's understanding of friendly behaviors by teaching them to greet each other in different languages. Some examples of greetings in various languages are: *Hallo* or *Guten Morgen* (German), *Halo* (Spanish), *Bonjour* (French), *Karo* (Nigerian), *Ohayo* (Japanese), and *ChaoEm* (Vietnamese).

6. *Friendly Phoning.* Furnish an area of the classroom with pretend telephones. Demonstrate a telephone conversation by inviting a child to answer the telephone. Stress things such as using an appropriate greeting, being polite, and saying goodbye. Suggest that children call each other or that they think of a friend to call.

7. *Moving Memories.* Read the book *My Friend William Moved Away* by Martha Hickman, in which loneliness and feelings of friendlessness are contrasted to memo-

ries of fun times the two main characters had together. Discuss with the children the emotions of the characters in various parts of the story and whether they have ever had those same feelings. Point out that people can still be friends even though they don't see each other every day. Help the children compose an imaginary letter to William from Jimmy based on events in the story.

8. *Letter for a Friend.* Suggest children write a letter to a friend. Ask them to think first of someone to write to and then of one or two things they'd like to tell that person. Either take dictation from them or encourage children to write their own letters the best way they know how using their own kind of writing. Provide paper without lines and a variety of writing tools. When children are finished, ask them to read their letter to you, or you read it to them.

Hints for Success:

- Get help from parents by sending home an empty envelope with a note of explanation, asking parents to help their child decide to whom he or she will write.

- Request that they attach a stamp and write the address of their child's friend on the envelope. Set a deadline for returning the prepared envelopes to school. Explain that the children will complete their letters at school and seal them into their envelopes. When everyone has written letters, walk to a nearby mailbox and mail them.

9. *My Friend Is.* Have children practice describing objects. Next, suggest that they play a game in which they describe a friend in the class using a variety of adjectives. See if others can guess who it is.

10. *Paw Paw Patch.* Using the traditional song "Paw Paw Patch," teach children the following circle game. A child who is "it" stands in the center. The group sings the first verse of the song, inserting the name of a child to whom "it" points. "It" will then wave to that child, who in turn will wave back. For the second verse, the whole group makes motions to match the words of the song. The child named becomes "it," and the cycle begins again.

Paw Paw Patch
Where, oh where is dear little _____?
(Repeat twice)
Way down yonder in the paw paw patch.
Pickin' up paws paws, put 'em in the basket.
(Repeat twice)
Way down yonder in the paw paw patch.

If you don't know the tune, recite the words as a chant; it works equally well.

11. *School Friends.* Read *My Friend Leslie* by Maxine Rosenberg to the children. This is a book about the friendship between two kindergartners, one who is multiply handicapped and one not handicapped at all. Prior to another reading later or on a different day, explain to the children that they will help you make a list of all the things the friends in the book did together. Hang a large piece of easel paper in plain sight of the group and begin reading the book. As the story unfolds, pause periodically, encouraging children to summarize the activities Leslie and Karen enjoyed together. Write these down. At the end, go over the list, discussing with the group the friends' common interests and the similar things the children like to do with their own friends. If this book seems too long for the children in your group, or you are unable to get a copy, conduct a similar activity using the book *Ira Sleeps Over* by Bernard Waber. Ask children to remember all the things the two friends did together on their sleep-over.

12. *Feelings Between Friends.* Explain that when people are friends, they sometimes worry about what the other person thinks of them. Tell the children you will read a story about two friends and ask them to listen carefully so they will know who felt worried and why. Read the story *Ira Sleeps Over* by Bernard Waber. At the end of the reading, show the group large cutout figures of the main characters (Ira, his sister, and Reggie). Give children a chance to talk about the characters and how they felt at various parts of the story. Ask questions such as "When Ira was asked to sleep over, how did he feel? Why?" "When Ira's sister reminded him that he never slept without his bear, how did he feel?" "What

did he decide to do? Why?" "When Reggie was telling the ghost story, how did he feel?" "How did Ira feel?" "When Ira learned that Reggie had a bear too, how did he feel?" Show children the pictures in the book at various points in the story and have them check expressions on faces. Finally ask, "Did you ever worry about what your friend would think about something you have? What did you do?"

13. *Yoo Hoo.*

General Purpose: For children to practice listening skills.

TFPs: 1, 9, 13, 14, 16, 17, 18, 23.

Materials: None

Procedure:

a. Explain that sometimes we can guess who a friend is from the sound of their voice. "Today you're going to play a game in which one friend hides and echoes part of the song, and the rest of us will try to guess who it is." Explain what an echo is and that there will be an echo in the song.

b. Introduce the game by teaching the following song. Make up a tune or use the words as a chant.

Yoo Hoo

There's someone living in the house next door,
I wonder who it can be.
There's someone living in the house next door,
Who always answers me.
Yoo Hoo, Yoo Hoo. (Group calls.)
Yoo Hoo, Yoo Hoo. (Echo answers.)
I wonder who it can be.

b. While children close their eyes, choose a child to hide behind a room divider or shelf. Sing (or chant) the song with the children, cuing the hiding child when to answer with the echo. Have the group try to guess who it is.

Hint for Success:

• Children may find it too challenging to play the game without peeking. Explain that it is more fun for everyone if they don't see who the "echo" is. Suggest that

they lower their heads and cover their eyes with their hands. Quickly tap someone and have them move very quietly "behind the wall."

How to Simplify this Activity:

• Remind the children of everyone's name each time before a new "echo" hides.

How to Extend this Activity:

• Choose more than one child to echo the song.

Physical

1. *Friendly Touches.* Discuss touching others in a friendly way. Remind children that while hugging is usually seen as friendly, some people don't like to be hugged by anyone except their family members. If a person wants to give a friendly hug, he or she could ask the person first. Emphasize that there are some ways of touching that people find friendly and others they don't like; make a list of these. Ask children to show some friendly ways to touch a teddy bear.

2. *Musical Hugs.* Precede this activity with Friendly Touches. Have children ask a friend to be their partner in this musical game. Tell them to choose an action that represents friendship, perhaps a hand hold, a clap, or a hug. Put on some bouncy music and invite children to walk around separately until the music stops. When this happens, they should find their friend and give each other their friendship sign.

3. *Friendly Leaders.* Have the children each choose a partner for a variation of the game Follow the Leader. In each pair, children take turns being the "leader" and the "follower," playing the game in the usual manner. The leader calls out a series of commands, such as "Hands on hips; open your mouth; touch your toes." The follower does everything that the leader says. To avoid feelings of competition, time the turns so each partner gets the same amount of time being the "leader" and the "follower."

4. *Friendly Pulling.* Introduce this activity with a discussion of ways in which friends help one another. Provide sleds or wagons

for children to use in friendship pairs or small groups. Suggest that they find ways to share the equipment and take turns being the puller and the rider.

5. ***Rise, Sugar, Rise.*** Teach the children the following song to the tune of "Skip to My Lou."

Up on the mountain, two by two.
(Repeat twice)
Rise, sugar, rise.

Let's see you make a motion, two by two.
(Repeat twice)
Rise, sugar, rise.

That's a mighty fine motion, two by two.
(Repeat twice)
Rise, sugar, rise.

Once children know the words, sing "Rise, Sugar, Rise" as part of a simple circle game. During verse one, the group holds hands and circles to the right as two children are selected to stand in the middle. During verse two, the children in the center create a motion together or in imitation of one another. During verse three, the children in the outer circle mimic the motions of the partners in the middle.

6. ***Outdoor Weaving.*** Collect cloth or burlap that can be cut into strips five to six feet long. One day, ask the children to help you cut or rip the cloth into strips. Another day, invite three or four friends to practice their fine motor skills by "weaving" the strips in and out of the mesh on a chain-link fence to create an outdoor decoration. Point out that such a project would be too big for one person to do alone. Working with friends makes the job go faster and makes it more fun. Older children could be encouraged to practice negotiation skills by agreeing on a pattern and then carrying it out.

7. ***Musical Hoops.*** Put several (seven or eight) large plastic hoops in the center of a large group of children. Then play music while the children move in a circle around the hoops. When the music stops, tell the children to get inside a hoop. Continue this game, calling out a different movement each time the music plays—walking, hopping, crawling, jumping, leaping, skipping, and so on. Remove hoops each time, until the entire class is in two or three hoops. Verbally point out the friendly and cooperative behaviors children exhibit throughout the game.

Pretend Play

1. ***Hospitable Homes.*** Arrange an area of the room as a pretend home using standard housekeeping play furniture or miniature dollhouse furniture and small figures. Provide at least one surface that represents the door and can be used for knocking. Discuss with the children ways people seek the company of friends. They may think of calling on the telephone or coming to visit and knocking on the door. Suggest things for them to say, model, or observe as children take the roles of visitor and friend at home.

2. ***Keeping in Touch.*** Set up two pretend houses in the same area or across the room from each other. Provide both with telephones, mailboxes, and doorbells. Suggest to the children that they could pretend to be friends living in the same neighborhood, or in neighborhoods far away from each other. Encourage them to act out ways to maintain their friendship. Expand the play by creating a central post office with stamping, sorting, and delivery areas. Further the fun by moving the entire setup outside and including tricycle "mail trucks" on which children can deliver letters to friends.

3. ***Picnicking Pals.*** Select an area of the room or a place outdoors to be the picnic site. Provide a picnic basket, eating props, a blanket or large towel, and other props to suggest an outdoor picnic. More elaborate settings could include trees, a pond, fishing poles, fish, a ball, books, a sun, clouds, puppet animals, birds, and so on. Ask the children to suggest things for the area and familiarize them with the idea of a picnic by using the chant described in the Language section of this unit. Encourage children to be part of a group of friends who decide to have a picnic together. As an alternative, arrange an area to look like the seashore. Provide water and sand toys,

blanket, towels, imaginary suntan lotion, a portable radio, books, and a swimming area. Ask the children to talk about some things they might do at the beach. Suggest that they pretend it is a warm sunny day at the beach, taking the roles of beach visitors, hot dog seller, lifeguard, and so on.

Social

1. *We Are Alike/We Are Different.* Invite two children at a time to look into a mirror at themselves and each other. Help them discover characteristics they have in common and things that are different about each of them. Record their names on paper and make two lists as they think of things that are the same ("We Are Alike") and things that are different ("We Are Different"). To extend the activity, suggest things that cannot be seen, such as skills, handedness, favorite foods, number of people in their families, and so on. Tell the partners that all day they can report to you other things to add to their list as they continue to learn more about each other and compare characteristics.

2. *Getting to Know You.* Tape-record a brief, individual interview with each child in your class (about five minutes each). Ask questions like "What is your favorite food . . . toy . . . place to visit?" "What makes you sad . . . happy . . . angry?" Introduce one interview to the class each day, or put the tape in a learning center. Ask the children to identify the mystery person. Emphasize the similarities and differences among the children interviewed or between the mystery person and themselves.

3. *Sociable Songs.* Reinforce children's understanding of how to initiate contacts with potential friends using the following songs.

Hello Song
(Tune: "Good Night Ladies")
Hello, *first child's name*
Hello, *second child's name*
Hello, *third child's name*
Today let's all be friends.

Repeat using the names of all the children in the group. To dismiss children, use a variation on these lyrics:

Good-bye, *first child's name*
Good-bye, *second child's name*
Good-bye, *third child's name*
Today we've all been friends.

Wave to the children as they leave the group.

Everybody Shake Hands
(Tune: "Everybody Do This")
Everybody shake hands, shake hands, shake hands.
Everybody shake hands, just like this.
Verse 2: Everybody wave hi.
Verse 3: Everybody smile awhile.
Verse 4: Everybody hug a friend.
Verse 5: Everybody hold hands.

If You're Friendly and You Know It
(Tune: "If You're Happy and You Know It")
If you're friendly and you know it say *Hello.*
(repeat)
If you're friendly and you know it then your words will surely show it.
If you're friendly and you know it say *hello.*
Verse 2: . . . say *play with me.*
Verse 3: . . . say *your turn.*
Verse 4: . . . say *sit by me.*
Verse 5: . . . say *here's some for you.*

Jenny's Here Today
(Tune: "Farmer in the Dell")
Jenny's here today
Jenny's here today
Let's all wave hello, 'cause
Jenny's here today.

4. *Pass It On.* Play this game with a small group or with the whole group sitting or standing in a circle. One person starts by looking directly to his or her right and saying "Hi" to the person there. Each person in turn does exactly the same thing, until the "Hi" has been passed all around

the circle. Try reversing the direction, speeding it up, slowing it down, or using a greeting in another language. Other variations are to pass a handshake, a hug, or a hand squeeze.

5. ***Our Friends Album.*** Take pictures of the children as they play at school together. Put the developed photographs into an album and ask children to dictate words that could be used for captions under each one. Keep the book in the reading area on the bookshelf for children to "read" to each other. Over time, add more pictures to the album. Have it available for parents to see.

6. ***Sign Here.*** Explain that sometimes friends like to have a special way to help them remember each other. One good way to remember friends is to collect their autographs (signatures). Make a simple blank autograph book for each child by stapling several pages together and attaching a cover. Encourage them to pass their books around and sign each other's. They could draw pictures on the pages or write a simple message to each friend. (Figure 3.6)

7. ***Fair Share.*** Give children a structured experience in sharing and cooperating as a group. To carry out this activity you will need: a two-pound lump of clay, a table with five chairs (one for an adult, four for children), and one plastic knife, one pair of child's scissors, and one twelve-inch length of wire to be used by the children to divide the clay if that is their solution for how to use it "fairly." Place a lump of clay in the center of the table. Neutralize the clay by keeping one hand on it. Say, "I have one big ball of clay, and there are four friends who want to use it. Tell me how everyone can have a chance." Listen to the children's ideas; elicit suggestions from everyone. Clarify each child's perspective by paraphrasing his or her ideas to the group. Follow up with, "and what do you think of that?" Remain impartial throughout this process. Do not show disapproval of any child's idea, regardless of its content. Remind children as necessary that the first step in playing with the clay is deciding as a group how that will take place. If children

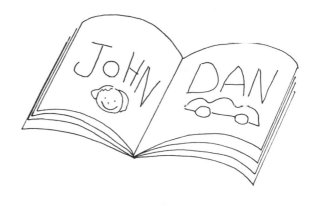

Figure 3.6 *Please Sign My Autograph Book*

become bogged down, repeat pertinent TFPs. Summarize the solution when it has been achieved. Praise children for figuring out a solution, then help them carry it out.

*8. ***Friendship Skits.***

General Purpose: To promote children's recognition and understanding of basic friendship skills.

TFPs: 1, 9, 12, 13, 14, 15, 16, 17, 32, 33, 34.

Materials: Two dolls (or people puppets); several small, colored blocks.

Procedure:

a. Seat children in a semicircle facing you. Make sure everyone can see your face and hands and the space directly in front of you. If you are sitting on the floor, kneel so you are more easily visible to the children. If you are sitting in a chair, use a low bench or table to display the props. As the script unfolds, manipulate the dolls in corresponding actions. Be expressive with your face and your voice. Use dialogue for the characters that seems appropriate for the situation; use different voices for each character.

b. Say, "Today, we are going to talk about friends. Here are two dolls. We are going to pretend that these dolls are real children just like you. Their names are Sarah and Cathy. They are five years old and go to a school just like ours.

Watch carefully and see what happens when Sarah and Cathy try to be friends."

c. Set up one doll (Sarah) as if "playing" with several blocks. Place the second doll (Cathy) facing Sarah but at least a foot away.

   Say, "Here is Sarah. She is playing alone with the blocks and is having a good time. Cathy sees Sarah and would really like to play with her, so she watches Sarah very carefully. Sarah keeps playing; she doesn't look up. Cathy feels sad. She thinks Sarah doesn't want to be friends.

d. Questions for discussion:

   1. Who was playing?
   2. Who wanted to play?
   3. Did Sarah know that Cathy wanted to play?

As children answer these questions, provide information to help in their deliberations: "Sarah was so busy playing, she didn't look up. That means she never even saw Cathy standing there. She didn't know Cathy wanted to play. Watch again and see what Cathy does differently this time."

e. Say, "Here is Sarah. She is playing alone with the blocks and is having a good time. Cathy sees Sarah and really would like to play with her. So she watches Sarah very carefully. Sarah keeps playing. She doesn't look up. Cathy walks over to Sarah and says, 'Hi. I like your building. I'll help you get some more blocks.'"

f. Questions for discussion:

   1. Who was playing?
   2. Who wanted to play?
   3. Did Sarah know Cathy wanted to play?
   4. How could she tell?
   5. What will Sarah do next?
   6. Let's think of some other ways Cathy could let Sarah know she wants to play.

g. As children suggest ideas, paraphrase them and write them down where all the children can see them. Accept all ideas regardless of originality, correctness, or feasibility.

h. If children have difficulty thinking of ideas, prompt them by providing information: "Sometimes, when people want to play, they can say 'Hi. I want to play.' Or, they can ask a question like, 'What are you building?' This lets the other person know they want to be friends. What do you think Cathy could do?"

i. Once children have suggested their ideas, replay the scene using each suggestion, one at a time. Ask the children to predict how Sarah will react in each case. Play out the scene as they suggest. Provide further information as appropriate. "John, you said Cathy could help Sarah build. Let's try that." (Maneuver the dolls and provide appropriate dialogue.) "Tell me what you think Sarah will do now."

j. Help children evaluate how well their solution worked. For example, "Sarah still doesn't know that Cathy wants to be friends. Tell us another way that Sarah could ask Cathy to play." Continue trying out their ideas.

k. As children find solutions, praise them for thinking of ways to help the friends figure out what to do. Summarize for them the ways that were tried and which ones proved more successful. As unfriendly solutions are suggested and role-played, point out that the results may be confusion, hurt feelings, sadness, and anger.

Hints for Success:

• The kind of puppets or dolls used for this activity can influence how much the children relate to the problems they are trying to solve. Use dolls that look like people, rather than animal figures. To make it easier for both sexes to relate to the characters, look for dolls that could be either boys or girls and are dressed and named neutrally. To help in manipulating objects, choose puppets or dolls with arms, rather than mouths, that can move easily.

• Demonstrate both effective and non-effective ways to make and keep friends. Vary the order in which you present these from day to day.

- Repeat the same scenario another day using different props.

How to Simplify this Activity:
- Carry out the activity with a very small group of children.
- Keep the scenarios short and simple. As children suggest solutions, act them out and point out the results.

How to Extend this Activity:
- Encourage the children to reenact on their own the scenario you demonstrated.
- Introduce open-ended scenarios in which a problem is posed, but no solution (effective or ineffective) is modeled. Invite the children to create a solution and then evaluate it.
- Make the dolls available to the children to role-play other scenarios of their own invention.

The preceding skit demonstrated ways children might try to *initiate* an interaction with another child. Additional sample scenarios illustrating *play initiation skills, acceptance of friendly overtures,* and *conflict negotiation* are provided below along with potential discussion questions for each.

Sample Skits
Skit 1: Michelle and John (three variations on initiating play)

Scene 1A: Michelle is building a train with the large blocks. John approaches and asks, "What are you building?"
M: A train.
J: I'll be the passenger.
M: I don't want any passengers.
J: Then I'll load the baggage car.
John and Michelle begin to play.

1. Who is playing?
2. Who wanted to play?
3. Tell me if you think they were playing together.
4. Do you think they will play together for a while?
5. How did Michelle know John wanted to play?

Scene 1B: Michelle is playing in the block area. John walks over and begins to add blocks to her building. Michelle looks up and smiles, saying, "Here are more blocks you can use." John continues playing with Michelle.

1. Who was playing?
2. Who wanted to play?
3. How did Michelle know John wanted to play?
4. Were the children playing together?
5. How did they feel?
6. Are they friends?

Scene 1C: Michelle is building a train out of blocks. John approaches and asks, "What are you building?"
M: A train.
J: I'll be the passenger.
M: OK, you can sit in the back.

1. Who was playing?
2. Who wanted to play?
3. Did Michelle want John to play?
4. How else could John let Michelle know he wanted to play?
5. Are they friends? Why?
6. Are the children happy?

Skit 2: Michi and Tamo (three variations on acceptance of friendly overtures)

Scene 2A: Michi is playing with the clay. Tamo approaches her and says, "Can I play?" Michi says, "There isn't enough, go away."

1. How did Michi feel when Tamo asked to play?
2. How did Tamo feel when Michi said no?
3. What could they have done differently so that each child would have been happy?

Scene 2B: Michi is playing with all the clay. Tamo says, "Can I have some?" Michi ignores him.

1. Tell me how these children feel.

2. How else could Tamo let Michi know he wanted some clay?

3. What could Michi have done if she didn't want to give up the clay?

4. How could both children have a chance to use the clay?

Scene 2C: Michi is playing with the clay? Tamo walks up and asks, "Can I play?" Michi answers, "Sure, here's some for you."

1. Who wanted to play?

2. How did Michi know Tamo wanted to play?

3. How did Tamo feel when Michi offered him some clay?

4. Tell me some other ways they could have played together.

5. Are they friends?

6. Do friends always agree?

Skit 3: Frank and Annie (two variations on conflict negotiation)

Scene 3A:

F: Oh, boy! Look at the clay. *(Moves toward it.)*

A: Oooh, clay. I'm going to use it all by myself. *(Takes it.)*

F: No you won't. If you do, then I won't have any to play with. That's a problem.

A: I don't care. I want it all to myself. You go away.

F: I want it too. Give it to me or else I'll hurt you! *(Grabs for object.)*

A: No! (Defends forcefully.) *(F. pushes A., she cries and hits F., he begins to cry.)*

1. Tell me what happened when Annie and Frank played together.

2. Were they having a good time?

3. Tell me how Annie and Frank felt when they played like this.

4. Tell me other ways they could find to play.

Scene 3B:

F: Oh, look, there's the clay in the art area.

A: I really like playing with clay. I'm going to make something really big with this clay so I need all of it for myself. *(Takes it.)*

F: We both really want the clay at the same time. This is a problem. What can we do about this problem, Annie?

A: I know one thing we could do. I'll take some for me and I'll give some to you. *(Annie divides the clay in half; gives part to Frank.)* Here's your part.

F: OK *(Takes his portion from Annie.)* Now we can each play with the clay. There are lots of things we can make.

1. Tell me what happened when Annie and Frank played together.

2. Were they having a good time?

3. Tell me how Annie and Frank felt when they played like this.

4. Tell me other ways they could find to play.

Skit 4: George and Mandy (two variations on conflict negotiation)

Scene 4A: George and Mandy both want to play with the same wagon.

M: It's mine. *(Hits George.)*

G: No, it's mine. *(Hits Mandy.)*

M: I'll hit you so hard. *(Both dolls begin to hit.)*

1. Tell me what happened when Mandy and George played together this time.

2. Were they having a good time?

3. Tell me how Mandy and George felt when they played together like that.

4. Tell me what other ways they could have found to solve their problem.

Scene 4B: George and Mandy both want to play with the same wagon.

M: It's mine.

G: No, it's mine.

M: We both want the wagon at the same time. That's a problem. What can we do?

G: I know, let's use it together. You can pull me for a while and then I'll pull you.

M: All right, climb in. Here we go. *(Repeat action with other doll.)*

1. Tell me what happened when Mandy and George played together this time.

2. Were they having a good time?

3. Tell me how Mandy and George felt when they played together this time.

4. Tell me what other ways they could have tried to solve their problem.

Skit 5: Aaron and Cindy (two variations on conflict negotiation)

Scene 5A: Aaron and Cindy are each playing with separate toys—by themselves. Aaron is playing happily with the boat; Cindy is using the puppets. After a short while, Cindy looks up from her play; she approaches Aaron.

C: Playing with that boat looks like fun. I want to play with it. Can I have it?

A: No.

C: But I like boats, too. I want it! *(Cindy grabs for and pulls at the boat. Aaron clutches it tightly.)*

A: You can't have it. Get away. *(The dolls continue to tug at the boat. The scene ends with them tugging at the boat.)*

1. Tell me what Aaron and Cindy did when they played.

2. Why did they play this way?

3. Were they having a good time? (You may want to talk about the differences in the way Aaron and Cindy felt; talk about the differences between good and bad times.)

4. How did Aaron feel about playing with the boat?

5. How did Cindy feel when Aaron did not give her the boat?

6. What other ways could they have played?

Scene 5B: Each doll is playing contentedly by itself. Aaron has the boat; Cindy has the puppets.

C: *(Walks over to Aaron.)* Playing with that boat looks like fun. I want to play with it. Can I have it?

A: If I give you the boat, then I won't have anything to play with. That would be a problem. Let's think of what we can do.
PAUSE

C: I know! If you give me the boat to play with, then I'll give you the puppets. We could trade!

A: OK, then we'll each have something to play with and we won't have a problem.
(Dolls trade the toys; they each—separately—resume play with the exchanged toys. Scene ends.)

1. Tell me what Aaron and Cindy did this time when they played. Sometimes when children play this way it is called trading. Sometimes children trade or bargain with their toys when they play. When people bargain they each agree to do something to or for each other. For example, you might say, "If you'll let me play puppets with you now, then I'll let you play with the boat later."

2. What other ways could Aaron and Cindy bargain?

3. What would you do if you wanted to trade with someone and they don't want to?

4. What would you do if you don't want to trade your toy for what another child has?

Skit 6: Tim and Amy (two variations on conflict negotiation)

Scene 6A: Tim and Amy enter area; one object is nearby.

T: I see the computer.

A: Oh, I see it too—and I'm going to use it.

T: No you won't. It's for me to play with. You get away from here.

A: No, I won't. I'm gonna tell on you. *(Tim pushes Amy forcefully; she falls and cries.)*

1. What kind of time did they have in this story?

2. How did they feel when they played this way?

3. Tell me other ways that Amy and Tim could play.

Scene 6B: Tim and Amy enter area; one object is nearby.

T: Amy, look at the computer.

A: Oh, I'm going to use it first.

T: No, I want it. I saw it first! *(Takes object.)*

A: Well, if you take the computer I won't have anything to play with. I really want the computer too. We have a problem. What can we do?

T: Hmmm, I'll think about it. . . . I know one thing we could do. I could use it now and you could use it when I'm finished with it.

A: OK, I'll go and play with something else for now. When you're done with the computer, remember to come and tell me!

T: OK. *(Amy walks away to another area. Tim plays with the computer for a while and then walks over to Amy. He hands her the object.)*

T: You can play with the computer now.

A: *(excitedly)* Oh, boy! Now I can play with it!

1. What kind of time were the children having?

2. How did they feel when they were playing?

3. Tell me other ways they could play. We can use these ideas in the story.

TEACHER RESOURCES

Field Trip Ideas

1. Plan a real picnic outing, including equipment for friendly games (such as ball games or kite flying) that two or more people could play at one time.

Classroom Visitors

1. Invite two adolescent or adult friends to visit the class to describe what they like to do together and what makes them friends.

2. Designate a day to be friends' day at school and have each child invite a friend to spend all or part of the day with the group. If this would make the group too large, divide the class into subgroups and have only a portion of the children bring a friend each day all week, until everyone has had a turn. Suggest they introduce their friend to everyone, tell something about them and invite them to choose an activity to do together.

Children's Books

Aliki. *We Are Best Friends.* New York: Mulberry Publishers, 1982.

Barkin, C., and E. James. *Are We Still Best Friends?* Milwaukee: Raintree, 1975.

Berger, T. *A Friend Can Help.* Chicago: Childrens Press, 1974.

Brandenberg, F. *Nice New Neighbors.* New York: Greenwillow, 1977.

Carlson, N. S. *Marie Louise & Christopher.* New York: Schribner's, 1974.

Clifton, L. *My Friend Jacob.* New York: Holt, Rinehart and Winston, 1980.

Crary, E. *I Want It.* Seattle: Parenting Press, 1982.

——. *I Want to Play.* Seattle: Parenting Press, 1982.

——. *My Name Is Not Dummy.* Seattle: Parenting Press, 1983.

Delton, J. *The New Girl at School.* New York: Dutton, 1979.

DeRegniers, B. S. *May I Bring a Friend?* New York: Atheneum, 1965.

Freeman, Don. *Corduroy.* New York: Viking, 1968.

Greenfield, E. *Me and Nessie.* New York: Crowell, 1975.

Hickman, M. *My Friend William Moved Away.* Nashville: Abingdon, 1980.

Hoban, R. *Best Friends for Frances.* New York: Harper and Row, 1969.

Hutchins, P. *The Doorbell Rang.* New York: Greenwillow, 1986.

Iwasaki, C. *Will You Be My Friend?* New York: McGraw-Hill, 1970.

Kellogg, S. *Best Friends.* New York: Dial, 1985.

Lobel, A. *Frog and Toad Are Friends.* New York: Harper and Row, 1970.

——. *Frog and Toad Together.* New York: Harper and Row, 1972.

Marshall, J. *George and Martha*. New York: Houghton Mifflin, 1972.

Rosenberg, M. *My Friend Leslie: The Story of a Handicapped Child*. New York: Lothrop, Lee, and Shepard, 1983.

Saltzberg, B. *What to Say to Clara*. New York: MacMillan, 1984.

Steig, W. *Amos and Boris*. New York: Farrar and Straus, 1970.

Stevenson, J. *Howard*. New York: Greenwillow, 1980.

Udry, J. M. *Let's Be Enemies*. New York: Harper Junior, 1961.

Vincent, G. *Ernest and Celestine*. New York: Greenwillow, 1982.

Viorst, J. *Rosie and Michael*. New York: Atheneum, 1974.

Waber, B. *Ira Sleeps Over*. Boston: Houghton Mifflin, 1972.

Zalben, J. B. *Will You Count the Stars Without Me?* Toronto: McGraw-Hill Ryerson Ltd., 1979.

Ziefert, M. *Mike and Tony: Best Friends*. New York: Viking, 1987.

Adult References

Adcock, D., and M. Segal. *Making Friends: Ways of Encouraging Social Development in Young Children*. Englewood Cliffs, NJ: Prentice-Hall Inc., 1983.

Hendrick, J. *The Whole Child*. Columbus, OH: Merrill Publishing Company, 1983.

Kostelnik, M., L. C. Stein, A. P. Whiren, and A. K. Soderman. *Guiding Children's Social Development*. Cincinnati: South-Western Publishers, 1988.

Miller, K. *The Outside Play and Learning Book*. Mt. Rainier, MD: Gryphon House, 1989.

Rubin, Z. *Children's Friendships*. Cambridge, MA: Harvard Press, 1988.

Smith, C. A. *Promoting the Social Development of Young Children*. Palo Alto, CA: Mayfield, 1982.

Stocking, S. H., D. Arezzo, and S. Leavitt. *Helping Kids Make Friends*. Allen, TX: Boys Town Center for the Study of Youth Development, 1980.

Zimbardo, P. G., and S. L. Radl. *The Shy Child*. Garden City, NY: Doubleday, 1982.

Chapter 4

Pets

The fascination of observing an aquarium filled with colorful fish; the joy of romping with a puppy or a kitten; the comfort derived from cuddling a bunny or a guinea pig; the pleasure of singing along with a parakeet: these are some of the rewards that come from having and caring for pets.

Children enjoy pets for many reasons. They like watching them, handling them, caring for them, and learning about them. For preschoolers and kindergartners, pets make gratifying companions; not only are they interesting and entertaining, but they are unconditionally loving. Moreover, for some children, too shy, too unsure, or too volatile to have productive interactions with peers, classroom pets offer social contact with other living beings. The gentle touch and soft voice to which an animal responds best may help children with emerging social skills to think of ways to approach and interact with their peers. Contacts with their classmates will naturally follow.

Teachers, too, consider pets a welcome addition to the classroom. Through these special animals children learn responsibility, and they learn to understand the natural world. Pets also introduce children to the life cycle in relevant, meaningful ways. Additionally, animals in the classroom help children better understand the interdependence of all of the Earth's living creatures as well as our common needs.

Evidence indicates that children's concepts of pets, pet behavior, and human actions related to pet care change in concert with their cognitive and emotional development. Three phases of understanding have been identified (Kellert and Westervelt, 1983). Initially, preschoolers and early elementary-aged children focus primarily on the affective nature of their relationships to pets. They are most interested in observing, talking to, and handling animals as a way to give or receive comfort and love. Gradually, as their understanding of animals expands, children become increasingly interested in how animals live, why they behave as they do, and how they should be cared for. Finally, as adolescents, young people become more sensitive to ethical concerns regarding animals and show greater appreciation for the ecological role of animals on the Earth.

PURPOSE

This unit emphasizes the first two phases of children's naturally developing understanding of pets. Many activities have been designed to help children gain awareness of the needs of all types of animals, as well as of their value. Understanding how best to meet those needs is also an integral part of the theme. Much attention has been devoted to interpreting cues in animal behavior that might provide feedback to children about their own actions. We hope children will learn to appreciate pets, as well as how to treat them in gentle, caring ways.

IMPLEMENTATION

There are several ways to implement a theme about pets. Teachers who work with three- and four-year-olds may wish to:

1. Introduce a one-week unit that concentrates on TFPs one through eight. Focus on some of the reasons people have for choosing to acquire pets, while identifying and discussing animals that make good ones.
2. Choose one or two common pets, such as cats or dogs, around which to build a unit. Invite a few parents to bring one pet a day to school for a brief visit.
3. Teach for a week about pretend pets. Invite children to share favorite stuffed-animal pets from home. Discuss how they are similar to and different from real pets.

For more experienced children, consider multiweek units:

Option One:
Week One: General overview using TFPs one through fourteen
Week Two: Pet selection
Week Three: What pets need
Week Four: Caring for pets

Option Two:
Week One: General Overview
Week Two: Mammals
Week Three: Reptiles and Amphibians
Week Four: Fish
Week Five: Insects
Week Six: Birds

Option Three:
Week One: Pets that live on land (cats, dogs, horses, rabbits)
Week Two: Pets that fly (parakeets, ducks, geese)
Week Three: Pets that live in or on the water (turtles, frogs, fish)

Option Four:
Week One: People who help others select pets (pet store, animal shelter employees)
Week Two: People who help others care for pets (veterinarians, groomers, trainers)

TERMS, FACTS, AND PRINCIPLES

General Information

1. A pet is an animal that is lovingly kept, primarily for fun and companionship.

2. Pets usually live at or near the home of the owner or at a place visited regularly by the owner.

3. A pet may be given a name by the owner.

*4. A special bond of love often develops between owner and pet.

5. Stuffed or imaginary animals may be used as pretend pets.

6. Many different kinds of animals can become pets.
   a. Mammals: cats, dogs, horses, guinea pigs, rabbits, sheep, goats, hamsters, gerbils
   b. Birds: parakeets, ducks, geese, chickens
   c. Reptiles: turtles, snakes, lizards
   d. Amphibians: frogs, toads, salamanders
   e. Fish: goldfish, guppies, tropical fish
   f. Insects: ants, crickets

7. Pets vary greatly in size, shape, color, and body covering.

8. Pets vary in their characteristics. Some pets:
   a. like to be handled
   b. are primarily to be observed and do not like to be handled or should not be handled
   c. are noisy
   d. are quiet
   e. move quickly
   f. move slowly
   g. sleep during the day and play at night

h. wake early in the morning and sleep at night
*i. have unique personalities
j. are very independent and need little care
k. are very dependent and need much care and companionship
l. like to be near children
m. are very nervous when around children who are moving quickly
*n may be very young and have not yet established behavior patterns with people
*o may be older and have established behavior patterns with people
p. eat meat
q. eat primarily vegetables or fruits
r. eat a combination of all kinds of food
s. require a warm living space
t. require a cold living space
u. require a very dry place to live
v. require a wet place to live
w. like or require much outdoor activity
x. prefer to be indoors
y. are very little and need only a little space
z. are very large and need lots of room.

*9. Pets begin life as babies, grow to be adults (which may reproduce), and eventually die.

*10. Pets often can show by their sounds or movements how they feel or what they need.
   a. Some pets pant when they are hot.
   b. Some pets hide when they are frightened.
   c. Some pets make special sounds when they are content, irritated, frightened, defensive.
   d. Some pets' hair stands on end when they are frightened or defensive.

Selection

11. Sometimes pets are purchased, sometimes found and adopted, and sometimes people receive them as gifts.

*12. People should select pets whose needs they can fulfill and avoid those they cannot care for properly.

*13. Some animals that are found in the woods, such as turtles or frogs, may be kept for a short while and then returned to their natural home.

*14. Some wild animals have difficulty surviving in captivity.

Needs of Pets

*15. Pets have needs that are similar to people's needs.

16. All pets need love and care.

17. All pets need food, water, and rest.

18. Pets need to be kept clean or groomed.

19. Pets need to be kept healthy.

20. Pets need to be kept safe.

21. Some pets need companionship.

22. Mammals and birds need play, exercise, and privacy.

Care of Pets

23. People are responsible for taking care of their pets.

24. People should take care of their pets by:
    *a. getting a license if required
    *b. learning about their pet's needs and habits
    c. providing food, water, and shelter every day
    d. playing with their pet gently and safely
    e. allowing the pet time to rest
    *f. keeping their pet safe
    g. keeping their pet's eating and sleeping area clean
    *h. training the pet
    *i. cleaning and grooming the pet
    j. playing with, exercising, petting, and talking to the pet in ways that it seems to like
    *k. taking the pet to the veterinarian for check-ups and shots
    *l. telling other people how to approach or play with the pet safely
    *m. telling people to stop when they are doing something that will harm or frighten their pet.

Illnesses and Injuries

25. Pets may become ill or hurt.

*26. There are many causes of pet illnesses: eating food that the pet cannot digest, eating poisonous materials, choking on sharp objects, being in places too warm or too cold for the pet's body, or "catching" a disease from another animal.

27. Injuries happen in different ways: being scratched or bitten by other animals, being hit by a car, or being dropped, squeezed, stepped upon, or otherwise mistreated by people or animals.

28. It is important that the pet is cared for quickly when it is ill or injured.

*29. The pet may act very differently when it is ill or injured than when it is feeling well.

30. A person should approach an ill or injured pet very slowly and gently.

31. A veterinarian can usually find the cause of an illness, treat it, and tell the owner the special kind of care it needs.

32. Sometimes pets become too ill or hurt to be cured.

33. People feel sad when their pets die.

34. People remember their pets even when they no longer have them.

*35. The lifespan of a pet is usually shorter than that of its owner.

ACTIVITY IDEAS

Aesthetics

1. *Pet Skins.* Provide a variety of textured materials that resemble fur or the scaly skins of reptiles, fish, and amphibians. Include some feathers. Cut large pet-shaped silhouettes out of construction paper or grocery sacks. Invite children to enjoy the various textures while gluing a decorative covering to the pet cut-out of their choice.

2. *Picture This.* Gather a selection of pet stamps of the type commonly used with ink pads. Provide modeling dough and invite the children to produce pictures on it, using uninked stamps.

3. *Rub-a-Pet.* First, cut out pet-shaped templates from the heavy cardboard of dismantled grocery boxes. Next, remove the paper wrapping from "fat" crayons. Show children how to lay a template flat on a table, then cover it with easel paper. Demonstrate how to rub crayons on their sides over the covered cutouts. Soon pictures of the pets underneath will emerge!

4. *Pets at the Easel.* Using heavy cardboard, create large stencils in simple animal shapes. Fasten the stencil over a sheet of

paper on the easel and invite children to paint inside the shape. Remove the stencil to reveal the picture underneath.

Affective

1. *If Wishes Were Fishes.* Invite children to ponder and then describe the pets they most wish they could have. Ask them to give reasons for their choices and prompt them to describe ways in which they would care for their pets. Record the group's ideas as an experience story or in the form of a graph.

2. *Pet-Care Pamphlets.* Provide children with booklets of blank pages. Prepare these by stapling or lacing two full-sized sheets of paper down the center, then folding them in the middle to produce a booklet. Encourage children to dictate or write a step-by-step procedure for the care of a chosen pet. Pages one and two might include when and what to feed the pet, pages three and four might describe the preparation of a sleeping place, and pages five and six might focus on grooming tips. Invite children to add illustrations and design a cover for their pet-care pamphlet.

3. *Pet Hugs.*

   General Purpose: To encourage children to share possessions with others.

   TFPs: 1–7, 15, 16, 18, 20, 21, 23, 24b, c, d, f, g.

   Materials: Compose a short note to send home, requesting that children bring a "toy pet" (stuffed animal or animal figurine of unbreakable material) to school on a specified day. Collect additional stuffed animals for children who are unable to bring one in or who forget to bring their own. Provide masking tape and a marking pen to make pet name tags.

   Procedure:

   a. Initiate a large-group discussion prior to "Pet Hug Day." Invite children to bring a favorite toy pet from home whose affection they wish to share with their friends. Explain that everyone will have a chance to experience the pleasures of another child's pretend pet. Talk about ways that children can give and receive affection with live pets. Encourage children to describe types of touch and methods of play that pets they've known seem to enjoy. What kinds of touch do the children especially enjoy from pets—licks, rubs against their legs, small animals scampering up their arms, or birds landing on their hands or shoulders? Suggest such examples only if children are unable to think of ideas on their own.

   b. On the designated Pet Hug Day, assign an adult to apply masking-tape name tags to toy animals as children arrive with them. Include the child's name as well as the name they've given the pet.

   c. Gather the children in a large-group area. Provide extra animals to children who have not brought one from home.

   d. Invite the children, one at a time, to stand and describe or introduce their pets. Encourage children to pass them or carry them around the group offering others a chance to pat, stroke, or gently hug them. Praise gentle touch, pointing out that live pets enjoy the same kind of treatment.

   e. Encourage children to tell their friends to *stop* if they think their pets would be hurt by or would not enjoy a particular kind of treatment. Explain that pet owners are responsible for the health and happiness of their animal friends. This includes teaching others how to approach and play with them, as well as telling them when to stop acting in a harmful or frightening way.

   f. Praise and thank children for sharing the pleasures of their pets with each other. Some children may want to put their pets away as soon as the activity ends; others may be willing to continue sharing them throughout the day.

Hint for Success:

• Discuss the sharing aspect of the activity in detail before Hug Day occurs. Explain that other children will want to hold or touch each animal, and in return will share their pets. Each child can decide when he or she wants his or her pet back.

How to Simplify this Activity:

- Collect rubber animal figures or stuffed animals from school stock rather than requesting home assistance. Allow children to choose a favorite one to describe, name, and share.

- Structure Hug Day around small group times. Have children share with four or five others rather than with the whole group. In addition to having them share their pet for hugs, interview each child about pet selection, pet food, and pet grooming.

How to Extend this Activity:

- Consider a construction activity to precede Hug Day. Children could create their own pets using fabric scraps, small cardboard boxes, and Styrofoam balls and then name them. These "personalized pets" could then be shared.

Cognition

1. *What Sorts of Pets?* Gather or make one or more sets of animals for children to sort. Sample materials could include animal figures, pictures from magazines, or animal stickers. Invite children to develop their own categories for sorting the animals. Some possibilities children might choose are:

   - pets and non-pets
   - indoor pets and outdoor pets
   - pets with and without tails (or fur, feathers, smooth skin, etc.)
   - four-legged pets, two-legged pets, and legless pets
   - favorite pets and non-favorite pets

2. *Match That.* Provide separate pictures of pets and of pet foods. Challenge children to match each pet with an appropriate food. Alternatively, purchase and display small amounts of appropriate pet foods. Provide pictures or figurines of pets that can be placed near the bowls of food that "match" each pet. Plan this activity after several days of talking about pets and their needs. Other possible matches might include pets and their living quarters (fish bowl, hamster cage, stable, etc.) or pets

and human living quarters that might be more or less suitable.

3. *Put-Together Pets.*

   General Purpose: For children to recognize or construct relationships among objects by comparing them.

   TFPs: 6, 7, 12.

   Materials: Create flannel-board animals out of flannel or some other cloth. Cut each one apart so that limbs, torsos, tails, heads, ears, feet, and wings are separate pieces. Or, cut out pictures of animals from magazines, mount them on cardboard, and cut into separate body parts as above. Choose animals that are often owned as pets. Provide a flannel board or table top.

   Procedure:

   a. Invite one or two children to examine the materials for a few moments. Children may begin constructing pets from the body parts on their own. If children have not begun to combine parts into wholes after a few minutes, explain that they can play a game with the pieces.

   b. Choose a body part from the group. Begin with an easily identified feature, such as a head or tail. Place the piece near the child. Ask the child to look carefully at the picture and tell you what he or she thinks is depicted. You may need to prompt some children: "This looks like a tail, I think. Tell me an animal that might have a tail like this. See if you can find a picture of a body that would go with this tail."

   c. Ask the child to place the part chosen next to the first body part. Ask him or her to evaluate the prediction: "Look at the two pictures now. Tell me if you still think they belong together."

   d. Encourage the child to find other parts of the same animal. Some children may enjoy combining parts in a silly way. Acknowledge and allow unique combinations: "You've decided that the frog needs wings! Tell me some special things this frog could do if his body looked like that."

   e. Vary the activity by placing pictures together in inaccurate groupings. Ask each child to decide if you are correct and to help you get it right. Praise children as they discover and correct your errors.

Hint for Success:
- Begin with very familiar animals (cat, dog, goldfish). Add less common ones as children grow comfortable with the procedure (lizard, parrot, goat).

How to Simplify this Activity:
- Cut animal pictures into two or three easily recognizable parts—head-body-tail or body-legs-wings are examples.
- Make sure that each animal is predominately a color that is different from the other animals chosen (brown dog, black cat, white rabbit, orange fish).

How to Extend this Activity:
- Invite older children to create silly combinations of animal parts. Challenge them to think of names for these "new" animals that suit their changed characteristics. What could the animal do in this changed form that wouldn't be possible in its real form? To introduce the game, suggest first a creature with a combined name (fish + bird = "fird"—a creature that can live underwater and fly into the treetops).

4. *What's Hiding Here?*

General Purpose: To increase children's visual discrimination skills.

Materials: Black, grey, and white construction paper; eight to ten camouflage overlays (directions follow); adult-sized scissors; pencil; coloring book, templates, or puzzle pieces of animals to trace.

Procedure:

a. Make the camouflage overlays (directions follow). Draw or trace pictures of pets onto the construction paper, varying the sizes from two to six inches high or wide. Cut them out. Find a box lid or make a cardboard tray with sides two inches high into which the acetate sheets will fit snugly.

b. Keeping the tray and camouflage overlays out of sight, show children the cut-out pictures. Encourage them to examine the shapes carefully by looking at them, handling them, naming the pets, and arranging them into groups.

c. Take away all the pictures saying, "Now we'll use these pictures to play a game." Out of children's view, arrange a few pictures in the tray. Choose one of the less densely patterned acetate sheets to lay over the pictures.

d. Show the tray to the children saying, "Tell me what's hiding here." Point to the pictures under the acetate and encourage children to find the hidden pictures.

e. Repeat, using different pictures and one or more overlays. Gradually increase the amount of camouflage children must see through. Each time encourage the children to tell what the pictures are and where they are located under the sheet or in relation to one another.

Directions for making Camouflage Sheets Made from Acetate

Materials:
8 acetate sheets, 8½-by-11 inches each
black indelible marker
colored indelible markers

Procedure:

a. Purchase the acetate sheets at an art supply store.

b. Use an indelible ink pen to draw an array of marks on each of the acetate sheets. Vary the number, thickness, and arrangement of the marks you make so that some sheets have only a few lines and others have more. Sample configurations might include:

Sheet 1 – lines two inches apart in a cross-hatch pattern

Sheet 2 – lines one inch apart in a crosshatch pattern

Sheet 3 – lines one-half inch apart in a cross-hatch pattern

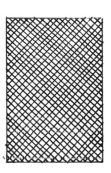

Sheet 4 – curved marks randomly drawn across the page

Sheet 5 – repeat sheet 4 adding more marks

Sheet 6 – alternating thick and thin lines

Sheet 7 – diagonal lines one-half inch apart

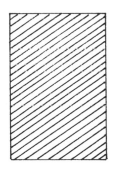

Sheet 8 – alternating thick and thin diagonal lines

Hint for Success:
• Allow children to arrange pictures for each other. Encourage them to take turns hiding pictures and finding them.

How to Simplify this Activity:
• Hide one picture at a time.
• Use cut-out shapes that are at least four inches high or wide.
• Select overlays that involve only a few marks.
• Hide pictures that are each a different color.

How to Extend this Activity:

- Increase the complexity of the camouflage by using pairs of colors other than black to mark the acetate. The following color combinations are ranked from the easiest to see through to ones that are more difficult to see through:

  a. red and blue
  b. green and yellow
  c. violet and orange
  d. blue and orange
  e. red and green
  f. yellow and violet

- Use cut-out shapes less than four inches high or wide.
- Hide several small pictures instead of a few large ones.
- Hide several pictures all the same color.

Construction

1. *Oh Give Me a Home.* Gather a range of art materials for children to use, including several kinds of small boxes (empty food containers, shoeboxes), small paper lunchbags, construction paper, glue or paste, scissors, and staplers. Initiate the activity by showing the children pictures of some structures used to house pets or by discussing various types of animal homes. Invite the children to construct their own notion of homes for pets. When their homes are completed, children may wish to construct animals to live in them.

2. *We're Off to See the Shelter.* Arrange a field trip to a humane society shelter or to an animal boarding facility. Prepare the children ahead of time by explaining that they are likely to encounter unusual smells and noises. Challenge them to watch for pets that they would enjoy caring for and to observe how the "experts" care for pets. After the field trip, invite children to create pictures of the facility and/or the animals, using a wide variety of materials that you provide (fabric, fake fur and feather scraps, markers, crayons, glue sticks, scissors, construction paper, pipe cleaners, yarn, etc....). Encourage children to recall their adventure by describing their art creations.

3. *Box Pets.*

   General Purpose: For children to construct their own representation of a pet.

   TFPs: 1, 2, 3, 5, 6, 7, 12.

   Materials: Collect a variety of boxes in several shapes and sizes. Ask families to help by sending discarded boxes to school. Look for round, square, rectangular, and heart-shaped boxes, as well as wrapping paper or paper towel rolls and empty food containers; quick-drying glue (wood glue works well); glue applicators and containers; fabric scraps, including fake fur, feathers, and yarn; art tables and chairs; marking pen for names and other labels.

   Procedure:

   a. Set up the area prior to children's participation. Pile all the boxes and containers in a large carton or on an extra table or shelf near the work area. Place containers of glue and applicators at each seat. Keep fabric, fur, and feather scraps nearby, but do not give them to the children until they have glued some boxes together.

   b. Invite the children to create pretend pets that they can take home to live with them. Point out the box collection, mentioning that they will find boxes that remind them of heads, tails, torsos, arms, legs, or wings as they examine the collection. Encourage the children to begin by choosing three or four boxes and to glue them together in a way that reminds them of a real or imaginary animal.

   c. Encourage the children to describe their pets and the various body parts they are adding as they work.

   d. Move the fabric assortment closer as children complete some box gluing. Invite them to create a hide, skin, shell, or other body covering that seems appropriate to their pet.

   e. Children may enjoy naming their pets or describing some special characteristics the pets possess. Write descriptions somewhere on the pets, if children wish. Some children may want to add facial features, or other attributes with crayons or markers.

Hint for Success:

• Display some pictures or figures of pets near the work area to encourage representation. Be careful not to insist that children replicate these exactly in their own work.

How to Simplify this Activity:

• Limit the selection of boxes to tubes of cardboard in various lengths: toilet paper rolls, paper towel rolls, and wrapping paper rolls cut in short sections.

• Set up the activity at a table with only two or three places when working with very young children who may need consistent help with scissors and glue applications.

How to Extend this Activity:

• First, invite children to think of what they would like to create. Next, ask them to decide what materials will be necessary to develop their creation, then to collect those items before getting underway. Remind them of such considerations as fastening parts together and of thinking about body coverings before searching for their materials. A fish or turtle, for example, might pose different sets of problems, especially as skin coverings are considered.

• Challenge all the children involved to create their own variation of a particular pet.

Language

1. *What Do You Mean By That?* Discuss the sounds that some pets make and reasons they may have for making them. Invite one child at a time to communicate as an animal would. Ask other children to identify the animal and the possible message. Let the sound-maker verify or explain the intended meaning (I'm hungry, I want to play, I'm sleepy, etc.).

2. *Sound-Off.* Make or procure a recording of pet sounds. Leave a few seconds of silence between each recorded sound if producing your own tape. Consider including some sounds of pets in action, such as a cat lapping milk, a collar bell jingling, a dog thumping his tail against the floor, or a rabbit munching a carrot. Challenge children to name each pet as its sound is heard.

How to Simplify this Activity:

Provide picture clues that are related to each sound. Show the children two pictures and ask them to choose the one that matches the sound they are hearing.

3. *This One's on Me.* Ask parents to send to school pictures of their children holding pets. Let children take turns showing and telling about their pictures to the group. Write down or record these descriptions and read or play them back to the children.

4. *Pet Riddles.* Prepare the children for this activity by first showing them pictures of the animals, describing them, and talking about them. Then read the following riddles to children one at a time, asking them to guess which pet answers the riddle.

   a. I like it when you stroke my head,
      or let me curl up on your bed.
      My happy noise sounds like a hum.
      I twitch my whiskers when I come
      to see if there's some food for me.
      My fur is soft—who could I be? (cat)

   b. My ears stand tall or sometimes flop.
      My way of moving is to hop.
      My house is sometimes called a hutch,
      and I like gardens very much.
      A crisp, orange treat is best for me.
      My tail is small and hard to see.
      What could I be? (rabbit)

   c. I live inside a watery home
      of windows made of glass.
      I like to have some shells or rocks
      between which I can pass.
      I won't invite you in to play,
      but watching me is fun,
      and though I move about a lot,
      I'll never learn to run.
      What am I? (fish)

   d. I live inside a cover
      that's like a tiny dome.
      There aren't too many like me,
      who grow themselves a home.
      And when I want some privacy,
      to think, or go to bed,
      I pull inside my arms and legs,
      and then tuck in my head.
      I'm known for moving slowly.

I like a sunny stone
to sunbathe on, after I swim.
I'll lie there all alone.
And if one ventures near me,
I'll catch a tasty fly,
and eat him for my supper.
Can you guess,
who am I? (turtle)

e. I never come into your house
I live in grassy fields,
and sometimes sleep in cozy barns
with walls that make windshields.
I'll sometimes take my people
out riding on my back.
I like it when they let me stop
to nibble on a stack
of tasty oats or hay bales
and apples make good treats.
You'll sometimes see me in parades
along the city streets.
What am I? (horse)

5. *Pet Songs and Fingerplays.*

I'm a Little Kitten
(Tune: "I'm a Little Teapot";
Words: Kit Payne)
I'm a little kitten,
fat and gray,
curled in the sun
on a warm spring day.
When a little mouse comes
creeping past.
I jump awake and
chase it fast!

My Puppy
(Words: Kit Payne)

(Hold up five fingers. Starting with the little finger, point to each as verse progresses.)

I have a little puppy.
She sleeps inside a box.
She likes to chase a ball around
and tug at old worn socks.
Each day, fresh food and water
I pour into her dish.
She wags her tail to thank me:
swish, swish, swish.

My Pets
(Author unknown)
I have five pets
That I'd like you to meet.
They all live on Mulberry Street.
This is my chicken,
The smallest of all.
He comes running whenever I call.
This is my duckling.
He says: "Quack, quack, quack,"
As he shakes the water from his back.

I Have a Little Poodle
(Author unknown)
I have a little poodle
(Hold up clenched fist for poodle.)
His coat is silver gray.
One day I thought I'd bathe him
to wash the dirt away.
I washed my little poodle.
(Scrub fist with other hand.)
Then dried him with a towel.
(Pat fist with other hand as if drying.)
My poodle seemed to like his bath.
He didn't even howl.

Little Turtle
(Author unknown)
There was a little turtle.
(Make small circle with thumb and index finger.)
He lived in a box.
(Cup hands to form box.)
He swam in a puddle.
(Swimming motions.)
He climbed on the rocks.
(Climbing motion with hands.)
He snapped at a mosquito.
(Snap with thumb and forefinger.)
He snapped at a flea.
(Repeat.)
He snapped at a minnow.
(Repeat.)
He snapped at me.
(Turn hand toward self and snap.)
He caught the mosquito.
(Catching motion with hands.)
He caught the flea.
(Repeat.)
He caught the minnow.
(Repeat.)
But he didn't catch me.
(Point to self and shake head, no!)

6. *Pets A-Plenty.* Prior to reading *The Pet Show* by Ezra Jack Keats to the children, gather magazine pictures corresponding to the pets mentioned in the book (parrot, frog, fish, canary, ant, goldfish, dog, mouse, puppy, turtle, cat, and an empty jar for the germ). Add two or three other animals not included, such as horse, goat, and pig. Read the story aloud. Later in the day, read the story a second time, asking the children to listen for all the pets

included in the pet show. When the story ends, show the children the picture cards and ask them whether each pet was or was not in the show. Refer back to the book to confirm the children's choices.

Another variation would be to remind children of the descriptions for each pet such as *noisiest* parrot or the most handsome frog. Invite them to create additional descriptions for the pets in the book and new ones for those animals not originally mentioned. Write these down for children to refer to and add to throughout the day.

7. *Sing a Song of Caring.*
   General Purpose: To encourage recall of verses in correct sequence and detail.

   TFPs: 1, 2, 4, 6, 11, 12, 15–24.

   Procedure:

   a. Gather the children in a large, open area. Tell them you have a song to teach them and that they will be able to add new words and create new verses after they learn the verse you know.

   (Tune: "Polly Wolly Doodle All the Day"; Words: Kit Payne)
   Oh, I wish I had a *little brown dog*
   to be my favorite friend.
   For games to play, and a place to stay,
   on me he could depend.
   I'd take him out to run about,
   and scratch him, as a treat.
   I'd give him toys and lots of love,
   and healthy food to eat.

   b. Sing the song once, then repeat it one line at a time, asking children to repeat each line after you sing it. Sing the whole song together two or three times.

   c. Invite children to name other pets to insert in the first line. They may wish to change the size, color, and gender, as well as the animal (a huge green frog, a tiny gray mouse, a big black horse, etc.) Sing "on me *she* could depend" alternately with "he." If an animal is chosen that could not be taken out running, change the verse to:

   Though I couldn't take her out,
   to run about,
   (I'd/or) scratch her as a treat,
   I'd give her toys and lots of love
   and healthy food to eat.

Or with the children's help, create a more appropriate sentence to describe care of the chosen pet.

d. Acknowledge children's ideas, even if the animals chosen would be inappropriate as pets. Later discuss whether all the animals named would really make appropriate pets.

Hint for Success:
- When first introducing this activity, sing the song as written above for several days. After children are comfortable with the tune and the verse, move to step c of the procedure.

How to Simplify this Activity:
- Ask children to choose new colors for the same pet, rather than new pets as well as new colors.

How to Extend this Activity:
- Invite older children to create whole verses to add to the song. Suggest a verse about specific grooming or feeding plans, or about naming the pet.

Physical

1. *Pet Food Preparation.* Arrange an opportunity for children to visit a farm or garden. Pick alfalfa or vegetables for the classroom guinea pig or rabbit. Emphasize other physical tasks such as grinding corn kernels into meal to mix with grains for chickens to eat, chopping or mixing together meat and vegetables for cats, or peeling carrots and feeding the scrapings to rabbits. Invite children to assist in making dog biscuits using the following recipe.

Ingredients:

1 T. yeast

¼ cup warm water

1 pint broth or gravy

3½ cups flour

2 cups whole wheat flour

2 cups rye flour

½ cup dry milk

2 cups bulgar

1 cup corn meal

4 tsp. salt

1 egg

1 T. milk

Procedure:

1. Dissolve yeast in water.

2. Mix other ingredients together.

3. Knead into a stiff dough.

4. Roll dough out ¼-inch thick, cut with small cookie cutter or shape 2-inch balls into dog bone shapes.

5. Beat egg and milk together, brush on the cookie tops.

6. Bake at 300° for 45 minutes.

7. Leave the biscuits out overnight, then store and serve one a day to a favorite pup.

2. *Handle with Care.* Invite a veterinarian or animal-shelter employee to visit the classroom. Ask them to demonstrate and explain appropriate ways to lift and carry various pets and to supervise a practice session with a classroom pet or a pet they've brought to show. Emphasize hand placement and pressure. Include some pointers about petting, scratching, or avoiding touch when appropriate to certain pets. (Salamanders should only be touched with wet hands, for example.)

3. *Look—No Hands!* Lead a discussion about the ways that pets eat and drink. Seldom can they use their "hands" to manipulate food. Invite children to try having their snack without using their hands. Serve a snack (including water) in shallow paper bowls rather than cups. Dry cereals or small pretzels are good (tidy) choices.

4. *Pet Tracings.* Using the same cardboard templates described as "tracing forms" for the Rub-a-Pet activity, show children how to hold a pencil or crayon tightly against the edge of a pet shape, then move it all the way around to produce an outline of the pet.

5. *Move Like a Pet.*

General Purpose: To enable children to practice a variety of motor skills.

TFPs: 6, 9, 12, 24, 25, 28, 29, 30.

Setting: Large open area (a grassy outdoor spot or a carpeted one indoors).

Procedure:

a. Ask children to take turns thinking of a pet they've seen or owned and show how that pet looked when it was sleepy, excited, or frightened.

b. Encourage the group to move like the animal mentioned. They may enjoy showing their own perceptions of the chosen pet's movements, or imitating the child who suggested the pet.

c. Move in an appropriate way yourself. Acknowledge or praise children's efforts: "Sarah is pretending to wag her tail. It looks like she's pretending to lick a face or hand just like a happy dog!" "Michael is tossing his head and mane. He is a proud horse!" "Victoria thought of leaping along like a frog. She is making frog sounds, too."

Hints for Success:

- Encourage all children to participate by calling on them by name, suggesting pets to those who aren't willing to share an idea out loud, or demonstrating movements yourself for children who have identified an animal but seem reluctant to imitate its movements.

- Show a film of animals in motion before introducing the activity.

How to Simplify this Activity:

- Very young children may find it easier to imitate an action that you demonstrate. In addition, moving all together can be more fun and involves less waiting for turns.

How to Extend this Activity:

- Encourage the group to watch carefully as one child demonstrates an animal's movements. Play Pet Charades by guessing what animal has been represented and what the animal might have been doing.

- Play Follow the Leader with one child at a time demonstrating a motion and the others moving along in a similar way. Give each interested child a turn as the leader.

Pretend Play

1. *Get the Vet.* Set up a pretend play area with some of the following props:

   - stuffed animals (cats, dogs, birds, hamsters, turtles, horses). Avoid jungle animals and other inappropriate pets.
   - laundry baskets that can be upended to represent pens or cages, boxes in which to "keep" puppies and kittens, old bird cages, plastic fish bowls.
   - white coats or men's shirts (medical garb).
   - surgical masks, stethoscopes, empty medicine bottles, hypodermic needle shells.
   - telephone, prescription pad and pencils, appointment book.
   - pet food and water dishes, grooming brushes.
   - magazines and pictures of pets.
   - signs: VETERINARIAN'S OFFICE. EXAMINING ROOM. OPERATING ROOM. THE DOCTOR IS IN/OUT.
   - a posted list of the terms, facts, and principles for adult reference.

   Encourage some children to take on the roles of pets, while others care for them.

2. *Pet Store.* Another pretend play area could include these items:

   - laundry basket or cardboard cages, plastic fish bowls, bird cages.
   - stuffed animals.
   - cash register and play money.
   - pet food boxes, pet dishes.
   - grooming tools, pet toys, collar, and tags.

   Encourage children to try out the roles of customer, cashier, and animal caretaker.

Social

1. *What Am I?* Invite children to participate in a guessing game. Tell them that you will take the first turn giving hints, and then each person who wants a turn can try to stump the audience. Describe a common pet without giving its name or making its sound. Start with relatively easy hints. ("I am brown and furry. I have a tail that I like to wag. Sometimes I lick my person's face or hand.") Add more hints after a moment, if no one can guess that you're a dog. Ask for a volunteer who would like to describe the next pet. Provide very young or inexperienced children with pictures to look at while they offer clues, or direct the hint-giver to make sounds or move like the animal. Emphasize the cooperative effort of working together to solve the puzzle of the pet.

2. *Help!* Tell a child to choose a partner for this game. Ask one child to choose a pet to be. Tell the other child that he or she is the caregiver. Encourage the "pet" to think of something that he or she would need help with from his or her human (getting food or water, being petted or played with, being let outside for fresh air or exercise, etc.). Invite the "pet child" to act out the need while the "human child" decides what message is being enacted and how to respond. The caregiver can either describe the kind of care he or she would give or act out the response. Other children can be invited to watch and add ideas about appropriate care.

3. *We Choose You.* Invite children to work together on two classroom murals. Write "Good House Pets" on the top of one long sheet of paper and "Poor House Pets" on the top of another. Provide markers or magazines with pictures of animals, scissors, and glue sticks. Encourage children to draw or cut out and glue pictures together. An adult can add labels of each pet chosen or drawn. Praise cooperative and helpful actions as the children create classroom decorations together.

4. *This Is the Place.* Draw large pictures of pet homes on mural paper: a bird cage, an aquarium, a doghouse, a large cage with crosshatch lines to represent wire sides, a smaller cage with an exercise wheel, a barn, a fenced-in farmyard, a pond. Cut out or draw small pictures of a variety of pets. Hang the murals on classroom walls at children's eye level. Invite children to

work together to place pets in their ideal environments.

5. *Pet Parade.* Invite children (and their families) to bring live or toy pets to school for a pet show and a parade. Encourage parents to accompany large or hard-to-handle pets. Small pets that are kept in cages or bowls could be dropped off with their child-owners. Borrow or gather a few wagons, if possible, to transport cages in the parade. Be sure that live, loose pets (cats and dogs) are on leashes. Obtain a record player or tape recorder and some march music. Arrange an outdoor area for this activity, if possible. Depending on the available facility, you may decide to limit the parade to stuffed animals, perhaps arranging for one or two live pets to visit for a part of the day.

6. *Welcome to Our World.*

   General Purpose: For children to practice negotiation skills while learning the reasons for classroom rules.

   TFPs: 1, 2, 6, 9, 12, 15–24.

   Materials: A current classroom pet in appropriate housing (a rabbit or guinea pig in a cage, a fish in a tank, a turtle in an aquarium/terrarium); two or three large sheets of paper; a marking pen.
   If your classroom does not have a pet, choose one to introduce through this activity.

   Procedure:
   a. Gather children in a large open area. Bring the pet to the area. Place the pet on a table or shelf where it is visible to the children.
   b. Explain that your classroom pet lives in the same place that the children do when they are at school and has many of the same needs for food and water, for safety, for companionship, and for love and communication.
      Point out that the children are responsible for seeing that these needs are met and that today's discussion will focus on the safety of their pet.
   c. Ask children to think about rules that will be necessary to ensure their pet's safety. Tell them to raise their hands if they have ideas to share.
   d. Call on children one at a time. Say, "Jessie, tell me one rule you've thought of to keep our pet safe." Paraphrase or repeat the rule. Ask other children to decide whether it is a good or necessary one. All ideas should be acknowledged. "Rachael, you've thought of an idea," or "you know that _____ is important for our pet." Avoid criticizing or ridiculing any idea.
   e. As rules are contributed, ask children to explain why they are important. The child who offers the suggestion can be encouraged to explain why it is important. More turns can be generated by asking others to raise their hands when they think of reasons. Encourage children to look at the pet as they think of ways to keep it safe and happy.
   f. Begin a list of the children's proposed rules. When three or four rules have been listed, encourage children to decide if all of them are necessary and if some are especially important. Again, allow several children to express ideas and debate their merits. Similarities and differences in opinion should be pointed out. "Ritika thinks that keeping your fingers out of the cage should be a rule. Trudy thinks that petting the pet through the holes in his cage is important. What do you think, Sam?"
   g. Narrow down or refine the list of rules as you continue guiding this activity. Create a final list on a new sheet of paper. Praise children for working together to think of ways to keep their pet safe.
   h. Make a simple line drawing to illustrate each rule. Hang the finished list behind the pet's permanent location in the classroom.

How to Simplify this Activity:

• Very young children may have trouble thinking of ideas. Suggest a first rule yourself if necessary. Ask children to raise their hands if they agree that it is an important one. Ask if any children don't think it's a necessary rule. Write the rule down if several children agree that it should be included.

- Describe simple scenarios to illustrate dangers that the pet might encounter. "Someone is shaking Fuzzy's cage! Fuzzy is very scared. Think of a rule that would keep Fuzzy from feeling frightened." You may want to include some "silly" rules to promote discussion of why they are unnecessary.

How to Extend this Activity:

- Begin this activity as a small-group experience. Have groups of four to six children each generate a set of rules with an adult mediator. Bring each list to a whole-group circle time. Have the group negotiate to combine the lists into one master list.

- Invite older children to recopy the final list onto a sign to be posted near the pet. Recruit volunteers to illustrate the rules with a picture that shows what each means.

- On this day or on subsequent days, extend the list to include rules related to other pet needs.

TEACHER RESOURCES

Field Trip Ideas

1. Visit a local pet store. Suggest that children make note of or list animal similarities and differences, such as animals with fur, scales, shells, or feathers. Ask the clerk or shop owner to discuss ways in which the various pets are fed, bedded, and/or handled.
2. Visit the local Humane Society or animal shelter. Encourage children to look carefully at the housing that is provided for different animals (cages, runs, fenced-in areas). Ask an attendant to tell the children about how different animals were acquired, and about the adoption process for acquiring them after they've been housed in the shelter.
3. Visit a teacher's home to meet his or her pet. Show the children where the animal sleeps, what and where it eats, and any other toys or grooming aids that are used to keep it healthy and happy.

4. Visit a petting zoo. Discuss the differences in accessibility to animals that they are likely to encounter: some animals might touch children or allow children to touch them; others, such as birds, might come very near but avoid direct contact.
5. Visit a veterinarian's office or clinic. Bring along a teacher's pet that can be examined while the children look on, if possible. Label and discuss the examination and treatment tools, or ask the vet to provide a running commentary of procedures and instruments.

Classroom Visitors

1. Invite a veterinarian or humane society representative to visit your classroom with a few pets. Ask the visitor to demonstrate proper handling and care of pets, as well as to describe the features of each animal.
2. Invite parents to bring family pets to school for a brief visit. Small pets in contained homes could all come on the same day (hamsters, gerbils, mice, goldfish). Larger pets or those who are intolerant of other animals might come one each day during the pet unit.
3. Invite a person with a seeing-eye or hearing-ear dog to visit. Ask him or her to describe the special training that the animal undergoes and the special help that the animal provides.
4. Ask a zoo or pet shop employee to bring one or two pets to school for a visit. Ask the person to emphasize one or more particular terms, facts, or principles, such as pet selection, pet handling, pet care, or pet breeding.

Children's Books

Aliki. *At Mary Bloom's.* New York: Greenwillow, 1984.

Anderson, C. W. *Billy and Blaze.* New York: Macmillan, 1936.

Brenner, B. *A Dog I Know.* New York: Harper and Row, 1983.

Bridwell, N. *Clifford, the Big Red Dog.* New York: Scholastic, 1972.

Carrick, C. *The Foundling*. New York: Seaburg, 1977.

Day, A. *Good Dog, Carl*. LaJolla, CA: Green Tiger Press, 1985.

Ellis, A. L. *Dabble Duck*. New York: Harper and Row, 1984.

Keats, E. J. *Pet Show*. New York: Macmillan, 1972.

Martin, P. M. *The Rice Bowl Pet*. New York: Crowell, 1962.

Ness, E. *Sam, Bangs and Moonshine*. New York: Holt, Rinehart and Winston, 1966.

Pender, L. *The Useless Donkeys*. New York: Frederick Warne, 1979.

Schertle, A. *That Olive!* New York: Lothrop, Lee, and Shepard Books, 1986.

Zion, G. *No Roses for Harry*. New York: Harper Junior, 1958.

Adult References

American Kennel Club. *The Complete Dog Book*. New York: Howell, 1985

Caras, R. *The Roger Caras Pet Book*. New York: Holt, Rinehart and Winston, 1976.

Clutton-Brock, J. *Domesticated Animals From Early Times*. Portsmouth, NH: Heinemann, 1981.

Kellert, S. R., and M. O. Westervelt. "Attitudes Toward Animals: Age Related Development Among Children." In *The Pet Connection*, edited by R. S. Anderson, B. Hart, and L. Hart. Minneapolis: Center to Study Human-Animal Relationships and Environments, 1983.

Pond, Grace, ed. *The Complete Cat Encyclopedia*. New York: Crown, 1972.

Sussman, N. B., ed. *Pets and the Family*. New York: Haworth Press, 1985.

Weber, W. J. *Care of Uncommon Pets*. New York: Holt, Rinehart and Winston, 1979.

Chapter 5

Homes

•

Oh, give me a home . . .

•

Home is where the heart is. As such, it is a state of mind as much as a physical structure. In our increasingly mobile world, families may relocate to another town, another neighborhood, or another domicile, but children soon recognize that once you put your possessions in a place, eat your meals there, and work there, it's home.

What an adventure it is for young children to venture out of their homes to the grocery store, the mall, the homes of others, and eventually, to school. Children who describe their school as "homey" pay it the highest compliment. They take home what they learn and create there, and loved ones delight in their accomplishments. In addition, people at home often reinforce what is learned in the neighborhood. Conversely, the larger community complements, recapitulates, or challenges that which is learned in the child's home.

Homes can take many forms. Some are mobile—house trailers, houseboats. Some homes bustle with shared lives—hotels, apartment complexes. Some homes offer isolated privacy—the single-family home or farm.

Children watch construction with fascination, awed by the undertaking of a crew as it creates a structure. At each stage of the building process, people use interesting tools and machines. As time goes on, children envision the completed structure more easily.

A home is a monument to cooperation. People build homes to house other people. People live together in homes, cooperatively caring for each other.

PURPOSE

The Homes theme takes the most concrete and familiar experience of the child and introduces a world of differences. Homes may differ the world over, but the fact that most people have one or yearn for one encourages children to value their own and to value diversity as well. We have developed activities that invite children to see their familiar environments in a new light. Focusing first on the natural categories of furniture, functions, and events that a study of homes invites, children can then venture beyond these familiar boundaries to explore the wondrous ways in which people differ while sharing the common experience of a home.

IMPLEMENTATION

The Homes theme can be explored and expanded to interest children of all ages. A suggested sequence of experiences from the concrete to the more abstract follows.

Option One: Develop single-week units that concentrate on the children's own homes. Invite families to share photos of their dwelling places, inside and out. We recommend that the teacher also share his or her home through photos or a field trip. Create multiweek units by featuring the home of one child each week. Make a bulletin board display that includes pictures, dictated stories, home-helper lists, and photos of pets and persons with whom the child shares his or her home. After featuring Homes as a central theme for a week or two, continue this as an ongoing project integrated into other themes.

Option Two: Select one type of home around which to build classroom activities. Explore homes that move: houseboats, trailers, tents. Introduce temporary versus permanent homes at the same time. Next, explore people who move. Arrange for a moving van to visit your school. Provide wagons, wheelbarrows, and boxes and ask children to pack and move school furniture, toys, and books. Invite them to create new arrangements in the room. Decide together if these changes should be permanent or temporary. Help children examine what stays the same when such moves are made and what actually changes.

Option Three: Design a unit around the processes involved in home construction. Equip the workbench with such materials as roofing tiles, insulation strips, and scraps of paneling. Pay weekly visits to a construction site; discuss the craftspeople and the tools that build the multilayered structure that emerges as a house. Invite children to replicate the processes as they cooperate to create models of homes or an actual playhouse with adult assistance.

Option Four: After a week spent exploring the physical characteristics of homes, take a week to concentrate on families or groups of people who share a dwelling. Discuss the reasons why some people dwell in more than one place. Explore what people must do to maintain their homes. How do people use their homes and why must people sometimes find new homes?

TERMS, FACTS, AND PRINCIPLES

1. A home is the place where a person or group of people live.

2. Homes provide shelter, private space, and security.

3. Homes are places where people keep their possessions.

4. Many physical structures can be used as homes: houses, apartment buildings, mobile homes/house trailers, condominiums, and houseboats.

5. Homes vary in size and shape and in the materials of which they are made.

6. Homes have roofs, walls, ceilings, floors, windows, and doors.

7. Homes consist of one or more rooms.

8. Rooms can be on one or more levels.

9. Different rooms have different uses.

10. Rooms have names, such as bathroom, kitchen, bedroom, or living room.

11. Rooms contain equipment and furniture.

12. Some homes have outdoor space: yard, driveway, balcony, porch, patio.

*13. Homes are found in cities, towns, suburbs, and rural areas.

14. A group of homes is sometimes called a neighborhood, a project, a community, a subdivision, a block, or a barrio.

*15. A home can be located on or under the ground, on or near water, in the mountains, deserts or plains, or in forests.

*16. The construction of a home depends on availability of materials and other resources, climate, the number of people who will live in it, the terrain, local laws, and peoples' preferences.

17. Homes are built by people.

*18. There are many jobs involved in building a home: designing, insulating, painting, carpentry, masonry, plumbing, wiring, excavating, roofing, and inspecting.

19. Home construction is often accomplished by many people working together.

20. Some people move into homes that no one has ever lived in. Some people move into homes that people have lived in before.

21. People eat, sleep, work, and play at home.

22. People work at home to maintain the home and its occupants. Some home jobs include: cooking, cleaning, raking, repairing, painting, serving, laundering, gardening, shoveling, and mowing.

23. People play at home alone or with family and/or friends.

24. Some people do jobs at home that are school, community, and/or occupation related.

25. People design, decorate, and furnish their homes to suit them.

*26. The spaces in a home in which people choose to eat, sleep, work, and play differ according to their needs and preferences.

27. People live in homes for different lengths of time.

28. Sometimes people leave their homes temporarily and live somewhere else (as when they visit, camp, travel, or evacuate).

29. Sometimes people leave one home and move to a new home.

*30. People have different feelings about leaving one home and moving to another.

31. Moving involves packing and transporting people, pets, and possessions.

*32. When people move they often leave familiar people, places, and things.

33. People who move discover new people, places, and things.

34. Some things about a new home are very different from the old home, while other things are very much the same.

35. Sometimes people visit their old neighborhood and/or communicate with the people who live there.

36. People move for different reasons.

ACTIVITY IDEAS

Aesthetics

1. *I'd Feel at Home.* With the children, make a mural that represents a neighborhood with a variety of homes. Include photos, magazine clippings, or simple drawings of houses, an apartment building, a mobile home, or perhaps a waterfront featuring a houseboat. Invite each child to study the various structures and to choose the one in which he or she would most like to live.

2. *The Art of the Architect.* Display reproductions of art that feature dwellings of the past and present. Include depictions of castles and cottages, igloos and tents. Include blueprints if possible. Focus children's attention on the environs as well as on the structures. Encourage them to think about the life-styles for which each design might have provided a setting. Older children might enjoy drawing their own ideal home plans. Provide graph paper and colored pencils for children to make their own blueprint designs.

*3. *Interior Motives.*

General Purpose: For children to derive pleasure from diverse art forms and to learn that people's tastes differ.

TFPs: 5, 7, 9, 10, 18, 25.

Materials: Glue and applicators, scissors, carpet squares, fabric scraps, wallpaper scraps, markers or watercolor paints, brushes, shoeboxes or similarly sized cardboard cartons, trays, baskets, large bowls.

Procedure:

a. Set up area prior to children's participation. Arrange displays of materials on a large table. Fill individual containers with carpet, fabric, and wallpaper scraps. Place markers and glue at each seat.

b. Invite the children to choose a box to represent a room in a home. Tell them that each of them can be an interior decorator; each box is a room that its decorator can design to his or her liking.

c. Point out the various materials. Mention that people have unique preferences for the areas in which they live. Every person may think of a different way to design a room that he or she would find comfortable.

d. Encourage children to explore and examine the materials as long as they wish, choosing pieces they particularly like. Offer to help with cutting if necessary. Children may enjoy describing some uses their rooms might have. (Some may be decorating bedrooms, others kitchens, living rooms, etc.)

Hints for Success:

- Display a collage of magazine photos that features rooms decorated in many styles. Explain that people plan rooms based on preferences and needs and then decorate them or hire others to carry out their plans.

- Point out that people sometimes combine a variety of materials (carpeting, fabric, paint, artwork) that share similar colors or have complementary designs. They imagine what the finished room will look like and then work to create a representation of what they imagine.

How to Simplify this Activity:

- Children who lack cutting skills may find it difficult to cut fabric and wallpaper. Precut many samples and invite children to choose favorites and attach them with glue sticks. Precut carpet samples can simply be laid in place in the bottom of the boxes.

How to Extend this Activity:

- Invite children to create several carton rooms, then attach them together with tape or glue to create one-story homes. Provide tiny boxes for children who wish to construct furniture for their rooms.

Affective

1. *A Home of One's Own.* Draw squares or rectangles on a large sheet of paper or poster board. Ask the children to help you think of the names of different rooms in a home. Label each square with the name of a room. Next, ask children to generate a list of furniture and equipment that might be found in each room. Encourage them to think about items found in their own homes, as well as things they would place in each room if they could add items. Invite children to illustrate the mural with colored pencils or pastel markers so that the dictated words remain visible. Some children might want to design their own furniture, others could be invited to draw toys, stamp-print wallpaper designs, or

add sketches of family members. You could use dollhouses and miniature furniture as well as items the children make themselves.

2. *The Best and the Rest.* Affix magazine cutouts or simple sketches of a variety of homes to a piece of poster board. Include a house, a mobile home, an apartment building, a motel, and a houseboat. Invite children to think of the best thing and the worst thing about living in each structure. Record the range of children's opinions near each illustration.

3. *Eating Us Out of House and Home.* Prepare plates or trays of several foods that are square, rectangular, or triangular in shape. Some examples would be quarter slices of bread, some cut as triangles, others as squares; crackers; or squares and triangles of hard cheese. Provide cream cheese and/or peanut butter to be used as "mortar." Give each child a paper plate on which to construct a "home of food." Provide plastic knives with serrated edges. Invite each child to plan and carry out a way to combine the foods so that they resemble a home. Encourage self-help skills, such as cutting bread or cheese slices into doors, windows, roofs, or shingles. Point out that the peanut butter or cream cheese "mortar" can be spread between food layers to stick them together and hold them in place. You may want to choose some leafy vegetables such as parsley, celery stalks, or broccoli flowerets that the children can use to create "landscapes." Package the homes in plastic bags or tinfoil for children to take home, or enjoy a "homey" lunch together!

4. *Home Rubbings.* Send a one-foot square piece of white paper and a crayon, with the paper peeled off, home with each child. In a note to parents, explain how to help children make a rubbing of an outside surface of their home. Position the bare crayon on its side on a piece of thin paper against a textured surface and then rub the crayon back and forth to transfer the design of the texture onto the paper. When children bring their home rubbings back to school, have them show their work and

compare the various effects created. The papers, labeled with their makers' names, could then be combined in a house or building shape to display in the classroom. This activity could also be adapted to inside home surfaces. In addition, parents could be asked to name the rooms from which the rubbings were taken.

Cognition

1. *Where I Come From.* Request that parents send photographs of their family's home to school. Protect the photos by placing them in plastic sleeves or in a photo album. Look through the photo collection with small or large groups of children. Invite each child to identify his or her own home when it appears. Encourage each one to tell others something about his or her home. Ask young children to describe pictured attributes of their homes. Invite older children to recall features of their homes that are not apparent in the photograph.

2. *By the Numbers.* Write each child's address (street number and street name) on a three-by-five index card. Spread out the photos of homes described above on a table top. Invite the children to examine the address cards; help them find their own if they are not able to recognize the numbers or street name. You may add children's names to the cards to make identifying them easier. As children find their addresses, direct them to place the addresses beneath their home photos. Extend the activity by inviting children to make personal mailboxes with address cards glued to the side. Children can produce mail for friends and deliver letters and pictures to the labeled mailboxes.

3. *It's a Nice Place to Visit But I Wouldn't Want to Live There.* Collect a variety of pictures of structures that could be homes and pictures that are not homes. Include structures that might house animals but not people: fishbowl or tank, doghouse, cage, rabbit hutch. Display pictures of stores, crates, vehicles, and cabinets. Invite children to sort pictures into homes

and nonhomes or into groups of different types of homes. Discuss why various structures would or would not make good homes for people.

4. *Neighborly Ways.* Obtain a map of your community. Mount it on corkboard or attach it to a bulletin board. Provide pins with decorative heads to mark the locations of children's homes. Bring to the children's attention other children who live in the same neighborhood, near the school or far from it, or near other familiar landmarks such as water, downtown, or an area shopping mall.

5. *Layer upon Layer.* Obtain or sketch drawings of a home in various stages of construction. One source is the children's picture book *Building a House* by Byron Barton. Another would be magazines that feature home building or remodeling. Trace or photocopy a sequence of pictures. Invite children to examine the pictures, deciding what comes first. An excavation site might be included to depict the first stage. Encourage children to work alone or in small groups to place the pictures in order of likely occurrence.

6. *That's About the Size of It.* Gather many pictures of homes. Real estate brochures and home improvement magazines provide a good source of such illustrations. Mount each picture on cardboard or on pieces of construction paper. Invite children to seriate the pictures by size of dwelling. A classification activity could also be planned. Children can sort pictures according to such attributes as number of doors or windows and type of roof, or whether the homes are mobile or immobile or single-family or multiple-family dwellings. Create a one-to-one correspondence activity by asking children to match people to homes, or chimneys to homes, or mailboxes to homes.

7. *What Have You?* Invite children to describe and compare a number of characteristics that their homes share or by which they vary. Possible questions to initiate the discussion include:

   • Tell me about the room in which cooking is done. Do you usually eat in the same room where you cook or in a different one?

   • What is the name of the room where you sleep? What else do you do in that room?

   • Where do you keep books in your home? Toys? Clothes?

   • How many people share your home? What spaces and items in your home do you share with others?

   • Do you take baths or showers? Where might you look for a clean towel?

   • Some people wash their clothing right in their homes. Others do laundry somewhere else. Tell how your family does laundry.

8. *Could You/Would You?* Mount pictures of rooms on poster board or construction paper. Hold up one picture at a time and name an activity associated with a room. Ask the children if it would be possible to do it in the room shown. Could you (or your parent) cook breakfast in the bathroom? How/Why or why not? Would you take a shower in the garage? Sleep in the bathroom? Do the laundry in the living room? Ask children to suggest a better room for each activity or a way to remodel the room shown so the activity could be accomplished there. Acknowledge and encourage creative ideas for adapting conventional uses of space.

9. *Pack It In.* Collect several boxes and cartons. Stack them in the classroom housekeeping area. Provide some suitcases for packing as well. Inform children that they can prepare to move to a new home today. Tell them that all the household goods must be packed. Encourage children to sort and pack the items according to their own notions of what belongs together. Invite youngsters to explain why they thought certain items fit well together.

10. *The Fun House.* Make flannel board homes with add-on doors, windows, trees for the yard, a mailbox, and so forth. Assemble homes in incongruous ways, challenging children to identify their "funny" features: doors halfway up the house or upside down, trees on the roof, mailbox sticking out of the side of the house, chimney at ground level.

*11. *I've Got This Feeling.*
    General Purpose: To enhance children's skills in discriminating textures by touch and visual examination.

TFPs: 4, 5, 6, 16, 17, 18, 25.

Materials: Bricks, stones, paneling scraps, shingles, drain tile, electrical wire, PVC pipes, shutters, gravel, Styrofoam, insulation. (Avoid fiberglass insulation. It has dangerous glass fragments embedded in it.) Optional: Carpet samples, linoleum squares, wallpaper scraps, paint sample chips.

Procedure:

a. Introduce the activity with a discussion of home construction techniques, materials, and professionals (bricklayers, stone masons, electricians, plumbers, painters, etc.).

b. Point out that many special materials are used to construct homes. These are chosen for special properties such as resistance to water or weather conditions, weight, flexibility, insulating qualities, etc.

c. Invite children to examine a display of the materials. Encourage both tactile and visual exploration.

d. Encourage and introduce descriptive words: "Find a smooth material; show me one that's rough." Children may enjoy speculating about various uses of materials or identifying ones that they recall seeing in their own homes.

Hint for Success:

- Contact a lumberyard, building contractor, or construction company. Ask a representative to save scraps of building materials for you. Scraps can be separated into small samples to allow several children to examine them at a time.

How to Simplify this Activity:

- Attach material samples to a piece of wood or cardboard. Young children will be able to focus better on texture if the materials are fixed in place and easy to examine by touch.

How to Extend this Activity:

- Invite children to use the material scraps for construction projects at the classroom workbench. Provide wood glue or putty along with hammers and nails.

- Explore the interior and exterior of the classroom and school building; match sample materials to those discovered.

Construction

1. *Inside These Walls.* Help children select and collect materials that can be used to make a home in the outdoor play yard. Blankets and rope, large boxes, cardboard, or hollow wooden blocks could serve as walls. Challenge the children to figure out ways to suspend or attach the materials. Help them to implement their plans as necessary. Allow plenty of time for the children to enjoy inhabiting their structure.

2. *Chill Out.* Call appliance stores to seek the donation of a refrigerator or freezer carton. Cut windows and doors as directed by the children. Provide paint and small paint rollers or wall-paint brushes for children to use to paint their "home." After the house has been painted, suggest that children decorate the inside walls with stamp prints, wallpaper scraps, or drawings. Provide fabric scraps to make curtains, if desired. Help children obtain other materials to create additional features that they think are desirable, such as a mailbox, a chimney, door knobs, or a "lawn."

3. *In a Cottage Small.* Collect an assortment of matchboxes, tiny gift boxes, spools, three- or four-ounce paper cups, and other odds and ends that suggest miniature furniture. Gather markers, crayons, glue sticks, and fabric scraps. Invite children to create a tiny home full of tables, chairs, beds, couches, and appliances.

4. *Add-Ons.* Gather several sizes of grocery boxes, masking tape, hole punches, and telephone wire or pipe cleaners. Initiate the activity by discussing the many rooms that make up most homes. Display pictures that show how rooms connect. Invite the children to choose an arrangement of boxes and to attach them together with wire or tape to make the rooms of a house. You may have to punch some holes in the "walls" through which children can lace the wire connectors. Provide dollhouse furniture to arrange in the completed rooms, or use child-constructed furniture from the previous activity.

5. *Blocks Around the Block.* Make all your wooden building blocks available to the children. Suggest that they construct a home with many rooms, or a neighborhood of structures. Encourage the chil-

dren to use lots of blocks. Toy vehicles, people, and pets could be added to populate the neighborhood.

*6. ***Sticks and Stones May Build Our Homes.***
General Purpose: To encourage children to explore building materials while representing a three-dimensional structure.

TFPs: 2–8, 12, 14, 16–19, 25.

Materials: Sticks, stones, brown clay, trays or linoleum tiles, water, spray bottles, newspaper. Optional: electrical wire, tongue depressors/craft sticks, toothpicks, berry baskets, pieces of roofing tile or paneling scraps, insulation strips.

Procedure:

a. Set up the area prior to children's participation. Moisten and knead clay to increase malleability. Cover table top with newspapers, and provide trays or linoleum tiles as individual work surfaces to facilitate cleanup. Place piles of sticks, stones, and other building materials at each seat or within easy reach of each child.

b. Invite the children to build structures with some materials that might be used in home construction. Provide each child with a ball of clay. Point out that the clay can be moistened by spraying it with water, so that it becomes softer and easier to mold into the desired shapes.

c. Encourage children to choose other available materials to add to their structures as they wish. Mention that people think of many different ways to use similar materials when they design and build homes.

d. Children may want to add other materials to their "buildings." Encourage new ideas and verbal descriptions of structures. Some children may want to combine their structures on a common base to display a neighborhood (project, community, barrio, or apartment complex).

e. Discuss the many jobs involved in building a home.

f. Encourage children to seek each other's help for some steps in the building process.

Hint for Success:

• Display pictures of homes constructed of a variety of materials for children to refer to as they work. Expect more successful representations of structures after several days of exploring the TFPs for this unit or after a field trip to a construction sight.

How to Simplify this Activity:

• Use a simple modeling dough recipe in place of brown clay. Prepare the modeling dough in a natural color: beige, brown, or brick red.

• Give each child a box or basket with his or her own share of building materials. Preform the clay or dough into cubes to represent homes. Children can then press or wrap various materials onto the cubes.

How to Extend this Activity:

• Invite older children to work together to construct a multilevel dwelling. Include sheets of plywood approximately eighteen inches square to provide a steady, sturdy base. Encourage children to "landscape" their homes with grass, wood chips, trees, or bushes that they create.

• Assist children as they build wooden boxes at the workbench to serve as roughed-in homes. Later or on another day, provide electrical wire, rubber tubing for plumbing, cellophane for windows, and paint and wallpaper to decorate interior and exterior walls.

Language

1. ***Who's That?*** This is a game that gives children opportunities to gauge the direction and location of sound. Provide a bell, triangle, or telephone that rings when dialed; four carpet squares; a chair; and an optional blindfold. The game may be played by three or more players. One child is designated as "at home" and sits in the chair. Other players sit on the carpet squares on each side behind or in front of the chair at various distances. Show the telephone or bell and let everyone ring it

for fun. Tell the child who is "at home" to close his or her eyes (or to wear the blindfold). Explain that he or she should listen for the sound of the bell or phone and point to who is ringing it. Quietly hand the bell or phone to one of the players and have him or her ring it. The person "at home" will try to hear where the sound is coming from and point to that person, who then becomes the person at home. Repeat the game until everyone has had at least one turn. Praise children for listening quietly. This game is most successful when played in an area relatively free of noise. Some children may feel more comfortable turning their backs with their hands over their eyes. Begin with three players. As they become more experienced, add more children to the game. In addition, provide a greater challenge by increasing the distance between the child "at home" and the others, or by grouping the "visitors" closer together.

2. *My Ideal.* Gather paper, pencils and markers, or a tape recorder and blank tape. Invite one child at a time to describe his or her ideal home while you record their words. Very young children respond best to an interview format. Ask them to complete such statements as, "My ideal home would be built of _____ ." (Explain that "ideal" means something they consider to be perfect or just right.) Follow up with more specific statements: "My home would have _____ bedrooms." "My home would have a _____ outdoors." After recording answers, read or play them back to the child or to the group. Extend the activity by inviting children to depict their "ideal" home using magazine pictures or doll furniture or to write about it in their own form of writing.

3. *The Bad, the Better, the Best.* Read one or more of the books about families moving listed in the teacher resource section of this unit. Invite children who recall making a move to a new home to describe it to others. Ask children to tell the best thing that happened as a result of their move. Did they acquire new friends or a larger yard? Next, suggest that children describe a loss that they felt as a result of their move. Did

they leave behind a favorite tree, a favorite hiding place or a playmate in their "old" neighborhood?

4. *From the Mountains to the Valleys to the Oceans.* Initiate this activity with one or several discussions of building materials and how their use is related to geographic factors as well as availability of natural resources. Point out that people who live on a mountaintop might find different materials with which to build a home than would people by the ocean. Similarly, people living on a body of water could choose to construct a mobile, floating home, while this would not be feasible for a mountain dweller. Display some pictures of differing geographic areas. Challenge children to examine the pictures and to identify naturally occurring materials from which they could build homes: rocks that appear in illustrations of mountainous environments; trees in forest settings; sand, shells, and palm fronds in an ocean scene. Ask children to describe methods and materials they might use to construct homes in each of these locations. Ask them how they might obtain materials that aren't indigenous to the named or pictured areas or what could be substituted.

5. *It's Where I Hang My Hat.* Show children pictures of various rooms, as well as pieces of furniture and equipment found in homes. Ask them to describe what they do in the room or with the item in their own home. Encourage children to think of other rooms or items that are not pictured, but that they rely on in their homes.

6. *The Sounds of Home.* Produce a tape recording of some sounds common to homes. Examples include running water, a toilet being flushed, a telephone ringing, a baby crying, a doorbell ringing, or a car being started. Direct children to listen carefully and identify the object or event that might produce each sound. You could make lotto boards (see Chapter 18 for the procedure) that picture each event or object represented in the tape recording. Give each child a lotto board and a set of markers (poker chips or cardboard shapes) to place on each picture as its related sound is identified.

7. **Story Rhythms.** Read an illustrated version of the poem, "This Is the House That Jack Built." Talk with children about the rhythm of the repetitive lines and how it adds to the enjoyment of the story. Invite children to gently slap their thighs in time to the words as you read the book a second time through. Make sure to maintain a steady verbal cadence rather than interrupting the text to point to the pictures or ask questions.

8. **Home Hums and Poems.** Introduce children to the following songs and finger plays related to living in homes.

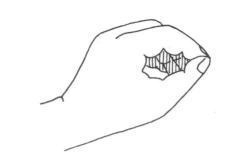

Figure 5.1 *Make a Mouse Shape with One Hand*

Little Mouse
(Traditional)
There was a little (brown) mouse, in a little (brown) house, as lonely as she could be. So the little (brown) mouse, in the little (brown) house, invited company!

Motions:
Represent a mouse by holding all four fingers against the thumb. (Figure 5.1)

Make a house by holding the fingertips of both hands together with the palm at angles to form a peaked roof. Gesture toward yourself with both hands when "inviting company." Invite children to suggest other colors for the mouse and the house.

Oh Give Me a Home
(Tune: "Home on the Range";
Words: Kit Payne)
Oh give me a home
Where my family can roam
All around in the rooms and the yard.
Where the lights brightly burn
Every time I return
When the work of my day
Leaves me tired.
Come, visit my home,
Where we'll eat and we'll sing
and we'll play
When we've finished the chores,
both in and outdoors,
for we all help each other
that way.

Some Folks Live
(Author: Kit Payne)
Some folks live in cabins, some folks in a tent.
Some folks purchase houses, some, apartments rent.
Homes can float on water, homes can drive away.
Homes can be forever, or only for a day.
But every home's where people sleep, and work and eat and play.

When I'm Big
(Author: Kit Payne)
When I grow big I'd like to make
a home to which my friends I'll take.
To show them all the things I keep;
Maybe they can stay and sleep,
or eat a meal inside with me—
how very pleasant that will be!

*9. **My Own Home.**

General Purpose: To encourage children's use of memory and descriptive language skills.

TFPs: 1, 2, 3, 4, 5, 6, 7, 8. 12, 13, 14, 21, 25, 26.

Materials: Tape recorder and blank tape or writing paper and pen or pencil. Optional: Drawing paper and markers or crayons.

Procedure:

a. Invite children to join you, one to three at a time, to write a story called *My Own Home.* Tell the children that one person can tell his or her story while others listen; then it will be someone else's turn.

b. Point out that you will record the story-teller's words (in writing or on tape). Some children may be ready to dictate descriptions of their homes with only a little encouragement. Others may respond best to an "interview" format.

c. Encourage each child's descriptions through comments and praise. "You remembered that your door has a shiny handle," or, "It sounds like you love your porch."

d. Label the top of each page as children describe aspects of their homes or introduce each item on the tape. "Tell me about the outside of your home." "Tell me the colors of your home." "What are some materials it is made of?"

Other possible subjects for children to describe include: the room where I sleep, the room we usually eat in, my favorite chair, the room where I keep my best toys, the people who live at my home, and my home jobs.

e. Some children may want to draw illustrations to accompany their story. Read or play back the stories to the children. Avoid comparisons of possessions or of size or desirability of living quarters.

Hint for Success:

• Describe your own home first. Play back the tape recording of your voice to demonstrate how your words have been preserved.

How to Simplify this Activity:

• Conduct a discussion of children's homes without recording children's individual statements.

• Collect photographs of the children's homes; invite children to describe what is pictured.

How to Extend this Activity:

• Make a classroom book entitled *All Our Homes* by laminating each child's story. Punch a hole in the top of each laminated page. Attach the pages together with a ring fastener or length of yarn. Make the book a permanent addition to your book corner. Each page could be cut into the shape of a house before dictated sentences are added. The sentences facilitate children's recognition and selection of the *All Our Homes* book during story times.

• Encourage children to use their own form of writing to complete the activity described above.

Physical

1. *Department of the Exterior.* Gather several tools and implements used for maintaining the exterior surfaces of homes: window-washing squeegees and chamois, large sponges, paint rollers and brushes, paint pans, buckets, and a small stepladder. At large-group time, initiate a discussion of the many ways people care for the buildings and structures that house them. Ask children to suggest reasons why homes require outside maintenance. Show the various implements to the children; pass them around for examination. Ask children to name them and/or explain their functions. If they are unable to do so, explain and demonstrate each item's use. Later, take the children and the materials outside. Put water in the paint pan and buckets. Invite the children to "paint" the school with water, trying both rollers and brushes. Suggest that someone can wash windows with a sponge, while an assistant dries them with a chamois. Offer another child the use of the squeegee; demonstrate and direct its use. If you have access to a very sturdy, low stepladder, assign one child at a time the task of painting above standing reach, or washing the top sections of windows. Discuss the physical effort involved in manipulating the tools and whether it is more or less than what would be required to carry out the tasks without special implements.

*2. *Drawn to Home.*
   General Purpose: To provide children with practice in grasping and controlling writing tools.

TFPs: 8–11, 16, 18.

Materials: Pictures that represent pipes through which water flows in a home. (Figure 5.2 shows some examples); pencils, markers, and/or crayons.

Procedure:

a. Invite children to join you at a table to trace the paths that water might take through the plumbing pipes in a home.

b. Provide each child with a pencil and a copy of the picture(s). (Figure 5.2)

c. Direct children to guide their pencils down the middle of the "paths," from a water tank to a laundry tub, toilet, sink, or other outlet. Introduce the straight path first because it is the easiest to follow, then a curved path, then one with corners. Paths followed from top to bottom of the page are more difficult than those drawn from side to side.

d. As children navigate the paths, encourage discussions of how accessibility to water is managed in various types of homes. Some homes are on one level, some have two or more levels. Often, water from one source is fed to many rooms in a home through plumbing pipes. Water must also drain from higher to lower levels. Children can share ideas about the appliances and fixtures in their homes that accommodate plumbing.

e. Comment on children's attempts to produce pencil trails within the boundaries of plumbing paths: "You've kept your pencil right between the lines." "You're trying hard to follow that path!"

Hint for Success:

• Invite children to negotiate the paths with a finger or a small object (like a car) before trying the activity with writing implements.

How to Simplify this Activity:

• Give children markers because they are easier to guide than pencils. Start with broad, washable markers, then move on to narrower tipped ones.

• Draw path pictures on large pieces of poster board so that the "pipes" can be very wide and can extend for some dis-

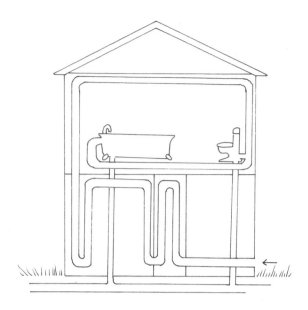

Figure 5.2 *Follow the Water Flowing Through Pipes in This House*

tance in a straight line before introducing curves and corners. Laminate or cover with clear contact; provide wax pencils or wipe-off markers so the posters can be used repeatedly and wiped clean.

How to Extend this Activity:

• Produce more intricately curved paths with many cross-overs and corners.

• Write the path tracer's name in "path-form" at the top right of his or her paper, for an exercise in producing letters. (Figure 5.3) Invite him or her to rewrite it inside the lines.

Social

1. ***Raise the Roof.*** Obtain two-by-four-inch planks, cut to lengths of four feet each. Present them, along with hollow wooden blocks or sturdy cardboard "brick" blocks to the children. Invite the children to work together to combine the materials into a home. Encourage them to negotiate and compromise as they carry out their home construction project. There should be at least twelve to eighteen planks and at least as many "cornerstone" blocks. After a structure has been formed, challenge the children to think of a way to make a roof

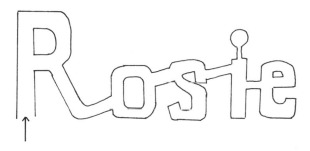

Figure 5.3 *Follow the Path Through Your Pipe-Name*

for their home. You might offer blankets or large pieces of cardboard produced by cutting large cartons apart. Accept the children's ideas and assist them with putting the roof in place and attaching it in some manner if they so desire. Use caution in deciding whether the children's structure is sturdy and stable enough to be safely "inhabited." You may wish to direct "demolition" and "remodeling" instead.

2. *We're in this Together.* Use the children's refrigerator carton home or tent, described in previous activities, as a space for which to develop rules for cooperative use. Initiate a discussion during a large-group time regarding the need to be considerate and to share the responsibility for maintenance and safety when people live together in the same home. Inform the children that since they will be pretending to live together in their new home-away-from-home, they should decide together on some rules for its use. If necessary, suggest some categories for rules to get the conversation going. "Decide, first, how many people can be in this home at a time." "How will others know when it's their turn to 'Come home'?" "What kinds of 'possessions' can be brought into the home?" Draw simple illustrations and/or write simple statements for each rule. Post the rules near the home for future reference.

3. *United We Sand.* Before using the two-by-four-foot planks described in the "Raise the Roof" activity, invite the children to work in teams to sand away rough edges. Affix coarse sandpaper to blocks of wood with carpet tacks or construction staples. Make some blocks suitable for one child to use at a time; make others that are large enough for two or three children to use together. If possible, clamp the planks into a workbench vise or anchor the ends with large stones in an outdoor area to make the sanding easier.

4. *Here We Are!* Take a small group of children on a walk around the neighborhood of the school, or if possible, around one of their own neighborhoods. As you walk, discuss mapmaking and inform the children that you will all work together to produce a neighborhood map. You may want to bring a small notebook and a pencil along on your walk or an instant camera to record your observations. Ask children to mention landmarks that they notice so that you can include them on the map when you get back to school.

After the walk, gather a large sheet of paper or poster board, a marking pen, and some crayons. At the children's direction, draw a map of the path you took on your walk. Invite the children to illustrate the map with pictures of some of the homes, trees, mailboxes, or other landmarks that you encountered. Different groups of children could be taken on map-walks of nearby neighborhoods each day of the unit. One group might produce a map of the school and playground, another of the inside of the school. Hang all the maps up as they are completed. Encourage children to describe the courses that are pictured on each map.

*5. *To Each Its Own.*

General Purpose: To provide children with a cooperative experience that encourages discussions of the names and functions of areas in a home.

TFPs: 1, 2, 4, 7–11, 25, 26.

Materials: A large sheet of paper (a roll of butcher paper or brown wrapping paper, approximately six feet long); glue sticks or white glue and applicators; scissors; lots of home-decorating or family life-style theme magazines; yardstick; dark marking pen.

Procedure:

a. Prepare the length of paper ahead of time by sectioning it into six or eight squares or rectangles. Vary the size of the "rooms." You could cut the paper to resemble a mobile home or houseboat, or add a roof line with an attic section, a basement, a patio, or a yard.

b. Invite children to decide what kinds of rooms their home mural will have; point out that most homes have a bathroom and kitchen. Ask the children where these rooms will be located. Ask children to tell you what the other rooms' uses will be. Use the marking pen to label each of the rooms.

c. Distribute magazines; encourage children to cooperate in small groups as they search for pictures that represent various rooms. Very young or inexperienced children could tear out pictures or choose pictures from a precut pile.

d. Encourage cooperation by pointing out opportunities for helping behavior: "It looks like Dennis has found a picture for the bathroom. Sarah, you can help by passing him some glue." "Aki, you noticed that Tommy needs scissors! I like the way you helped by sharing yours." (Providing a limited number of scissors and glue sticks will encourage problem solving and sharing, with adult guidance).

e. Encourage children's discussions of the functions of rooms and the equipment, furniture, or activities associated with them. Children may want to share examples of ways that areas of their own homes are used. As they choose pictures of furniture or appliances, ask children to decide together in what rooms objects might be found.

Hints for Success:

• Demonstrate and direct applying glue to the back of the picture that the child wants to show.

• Accept the placement of many similar pictures of objects in the appropriate rooms: several toilets or more than one bathtub in each bathroom.

How to Simplify this Activity:

• Cut out pictures of furniture and appliances ahead of time. Place them in groups that would go in the same room. Ask children to look through a set of pictures together and decide which room the set might represent. Point out which area has been labeled as that room.

Invite children to work together to place all the furniture in one room at a time.

• Have children arrange pictures on separate sheets of paper to represent each room in a home. Tape all the pictures together to produce one large home mural after each room is completed.

How to Extend this Activity:

• Introduce the activity with a discussion of the divisions of space common to most rooms. Ask children to generate reasons why particular rooms feature particular groupings of furniture and equipment. Encourage discussion of equipment that might be found in different rooms in the homes of different people. For instance, laundry equipment might be located in the basement in one home, in the kitchen of another, in a special laundry room near the kitchen, or absent altogether. Model and direct negotiation among the children as to where it will be placed in *their* home.

• Prepare a similar activity with flannelboard figures. The entire board can represent the home; cut strips of flannel to serve as room dividers. Cut out a set of furniture. Together children can arrange and rearrange the house in many combinations of rooms and furniture.

• Add a yard and some catalogues of play equipment. Invite the children to plan an outdoor play space for their home and to affix pictures of slides, climbers, or sandboxes to the area that represents the yard.

• Encourage older children to lay out the furniture and equipment cutouts logically within the rooms rather than attaching many pictures at random within the "walls."

• Encourage group decisions about how much furniture each room would need; decide together how many people and pets are in the family for whom the home is being arranged.

Pretend Play

1. *Real Estate.* Set up a pretend play area as a real estate office. Include pictures of many kinds of homes, home magazines, and real estate brochures. Arrange a desk with a

telephone, pads of paper and pencils, and some chairs. Suggest that one child serve as the real estate agent. Another child can sit in the client's chair and describe the kind of home for which he or she is shopping. You can direct the agent to display pictures and "write" a list of requirements to suit the client. Provide clients with graph paper and pencils to sketch drawings that augment their descriptions of desirable dwellings. Encourage them to list the types of rooms and outdoor features they might desire. Extend the activity by encouraging the agent and customers to "visit" some of the homes for sale that the children create in the Dollhouse Dream Homes activity described next.

2. ***Dollhouse Dream Homes.*** Set up one or more dollhouses on tables or on the floor. Wooden or cardboard crates stacked side-by-side and on top of each other can serve as dollhouses as well. Provide a collection of dollhouse furniture or small boxes, spools, and empty film canisters. Invite children to set up rooms with complementary arrangements of furniture. Ask why they make certain groupings of furniture. Encourage explanations of the functions of particular rooms.

3. ***At Home in the Woods.*** Obtain a camping tent, preferably with flexible frame construction. Invite children to accompany you on a pretend camping trip. With the children's assistance, set up the tent indoors or outdoors. Pack the equipment that the children feel would be necessary. Remind them that camping, like living in a permanent home, involves cooking, cleaning, sleeping, dressing for the weather, and playing. Make a child-dictated list of necessary equipment, if you wish. Collect duffel bags, suitcases, or boxes to pack materials. Small lawn chairs, an inexpensive barbecue grill, sleeping bags, flashlights and insect-collecting containers, binoculars, hats, and sunglasses will add to the pleasure of a pretend camping excursion. If weather and environment permit, take all the supplies outdoors. Set up camp and enjoy a picnic lunch or snack prepared in "the great outdoors." Encourage children to act out a campfire singing session and preparing for bedtime. Go on a nature hunt to collect bugs, look for birds, and enjoy the wonders of living close to nature.

4. ***It's a Deal.*** Prepare for a pretend yard or garage sale with the children. Invite the children to choose classroom materials or personal possessions that are no longer needed in anticipation of an imaginary move to new quarters. Provide dot stickers or tags and markers to affix to items as they are priced. Display the tagged items on tables or in an open area. Inform children that some of them can be the movers and sellers while others are the prospective buyers. Supply a cash box, sales pad and pencil, play money, and grocery sacks to pack up their purchases. Encourage exchange of play money for goods. Customers can take their treasures "home" and unpack them into their original storage spaces and containers, pretending to stock the classroom with new-found toys and furniture.

*5. ***Modern Moves.***

General Purpose: To provide an opportunity for children to discuss and enact some feelings and experiences associated with moving.

TFPs: 1, 3, 4, 11, 13, 25–36.

Materials: Wagons, small moving dollies, and/or sturdy boxes with ropes attached for pulling; smaller boxes, diapers, rags, or small blankets for wrapping and padding; telephones; "work-order" pads; pencils; MOVING SERVICE sign; child-sized furniture; clothing; stuffed animals; dolls.

Procedure:

a. Initiate a discussion about moving. Invite children who have moved to share their feelings and experiences. Point out that people often take furniture, pets, and other possessions with them when they move. People may move a short distance, maintaining many of the same friendships and routines, or long distances that cause many changes in lifestyle. Although people don't "lose" friends, it may be difficult to see them often after a distant move. People can keep in touch with friends by mail or telephone.

b. Announce that the children will be able to run a moving service. Set up an area of the room prior to their arrival. Hang MOVERS sign on a table. Place a phone, work-order pad, and pencil on the table. Arrange an area to represent the home. Place clothing on shelves or in dresser drawers, dishes in cupboards, and so forth. Stack several boxes in the area. Park wagons, moving dollies, and/or moving-van cartons nearby.

c. Invite the children to join you in the area. Explain that the family must move to a new home. Create a story to explain why. Go on to say that now the family needs the services of a moving company to help take their furniture and other possessions to their new home. (Focus on this as a positive experience.)

d. Suggest that some children play the roles of family members. One may want to place a call to the moving service, announcing the day they would like to move. Another child can answer the call and write up a work order. The "family" can begin unloading shelves and drawers and neatly packing the materials into boxes. The "movers" can arrive and begin loading furniture into/onto the "moving vans"; encourage packing with padding. If possible, relocate your pretend play area with "child labor" to another place in your room. Then have the children return the materials to their original location at session's end.

e. Allow children to direct the play as much as possible, intervening to introduce additional facts and principles or playing the role of a new neighbor or "moving supervisor" only if children become bored or begin using props inappropriately.

Hint for Success:

- Read one of the stories about moving noted at the end of this unit. Follow up with a discussion of events in the story to provide children with some of the information they will need for their play.

How to Simplify this Activity:

- Invite children to enact moves to new quarters with dollhouses and miniature furniture instead of school furniture. Select wooden or plastic trucks to serve as moving vans. Provide small shoe

boxes or gift boxes into which possessions and furniture can be loaded. Choose some animal and people figures with which the movers can work as well.

How to Extend this Activity:

- Invite children to plan a new room arrangement for the classroom. Draw the plan on paper before proceeding with the move. Pack and move one area at a time, referring to the drawn plans. This activity could be extended over several days, moving one area at a time and constructing blueprints of the new arrangements with movable symbols to represent each piece of furniture.

TEACHER RESOURCES

Field Trip Ideas

1. Visit the home of one or more teachers.
2. If some of the children in the classroom live in the neighborhood of the school, take a walking "homes tour" to see their homes from the outside. If family members are at home during the day and are willing, perhaps the children could tour the inside as well. Invite the child whose home you are visiting to explain some functions of different spaces in the home.
3. Visit a construction site to view some of the materials, equipment, and strategies that are involved in building a home. If possible, arrange to visit the building sites of more than one kind of structure; compare the emerging features and the materials being used.
4. Visit a household that is preparing to move. Call a moving service and inquire if it would be possible to watch a van being loaded with furniture.
5. Take a bus tour or walking tour around one or several residential blocks, a mobile home park, or through a campground. Note the many variations in structures and equipment along the way.

Classroom Visitors

1. Invite a representative of a construction company to visit. Suggest that he or she bring some tools or materials to show: a tool belt, measuring tape, hammer, screwdriver, scraps of lumber, roofing tile, insu-

lation strips, plumbing pipes, electrical wire, and so forth.

2. Ask families if they or any relatives or close friends own a motor home. Arrange for them to drive it to school. Take a few children at a time inside for a look around. Point out such common features as a stove, a bathroom, a bed. Ask children to tell you what features a motor home has that their homes have or lack.

3. Arrange for a moving van to visit your school. Ask if a company representative would be willing to describe his or her job and to show the children a rolling dolly, some furniture pads, and the way that the van doors function. Perhaps the children could walk up the loading ramp and into the van.

4. Invite an exterminator to visit. Ask that he or she bring pictures of "household pests" that cause problems to homeowners and to explain how and why they are discouraged from taking up or maintaining residence in people's homes.

Children's Books

Adams, P. *This Is the House That Jack Built*. Wilts, England: Child's Play (International), 1977.

Barton, B. *Building a House*. New York: Greenwillow, 1981.

Bour, D. *The House from Morning to Night*. New York: Kane Miller, 1978.

Burton, V. L. *The Little House*. Boston: Houghton Mifflin, 1942.

Cannon, C. *Kirt's New House*. New York: Coward, McCann, Geoghegan, 1972.

Civardi, A. *Moving House*. Tulsa, OK: EDC Publishing, 1985.

Clark, A. N. *In My Mother's House*. New York: Viking, 1941.

Davidson, A. *Teddy Cleans the House*. New York: Holt, Rinehart and Winston, 1985.

Duke, K. *Clean-Up Day*. New York: Dutton, 1986.

Duvoisin, R. *The House of Four Seasons*. New York: Lothrop, Lee and Shepard, 1956.

Hill, E. S. *Evan's Corner*. New York: Holt, Rinehart and Winston, 1967.

Hoberman, M. A. *A House Is A House for Me*. New York: Viking, 1978.

Larsson, C. *A Home*. New York: Putnam's, 1975.

Miles, B. *A House for Everyone*. New York: Knopf, 1958.

Moore, E. *Grandma's House*. New York: Lothrop, Lee and Shepard, 1985.

Murphy, S. and Murphy, P. *Mrs. Tortino's Return to the Sun*. New York: Lothrop, Lee and Shepard, 1980.

Prather, R. *New Neighbors*. New York: McGraw-Hill, 1975.

Reish, J. *Hannah's Alaska*. Milwaukee: Raintree, 1983.

Rockwell, A., and H. Rockwell. *Nice and Clean*. New York: Macmillan, 1984.

Schick, E. *One Summer Night*. New York: Greenwillow, 1977.

Sharmat, M. W. *Mitchell Is Moving*. New York: Collier, 1978.

Slobodkina, E. *Billy the Condominium Cat*. Reading, MA: Addison-Wesley, 1980.

Sobol, H. L. *Pete's House*. New York: Macmillan, 1978.

Williams, V. B. *A Chair for My Mother*. New York: Greenwillow, 1982.

Adult References

Bowyer, Carol. *The Children's Book of Houses and Homes*. London: Usborne, 1978.

Faulkner, R., L. Nissen, and S. Faulkner. *Inside Today's Home*. New York: Holt, Rinehart and Winston, 1986.

Kidder, T. *House*. Boston: Houghton Mifflin, 1985.

McAlester, V., and L. McAlester. *A Field Guide to American Houses*. New York: Knopf, 1980.

Roske, M. D. *Housing in Transition*. New York: Holt, Rinehart and Winston, 1983.

Vila, B., and J. Davidson. *This Old House: Restoring, Rehabilitating & Renovating*, Boston: Little, Brown, 1980.

Chapter 6

Clothing

●

Mary wore her red dress,
red dress, red dress.
Mary wore her red dress,
all day long.

●

This familiar song is a favorite of children the world over. They easily relate to the words because they think of themselves not only in terms of their names but in terms of their clothing as well. When asked to describe themselves, most children mention what they are wearing as an integral part of who they are.

Moreover, everyone in the world wears clothes. Whether to cover and protect the body or to decorate and draw attention to it, clothing is a universal aspect of human society. Our wearing apparel comes in many forms and is used for a multitude of purposes. Some clothing identifies a person's occupation or recreational activity; some is indicative of certain cultural or national groups; many garments are designed in response to climatic or other environmental conditions; some articles of clothing are worn every day, while some are worn only on special occasions; most clothing represents a person's individual taste and style. Clothing brings people together in its similarity and sets us apart from one another by its differences. As a consequence, the study of clothing can be viewed as a logical extension of the study of people themselves.

PURPOSE

Within this theme, we have focused on ways in which people use clothing, how clothing is constructed, and how it is worn. This approach allows us to integrate many multicultural activities throughout the unit in a natural, unforced manner. In addition, we have been cognizant of children's gender stereotypes with respect to what males and females wear, or are "supposed" to wear, and have taken pains to address them. Our ultimate goal is to increase children's awareness of themselves and others while exploring a sound information base related to the many facets of clothing.

IMPLEMENTATION

There are numerous ways to implement a clothing unit.

Option One: Plan this theme as a follow-up to one on self-awareness or the human body. Younger, less experienced children will benefit from the inclusion of lessons on dressing and self-help skills (buttoning, zipping, etc.) and on the appropriate order of dressing (especially winter or outdoor garments as appropriate). For older children, extend the study to incorporate the influence of personal taste and other aspects of decision making with respect to clothing choices.

Option Two: Develop a multiweek unit beginning with what is most familiar to the children and then moving on to more abstract, less familiar ideas. The first week should focus on the function and uses of clothing. Clothing construction should be the topic of week two, while the origins of clothing materials would occupy week three. Dressing could be incorporated at any logical point, or, if the children are already adept at dressing, simply disregarded.

Option Three: Select only a portion of this clothing unit on which to focus intently. For example, study the origins of clothing, using as many firsthand experiences as possible. This may be more easily accomplished in a farming community, but urban museums and libraries should not be overlooked as resources. Clothing factories and outlet stores may be additional valuable sources of material. Younger children might examine and analyze their own clothing, while older or more experienced children could focus on multicultural articles of apparel. The latter group could delve deeper by learning how the sources of clothing materials vary in different countries according to the natural resources available locally.

TERMS, FACTS, AND PRINCIPLES

General Information

1. Clothes are the items people have specially designed and made to cover, protect, or decorate their bodies.
2. People in all cultures wear clothing.
3. The clothes people wear are influenced by many factors, such as weather, availability, activities, social customs, and personal preferences.
4. Clothing is usually meant to be worn on particular parts of the body.
   a. Feet: shoes, socks, boots, snowshoes, sandals, slippers, clogs, thongs.

b. Head: hats, helmets, caps, crowns, wimples, miters, yarmulkes, veils, turbans, fezes.

c. Arms, torso, legs: capes, shirts, blouses, pants, jackets, coats, sweaters, vests, parkas, snowsuits, slickers, habits, cassocks, dresses, trousers, skirts, kilts, shorts, culottes, chaps, jeans, overalls, tutus, tuxedos, leggings, leg warmers, kimonos, leotards, shawls, serapes, ponchos, tights, robes, pajamas, nightgowns, diapers, training pants, burnooses.

d. Hands: mittens, muffs, gloves, (oven mitts, rubber gloves, work gloves, winter gloves).

5. Most clothing keeps parts of the body hidden from view.

6. People wear certain articles of clothing, such as underwear or bathing suits, to cover private parts of their bodies.

7. People often wear clothes to keep their bodies safe and comfortable.

8. Clothes that help people keep their bodies safe include: long pants, long-sleeved shirts, work gloves, boots, helmets, life jackets, shoes, sunglasses, safety goggles, knee and elbow pads, face masks, chaps.

9. Clothes that help people keep their bodies comfortable include:

a. For warmth: hats, mittens, scarves, coats, snowsuits, pants, socks, boots, tights, overalls, serapes, burnooses.

b. For dryness: raincoats, slickers, ponchos, rubbers, boots, galoshes, rain hats.

c. For coolness: mesh shirts, sun hats, shorts, sandals, sun visors, sunsuits, burnooses.

10. In general, people wear more and/or heavier clothes in cold weather and fewer and/or lighter clothes in warm weather.

11. People reserve some clothing for special times, such as holidays; parties, religious ceremonies; celebrations of local, regional, or national events; and ethnic festivals or historical commemorations.

12. All people have clothing preferences.

*13. People sometimes change their minds about the kinds of clothes they like. They may be influenced by what others think, or by what they have seen or read.

*14. People often wear an article of clothing because they think it makes them look beautiful, handsome, silly, conspicuous, inconspicuous, like their friends, different from their friends, similar to someone they admire, or different from someone they don't like.

*15. People sometimes wear clothing to mask or call attention to particular parts of their body.

*16. People often wear clothes that make them feel relaxed, confident, special, happy, or unique.

17. Some clothing items have such particular religious, occupational, or ethnic significance that they are appropriate to wear only at special times or to be worn only by the people for whom they were intended.

*18. People's ethnicity, character, and gender cannot necessarily be discerned by the clothes they wear.

*19. People's aesthetic tastes are often reflected in the clothes they wear. People combine items of clothing in ways unique to them.

20. Some types of clothing reflect a person's occupation. These are called uniforms.

21. Some types of clothing are entirely ornamental.

22. Sometimes people wear jewelry or other decorations along with their clothing.

Clothing Origins

23. People make clothing for themselves or others.

24. People use many kinds of materials to make clothing.

25. Materials used for clothing are made in a variety of colors, patterns, textures, weights, and drapes.

26. People use a variety of tools and/or machines to make clothing, such as scissors, needles, thread, awls, knitting machines, spinning wheels, looms, pins, cutting machines, and sewing machines.

27. Clothing is often made from cloth.

28. Cloth is a woven, knitted, or pressed material made of natural (wool, hair, cotton, silk, flax, hemp, leather) or synthetic fibers or a combination of both.

29. People get natural fibers from plants and animals.

*30. People shear wool from sheep; spin wool into yarn; dye the yarn; and weave, knit, or crochet the yarn into cloth or clothing.

*31. People make leather from the skins of various animals.

*32. People process the raw leather so that it can be made into clothing.

*33 Cotton cloth is made from the cotton plant. People plant the cotton, pick the cotton, clean it, spin it into thread, color the thread, and weave it into cloth.

34. People create synthetic fibers, such as plastic, nylon, rayon, and dacron, in factories.

*35. People invented synthetic fabrics for many reasons: strength, durability, ease of care.

36. Sometimes people stamp or paint designs on cloth.

Clothing Construction

37. People make cloth into clothing in various ways.

38. People use patterns to make parts of each piece of clothing.

39. People cut out the pieces of cloth using scissors or cutting machines.

40. People sew or lace the pieces of cut cloth together in a particular way and in a special sequence.

*41. When two pieces of fabric are sewn together, the joining point is called a seam.

*42. The bottom of a dress, pants, or robe is called the hem. This can be shortened or lengthened to suit a person's height.

43. Sometimes people add decorations to clothes after they have been put together.

44. Once the fiber has been made, the process of making clothing is similar for both natural and synthetic fabrics.

*45. As a person's body size changes, the size of the clothing he or she needs will also change.

Dressing

46. The process of putting clothing on the body is called dressing.

47. Some clothing is held together on the body with fasteners: zippers, buttons, snaps, ties, buckles, Velcro®.

48. People learn to use the fasteners on clothing.

49. Each piece of clothing has an inside and an outside, a back and a front, a top and a bottom; some articles of clothing may have a right and a left side.

50. Sometimes the order in which clothing is put on makes a difference.

51. The way a person attempts to put on his or her clothes makes it easier or harder to get dressed.

*52. Certain articles of clothing can be put on comfortably or effectively in only one way.

*53. Certain articles of clothing may be put on in a number of ways (scarves, sarongs, hats, ties).

54. Clothing is made in different sizes to fit people of varying shapes and dimensions.

55. Having to wear certain clothing for one purpose may make achieving another goal more difficult. For instance, wearing a snowsuit for warmth may make it more difficult to run.

*56. Clothes must be cleaned to maintain their appearance and durability.

ACTIVITY IDEAS

Aesthetics

1. *The Chosen Few.* Arrange a collection of fabric scraps on a tray or table top. Choose fabrics with varying designs and textures, such as velvet, corduroy in different wales, piqué, seersucker, satin, and fake fur. Make sure to include both natural and synthetic pieces as well. Encourage children to examine the articles closely by

touch, smell, sight, and sound (as when rubbed or shaken). Then ask them to select their favorite from among the group. To extend this activity, ask each child to rank the materials from least to most favorite, and vice versa. Older children could also compare their preferences with one another and discuss the reasons for their choices.

2. *Silly Dress-up.* Invite children to combine provided articles of clothing in ways that seem amusing to them, such as high heels worn with cowboy's chaps, a rhinestone tiara with gardening gloves, or a man's tie with a fancy skirt. Take photographs of the fun for a classroom picture gallery.

3. *Fabric Painting.* Provide a collection of fabric scraps of varying textures at the art table. Also make available different colors of tempera paint in pie tins. Invite children to dip a piece of the material into the paint, cautioning them to use only a little paint rather than soaking the fabric through. Then show them how to press the painted fabric onto pieces of construction or manila paper to make a print. Point out the interesting designs that the various fabrics produce.

4. *Personal Wardrobe Design.* Trace life-sized silhouettes of the children's bodies onto paper or provide smaller body shapes drawn on paper. (Make each one at least 8½ by 11 inches to provide a large enough coloring surface for small hands.) Provide markers or crayons in many colors. Invite children to "dress" the figures in any way they wish. Have available glitter or trimming scraps (ribbon, lace, small buttons) and glue sticks for children to use.

5. *Fashions on Parade.* From books and magazines, make a collection of pictures of clothing from various periods in history, including different decades of this century. Focus on entire outfits (for men, women, and children) or on specific articles of clothing, such as hats or shoes. Present these to children for a discussion of changing fashions. Ask children to talk about what they see in the pictures and what differences and similarities they observe. An extension would be to solicit a discussion of the children's current clothing preferences. Invite them to talk about some reasons why they think clothing styles might change. Make some suggestions of your own (taste, availability, social pressure, adaptability to different activities and life-styles).

Affective

1. *Dandy Dress-up.* Supply a variety of hats, scarves, costume jewelry, feathers, ties, glasses frames, gloves, and colorful cloth remnants. Tell children to adorn themselves in ways that please them, so that they look beautiful, handsome, interesting, and so on. Older children could dictate, write, or record on tape how the clothing expresses their personality or personal taste.

2. *Pick a Pocket.* Provide articles of clothing that have pockets or that could be draped to make a pouch. Ask children individually to think of and talk about the special things they would like to keep in their pockets. These can be real or fantasy items. The emphasis should be on individual choice. Record the children's selections in some way. Ask older children to explain the reasons for their choices and how they would use the things in their pockets. In an alternate approach, talk about the pockets each child has on his or her clothing.

3. *Private Lives.* Talk with children about clothing that is designed to keep their private parts from public view and why. This category includes underwear and bathing suits. Have available models or drawings of a naked male child and a naked female child and articles of clothing cut out of felt or paper. Ask children to identify which clothing would be appropriate for each figure and encourage them to dress the figures for privacy.

*4. *Outgrown Clothes.*

General Purpose: To provide children with opportunities to learn about themselves.

TFPs: 52, 53

Materials: Outgrown children's clothing, additional clothing in a variety of sizes and styles, a full-length mirror.

Procedure:

a. Introduce the activity by discussing how children's needs for clothing change as a result of children's growth or weather conditions.

b. Invite children to try on the articles of clothing provided.

c. Stimulate children's conversations about growth over time, how they can tell they are growing, and the significance to individuals of their own growth. Some children may compare themselves to others. Help children observe and articulate similarities and differences.

Hint for Success:

• Supply clothing traditionally worn by boys and girls as well as androgynous items.

How to Simplify this Activity:

• Present a few clothes at a time. Allow children time to explore these items before adding or changing any articles.

• Select only one type of clothing at a time, hats or shoes, for example.

• Initially, focus on the physical aspect of "trying on," gradually incorporating more verbalizations.

How to Extend this Activity:

• Use a larger number and wider variety of clothing types.

• Help children record their observations on a chart or in an experience story.

• Probe children's ideas in more depth about how they feel being bigger than they were. Talk about how big or old they think they might have to be to fit into adult or teenage clothing.

Cognition

1. *From Sheep to Shawl.* Introduce the activity by reading *Pelle's New Suit* by Ella Beskow or *From Sheep to Shawl* by Ali Mitgutsch. Re-create some parts of either story in the following ways. Get some raw sheep's wool or a sheepskin and encourage children to explore its properties. Give children carding combs or two dog brushes and instruct them to brush the fibers of the wool so that they become straight and smooth. Try to procure a drop spindle. If you cannot, have children take a few fibers of wool and twist them between their fingers to simulate the action of a spinning wheel or machine.

Show children woolen yarn (in a natural color) and explain that this is the product of the spinning process. Next, demonstrate knitting or crocheting (if you can) or describe them using actual needles. Allow children to try. Have available woolen knitted or crocheted items and explain how they were made (by hand or machine). The parts of this lesson could be presented as individual activities all on the same day or on sequential days.

2. *Try It/Dye It.* Find pieces of cloth made of as wide a range of materials as possible—include such things as leather, plastic, nylon, mesh, cotton, wool, burlap, and so on. Purchase one or two packages of cold water commercial dye and prepare it according to the directions. Show the children how to use the dye. Then ask them to try dyeing each of the material samples using both types of dye. Help them chart the results. Ask them to figure out what attributes of the material made differences in the outcomes. Bring out some materials they hadn't used before and ask them to predict what would happen if they tried to dye them. Have them test out their predictions. Older children could be instructed to do this activity independently if you set up the experiments in a series of stations with pictographs available at each.

Or, they can record their results in notebooks as they work in teams of two or three. Younger children will require more supervision. Be sure to provide smocks or aprons for all participants.

3. *Telltale Togs.* The purpose of this activity is to help children figure out what they can and cannot discover about people by looking only at their clothing. Bring in examples or pictures of clothing that are not gender specific, such as jeans, coats, gloves, scarves, sunglasses, work shoes, and so on. Ask the children to identify each item and to speculate about the person who might wear it. Is it a man or a woman? Does he or she do a particular

job? Focus the children's attention on generating a variety of responses rather than any one correct answer. Ask for clarification from each child and responses from others engaged in the activity. Write down all of the ideas children suggest.

To vary this activity, use pictures of people in uniforms and have the children guess the gender of the wearer. Be sure to represent different jobs or occupations.

4. *Uniformity.* Show children a variety of pictures of people wearing different types of uniforms (bus drivers, waitpersons, physicians, firefighters, police officers, store clerks, mail carriers, telephone repairers, etc.). Help them figure out what jobs the people do. Then have them examine the uniforms and how the design of each enables people to do their work. Also draw the children's attention to the safety features of each outfit and explain how they provide protection against job-related hazards. Record the children's answers using a tape recorder, chart, or experience story format. Use common or familiar occupations with younger children; older children may be challenged by more unusual examples, such as rock climbers, assembly-line workers, landscape gardeners, or painters.

5. *Weather Match-ups.* Provide real clothing items appropriate to different types of weather. Use pictures of weather conditions, such as rain, snow, and sunshine, to generate a discussion of how weather affects clothing choices. Ask the children to sort the clothing into piles that match the conditions under which they would wear them.

6. *From Cloth to Clothes.* Show children samples of a fabric (cotton, wool, etc.) and an article of clothing made from that fabric. Provide paper patterns that correspond to the finished article of clothing. Cut out some pieces of cloth using the pattern. Have children identify which parts of the pattern were used to make up which parts of the clothing.

*7. *Feel and Find.*
   General Purpose: To provide children practice in discriminating among objects with and without visual cues.

   TFPs: 4d.

   Materials: Several pairs of gloves with distinctly different functions and attributes: rubber gloves, surgical gloves, heavy leather gloves, thin-knitted or fabric gloves, oven mitts; a purchased "feely box" or a box closed on all sides with a hole cut in one end through which a child's hand could pass; table and chairs.

   Procedure:
   a. Put one of each pair of gloves inside the feely box. Put the other gloves out on a table top.
   b. Ask children to examine the exposed gloves by handling them. As the youngsters do this, point out that gloves are designed and constructed for many different purposes and of many different materials.
   c. Invite the children, one at a time, to discover what's in the box using only their sense of touch.
   d. Direct children to put one hand in the box and use their fingers to explore the first glove they feel.
   e. Ask children to show you which glove on the table matches the one they are feeling. Have the child pull out the hidden glove to see if a correct match was made. If the answer is yes, continue with a new pair; if the match is incorrect, ask the child to try again.

How to Simplify this Activity:

• Choose gloves that have very distinctive textures, sizes, or shapes. Only use a few at a time, changing the assortment periodically and gradually adding more samples.

How to Extend this Activity:

• Choose gloves that are similar in feel, so that children have to make finer distinctions. Ask children how the gloves might be used. Explore the reasons behind their answers.

*8. *Clothing Classification.*
   General Purpose: To provide children with practice in grouping objects according to perceived similarities and differences.

   TFPs: 4, 7, 8, 9, 10, 12.

Materials: Mount at least twenty-four pictures of clothing articles on oak tag paper and cover them with clear contact paper. Include several pairs of identical pictures.

Procedure:

a. Place the pictures on the table with the following instructions: "Here is an assortment of clothing pictures. Today we can play some games with them. Look at them, touch them, handle them, and talk about them so you can learn about them." The above process may take a few minutes or several days depending on the children's prior experience with objects and with classification activities.

b. Point to one of a pair of pictures and say, "Show me the picture that looks just like this one." Repeat for the other pairs.

c. When you have determined that children can match the pictures, select a small number of pictures (six to eight) and say, "Put together all the pictures that are alike in some way." Allow the children time to do this.

d. Point to each group of pictures in turn. "Tell me one way in which these are the same." Be receptive to all answers by acknowledging and paraphrasing what each child says.

e. Point to a card not included in the group and ask why it doesn't belong.

f. Scramble the pictures in the middle of the table, then say, "Show me a different way to put together the pictures that are alike. Tell me why these belong together."

g. Repeat the preceding steps, adding additional pictures.

h. When children seem comfortable sorting in different ways, say the following: "Put together the pictures that are alike in two ways—or that have two things in common. Tell me why you put them together this way."

i. Next, point to one group of pictures and say, "Here are some pictures that are alike. Show me how you can divide this group into other groups that are alike."

j. Then, point to two groups of pictures as sorted by any child. Ask the child to tell

you something that is alike about both groups.

k. Offer a new picture. Ask the same child to put it in one of the groups he or she has made and to tell you why it belongs.

l. Finally, point to some pictures that the child has not grouped and say, "Tell me why you didn't put those pictures in one of your groups."

Hints for Success:

- This plan should be carried out over a long period of time—several weeks or months.

- Don't hurry children through the steps. They will require lots of opportunities to go from one to another.

How to Simplify this Activity:

- This plan is written in steps of increasing difficulty. Use only the first few parts for younger or less experienced children.

- Use only one type of clothing at a time, hats, shoes, or shirts, and so on.

How to Extend this Activity:

- Choose pictures that have subtle distinctions and more detail in their drawing.

- Substitute real objects for the picture cards.

Construction

1. *Clothing Cut-ups.* Introduce this activity with a discussion of the various kinds of clothing different people wear. Show children samples of simple clothing patterns and how they are used. Demonstrate by actually cutting out a simple item from cloth and basting it together. Tell children they can create their own pattern to make a *sash.* Show a sash and demonstrate how it might be worn. Provide precut or drawn outline shapes representing a sash for children to cut out themselves. Supply markers, scissors, glue, feathers, sequins, and fabric scraps for children to use in making their sashes.

2. *Presto Prints.* Show children several cloth samples decorated with a variety of designs. Explain that people all over the world like to decorate cloth so that the

clothes that are made from it are pleasing. Cut thin sponges in several shapes and distribute to the children. Soak large, thick sponges in paints of various colors and place them in open containers. Show children how to soak up paint by pressing their thin sponge shapes onto the large sponges. This method will ensure that the children's smaller sponges will not soak up too much paint. Assist children as they use their small sponges to print on a sheet of cloth. Children can be given a choice of shapes and colors to make their "printed cloth" design.

3. *Body Wraps.* Provide illustrations or pictures of people in different countries wearing lengths of cloth as articles of clothing. Have available large pieces of fabric, such as sheets, and encourage children to experiment with different ways of wrapping the cloth around their own bodies.

4. *Gingerbread People.* Follow any standard gingerbread recipe or use this one:

Ingredients:
½ cup butter
1 cup molasses
1 egg
1 tsp. baking soda
2 tsp. baking powder
½ tsp. cloves
½ tsp. ginger
1 rounded tsp. cinnamon
½ tsp. salt
1 T. orange rind
2½ cups whole wheat flour

Procedure:
Cream butter and molasses. Beat egg into batter. Slowly mix in dry ingredients. Chill dough in the freezer for 20 minutes. Roll dough out thin, cut using people-shaped cookie cutters. Bake at 350° for 8 minutes. Makes 4 to 6 dozen cookies.

Icing:
3 oz. cream cheese, creamed with 1½ T. milk. Beat in ¼ cup confectioner's sugar. Add 1 tsp. vanilla and ½ tsp. cinnamon.

Have children spread the icing on the cookies where the clothing is supposed to be and decorate their own cookies with raisins and shredded coconut. If you wish, add a few drops of food coloring to the icing.

*5. *Very Best Vests.*
General Purpose: To provide children with an opportunity to represent a single object using combinations of materials or techniques.

TFPs: 4c, 5, 12, 14, 21, 39, 48.

Materials: Paper grocery bags (at least one per child); glue; paper; scissors; fabric scraps; an assortment of feathers, beads, yarn, string, glitter, buttons, markers, crayons.

Procedure:
a. Set up the activity prior to the children's participation.
b. Introduce the activity with pictures of people wearing vests for decoration, for warmth, and so on. Use pictures of people from different countries displaying a variety of color and patterns in their vests. Provide some real vests for children to try on. Explain that they will have a chance to create their own vests out of paper.
c. Point out the array of materials available. If necessary demonstrate how to use the glue or cut out the vest. (Figure 6.1)
d. Encourage children to develop their own creations. Point out the many differences in finished products. Discuss the many ways children chose to decorate their vests and emphasize that people have different preferences for colors, texture, and styles when they choose clothing.
e. Invite children to try on their vests and view themselves in a full-length mirror.

Hints for Success:
• Wear a vest yourself, either an actual piece of clothing, or one you've constructed ahead of time using the same materials available to the children.

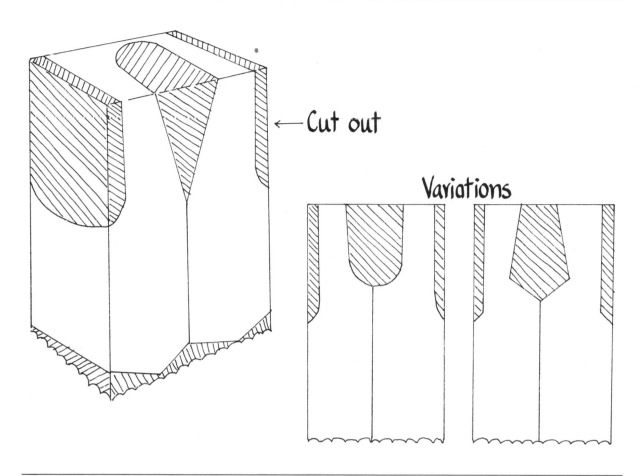

Cut out ←

Variations

Figure 6.1 *Paper Bag Vests*

- Avoid complex or fancy decorations if you choose to construct a model. Children hesitate to make their own product if a model is available that looks difficult to re-create.

- Use decorations representing a number of cultures.

How to Simplify this Activity:
- Cut the vests yourself so children can concentrate on decorations.

How to Extend the Activity:
- Invite several children to participate in decorating a vest for the teacher to wear.

- Have children make vests out of actual cloth. Children can either glue or sew on the decorations.

*6. **Hats Off**.
General Purpose: To provide children with an opportunity to represent a single object using various combinations of materials or techniques.

TFPs: 4, 9, 12, 14, 21, 24.

Materials: Newspaper, easel paper, yarn, markers, stickers, ribbons, feathers, fabric scraps, stapler, glue (or glue sticks).

Procedure:
a. Bring in a variety of hats for children to try on.
b. Invite the children to make their own hats. Tell them that they will be able to wear them and/or take them home when they are finished.
c. Take a single sheet of newspaper and double it. With the open edge down,

Figure 6.2 *Make Hats from Pieces of Newspaper*

fold the top two corners together (see Figure 6.2).

Fold up the edges. A double fold will make the bottom more stable. Staple the corners.

d. Point out the glue sticks and decorations, inviting children to decorate hats in any way they would like. Some may prefer coloring with crayons or markers. Ask children to add their name, or to show you where they would like you to write it for them.

Hint for Success:

- Separate the sheets of newspaper in advance. Place the decorations in small containers arranged on the table so that children can reach them.

How to Simplify this Activity:

- Prefold and/or prestaple the hats.

How to Extend this Activity:

- Make a diagram for children to follow in folding their hats.
- Allow children to use the stapler independently.

Language

1. *Fabric Fundamentals.* Display a wide variety of fabric scraps for the children to examine. Once the children have explored the materials, ask them to describe individual scraps using as many adjectives as possible. Record their ideas on a separate sheet of paper for each fabric sample. Finally, staple the materials to the corresponding descriptive list. To vary this activity, don't attach the fabric to the list. Instead, read the description out loud and have children guess which sample is being described.

2. *Button Box Stories.* Give children an assortment of buttons to look at and handle. Then tell them to close their eyes as they think of how the buttons feel. Ask them to choose their favorite button and dictate a story about it. Prompt the storyteller by such phrases as, "Once upon a time . . .," "And then . . . ." Record the story on audio tape or on paper. Play back or read each story to its author. If possible, allow children to keep the buttons they selected.

3. *Why Wear It?* Present children with illustrations or photographs of people in various recreational, climatic, or work-related circumstances. Ask children to describe the clothing that is being worn and to explain why the person is wearing it, within the context of the picture. Children's answers can be taken down as dictation or recorded on tape. This activity can be done with children individually or in groups.

4. *Special Clothes for Special Occasions.* Send a note home to parents asking them to allow children to bring to school (in a bag) an outfit or article of clothing that

they wear on special occasions. This might be party clothes, pajamas, a uniform, or a costume. Accept anything the child feels is special. Set aside a time of the day for children (either in a small group or in front of the class) to talk about the item or outfit that they brought and to tell when they wear it and why it is special. Children could be assigned on different days so that not all the clothes arrive at once.

5. *Clothing Riddles.*

Boots

For playing in the squishy mud,
there's nothing quite as fine.
And when there are a lot of them,
I know that *two* are mine.
I wear them on a rainy day,
and often with snowsuits.
They zip or snap or get pulled on.
They are called my _____ .

Umbrella

I'm like a bowl held upside down,
my handles holds me high
above your head on cloudy days,
when rain falls from the sky.
But when the sun comes out again,
or back inside you skip,
you shake me out and fold me up,
and leave me there to drip.
What am I?

Sunglasses

You wear these on your face when it's a sunny day.
And you put them in your pocket when the sun has gone away.
On bright days in the out-of-doors,
they help your eyes feel cool.
But people usually take them off when coming into school.
What are they?

Gloves

You put these on two body parts when snow begins to fall.
They have a special chamber for your fingers, one and all.
They're sometimes tied together, or fastened to your sleeve.
So you can always find them when it's time for you to leave.
What are they?

*6. *Tell Me How.*

General Purpose: To provide children with practice in giving precise verbal directions.

TFPs: 4, 5, 47, 48, 50, 51.

Materials: A set of adult-sized outdoor clothing, such as a hooded jacket, boots, gloves, snowpants, scarf, hat.

Procedure:

a. Gather the children into a group. Invite them to help you plan and learn a good way to get ready to go outdoors. Put the clothing in a pile near you.

b. Introduce the activity by saying, "I was having a real problem putting on my (jacket) (snowsuit) today. I would like some help from you. You tell me what to do, and I will do exactly as you say."

c. "Tell me what I should do first." Follow exactly the directions the children give you. If they say, "Put your hands in the sleeves," do precisely that—no more, no less. Unless children tell you otherwise, put things on backwards or upside down.

d. Play up to their laughter. Look surprised when something goes wrong.

e. Repeat the correct sequence as soon as children are able to articulate it.

f. Applaud their efforts as well as your own.

Hints for Success:

• Do this demonstration shortly before children will be getting into their own outdoor things so the lesson is fresh in their minds.

• While this can be used to teach many things (independence in dressing, etc.), concentrate on the verbal aspects.

How to Simplify this Activity:

• For younger children, follow their approximations of precise directions.

• Take only a few moments between steps so they don't get bored or frustrated.

How to Extend this Activity:

• Choose a child to be the one to dress. Secretly explain the "point" of the activity, namely to follow the verbal instructions to the letter. Select a youngster you think can get into the fun of the activity. Children may be paired for these activities, each taking a turn at being the giver and the receiver of the directions.

7. ***Chants, Songs, and Fingerplays.***
Mary Wore a Red Dress
(Traditional)
Mary wore a *red dress*, red dress, red dress.
Mary wore a red dress, all day long.
Directions:
Substitute a different child's name and an article of clothing the child is wearing each time you sing the song. This verse may be used as a greeting song at the beginning of the day. Ask children to identify the piece of clothing they wish to sing about.

This song has its own traditional tune, or sing to the tune of "Down by the Station."

Hokey Pokey
(Traditional)
Directions:
Play this familiar game substituting clothing parts for body parts. For instance, "You put your sleeves in, you take your sleeves out." The final verse should be: "You put all your clothes in . . . etc." Accompany the singing with appropriate motions.

Miss Mary Mack
Chant:
M̲iss Ma̲ry Mack̲, Mack̲, Mack
A̲ll dressed i̲n black̲, black̲, black
W̲ith silver buttons̲, buttons̲, buttons
A̲ll down her back̲, back̲, back.
Directions:
Clap to the chant on the u̲nderlined syllable.

Baa Baa Black Sheep
(Traditional)
Baa Baa black sheep,
Have you any wool?
Yes, sir. Yes, sir,
three bags full.
One for my master,
one for my dame.
And one for the little boy (girl)
who lives down the lane.

Jenny Jenkins
Will you wear *red*, oh my dear, oh my dear?
Will you wear red, Jenny Jenkins?
No, I won't wear red, 'cause it's the color of my *head*.
Chorus:
And I'll buy me a foldy, roldy, tildy, toldy, seek-a-double, use a cause-a-roll, to find me. Roll, Jenny Jenkins roll.
Directions:
The tune to this is traditional, however it is easily done as a chant. Substitute different colors and a corresponding rhyme. At first, ask children to choose a color, and you supply the rhyme. As children become familiar with rhymes, they can generate both the color and the appropriate rhyming word.

My Hat It Has Three Corners
My hat it has three corners,
three corners has my hat.
And had it not three corners,
it would not be my hat.
Directions:
Sing, chant this, with appropriate accompanying gestures on the words:
"My" (touch chest)
"hat" (touch top of head)
"three" (hold up three fingers)
"corners" (make a triangle shape in the air with your fingers)
Repeat this song several times. Each time through, leave out one word, substituting the motion instead. Continue doing the motions until all four words are left out.

Physical

1. *Sew Many.* Cut doll-sized pieces of fabric. Describe how the pieces should be sewn together to create an article of clothing. (Or make a chart that outlines the steps.) Provide real needles with large eyes and embroidery floss or other firm thread. Knotting both ends of the thread together makes it easier for children to manage.

2. ***Folding Laundry.*** Present articles of clothing, such as socks, shirts, pants, and so on. Tell children that the purpose of the game

Start with two plates.   Cut one in half.   Lace the half to the whole.

Figure 6.3 *A Paper Plate Pocket*

is to fold the laundry so it can be put in drawers or baskets. Demonstrate pairing socks or folding shirts if necessary.

3. ***Catch the Hat.*** Play a game of toss and catch using a hat in pairs or as a group. The hat is tossed in the air, and the children try to catch it. The one who does tosses it the next time.

4. ***The Braid Brigade.*** Tie three one-foot lengths of yarn or ribbon to the back of a chair. Teach children the process of braiding. Provide lots of opportunity for them to practice. The finished braid can be worn as an ornament, such as a belt, or can be glued or sewn to fabric as a decoration.

5. ***The Mitten Tree.*** Draw a 5½-by-7-inch mitten outline on stiff construction paper or tagboard and make enough for each child. Give children scissors to cut around the outline. Provide stickers, glue, and other items for children to use to decorate their mitten(s). Cut out a tree and staple it to a bulletin board. Tack children's cut-out mittens onto the tree. More skilled children can draw their own outlines. The activity could be adapted to a hat, coat, shirt, or shoe "tree."

6. ***Pocket Sew-up.*** Use paper plates, large blunt needles, yarn, and a hole punch. (Figure 6.3) Cut one plate in half. Place it over the lower half of a second plate and hold it steady. Help children punch holes around the outer rims of the plates. Then,

allow them to select a piece of colored yarn and help them thread a needle. Tie one end to a punched hole. Demonstrate how to sew. Secure the yarn to the plate when the child completes the last hole. In a variation of this activity, attach a piece of yarn to the top or sides of the pocket so children can tie it around their waist or wear it over their shoulder. Suggest that children actually use the pocket to carry something.

*7. ***Belt It Up.***

General Purpose: to help children develop small muscle skills and eye-hand coordination.

TFPs: 1, 4, 26, 40.

Materials: Poster board, cut into strips approximately twenty inches long and two inches wide; yarn or lightweight string in a variety of colors; blunt-tipped, large-eye needles; hole punches; marker to add names and/or decorate belts. Optional: Small beads (¼ to ½ inch) with holes for stringing; table and chairs.

Procedures:

a. Set up the area prior to children's participation. Pile the poster board strips in the center of a table. Place a hole punch at each child's seat. Cut the yarn into pieces approximately twenty-eight inches long, or supply scissors for children to cut the yarn themselves. Provide

Making a Belt

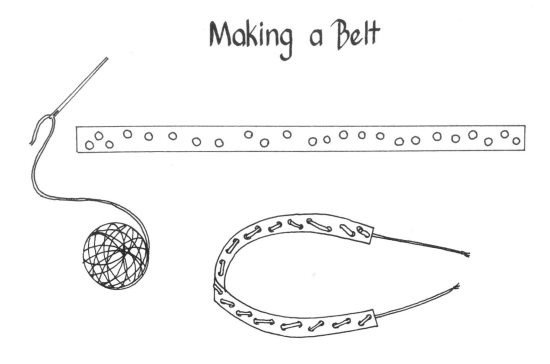

Figure 6.4 *Children Can Make a Belt to Wear*

containers of markers and beads if you wish.

b. Invite the children to make their own belts to wear. (Figure 6.4) Distribute a poster-board strip to each child. Show children how to punch holes along each edge of the poster-board strip, allowing them to space the holes as they desire. Note that inexperienced children may need an adult to hold the poster board while they use both hands to squeeze the hole punch together.

c. Distribute needles to the children. Invite them to choose yarn (string) colors. Help with needle threading if necessary. Double the string/yarn and knot to help keep it in the needle as children work.

d. Direct the children to begin "sewing" the yarn in and out of the holes in the poster board, weaving a design along the edges of the "belt." Leave about six inches extending at each end. Help children tie knots at each end of the yarn to keep it from pulling through the belt at the ends.

Hints for Success:

• Provide beads to be threaded onto the yarn at each end of the belt. Tie knots to keep the yarn in place. The belts can be fastened around the children's waists by tying the yarn ends together. Some children may enjoy adding additional decoration with markers.

• Talk about some functions of belts as children work: Some are pretty and decorative, some are necessary to keep pants in place. Point out similarities and differences in colors and patterns as children finish their products.

How to Simplify this Activity:

• Very young children can be given precut belt strips and stickers, or glue sticks and paper scraps, with which to decorate them. This requires less dexterity than hole punching and lacing and still results in a decorative product that allows practice of fine motor skills. The adult can add one hole to each end of the belt, then attach yarn ties as a fastener.

How to Extend this Activity:

- Allow older, more experienced children the opportunity to do all parts of this activity independently. The greater their skill, the more they can do.

Pretend Play

1. *Suds 'n' Duds.* Allow children to actually wash doll clothes. Provide a water source (sink, water table, small plastic tub on table), soap, a scrubbing board, and smocks. Newspaper or rag rugs under the water container will absorb spills. Provide a place to hang clean clothes. (A drying rack or a line with clothes pins across a corner of the area will do.) Encourage the children to hang up the clothes by themselves.

2. *Trips Ahoy!* Make available various articles of clothing and small suitcases. Tell children that when people go on a trip they usually have to take their clothing with them. Encourage the children to pretend that they are going to travel and to choose and pack the things they will need.

3. *What Can I Be?* In a corner of the room, provide simple materials for dressing up. One day have scarves, another day hats, another day coats and capes, another day shoes, and so on. Make a mirror available for children to see themselves.

4. *Clothing Store.* Set up an area of the room to look like a clothing (or shoe) store. Provide a variety of actual clothes or shoes for children to try on, a mirror, a "dressing room," and a cash register, as well as accessories, such as necklaces and hats. Prior to this, discuss some of the roles children might assume (customer, salesperson, shop assistant) and some appropriate behaviors for each. Inexperienced children do better with a more limited selection of items or by focusing on only one type of clothing at a time.

5. *Clothing Factory.* Using real sewing machines (without needles), clothes forms, and fabric cut into parts of clothes, set up an area as a clothing factory. Furnish the area with threaded blunt needles and canvas, dolls to dress, mirrors, a child-sized ironing board with toy iron, tape measures, scissors, and so forth. Children can play the roles of clothing designer, clothing maker, customer, and clothing fitter.

*6. *Laundromat/Laundry Room.*

General Purpose: To provide children with opportunities to create play themes and to experiment with a variety of objects, roles, and characterizations as they pretend.

TFPs: 1, 56.

Materials: A cardboard washer and dryer or standard, child-sized housekeeping furniture that could represent a washer and dryer, such as a stove and a cupboard; laundry baskets, a variety of clothing in several sizes; a table; empty detergent containers; a cash register; tokens or play money; a "laundromat" sign. Optional: toy iron and ironing board, telephone, hangers, dressers or shelves, wash tubs.

Procedure:

a. Set up the area prior to children's participation. Pile clothes in two or three laundry baskets. Place pieces of furniture in a row to represent washers and dryers, or cut and decorate large cartons to achieve this effect. Display detergent boxes or bottles on a table or shelf.

b. Invite children to come into the laundromat and bring their baskets of dirty clothes. Suggest that one or two children may want to be "laundry workers" who make change, help people learn how to operate the equipment, charge fees to wash and/or iron people's clothes, answer telephone calls, and so forth.

c. Allow children to direct the play as much as possible, intervening to provide additional information or demonstrate procedures only as boredom or inappropriate uses of materials dictate.

Hints for Success:

- Before opening the area, talk with the children about their experiences or observations regarding clothes washing, either at home or at a laundromat. This will remind them of some things they already know and provide a foundation on which they can base their play. Explain how to put clothes in the machine or tub, how to remove them, what to do next, and so forth.

- If possible, schedule a trip to a laundromat so children can see actual machines at work.

How to Simplify this Activity:

- Use a few simple props, such as doll clothes and a washtub. Add new items gradually over time.

How to Extend this Activity:

- Expand the area to include pretend dry cleaning. Provide a uniform for the caretaker and cash and cash registers for making "change" for the machines.

Social

1. *I Packed My Grandmother's Trunk.* This old parlor game becomes a true social activity when it is adapted so children can work together rather than in competition. It is best done with a few children at first. As children's memory and familiarity with the game increases, more children can be added. Each round of the game goes as follows: The leader says, "I packed my grandmother's trunk and in it I put _____ ." Each child in turn verbally supplies an item of clothing. At the end of the round, the children help each other remember what was in the trunk. A variation of this game might be to provide actual clothing items for children to select and then put into a cardboard "trunk" in turn. Each child would describe the item he or she picked as well as the others' choices. At the end of the round, the "packed" items could be used to prompt the children's memories as needed.

2. *Friendly Fashions.* Ask children to think of a person in the class that they like (child or adult). Tell them to find out this person's favorite color and favorite article of clothing. Using shapes (precut for younger children) representing hats, shoes, belts, shirts, dresses, pants, and so on, instruct each child to create a representation of that favorite piece of clothing and give it to the person they chose.

3. *Fave Raves.* A few days before you plan to do this activity, ask each child to wear some favorite article of clothing or accessory to school. With a large or small group of children, have each identify the item and explain why it is their favorite. Ask other children, one at a time, to tell something they also like about the other child's favorite item. Focus on the positive. If children laugh at a particular article, say something like, "What you like about Sam's sneakers is that they make you laugh."

4. *Celebrity Scarecrow.* This is an activity to be done over several days or even weeks. First, construct on your own, or with child assistance, a scarecrow. Use straw or hay, if the materials are available, or use wadded newspaper in paper bags tied together to represent a person's body. The object is for the children to work together to design and make clothing for the scarecrow. Encourage the children to work together to create the pants, the shirt, the hat, and so on. You may have to cut the material, but children of all ages can be involved in putting together the parts of each garment. Dress the scarecrow at a time when all the children can participate. Focus on the cooperative efforts of each child. Another option is for children to contribute articles of clothing from home to dress the scarecrow.

*5. *Common Clothing.*

General Purpose: To offer children opportunities to find similarities between themselves and others (a friendship-promoting activity).

TFPs: 12, 13, 14, 16.

Materials: Large group of children in an area that allows free movement.

Procedure:

a. Gather the children for a large-group experience. Introduce the activity with a discussion of clothing. Refer especially to the terms and facts listed above.

b. Tell children that you will teach them a "clothing game." They will each have to listen and look carefully at themselves and their friends, to understand the clues. Assure them that each child will get a turn, but that they may have to wait and watch awhile first. Encourage them to watch without talking and let each child solve the mystery on his or her own.

c. Beginning at one side of the group, choose a child by name. Tell the child that you've noticed that he or she is wearing overalls (jeans, tennis shoes, or a belt). Tell the child to find another person who is also wearing overalls and to stand beside that person.

d. Continue calling on one child at a time to find someone else with a similar piece of clothing.

e. The game ends when each child has had an opportunity to find a "match."

Hint for Success:

• Pay attention to groupings as they form. You may want to use color-only clues or clothes-fastener clues to increase difficulty or to be sure of including all children. "Find another child with buttons on his or her shirt." "Find a person with a zipper that is *not* on his or her pants." "Find another *girl* who is wearing stripes." Comment on the similarities that children are discovering.

How to Simplify this Activity:

• At first, use obvious clues such as color or pattern. Focus the children's attention on a body part, then on the article of clothing that covers it: "Look at your feet. Find someone else that has socks just like yours."

How to Extend this Activity:

• Introduce less obvious attributes, like matching the number of buttons on a garment, or matching the number of individual pieces that comprise an outfit. Shades of particular colors can also be matched, as well as specific patterns (stripes, flowers, etc.).

TEACHER RESOURCES
Field Trip Ideas
1. Take the children to visit a tailoring or dressmaking establishment.
2. Visit a laundromat.
3. Take a trip to a clothing store (general clothes or specialty shop).
4. Visit a farm to see cotton, wool, or flax.

Classroom Visitors
1. Invite someone to the classroom who will actually sew a garment together using a sewing machine.
2. Ask a spinner or weaver to demonstrate these processes on their machines.
3. Find a knitter (a parent) who could make a pair of mittens or scarf over a few days' time in your classroom so children could watch.

Children's Books
Anderson, L. C. *The Wonderful Shrinking Shirt.* Niles, Il.: Whitman, 1983.

Baylor, B. *They Put on Masks.* New York: Scribner's, 1975.

Beskow, E. *Pelle's New Suit.* New York: Harper and Bros., 1929.

Blood, C. L., and M. A. Link. *The Goat in the Rug.* New York: Four Winds Press, 1976.

Blos, J. W. *Martin's Hats.* New York: William Morrow, 1984.

Charlip, R., and B. Supree. *Harlequin and the Gift of Many Colors.* New York: Parents, 1973.

dePaola, T. *Charlie Needs a Cloak.* Englewood Cliffs, NJ: Prentice-Hall, Treehouse, 1982.

Freeman, D. *A Pocket for Corduroy.* New York: Scholastic, 1978.

Hall, A. *The Runaway Hat.* Singer, 1969.

Hoberman, M. A. *I Like Old Clothes.* New York: Knopf, 1976.

Keats, E. J. *Goggles.* New York: Macmillan, 1969.

Klimowitz, B. *When Shoes Eat Socks.* Nashville: Abingdon, 1971.

Kuskin, K. *The Dallas Titans Get Ready for Bed.* New York: Harper and Row, 1982.

———. *The Philharmonic Gets Dressed.* New York: Harper and Row, 1982.

Littledale, F. *The Elves and the Shoemaker.* New York: Macmillan, 1975.

Matsuno, M. *A Pair of Red Clogs.* London: World, 1960.

Mitgutsch, A. *From Cotton to Pants.* Minneapolis: Carolrhoda, 1977.

———. *From Sheep to Shawl.* Minneapolis: Carolrhoda, 1977.

Potter, B. *The Tailor of Gloucester.* New York: Frederick Warne, 1973.

———. *The Tale of Mrs. Tiggy-Winkle,* New York: Frederick Warne, 1973.

Ricklen, N. *Baby's Clothes.* New York: Simon and Schuster, 1986.

Robinson, D. *Anthony's Hat.* New York: Scholastic, 1976.

Seuss, Dr. *The Five Hundred Hats of Bartholemew Cubbins.* New York: Random House, 1938.

Slobodkina, E. *Caps for Sale.* Reading, MA: Addison-Wesley, 1940.

Stinson, K. *Red is Best.* Toronto: Annick, 1982.

Watanabe, S. *How Do I Put It On?* New York: Philomel, 1977.

Wells, R. *Timothy Goes to School.* New York: Dial, 1981.

Willis, J., and S. Varley. *The Long Blue Blazer.* London: Anderson Press, 1987.

Winthrop, E. *Shoes.* New York: Harper and Row, 1986.

Adult References

Davenport, M. *The Book of Costume.* New York: Crown, 1948.

Dines, G. *Sun, Sand and Steel: Costumes and Equipment of the Spanish/Mexican Southwest.* New York: Putnam, 1972.

Gorslinge, D. *What People Wore.* New York: Viking, 1952.

Hofsinde, R. (Gray Wolf). *Indian Costumes.* New York: William Morrow, 1968.

Lurie, A. *The Language of Clothes.* New York: Random House, 1981.

Russell, D. A. *Costume History and Style.* Englewood Cliffs, N.J.: Prentice-Hall, 1983.

Worrell, E. A. *Children's Costume in America 1607-1918.* New York: Scribner's, 1980.

Chapter 7

Dental Health

•

Many milestones in children's lives indicate to themselves and to others that they are changing: the child's first steps, the child's first words, the first tooth to come in, the first tooth to fall out.

•

Teeth play a major role in many aspects of people's lives and serve three major functions. First, they provide a necessary aid in the digestive process as food is taken in, chewed, and swallowed. Second, teeth assist in the pronunciation of words. As we talk, our tongues move around to different parts of the mouth affecting the sounds we make. And third, teeth provide part of the necessary framework for the inside of the mouth as well as for the mouth's outside structure, thereby enhancing personal appearance.

Children are proud of their teeth and take great pride in caring for them. Toothbrushing is one of the first personal hygiene activities in which parents involve their children, and children can feel reasonably successful at it with minimal training.

Yet it is a skill which, if practiced often in conjunction with regular care from a dentist, will contribute to the development of a healthy life-style. For example, we know that the overall quality of children's secondary teeth is related to the maintenance of their "baby" teeth. Moreover, the degree to which young children develop appropriate self-care routines tends to stabilize in early childhood and greatly influences their adult practices.

PURPOSE

Many teachers are required to, or have a great interest in, teaching children about dental health. This unit was developed in direct response to their requests for meaningful ways to expand children's understanding of the importance of their teeth and their own role in tooth care. In addition, its aim is to help children explore "visiting the dentist" within the familiar boundaries of their own classroom.

Consequently, the unit outlined in the following pages provides a comprehensive selection of activities designed to build children's awareness and understanding of healthy dental practices in an enjoyable, informative manner.

None of the activities entails adults or children actually putting instruments or fingers in each other's mouths. Children are cautioned to simply "pretend" such actions as a way to maintain safety and appropriate sanitation. Finally, although dental floss is introduced as a potential dental tool, it is used only in an exploratory fashion outside the mouth, since the age at which children can use it safely varies depending on their abilities.

IMPLEMENTATION

The Dental Health theme can be introduced to children in any one of several ways.

Option One: Present this unit early in the year as an outgrowth of familiarizing children with classroom routines, including toothbrushing after meals.

Option Two: Make note of National Dental Health Month (declared each February) by presenting this theme at that time.

Option Three:
Weeks One and Two: Focus on body awareness (parts and functions). Incorporate teeth into this segment.
Weeks Three and Four: Emphasize caring for the body, including oral hygiene practices.

Option Four:
Week One: Concentrate on teeth and personal hygiene.
Week Two: Add information about going to the dentist.
The study of dental health could logically precede or follow a unit on healthy foods, one on fitness, one on hand tools, or it could be prompted by children losing or gaining new teeth.

TERMS, FACTS, AND PRINCIPLES
The Mouth
1. People's mouths are an important part of their bodies.
2. People use their mouths to take in food, speak and sing, whistle, sometimes to breathe, and to display their emotions.
3. All people have mouths.
4. The mouth has several parts: bones, teeth, gums, and tongue.
*5. The two bones that make up the framework of the mouth are called the jawbones.
*6. The maxilla is the upper jawbone and it does not move.

*7. The mandible, or lower jawbone, is hinged, making it movable. It enables people to open their mouths.

8. The tongue is used to speak, taste foods, help identify textures of objects, or move food around in the mouth.

9. The gums are made up of soft pink tissue covering the jawbone and surrounding the base of the teeth.

Teeth

10. Teeth are the hard, white, bonelike protrusions through the gums.

11. Teeth serve three main functions: to help people chew food, to aid in speaking, and to enhance a person's appearance.

12. Sometimes a tooth can hurt due to injury or decay; this is called a toothache.

*13. Children usually have twenty primary, or baby, teeth by the time they are about four years old.

14. Teeth grow from tooth buds that are present at birth.

*15. Adults usually have thirty-two permanent teeth that replace and add to the primary teeth.

16. All primary teeth fall out and are replaced by teeth that are intended to be permanent.

*17. There are four basic types of teeth: incisors, cuspids, bicuspids, and molars. Each serves a different purpose in eating food. Incisors cut and bite, cuspids tear, and bicuspids and molars mash or grind.

18. Each tooth has two parts: the crown is above the surface of the gums; the root is below the surface of the gums.

19. The crown is the part of the tooth that is brushed; the root holds the tooth in place.

Dental Care

20. Dentists recommend that to brush, sweep the toothbrush along the tooth in a motion heading away from the gum line.

21. A dentist is trained to help people maintain, repair, or clean teeth.

22. A dentist uses many instruments and tools to examine, clean, and repair teeth, such as lights, mouth mirror, probe, chisels, excavators, X-ray machines, and so on.

23. Brushing teeth helps keep them clean.

24. Brushing teeth helps keep them white.

25. Small pieces of food stay in the mouth after a person eats.

26. Brushing teeth helps remove small pieces of food from the mouth and the teeth.

*27. A sticky film called plaque is always forming on the teeth.

*28. Plaque eats away the enamel, the hard, smooth outer layer of the teeth, causing cavities to form. A cavity is a hole in the tooth.

*29. Brushing helps prevent plaque from building up on the teeth and causing cavities to form.

*30. Sometimes food gets stuck between the teeth or at the base of the teeth near the gums.

*31. Flossing teeth helps remove food particles between teeth that can't be reached by the bristles of the toothbrush.

32. Brushing teeth after each meal, or at least in the morning and at night, helps keep teeth healthy and cavity-free.

Food and Teeth

33. Eating a raw vegetable or fruit, such as a carrot, celery, or apple, after a meal helps clean the teeth.

34. Foods that contain a lot of sugar contribute more to cavity formation than other types of food.

35. Cutting down on sugary foods may help cut down on the number of cavities a person gets.

36. A person can make some food choices that lead to improved dental health.

37. It can be dangerous to put small, nonfood objects in the mouth.

Professional Care

38. It is important to visit the dentist for dental checkups twice a year to be sure that the teeth are healthy and cavity-free.

39. When being examined by a dentist or dental hygienist, the patient sits in a reclining chair, holds open his or her mouth, and allows the examiner to look in the mouth

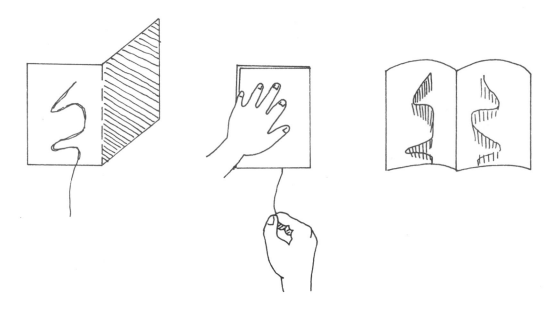

Figure 7.1 *Painting with Dental Floss*

and work on the teeth and gums using special instruments.

40. Only foods should be put into the mouth.

41. A dental hygienist or dental assistant is trained to clean and polish teeth or to assist the dentist when he or she is examining a patient.

42. Teeth feel clean and smooth after a cleaning.

43. If a toothbrush is not available, it is beneficial to eat a cleaning food such as a raw fruit or vegetable.

44. Swishing water in the mouth is another way of cleaning the mouth and rinsing away some of the germs, although it is not as effective as brushing.

45. A toothbrush is a small, thin brush with bristles on the side of one end. It is used for cleaning the teeth.

46. Dental floss is thin, strong thread that older children and grown-ups use to remove food particles from between their teeth.

47. Toothpaste is a cleaning paste people use to help them clean their teeth and make their mouth feel good.

48. Different people prefer different toothpastes.

ACTIVITY IDEAS

Aesthetics

1. ***Painting with Dental Floss.*** Set out *unwaxed* dental floss which has been cut into a variety of lengths. Show the children how to dip the floss into paint, then drag it across paper to make a mark. Encourage children to experiment with making a variety of motions with the floss. It will be necessary for them to dip the floss into the paint often. A variation is to show children how to lay the paint-covered floss in a design on one half of the paper and then fold the other half over it. Next, have them press down on the paper and then open it up to reveal the design printed on both sides. A different effect can be achieved if children lay the floss on the paper with a three-inch length extending beyond the fold. (Figure 7.1) Children can then hold the paper closed with one hand and pull the exposed floss with the other until the entire length has been removed. Inside, both the print from the original design as well as the effect made by the moving floss will be visible.

2. ***Painting with Toothbrushes.*** Provide toothbrushes for the children to use instead of paintbrushes when painting. The

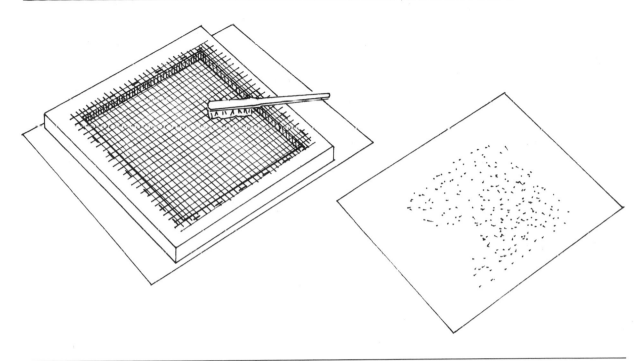

Figure 7.2 *Create a Spatter Design with Toothbrush and Paint*

location of the bristles on the side of the shaft rather than at the end will affect their method of holding the brush. Encourage children to experiment by making different motions to spread the paint. Also, use toothbrushes to splatter paint. Make a wire screen mounted in a frame that holds the screen approximately one inch above a piece of paper. (Figure 7.2)

Show children how to create a dappled effect by brushing paint across the screen and onto the paper below with a toothbrush.

3. *Smiling Faces.* Show children a variety of artists' portraits of people smiling. Draw their attention to people's facial features. Ask children which picture they like best and why.

Affective

1. *Preparing a Healthy Snack.* Involve the children in making a snack. Have them help you prepare raw vegetables, such as celery or carrots, and fruits, such as apples or pears. Point out that these are some of the foods that help clean teeth. Consider

making a dip, following one of the recipes provided below, to provide a contrast between the effects of food on teeth. Have the children dip their foods into either the fruit or vegetable dip. Point out that the dip sticks to the raw foods much as it does to their teeth. As the children eat, have them feel their own teeth often to find out if they are sticky or clean.

Fruit Dip
Ingredients:
1 pkg. frozen strawberries
⅔ cup mayonnaise
1 cup strawberry yogurt

Procedure:
Combine strawberries and mayonnaise, then fold in yogurt. Chill for 1 hour.

Vegetable Dip
Ingredients:
1 pt. plain yogurt
1 (1¼ oz.) pkg. ranch dressing

Procedure:
Season yogurt to taste with dressing mix.

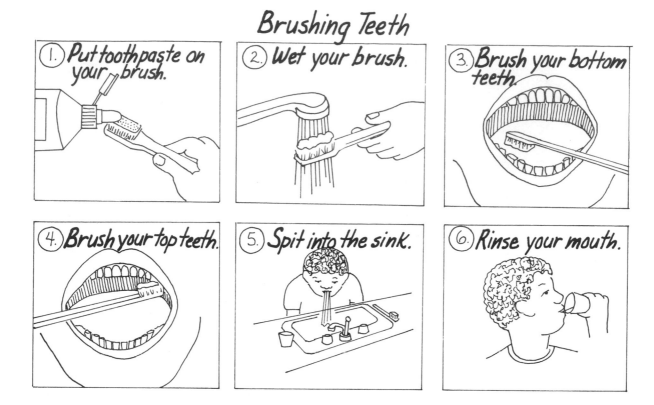

Figure 7.3 *A Picture Sequence of Brushing Teeth*

2. *My Favorite Toothpaste.* Select a variety of toothpaste brands for children to sample. Place a small drop of one kind of toothpaste on the end of a popsicle stick. Have the child taste the toothpaste. Follow the same procedure with each variety. Ask each child to choose a favorite. Write the name of each child's selection on a large piece of paper and include any comments about why he or she chose it. Post the paper on the wall. Later, encourage children to refer to the chart as a reminder of which paste they will use to brush their teeth at school.

3. *Brushing Teeth.* Most of the children, if not all, have probably been exposed to toothbrushing before. Therefore, your purpose is to teach correct methods, reasons, and personal care. Provide a toothbrush for each child in the class. Invite children to decorate their brushes with stickers or markers to make identification easier. Set aside a portion of the day following either a snack or meal for Toothbrushing. As a part of the children's routine, it will be easier to ensure that all of the children have an opportunity to participate. Toothbrush racks that allow for easy storage are available for classroom use and will hold as many as twenty toothbrushes.

Introduce the activity by singing with the children "This Is the Way We Brush Our Teeth" to the tune of "Here We Go Round the Mulberry Bush." While singing, model or demonstrate each of the brushing motions used to clean teeth—top, side, front, under the teeth.

As you sing the song and change the motions, assist the children in identifying and imitating the proper movements by calling out "front teeth, back teeth, sides" and so on before each change or new verse.

Vary this activity another day by brushing *your* teeth in front of the children. First, explain the steps you'll do, pointing

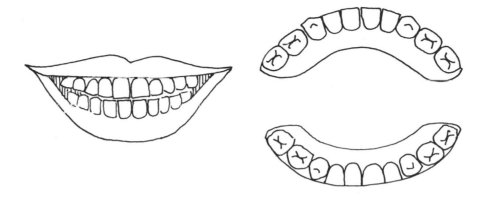

Figure 7.4 *What Children See When They Look at Their Teeth*

to a picture chart as you do so. Then, actually follow these steps in brushing your teeth. Finally, have the children try to follow the steps on the chart themselves. Consider having them go through the process using wet brushes only, then end by adding toothpaste. (Figure 7.3)

4. *See My Teeth!* Read one of the children's stories listed in the teacher resource section that describes a visit to a dentist. Highlight the part where the dentist counts and examines the child's teeth. Following the story, set up the activity by placing several tooth picture charts near a mirror for the children to see. (Figure 7.4) Point out that each person has the same types of teeth that are found in the same location in everyone's mouth. Ask the children to look at their teeth in the mirror and compare what they see with the tooth chart. As the children locate various teeth in their mouths, help them find the corresponding teeth on a chart designated as their own and mark them with a pencil or crayon. Write the children's names on their papers so they will have a record of how many teeth they have. Post these on the wall for future reference.

5. *A Sticky Mess.* Cornstarch Surprise is another name for this enjoyable mixture. As children play with the mixture, talk about how the residue left on their hands is much like plaque left on teeth.

   Slowly add water and food coloring to dry cornstarch until the mixture achieves a smooth, pastelike consistency. Do not add all of the cornstarch at first so that you can compensate if too much water is added. The mixture is unique in its response to pressure or the lack of it. When held in a flat hand, the cornstarch will become more fluid and will seep and drip from the fingers. When compressed, it will become hard and crack and crumble into pieces.

6. *Get the Red Out.* Disclosure tablets are small, red or purple tablets, which, when chewed, temporarily color clean teeth light red or purple and plaque-laden teeth a deeper red or purple. Their function is to help children become aware of how to brush their teeth more thoroughly. These tablets may be obtained from a dentist or over the counter at a drugstore. Notify parents in advance that you are going to use disclosure tablets so that they can let you know if their children are allergic to them. Provide hand-held mirrors for the children to use in examining their own teeth. Give each child a disclosure tablet and direct him or her to chew it. Do this near a sink so that children will be able to spit out the excess color. Give children their own toothbrushes and instruct them to brush their teeth. When they are finished, ask the children to examine their teeth in the mirror. If any dark red color is visible, encourage the child to brush again until the teeth are clean. Consider sending some tablets and instructions home so parents can reinforce thorough brushing.

As a variation on this activity, ask four children to chew a disclosing tablet. Then have one student eat a cracker, another a carrot, a third an apple, and a fourth some soft candy. Ask the other children to look at the four sets of teeth and compare the results.

7. *Hinges Song.* Sing the following song at group time. If you do not know the actual tune, substitute the tune "I Am a Fine Musician."

Hinges* by Arleen Fisher
I'm all made of hinges because everything bends,
From the top of my neck way down to my ends.
I'm hinges in front and I'm hinges in back.
But I have to be hinges or else I would crack!

This is a great way to help children become more familiar with their bodies and the function of joints. Focus on the jaw as an example of a body hinge. As children sing the words, ask them to place their fingertips on the spot on their face where their jaw is "hinged" to enable it to open and close. Point out the movement that occurs. Follow up by encouraging children to keep their fingertips in place as they "open their mouths wide," "pretend to bite," and "pretend to chew." Talk with them about how these movements feel.

8. *Make Toothpowder.* Make a picture chart illustrating the following recipe. Help children follow it to create their own tooth-cleaning powder. This recipe makes small amounts that can be placed in individual jars, such as baby food jars or other small containers, for use at school or for the child to take home.

Combine:

1 T. salt
2 T. baking powder
a little peppermint flavoring

To use, wet the toothbrush and put some of the powder on the bristles.

*From *Up the Windy Hill,* published by Abeland Press, New York, 1953. Copyright renewed 1981. Author controls all rights.

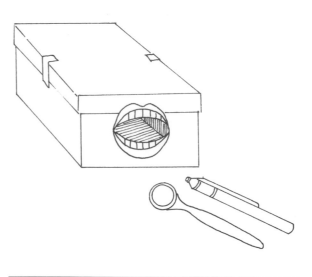

Figure 7.5 *What Can You See in the Looking Box Mouth?*

Cognition

1. *What Goes in Your Mouth?* Select a variety of objects including tools, foods, and other materials that could fit in a person's mouth but that may or may not be appropriate there. Include objects in a variety of sizes so that size is not the only criterion influencing children's decisions. Invite the children to identify what they should and should not put into their mouths and the reasons for those decisions. Use the "looking" box described below as a receptacle for all the items that go in the mouth and a plain shoebox for the others.

2. *A Looking Box.* Provide mouth mirrors (obtained from a health supply store or on temporary loan from a dentist or your local dental health association) and small penlights for the children to use to examine things that are hidden from view in a covered box. Cut a hole in one end of the box and surround it on the outside with pretend teeth and lips. (Figure 7.5) Put several objects in the box so that children cannot see them directly. Encourage them to use the tools offered to discover what's inside without lifting the lid. Make the activity more challenging by placing stickers on the inside walls of the box. Make a set of matching sticker cards. Invite children to find the sticker in the box that matches cards they choose from a pile.

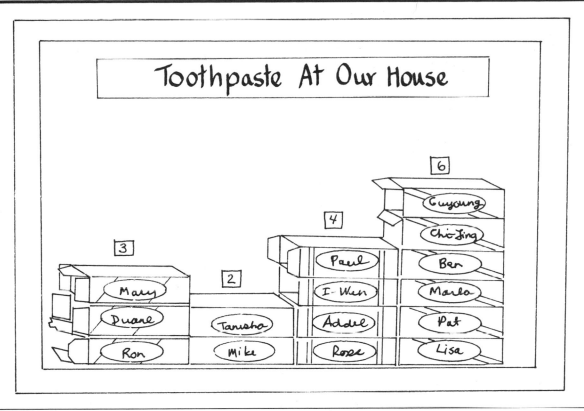

Figure 7.6 *A Toothpaste Graph*

3. **Count and Match Teeth.** Gather pictures of people's faces and make number cards that correspond to the number of teeth visible in each picture. Tell children to look at the picture, count the teeth, and then match the picture to a card with the numeral identifying the number of teeth. It may be helpful to provide a magnifying glass to allow children to clearly distinguish the individual teeth.

4. **Collage of Sticky vs. Cleaning Foods.** Gather magazine pictures of a wide variety of foods, together with paste, paper, and a selection of real foods such as fruits, vegetables, and candy. Explain that some foods act as teeth cleaners because they do not leave sticky remains on the teeth. Give each child a portion of a sticky food such as a cracker with peanut butter. Encourage the children to feel their teeth with their tongues to determine if the food is still there. Have the children open their mouths to show each other their teeth or have them look in a mirror at their own teeth. Next give each of the children a small portion of a cleansing fruit or vegetable such as a slice of an apple or a carrot. After they have chewed and swallowed it, have them repeat the procedure of feeling their teeth and looking at them. Next, set out the pictures and explain that some of them are of cleansing foods and others are of foods that will leave a sticky residue. Be sure to emphasize that brushing should follow eating any of the foods, but that it is especially important after eating sticky foods. Give each child a paper divided in half—one portion headed "cleaning," the other, "sticky." Help them find both kinds of foods and make a collage of them under the corresponding categories.

5. **Toothpaste Graph.** In a note sent home to families, ask each child to bring an empty toothpaste box to school. Be sure to allow plenty of time; parents will need at least a week to send these in. Put each child's name on his or her box when it comes in, so the child can identify it. Help children create a graph by gluing or taping their containers to a piece of cardboard. Group identical brands so that children can compare the number of each. (Figure 7.6)

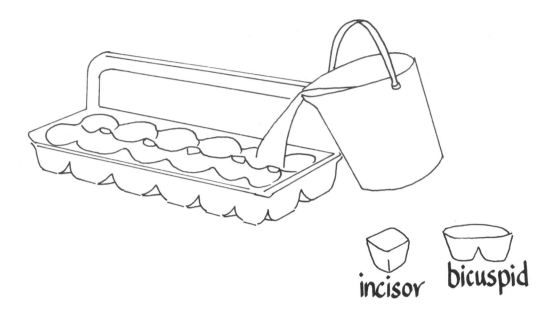

incisor   bicuspid

Figure 7.7 *Make Plaster Teeth in an Egg Carton*

6. ***Plaque's Back.*** Draw a mouth full of teeth on a round piece of paper cut out to fit the bottom of the inside of a round baking pan. Show the children how to dip a marble into paint and then roll it around the pictured teeth to color them with paint "plaque."

7. ***Deciduous Objects.*** Primary, or baby, teeth, also known as deciduous teeth, fall out beginning around the age of six. The word deciduous means to fall out or off and may be applied to a variety of objects, such as leaves, pinecones, hair, and so forth. Place a variety of these objects on a tray and encourage the children to examine each and identify *where* it was attached to the host object.

8. ***What Else Has Teeth?*** Teeth or tooth shapes can be found in many places. Provide an assortment of objects or pictures of objects that have teeth and some that do not. Examples of toothed objects are gears, rakes, saws, stalagmites and stalactites, and animals. Direct children to find all the objects that have teeth.

Construction

1. ***Plaster Teeth.*** Help children make their own set of plaster teeth and then work on them as a dentist would. Use one egg carton box to set up six pairs of "teeth." Make liquid plaster of paris using the recipe below and pour it into the egg carton sections, filling to the top. When the plaster hardens completely, turn the mold over and pop the "teeth" out, separating the pairs. Discuss ways dentists scrape and drill teeth to remove plaque and decay. Provide children with tools they can use to care for their plaster teeth, such as toothpicks and craft sticks (for drills) and modeling dough (for fillings). To make plaster of paris, pour powdered plaster into a container less than half full of water. Avoid mixing until enough powder has been added to make a hill under the water's surface and no more can be added. Then use a stick to mix well. Continue mixing until a slight film forms on top. Hint: Excessive mixing helps the plaster set fast (within minutes); too little mixing

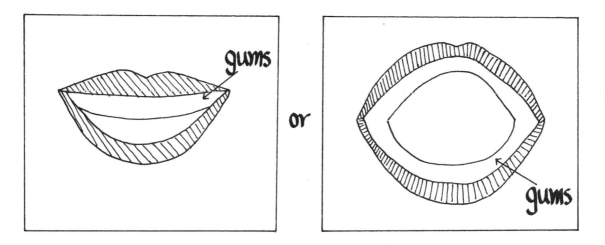

Figure 7.8 *Simple Outlines for Making a Mouth*

makes hardening take longer (hours). Do not mix more than can be used in fifteen or twenty minutes. Hint: Be aware that plaster can clog drains easily and should be kept away from sinks, even in liquid form. Use a flexible plastic container to mix it and allow residue to dry up. Squeeze the sides to crack and remove plaster that remains or throw the container away. (Figure 7.7)

2. *Make a Mouth.* Draw mouth shapes on construction paper similar to the example provided in Figure 7.8.

    Give each child a picture and a small amount of school glue that is tinted pink. Invite each child to cover the gum outline with the glue. Provide white popcorn seeds for children to place into the glue as teeth.

Language

1. *Mouth Sounds.* Make a tape recording of sounds made by the mouth being used for different purposes, such as chewing, coughing, biting, swishing, gargling, brushing teeth, drinking, whistling, talking, and singing. Show the children pictures of people involved in these actions. As you play the tape, encourage the children to listen to the sounds, locate the picture, and tell how they know it illustrates that sound.

2. *Which Brush and Why?* Bring in a variety of brushes for the children to examine, including hair, tooth, lint, fingernail, dog, and paint brushes. As each is introduced, explain its name and its purpose. Encourage the children to use the correct names when passing the brushes around or when using them in their play.

3. *Talk Without Teeth.* Show the children how your face looks when your lips are stretched over your teeth. Explain that this is similar to what it would be like if you did not have teeth. One of the functions teeth perform is to help with speech. Talk with your lips over your teeth to demonstrate. Encourage the children to imitate you as you sing together one of the children's favorite songs. Discuss with the children how not using teeth changed the song and what it sounded like.

4. *Going to the Dentist.* Discuss with the children what they see at a dentist's office and what happens there. Show them a picture of a dentist's office or equipment that they might see there. On a large piece of paper, list the things that the children say they see

when visiting their dentist, or list what they say they see in the picture. Some examples are: chair, machines, X-ray, books, receptionist. Read the book *At the Dentist: What Did Christopher See?* by Sandra Ziegler. Then begin a new list of the things that the children remember from the story. Compare the two lists with the children.

5. **The Lost Tooth.** Read the story *Airmail to the Moon* by Tom Birdseye. Discuss with the children all of the places that Amy looked for her tooth. Hand each child a white popcorn seed (tooth) and tell them to put it somewhere in their clothing, such as in a pocket. Read the story again and then direct the children to find their "tooth" again.

Physical

1. **Painting Plaque on Teeth.** Draw a tooth shape on paper used for painting. Provide paints labeled with the name of a food. For example, red paint may be labeled as tomato, brown as chocolate, pink as strawberry, and so on. Encourage the children to paint the tooth with the foods to represent food particles on the tooth.

2. **Magnet Food on Teeth.** Cover an 8-by-11-inch piece of sheet metal with white contact paper. On the contact paper draw a picture of teeth in a mouthlike shape. Next, cut a magnet strip into very small pieces to serve as food particles. Scatter these over the teeth. Provide a magnet wand or regular magnet to the children explaining that it will serve as a pretend toothbrush. Show them how to remove the food particles by maneuvering the magnet over the drawing. Encourage the children to clean the teeth completely.

3. **Bead Stringing on Dental Floss.** Substitute dental floss for the more typical string or shoelaces used in stringing wooden beads. Encourage the children to string a temporary necklace or bracelet.

4. **Humpty Dumpty Gets Cleaned.** Empty an egg of its contents without damaging the shell. This can be accomplished by poking a small hole in both ends of the egg and then blowing out the contents. Set the egg shell in a cup of a carbonated soda drink overnight. The sugar from the soda will color the egg. Provide one egg and a toothbrush for each child and encourage them to clean their egg by brushing away the dirt. Note that the enamel of the egg in many ways is similar to the enamel on teeth. This activity is suggested for older children.

5. **Cleaning Rocks.** Prior to this activity, instruct children in toothbrushing and mouth rinsing. Provide rocks that are about the size of a baseball or softball, toothpaste, and toothbrushes. Encourage the children to brush the rocks as they would their teeth. Point out the changes that occur to the rocks' surface. Be sure to have water available for rinsing.

6. **Feel It with Your Tongue.** At snack- or mealtime ask the children to notice the way each food feels as they eat it. Ask them to notice what it feels like when they first put into their mouths and how it changes as they chew. Focus on the tongue as a sensory organ and as a means of manipulating the contents of the mouth. This activity is not suggested for toddlers because it is difficult for them to control the food in their mouths if they are concentrating on the texture.

7. **Bite, Tear, and Mash.** Each tooth serves a different purpose. With a food such as Fruit Leather Roll Ups, the children can experience all three basic uses of teeth as well as see the impression of their teeth. After making the fruit leather, ask the children to bite down on it to see the marks made by their teeth. Next, encourage the children to first bite with the front teeth, or incisors, then, to tear with the canine teeth, and lastly, to mash the food with the bicuspids or molars prior to swallowing.

Fruit Leather Roll Ups
1. Puree fresh fruit or drained canned fruit in a blender. Add one tablespoon of lemon juice to each quart of fresh fruit.

2. Cover an inverted baking sheet with plastic wrap and tape down the edges to avoid shrinkage.

3. Pour puree about ¼-inch thick over the bottom of the baking sheet (on top of the plastic wrap), leaving about 1 inch free around the edges.

4. Dry in an oven at 140° with the oven door open at least 2 inches. Dry until puree is leathery, but still pliable and not sticky to the touch. It will take several hours.

5. Roll up fruit leather and store in an airtight container.

Pretend Play

1. *Dentist's Office.* Provide props commonly associated with a dentist's office, such as mirrors, lights, a chair, bibs, and cups for water. Additional props such as an X-ray of a mouth, plastic gloves, and popsicle sticks for tools will also help to enhance the play. Encourage the children to take on the roles of dentist, patient, assistant, and receptionist. Caution them to avoid actually putting fingers or instruments in each other's mouths. These are actions they should pretend instead. As an alternative, use dolls as patients or provide puppets with mouths that open.

2. *Restaurant/Home.* Set up a play area to look like a restaurant. Provide picture menus and other appropriate props. Invite the children to play the roles of waiter or waitress, cook, and customer. Emphasize the importance of choosing and selecting foods that clean the teeth as well as remembering to swish or brush the teeth after a meal. Extend this activity by adding a house with a bathroom area. Encourage children to pretend to brush their teeth after coming back from the restaurant or throughout a day at home.

Social

1. *Brush Plus.* In small groups, ask the children to sample the taste of each of four varieties of toothpaste you have provided. Ask each child to indicate which one he or she liked best. Review the individual choices with the children and then work with them to agree as a group on selecting one toothpaste to be used by that group for the day. Consider using the rating plan offered in Chapter 22 as a guide for your teaching. Explain to the children that tomorrow they will have a chance to continue or change their preference.

2. *"Get the Red Out" Circle Game.* Introduce disclosure tablets as a regular part of the toothbrushing routine. (See the Affective section of this unit for more information about these.) After the children have had an opportunity to use the tablets for a couple of days and have seen how their teeth look before and after, gather them together for this circle game. Begin by looking at all of the children's clothes and helping them to identify the colors in what they are wearing. Tell the children that the group is going to listen to a record and that when the music stops the teacher or an assigned child will call out a color saying, "Get the *red* out," or "Get the *blue* out." All of the children in the group who are wearing that color will then put that portion of their bodies on the outside of the circle area.

TEACHER RESOURCES

Field Trip Ideas

1. Visit a dentist's office to view some of the equipment and instruments used. Ask a dentist or dental hygienist to explain why people come to the dentist and to describe what the dentist and dental hygienist do.

2. Visit a zoo where one of the animal keepers could explain how animals keep their own teeth healthy and what zoo personnel do to help.

Classroom Visitors

1. Invite a dental worker to visit the class to discuss and show materials related to dental health.

Children's Books

Bate, L. *Little Rabbit's Loose Tooth.* New York: Crown, 1975.

Birdseye, T. *Airmail to the Moon.* New York: Holiday House, 1988.

Brenner, B. *Faces*. New York: Dutton, 1970.

Cooney, N. E. *The Wobbly Tooth*. New York: Putnam, 1978.

DeGroat, D. *Alligator's Toothache*. New York: Crown, 1977.

Doss, H. *All the Better to Bite With*. New York: Messner, 1976.

Duvoisin, R. A. *Crocus*. New York: Random House, 1977.

Kessler, E., and L. Kessler. *Our Tooth Story: A Tale of Twenty Teeth*. New York: Dodd, Mead and Company, 1972.

LeSieg, T. *The Tooth Book*. New York: Random House, Beginner Books, 1981.

Nourse, A. E. *The Tooth Book*. New York: McKay, 1962.

Pomerantz, C. *The Mango Tooth*. New York: Greenwillow, 1977.

Showers, P. *How Many Teeth?* New York: H. W. Wilson Co., 1962.

Ziegler, S. *At the Dentist: What Did Christopher See?* Chicago: The Child's World, 1976.

Adult References

Barr, G. *Young Scientist and the Dentist*. New York: McGraw-Hill, 1970.

Lauber, P. *What Big Teeth You Have*. New York: Crowell, 1986.

Mason, G. F. *Animal Teeth*. New York: William Morrow, 1965.

Schloat, G. W. *Your Wonderful Teeth*. New York: Scribner's, 1954.

Wilkin, R. *Dental Health*. New York: Franklin Watts, 1976.

Chapter 8

Vehicles

.

Big, shiny, powerful, and noisy; varied in color, size, shape, type, and function, vehicles are a constant presence in children's daily lives. Children see, hear, and smell vehicles every day. They experience them at home, on the streets, in the fields, in parking lots, at construction sites, and along the tracks. Children ride in vehicles, eat, talk, and even sleep in them. It is no wonder that vehicles are especially important to young children, both in real life and in their play.

PURPOSE

The Vehicles unit is a response to children's natural curiosity about the topic. It includes information and activities regarding types of vehicles; how they move and sound; how they are designed, made, maintained, sold, and disposed of; and safety procedures. Our intent is to expand children's notions of the activities and occupations related to vehicles as well as their understanding of what vehicles are and how they work. Consequently, we have chosen to concentrate only on vehicles rather than including all forms of transportation such as boats and planes. The study of these vessels could follow this unit.

IMPLEMENTATION

Option One: Spend a week or two focusing on vehicle exploration. Provide toy vehicles for children to sort, match, seriate, count, and play with. Offer vehicle-shaped paper for children to paint on, give them miniature vehicles to dip in paint to make tracks, encourage children to make roads in the block area, and give children plenty of opportunities to ride child-sized vehicles such as trikes and wagons. Follow this general introduction with a more focused exploration of the TFPs and activities offered in this chapter.

Option Two:
Week One: General introduction to vehicles.
Week Two: Focus on vehicles that move on roads: cars, buses, and trucks.
Week Three: Focus on vehicles that move on rails: trains, trolleys, and monorails.

Option Three:
Week One: Focus on passenger vehicles.
Week Two: Focus on cargo vehicles.

Option Four:
Week One: Carry out a study of "machines."
Week Two: Study vehicles as particular types of machines.

Option Five:
Week One: Introduce a number of different types of vehicles.
Week Two: Study how vehicles work.
Week Three: Concentrate on people who use vehicles and people who monitor their use.
Week Four: Focus on the people who make and repair vehicles.

In addition to the options described above, a general introduction to vehicles could be followed by a more in-depth study of a particular type of vehicle such as trains. The latter choice could be determined based on the interests of the children in your group and in light of vehicles prevalent in your community.

Finally, all of these options would be greatly enhanced by giving children a firsthand opportunity to examine and study a real vehicle and by using this as the basis for developing related activities.

TERMS, FACTS, AND PRINCIPLES

General Information

1. A vehicle is a device having wheels or runners that is used to transport people or objects from one place to another.

2. Vehicles travel on land; vessels such as planes and boats operate mainly in the air or on the water.

3. A vehicle requires a person to operate it.

4. Examples of vehicles are wagons, scooters, tricycles, bicycles, motorcycles, automobiles, trucks, buses, tractors, road workers, trolleys, trains, sleighs, snowmobiles, and sleds.

5. Vehicles come in a variety of sizes, shapes, and colors.

6. Vehicles have specialized parts that enable them to be used for certain jobs.

7. There are special names for people who operate vehicles: drivers operate cars, buses, sleds, and trucks; engineers operate trains and trolleys.

*8. The distances vehicles travel are described in units of measure called miles or kilometers.

9. Some vehicles, such as bicycles, tricycles, and wagons, are powered by people's energy.

10. Some vehicles, such as automobiles, trucks, buses, and trains, are powered by engines.

11. Vehicles travel at different rates of speed.

12. Some vehicles, such as tricycles and scooters, are operated primarily for fun.

13. Some vehicles, such as fire trucks and tractors, are designed to perform work.

14. Some vehicles, such as automobiles and jeeps, are used for both fun and work.

15. Some vehicles, such as buses and passenger trains, are used primarily to carry people.

16. Some vehicles, such as trucks and freight trains, are used primarily for carrying objects.

17. Some vehicles produce distinctive noises; trains whistle, buses honk, emergency vehicle sirens wail, and automobile engines clatter.

Vehicle Maintenance

18. It is important that owners of vehicles keep them in good repair so the vehicles are safe to operate.

19. At times vehicles break down because some part no longer works.

20. Sometimes vehicles are damaged in accidents.

21. Some vehicles can be repaired; some are beyond repair.

22. People who fix or help take care of other people's vehicles for a living are called mechanics.

23. Some owners fix or take care of their own vehicles.

24. Special stores or sections of stores sell the parts and materials people use to repair and care for vehicles.

25. Special places in the community are designed to help owners care for their cars: car washes, gas stations, car repair shops, auto parts stores, and specialty stores such as oil change or muffler shops.

*26. When owners decide they don't want their cars anymore they may sell them to other people or trade them in when buying a new car.

*27. People may buy new or used cars.

*28. Cars that are so old or broken that they are unsafe are scrapped or junked.

*29. Places that scrap or junk cars are called scrap yards or junkyards.

*30. Junkyards are places where old cars are kept so that people who need a part might find one.

*31. Scrap yards are places where cars are crushed so that the metal can be used to make new cars.

*32. Some places serve as both junkyards and scrap yards at the same time.

Vehicle Safety and Laws

33. People who ride in vehicles are called passengers.

34. People who walk from one place to another near a road are called pedestrians.

*35. Traffic rules (laws) have been developed for pedestrians, vehicle operators, and passengers to follow in order to protect the safety of all.

36. Traffic safety rules for pedestrians include:
a. Walk on the sidewalk.
b. If there is no sidewalk, pedestrians should walk on the left side of the road facing the oncoming cars, so that drivers are able to see the pedestrian and the pedestrian is able to see the cars.
c. When crossing a road, pedestrians should cross at an intersection following the walk/don't walk signals when they are available.

d. Pedestrians should look both ways up and down a road to see if any vehicles are coming before crossing the road. If a vehicle is coming, they should wait until it has passed to cross the road.

37. People learn how to operate most vehicles by:
    a. Watching others do it.
    b. Reading about how to do it.
    c. Having someone teach them how to do it.
    d. Practicing, with supervision.

38. People prove that they know how to operate a vehicle by passing a test and by continuing to operate it correctly and safely.

39. People in the community have made up rules to ensure that vehicles are operated safely.

*40. Some rules are so important that people make them into laws.

*41. Laws are rules that communities hire special people to enforce. Some of the community helpers who are directly responsible for enforcing vehicle laws are police officers and inspectors.

*42. Certain people inspect trains, cars, and trucks for safety and enforce laws about how those vehicles are used.

*43. When people break the law, inspectors or law enforcement officers penalize them in some way.

*44. Most people obey traffic laws even when no one is around to watch them.

45. People who obey the laws keep themselves and others safe.

*46. A driver's manual explains what the traffic laws are.

*47. Traffic safety includes such rules for road vehicles as:
    a. Vehicle operators are responsible for following the speed limit.
    b. Cars are to be kept in safe operating order.
    c. Vehicle operators are responsible for knowing what the posted traffic signs are and how to follow the rules they stand for (yield, school zone, pedestrian crossing, railroad crossing, intersection indicators, etc.).
    d. The driver must be a certain age.

Making, Selling, and Buying Vehicles

*48. Vehicles are complex machines, made up of several of the six simple machines (wheel, screw, lever, pulley, wedge, and inclined plane).

49. People design vehicles to do different jobs.

*50. The same type of vehicle will have different designs at different points in time.

*51. Designing a vehicle begins when a person has an idea. Based on the idea:
    a. A picture is drawn.
    b. A model is built.
    c. The model is tested.
    d. The model is redesigned.
    e. The vehicle is produced for sale.

*52. Some vehicles are made by a few people.

*53. Some vehicles are made by many people working together.

*54. Sometimes vehicle parts are made in one place and assembled in another.

*55. People have invented tools and machines to help them build vehicles.

*56. People buy vehicles.

*57. People choose to buy vehicles for different reasons:
    a. Suitability for type of job to be done
    b. Perceived attractiveness
    c. Price
    d. Ease of repair
    e. Ease of operation
    f. Environmental issues

*58. People advertise vehicles so other people will know about them and want to buy them.

59. People all over the world use some form of vehicle transportation.

*60. People build and choose to buy vehicles to suit the places in which they will be used.

*61. Some vehicles are found in many parts of the world; some are unique to a particular locale.

*62. Terrain, weather conditions, available materials, and life-styles influence what vehicles people use.

ACTIVITY IDEAS

Aesthetics

1. ***Driving Through Textures.*** Put sand, salt, cornmeal, water, snow, or gravel in a large tub. Give children a variety of small vehicles to drive through, around, and over the material. As the children explore the movement of the vehicles through the texture and express their pleasure in doing so, comment on their curiosity and enjoyment. "Casey, you like driving the truck through the sand to make tracks."

2. ***Vehicle Songs.*** After children are familiar with the children's song "The Wheels on the Bus," try the following variations.

   - The wheels on the car/truck/motorcycle go round and round.

   - The windows on the cars go up and down.

   - The passengers in the car put on their seat belts.

   - Police officers in the town help the drivers.

   - The runners on the sleigh slide across the snow.

Twinkle, Twinkle, Crossing Light
(Tune: "Twinkle, Twinkle, Little Star")
Twinkle, twinkle crossing light
Shining on the corner bright.
When it's green, it's time to go,
When it's red, it's stop you know.
Twinkle, twinkle crossing light,
Shining on the corner bright.

Bike Ride
(Tune: "Row, Row, Row Your Boat")
Pedal, pedal, pedal your bike
carefully down the street.
Round and round and round it goes,
pedal with your feet.

Train is a' Comin'
(Author unknown; This traditional song has a tune of its own. If you don't know it, substitute "Skip to My Lou.")

Chorus:
Train is a' comin', Oh yes.
Train is a' comin', Oh yes.
Train is a' comin', train is a' comin',
Train is a' comin', Oh yes.

Verse:
Sara is the engineer, Oh yes.
Michael is the conductor, Oh yes.
Gwen is the passenger, Oh yes.
Train is a' comin', Oh yes.

Substitute different children's names for each verse as they act out the song.

Construction Vehicle Song
(Tune: "London Bridge";
Words by Patricia Duffy)
A front-end loader scoops up rocks,
scoops up rocks, scoops up rocks.
A front-end loader scoops up rocks and
dumps them into trucks.

A crane is used to lift and carry, lift
and carry, lift and carry.
A crane is used to lift and carry
materials used for building.

Off-road trucks are very big, very big,
very big.
Off-road trucks are very big and can haul
huge loads.

3. ***License Plate Rubbings.*** Collect old license plates, either from parents or gathered from a junkyard. Have the children place the license plate with the numerals and letters facing up. Discuss the significance of the plates, that every vehicle must have one before a driver can use the vehicle on the road, and that each vehicle has a different set of numerals and letters to identify it. First, show children how to place a piece of paper on top of the license plate. Then, demonstrate how to hold an unwrapped crayon, moving it sideways

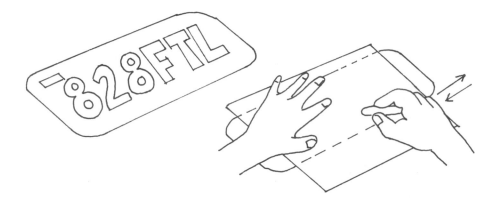

Figure 8.1 *License Plate Rubbings*

back and forth over the paper and license plate to make a "rubbing." (Figure 8.1)

Affective

1. *Knowing When the Job is Done.* Provide soap, water, sponges, and rags for children to use to wash tricycles and wagons on the playground. Before the children begin washing, gather them together and explain the task. End this brief discussion by asking them what criteria they will use to judge the job "complete." Write down their ideas on a large piece of easel paper. Read the list back to them, then post it near their "work" area. Help the children get started. Later, as children indicate that the trikes are washed, help them use their chart to figure out if the job is complete. If it isn't, encourage children to "fill in" the missing actions. If they have met their criteria for completeness, point this out to them and praise them for seeing the job through to its completion.

2. *Familiar Family Vehicles.* Provide children with magazines, scissors, and markers or crayons as well as booklets made from 8½-by-11-inch pieces of construction paper cut in half and stapled together. Ask the children to think about the vehicles their family has at home and then describe them. Children may dictate their ideas or write them out in their own version of writing. Afterward, they could illustrate their work using pictures from magazines.

3. *Choosing a Vehicle for Myself.* Prepare a booklet in which children describe the characteristics of their favorite vehicle. On the cover leave a space for the child's name and write "_____'s Favorite Vehicle." At the top of each following page write:

(p. 1) My favorite vehicle is . . .
(p. 2) It is my favorite because . . .
(p. 3) I would use my vehicle to . . .
(p. 4) The sound my vehicle would make is . . .

Either have the children dictate the ending to each sentence or fill in the spaces by themselves. After the sentences have been written, ask children to draw a picture to illustrate the text. Once the books are finished, read each child's book to the group. Highlight the similarities and differences between them.

*4. *Make a Driver's License.*
General Purpose: For children to identify the characteristics and qualities that make each of them unique.

TFPs: 38.

Materials: Five-by-seven-inch piece of tagboard for each child, clear contact paper, two-foot lengths of yarn. Optional: wallet-sized photograph of each child, one pencil for each child.

Procedure:
a. Prepare forms on the tagboard for the children to fill out to describe themselves using information that would be included on a driver's license, such as:
My name is _____ .
My address is _____ .

Figure 8.2 *Make Your Own Driver's License*

My birthday is _____ .
I am a girl/boy (circle one).
My hair color is _____ .
My weight is _____ .
My height is _____ .
If the photo is to be included, make a space for it in the lower left-hand corner of the license.

b. Introduce the activity to the children by telling them that all people who operate motorized vehicles are required to have a driver's license. Show children an actual driver's license. Point out the information on the license and explain that it describes the person. Give the children the prepared form and let them know they are going to make a driver's license for tricycle operators.

c. Hand each child a pencil and read them the lines on the form. Have them verbally answer the information and write it down. (Pretend writing is fully acceptable.)

d. When the children are done, if desired, glue on the photograph and cover each license with clear contact paper.

e. Attach yarn to their licenses so the children can wear them. (Figure 8.2)

Hints for Success:
• Have a scale and tape measure available so you can weigh and measure the children.

• Provide a full-length mirror for children to view themselves as they describe their physical traits.

How to Simplify this Activity:
• Ask children to write their name on the form. Take the children's dictation for the rest of the information.

How to Extend this Activity:
• To teach children more about the process of getting a driver's license, prepare a simple driving test for them to "earn" their license. For example, have them ride a trike around a line of cones, stop at a stop sign, and park in a parking space. Once the child takes the test, give him or her a license.

Cognition

1. *What Vehicle Would I Use?* Describe a situation to the children requiring the use of a vehicle. Ask them what vehicle they might pick for the job and why. Change the scenario each time so that a different vehicle might become necessary. Provide pictures or models for children to consider and choose from.

Problem	Potential Vehicle to Use
Large load to carry	Van, pickup truck, train's boxcar, moving van, station wagon, tractor-trailer
Circus to be moved	Train, convoy of trucks
Race	Bicycles, fast car, boxcar
Getting to school or work	Bicycle, bus, car, subway, taxi, motorcycle
Traveling in the city	Rickshaw, taxi, double-decker bus, trolley car
Traveling in the country	Horse-pulled wagon, tractor, truck, three-wheeler, ox cart
Traveling on rocky terrain	Jeep, logging truck, off-road truck
Fire to put out	Fire truck
Large group of people to carry	Passenger train, bus, trolley
Traveling on snowy roads	Snowplow, snowmobile
Pile of dirt to move	Bulldozer, backhoe, front-end loader

Summarize what the children have learned: there are many types of vehicles that people use to get jobs done. Some vehicles can be used for several different purposes; others have one main function. Include children in the summary by having them find vehicles that fit within the multipurpose and single-purpose categories. Ask them to explain why they placed each one where they did.

2. ***Out Our Window.*** Conduct this activity near a window that has a clear view of the street. Following a discussion of different types of road vehicles, ask children to watch out the window and identify the kinds of vehicles they see go by. Identification could be by type (truck, car, bus, etc.), by color, or by the number of wheels. A chart could be made of the results. Next, ask children to predict what vehicles might go by in the next few minutes. Record their ideas in words or make a picture chart showing their predictions. Using a timer to signal one to three minutes, ask children to watch the traffic and to contrast their predictions with the actual vehicles they see.

3. ***Junkyard Problem Solving.*** Gather a collection of broken toy vehicles. (Ask children to bring some from home.) Have children choose which parts are usable, which vehicles are reparable, and which vehicles should be scrapped. Encourage children to decide how vehicles and pieces could be combined in order to make a complete vehicle.

4. ***Vehicle-to-Terrain Match.*** Show the children pictures of various weather and ground conditions. Have available models of vehicles: train, pickup truck, motorcycle, all-terrain vehicle, car, convertible, snowplow. Ask children which vehicles would be best to use in each circumstance, and ask them to explain the reasoning behind their ideas.

5. ***Vehicles that Do a Job.*** In the block area or on the playground have available several types of toy vehicles, such as a fire truck, tank truck, tractor, bulldozer, train, moving van, all-terrain vehicle, bus, car, ambulance, and tow truck. Set up scenarios that require vehicles to do a particular job such as:

   • move a large load of rocks, sand, blocks, or furniture

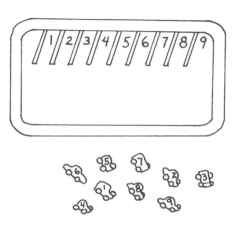

Figure 8.3 *"Park Your Car" Game*

   • clear snow
   • put out a fire
   • pull a wagon
   • move a broken-down car
   • deliver new cars
   • rescue people from a car crash

Ask the children to decide which vehicle could do the job and encourage them to carry out the task with the model vehicles.

6. ***How Do We Get There?*** Introduce the use of road maps to the children by first drawing a simple map of your classroom, school, or playground. Draw outlines corresponding to furniture and equipment and label each item. Plot a course for the children to follow using a toy vehicle, and encourage them to get to a specified location using the map.

7. ***May I Park Your Car?*** Make parking lots on cafeteria-type trays using thin strips of masking tape to designate parking spaces. Number each space. Put corresponding numbers on the tops of small toy cars. Have children park the cars in the spaces by matching numbers. (Figure 8.3)

8. ***In the Driver's Seat.*** This circle game can be played in three ways.

Option One (emphasis on rhythmic language): Begin a rhythmic chant. "Sitting in the driver's seat what do I see? I see a (adjective noun) looking at me." Insert a color name and an object name (such as brown car, yellow truck, red sign, green light) to complete the sentence. Continue in this fashion around the circle, with each child thinking up a different color/object combination. Repeat the chant another day using size/object or texture/object combinations.

Option Two (emphasis on visual memory): Gather an array of objects or pictures depicting things one might see along the highway. Collect as many as there are children in the group. Conceal them in a bag or "feely" box. Start the game by saying, "Sitting in the driver's seat I saw _____." Select one of the objects/pictures, hold it up for all to see, then say its name. Cover the item with a towel and move on to the next person in the circle. Repeat the chant and ask that person to select an item, name it, and try to remember the covered items as well. Continue this process until all of the items are revealed.

Option Three (emphasis on auditory memory): Carry out the circle game as described above without using objects or pictures. Instead have children focus on remembering what they heard and repeating the cumulative list of items.

9. ***Vehicles Around the World.*** This activity will give the children the opportunity to increase their understanding of what features characterize a vehicle while learning about transportation in different parts of the world. Present the children with models and pictures of modes of transportation that are different from the ones with which they are familiar. Guided by the first two TFPs, which explain what characterizes a vehicle, have the children decide whether or not each example is a vehicle. You might show an ox cart, rickshaw, sedan chair, elephant with a person riding, double-decker bus, three-wheeled cars, horse with rider, or cars and trucks of various countries.

*10. ***The Bus Trip.***
   General Purpose: To increase children's memory skills.
   TFPs: 1–14.
   Materials: Camera and film, city/town bus service.
   Procedure:
   a. Prepare for this activity by taking a ride on a local bus route yourself. Later,

retrace the route and take pictures of obvious landmarks.
   b. Once the pictures have been processed, show them to the children. Explain that all of you will be taking a ride on a bus together and that during the ride you will see these landmarks.
   c. Go on the bus ride as a group. Encourage the children to look for some of the landmarks featured in the photographs.
   d. Once back at school, show the children the pictures again. Ask them to arrange the pictures into the order they were seen on the trip.
   e. Post the pictures in the classroom.

How to Simplify this Activity:
- Take a field trip by bus to a location familiar to the children. While on the trip, take three to five Polaroid pictures of favorite landmarks the group points out. As above, have the children order the pictures once the group is back at school.

How to Extend this Activity:
- Post a large map of your town. With the children, highlight the bus route you took. Use colored dots on the pictures to match colored plastic thumbtacks. Work with the children to place the thumbtacks on the map to identify the locations of pictured landmarks.

Construction

1. ***Construct a Vehicle.*** Gather scrap materials that could be used by the children to create a vehicle—container tops for wheels, meat trays for truck and train beds, wooden blocks for vehicle bodies, wooden cylindrical shapes, hammers and nails or a mixture of equal parts of wood glue and white paste. Introduce the activity by letting the children know that materials are available for them to use to build any kind of vehicle they choose. Have them consider ways the materials could be put together to form their vehicle. Encourage children to carry out their ideas and to think of names for their creations.

2. ***Build a Traffic Pattern.*** Have children pretend that an area of the room (or outdoor sidewalk or sandbox) is a small town. Ask

Figure 8.4 *A Milk Jug Helmet*

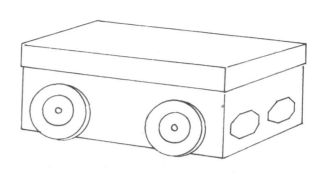

Figure 8.5 *Use a Shoe Box as the Basis for Designing Simple Cars*

them to think first about what features they want in the town, such as buildings, parks, stores, homes, factories, and so on. Next, have them decide where the people need to go and how roads can be built without disrupting existing trees and buildings. Show children the materials available to make roads and have them begin the process of "building" a road with blocks, tape on the floor, chalk on the sidewalk, or by digging with shovels in the sand. Provide children with model vehicles to use in the town.

3. *Vehicle Design Using Felt Shapes.* Provide the children with a flannel board and cutout felt shapes of varying sizes: circles, triangles, rectangles, diamonds, and so on. Invite the children to put the shapes together to create a vehicle.

4. *Make a Helmet.* Cut enough gallon-sized milk jugs into helmet shapes for everyone in the class. Give children markers, glue, stickers, bits of paper, and so on to decorate their helmets.

   Discuss with them why people who ride certain vehicles such as motorcycles and bicycles wear helmets. Take the helmets outside for children to use when operating playground vehicles. (Figure 8.4)

5. *Loading Ramp.* Provide several sizes of triangular blocks for the children to use as loading ramps. Also make available a variety of toy vehicles with additional small objects to be used as cargo. Point out that the ramp (or inclined plane) makes the job of getting cattle, large boxes, new cars, or scrap metal onto trailer trucks or trains much easier. Encourage the children to choose how to construct the most appropriate loading ramp for the vehicle being loaded and the cargo to be put on the vehicle.

6. *Designing a Car.* Before manufacturers produce a car, a design is drawn to represent the final product and a model is created from that design. If changes in the plan are needed, they are made in this early stage. To acquaint children with this phase of car manufacturing, draw a simple car design to make from a box. (Figure 8.5) Show this design to the children. Present each child with a cardboard box approximately eight inches long, four inches wide, three inches tall (poke out two holes in both sides for axles one-half inch from bottom), two thin dowels three-eighth inch in diameter and about 5½ inches long (axles), four wooden wheels 1½ inches in diameter with three-eighth-inch holes drilled in the centers. Invite them to create a model car with the materials based on the pictured design. Once they have accomplished this task, ask the children if they would like to make any changes in the design. Have everyone consider ways to implement these changes in their models. This activity is an excellent introduction to Assembly Line.

*7. *Assembly Line.*

   General Purpose: For children to explore the concepts of specialization and interdependence.

Assembly Line

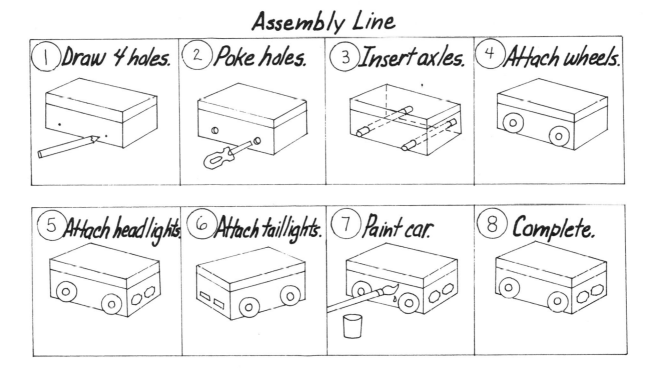

Figure 8.6 *Assembly Line Steps for Car Production*

TFPs: 47–54.

Materials: Paper and pencils, several small rectangular boxes, all the same size (approximately eight inches long, four inches wide, three inches tall), thin dowels (three-eighth inch) cut to extend beyond the width of the rectangular boxes by about one inch (to serve as axles), several wooden wheels 1½ inches in diameter with three-eighth-inch holes drilled in the centers, small silver circles to be used as headlights (one-half inch in diameter), glue, markers or liquid tempera paint and brushes, tables set up in a long line, if possible.

Procedure:

a. Explain to children that some vehicles are made in factories on assembly lines. Many people work together to make cars that look exactly the same. Each person has one job to do in putting the whole car together. Today, the group will have the opportunity to construct cars on an assembly line.

b. Set up the assembly line. Place the materials in a row in the order they are to be put on. Make the following chart available so children can see this sequence of steps.

Assembly Line Steps:

1. Mark placement for axle hole in box body.

2. Use tool to make hole in body as marked for axle.

3. Put axle in hole.

4. Attach wheels.

5. Put on headlights.

6. Create taillights using a marker.

7. Paint car body. (Figure 8.6)

c. Assist children in deciding who will do each job.

d. Assign one child to inspect the operation of the assembly line as a way to ensure that a safe vehicle is being built.

e. Test the completed vehicles.

f. Deliver cars to a dealership to be sold.

Hint for Success:

• Allow children to change jobs, if they so desire.

How to Simplify this Activity:

- Rather than attaching wheels to axles, simply have children paste circle shapes on each box to represent wheels.

How to Extend this Activity:

- Have children evaluate the car that was designed. Ask what they could do to make the car better. Have them carry out the plan to redesign the car.

- After children have participated in the assembly line, invite them to make the whole car on their own. Lead a discussion in which children compare working on the assembly line, doing one job over and over again, with doing the whole job by themselves.

Language

1. *Write and Illustrate a Driver's Manual.* Following discussion of traffic safety and the importance of traffic laws, provide the children with construction paper and markers. Explain that people learn traffic safety laws by reading a driver's manual. Direct each child to think of a traffic safety law to dictate to an adult writer or to write themselves. Children could illustrate their laws by drawing or using magazine pictures. Compile the finished papers into a classroom Driver's Manual. Create a cover for the manual and make it available on the bookshelf for children's reference.

2. *Identify Traffic Signals.* Show the children traffic signals such as a traffic light, stop sign, yield sign, walk/don't walk light, railroad crossing sign, pedestrian crossing sign, and school zone sign. Explain the meaning of each sign. Give the children an opportunity to practice using these signals by incorporating them into the block area where toy vehicles are being used or outside where children are riding and/or running.

3. *Vehicle Flannel-Board Story.* Using a flannel board and felt pieces, tell the children a story depicting the part vehicles played in getting some item to their home or school. Below is a sample story featuring apples.

Flannel pieces:

apple tree, box of apples, several people, tractor with trailer, barn, sun and moon, two trucks, train with refrigerator car, grocery store with a produce department, shopping cart, car, home or school.

Basic story outline:

- One day at an apple orchard someone picked apples and carefully put them in a box. When the box was full, the worker put the box on a tractor-trailer. The tractor was driven to the barn and the box of apples was piled with others.

- The next day a large truck drove up to the barn. Workers loaded the truck with all the apple boxes. When the truck was full, the driver drove it to a train station. The driver waited for the train to come and then helped the railway workers load the boxes into a refrigerator car.

- The train traveled for many miles, from morning (sun shining) into the night (moon) and was still going the next day, until it came to (railroad station nearest your location).

- At the station, the workers unloaded the apples from the refrigerator car and onto another truck.

- The truck driver drove the truck to (local grocery store). The produce worker at the store took the apples and put them on the fruit counter.

- On Wednesday, (person familiar to the children) drove to the grocery store, got a shopping cart, and went to the produce area to choose some apples. After paying for the apples, (same person) pushed the cart to the car and drove to school. Now we have apples to eat. The end.

Prior to telling this story, explain to the children that their job will be to listen for all the vehicles used to deliver the apples. Afterward, cover the flannel board with a cloth and ask children to name the vehicles they remember. Write them on a large piece of paper in full view of the group. Once the children have finished, compare their list with the flannel-board vehicles. Have the children evaluate the results, adding forgotten vehicles or crossing out ones that didn't belong.

4. *Writing Advertisements.* After the children have had an opportunity to see car advertisements (post some on walls, sing familiar "chants" from TV car commercials, display vehicle advertising pamphlets in book area), encourage them to write their own advertisement in order to "sell" a vehicle from home, a model from school, or a vehicle they have designed and created at school. Tell children that their advertisements should let people know the vehicle is for sale and why someone would want to buy it. Post the finished "ads" around the room.

5. *Follow That Car!* Using masking tape for roads and blocks for buildings, create a town with two or more streets. Make each building distinctive, using tape, colored paper, or magazine pictures to differentiate one from another. Give each player a toy car or truck of their choice. Begin the game by verbally describing a route your car is taking in the town as you maneuver it through the streets. Emphasize the terms "first, next, and last." For example, "First I'll stop at the bakery, next I'll stop at the post office, and last I'll drive home." Invite children to retrace your route, physically with their own cars and verbally using the words "first, next, and last." Once they get the idea, encourage children to establish their own routes for others to follow. To add interest, pretend to follow their routes yourself and "make mistakes" that they can then correct. Also, vary the terms used such as "first, second, third" or "over, under, around" and so forth.

*6. *Listening for the Main Idea: The Little Engine That Could.*
General Purpose: For children to become more familiar with the elements of a story.
TFPs: 5, 10, 13.
Materials: The book, *The Little Engine That Could* by W. Piper; pictures of the following items large enough for children to identify easily: train, boat,

mountain, tunnel, a group of children, a group of animals. These pictures should not exactly duplicate those used in the actual story.

Procedure:

a. Introduce the activity by telling the children that you are going to read a book. Explain that when you are finished you will all discuss the story.

b. Read the story to the children.

c. When you finish, show them the pictures of the train and the boat and ask them whether the story was about a train or a boat.

d. Next, show the pictures of the mountain and the tunnel and ask, "Was this a story about a train going over a mountain or through a tunnel?"

e. Next, ask, "Was the story about taking something to children or taking something to animals?"

f. As children respond, acknowledge their answers. "You think the story was about a _____ ." Allow other children to give their ideas by saying, "What do you think?" Summarize the children's answers and then say, "Let's look in the book and see." Have children evaluate the accuracy of their responses.

g. Continue without pictures by asking if the story was about: 1) an engine too big or an engine too small, 2) helping or telling the truth, 3) trying hard or doing nothing.

h. Summarize the main points the children identified in the story.

Hint for Success:

• The choices here progress from concrete to more abstract content ideas. If the children have difficulty determining the main concepts of the story, read the story again and repeat the choices.

How to Simplify this Activity:

• Use a simpler story, with a shorter text.

• Use pictures for each pair of choices until the children have mastered listening for content.

How to Extend this Activity:

• Give children more than two alternatives from which to choose.

• Ask children to retell the story using the picture cues as a way to remember major points.

*7. *Vehicle Sound Stories.*

General Purpose: For children to practice listening for content and details.

TFPs: 1, 2, 4, 17.

Materials: Large carpeted area, story idea for teacher's use (prepared prior to experience). Optional: tape recorder or record player with a recording of soft instrumental music.

Procedure:

a. Gather the children in a large area. Play soft background music if desired. Tell the group that you will all be taking a pretend trip. Explain to them that they will have an important part in telling the story because they will make the sounds of the vehicles as you mention them.

b. Begin the story.

c. Base the story on traveling to a place with which the children are familiar, such as the zoo, a local park, or the grocery store. Include as many vehicles as possible. For example, riding a tricycle to the car; starting off in the car until it breaks down; riding in a tow truck to the repair shop; going to the shop; seeing a motorcycle, bicycle, and truck go by; riding the bus to the destination.

d. As each vehicle is mentioned, pause so the children have a chance to make the vehicle sounds.

Hint for Success:

• Invite the children to practice some vehicle sounds before you start the story. Encourage them to make any sound they think represents each vehicle you mention. During this time, point out that people may think of different ways to sound like the same vehicle.

How to Simplify this Activity:

• Do this activity in two parts. First, make the vehicle sounds without the story. On another occasion, tell the story accompanied by the children's sounds.

• Limit the number of vehicles mentioned.

How to Extend this Activity:

• Increase the number and the variety of vehicles mentioned.

• Ask children to carry out vehicle-type actions as well as making sounds.

• Encourage one child at a time to lead the group in a story about vehicle travel in which the group produces sounds as before.

Physical

1. *Vehicle Stickers.* Gather magazine pages containing small pictures of vehicles. Encourage children to tear or cut them out. Provide the following sticker solution or get the children to help you make it.

Sticker solution:
Boil: 8 T. of vinegar
Add: 4 packets of unflavored gelatin
Reduce heat to low. Stir until the gelatin is dissolved.
Add: 1 T. of flavored extract
This solution will last for months and can be reheated before each use.

Give the children small brushes to apply the sticker solution to the back of each picture. When dry the sticker will be ready to be licked and "stuck." Since this sticker solution hardens as it cools, keep the container in hot water to maintain it in liquid form.

2. *Traffic Safety Walk.* Prepare children for this walk by discussing pedestrian safety using the TFPs for this unit. Take a walk around the school area using a variety of movements, such as hopping on one foot then the other. As children move, remind them of pedestrian safety rules. Back at school, have the children recall the rules they followed.

*3. *Scooter Boards.*

General Purpose: To help children improve their coordination skills.

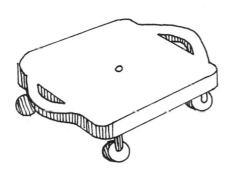

Figure 8.7 *A Typical Scooter Board*

TFPs: 1, 3, 4, 5.

Materials: Commercially available scooter boards. (Figure 8.7) Four to six traffic cones.

Procedure:

a. Invite children to try using the scooter boards any way they wish.

b. Once children have experimented with using the boards in their own way, introduce the following variations:

- Sit on the scooter—push forward using hands only, push backward using hands only, push forward using feet only, push backward using feet only.

- Put one knee on the scooter—propel forward with other leg holding hands up in the air, propel forward with other leg keeping both hands on the scooter.

- Lie on scooter on stomach—holding arms out straight, push off wall with feet and guide, push forward using hands only, push forward using feet only.

- Bend forward keeping two hands on the scooter and two feet on the floor, then run forward.

Hints For Success:

- Use the scooter boards on a flat, smooth surface.

- Maintain children's interest by calling the scooters vehicles and the children drivers.

- Make up scenarios related to drivers and vehicles as children try variations.

- Establish the following ground rules for using the scooters:

  One child at a time on each scooter.

  Sit or lie on the scooters, do not stand on them.

  Scooter drivers should steer clear of other scooters rather than "crashing" into them.

  Give beginners gloves to wear until they are accustomed to the boards.

How to Simplify this Activity:

- Focus on forward movements only.

- Introduce only one variation at a time.

How to Extend this Activity:

- Put the cones in a line for children to weave through.

Pretend Play

1. *Gas Station.* Set up gas pumps with hoses, windshield washing equipment, cash register, tires, tire pump, cars/tricycles, wrenches, screwdrivers, and fan belts. Invite children to play the roles of mechanic, cashier, customer, and so on.

2. *Car Wash.* Set out washable riding vehicles, hoses, sponges, brushes, soap and water, towels, and cash box. This could be done on a washable floor indoors or outside in a play yard. Children can be customers, cashiers, and car washers.

3. *Officer/Inspector in Charge.* Create police and inspector badges, hats, and/or coats for children to wear indoors or outdoors. Allow children to take turns as the officers who oversee the safety of the vehicle operators, passengers, and pedestrians. Have the officers watch over the speed at which vehicles are traveling and the operating order of vehicles and make sure drivers are following the traffic signs. Post signs such as STOP, WALK/DON'T WALK, PEDESTRIAN CROSSING, and RAILROAD CROSSING. Have available

"tickets" that the officers can give out in case someone is traveling in an unsafe manner.

4. ***Auto Parts Store/Repair Shop.*** Create a pretend play area in which children (pretend car owners) have a choice of having a mechanic fix their car or of buying parts to fix it by themselves. Divide the area in two. In the "car parts section," "sell" tools and parts, such as car washing materials, oil pans, empty plastic oil containers, wrenches, rubber gaskets, screwdrivers, rubber mallets, nuts and bolts, air filters, washers, screws, and tires from broken toy cars and trucks. In the "garage" segment of the area, set up riding cars, trucks, or motorcycles that the children can fix. Include coveralls to wear, rags, telephones, repair sheets, pencils, clipboards, and name tags for the children acting as professional mechanics. Show children the two areas. (Have signs up reading, AUTO PARTS STORE, REPAIR SHOP.) Tell them about the possible roles in each area and encourage them to begin playing.

5. ***Pedestrian Safety.*** To familiarize the children with pedestrian safety, start by introducing traffic lights, stop signs, and pedestrian signs within the classroom. For example, have the children create a town or city in the block area which includes both human figures and vehicles. Ask children to find safe places for pedestrians to cross the road and to designate a way for drivers and walkers to recognize these crossings. Encourage children to practice using these signals as they play.

6. ***Driver Training School.*** To help children discover that operating a motorized vehicle is a learned skill, create a driver training school in the pretend play area. Set up stationary vehicles, either ready-made ones or chairs set up with pretend steering wheels. Also, provide seat belts made from two heavy cloth strips tied to each side of a chair with Velcro® fasteners in the middle. (Figure 8.8) Put out the driver training manuals children developed earlier in the unit. Tell the children about the possible roles they could take: the driver training instructor or the new driver who listens to the instructor and follows his or her direc-

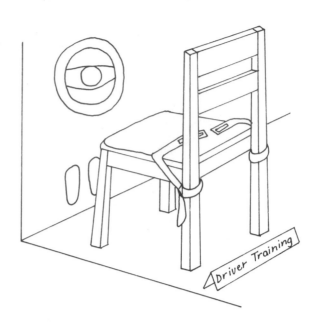

Figure 8.8 *Learning to Drive at the Driver Training School*

tions. Let the children know that the new driver learns about how to drive a car by reading an instruction manual. Direct their attention to the manuals you have provided. Differentiate the roles by providing the driving instructors with a special name tag. Encourage children to switch roles periodically.

7. ***Vehicle Showroom.*** Set up the pretend play area as a vehicle showroom. Display model vehicles—large and/or small—as well as vehicles the children have constructed. Obtain and/or have children produce sales brochures to advertise the vehicles. Post advertisements children have drawn around the classroom. Encourage children to figure out what about the vehicles will "entice" others to want to buy them. Possible roles are the salesperson, customer, and manager. Props to include are calculators, pencils, license plates, purchase forms, and registration forms.

*8. ***All Aboard!***
   General Purpose: For children to experiment with a variety of objects, roles, and characterizations.

   TFPs: 4, 6, 7, 10, 15, 16.

Materials: Large appliance box, chairs, pillows, blankets, and smaller boxes to serve as "cargo."

Procedure:

a. This is a "progressive" pretend play plan. It will give the children an opportunity to take on the actions and roles of railroad personnel and passengers while also teaching them about the purposes of railroad cars.

b. Introduce one type of railway car each day. For example, on Monday set up the pretend play area as an engine and passenger car. Arrange a space up front for the engineer and lines of paired chairs to serve as the passenger car.

c. On Tuesday, create a sleeper car and dining car. Set up sleeping mats with pillows and blankets to represent berths. In the dining area provide menus, order forms, dishes, and pretend food so the wait staff can serve customers.

d. On Wednesday, create a boxcar with freight. Provide empty boxes from a local grocery store for children to load. Ramps, scales, wheelbarrows, and small dollies could also be added.

e. On Thursday, make a refrigerator car. Provide children with coats and gloves to wear as they load and unload freight.

f. On Friday, set up a caboose.

Hints for Success:

• Label the outside of each railway car.

• Provide name tags for the children to help define the roles they are playing on the train.

How to Simplify this Activity:

• Set up and use only one railroad car each day. Keep the same type of car out for several days.

How to Extend this Activity:

• One week, make the train a passenger train with engine, passenger car, and dining car.

• The next week, set up a freight train with an engine (or two engines), boxcar, refrigerator car, tank car, flatcar, gon-dola car, and caboose. Encourage children to decide which cars to include in the freight train and invite them to take part in creating the railway cars.

Social

1. *Let's Ride Together!* Provide vehicles that require cooperation to run for the children to ride in together (wagons, sleds, two-person scooters, etc.).

2. *Cooperative Vehicle Construction.* Have the children work together to decorate a large box as a bus, train, car, or wagon. Decorating could be done with markers, crayons, wallpaper scraps, pipe cleaners, paper, glue, and paint. Encourage children to plan together about how to do the job. Have children decide who will do the different tasks. When the work is done, add the vehicle to the pretend play area for the children to use together.

3. *Ka Choo Circle Game.* Have children spread out across a large area, making a circle without holding hands. Choose one child to be the "engine" in the center. As the children chant and clap the following verse, the "engine" picks up passengers from among the children in the circle. As each passenger is selected, he or she holds onto the waist or the shoulders of the last child in the "train" or "trolley." The train/trolley continues to move around the circle, weaving in and out until *all* the children are included.

Here Comes the Train/Trolley
(Traditional chant; Author unknown)
Chant the verse three times and then the chorus twice. Repeat the verse and chorus until all names have been called.

Verse:
Here comes the train (or trolley).
It's coming down the track.
It's coming to take our Sandra back.
(Substitute a different child's name each time the verse is chanted.)

Chorus:
Ka Choo, Ka Choo,
Ka Choo, Ka Choo, Ka Choo

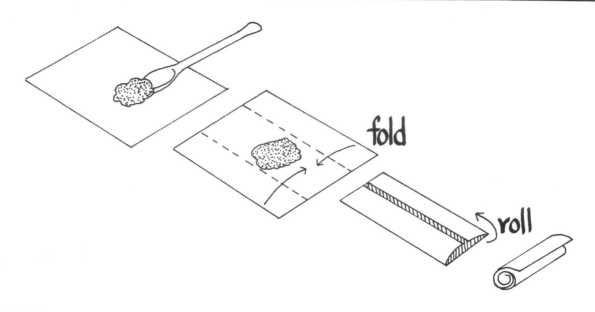

Figure 8.9 *Making Sanbusa*

4. ***Who Can Drive?*** Prior to the children's arrival, gather pictures of a wide variety of vehicles. In addition, cut out faces of men, women, and children of varying ages and culture groups. Put the vehicle pictures in one "feely box" and the people in another. Have children pick one item from each box. Ask them to decide whether that person could drive the vehicle selected and to offer a rationale for their decision. As the game proceeds, explore the notion that both males and females can be drivers as can people of all culture groups.

5. ***Red Light, Green Light.*** This exercise will allow the children to engage in a social activity while practicing traffic safety rules. One person acts as the traffic light, holding up either a green paper circle as the green light or a red circle as the red light. All others start out in a line facing the traffic light person. As the green light shows, everyone moves forward. When the red light shows, everyone stops. Continue until the group reaches the traffic light. Have an adult be the traffic light first to demonstrate how to play the game, then let children take turns in this position. To extend the activity, change the red light/green light signal to the walk/don't walk signal seen at pedestrian crossings.

*6. ***Box Lunches.***

General Purpose: For children to develop a greater appreciation of the ethnic background and culture of others.

TFPs: 15.

Materials: Container to hold food, such as a bag or box; ingredients and tools as listed in one of the following lunches.

Procedure:

a. Explain to the children that sometimes when people travel on a vehicle, they are away from home during a mealtime. Many times, people bring food with them to eat while traveling. Around the world, people travel and people eat. The vehicle they travel in or the food they pack may differ from one cultural group to another.

b. Include children as much as possible in the preparation of one or more of the following "box" lunches:

Danish Open-faced Sandwiches
Ingredients:

Bread

Sliced lunch meat or sliced cheese

Sliced cucumber or pickles

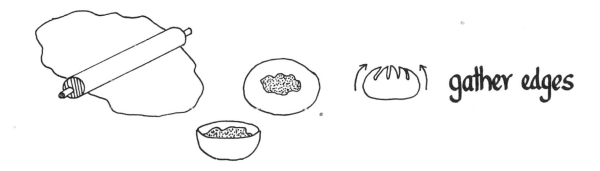

Figure 8.10 *Making Pasties*

Procedure:
Combine ingredients into open-faced sandwiches. Provide juice or fruit and a cookie.

Sanbusa
Ingredients:
Uncooked eggroll wrappers (found in the specialty section of your local supermarket or at an oriental market)
Spinach or grated cheese
Ground beef
Oil

Procedure:
1. Brown the ground beef, add spinach.
2. Place a spoonful of mixture onto eggroll wrapper. Fold wrapper and roll as shown. (Figure 8.9)
3. Deep fry until wrapper is browned, place on paper towel to cool or bake in 350° oven for 10 to 15 minutes.
4. Accompany with dried fruit and a drink.

Scottish, English, or Finnish Pasties
Short Crust Pastry Ingredients:
1 lb. flour
½ to ¾ lb. margarine
½ tsp. salt
Cold water

Procedure:
1. Rub the margarine into the flour until mixture is as fine as bread crumbs.

2. Add the salt and enough cold water to make a stiff dough.
3. Roll out at once.
4. Cut into 6-inch squares or circles.

Filling Ingredients:
½ lb. flank or round steak*
1 onion
½ lb. potatoes (parboiled)
*Brown meat in a skillet ahead of children's arrival.

Procedure:
1. Cut the meat into small pieces, dice the potatoes, chop the onion.
2. Mix all ingredients in a bowl with seasoning (garlic powder, pepper) and 2 tablespoons of water.
3. Place a scoopful of the filling mixture on each pastry shape.
4. Wet the edges and pull the sides up over the meat, joining them on the top. (Figure 8.10)
5. Brush with beaten egg and bake for 45 minutes at 350°.
6. Wrap in aluminum foil and pack.

Mrs. Lee's Korean Sushi
Ingredients:
1 cup "sweet" rice
6 sheets packaged nori or kim (fresh dried scaweed)
2 hardboiled eggs
1 cucumber
1 carrot (parboiled)

Figure 8.11 *Making Sushi*

Procedure:

1. Cook the raw rice for 20–30 minutes in 2 cups of water. Rice is done when water is all absorbed.

2. Cool the rice.

3. Mince the eggs, cucumber, and carrot separately.

4. To assemble,
   a. Take one sheet of the nori and lay it flat on a clean towel.
   b. Spread ⅙ of the rice evenly over the nori/kim leaving a ¼- to ½-inch margin around each edge.
   c. Sprinkle the egg over all. Place cucumber and/or carrot in lines across the center of the rice.
   d. Roll the entire sheet, from left to right. (Figure 8.11)
   e. Unroll the cloth and slice the roll into ½-inch circles.
   f. Serve at room temperature.

5. Accompany this meal with shrimp chips (found in oriental specialty stores), celery sticks, cucumber slices, and some soy sauce for dipping.

Hint for Success:

• Ask parents of children in the classroom for favorite "box lunches" from their families or cultures. The lunches could be prepared and eaten on a field trip or as a regular meal at school, possibly a picnic.

How to Simplify this Activity:

• Prepare the lunches with the children helping as much as possible. Go on a pretend trip to a favorite spot and eat the lunches outside.

How to Extend this Activity:

• Have a person that represents the culture reflected in each box lunch visit the class, either to fix the lunches with the children or to eat with them. Invite the person to talk about the vehicles used in their country and trips they might take with such a box lunch.

TEACHER RESOURCES

Field Trip Ideas

1. If there is a local vehicle assembly plant with safe visitor access, arrange for children to visit to observe how an actual vehicle assembly line works.

   If your children are six and older, before the field trip, ask children to predict the order in which the vehicle parts will be assembled. During the trip, with the children, write down the actual order. Following the field trip, compare the lists and have children evaluate their prediction.

2. Arrange for a salesperson or manager of a car dealership to show the children some features of their sales work. Possible items to be explored could be:

a. how advertising is used to draw potential customers to the dealership or give them information about the vehicles
b. how people decide on what car to buy
c. how vehicles are displayed to make people want to buy them

3. Find out if there is a museum in the area that features vehicles. Visit the museum in advance to be sure that the displays are easy for children to see.
4. Take the children to a train station to see and hear as well as observe people working at the station. Arrange for a time that the children can observe the ticket salesperson selling tickets to passengers, meet a conductor, engineer or other railway worker. Ask if there might be one worker who could tell interesting, short stories about working on a train.
5. Take a trip to the local police or fire station and focus on the types of vehicles police officers and firefighters use in their work and what functions these vehicles perform.
6. Visit a junkyard to explore old vehicles and vehicle parts. Ask the owners or managers what parts of the yard can be safely viewed by the children. Consider looking at the cars that have been in accidents and discuss vehicle safety.

Classroom Visitors

1. Invite a police officer to describe the work she or he does in assuring traffic and pedestrian safety.
2. Ask a vehicle inspector to discuss his or her role in keeping people safe by testing and checking vehicles.
3. Find an automobile designer to talk about what goes into designing a new automobile. Request that he or she bring sample drawings or models to show the children.
4. Ask a person who drives a vehicle professionally to talk about what he or she does to assure the safety of passengers as well as others on the road.

Children's Books

Alexander, A. *ABC of Cars and Trucks.* Garden City, NY: Doubleday, 1971.

Baker, E. *I Want to Be a Taxi Driver.* Chicago: Childrens Press, 1969.

Barr, J. *Mr. Zip and the U.S. Mail.* Niles, IL: Whitman, 1964.

Burningham, J. *Mr. Gumpy's Motor Car.* New York: Crowell, 1973.

Burton, V. L. *Maybelle the Cable Car.* Boston: Houghton Mifflin, 1952.

Cameron, E. *The Big Book of Real Trucks.* New York: Grosset and Dunlap, 1970.

Cole, J. *Cars and How They Go.* New York: Crowell, 1983.

Crews, D. *School Bus.* New York: Puffin Books, 1984.

———. *Freight Train.* New York: Greenwillow, 1978.

———. *Truck.* New York: Greenwillow, 1980.

Ehrlich, A. *The Everyday Train.* New York: Dial, 1977.

Gackenback, D. *Binky Gets A Car.* New York: Clarion, 1983.

Hitte, K. *A Letter for Cathy.* Nashville: Abingdon Press, 1953.

Holl, A. *ABC of Cars, Trucks, and Machines.* New York: McGraw-Hill, 1970.

Jewell, N. *The Bus Ride.* New York: Harper and Row, 1978.

Keats, E. J. *A Letter to Amy.* New York: Harper and Row, 1968.

Kessler, E., and L. Kessler. *Big Red Bus.* Garden City, NY: Doubleday, 1964.

MacDonald, G. *Red Light, Green Light.* Garden City, NY: Doubleday, 1944.

McLean, A., and J. McLean. *The Steam Train Crew.* New York: Oxford University Press, 1981.

McMillan, B. *The Remarkable Riderless Runaway Tricycle.* Boston: Houghton Mifflin, 1978.

Mathiew, J. *Big Joe's Trailer Truck.* New York: Random House, 1974.

Miner, I. *The True Book of Our Post Office.* Chicago: Childrens Press, 1955.

Neville, E. C. *The Bridge.* New York: Harper and Row, 1988.

Oppenheim, J. *Have You Seen Roads?* Reading, MA: Addison-Wesley, 1969.

Penick, I. *The Pop-up Book of Trucks.* New York: Random House, 1974.

Piper, W. *The Little Engine That Could.* New York: Platt and Munk, 1980.

Retan, W. *The Big Book of Real Trucks.* New York: Grosset and Dunlap, 1987.

Scarry, R. *Cars and Trucks and Things That Go.* New York: Golden, 1974.

———. *The Great Big Car and Truck Book.* New York: Western Publishing, 1951.

Shuttlesworth, D. *ABC of Buses.* Garden City, NY: Doubleday, 1965.

Siebert, D. *Truck Song.* New York: Harper and Row, 1984.

Spier, P. *Tin Lizzie.* Garden City, NY: Doubleday, 1975.

Zaffo, G. *The Great Big Book of Real Fire Engines.* New York: Grosset and Dunlap, 1958.

Adult References

Jackson, J. *Man and the Automobile.* New York: McGraw-Hill, 1979.

Ogburn, C. *Railroads.* Washington, D.C.: National Geographic Society, 1977.

Chapter 9

Exploring Space

•

Starlight, starbright.
First star I see tonight. . . .

•

People have looked up at the sky with awe and wonder since the beginning of time, marveling at the objects they see and yearning to travel to the far reaches of space. Many ancient myths and legends attempt to explain the heavenly bodies and their origins. Modern humans, too, speculate on the origins and make-up of the objects in the sky. Over the years, people have developed sophisticated techniques for exploring the marvels of space, indirectly through observations with highly sensitive telescopes, as well as directly, through actual space travel and deep space probes that return a wealth of data to earth. Much media attention has been focused on these exploits, stimulating a sense of adventure in both young and old. Children often imagine themselves heading off into space to explore new frontiers, perhaps to find intelligent life somewhere beyond the earth.

PURPOSE

A theme about space exploration, therefore, offers an opportunity to capitalize on children's budding curiosity about the natural world. Furthermore, it presents a positive introduction to both a scientific and social studies topic in which the various roles played by human beings are well defined. In this study, children will learn facts about the exploration of space, begin to understand and appreciate the work that astronomers and astronauts do, and recognize the value of people working together to accomplish an enormous and challenging task. A conscious effort should be made to emphasize that both men and women have been involved in space exploration for a long time. For example, female astronomers, such as Cecilia Payne Gaposhkin, Ann Cannon, and Margaret Burbage, have made significant contributions to our understanding of the universe, and the space trips of Terashkova and Sally Ride are an inspiration to young girls everywhere. Finally, mention must be made of the need to treat space and the objects in space with respect in order to preserve them for the future. Space trash, for example, is only one of the potential problems humans will have to face in the years to come.

IMPLEMENTATION

This unit is best implemented following a study of this book's Sky unit since it is based on introductory information about stars, planets, and moons that should be familiar to children before they can focus on space exploration. Furthermore, it is a natural follow-up.

Within this guideline, several options are available for presentation.

Option One: Spend one week on an overview of space exploration, including discussion of direct and indirect methods.

Option Two: Plan to carry out the Exploring Space unit over two weeks. In week one, focus on astronomers and the tools and methods they use to study space. In week two, move on to astronauts and actual space.

Option Three: If you wish to extend this study over several more weeks, add a week to examine the future of space exploration to Option Two. Plan another week that focuses on intelligent life in space. How might such creatures look and behave? How can we develop communication systems with them? How can we live peacefully with alien beings?

TERMS, FACTS, AND PRINCIPLES

General Information

1. Space is the region beyond the earth's atmosphere.

2. Space is vast, no one knows how big it is.

3. There are many objects in space. Some that we can see are planets, moons, and stars.

4. There are empty places in space between the planets, moons, and stars.

5. People know many things about space and the objects in space; there is still much to learn.

Stars, Planets, and Moons

6. A star is an object in space that produces heat and light.

7. The sun is a star around which nine planets orbit.

8. An orbit is the special path followed by a planet or moon. No two planets or moons have the same orbit.

9. A planet is a large object that moves around a star and is too small to produce heat and light by itself.

10. The planets that orbit the sun are (in order of increasing distance from the sun): Mercury, Venus, Earth, Mars, Jupiter, Saturn, Uranus, Neptune, and Pluto.

11. We live on the planet called Earth.

12. The planets vary in size, shape, color, and make-up. Each planet has unique physical characteristics by which it can be identified.

13. The planets closest to the sun are hot; the planets farther away from the sun are cooler.

14. People on Earth can sometimes see Mercury, Venus, Mars, Jupiter, and Saturn without using telescopes.

15. Planets spin, or rotate, around themselves on an axis as they orbit the sun.

16. It takes each planet a different amount of time to orbit the sun. It takes Earth one year.

17. Many planets have moons that orbit them.

Indirect Space Exploration

18. People explore space indirectly by observing it from a distance.

19. It is sometimes possible to look at objects in space without any special instruments.

20. The best time to observe the stars, planets, and moons is at night when it is very dark and very clear.

*21. The earth, other planets, and stars are in constant motion.

22. Astronomers are scientists who study space and the objects in it.

23. Both men and women can be astronomers.

24. Astronomers use a variety of instruments to help them.
   a. *Telescopes* are instruments that make objects in space appear brighter (and larger) by gathering light and focusing it.
   b. A *camera* attached to a telescope takes a picture of objects in space. Astronomers study the pictures to find out more about the objects.
   c. *Computers* help scientists understand the information they are gathering.

25. Astronomers work in observatories and laboratories.

26. An observatory is a building that houses a telescope. The moon, planets, and stars are viewed with a telescope through an opening in the dome of the observatory.

27. Observatories are usually located on mountains far from the city lights.

28. Astronomers and other people working with telescopes sometimes live at observatories for days or weeks at a time. Because they work mostly at night, they sleep during the day. There are beds for them to sleep in and places to prepare and eat food.

29. People who are not astronomers learn about space by watching the sky, reading books, viewing TV programs, and visiting planetariums.

*30. A planetarium is a room in which images of stars and other objects in the sky are projected on a domed ceiling for people to see.

*31. People who work at a planetarium develop exhibits there that give people information about space.

Direct Space Exploration

32. People explore space directly through space travel.

33. A pioneer is a person who explores and tries out new things.

34. Astronauts are pioneers who explore space.

35. An astronaut is a person who is specially trained to fly spacecraft and explore space.

36. Both men and women can be astronauts.

37. To become an astronaut a person must learn many things, such as navigation, facts about the planets, how to operate spacecraft, how to use equipment, and how to take care of and control their bodies in space.

38. Astronauts undergo intensive training prior to going into space.

*39. Some astronauts have traveled in a space shuttle. This large spacecraft combines a rocket and glider airplane that can carry passengers and equipment into orbit and back.

*40. Some astronauts have traveled to a space station. From this orbiting human-made satellite, space can be explored.

41. When two or more space vehicles meet in space at a planned time and place it is called a rendezvous.

42. During a link-up, contact is established between space vehicles meeting in space.

43. Some astronauts have landed on and explored parts of the moon.

44. Astronauts found no plants, animals, or water on the moon. They found mountains, valleys, and plains of rocks.

*45. People weigh nothing in space. This means that they float freely and are not pulled down to the floor of the spacecraft by gravity.

46. There is no air to breathe or water to drink in space.

47. When astronauts go into space they must take their own air, water, and food.

48. Food for use in space must be specially prepared to be eaten when there is no gravity.

49. Astronauts eat food in space that provides the same nutrients as the food people eat on earth.

50. Space food is either freeze-dried or in a liquid or semiliquid state because it stores better and is easier for astronauts to eat in a weightless atmosphere.

51. Astronauts squeeze some of their food from packages through special nozzles.

52. To go outside their spacecraft, astronauts put on special clothes. These include spacesuits, moon boots, helmets, oxygen tanks, gloves, and lifelines to connect them to their spacecraft.

*53. People use the space shuttle to put satellites into space, to perform experiments, and to find out more about how people and animals can live in space.

54. Some people who are not astronauts can now travel into space on the space shuttle.

55. Spacecrafts travel at faster speeds than vehicles on earth so they go farther in less time.

56. There are many different kinds of space vehicles. Some can be used again; others cannot.

*57. Some of the tools astronauts use in space are different from tools people use on earth; others are similar to those on earth.

Mission Control

58. Mission Control is the headquarters for space exploration by American astronauts.

59. The people at Mission Control talk to the astronauts and help guide their journey.

60. People in space use radios and TV to communicate with the people on Earth.

61. People at Mission Control have many different jobs, such as plotting the course, figuring out where the spacecraft is located, checking on the equipment, checking the health of the astronauts, and talking to the astronauts.

62. Some people at Mission Control use computers to figure out how high the spacecraft is, where it is going, where it has been, how fast it is going, and where and when it will land on Earth.

63. Some people at Mission Control keep track of the weather to aid in determining when the spacecraft should take off and land.

64. Some people at Mission Control talk to the astronauts to give them information, to get information from them, and to keep them company.

65. Many people on Earth have watched pictures of astronauts in space on television.

66. Astronauts often take pictures of how Earth looks from space. They send these to Earth for people to look at.

Lift-off and Landing

67. A spacecraft is carried into space at the front end of a rocket.

*68. A rocket works by pushing gas out of the back at a very high speed. This propels it forward.

69. Before lift-off people make sure everything on the rocket and spacecraft is working. This is called the "countdown." People count backwards on a countdown.

70. When the countdown reaches zero, the rocket and the spacecraft lift off.

*71. When the spacecraft is moving fast enough, the rocket drops off because the spacecraft no longer needs to be pushed.

*72. Pilots steer the spacecraft by using little rockets to push it in one direction or another.

*73. To land the spacecraft, pilots make it head back to earth by slowing it down with a rocket that is pointed forward.

74. Some spacecraft use parachutes as they come close to the ground or water, others use wings to help them glide in for a landing.

Life in Space

75. The only life forms we know of are on Earth.

76. Some people think there might be life in other parts of space.

ACTIVITY IDEAS

Aesthetic

1. *Space Music.* From a library, borrow recordings that have been inspired by space, such as *The Planets* (by Holst) or the *Jupiter Symphony* (by Beethoven). New age music (by Windham Hill artists, for instance) would be appropriate also, as much of it has an eerie or "spacey" feeling. Play these for children at quiet times. Ask them to imagine being in space or looking into space as they listen. Find out what sights they are imagining and, if possible, make note of these. Stimulate their ideas with comments of your own: "Oh, now I can see _____" or "this makes me feel _____." To extend this activity, have children move to the music once they are familiar with a particular selection.

2. *Sky Watch.* In a note home, explain to parents that children are studying space. Ask parents to permit children to stay up late one evening to watch the moon and the stars (if such viewing is possible in your locale). Send home a sky chart depicting the night sky during specific months. (These are available from museums, libraries, and planetariums.) Ask parents to look at the sky with their children. No real knowledge of the stars is necessary, since the focus of this activity is appreciation of nature.

*3. *Kaleidoscopes.*

General Purpose: To encourage curiosity and wonder.

TFPs: 2, 4, 5.

Materials: Two or more kaleidoscopes.

Procedure:

a. Introduce the activity with a discussion of the unknown vastness of space. Mention that although people are developing more powerful instruments all the time, they are still unable to "see" most of space. Because people cannot go to the stars, they have made objects like kaleidoscopes that remind them of stars and starlight.

b. Offer kaleidoscopes to the children. Show them that by pointing them toward a light source (a window or light) and looking into the appropriate end, they can see wonderful sights. Instruct them to turn the barrel and tell you what they notice is happening.

c. Mention that although astronomers, astronauts, and others who use telescopes often make predictions about what will be revealed, they are often surprised, awed, and amazed at what they see.

d. Encourage children to experience and/or express joy in the beauty of the designs they discover. Suggest that they trade kaleidoscopes with each other to compare the patterns and colors.

Hints for Success:

- Kaleidoscopes are very popular. Be sure that they are available for several days so that all children who wish to can have several chances to use them.

- Make a list so that children can sign up for a turn and can judge how long they have to wait.

How to Simplify this Activity:

- Adult help may be required to hold and turn the kaleidoscope when younger children are using it.

How to Extend this Activity:

- Suggest that children re-create the designs they have seen using markers, crayons, or parquetry pieces.

- Explain that both kaleidoscopes and telescopes employ mirrors to make their images. Point out the similarities in their names. Compare a real telescope with a kaleidoscope.

Affective

1. *Pioneers in Space.* Carry out a discussion with children focused on how they would feel being the first person to a) go to the moon, b) live in a space shuttle, or c) travel beyond the solar system. Use such emotion descriptors as excited, fearful, anticipating, nervous, exhilarated, unsure, and so on to help children identify their feelings. Explain that being brave does not mean people have no fear, but rather that, in spite of fear, they do their job. Explore the circumstances, such as traveling alone or with others; being lost; landing on a planet; hearing the voices from Mission Control; or losing contact with Mission Control, that might stimulate particular emotions.

2. *"If I Were an Astronomer/Astronaut...."* This activity works best when carried out after children have become familiar with the actual roles of astronomers and astronauts. Ask the children to imagine being an astronomer or astronaut. Ask them to tell you or a small group of children what they would like best, what they would like least, and, for older children, which skills they already possess that would be useful in their job. Have them also talk about what they would have to learn.

*3. *Packing for a Trip to the Moon.*
   General Purpose: For children to prioritize things that are special to them.

   TFPs: 3, 32, 43–47, 50, 51.

   Materials: A list of space TFPs highlighting those listed above; about ten or twelve pictures (hand drawn or cut from magazines) of "special things," such as a tricycle, tree, apple, house, pajamas, wagon, teddy bear, pet, camera, food, clothing; a small box representing a suitcase.

   Procedure:

   a. Introduce the activity with a discussion of astronauts and "civilians" who have traveled into space and/or landed on the moon. Talk about the many things they had to leave behind and the length of time they were gone.

   b. Invite the children (or one child) to look through the pictures you have provided and decide which four items they would pack for a trip to the moon. Remind them that space on the ship would be limited and they would not be able to take everything they wanted.

   c. Encourage each child to discuss why he or she would or would not choose each of the items, as the pictures are separated into a "take along" group and a "leave behind" group. Accept several changes of mind as items are placed in the "suitcase."

   d. Suggest that the children think of *one* other thing each one would *really* want to take along. They may want to draw their own pictures of that item.

Hints for Success:

- Make sure the pictures include objects that are familiar to children.
- Limit the number of children participating at any one time to two.

How to Simplify this Activity:

- Use real objects and a real suitcase.
- Limit the number of choices to six or seven at first.

How to Extend this Activity:

- Discuss with children some of the items real astronauts take into space.
- Have children generate their own individual lists and then put the items into first-, second-, and third-choice groups.
- Discuss the items several children listed in common; help children figure out how these might be shared.

Cognition

1. *Countdown.* Practice counting to five (with younger children) or ten or twenty (with older children). Explain that when a spacecraft is ready to be launched, the people in charge count down (backward) as they check to make sure everything on the spacecraft and the rocket is working properly. Demonstrate how to count backward from five, ten, or twenty, to zero. Ask the children to follow suit. After zero, say "blast-off" or "lift-off." Throughout the day, use a countdown to designate transitions (going outdoors, going home, clean-up time, snack time, etc.). Instead of "blast-off," chant the name of the activity coming next ("10, 9, 8, . . . clean-up!"). When children are waiting for a turn, the same countdown may be used.

2. *Balloon Launch.* This activity is designed to show children how a rocket works. Blow up a balloon while children watch. Hold the end so no air escapes. Ask the children to predict what will happen when you let go. Paraphrase their responses. Let go of the balloon. Watch it fly around. Retrieve the balloon. Ask children to tell you what they saw and why they think it occurred. Explain that the gas (CO_2) that you blew into the balloon rushed backwards out of the balloon's neck and pushed the balloon forward. This is like a rocket pushing a spacecraft. Because the balloon was not pushed fast enough to get past the earth's atmosphere, it fell down when there was no more gas escaping fast. Give older children balloons with which to experiment.

3. *Where's the Weight?* A kinesthetic sense of weightlessness can be experienced even on Earth. Purchase or borrow a set of leg and arm exercise weights. Ask a volunteer child to wear them for a period of five to ten minutes. Have the child move around the room or playground during this time. Remove the weights and ask the child to describe the difference in ease of movement and sensation of lightness. Have onlookers also describe the differences they can see in the child's movements.

4. *Jump the Planets.* Beginning with the sun at the center, place cardboard shapes representing each planet in the proper order on the floor or rug: Mercury, Venus, Earth, Mars, Jupiter, Saturn, Uranus, Neptune, and Pluto. Make the planet representations as realistic as possible so children can easily distinguish them. Instruct children, one at a time, to step on each "planet" in turn. As they step on Mercury, they should say "Mercury, jump one" and jump once. Next, they step on Venus and say, "Mercury, jump one" (and do it); "Venus, jump two" (and do that motion). Each time they step on a "planet" they add its name and the appropriate number of jumps. In this way children learn the order of the planets outward from the sun. For older children or children who have learned more about planets, the actions as they move farther away from the sun should be less vigorous. This represents the decreasing amount of solar energy reaching planets as their distance from the sun increases.

5. *Sifting Moon Rocks.* The aim of this activity is to encourage problem solving. Fill a sand table or other large container with a mixture of sand, gravel, and pebbles. Put

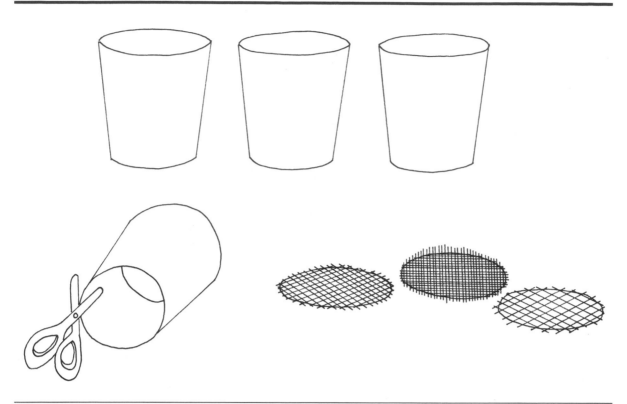

Figure 9.1a *Cut the Bottoms Out of the Cups to Make Sifters*

aside. Purchase screening of various-sized mesh. Cut the bottoms out of several thin plastic containers (for example, yogurt, sour cream, or cottage cheese containers). (Figure 9.1a)

Using duct tape, tape the screen along the outside edge of the bottom of each container. (Figure 9.1b)

Be sure that there are no sharp edges left untaped. Tell children that when astronauts went to the moon, they brought back samples of the surface and that they sifted the sand they found. Ask them to look at the different sieves and to look at the sand mixture. Then ask them to predict, by looking at the materials, which sieves will trap the largest pebbles, which the smallest, and which the tiny sand particles. Allow children to test out their predictions by using the sieves. Ask children to evaluate their predictions based on their experience.

*6. **Space Food.**
General Purpose: To increase children's sensory acuity.

TFPs: 47–51.

Materials: Plastic locking bags, straws, small paper plates, clothespins or clips to reseal bags, scissors, Earth food (bananas, apples, grapes, oatmeal, hardened gelatin, orange juice); space food (dried banana chips, apples, raisins, semiliquid gelatin in bags with hole for straw, orange juice crystals, granola bars, fruit rolls, space cookies).

Procedure:

a. Introduce the activity by explaining to children that before astronauts go into space, food has to be prepared for them in special ways. Tell them they will have a chance to eat the food prepared for astronauts and also to eat the same food in its natural state (as they might eat it on Earth).

b. Place samples of the "space" food on children's plates. Instruct the children to explore the food by looking, smelling, touching, and tasting. Allow time for children to guess each food. Paraphrase their descriptions, holding up

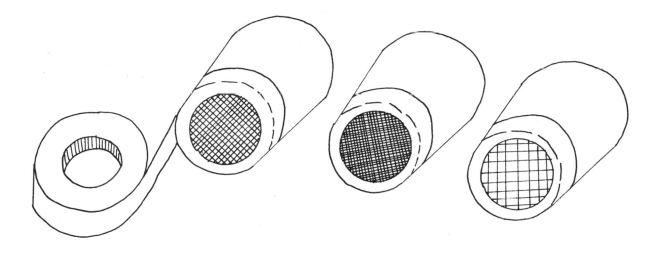

Figure 9.1b *Fasten the Screen Pieces with Tape*

the particular food item they are discussing from your own sample.

c. Distribute samples of the natural food items. Ask children to look at, smell, touch, and taste these.

d. Instruct the children to match up the items, one at a time. Children should then be permitted to eat the food if they wish.

e. As they eat, ask the children to describe the similarities and differences between the food items.

Hints for Success:

• Have enough of each food for every child to try.

• Instruct children to refrain from eating the food right away.

• Cut hard food into bite-sized pieces before beginning the activity.

• Cover the table with newspaper and have a sponge and bucket of water handy for clean-up.

• Premeasure crystals in baggies before children add water.

How to Simplify this Activity:

• Try one or two items at a time.

• Use the most familiar foods first, such as bananas and apples.

How to Extend this Activity:

• Involve older children in preparing food for space (making gelatin, adding water to make juice from crystals, etc.).

• Have them package the food (putting liquid into baggies, cutting hole for straw, etc.).

Space Cookies
Ingredients:

1 egg

½ cup margarine

½ tsp. molasses

⅔ cup honey

1 tsp. vanilla or almond extract

1 cup whole wheat flour

½ tsp. salt

1½ tsp. baking powder

½ cup raisins or other soft, dried fruit.

2½ cups granola

Procedure:

1. Cream margarine, honey, and eggs.

2. Add dry ingredients and mix.

3. Drop by heaping teaspoonful on a greased cookie sheet.

4. Bake at 375° for 10 to 12 minutes.

Granola

Ingredients:

3 cups rolled wheat or oat bran

3 cups rolled oats

1 cup sunflower seeds

½ cup sesame seeds

½ cup wheat germ

1½ cups coconut

½ tsp. salt

1 cup peanuts or almonds

¾ cup vegetable oil

¾ cup honey

2 tsp. vanilla or almond extract

raisins or other soft, dried fruit

Procedure:

1. Measure all of the dry ingredients into a large cake pan.

2. Mix the liquid ingredients together; pour over the mix.

3. Bake at 350° for 30 to 45 minutes; stir once or twice while cooking for even browning.

4. Add raisins or other soft, dried fruits after baking if you like.

5. Store in an airtight container.

6. Eat plain as a snack, for breakfast over fruit and milk, as a topping for yogurt, or in cookies.

Construction

1. *Moonscape.* Provide a large container of damp sand (in a sand table, if available), small plastic vehicles (such as dune buggies), a variety of rocks and pebbles, and illustrations or photographs of the moon's surface. Precede this activity with a discussion of what astronauts found on the moon (see TFPs). Allow two or three children at a time to re-create a lunar landscape in the sand, as they imagine it might look.

2. *Spinning Satellites.* After children have had opportunities to learn about various kinds of spacecraft and satellites, provide materials for them to make their own versions. Include such items as Styrofoam balls, chunks of Styrofoam (that older children can shape), pipe cleaners, toothpicks, nails, aluminum foil, and wire. (Variously colored telephone wire is especially good.) When children have finished their spacecrafts, hang them from the ceiling, if possible, so that the entire room is transformed into a spacescape.

3. *Creatures from Space.* Introduce this activity with a discussion about life in other parts of space or by reading stories to children on the subject. Emphasize that if there are other creatures in space, they are likely to be peaceful rather than fearsome, as they are so often depicted. Provide self-hardening clay or plasticine for children to use in making their notion of an alien. If hardening clay is used, provide each child with a soft ball of clay on a plastic mat, a smock, and a small amount of water in a dish (or a damp sponge). Caution the children not to get the clay too wet, or it will not hold its shape. Dry the completed projects on cardboard or absorbent paper. After several days of drying, children may paint these with water-based paints. Older children could also use acrylic paint.

4. *Navigating through Space.* After children have learned about the roles of astronomers and astronauts, present them with the idea of planning an imaginary journey through space. Talk with them about the objects they will find there and how to avoid crashing into them. Provide children with paper, markers, star stickers, and sticky dots. Tell them to create their own space picture out of these and then chart a course through space with a marker around the stars, planets, and moons.

5. *Star Patterns.* Give children heavy blunt needles and black construction paper. Tell them to poke out holes in the shape of a constellation. The constellation should be of each child's own design. Tape the "sky" pictures to a window so that light shines through the star holes. Children can then view their constellations through homemade, paper towel roll "telescopes" that they have decorated in various ways.

6. *Space Pack.* Gather two or three child-sized backpacks. Provide paper towel rolls, tape, string or rubber bands, and hole punches. Give children pictures of astronauts in full gear to study. Explain that when astronauts leave their ship they must take their oxygen with them. Tell children to make their own life-support systems by taping, tying, or fastening paper rolls together in a small bundle. These they can decorate as they wish so they can tell them apart. When the child astronaut goes on a "mission," he or she can put a space pack into a backpack for the journey.

*7. *Making a Space Suit.*

General Purpose: For children to reconstruct something in their own way.

TFPs: 37–52.

Materials: Large cardboard cartons, scissors or box knife for adult use, duct or masking tape, markers or crayons. Optional: discarded inner tubes, cleaned bleach bottles, brass brads, pictures of astronauts in suits, glue sticks, etc.

Procedure:

a. Gather the space materials in an open area. (This activity may be done more easily on the floor than on a table.) Have adult scissors and/or box knife available but beyond children's reach.

b. Invite children to examine pictures of astronauts and/or discuss the above listed TFPs. Point out that people need special equipment to venture outside their spacecraft in order to stay warm, to breathe, and to communicate with other people. Mention that an astronaut's suits must cover all of their body to keep warm, breathable air inside.

c. Tell children that they can help design and construct a space suit. Suggest that they use the displayed materials, as well as others they may think of and ask for. Some children may begin exploring and manipulating the materials with few directions. Other children may require more guidance: "Look at these boxes. Show me one that you think would cover your body. You will want your head and arms to be free. Let's make a hole for your head first. Someone can

put this box on so that we can mark places for arm holes. I'll cut two holes, here and here, for arms. Now you can decorate the suit. Here are some markers. You may think of other ways to decorate it. You can ask me to help you find other materials if you'd like."

d. Offer a small box for the helmet/head cover. Cut a window for the face and tape it to the larger box. Or, cut a bleach bottle, spout up, so that it has a face window.

Hints for Success:

• Construct more than one suit so that children can act out astronaut exploration in pairs or groups.

• Leave suit(s) out for several days, as they will be popular.

How to Simplify this Activity:

• Give children cut out pieces of cardboard to serve as dials and knobs. Punch holes in these pieces and attach them to suit with brads so they will turn.

How to Extend this Activity:

• Encourage children to cooperate in decorating the various cardboard parts in any way they wish. Suggest that the inner tube sections be attached for breathing tubes or speaking hoses. Punch holes to thread them through. Tape them in place.

*8. *Making Telescopes.*

General Purpose: To create a tangible product using a variety of materials.

TFPs: 3, 6, 12.

Materials: Paper towel tubes or cardboard tubes from wrapping paper cut in half; black drawing or construction paper or black fabric; hole punch; heavy needle, sharp pencil, or nail; tape or paste. Optional: aluminum foil.

Procedure:

a. Introduce the activity with a large-group discussion of instruments, such as telescopes, used to view distant objects. Explain that telescopes are often constructed of long, narrow tubes that provide a dark chamber through which to peer. By keeping surrounding light away from the eye, the light coming in the end appears in sharp focus.

b. Invite the children to make a telescope with you. Provide each child with a black circle (paper or fabric) that is larger than the end of a tube and can be easily taped or pasted in place.

c. Instruct or help children punch holes of various sizes in the black circles. Make five or six holes spaced far enough apart so that the circles won't tear.

d. Each child may wish to decorate a tube in some way, to form the chamber of the telescope. Point out the tinfoil, or offer crayons or markers for this purpose. Encourage children to be creative with this step. (One possibility is to wrap the whole tube with aluminum foil, taping or pasting the ends in place.)

e. When the tube has been decorated, help the child tape the black, hole-punched material firmly across one open end. (This can also be done with paste or a rubber band.)

f. Direct each child to a light source (window or electrical fixture). By looking into the open end of the tube, they will see simulated "stars" of light where holes have been punched. Reinforce the concept of a dark chamber that helps the light viewed appear more vivid. Introduce or reinforce facts about astronomers and observatories.

Hints for Success:

• If possible, show children an actual telescope before expecting them to construct one.

• Put each type of material in a separate container or tray so children can find what they need.

• Allow children to use the telescopes in their play.

How to Simplify this Activity:

• Prepunch the holes in the fabric or paper.

• In additional or alternative activity, tape two toilet paper rolls together for a pair of binoculars, with or without using the black paper to cover the ends.

How to Extend this Activity:

• Have children keep a chart of the planets and stars they "see" through their telescopes.

• Children can write a diary of their "nightly" observations.

Language

1. *Star Travel Fantasy.* After reading one of the children's books listed in the teacher resource section of this unit, tell children to imagine traveling far into space to a distant star. Explain that it will take a long time to get there. Ask them to describe the trip and also the fantastic things they might encounter when they arrive. Record these responses on tape for children to hear at a later time.

2. *Space Journey Journal.* Prepare a booklet for each child in the group by stapling four or five pages inside a manila folder, or use a sheet of construction paper as a cover. Tell children that when astronauts go into space, they keep a journal or diary of everything they do each day.

   Explain that they should imagine a journey through space and describe what they hear, see, and feel as they go. Suggest that they also include notes about other travelers, the scientific work they are carrying out, and how they are operating and maintaining their spacecraft.

   Set aside some time every day of the week for children to dictate the stories of their space journeys to you or another adult or invite older children to "write" their own.

   Pictures of life in a spacecraft may stimulate the thinking of younger children. Children may also wish to illustrate their journals.

3. *Wondrous Words.* Prepare a list of compound words related to space travel. This list might include spacecraft, spaceship, space shuttle, and space probe. Write the second part of each word on separate oak tag strips. Place the word "space" on a chart or flannel board. Ask children to think of as many words as they can that begin with "space." As they say the words, place the appropriate oak tags next to

"space." Say the word out loud as you do this. Another time, use a different beginning word, such as "rocket." To extend this activity, have children create new compound words relevant to the topic ("spacerock" or "moonjump").

4. ***Chants, Songs, and Fingerplays.***
   a. "Let's Go On a Space Trip." This is a variant of "Let's Go on a Bear Hunt." Seat the children in a circle or group around the leader. After the leader chants a line, the group repeats the words (and any appropriate motions, if you wish). A sample of a chant follows. Feel free to edit or add to it.

   Let's go on a space trip.
   Let's pack our bags.
   Don't forget your toothbrush.
   Let's climb aboard.
   Strap yourself in.
   Count down—10, 9, 8, 7, 6, 5, 4, 3, 2, 1, zero, lift-off!
   We're going faster! Hold tight!
   Now we're in space.
   Oh look I see the moon!
   It's big:
   Can't go over it, can't go under it, let's go around it.
   Now I see a planet.
   Can't go over it, can't go under it, let's go around it.
   Look, there's the sun.
   It's so bright it hurts my eyes
   We're turning back.
   I see the planet;
   I see the moon.
   Look, there's the earth.
   It's getting closer
   The parachute is open.
   We're floating down to a soft landing on Earth.

   b. "Stars Shining." This adaptation of a simple counting song from Texas easily lends itself to a chant.

   By 'n by, By 'n by
   Stars shining
   Number, number one, number two, number three
   Oh my, by'n by, by'n by
   Oh my, by'n by

Repeat, counting up to ten. (The last verse will have four numbers instead of three.)

Children enjoy counting their fingers, or give each of ten children a star to hold, and children can count these.

   c. "Hickory, Dickory, Dare." This is an adaptation of an old counting-out rhyme.

   Hickory, dickory, dare.
   A spaceship flew up in the air.
   An astronaut in white guided its flight.
   Hickory, dickory, dare.

   d. "Sally Go Round the Sun." This old children's singing game from South Carolina works well as a chant. Children join hands in a circle. They skip (or jog) around to the left for the first line, change direction, and skip (or jog) to the right for the second line. At the word "boom," everyone squats down or falls to the ground.

   Sally go round the sun, Sally go round the moon,
   Sally go round the sunshine every afternoon. Boom!

   e. "We're Flying to the Moon." Sing this to the tune of "The Farmer in the Dell." Accompany the song with appropriate hand or body motions. Below is the first line of each verse.

   We're flying to the moon. . . .
   We're going in a spacecraft. . . .
   We're flying to the moon. . . .
   We're walking in space. . . .
   We're landing on the moon. . . .
   We're walking on the moon. . . .
   We're Collecting rocks. . . .
   We're Flying back to Earth. . . .
   We're Landing on the Earth. . . .
   This tune is a natural for teachers and children to adapt. Another version might focus on how astronomers use telescopes to observe space:
   We want to see the planets. . . .
   We're focusing our telescopes. . . .
   We're looking through our telescopes. . . .

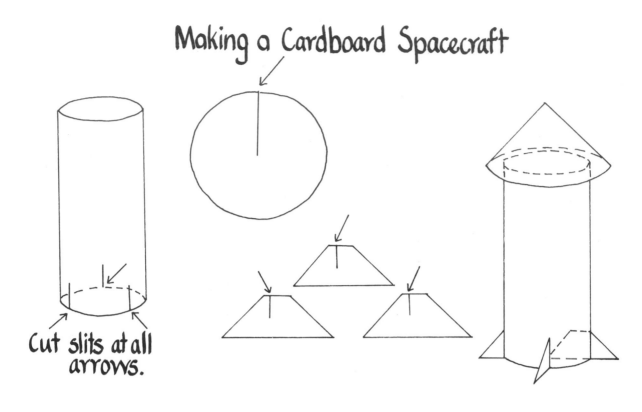

Making a Cardboard Spacecraft

Cut slits at all arrows.

Figure 9.2 *Cardboard Tubes Make Simple Spacecraft*

5. ***Creating a Predictable Book.*** Read the book *Brown Bear, Brown Bear, What Do You See?* by Bill Martin, Jr. Emphasize the rhythm of the sentences as you read. Explain to children that today they are going to write a book with the same kind of rhythm, only theirs will be about space. Begin with the words, "Astronomer, astronomer, what do you see? I see a red planet looking at me. Red planet, red planet what do you see? I see a _____ ." Encourage children to fill in a color and an object that may be seen in space. Write down the children's ideas, adding new stanzas. When the last stanza has been written, repeat each of the objects, from first to last. ("I see a red planet, a silver star, and so on, looking at me.")

*6. ***Tour for an Alien.***
   General Purpose: For children to gain experience with written language.

   TFPs: 5, 75, 76.

   Materials: Writing paper, drawing paper, crayons or markers; a list of space concepts to use as a reference. *The Little*

Prince by Antoine de Saint-Exupery could be read as an introduction to this activity. (Point out that it is a fantasy.)

Procedure:
a. Explain that you're pretending that an alien from another world is coming to visit Earth. Point out that no one has evidence, so far, that people or other creatures live in other parts of space, but that humans are very curious about whether life-forms exist in places we've not discovered yet.

b. Challenge the children to think about things in their world that they would especially want to explain or show to aliens. Suggest that they describe their favorite places to go, things to see, foods, toys, and so on.

c. Begin making a list, headed "Tour of Our Earth," as children offer suggestions. Some children may need little prompting beyond the above categories. Other children may require lots of encouragement. Respond to each idea with enthusiasm or praise: "You thought of showing our visitor the amusement park! Good idea! What places in the park would you visit first?" "Margaret would want the visitor to taste a hamburger. Tell me how you think this alien would eat food."

d. Offer drawing paper to children who wish to illustrate their ideas. Paste or staple parts of the list to each picture.

e. Some children may want to draw pictures of the space alien or describe how it might look.

Hint for Success:

• Carry out this activity with a small number of children at a time. Then read the tour itinerary to the rest of the children.

How to Simplify this Activity:

• Provide pictures of familiar places to stimulate children's ideas.

How to Extend this Activity:

• Introduce space TFPs when possible to encourage children's ideas. Talk about the many stars and planets people have seen but have been unable to explore up close. Talk about the new techniques to learn more about space that are being developed every day. Talk about the special needs of humans during space exploration (for cooling or warming the body, for an oxygen source, for special foods and clothes that are functional in zero gravity, etc.). How might space aliens deal with these conditions?

Physical

1. *Cardboard Spacecraft.* Collect enough toilet paper rolls for each child to have at least two. Draw circles on cardboard that are one inch larger in diameter than the end of the toilet paper roll. Draw a line from the edge of the circles to the centers. Ask children to cut out the circles and slit them along the line. Help them bend their circles into a cone shape and tape them in place. Dip the end of the rolls in glue. Attach them to the nose cones. Cut out three small flat-topped cardboard triangles. Make a slit in each and a corresponding slit in the open end of each roll. Put them together to act as wings to stabilize the spacecraft. (Figure 9.2)

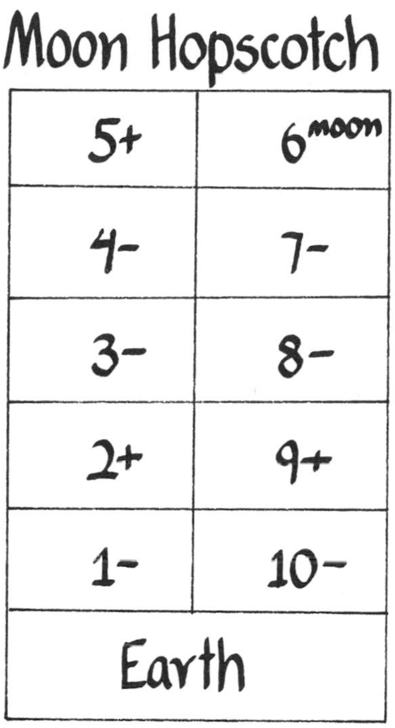

Moon Hopscotch

5+	6 moon
4-	7-
3-	8-
2+	9+
1-	10-
Earth	

Figure 9.3 *A Variation on the Traditional Hopscotch Game*

2. *Starlight.* Draw star shapes of various sizes on construction paper or oak tag. Make a variety of shapes so that children understand that stars in space are not five-pointed objects. Have children cut out the shapes. Hang them around the room and from the ceiling. Make mobiles of stars by attaching strings and hanging them from hangers. Older children can trace the shapes themselves or draw them freehand. Provide aluminum foil to wrap around the oak tag stars or have glitter available to decorate them.

3. *Moon Hopscotch.* Hopscotch is an ancient game whose origins are unclear. Variants have been found all over the world. The diagram in Figure 9.3 is from Holland. The general rules are that players toss a pebble or other marker into a square and hop or jump around it and over it, turning back at the top. They retrieve the marker on the way back and continue by tossing it to the next box. Under no circumstances is the player to hop into the square that contains the marker. Rather than playing this game competitively, give each child a turn. In this version of the game, the boxes

marked (–) must be hopped on using one foot, the boxes marked (+), using two feet. The "moon" box is out of bounds. Ignore these signs with younger children.

4. **Parachute Lift-Off.** In an open area, instruct children to hold on to the edges of a parachute or a large sheet. Explain that children will work together at a signal to pretend to lift-off, just as spacecraft do. Have children squat down and then count down. On the words "Lift-Off" children stand up and lift the parachute high in the air, allowing it to hang there as long as possible. Repeat the activity using balls or balloons in the center. The object is to keep the balls or balloons bouncing, so vigorous shaking is necessary. Explain that spacecraft use lots of energy to get into space. Have children try to keep one ball or balloon in an orbit around the edge of the parachute by tilting the parachute.

5. **Astronaut Training.** Explain to children the importance of physical fitness in space. Discuss exercises that astronauts do while in weightless conditions in order to keep their muscle tone firm. Choose two or three common fitness exercises, such as jogging in place, jumping jacks, toe touches, and stretches. To recorded music, demonstrate these for children and have them imitate your movements. Carry this out for only a few minutes at first, then gradually increase the number of times children do each exercise. To extend this activity, schedule a specific time for astronaut training exercises each day.

6. **Orbit Game.** This can be done with a small group of children or with the entire class in an area large enough for everyone to move around. Remind children that planets move in orbits around the sun and that they never crash into each other. Tell them that they will pretend to be planets, each moving in his or her own orbit around the sun. (One child may be designated as the sun.) Have ready a record or tape of slow music that sounds "spacelike." Instruct children to begin when the music starts and to stop when the music stops. Describe how a planet turns on its axis while orbiting the sun. This latter step should be introduced after children have had some

practice. Begin the music. Praise children for moving without interfering with the other planets' orbits.

*7. **Space Struts.**
   General Purpose: To engage in activities that require balance.

   TFPs: 35, 37, 45, 52.

   Materials: "Stilts" constructed from large coffee cans in pairs of identical size. Punch holes near the top edge of each with a nail. Thread rope through the holes. Measure rope to a length that children can grasp with elbows slightly bent while standing on top of cans. Knot the rope, to serve as handles. Fill the cans with gravel. Apply plastic covers and tape firmly in place. A grassy area provides some padding in case of falls, though a hard surface (with adult spotters) may be easier to navigate.

   Procedure:
   a. Discuss the effects of wearing space gear. Talk about everyday tasks that are radically affected, such as walking and running. Explain that astronauts feel awkward at first, just as children do.
   b. Invite the children to explore walking on stilts. Instruct them to pull up firmly on the ropes of the stilts, allowing their arms to assist in "lifting" their legs. Very young/inexperienced children will need an adult hand to "walk." Older children may be able to move about quite skillfully. Experiment with different amounts of weight by varying the substances with which you fill pairs of cans.

Hint for Success:
- Children may take many attempts before using the stilts successfully, so have them available for several days.

How to Simplify this Activity:
- Begin with unweighted cans, until children are able to coordinate their hands and legs.

How to Extend this Activity:
- Encourage children to walk on a taped or chalk-marked path; draw curved lines for them to follow and corners for them to turn as they become more skilled.

Pretend Play

1. *Space Station/Spaceship/Satellite.* Set up an area of the room to resemble a space vehicle. Provide a place where the pilot or commander steers the craft (include a panel with real or pretend dials, headphones, a "viewing screen," microphone, star charts, and maps); an area where the astronauts eat and sleep (include mats or lounging chairs with belts attached as seat belts, cubbies to store pretend food, small baggies with straws); lifelines from the "inside" of the spacecraft reaching "outside" into space; and pretend helmets and large coats and boots for out-of-ship exploration. If possible, hang a few items from the ceiling, such as pencils or headphones, to suggest weightless conditions. Prior to the children's play, discuss the roles they might take: pilot, star mapper, journal writer, planet explorer, repair person, and communication person.

2. *Mount (your school's name) Observatory.* The observatory should be set up in two sections: the dome for viewing the sky and the astronomer's living quarters. (A standard, one-room "house" area is appropriate for this, but eliminate the dolls and doll equipment.) In the observatory, put black paper on the windows or on a wall designated as "space." Glue or tape stars and planets on the paper. If you wish, also include pictures or drawings of spacecraft, comets, and so on. Provide a table with paper and pencils for making sky charts, kaleidoscopes, magnifying glasses, and prisms. A "computer" set-up is also appropriate. Provide small tube telescopes (made from paper towel rolls) and, if possible, a large telescope made from a rug roll tube or a mural paper roll. Mount this on an angle (braced by chairs) so that it points toward the window or sky wall. A discarded radio makes a good instrument for "aiming" the telescope. (Figure 9.4) Include children's reference books or picture books that depict the sky. Encourage children to take on a variety of roles: astronomers, night assistants (who help run the telescope), data reduction specialists (who analyze what has been observed), food preparers, and servers. Involve older chil-

Telescope for Observatory

Fasten with rope or tape.

Figure 9.4 *A Mailing Tube Makes a Great Pretend Telescope*

dren in making the props. Each day add new ones that children have constructed.

3. *Astronaut Training Center.* Introduce this activity with a discussion of how astronauts train to make sure they are physically fit for the rigors of space travel. Set aside an area for a fitness center, with several of the following props: mats, mirrors, a stationary bicycle (if available), scales, pretend weights (made of tubes and cardboard wheels), an area for aerobic workouts (records or tapes may be included), and an obstacle course. Remind children that flexibility and agility are as important for astronauts as strength. To extend this activity, include a good nutrition area, in which budding astronauts can sample dried fruits and vegetables and reconstituted beverages or camping food.

4. *Lunar Surface.* Set up a sample planetary or lunar surface (for Mars use red sand; for the moon, grey or brown sand, gravel, and rocks) in a sand table or similar container. Provide shovels, screens or sieves, and small bags (for collecting). Tell children that they have just landed on Mars, or the moon, and that their job is to collect samples to bring back to Earth. Children can also be encouraged to explore the surface,

to study the impact of meteors (small rocks dropped onto the sand from a foot or two above), or to discover other living creatures on some unnamed and, as yet, undiscovered planet far out in space.

5. ***Mission Control.***
General Purpose: To encourage children's enactment.
TFPs: 24, 58–66, 69, 70.

Materials: Pictures of mission control, construction or actual space maps, cardboard boxes with attached or illustrated knobs, dials, viewing screens; headphones (these can be discarded sets from radios, etc., or constructed with plastic headbands or long pipe cleaners with Styrofoam cups, cut about 2″ tall and attached), microphones (sections of hose can be used), clipboards, paper and writing tools, telephones, uniform hats and/or coats. You can provide some or all of the preceding props, as well as any other space-related pictures or materials. Tables and chairs can also be provided. Post a list of TFPs for adult reference.

Procedure:
a. Set up an area prior to children's arrival. Make a MISSION CONTROL sign with a sheet of the paper and hang it over the area. Display pictures at child's-eye level. Set "control boxes" on tables, hang "uniforms" on chair backs, and so on.
b. Invite children to explore the area. Offer occasional mention of the above TFPs, as necessary to extend play. Encourage children's imaginations, while modeling some appropriate behavior, dialogue, and uses of materials. "This is shuttle commander Smith calling Mission Control: Could you give me an update on the weather there in Michigan? How is it looking for our scheduled landing?" (Wait for replies.) Turn roles over to observing children, when possible: Handing a section of microphone-hose to a child, say "Mission Control, Astronaut LaToya has an amazing view out of her spaceship window to tell you about. Go ahead La-Toya, tell them about that planet we're looking at!"

Hint for Success:
• Limit the number of children permitted to play in Mission Control at any one time. Provide four or five tags or Mission Control badges for children to wear in the area. Children should hang these near the entrance to the play area when they are finished playing there so others will know that play spaces are available.

How to Simplify this Activity:
• Provide a less elaborate set-up with fewer props.

How to Extend this Activity:
• Conduct an "interview" of a Mission Control expert. Introduce yourself as a television or newspaper reporter. Request time to clear up some questions your viewers/readers have. Refer to TFP list for question ideas, or ask about the function of their equipment. Carry a clipboard or tape recorder, to record the answers. Model this role, then turn it over to a child.

Social

1. ***Friendly Contact.*** Select a piece of music that has a space theme or feeling. Tell children that each one of them is going to be a spacecraft moving in space. When the music stops, they are to quickly find another spacecraft to rendezvous with. They can "hook up" by linking arms, touching shoulders, standing back-to-back, or by any other means of physical contact that is agreeable to both. Remind children that real spacecraft do not collide with each other or with other objects in space.
2. ***Travel Tips.*** Involve children in making rules regarding the number of youngsters allowed in pretend play. At the beginning

of the unit, discuss the set-up for the week with the entire group. Explain the type of toys or props that will be available and tell children that they can decide now how many people can play in the area at a time and what their conduct should be. Discuss also how new people who want a chance to play can get involved. Solicit suggestions from the group and write them down on a large sheet of paper. Limit the number of rules to four or five so children can remember them. Post the list of rules in the play area and, whenever necessary, remind children of them and help children carry out the terms of the rules (how long one mission is to last, etc.). At the end of the day (or week), evaluate the rules with the group and make suggested modifications.

3. ***Mission Possible.*** Ask each child to choose two other children to go along with him or her on a space mission. Explain that real space journeys require people with many different skills and capabilities. Find out on what basis children have made their choices. You can obtain interesting information about children's friendships from these groupings. Group children's preferred playmates together when assigning children to small-group projects. Point out to children similarities in their choices. Each of these will promote greater friendships among the children.

*4. ***Link-ups in Space.***

General Purpose: To help children develop cooperative behaviors.

TFPs: 35, 37–42, 52.

Materials: Discarded bicycle inner tubes in the largest available size or stretch ropes, purchased or constructed from heavy-weight elastic knotted to form a loop about six feet in diameter, or large plastic hoops.

Procedure:

a. Introduce the activity by describing a rendezvous in space, a carefully planned meeting of vehicles and/or persons. Discuss the "link-ups" that can be accomplished, either with special equipment built into the vehicles, or when two or more astronauts secure themselves together to explore space without becoming separated from each other or their vehicle. Discuss the level of cooperation necessary to the success of these missions.

b. Pair the children and give each two an inner tube or plastic hoop. Demonstrate that two children can stand inside the tube together. In order to move as a team, communication and planning are important. If one person goes right and the other left, no progress is made.

c. Help children figure out what signals they will give to each other.

Hint for Success:
- This activity requires considerable space if many pairs are involved at once. It can be done outside, winter or summer, or as a free-choice offering, limited to two or three pairs at a time.

How to Simplify this Activity:
- Instruct both children to face the same direction. As they become more skillful, have them try to move while facing one another.

How to Extend this Activity:
- Encourage pairs of children to take turns as leader and assistant. The leader tells the other where they will go.
- Explain about orbiting objects in space and encourage children to try this. Have one child in the pair orbit the other and then have pairs of children orbit the other pairs.

TEACHER RESOURCES

Field Trip Ideas
1. Take the children to visit a planetarium. (Make sure that the show is appropriate for your age group. Let the director know what the children have been studying).
2. Take the children to a science or space center.

Classroom Visitors

1. Invite an amateur or professional astronomer to bring in a telescope for children to examine and look through. Contact the Astronomical League, P.O. Box 3332, Des Moines, Iowa 50316, for information about astronomy groups in your area.
2. Ask a meteorologist to describe how pictures from space are used in weather prediction, tracking storms, and so on.
3. Find a science-fiction writer (or avid science-fiction reader) to discuss the relationship between real science and science fantasy.

Children's Books

Asimov, I. *The Best New Thing*. Winter Park, FL: World, 1971.

Barton, B. *I Want to be an Astronaut*. New York: Crowell, 1988.

Fuchs, E. *Journey to the Moon*. New York: Delacorte, 1969.

Henbest, N. *Spotter's Guide to the Night Sky*. New York: Usborne, 1979.

Hillert, M. *Up, Up and Away*. Chicago: Follett, 1982.

Langseth, M., and L. Langseth. *Apollo Moon Rocks*. New York: Coward, McCann and Geoghegan, 1981.

Lord, S., and J. Epstein. *A Day in Space*. New York: Scholastic, 1986.

Martin, B., Jr. *Brown Bear, Brown Bear, What Do You See?* Toronto: Holt, Rinehart and Winston, 1982.

Moché, D. L. *The Astronauts*. New York: Random House, 1978.

——. *If You Were an Astronaut*. New York: Golden, 1985.

——. *My First Book About Space*. New York: Golden, 1982.

The Moon. London: Macdonald and Co., 1971.

Myring, L. *Finding Out About Rockets and Spacelight*. New York: Hayes Books, 1982.

Oxenbury, H. *Tom and Pippo See the Moon*. New York: Aladdin Books, 1988.

Patton, J. *Astronomy*. Chicago: Rand McNally, 1982.

Petty, K. *The Planets*. New York: Franklin Watts, 1984.

Quakenbush, R. *The Boy Who Dreamed of Rockets*. New York: Parents, 1978.

Reigot, B. P. *A Book About Planets*. New York: Scholastic, 1981.

Ride, S., and S. Okie. *To Space and Back*. New York: Lothrop, Lee and Shepard, 1986.

de Saint-Exupery, A. *The Little Prince*. New York: Reynel and Hitchcock, 1943.

Snowden, S. *The Young Astronomer*. Tulsa, OK: Hayes Books, EDC, 1983.

Tabrah, R. *The Old Man and the Astronauts*. Honolulu: Island Heritage, 1975.

Wheat, J. K. *Let's Go to the Moon*. Washington, DC: National Geographic Society, 1977.

Adult References

Apfel, N. H. *The Moon and Its Exploration*. New York: Franklin Watts, 1982.

Cowley, S. *Space Flight*. Chicago: Rand McNally, 1982.

DiCerto, J. J. *From Earth to Infinity*. New York: Messner, 1980.

Maurer, R. *The NOVA Space Explorer's Guide*. New York: Clarkson N. Potter, 1985.

Oberg, A. *Spacefarers of the '80s and '90s*. New York: Columbia University Press, 1985.

Schulke, F., D. Schulke, P. McPhee, and R. McPhee. *Your Future in Space*. New York: Crown, 1986.

Part II

Science
Concepts

Chapter 10

Plants

Plants are part of each child's natural environment. Children come into contact with plants every day—picking dandelions, examining withered blossoms on the windowsill, smelling freshly cut grass, biting into a crunchy apple, helping peel potatoes, or swishing through newly fallen leaves. Through hundreds of similar day-to-day experiences children first become aware of plants, and through the active use of all their senses they learn more about them. Some lucky youngsters have access to knowledgeable persons eager to share what they know about the plant world.

PURPOSE

Our aim in developing a unit on plants is to help teachers create an environment in which all of these learning elements are present. Consequently, the activities focus on giving children numerous firsthand opportunities to experience plant life. They also take advantage of children's natural inclinations to touch, smell, taste, and explore. Simultaneously, the activities are designed to help children understand how plants grow and how they benefit the world. This is accomplished both through self-discovery and through the receipt of relevant information from adults and peers.

Since the potential pool of information related to the concept "plants" is immense, one might pursue many different directions in creating a theme on the topic. To make the material more manageable, we have chosen to limit our focus to seed plants. We highlight the characteristics of such plants and what they require to grow and flourish, as well as people's reliance on plants as a source of food.

IMPLEMENTATION

We expect that teachers will explore these introductory ideas using plants common to their locale, thereby enhancing the relevance of the children's experience. Moreover, we assume that depending on the interests of the children, the prologue to plant life offered in this chapter could be expanded to include:

• The study of particular types of plants (cacti, trees, grains, grasses, fruits and vegetables, etc.).

• The propagation and cultivation of plants (from seeds, bulbs, corms, cuttings, or a study comparing plants that grow in the soil with those that grow in water).

• Plants as a food source for particular animals.

• Plants as a source of clothing and shelter for people.

• The role of plants in the ecological balance.

Finally, we realize teachers will not confine the study of plants to only one segment of the school year. Related activities (such as charting the growth of a fast-growing plant, making leaf rubbings, or going on a nature walk) can and should be integrated into the context of everyday classroom life.

However, we also know that the concentrated study of plants piques children's interest in subsequent nature-based activities and that it is a favorite theme for children and grown-ups alike. The following options offer ways in which a plant unit might be structured.

Option One: Focus on TFPs 1 through 27 plus a few TFPs from the other subsections. This will provide children with a general overview to plants lasting two or three weeks.

Option Two:
Week One: Provide a general introduction to plants.
Week Two: Focus on roots and stems.
Week Three: Focus on leaves.
Week Four: Focus on flowers and seeds.

Option Three: Select one subtopic, such as leaves, to focus on for a week or two. Introduce that unit in the fall, then repeat it in the spring, building on what children have learned as well as contrasting leaves and leaf growth during two different seasons.

TERMS, FACTS, AND PRINCIPLES

General Information

1. Plants are living things that have no sensory organs and cannot move from place to place on their own.

2. Plants grow; they change in size and develop more parts.

3. In order to grow, plants require light, water, air, and nutrients.

4. Green plants make their own food using air, water, and nutrients.

5. Plants get nutrients from water and the soil.

6. Plants vary in size from tiny algae to huge trees.

7. Different plants have various growing habits: some grow upright, others grow along the ground, others need some sort of physical support in order to flourish.

8. Plants grow toward sunlight and around obstacles.

9. Some parts of plants move from one place to another by riding on the wind, or being carried on insects, animals, and people.

10. Plants grow in most places on the earth.

11. The same plants grow in different parts of the world.

*12. Most plants need particular outdoor conditions of rainfall, soil, and temperature (arid, temperate, tropical) to grow well.

13. Plants are called by a variety of common names, depending on the culture of the people who live in that region.

14. Some plants grow in the wild, others must be planted by people.

15. Plants may be planted indoors or outdoors.

*16. All plants have a Latin first and last name that is the same all over the world.

*17. Transplanting involves carefully taking the plant out of its container and putting it into a larger container or into the ground.

18. Outdoor gardening often requires special tools—shovels, hoes, rakes, and trowels— to prepare the ground for planting.

19. When people pull unwanted plants from gardens they are weeding.

20. When people collect plants they want or need they are harvesting.

21. The edible parts of some plants are called vegetables.

22. The part of a plant that encases the seeds and can be eaten is the fruit.

23. Some plants and fruits are not safe to eat.

24. Plants are used as food by other plants, insects, animals, and people.

25. People use parts of plants to make things (furniture, paper, chewing gum, glue, cloth, medicines, and lumber).

26. Many animals use plants to construct their homes (squirrel and bird nests, insect hives, deer shelters).

Parts of Plants

27. Plants have many parts (roots, stems, leaves, flowers, seeds).

Roots

28. Roots of most plants grow in the ground or under the surface of the ground.

29. Roots grow away from light and where water is available.

30. The roots hold the plant in place so wind and water can't carry it away.

31. Roots absorb water and nutrients from the soil and carry them to the stems of the plant.

32. People and animals eat the roots of some plants (carrots, potatoes, radishes).

Stems

33. Stems grow above the ground.

34. Stems support the leaves and flowers of plants.

35. Some stems are stiff and hard (tree trunks); some stems are soft and bendable (ivy vines).

36. Stems carry water and nutrients from the roots to other parts of the plant.

37. People and animals eat the stems of some plants (celery, asparagus, sugar cane, bamboo).

Leaves

38. Leaves grow on the stems of plants.

39. Leaves vary in many ways (size, shape, color, texture, thickness).

40. Each type of plant has its own special kind of leaves.

41. Differences in leaves help people identify plants.

*42. Leaves may grow in simple form (single leaves, such as on maple or oak trees), or compound form (several leaves growing from a single stem, such as on elder or locust trees).

43. Leaves begin as tiny buds and grow larger as the plant matures.

44. Leaves make food for the rest of the plant.

45. Most leaves are flat so they have a surface exposed to the sun.

*46. Leaves contain a substance called chlorophyll that helps turn water, air, and light energy into food for the plant.

*47. The process by which a plant turns water, air, and the sun's energy into food for the plant is called photosynthesis.

*48. When a plant contains lots of chlorophyll, it looks green; when it has less chlorophyll, other colors show in the leaves and stems.

49. Leaves may change color during different seasons.

*50. Many trees stop making food in the fall, and the green chlorophyll goes away, allowing other colors to show (yellow, orange, brown, red).

51. Many trees lose their leaves in the fall. When the earth around the tree gets colder there is less water for the tree to use, and it begins to store moisture for the winter. The tree grows a layer of cork at each leaf stem to block any water from leaving the tree through its leaves. The leaves dry up and wind blows them to the ground.

52. Some trees do not lose their leaves and their leaves do not change color. They are called evergreen trees.

53. People and animals eat the leaves of some plants (lettuce, spinach, collard greens).

Flowers

54. All seed plants grow flowers.

55. Flowers produce seeds that can grow into new plants.

56. Flowers vary in size, shape, color, and number.

57. Buds may contain tiny flowers that have not opened yet.

58. When flower buds grow bigger and are ready to open they bloom.

59. Different flowers bloom at different times of the year, depending on how warm it is and how much light is available.

60. Flowers have parts on the outside (petals) and the inside (ovule, pistil, stamen, stigma).

61. Flower petals are separate and often colorful flaps that attract insects and protect the internal flower parts.

62. The internal parts of a flower together make seeds that can produce new plants and flowers.

63. Flowers produce a substance called pollen that is used by other flowers to make seeds.

64. Insects, birds, and animals help flowers by carrying pollen from flower to flower.

*65. Flowers attract insects, birds, and animals by their color, scent, or nectar (a liquid inside the flower).

*66. Some pollen is very dry and blows from flower to flower.

67. Pollen is often yellow (a color that attracts insects).

*68. Some pollen is sticky and sticks to creatures who visit the flower. It then rubs off on other flowers they visit.

69. Many flowers can close up tightly to keep their pollen safe and dry.

70. People and animals eat the flowers of some plants (zucchini blossoms, broccoli tops).

Seeds

71. Seeds come from the flowers or fruits of plants and can grow into new plants.

72. Seeds look different from each other in size, shape, color, and texture.

73. Some seeds have two halves (dicot), such as peanuts, beans, and peas. Other seeds do not (monocot), such as corn, grasses, wheat, and oats.

74. Inside the seed coat is food for the plant and a baby plant (embryo).

75. When seeds begin to grow they are sprouting or germinating.

Leaf Painting

Paint the leaf well.

Press painted side down with cardboard.

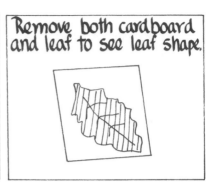
Remove both cardboard and leaf to see leaf shape.

Figure 10.1 *Leaf Prints Made Simple*

76. Seeds need water, warmth, and air to sprout.

77. Some kinds of seeds sprout more quickly than others.

*78. Seed growth follows a predictable pattern: soak up water, seed case breaks open, roots form, stem begins to grow, and finally leaves begin to develop.

*79. Seeds can be planted and grow indoors in pots of soil, or outdoors in the ground as long as it is warm enough.

*80. The size of a seed is not related to the size of the mature plant that grows from it. (Tiny acorns grow into huge oak trees.)

81. People and animals eat the seeds of some plants (pecans, rice, peas, popcorn, peanuts, coconuts).

82. People use the seeds of some plants to make other foods. (Wheat, oats, corn, and rice are used to make bread and cereals.)

83. People and animals eat some fruits that contain seeds that can be eaten (tomatoes, strawberries, blackberries, okra, bananas).

*84. Seeds are scattered by nature in many different ways. Some stick to animal fur and are dropped, some are blown by the wind, some seeds scatter as their cases pop open, some seeds are eaten by birds and excreted elsewhere.

*85. Some plants produce seeds year after year; some plants die after they have produced seeds only once.

ACTIVITY IDEAS

Aesthetic

1. *Plant Prints.* Gather several healthy green leaves that have prominent veins and interesting shapes. Point out the parts of a leaf, paying particular attention to the veins. Offer children lumps of plasticine (nondrying clay), potter's clay (the kind that dries), or modeling dough. Using a rolling pin, demonstrate how the children can roll the clay out flat, lay a leaf on the flattened surface, and roll over the leaf surface. Remove the leaf. This will press the leaf into the clay and leave an impression. For a permanent print, allow the clay to dry and harden.

2. *Leaf Paintings.* Collect fresh green leaves that have interesting shapes and well-defined veins. Using thick poster paints in a variety of colors, demonstrate how to brush paint directly onto the leaves, then turn them over and press the wet leaves onto paper. Suggest that children paint the whole leaf especially the edges, on a newspaper-covered table. When they are ready to print the leaf, carefully place it painted side down on clean white paper, cover it with newspaper or cardboard, and press hard. A different way to apply color to the leaf is to use rollers (brayers) and water-soluble printer's ink. This method will give a crisp, satisfying print. (Figure 10.1)

3. *In the Eye of the Beholder.* Select reproductions of two or more famous paint-

ings of plants. (Libraries or schools often have collections from which to borrow.) Choose paintings that show artist's different interpretations of plants. Show children one reproduction at a time. Talk about the way the artist made the picture; ask children to look at the colors and to find the various parts of each plant. Then ask them to compare the paintings, telling which they like more and why. Paintings that would work well are: Van Gogh's *Sunflowers* (1888), Klee's abstract *Flowers in Stone* (1939), and Renoir's *Still Life* (1869). Others to consider are: Picasso's *Fruit Dish* (1908) and Cezanne's *Jug of Milk and Fruit* (1888).

4. *Bark Rubbing.* Outdoors, give each child a piece of white construction paper and large crayons with the paper peeled off. Demonstrate how to hold the construction paper against a tree trunk while rubbing the crayon sideways over it to make an "impression" of the bark. Encourage children to try more than one tree on various parts of their paper, then contrast the different effects.

5. *Hi/Lo Plant Song.* Sing this simple song using the eight notes of the scale. Use hand signals to emphasize ascending and descending pitches.

I Know A Little Pussy
(Author unknown)
I know a lit tle pus sy,
(do do do do do do do)
Her coat is sil ver grey.
(re re re re re re)
She lives down in the mea dow,
(mi mi   mi mi mi mi mi)
Not ve ry far a way.
(fa fa fa fa fa fa)
She'll al ways be a pus sy;
(so   so so so so so so)
She'll nev er be a cat.
(la   la la la la la)
For she's a pus sy wil low;
(ti   ti ti ti ti ti ti)
Now what do you think of that?
(do   do do do do do do)
Meow, meow, meow, meow, meow, meow,
(do   ti   la   so   fa   me
meow . . . Scat!
   re   do)

To emphasize the change in pitch in another way, have children begin singing the song in a crouching position and slowly extend their legs and bodies as the pitch becomes higher, gradually returning to their original crouch on the descending portion of the tune. They can pop up and clap hands on "scat!" In the spring, show children examples of pussywillow branches. Take the children on a walk to find some growing, or ask parents if anyone has some to donate. Encourage children to touch the soft buds developing on the tips of new growth. Repeat the song, focusing on the meanings of the words and the word trick. (The word pussy, meaning cat, is also used to describe this type of plant.) Pussy willow branches will force very easily in a glass or vase of water. In most cases they will develop roots and eventually leaves, and they can then be planted outside.

6. *Plant Collages.* Numerous plant parts could be offered singly or in combination for children to use in making collages or as tools in open-ended art experiences. Sample materials are:

seed casings or seed pods
seeds
leaves from flowers, trees, or shrubs
pine needles
dried flowers
inedible berries from bushes
petals
twigs, bark
stems
roots
grasses
wood shavings, sawdust

For gluing and printing activities, we do not suggest using plant parts that people rely on as primary food sources, such as rice, beans, fruits, or vegetables. We believe it is contradictory to teach children about the importance of such resources in supporting life and then offer them as play materials.

*7. *Flower Pressing.*
General Purpose: For children to use tools and techniques related to the arts to achieve a desired aesthetic effect.
TFPs: 1, 2, 6, 14, 53, 55, 56, 57, 58, 62.

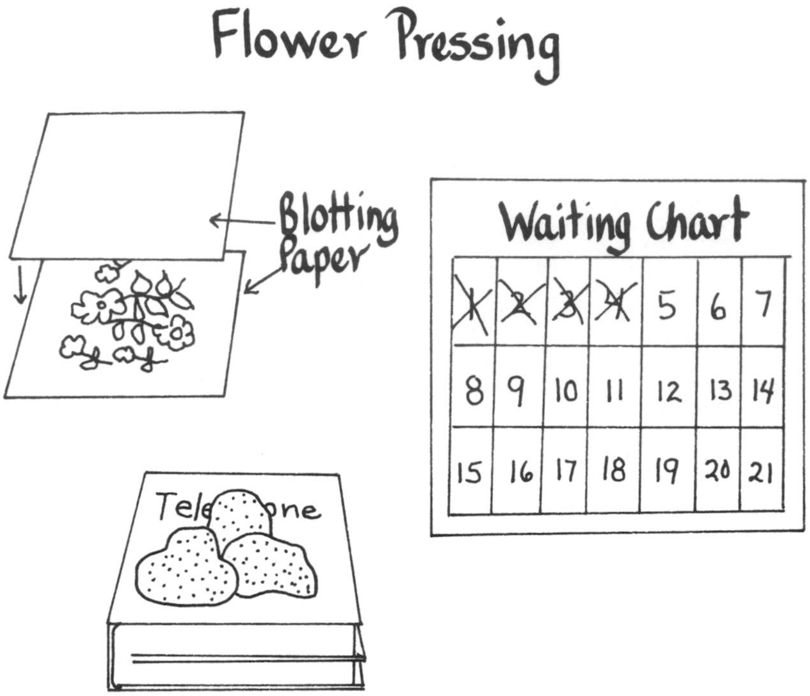

Flower Pressing

Figure 10.2 *Pressing Flowers is Easy and Fun*

Materials: A sample of a pressed flower, absorbent paper such as blotting paper, a flower press (optional) or heavy books (telephone directories work well), flowers, bricks.

Procedure:

a. Explain to the children that flowers wilt and die quickly after being picked. Some people like to preserve their beauty by "pressing" them. Show them a fresh flower, a wilted flower, and a pressed flower. Explain that to preserve flowers, they must be completely dried out. Fresh flowers contain lots of moisture. Pressing them squeezes most of the water out, but it takes a long time.

b. Have the children select flowers for this activity. Take them on a walk to pick some if possible, or bring some to class. Suggest they each choose two or three to preserve.

c. Ask each child to write his or her name on a piece of blotting paper about the size of a telephone book page. Encourage them to arrange their flowers facedown on the paper without overlapping. (Figure 10.2)

Cover the flowers with another piece of blotting paper and carefully place them inside a heavy book such as an old telephone directory. Pile several stones or bricks on top of the book to keep the pressure even. Leave the drying flowers untouched for at least three weeks.

d. Construct a calendar showing the day everyone's flowers can be checked. Mark off the days as the children wait.

e. Pressed flowers are delicate; assist children in removing the top blotting paper. If the flower has not completely dried, suggest that children return them to the book.

f. Dried flowers can be affixed to paper using clear-drying white glue to make a pretty picture.

Hints for Success:

- Thin flowers (forget-me-nots, baby's breath, sea lavender, and pansies) will be nearly dry and flat in three weeks; thicker flowers will take longer.

- Plants for this activity should be gathered on a dry day.

How to Simplify this Activity:

• Use a flower press to dry the flowers following the directions provided.

How to Extend this Activity:

• Suggest children use their pressed flowers to make pretty greeting cards or invitations for a special classroom occasion.

Affective

1. *Fruit Favorites.* Provide a variety of real fruits, suggesting that children handle them, peel or cut them open, taste them, and tell which ones they like the best. Follow up by teaching children the following fingerplay. Give each child a chance to insert the name of his or her favorite fruit in the blanks.

Way Up High in the *Fruit* Tree
Way up high in the (fruit name) tree (bush).
(Point up.)
Two little (fruit name) smiled at me.
I shook that tree (bush) as hard as I could,
(Pretend to shake the plant.)
Down came the (fruit name)
(Fingers flutter downward.)
Umm . . . Were They Good!
(Rub stomach and smile.)

2. *My Own Vegetable Salad.* Either provide salad ingredients and prepare them, or ask parents to send in a sandwich-sized plastic bag containing one ingredient. Include such items as torn lettuce, chopped celery, sliced radishes, chopped tomato, chopped green pepper, and bean sprouts. Explain that each child can choose ingredients to make a personal salad. Give each child a small bowl and invite them to select a variety of ingredients to combine into a salad. Place salad dressings (in squeeze bottles) on the snack table for an additional choice opportunity. As children make their choices, discuss with them what they chose and why.

3. *Seed Taste Test.* Arrange a display of edible seeds (peanuts, sunflower seeds, popped corn, coconuts). Place small individual servings of each in tiny paper cups or muffin papers. Tell children they can take a container of each and taste what's inside. Make a chart showing the seeds and have children put a sticker near the kinds they like best. At the end of the tasting activity, show the chart to the whole group and have them count how many people liked each kind of seed.

4. *How We Use Garden Tools.* Collect some real or toy gardening tools that the group could use to make a garden (shovel, hoe, rake, trowel). Hold up each one, naming it and explaining what kind of work it does in the garden. Ask the children to show with their bodies how they think people use the various tools. Take the group outdoors to your garden site. Demonstrate the actual way to use the tools and invite the children to practice, with adult supervision. Praise all efforts at learning to use the tools appropriately.

5. *My Plant Name.* Teach the children some names of flowers and trees that sound interesting and are fun to say (geranium, snapdragon, leadwort, bellflower, boxwood, morning glory, elderberry, foxglove, etc.). Show them pictures or real specimens of each one. Suggest children choose a flower or tree name to add to their own. Choose one to add to your own name and use it as an example: Blueberry Barb, Goatsbeard Gerry, or Boxwood Bill. Allow children to choose the combination that sounds good to them. Make new nametags for anyone who wants to wear their plant name. Another way to vary this activity is to use the Latin names for different plants along with the children's names.

*6. *My Leaf Study.* After several days of working with plants and plant parts, suggest that the children begin a Leaf Study. Tell them they are going to learn a lot about one leaf by looking at it very carefully just as scientists do. Have the group generate ideas about what to look for in studying their leaves (colors, shape, texture, veins, holes, dirt, insect bites, etc.). Provide a selection of leaves and collect leaves that vary greatly in size, texture, color, and shape. Provide several more leaves than there are children in your group, so that everyone has a "real" choice. Encourage careful examination.

Remind children of some of the things to look for on their leaves. Help them speculate as to why each leaf looks like it does. Ask children to dictate to you some things they noticed about their leaves. Conclude the study by making a rubbing of their leaves or by taping the actual leaf onto the paper.

Cognition

1. *Let's Eat Plant Parts.* Collect a variety of real plant parts eaten by people (lettuce leaves, carrot roots, tomato fruits, celery stems, and so on). Also, gather pictures that correspond to your examples. Show the children each item in its natural state and discuss what part of the plant it represents. Wash and cut up some of each for the children to taste. Put the pile of pictures face down in the center of the table. Ask each child to select one and to taste the corresponding sample. Continue this matching process until the child has had a chance to try several items.

2. *What's Missing? Part I.* Help children locate plant parts by giving each of them a simple plant to take apart. Dandelions (with the roots attached) or inexpensive bedding plants such as marigolds would work well for this activity. Instruct the children to find and remove the plant parts as you name them. Provide a paper plate to catch the soil and plant pieces the children pull off. Next, ask the children to line up all the plant parts they discover, count them, and tell how many of each they found.

3. *What's Missing? Part II.* As a follow-up to the previous activity, display a set of What's Missing? pictures, such as those depicted in Figures 10.3a, 10.3b, and 10.3c, near a tray containing a real plant that has been taken apart. The pictured plant should match the plant on the tray. Suggest that children try to figure out what plant part is missing in each picture by first examining the real plant and then comparing it to those depicted.

4. *Leaf Touch.* Show children a variety of leaves that differ in texture. Have them feel them and compare their surfaces. Some examples of common leaves that would provide variations are: jade (smooth), coral berry (leathery), asparagus fern (soft and feathery), iron cross begonia (bristly), and cryptanthus starlite (prickly).

5. *Leaf Silhouettes.* Collect some fresh leaves that vary in size and shape. Trace them onto black construction paper, cut them out, and mount the black paper silhouettes on a colored background. Ask the children to match each leaf to its silhouette. To keep the fresh leaves from drying out and curling, cover each one with clear contact paper, then cut them out. You could use flower blossoms in this activity as well.

6. *Leaf Treasure Hunt.* Introduce the activity by discussing the fact that leaves are different shapes and by showing the children a sample of leaves they might find outdoors on a Leaf Treasure Hunt. Take the class outside. Give small groups of children a paper bag on which a leaf shape has been glued. Instruct them to find as many real leaves of that shape as they can.

    Encourage children to help each other, rather than making the activity a race or a competition. Point out that leaves of the same shape can be different sizes and colors. Discourage children from picking healthy leaves from trees that need them to produce food. Autumn is a good time to do this activity since the leaves are more likely to be falling and are easily found on the ground.

7. *Traveling Seeds.* Point out that the seeds produced by the "mother plant" need to be carried away to another place so they can start to grow new plants. Show children examples of seeds that travel from place to place by various methods. In the fall, investigate Queen Anne's lace, milkweed, and burdock. In spring, help children discover seeds in dandelions and maple wings. Demonstrate how the seeds may be dispersed by wind, by getting caught on animal fur, or by other means of traveling from the mother plant. Encourage children to participate in seed dispersal by blowing on various seeds or pretending to be seeds traveling away from the mother plant.

8. *Dandelion Circles.* Some fine spring day when the dandelions abound in full bloom, take the children outdoors to a place

What's Missing? ~ Complete Picture

Figure 10.3a *A Complete Picture for the "What's Missing?" Game*

where dandelions are growing. Give all the children an eighteen-inch length of thick, colorful (not green) yarn. Tell each child to make a circle with the yarn on the grass surrounding a bunch of dandelions. Help them to count the number of dandelions in their circles and to record the numbers on a chart. Leaving the yarn on the grass, ask the children to walk all around, looking at the various circles. Tell them to find the circle with the most dandelions, the circle with the fewest dandelions, and so on. Record their ideas, then help them count to see if they were correct.

What's Missing?

Figure 10.3b *What's Missing in These Pictures?*

What's Missing?

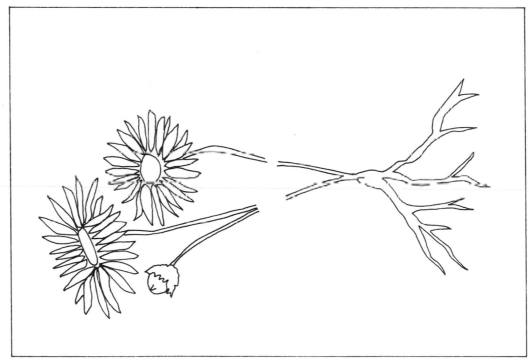

Figure 10.3c *Something Else Is Missing*

9. *Seeds and Not Seeds.* Give children a collection of materials that contain seeds and objects that are not seeds. Provide two trays with signs marked SEEDS and NOT SEEDS. Encourage children to decide on what tray each item should go. After the children have tried this on their own for a few days, do the task as a group to clarify their answers and clear up any misconceptions. Your collection could contain such things as peanuts (in and out of the shell), a whole coconut, peppercorns, kernels of canned corn, pinecones, pebbles, small bits of wood, twigs, chalk pieces, Styrofoam pellets, leaves, peach pits, cherry pits, avocado pits, and so on.

10. *Green is the Color.* Suggest that children can disguise colors just as green chlorophyll hides other colors in leaves of plants. Have children choose several colors of construction paper leaf shapes (any color but green) and paste them onto a background paper. Supply them with thin (but not watery) green poster paint and wide brushes. Have children paint over their pasted leaves, pretending this is chlorophyll, and see what colors show through. Point out that the more paint they apply the greener their leaves will look, just as the more chlorophyll leaves contain, the greener they appear.

11. *Our Seed Collection.* Ask children to bring seeds from home. They could find seeds in fruits, vegetables, or fully developed flowers, or they might purchase seeds. Some families may have partially used seed packets they would be willing to donate. Each day have the children add their seeds to the collection. Display the variety on a large tray. Encourage children to touch, smell, and compare the seeds. You could also make seed packets into a display nearby. Attach one seed with clear tape to the seed packet picture of the plant so children can identify different kinds of seeds in the collection. Offer egg cartons for sorting when the collection gets large and children have investigated the seeds for several days.

12. *Shakedown Survey.* Give each child a one-foot-square piece of black or white felt. Take the group outside, showing children how to gently shake tree and bush branches or flower stalks as they hold their felt piece underneath the plant. After each child has collected several plant "droppings," return indoors. Provide magnifiers and sorting trays for children to use in examining, grouping, and comparing the results of their shakedown survey.

13. *Seed Predictions.* Gather some common fruits and vegetables as well as a few less familiar to the children. Explain that today the group will be doing an experiment to find the seeds within the fruits of certain plants. Hold up each item one at a time and ask children to predict how many seeds it contains. Write down each child's prediction next to his or her name on a chart to help children remember their ideas.

Peel or cut each fruit/vegetable, or have the children do this, and examine and count the seeds. Record their number on your original chart. Once all the fruits/vegetables have been examined, eat them, but keep the seeds to count again.

14. *Leaf Sniffs.* Show children a selection of leaves that have distinctive smells, such as bay leaves, pine needles, mint leaves, and other herbs. Encourage them to sample each fragrance and then match each one by scent to a set of identical leaves that cannot be seen.

15. *Fruits and Vegetables A to Z.* With the children, go through the book *Eating the Alphabet* by Lois Ehlert. (If this book is unavailable to you, collect pictures of fruits and vegetables and label each one, highlighting the first letter of each name. Encourage children to explore these.) Follow up by offering children a set of alphabet letters and a set of fruit/vegetable picture cards, plastic representations, or real fruits and vegetables. Invite children to match the letters to the fruits and vegetables whose names begin with them. Refer children to the book (or the original cards) as a resource and as a way to confirm their ideas.

Extend the activity by assisting children in making a frieze in which each letter is illustrated using the fruit and vegetable pictures. **Note:** Q can be represented by Quince; U can be represented by Ugli fruit; X can be represented by Xigua (pronounced *she gwah*), the Chinese name for watermelon, or X can be skipped.

16. *Flower Visitors.* Provide some actual experience in a flower garden, where children can observe insects flitting from flower to flower. After they are familiar with the terms "pollen" and "nectar," suggest that some children be the flowers growing in the garden. Others could be the insects, birds, or animals that drink the nectar and take the pollen to other flowers. Help the children make "pollen" by tearing yellow construction paper into small pieces. Attach tape rolls to the back of each piece and fasten the "pollen" to those children taking the role of the flowers. Ask children what kind of visitor they are pretending to be. Make suggestions such as a bee, butterfly, beetle, bird, squirrel, and so on. Remind children that when a visitor comes to a flower to smell or nibble, it might take some pollen and put it on the next flower to help that flower make seeds that grow.

*17. *Making Natural Dyes.*

General Purpose: For children to become aware of the wonders of the natural world.

TFPs: 25, 28.

Materials: A variety of plants for making dyes (white or yellow onion skins, yellow or orange marigolds, red beets, blueberries), can opener, white string or strips of white cloth, bowl, waxed paper. Optional: blender.

Procedure:

a. Explain to children that dyes are liquids used to color cloth. Long ago, people used plant parts to make dyes, and such dyes are still used today. Show them the collection of plant parts, naming and discussing each one.

b. Suggest that children may dye some cloth themselves. First, colored liquid must be prepared from the plant. For beet dye, use the liquid from a can of beets or prepare beet dye from scratch (cook fresh beets until soft, peel and cut the beets into pieces, put the beet pieces and a little of the hot cooking water into a blender set on "liquify," strain the liquid).

c. Give each child a chance to dip string and cloth strips into the juice. Explain that the cloth will absorb the color slowly. The longer it sits in the juice, the darker the color. Wait for ten minutes for good color.

d. Suggest that children hang or lay the strings and cloth strips to dry on non-absorbent paper such as waxed paper.

e. When the cloth pieces and strings are dry, show children how to use them for simple weaving or decorating packages.

Hints for Success:

• Soak the materials to be dyed for one hour in a mixture of one gallon hot water, several tablespoons of white vinegar, and at least 1 teaspoon of cream of tartar dissolved in a cup of cool water. This will allow the fibers to absorb the color better and make the color "fast."

• Point out to the children that their fingers and anything else that touches the dye will also turn red for a short while.

• Provide children with smocks and encourage them to wash their hands as soon as possible after handling the fabric pieces.

How to Simplify this Activity:

• Do this in small groups or with only a few children at a time.

How to Extend this Activity:

• For children who show high interest, use the other plants suggested (see materials) to make other dyes. Crush the plants and place each one into a jar with hot water. Stir and allow to sit over night; strain the liquid before using it as a dye.

• The dyes could also be brushed onto the cloth like paint.

*18. *Plant Experiments.*

General Purpose: For children to develop inquiry skills using the scientific method (observe, hypothesize, predict, test, evaluate).

TFPs: Vary according to the experiment chosen.

Materials: Vary according to the experiment chosen.

Experiment E

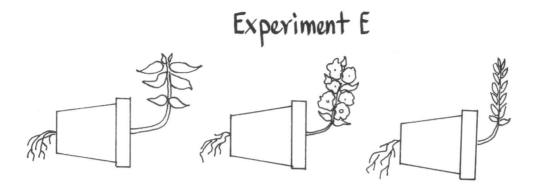

Figure 10.4 *Plant Experiment E*

Experiment A: Do plants really grow toward the light? Materials: a leafy plant, water.

Experiment B: How much water is best for this plant? Materials: three identical plants, three signs indicating three different water amounts (NONE, LITTLE, A LOT), a measuring cup, water.

Experiment C: How much light does this plant need to grow well? Materials: three identical plants, three signs indicating three different light levels (SHADE, LOW LIGHT, BRIGHT LIGHT), water.

Experiment D: What will happen to the flower that we picked? Materials: a fresh blossom, a clear plastic or glass container with a cover.

Experiment E: Do roots always grow down and stems (shoots) on plants always grow up? Materials: three different plants to lay on their sides, water, light. (Figure 10.4)

Experiment F: Will this plant grow without leaves? Materials: a leafy plant, water.

Experiment G: Which seeds will sprout first? Materials: three or four kinds of seeds (radish, bean, marigold), soilless media for planting (available from a greenhouse), cups or pots, pebbles for drainage, labels telling which seeds are in each container, water.

Procedure:

a. Decide which experiment you will try. Gather the necessary materials and encourage children to explore them. After the children have had some time to investigate and handle most of the objects involved, collect and reorganize the materials in a way that focuses the children's attention on the experiment. Tell them that today you will all begin an experiment using these things.

b. Encourage the children to observe and look carefully at the details that pertain to your experiment. Ask them to tell about what they see. (For experiment A they see a healthy, growing plant, sunlight coming through the window, a cardboard box with a hole in it, and a container of water.) Ask questions that will really encourage them to notice things, such as "How do you know this plant is healthy?"

c. Ask the main question of the experiment you have chosen to present. Listen to the answers the children give. Record their guesses or predictions on a chart. Follow up by asking each child to tell why he or she thinks this will happen (to give a hypothesis) and record that on the chart.

d. Carry out the experiment. Be sure to control the circumstances of the test. In experiment A, for instance, be sure to use a healthy plant and put it in a place where it must seek light (such as in a cardboard box as shown in Figure 10.5).

e. Help children evaluate the results of the experiment. What actually happened? Why do they think that happened?

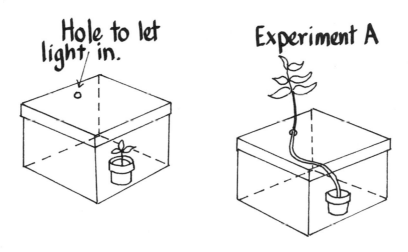

Figure 10.5 *Plant Experiment A*

Review the chart. Were their guesses correct? What do they think now?

Hint for Success:
- Use a simple chart to record the children's guesses and reasoning.

How to Simplify this Activity:
- Carry out one experiment with the whole class. Choose one that is simple and yields quick results, such as experiment A or F.

How to Extend this Activity:
- Divide the class into small groups and carry out one experiment in each. Have each group make its own prediction chart and report to the others after its experiment is completed. Suggest group members dictate a group experience story telling what they did and what happened.

*19. *What's Inside a Seed?*
General Purpose: For children to acquire factual information.

TFPs: 71, 72, 74, 78.

Materials: Large dry lima beans (keep a few dry and soak the rest overnight in water), fruits that have seeds (apples and avocados), table knives, a simple diagram of the inside of a seed.

Procedure:
a. Show children the fruits and have them cut them open to find the seeds inside. Point out the different sizes and kinds of seeds they've discovered.
b. Discuss the fact that there is a baby plant inside each seed that can grow into a new plant. Show the diagram and point to the embryo.
c. Give a few children the dry lima beans to open. They'll discover that this is difficult since the beans have so little moisture in them. Explain that seeds must absorb water before they can open and begin to grow.
d. Show the group how you soaked the lima beans overnight. Give each a presoaked lima bean. Have them carefully remove the seed coat, gently pull apart the two plant food sacks, and find the embryo. Have them compare their discoveries to the diagram. (To avoid soaking, use peanuts instead.)

Hints for Success:
- Demonstrate how to open the seeds before passing them out to the children.
- Select the largest dried limas you can find.

How to Simplify this Activity:
- Show children how the seeds can be opened, then give each child an open seed to examine more closely.

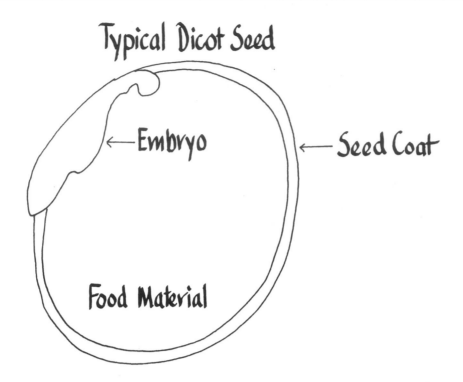

Figure 10.6 *Look Inside the Seed*

How to Extend this Activity:

- Allow the children to discover the seed parts before showing them the diagram. After discovering the various components, suggest they make a picture of their own kind of seed. (Figure 10.6)

- Point out that the "food" for the embryo is also food for people and animals.

- Give children examples of dicot seeds (beans, peanuts, peas) and monocot seeds (corn, wheat, oats, barley) to explore and/or sort.

Construction

1. *Flowers Are Beautiful!* Take the class to visit a greenhouse or garden to see the variety and beauty of the plants and flowers. Ask a knowledgeable person to tour the area with you and the children and offer information about the names of the flowers, what kind of conditions they need, and when they bloom outdoors. Point out the inside and outside of the flowers, the different colors, sizes of blossoms, and fragrances. Return to the classroom and offer paints, crayons, or markers to the children so they can make pictures of their impressions of the plants. Note that the emphasis here is on the children's interpretations rather than on realistic drawings of the plants they saw.

2. *Mix and Match Plants.* Provide children with a variety of pictures of individual plant parts (trunks, stems, branches, leaves, flowers, roots, etc.) made out of construction paper or cut from gardening catalogues. Explain that today everyone will get to invent his or her own plant. Encourage youngsters to select all the parts they will need to make a complete plant and combine them in any way they choose. The final products could be pasted on paper or traded to a friend to be recombined into a new construction.

3. *Support Your Local Plant.* Give children experience seeing and handling roots of plants. Offer them building materials that permit linear constructions, such as plastic connecting blocks or pipe cleaners. Make a cardboard or paper plant and suggest that children build the root system for the plant out of the materials provided.

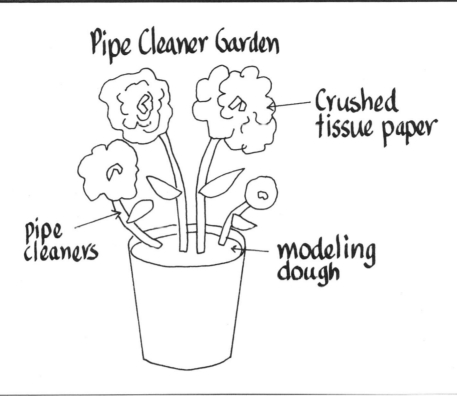

Figure 10.7 *Pipe Cleaner Garden in a Cup*

4. *Up and Down Garden.* Give children experience with a garden by visiting one, by looking at pictures of one, or by growing one. Later, read the book *Planting a Rainbow* by Lois Ehlert, emphasizing the illustrated plant parts above and below the ground. Divide a large mural-sized paper horizontally across the middle to suggest above the ground and below the ground. Tell children that this is a special paper garden where they can see both above and below the ground. Point out the two areas, asking children to think of things they might see in each. Provide materials such as markers, paste, and construction paper pieces or magazine pictures. Ask the children to create their own Up and Down Garden where both the above-ground and below-ground parts of the plants show.

5. *Pipe Cleaner Garden.* After children have experienced a garden, provide materials for them to make their own miniature three-dimensional garden. Offer hardening modeling dough in paper cups, pipe cleaners, tissue paper, and a variety of scrap-paper colors. (Figure 10.7) Demon-strate how to stick the pipe cleaners into the modeling dough to represent stems. Encourage the children to create the rest of the plant using the stems they have made.

Language

1. *Enormous Turnip.* Read *The Great Big Enormous Turnip* by Alexel Tolstoy to the children. Show them a real turnip (preferably with the leaves attached). Discuss how the series of characters worked together to accomplish a task. Act out the story, having volunteers take on roles. Finally, suggest that the children make up their own story incorporating characters who work on a common task.

2. *Plant Detective.* Play a game that encourages children to use words to describe details they notice. Make available two very different-looking plants. Have children generate two lists about the plants, one describing the similarities and the other describing the differences between them.

3. ***This Year's Garden.*** The book *This Year's Garden* by Cynthia Rylant can be a starting point for planning a class garden. Be sure to recruit experienced parents to help with this project. It is critical to select a spot with adequate light, available water, and soil that can be prepared, amended, and fertilized. Read the story to the children and discuss some of the things the family did to prepare for their garden. Help the children make a list of things to do before planting a garden. Draw a diagram of the area you have for planting and ask the children to help plan what to plant. Carry out your plan.

*4. ***We Visited a Flower Shop.*** After visiting a flower shop with the children, ask them to recall some things they saw, heard, smelled, touched, and did there. Explain that they can describe their trip to the flower shop and that you will write it down. Gather the children into a central place and position the large paper where all can see it. Ask questions such as, "Where did we go? Who went? What did we do first?" Write their ideas in sentences using as many of their exact words as possible to help children develop the concept that stories can be their words written down. Read the completed story to them. Display the finished story.

Physical

1. ***Sock Walk.*** In the summer or early fall, discuss the way seeds travel away from the mother plant and are deposited elsewhere. Demonstrate one way this happens by taking children on a Sock Walk. Collect enough old large socks for everyone to have one or two. Have the children wear the socks over their shoes while on a walk outdoors. Tell them to swish their feet in dry leaves, across an open field, or through the natural parts of a playground. Have them carefully remove the socks and notice any seeds that may be sticking to them. Examine the seeds; try planting some.

2. ***Stem Streaming.*** After learning the parts of plants and what they do, have the children pretend to be the stem of a plant.

Help them stand in a line and try to pass cups of water up to the leaves and flowers without spilling any. This is a good activity to do outdoors on a warm day.

3. ***Sunlight-Grow.*** Play a game similar to the traditional one of Red Light, Green Light. Have one child be the leader, holding a sign with a bright sun on one side and a cloud on the other. Everyone else pretends to be a plant that can grow a little whenever the sun shines. To play the game, ask the leader to stand in front of the group holding the sign. When the leader shows the sun and says "Sunlight-Grow," the plants crouch low and grow by coming up slowly and developing branches until the sign is turned around to show a cloud. When the leader says "Cloudy-Stop," everyone must stop growing until the sun shines again. Have children take turns being the leader. Avoid the competition of the original version of this game by not eliminating those who fail to stop growing. Praise all children for growing and trying to stop according to the signals.

4. ***Leaf Bounce.*** Get the children to rake up a pile of dry leaves outdoors. Have everyone hold the edges of a parachute or large sheet; fill the parachute with leaves and have fun bouncing the leaves out by making wave motions.

5. ***Mighty Fine Finger Foods.*** All of the following recipes can be used to enhance children's fine motor skills. In carrying them out, encourage youngsters to do as much as they can on their own. Also, talk about what part of the plant each recipe features.

Leafy Green Salad
Ingredients:
Choose three or more of the following greens:
Spinach
Leaf lettuce
Iceberg lettuce
Red lettuce
Dandelions greens
Endive

Procedure:

1. Wash leaves.
2. Tear into bite-sized pieces.
3. Toss together in a bowl.
4. Serve plain or with a simple olive oil and wine vinegar dressing.

Seed Pod Treats

Ingredients:

Snow peas or sugar snap peas

Utensils:

Large covered pot

Slotted ladle or large spoon

Wire basket

Procedure:

1. Wash vegetables.
2. Show children how to remove the "string" and tips from each pod.
3. Bring water to a rolling boil.
4. Blanch (dunk in boiling water) peas 15–30 seconds.
5. Drain.
6. Run cold water over pods.
7. Drain a second time.
8. Serve and eat.

Peeled Fruits

Offer children different varieties of oranges, tangerines, and/or tangelos to peel and then break into segments. Ask children to compare the relative ease with which they are able to peel the various fruits.

Roll-Cut Roots/Stems

Ingredients:

1½ lb. carrots or

1½ lb. asparagus

Vegetable peeler

Butter knives

Large covered pot

Procedure:

"Roll-cutting" is a classic Chinese method for cutting long, cylindrical vegetables. To roll cut, first slice off the bottom end of the vegetable at a 25° angle. Roll the stalk a quarter turn away from you, then cut on the diagonal 1½ inches farther up the stem/root. Continue rolling and cutting on the diagonal until the entire stalk is cut into segments.

1. Assist children in washing and scraping the vegetables.
2. Blanch (dunk in boiling water) the vegetables 30–60 seconds yourself, drain and run cold water over them.
3. Show children how to roll-cut and let them do it.
4. Combine the following ingredients to make a dressing:

    1 T. plus 2 tsp. of sesame oil (found in Asian groceries)

    4 T. brown or white sugar

    2 tsp. white vinegar

    2 tsp. regular soy sauce

5. Toss dressing with vegetables.
6. Chill one hour.
7. Serve.

*6. ***Plant Mazes.***

General Purpose: For children to coordinate digital, finger-thumb, and eye-hand movement.

TFPs: 6, 7, 28.

Materials: Teacher-made mazes, writing instruments (markers, crayons, pencils).

Procedure:

a. Show the plant mazes to the children, pointing out the roots, stems, and other plant parts. Tell them that these are special plants that show the path inside where the water moves. Point to the maze part.

b. Suggest that each child choose a writing instrument to trace the maze inside the plant picture. Encourage them to find the root end and stay within the stem until they arrive at the flower.

c. Praise all attempts to stay within the paths.

Hint for Success:

- Make a sequence of mazes that become increasingly more difficult. If a child is having great difficulty staying within the lines of one of the mazes, this may indicate that he or she needs a less complex one. If so, provide it.

How to Simplify this Activity:

- Suggest that children trace the path with their finger before giving them a writing instrument.

- Provide fat writing instruments such as magic markers for very young or inexperienced children.

- Make the paths wider and shorter.

How to Extend this Activity:

- Make the paths narrower and longer. Create complex paths or mazes with several choices of which way to go. Suggest that older children make their own paths to trace. (Figure 10.8)

Pretend Play

1. *Our Orchard.* Arrange an area of the room to be a fruit orchard. Line up pails of sand or dirt with branches stuck into them to create the trees. Have the children cut out pretend fruits to attach to the branches. Nearby provide a pretend kitchen for preparing the harvested fruits. Include baskets, buckets, and pretend cooking utensils. Pie tins and rolling pins may suggest pie-making to the children. Follow up by arranging a place where children can pretend to sell the produce from the orchard. Discuss and act out the roles of orchard farmer, seller, and buyer. As a variation, make a market or a florist's stand.

2. *Photosynthesis Fun.* Have the children act out the process of photosynthesis. Prepare several blue paper "water droplets," many yellow "sunlight energy rays," and many green paper "chlorophyll kernels." Form a circle of children, telling them they are a giant leaf. Explain that this leaf can make food for the plant to live and grow but it needs certain things, such as chlorophyll. Pass out "chlorophyll kernels" to everyone. Have someone be the leaf stem and give that person the "water droplets" to send up to the other parts of the leaf. Suggest that all the leaf parts pretend to absorb sunlight. (Have one person be the sun and give each child a sunlight energy ray.) Then have them mix their substances with the water that is being passed to them and—Hurrah!—they've made food for the plant.

3. *Garden Plot Pretend.* Teach children the following poems about gardening. As they recite them, ask them to make up actions to fit the words.

Growing
(Author unknown)
A little garden flower
is lying in its bed.
A warm spring sun
Is shining overhead.
Down came the raindrops
Dancing to and fro.
The little flower wakens
And starts to grow.

My Garden
(Author unknown)
I dig, dig, dig, and plant some seeds.
(digging and planting motions)

I rake, rake, rake, and pull some weeds.
(raking and pulling)

I wait and watch and soon I know
(waiting)

My garden sprouts and starts to grow.
(sprouting)

4. *Greenhouse.* Take the children to visit a greenhouse where plants are grown indoors in containers. Furnish an area of the classroom with props to suggest a greenhouse where they can act out what they saw. Use a piece of clear plastic, a plastic tablecloth, or opened plastic garbage bags to imitate the roof on the greenhouse. (Suspend these from table to wall or be-

Sample Plant Mazes

Figure 10.8 *Trace the Path Water Takes Inside Each Plant*

Figure 10.9 *A Place to Pretend About Plants*

tween chairs.) (Figure 10.9) Provide pots, plant flats, watering cans, pretend gardening tools, and plants made of cardboard or plastic. Making available sets of gardening gloves and aprons may encourage children to take on the roles of greenhouse workers and horticulturists.

5. *Flower Show.* Show pictures of people at a flower show. (Ask a local gardening group to provide information, pictures, posters, and examples of ribbons won.) Give children a place to set up their own flower show. In one area, children could "produce" the flowers and make the ribbons and other awards. Elsewhere they could mount the "show." Explain some of the various categories in which to enter flowers and provide materials so that children could take on roles of flower growers, guides, and judges in the show.

6. *Vegetarian Restaurant.* Arrange an area of the classroom as a restaurant that serves dishes made exclusively from plants. Provide simple props for the cook (a chef's hat, apron, cooking pots), the customers (purses, wallets, hats), and the waitpeople (menus, plates, cups, pad, and pencil). Help children focus on how the vegetables

are prepared by offering the same food on the menu cooked in various ways, such as fried, baked, or boiled potatoes. Pictures of these foods glued on paper plates would further enhance children's play.

Social

1. *What to Plant?* Divide the class into small groups. Give each small group a choice of several kinds of seeds to plant. Tell them they can only plant one kind and must decide together what to plant. Help them brainstorm, listen to each other's ideas, and choose a way to decide. If a group is having difficulty deciding, suggest that sometimes groups come to a decision by voting, picking a seed out of a bowl, or allowing one person in the group to make the decision. Help children settle on a plan and then try it.

2. *Our Class Bush.* Provide a way for children to contribute to the making of a class bush. You might anchor real branches into a bucket of sand or plaster and have children add real or paper leaves, berries, and other details to make it look the way they want. To add interest, suggest that chil-

dren investigate real bushes and other shrubs outdoors, looking for ideas for things to add to their own bush (insects, spider webs, nests, etc.). Provide a variety of materials near their work area so that children can make and add things as they think of them over several days. Have the group name their completed bush and decide together where it will be placed in the room.

3. *Plant Photo Walk.* Divide the class into two groups. Taking different routes, escort each group on a walk through a nearby neighborhood. Take photographs of some of the plants children notice along the way. After the pictures are developed, number them in two sequences according to each route taken. Have the groups swap photos and then walk the alternate route, using the photos to find the same plants the other group found.

4. *Invite a Gardener.* Seek out a parent or friend who has a garden and lots of experience with gardening. Have the children design an invitation asking that person to visit the class. The invitation could suggest that the visitor show his or her tools, work clothes, and some of the plants grown in a home garden, and ask the visitor to tell about what home gardeners do and how much pleasure he or she gets from gardening.

*5. *Unwanted Visitors.*

General Purpose: For children to develop awareness and concern for the rights of others.

TFPs: 1, 15, 19, 20, 24, 26.

Materials: *The Tale of Peter Rabbit* by Beatrix Potter, paper, and dark marker. Other materials will vary depending on the plan developed by the children. This activity would be an excellent follow-up to the planting of a real garden.

Procedure:

a. Read the story of Peter Rabbit to the group and have children figure out Mr. McGregor's problem and how he solved it. Discuss different kinds of pests in a garden, such as animals and birds who eat the plants and careless people who step on plants or take things that don't belong to them.

b. Suggest that children plan some ways to prevent garden pests from spoiling their garden. Help them brainstorm ideas about what kind of pests may be a problem and some ways to deal with them. Focus on the rights of the group and those of individuals.

c. Help the children come to an agreement about one or more ways they might prevent their garden from being disturbed. They could put up signs, construct a fence, or build a scarecrow. Plan what will have to be done and who will do each part of the job. Divide the class into work groups to carry out the plans.

d. After the prevention strategy is in place, help the children evaluate whether their plan is working or not. Revise the plan as needed.

Hint for Success:

- If children suggest inappropriate strategies for dealing with potential problems, take the opportunity to point out what negative results may occur as a result. Steer them toward more appropriate suggestions.

How to Simplify this Activity:

- Give children some ideas for possible problems and propose several acceptable solutions from which they could choose.

How to Extend this Activity:

- Have children write or dictate stories about the problems and solutions.

TEACHER RESOURCES

Field Trip Ideas

1. Locate a nearby farm that grows various crops. Take children walking through the fields, pointing out plant parts, how plants grow, and which parts will be harvested. Show the machinery needed to do the work and ask the farmer to describe a typical day on the farm. If possible, have the children pick some vegetables to take back to school to prepare for a meal.

2. Visit a local greenhouse, showing children the variety of plants grown there. Ask a

knowledgeable person to show the children equipment used, seed varieties, and ways plants are treated when diseased.

3. Take the class to visit a nearby arboretum, where plants are grown and displayed outdoors. On a walk, look at the variety of sizes, shapes, colors, textures, and positions of plants. Take pictures of the various plants and display them in an album that children may use to tell the story of their field trip.

4. Organize a trip to a nearby flower store. Ask children to help you choose some flowers to buy for the classroom. Point out the care that the florist uses when handling flowers. Tell children to find their favorite flower on display.

5. Visit a tree farm where seedlings are grown. Point out the variety of trees and how they are produced, and purchase one to plant near your school if possible.

6. Locate a lumber seller in your community. Take the children to visit, showing them piles of lumber, how the lumber is sawed, what people do with lumber when they buy it, and other interesting aspects of the lumber business.

7. Focus on the produce section of a local market. Ask children to identify different fruits and vegetables and to tell what part of the plant each is. Notice the variety and show some plants with which the children may be unfamiliar. Purchase some vegetables or fruits to take back to school for a meal or special treat.

Classroom Visitors

1. Ask a community resident who works with plants and/or the products of plants to come to your classroom. Ask him or her to bring tools to show the children and to demonstrate several aspects of working with plants. Let the visitor know the kinds of things you think he or she could contribute and discuss the amount of time available. Suggestions for resource people might be: woodcarver, flower arranger, farmer, gardener, forest ranger, tree nursery worker, garden club member, horticulturist.

Children's Books

Budbill, D. *Christmas Tree Farm.* New York: Macmillan, 1974.

Ehlert, L. *Growing Vegetable Soup.* New York: Harcourt Brace Jovanovich, 1987.

———. *Planting a Rainbow.* New York: Harcourt Brace Jovanovich, 1988.

———. *Eating the Alphabet.* New York: Harcourt Brace Jovanovich, 1989.

Freschet, B. *Owl in the Garden.* New York: Lothrop, Lee and Shepard, 1985.

Heller, R. *The Reason for a Flower.* New York: Grosset and Dunlap, 1983.

———. *Plants That Never Ever Bloom.* New York: Grosset and Dunlap, 1984.

Jordan, H. J. *How a Seed Grows.* New York: Crowell, 1960.

Kachalla, S. *All About Seeds.* Mahwah, NJ: Troll, 1982.

Krauss, R. *The Carrot Seed.* New York: Harper and Row, 1945.

Lobel, A. *The Rose in My Garden.* New York: Greenwillow, 1984.

Mabey, R. *Oak and Company.* New York: Greenwillow, 1983.

Mitgutsch, A. *From Seed to Pear.* Minneapolis: Carolrhoda, 1971.

Petie, H. *The Seed the Squirrel Dropped.* Englewood Cliffs, NJ: Prentice-Hall, 1976.

Potter, B. *The Tale of Peter Rabbit.* New York: Crown, 1988.

Quackenbush, R. *Here a Plant, There a Plant, Everywhere a Plant, Plant.* Englewood Cliffs, NJ: Prentice-Hall, 1982.

Rockwell, A., and H. Rockwell. *How My Garden Grows.* New York: Macmillan, 1982.

Romanova, N. *Once There Was a Tree.* New York: Dial, 1985.

Ryder, J. *The Snail Spell.* New York: Warner, 1982.

Rylant, C. *This Year's Garden.* New York: Macmillan, 1984.

Starton, M. *A Walk Through the Woods.* New York: Harper and Row, 1976.

Tolstoy, A. *The Great Big Enormous Turnip.* New York: Franklin Watts, 1968.

Tresselt, A. *The Dead Tree*. New York: Parents, 1972.

Weil, L. *The Little Chestnut Tree*. New York: Scholastic, 1973.

Wheeler, C. *Marmalade's Yellow Leaf*. New York: Knopf, 1982.

Wood, J. N., and K. Dean. *Nature Hide and Seek: Jungles*. New York: Knopf, 1987.

Worthington, P., and J. Worthington. *Teddy Bear Gardener*. New York: Viking, 1986.

Zion, G. *The Plant Sitter*. New York: Harper and Row, 1959.

Adult References

Bowden, M. *Nature for the Very Young*. New York: John Wiley and Sons, 1989.

Crockett, J. U. *The Time-Life Book of Perennials*. New York: Henry Holt and Company, 1972.

Dowden, A. O. *The Nobel Harvest: A Chronicle of Herbs*. New York: Collins, 1979.

Lauber, P. *Seeds: Pop, Stick, Glide*. New York: Crown, 1981.

Little, E. L. *The Audubon Society Field Guide to North American Trees*. New York: Knopf, 1980.

Moggi, G., and L. Giugnolini. *Simon and Schuster's Guide to Garden Flowers*. New York: Simon and Schuster, 1983.

Peterson, L. A. *A Field Guide to Edible Wild Plants*. Boston: Houghton Mifflin, 1977.

Peterson, R. T., and M. McKenny. *A Field Guide to Wild Flowers of Northwestern and North-Central North America*. Boston: Houghton Mifflin, 1974.

Selsam, M. E. *The Plants We Eat*. New York: William Morrow, 1981.

Suzuki, D. *Looking at Plants*. New York: Warner, 1985.

Symonds, G. W. D. *The Tree Identification Book*. New York: William Morrow, 1973.

Zimm, H. S., and A. C. Martin. *Flowers*. New York: Golden, 1950.

Chapter 11

Insects

•

nsects are everywhere! Readers who have seen the shimmering beauty of butterflies in the summer sun, brushed away a buzzing bee, listened to the chirping of crickets at dusk, awakened to plants ravaged by beetles or caterpillars, watched ants swarm over a melted sweet, or chased fireflies in the darkness know that this is true.

Because insects are so numerous and such a pervasive presence in the environment, young children too, are soon aware of these tiny creatures and want to know more about them. Thus, our purpose in developing a theme on insects is to enhance children's natural curiosity about the flying, buzzing, whirring, jumping animals they call "bugs."

PURPOSE

This unit has been designed to introduce children to common characteristics of insects in general and to offer them more in-depth information and experiences about four specific kinds of insects:

- butterflies and moths
- bees
- ants
- grasshoppers and crickets

We chose to concentrate on these four insect types because they are interesting to study, they are known to children all over the country, and they are readily available and easily observable in the natural environment.

As children participate in the activities that accompany this unit, they will have opportunities to make many discoveries about the natural world. They will be introduced to:

- the color, beauty, and diversity of insects
- the wonder of metamorphosis
- characteristics of cooperative living
- the interrelationships among all living creatures on the planet

IMPLEMENTATION

It is possible to teach the insect unit in several different ways. For students and practitioners working with children not experienced in the theme, we suggest one of these strategies.

1. Teach a one-week unit that introduces general information about the common characteristics of insects. Use TFPs 1–15 as well as the TFPs that focus on the physical descriptions of butterflies and moths, bees, ants, and/or grasshoppers and crickets.
2. Develop a one-week unit concentrating on only one of the insects presented here. Select the one that is found most readily in your area.
3. Teach a unit about an insect featured prominently in a story you have read or a song you have sung to your group. Samples might include bees, previously introduced in *Winnie the Pooh and The Honey Tree* by A. A. Milne, or butterflies, featured in *The Very Hungry Caterpillar* by Eric Carle.

For more experienced children we recommend that teachers present multiweek units. Possible foci could include:

Option One:
Week One: General overview using TFPs 1–15
Week Two: Butterflies and moths
Week Three: Bees
Week Four: Ants
Week Five: Grasshoppers and crickets

Children's interest should be the determining factor in deciding whether a five-week unit is desirable. While some groups may want to study all four insect types, others may be better served if teachers focus on only one or two following the general overview.

Option Two:
Week One: General overview
Week Two: Flying insects (bees, butterflies, and moths)
Week Three: Ground insects (ants, grasshoppers, and crickets)

Option Three:
Week One: General overview
Week Two: Social insects (ants and bees)

Option Four: (comparing insect behaviors across many types):
Week One: How insects eat
Week Two: How insects move
Week Three: How insects communicate

TERMS, FACTS, AND PRINCIPLES

General Information

1. An insect is a small animal with a hard-shelled body.

2. All insects hatch from eggs.

3. The body of an insect has three parts: head, thorax, and abdomen.

4. The head of an insect has a mouth, antennae, and several eyes.

*5. The mouth of an insect has teeth, a tongue, and a sucking tube that is used for eating.

6. The antennae of an insect are used to smell, touch, hear, or taste.

*7. Most insects have two sets of eyes: the outer set can see in many directions at once, the inner set can detect light and shadow.

*8. The thorax of an insect consists of three segments, each with a pair of legs.

9. Some insects have one or two pairs of wings connected to their bodies at the thorax.

*10. Insects have no bones. They have an outside skeleton that protects their soft body parts.

11. Insects are food for other insects, birds, reptiles, and some mammals.

12. Insects have many enemies: severe weather, birds, squirrels, frogs, fish, bats, and other animals who eat them, and humans who collect them or destroy their natural environments.

13. Insects are fragile and must be handled with care and respect.

14. Insects are found everywhere on the earth; some species live in every country in the world.

15. There are more than a million species of insects on the earth. Some of the common ones are: ants, butterflies, moths, bees, beetles, grasshoppers, fleas, crickets, roaches, flies, mosquitoes, gnats, hornets, wasps, locusts, termites, fireflies, sowbugs, and earwigs.

Butterflies and Moths

16. Adult moths and butterflies are harmless insects.

17. Butterflies and moths have four wings arranged in a front pair and hind pair.

18. Butterflies and moths come in many shapes, colors, and sizes.

*19. Butterflies and moths have thousands of tiny scales covering their bodies and wings which give them color.

*20. Butterflies and moths are cold-blooded and depend on outside warmth for their body heat. They are only active when warm.

*21. Adult moths and butterflies do not look at all like they did at birth.

*22. Butterflies and moths change in form and structure, as well as in size, as they mature. This is called metamorphosis.

*23. The stages of metamorphosis are:
   a. Egg
   b. Larva or caterpillar: The newly hatched larva resembles a worm or grub. The main job of the larva is to eat and grow.
   c. Pupa: The larva begins forming a casing within which the insect rests in the pupal stage. The casing is called a cocoon if a moth is developing, or a chrysalis if a butterfly is developing. The pupa may spin its entire casing, or build it of leaves, twigs, and soil. Depending on the species, the pupal stage may last a few days or an entire winter.
   d. Adult

24. Butterflies and moths suck the nectar of flowers.

*25. Butterflies and moths suck water or nectar with a special tongue called a proboscis.

*26. Some butterflies and moths are fond of other liquids: honey, sap, juice from fruit, or honeydew secreted by insects called aphids.

*27. Butterflies and moths taste with special organs on the bottoms of their feet.

28. Sometimes it is difficult to tell a butterfly from a moth.

*29. Most moths fly during the night. Most butterflies fly during the day.

*30. A moth's antennae are usually wide and feathery. A butterfly's antennae are long, slender, and knob-ended.

*31. Butterflies usually fold their wings together in an upright position when they land. Moths spread their wings out wide and flat.

*32. Moths usually have stouter, furrier bodies than butterflies.

Bees

33. Bees have wings.

*34. Bees have an egg-laying organ that also serves as a stinger.

35. Bees live together in colonies called nests or hives.

36. Bees do special dances that communicate messages to other bees.

37. Two of the several varieties of bees found in North America are honeybees and bumblebees.

38. Honeybees and bumblebees gather pollen and nectar from flowers.

39. Pollen and nectar are combined to make honey.

*40. To carry pollen, honeybees and bumblebees pack it into small pockets on their hind legs.

41. The bumblebee is yellow and black and has a fuzzy body.

*42. The bumblebee often builds its nest in another animal's deserted nest.

*43. The bumblebee may dig an underground chamber in which to build a nest.

*44. The bumblebee secretes wax from her body and uses it to build small pots in which to store honey.

45. The female bumblebee's main job is to gather pollen and nectar as food for her babies.

*46. The male bumblebee's main job is to mate with the female, after which the male dies.

47. The honeybee has a shiny, brown, hairy body.

*48. There are three types of honeybees: queens and workers are female, drones are male.

49. The honeybee builds a complex nest called a hive.

*50. Workers tend the young, clean the hive, forage for food, and feed the queen and her babies.

*51. The honeybee brings its pollen and nectar to the hive where the combination is converted into both honey and beeswax.

52. Humans enjoy eating both honey and beeswax.

*53. An apiary is a place where honeybees are housed, generally in their own hives, so that an apiarist, or beekeeper, can harvest some of the honey that bees produce.

Ants

54. Ants are very small insects.

55. Most ants do not have wings.

*56. The queen, or mother ant, in each family and the drone, or father ant, have wings until after they mate.

*57. Soon after mating, the drone dies and the queen pulls off her wings before settling into her nest to lay eggs.

58. Most ants are black, brown, or rust. Some ants are yellow, green, blue, purple, or red.

59. Ants are very strong for their size.

*60. Most ants can lift objects that are ten times heavier than their bodies. Some ants can lift fifty times their body weight.

61. Ants have two "feelers," sensitive antennae attached to the front of the head.

62. The antennae of an active ant move constantly as their organs of smell, touch, taste, and hearing operate.

63. Ants can see moving objects better than still objects.

64. Ants use their mouthparts to grasp food, carry their young, fight enemies, dig soil, and cut through wood.

65. Each of an ant's six legs has a foot with two hooked claws.

66. An ant's claws allow it to climb up surfaces.

*67. Ants have a big stomach called a crop in which they carry food home to share with other ants.

68. Ants eat dead insects, bruised fruit, seeds, berries, and sap.

*69. When an ant arrives home and a hungry ant begs for food by stroking the food-gatherer's head, they stand mouth to mouth and food is exchanged.

*70. When a food-gathering ant needs food, the food passes from its crop into a smaller stomach for digestion.

*71. Ants do not have ears but can sense sound vibrations with special organs on their antennae, legs, trunk, and head.

72. Ants are known as social insects. They live together in organized communities called colonies.

*73. Most members of an ant colony are workers. Workers are female but do not lay eggs as does the queen.

*74. Worker ants' jobs are to build the nest, search for food, care for the young, and fight enemies.

*75. Male ants have only one job: to mate with young queens. The males die soon after mating.

*76. Each queen starts a new colony after mating by digging into the ground or under a stone, laying her eggs, and waiting for her new family to arrive and continue building the nest.

*77. Ants have no voice and do not communicate with sounds.

*78. Ants give messages through secretions which they pass throughout the colony by touching each other.

*79. Secretions help ants to recognize others from their colony and to tell which jobs need doing.

*80. Ants leave secretions as a trail to help other ants find food.

Grasshoppers and Crickets

81. Grasshoppers and crickets are insects with long, strong rear legs that enable them to jump long distances.

82. Grasshoppers and crickets have mouthparts that are suitable for chewing through grass.

83. Grasshoppers and crickets have spined forelegs that are useful for climbing.

*84. Grasshoppers and crickets resemble their parents when hatched but lack wings.

*85. Grasshoppers and crickets molt. This means they outgrow and shed their skeleton and form new, larger ones.

*86. Molting is not painful and does not hurt the insect.

*87. Baby grasshoppers and crickets have tiny wingpads that enlarge with each molt until, as adults, they have functional wings.

88. Grasshoppers and crickets find food and shelter in tall grass.

89. Grasshoppers and crickets are usually green when the grasses are green and turn tan when the pastures and fields begin to turn brown.

90. Grasshoppers and crickets have no voice but make sounds by rubbing their rear legs against the edges of their wings, or by rubbing one leg or one wing against another. These sounds are called chirps.

*91. Some grasshoppers and crickets hear with organs situated on the rear part of their bodies just below the wings.

92. Grasshoppers differ from crickets in several ways.

93. Grasshoppers have antennae that are shorter than their heads. Crickets have very long, slender antennae.

*94. Grasshoppers have heads placed at right angles to the body with mouthparts facing the ground. Crickets have stout heads that extend from the thorax with mouthparts facing forward.

95. Grasshoppers chirp in the day. Crickets chirp at night.

*96. Grasshoppers have wings that stand up from the top of the body. Crickets have wings that lie tightly against the sides of the body.

ACTIVITY IDEAS

Aesthetics

1. *Painting on Insect Shapes.* Cut easel paper into the shapes of common, easily outlined insects such as butterflies or ladybugs. (Refer to the teacher resource section for

some examples of these.) For variety, provide children with a top or front view as well as a side view of each insect. Or, simply outline the shapes with a heavy marker on the paper rather than actually cutting silhouettes. Make available markers, crayons, paint, or chalk for children to use to decorate their insects. One day provide colors that correspond to the insects' real coloration, another day offer "fantasy colors" that bear no resemblance to the true colors of the insects. In both cases, treat this as an exercise in imagination rather than a realistic depiction of insect life.

2. *Beautiful Insects.* Share colorful pictures of insects or real insect specimens with the children. Talk with them about the beauty (color, shape, texture, patterns) they observe.

3. *Insect Songs and Poems.* Teach children the following songs and poems, emphasizing the enjoyment that comes from the rhythm of the words.

Twinkle, Twinkle Firefly
(Tune: "Twinkle, Twinkle, Little Star"; Words: Kit Payne)
Twinkle, twinkle firefly,
flying in the evening sky.
Flashing on and off your light
adding beauty to the night.
Twinkle, twinkle firefly,
flying in the evening sky.

Bee's Eyes
(Tune: First verse of "For He's A Jolly Good Fellow"; Words: Kit Payne)
I'm seeing the world through bee's eyes,
(Sing three times.)
and honey's on my mind.

I'm buzzing around some flowers,
(Sing three times.)
and honey's on my mind.

I'm sipping my fill of nectar,
(Sing three times.)
and honey's on my mind.

I'm packing my legs with pollen,
(Sing three times.)
and honey's on my mind.

I'm mixing a batch of beeswax,
(Sing three times.)
and honey's on my mind.

I'm filling the hive with honey,
(Sing three times.)
and honey's on my mind.

I'll share my honey with you dear,
(Sing three times.)
'cause honey's on your mind!

(Sing the following lines to the tune of the last verse of "For He's a Jolly Good Fellow.")
'cause honey's on your mind,
'cause honey's on your mind,
I'll share my honey with you dear,
'cause honey's on *your* mind.

The Ants Go Marching
(Variation on traditional rhyme; sing to the tune of "When Johnny Comes Marching Home.")
The ants go marching one by one,
Hoorah, Hooray
The ants go marching one by one,
Hoorah, Hooray
The ants go marching one by one,
the last one stops to work in the sun.
The ants go marching, around and around,
and under the ground,
and out in the rain.
(Increase the number of ants and give the last one a new activity with each verse.)
The ants go marching two by two . . . etc.

two   - drink some dew
three   - climb a tree
four   - crawl under a door
five   - burrow and dive
six   - pick up a stick
seven   - check tunnel eleven
eight   - lick my plate
nine   - crawl over a vine
ten   - signal THE END!

Five Little Grasshoppers
(Adapted from a traditional rhyme)

Words:
Five little grasshoppers playing near my door; one saw a honeybee, then there were four.

Four little grasshoppers playing near a tree; one chased a busy fly, then there were three.

Three little grasshoppers looked for pastures new; one met a cricket, then there were two.

Two little grasshoppers sitting in the sun; a ladybug called "play with me," then there was one.

One little grasshopper said I'll have some fun; she went to find her brothers, then there were none.

Actions:

Hold up one hand with fingers extended. Starting with your little finger, put your fingers down one at a time in accordance with the words.

4. *Bee Dances.*

General Purpose: For children to respond spontaneously to moods and feelings prompted by the arts and nature.

TFPs: 34–53.

Materials: None.

Procedure:

a. Introduce the activity with a discussion of bees. Ask children to make the sounds they think bees might make. Point out that their buzz doesn't tell a message, but that bees do have a way to communicate: they dance a story that other bees can "read" by watching.

b. Invite children to imagine that it is a sunny spring morning. They are bees, leaving their homes to explore the glorious day. Encourage children to create bee dances that "tell" how the day makes them feel.

c. Introduce soft music (if desired), or invite the children to buzz an accompaniment for their dances.

d. Some children may enjoy explaining the message their dances tell.

e. Dance uninhibitedly with the children! Explain your message, if you wish. Make it one of joy.

Hints for Success:

• Before trying this activity, expose children to information about bees in pictures, films, filmstrips, or descriptions so that they know what you are talking

about and can become involved more easily.

• Plan this activity for a large, open area indoors or outdoors.

• Provide music to help set the scene. Select portions from instrumental pieces that do not contain lyrics or directions. Tchaikovsky's *Nutcracker Suite* and the "Flight of the Bumble Bee" by Peter Ilich Tchaikovsky or other classical flute pieces can be used successfully.

How to Simplify this Activity:

• Younger children can do the same dance sitting down. Show them how to use their hands as bees and move to the music.

How to Extend this Activity:

• To enrich older children's experience, provide bee props such as antennae and wings.

Affective

1. *What Am I?* Following a discussion of how insects move and communicate, ask each child to think of the kind of insects they'd like to be. Invite the children, as a group or one at a time, to demonstrate the insect they've chosen. Caution them not to tell what it is. Have class members guess which insect individual children are portraying.

2. *Caring for a Caterpillar through Metamorphosis.*

General Purpose: For children to experience the pleasure of work through a real-life task.

TFPs: 16, 18, 21, 22, 23.

Materials: A pail covered with cheesecloth or mosquito netting or a wide-mouth plastic container with a few small holes punched in the lid; a "caterpillar home" (see sidebar for instructions) or a terrarium with a tight-fitting lid); a twenty-by-thirty-inch sheet of poster board; one three-by-five-inch index card for each child in the class printed with his or her name; magnifying glasses; an 8½-by-11-inch notebook. Optional: individual notebooks for each child; markers or crayons.

Caring for Our Caterpillar					
Tasks	Mon	Tues	Wed	Thur	Fri
Fresh Leaves					
Clean Home					
Observe and Report					

Figure 11.1 *Who Will Help Care for the Caterpillar Today?*

Procedure:

a. Prepare caterpillar home(s) and job chart before introducing the activity to the children. Across the top of the poster board list the days of the week. On the left-hand side write the tasks related to caterpillar care: provide fresh leaves, clean home, observe and report. (Figure 11.1)

b. Take the children on a caterpillar hunt. Look for caterpillars on the leaves and stems of plants. Look closely at leaves with holes. Caterpillars may be feeding there.

c. Once found, carefully remove the caterpillar from the plant. Transport the caterpillar to the classroom in the covered pail or wide-mouth container. In addition, take a supply of leaves from the plant on which you found the caterpillar. These leaves may be the only type the insect will eat.

d. Put a fresh twig in the caterpillar home or terrarium to serve as a secure base for pupation.

e. Encourage the children to handle the caterpillar gently and watch as it crawls over their hands.

f. Put the caterpillar in the home or terrarium you have prepared.

g. Review the process of metamorphosis with the children.

h. Explain that the responsibility of caring for the caterpillar now belongs to them. Explain the jobs that children will be performing:

- Keeping the container clean by removing dead leaves, excrement, and the molted skin of the caterpillar each day.
- Providing fresh leaves to the caterpillar every day.
- Observing how the caterpillar looks, eats, and moves, how it forms its cocoon or chrysalis, and finally how it emerges as a butterfly or moth.

i. Show children the job chart. Tell them that each day over the next several weeks individuals will be assigned tasks to work on. Children can tell whose turn it is by looking for their names and seeing which job is theirs on what day.

j. Show the group how to carry out each task. Offer appropriate reminders to individual children as they attempt their jobs.

k. Refer to the job chart every day and assist children in "reading" it.

l. Provide an opportunity for the "observer" to report his or her findings to the group on a daily basis. Write down the observations. Add other children's observations as well.

m. Periodically review with the class all the observations gathered up to that point.

n. Once the butterfly or moth emerges and begins to spread its wings, observe it briefly, release it, and watch it fly away.

o. Praise children periodically for their ability to carry out the tasks of caring for their caterpillar. Do this throughout the entire process.

Hints for Success:

- Once a caterpillar is in the pupa stage, food is no longer necessary. If you found your caterpillar anywhere other than on a plant, assume it is about to enter this stage.

- Environmental conditions important for the caterpillar's survival include:

1. adequate ventilation around the home or terrarium

2. moderate temperatures

3. indirect sunlight

4. avoiding extreme fluctuations in any of these conditions

- If you find your caterpillar on a plant, supply fresh leaves from the same plant or at least from one of the same species every day. The leaves contain enough moisture so that no additional water is required.

- If you find more than one caterpillar, create a separate "home" for each.

- Rotate children's names among the three jobs so that each child has a chance to complete more than one task.

- Provide pictures of the caterpillar, pupa, and adult stages as a cue to children about what will happen next.

- If the caterpillar dies or fails to emerge as an adult, talk with the children about their reactions. Be careful not to imply that they were at fault for the insect's

demise. Instead, emphasize that sometimes people work hard at a task yet it doesn't turn out as they hope it will.

How to Simplify this Activity:

- Carry out the daily jobs as part of a circle-time or large-group experience.

- Ask the group as a whole to volunteer observations rather than asking particular children to do so on their own. The child whose job it is to report can simply be the first one asked for an idea.

How to Extend this Activity:

- Help children keep their own notebooks in which you write their personal observations as dictated to you on a weekly basis. Rather than doing the whole group at once, record a few children's notes each day.

- Allow children to keep their own notebooks in which they draw or write their own observations on a daily basis.

Caterpillar Home

Materials for each home: Scissors, a quart-sized paper milk carton, one leg cut from a pair of pantyhose, a forked twig, one wire tie for fastening.

Procedure:

a. Cut a four-by-eight-inch window in one side of the milk carton.

b. Pull the pantyhose over the bottom of the container to the top, so that the entire container is covered.

c. Put a forked twig in the container.

d. Gently place the caterpillar inside its new home.

e. Fasten the stocking at the top with the wire tie. (Figure 11.2)

Cognition

1. *Ant Farm.* Ant farms are relatively inexpensive and are available in most toy or hobby shops. Purchase one. Send for ants or collect them with the children. Observe,

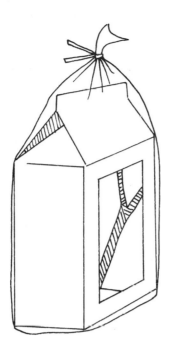

Figure 11.2 *A Simple Caterpillar Cage*

describe, and graph information about the ants.

2. *Insect Counting.* Show children pictures or models of various insects that clearly show legs and body parts. Work with the children to count the insects, their legs, wings, antennae, eyes, heads, and so forth.

3. *Insect Pairs.* Invite children to create a one-to-one correspondence between pictures of bees and flowers or between other insect pairs, such as fruitflies, dragonflies, ladybugs, ants, or crickets.

4. *The Insect Line.* Make available pictures or models of insects that children can order according to a variety of dimensions: largest to smallest, brightest to dullest, prettiest to least attractive, and so forth.

5. *Who Lives Here?* Provide children with pictures of insect homes (garden, meadow, tree, rotting log, nest, hive). Also offer individual insect pictures that have been cut from magazines. Have youngsters match each insect to its home. Note that the insect illustrations pictured at the end of this unit could be cut out for this activity. Insect "stamps" are also available commercially and can be used.

6. *Insect Babies and Adults.* Show children pictures of insects in their early stages, as well as in the adult stage. Ask children to match each baby insect with its adult. Suitable photos and drawings are readily available in many gardening magazines, especially those that come out in the early spring.

7. *Metamorphosis.* Give children photographs or drawings depicting the metamorphosis of a moth or butterfly. Several puzzles and other commercial materials depict this process and could be used to add interest and variety. Ask children to arrange the pictures or pieces in order from egg to adult. Rearrange them out of sequence and tell children to find the mistake. Encourage older children to speculate on why the egg comes first, or why the caterpillar precedes the butterfly and what they think would happen if the order was changed. Focus on the thinking processes children display, not on the correctness or feasibility of their answers.

8. *Insect Observations.* Look for ladybugs on leaves, butterflies on the wing, bees near flowers, flies on windowsills, ants in slightly raised clear patches on the ground, and crickets or grasshoppers in tall grass. Help children observe these insects in the natural environment. Note their colorations, movements, and observable body parts.

9. *Insect Observations in the Classroom.* Attempt to capture harmless insects such as ladybugs or grasshoppers for closer scrutiny. Use a butterfly net or widemouth jar as a "bug catcher." Keep grasshoppers and crickets in a see-through plastic container or bowl that is covered with mesh to allow air inside. Provide fresh green leaves and grass every day. No additional water is necessary. Keep ladybugs in a clear, loosely covered jar or terrarium, the bottom of which is covered with a thin layer of soil. Add twigs or small stones to serve as hiding places for these insects. Feed ladybugs aphids, which can be found on the branches of infested plants. Cut a

small portion of such a branch and place it in the container. Additional water will not be required since the aphids themselves are high in moisture. Give children magnifying glasses with which to observe the insects. Point out physical attributes as well as eating and resting habits. If you have more than one insect of the same type, note their methods of interaction. After a few days, release the insects into a suitable outdoor environment.

10. *Just for Fun.* Gather a selection of children's fictional storybooks about insects. You might include *The Very Hungry Caterpillar* by Eric Carle, *Ladybug, Ladybug* by Kathleen Daly, and *The Honeybee and the Robber* by Eric Carle. First, ask children to generate a list of all the facts they know about the insect in question. Write these down and post them where you and the children can refer to them later. Then read the story out loud. Ask children to identify parts of the story that are pretend and parts of the story that are true. Refer to the children's list to help clarify the truths.

11. *Honey Yum!* Provide children with an opportunity to taste honey and beeswax. Try different types of honey derived from varying flowers. Compare the tastes.

12. *Insect Riddles.*

    General Purpose: To enable children to apply knowledge gained from previous experience to new situations.

    TFPs: All.

    Materials: Riddles in box on page 229. Optional: picture cards of insects and noninsects at least 8½-by-11 inches in size.

    Procedure:
    a. This activity is suitable for both small and large groups of children.
    b. Explain that the group will be playing a guessing game. You will tell a short story about an insect or an animal who eats insects; children are to guess which insect or insect-eating animal you are describing.
    c. Caution children to listen to the entire riddle before making a guess. Tell them that after you have said, "What am I?" the riddle will be over. Then, they can say their ideas.

    d. Alert children that a riddle is about to begin by using words such as, "See if you can guess this one . . . ," "Here's another one . . . ," "Ready . . . ," "Try to figure this one out . . . ."
    e. Paraphrase children's answers. Ask them how they decided what the riddle was about.
    f. If children guess incorrectly, repeat the riddle, highlighting critical information using exaggerated facial and vocal expressions.
    g. If children cannot figure out the answer, show them two pictures, one that corresponds to the answer and one that does not. Tell them to study the pictures closely and to listen one last time. If the answer is not obvious at this step, tell them what it is and explain why, using the pictures as an aid.
    h. Praise children throughout the activity for listening and for working hard at figuring out each riddle.

Hints for Success:
- Implement this activity only after children have had numerous opportunities to hear, talk about, and experience the TFPs for this unit.
- Define a riddle as a story or poem that asks a question.
- Decide in advance whether children may call out an answer or whether they must raise their hands. Explain your expectations before you present the first riddle.
- Use animated facial expressions and varied vocal tones to enhance your presentation.

How to Simplify this Activity:
- Introduce the activity as described in steps 1–4. Show children a picture of the insect/animal in question as you describe it. Ask them to name the insect/animal.
- Repeat the activity another time, focusing on step g of this plan.

How to Extend this Activity:
- Invite children to make up their own riddles. Write each one down, reading them aloud to check for accuracy. Ask other children in the group to guess the answers.

Insect Riddles

1. I make a food that's sticky sweet,
    that bears and people like to eat.
    I mix a pollen-nectar batch
    and store it in a special wax.
    What am I? **Bee**

2. I flutter by the flowers,
    sipping up my lunch.
    My babies look like little worms
    and leaves are what they munch.
    What am I? **Butterfly**

3. I hop about in meadows
    when grass is green and tall
    and make a cheerful chirping sound
    in summer, spring, and fall.
    What am I? **Grasshopper**

4. I buzz by your screen door,
    I land on your clothes,
    I sample your lunch,
    and I tickle your nose.
    I fly by so fast and I'm so hard to swat.
    Some call me a pest and dislike me a lot!
    What am I? **Fly**

5. I'm *not* an insect, but I spin
    a trap to catch an insect in.
    I have too many legs to be a real insect:
    count and see!
    What am I? **Spider**

6. I crawl along so slowly,
    as quiet as a mouse,
    then quickly catch an insect
    and take it in my house.
    My house is hard and rounded
    and grows upon my back.
    I take my home along with me
    and never have to pack!
    What am I? **Turtle**

13. ***Insects—Yes or No?***

    General Purpose: For children to recognize similarities and differences among living things.

    TFPs: 3–9, 17–20, 22, 23, 41, 47, 54, 56, 58, 59, 62, 63, 82–85, 94, 95, 97.

    Materials: Pictures of many varieties of insects (bees, butterflies, moths, ants, grasshoppers, mosquitoes, and so on); pictures of a variety of birds and other small animals (mice, chipmunks, lizards, bats, and so on); two trays or baskets, one designated by a small sign reading INSECTS, the other by a sign reading NOT INSECTS; list of insect terms, facts, and principles for adult reference.

    Procedure:

    a. Arrange the pictures on a tabletop. Keep the trays or baskets in reserve for the moment.

    b. Invite a few children to examine the pictures. Some may wish simply to look at the pictures, others may spontaneously sort them by such attributes as color, winged versus nonwinged insects, size, or personal preferences (favorite versus less favorite).

    c. Invite the children to play a game with the pictures. Bring out the trays or baskets designated INSECTS and NOT INSECTS. Explain their purpose in the sorting process. Direct the children to choose a picture that would belong in the INSECT pile. Encourage the children to explain why they've characterized their choice as an insect. "Tell me something about this picture that lets you know it's an insect." Some children may recall accurate facts about insects. Acknowledge the reason they give for having chosen it, then extend their knowledge: "You noticed that this animal has wings and many insects have wings! Insects all have six legs. Count this animal's legs with me. This animal has two legs. It's a bird. Put the bird in the NOT INSECT pile."

    d. Direct the children to find another picture of an insect. Acknowledge the characteristic by which individual children select the next picture: "You remembered to look for an animal with six legs. That *is* an insect you chose!"

    e. Periodically ask children to find a noninsect. Ask them how they decided which card to choose. Follow up as described in steps c and d.

    f. Continue the procedure as the children's interest dictates. Repeat the activity another day without direct adult supervision.

Hints for Success:

• Present this activity after children have had numerous opportunities to become familiar with the attributes all insects share: six legs all arranged in pairs, small three-part bodies, antennae, often winged, often two sets of eyes.

- Choose pictures in which only one type of insect or noninsect is depicted at a time. This will make it easier for children to focus on relevant details.

- Mount pictures on construction paper and/or laminate them or cover them with clear contact paper to make them more durable and attractive.

- Use some of the same pictures you made for the Insect Memory Game.

How to Simplify this Activity:

- Use only a few pictures. Also, begin by comparing insects to plants, vehicles, toys, furniture, or people. Gradually introduce animals such as mammals, reptiles, fish, and amphibians. After children are successful in distinguishing these from insects, introduce winged creatures and spiders.

How to Extend this Activity:

- Provide many pictures including some of insects that are unfamiliar or that may be confusing (that appear to have more than six legs or are in a stage of development that looks different from the adult insect). Challenge children by including a picture of a spider or by including pictures of machines, sculptures, or other inanimate objects that look similar to an insect.

Construction

1. *Making an Ant Colony or Bees' Nest.* Tell children to create their own interpretation of an ant colony or bees' nest using a climber, jungle gym, or arrangement of boxes as the nucleus. Provide additional materials such as blankets, sheets of newspaper, and large hollow blocks with which children can build.

2. *Sandbox Ant Hills.* Tell children that today the sandbox or sand table is an ant hill. Encourage them to figure out what to use for pretend ants and how to make ant nests, trails, and food supplies.

3. *Making Folded-Wing Butterflies.* Gather the following materials: Egg carton sections two to six units long; pairs of wings in various sizes made from folded construction paper; markers and crayons; glue; bits of colored paper for decorating; pipe cleaners; scissors; a selection of pictures of butterflies.

Start by showing children the butterfly pictures. Point out the pairs of double wings that are identical on both sides. Talk about the colors and patterns. Look at antennae, legs, and sectional bodies. Next, bring out the materials. Point out the variety and encourage the children to select some materials to work with to make their own butterflies, including at least one set of wings. Open the wings to display a mirror-image design. Help children as needed with folding, cutting, gluing, poking holes, or other techniques they may not yet have mastered. Avoid doing too much for them or suggesting that all butterflies be constructed in exactly the same way.

Praise the children as they work, and make sure to allow them to create their own butterfly designs rather than insisting that they try to replicate them from real life.

4. *Child-Sized Butterfly Wings.*

General Purpose: For children to represent a single object using various combinations of materials or techniques.

TFPs: 16–32.

Materials: Sheets of packing foam (the type in which new stereo equipment or small appliances frequently are wrapped), scissors, glue, glitter, scraps of tissue paper, lightweight fabric or sewing trims, markers, strapping tape.

Procedure:

a. Cut sheets of packing foam to resemble butterfly wings approximately 30 inches high by 30 inches long. (Figure 11.3)

b. At the midpoint of each wing, cut two 8-inch long slots, 5 inches apart, through which children can place their arms. Reinforce ends of slots with strapping tape to prolong life.

Figure 11.3 *Child-Sized Butterfly Wings*

c. After a discussion of butterflies and their beautiful markings, provide children with wing cutouts. Invite them to decorate the wings using the materials provided.

Hints for Success:

- Have two children work together, one decorating each side of a wing pair.

- Post pictures of a variety of types of butterflies for the children to enjoy as they work.

How to Expand this Activity:

- Add the wings to a pretend play area, or take them outdoors for children to wear and enjoy. Point out that the children have produced many different designs, just like the variety of patterns that adorns real butterflies.

- Have children make the wings themselves by cutting along an outline you have drawn on the foam.

Language

1. *Cricket Sounds.* Use masking tape to attach a pair of rhythm sticks, wood blocks, or sandpaper blocks to the underside of children's forearms or on the inner part of their lower legs. Do this over clothing so that the tape does not hurt coming off.

Suggest that children "chirp" a tune by rubbing the sticks or blocks together. Ask other children what they think their "cricket tunes" might mean.

Create the same effect by gluing, sewing, or taping the sticks or blocks to elastic bicycle bands with Velcro® fasteners (available in most bike shops). Children can slip these onto their arms or legs.

2. *If I Were a Butterfly.* Ask children to describe what it would be like to be a butterfly. Write each child's answer exactly as stated on a separate, butterfly-shaped piece of easel paper. Read each child's story back to him or her. Post all stories where children can refer to them easily.

3. *Comparing Insect Habitats.* Select two different outdoor habitats—lawn, vegetable garden, flower garden, meadow, riverbank, seashore, marsh, wooded glen, rotting log, sunny glade, or shaded glade. Take children to both on the same day or on two consecutive days. Keep a record of all the insects they see. Return to the classroom and invite the children as a group to dictate a story comparing the two habitats. Refer to the children's "field observations" as necessary.

4. *Insect Memory Game.*

   General Purpose: To increase children's vocabulary and memory skills.

   TFPs: 16–18, 33, 41, 47, 54, 58, 82, 90, 94, 95, 97.

   Materials: Realistic pictures of many varieties of insects.

   Procedure:

   a. Invite two to five children to join you to talk about insects and to play an insect game.

   b. Spread out several pictures, face up, in front of the children. Point out or ask the children to name some of the insects. Label the insect pictures not yet mentioned.

   c. Explain that now the group will play a memory game. It will begin with one person naming an insect that he or she might find. The next person will try to remember what the first child found and then add another kind he or she might see. This process will continue until the list gets too long for anyone to remember.

d. Ask a child to say, "I went on an insect hunt, and I found a *(insect)*." If children seem uncertain about how to proceed, take the second turn yourself, to model recalling the first answer. "I went on an insect hunt, and I found a *(first child's insect);* then I found a *(your own insect)*." Invite another child to try to remember both insects and then to add his or her own selection.

e. Help children figure out ways to improve their recall of the list. For instance, at first encourage children to line up the picture cards as a way to remember. Repeat the activity telling children that they can look at the scattered array of cards for reference, but that they can't rearrange them. Finally, try the game without picture prompts.

f. Praise children often as the game proceeds.

Hints for Success:

• Choose pictures that depict only one type of insect per picture.

• Use some of the same pictures you made for Insects—Yes or No?

• Allow children to name the same insect in the sequence more than once.

• Remind children to give each other plenty of time to remember the list before blurting out answers. Tell excited children, whose turn it is not, to say the names silently to themselves.

• Periodically repeat the whole list yourself as a way to remind children of the sequence. "So far we've found a bee, a fly, a ladybug, a bee, and an ant."

How to Simplify this Activity:

• Use only a few pictures at a time. Confine these to the most common insects children see, such as bees, butterflies, ladybugs, flies, and ants.

• Ask children simply to name an insect they might find without introducing the cumulative component of the activity.

How to Extend this Activity:

• When it is your turn, introduce insects that are less commonly named, such as mosquito, dragonfly, lightning bug, or moth.

• Ask children to name an insect and the habitat in which they found it. For example, "I went on an insect hunt and found a ladybug on a leaf, a butterfly in a garden, a cricket in the grass," and so on.

5. ***Stamping Ant Messages.***

General Purpose: To increase children's awareness of nonverbal communication in the animal world and to give them practice in communicating with others.

TFPs: 54–81.

Materials: Empty roll-on deodorant bottles and/or bottles with squeeze-type applicators, such as small glue bottles or empty shampoo bottles with flip-up caps and small dispensing holes; tempera paint; construction paper; manila paper or butcher paper; markers.

Procedure:

a. Introduce the activity with a discussion of communication in the ant world. Refer to the TFPs for this information.

b. Invite children to "secrete" ant trails on paper. Provide paper and a dispenser filled with paint. Briefly demonstrate how to make dots on the paper using the dispensers.

c. Invite the children to secrete any kind of trail they wish. Some may want to secrete a straight line of dots across their paper; others may produce a sheet full of dot designs.

d. Provide markers for additional drawing and for putting children's names on their papers.

e. Encourage children to explain the message the secretions represent. "Tell me what your secretions are telling your ant friends. What will they find at the end?" Write this "translation" on the bottom or back of each child's paper. Read the message back to the child so he or she can confirm its accuracy.

Hint for Success:

- Test the dispensers prior to the children's arrival. Paint that is too thin or dispensing holes that are too big will interfere with children's ability to control the paint.

How to Simplify this Activity:

- Make the activity simpler by giving less information about ants and using large (at least eleven-by-fourteen-inch) pieces of paper.

How to Extend this Activity:

- If children are interested in drawing, you may mention that ants eat other (dead) insects, bruised fruit that has fallen to the ground or to a surface to which they can climb, seeds, berries, and sap. The children may want to draw a food on one area of their paper, then make a trail that leads to and from the food.
- Ask someone to try to decipher another child's message before hearing the translation. Encourage the two children to discuss similarities and differences between the intended meaning and the interpretation.

Physical

1. **Pollen Pockets.** Make four to six pollen pockets using four-ounce paper cups and six-inch strips of elastic a half inch wide. Punch two holes (one inch apart) near the rim of each cup. Thread the elastic through the holes. Have children tie one pollen pocket to each leg. Ask them to carry pollen (confetti, sand, or Styrofoam bits) from place to place with as few spills as possible. As children become more adept at moving without losing "pollen," introduce new challenges such as having them crawl over or under something. (Figure 11.4)

2. **Butterfly Flutter.** Give children colorful, flowing scarves or crepe-paper streamers. Show them how to use these props and their bodies to make fluttering, gliding, or gentle flying movements. Encourage chil-

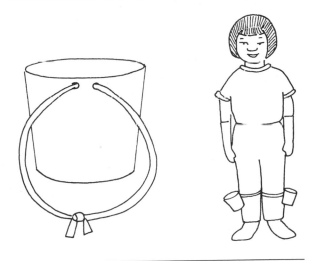

Figure 11.4 *Children Can Do Bee Work with Pollen Pockets*

dren to think of their own ways to mimic the butterfly movements they have observed. Add soft music as a way to enhance the quiet mood.

3. **Anthill or Beehive Mazes.** Create mazes on paper so that children can help the ant find his way through the nest to the outdoors, or help the bee find her way from the flower to the inside of the hive. To make bees and ants, trace the insect shapes in the teacher resource portion of this unit.

4. **Insects on Parade.** After talking with the children about how various insects move, invite each child to pick one and mimic its movements in a joyous parade around the room or playground (butterflies/moths flying or fluttering; crickets/grasshoppers hopping, jumping, and springing; ants scurrying, crawling on all fours).

5. **Grasshopper Day.** Announce that today is Grasshopper Day! This means that during a brief, designated portion of the session, children may move from one spot to another by hopping or jumping only. Let children know when to begin and give them a clear signal when you want them to stop. Fifteen to twenty minutes is a good length of time for this experience. It is best suited for a time in the day when children are usually allowed to move about freely. Join in the giggles and fun by remembering to hop and jump yourself!

6. *Grasshopper Long Jump.*

General Purpose: For children to practice fundamental motor skills.

TFPs: 82–97.

Materials: Live grasshoppers or crickets, if available; string; measuring tape or yardstick. Optional: pictures of crickets or grasshoppers.

Procedure:

a. Introduce the activity with an observation of live grasshoppers/crickets, if possible.

b. Observe the insects jumping. Note the way the adults use their wings to extend the distance jumped.

c. Demonstrate the standing long jump. Flex slightly at the knees. Bend your body forward. Extend your arms forward, then back. Push off with feet, stretch arms forward. Jump with extended legs. Land with knees bent.

d. Encourage children to squat and jump in a similar manner. If children are jumping with straight legs show them how to bend their knees. Suggest various strategies for using arms as "wings" to increase balance and stability. Praise all efforts.

Hints for Success:

• You may be able to purchase grasshoppers or crickets at live bait stores or in pet stores. Also, look for them in tall grass during warm weather. Handle them very gently and set them free in a meadow or grassy environment after observation.

• Children or adults may be able to catch grasshoppers or crickets in a butterfly net or a large wide-mouth jar placed with the open end a foot or so in front of the insect. Note that crickets and grasshoppers jump high and erratically, so several attempts may be necessary to capture one.

How to Simplify this Activity:

• Introduce jumping to inexperienced children by having them first rock back and forth on their heels and toes until they roll onto tiptoes. Then encourage children to flex and extend their knees rhythmically, rising higher and higher until their feet leave the ground.

• Younger children, or children at less advanced stages of jumping, typically do not use arms for thrust or balance very well. Encourage each child to use his or her arms to help them jump a greater distance. Tape grasshopper or cricket pictures to the floor and show youngsters how to jump from one to the next to motivate them to try this activity.

How to Extend this Activity:

• For children who demonstrate interest, measure and compare the jumping distance of grasshoppers/crickets (with and without wings if both adults and young are available) and of children. Mark the approximate distance with string; measure it afterward with a yardstick or tape measure.

• Encourage children to jump from one level to another: down to up, up to down, from mat to floor, floor to mat, step to floor, floor to step.

• Place a slender object, such as a rhythm stick or a jumprope, on the ground. Ask children to jump over it. Increase the number of objects and widen the jump, encouraging children to practice increasing the distance they can jump.

Pretend Play

1. *Bees in the Hive.* Arrange a pretend area where children assume the role of bees (queen, drones, workers). Provide places where the bees can gather nectar from flowers, get pollen, lay eggs, feed, and make honey. Add props such as paper flowers to sniff, buckets in which to carry pollen, a card table covered with a blanket for the hive, and tubs in which to mix the pollen and honey. Consider providing bee costumes to enhance the play.

2. *Entomologist's Laboratory.* Supply a make-believe area with insect pictures and specimens, magnifying glasses, a tripod microscope, white coats, insect books, paper to write on, and markers, pencils, or crayons. Add an ant farm, a cross-section of an abandoned hive, a cricket or a caterpillar in a container, or a dried out wasp's nest to give the children real insects and

insect homes to explore. Explain what a laboratory is and why people might want to study insects. Help children take on roles observing and recording insect behavior. Include a kitchen, explaining that scientists get hungry and sometimes cook their own meals. Add butterfly nets, paper flowers taped on a wall as if in a garden or field, and cricket cages. Show children how people who study insects often gather their own specimens, being careful to treat them gently.

3. **Butterfly Dress-up.** Make butterfly wings out of cardboard or help children make their own. Provide antennae made from hair bands and pipe cleaners. Post pictures of flowers for the butterflies to sip nectar from. Read *Where Does the Butterfly Go When It Rains?* by May Garelick as an introduction to the activity and to give children ideas about how to pretend to be butterflies or moths.

4. **Picnic Partners.** Set up a picnic with dishes, pretend food, a tablecloth on the ground, bug jars, and magnifying glasses. Place paper insects or models of insects in various spots throughout the area. Encourage children to pretend they are on a picnic and must contend with a host of insect visitors. Periodically replenish the insects as children collect the original specimens. Extend the play by having youngsters take their insects to the entomology laboratory for study.

5. **Moving through Metamorphosis.** Prepare in advance a pillowcase "chrysalis" for each child. These consist of a plain pillowcase with four paper streamers approximately twenty-four inches long inside. Put the pillowcases on the floor a slight distance from where the children will gather. Conduct this activity with or without music. Begin by inviting the children to pretend that they are tiny eggs resting on leaves. Tell them to gradually develop into caterpillars which can crawl and creep. Then ask the children to crawl into their "pillowcase" cocoons or chrysalises and rest. Next, instruct them to emerge as butterflies or moths waving their "streamer" wings. Finally, direct children to fly away, eventually finding imaginary flowers on which to rest and suck nectar.

6. **Flower Walk.** Take children on a pretend or real walk indoors or outdoors. Encourage them to flit from bloom to bloom in the manner of a butterfly or moth by demonstrating or describing the action.

7. **Ant Colony.** Create a place in your room where children can pretend to be ants living in a colony. Help children establish a variety of roles: nest builders, food gatherers, scouts, tenders of the young, and the queen. Remind children of the ant behaviors referred to in TFPs 54–81. Make "feelers" by attaching pipe cleaners to head bands. Add a sand table where the "ants" can pretend to store food or protect the young. Offer plastic fruit, large hollow wooden blocks, and other "nesting" materials to support children's play further. Extend the activity by incorporating some of the other plans described in this unit such as Stamping Ant Messages.

Bee Costumes

Antennae (Figure 11.5)
Materials for each set of antennae:

1. One hard plastic headband of a dark color (available inexpensively at most variety stores).
2. Two pipe cleaners, any color.
3. Half-inch-wide cloth tape, brown or black.

Procedure:
Tape one end of each of the pipe cleaners securely to the headband. Gently bend the unsecured ends out to the side or around in a

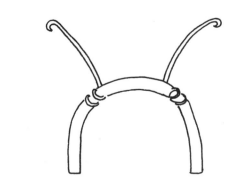

Figure 11.5 *Easy Bee Antennae*

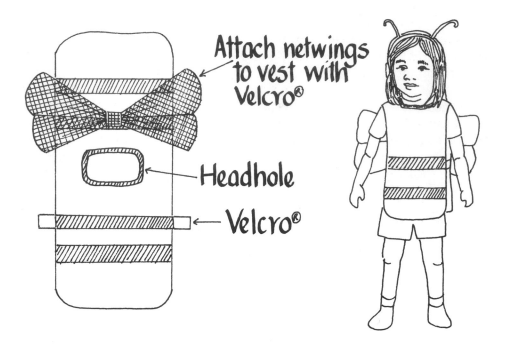

Attach netwings to vest with Velcro®

Headhole

Velcro®

Figure 11.6 *Winged Vests Make Children Look and Feel Like Bees*

circle to represent knobbed antennae. You could also thread a bead onto each antenna as a knob.

Winged Vest (Figure 11.6)
For *each* vest, you will need the following materials:

1. A rectangle of heavy, bright yellow, fabric, about one yard long by ⅓ yard wide. Vinyl with cotton backing (as for tablecloths or upholstering) works especially well.
2. Two thirds of a yard of black or yellow binding tape to finish the neckline.
3. One quarter of a yard of black Velcro®-type fastening material.
4. Two yards of black trim to create a striped effect on the body: ¾ inch width grosgrain ribbon is one possibility.
   Note: you may be able to find material that is already black and yellow striped. If so, omit this trim.
5. A sewing machine, black or yellow thread, and a sharp pair of scissors.

To construct *wings* for each vest, you will also need:

6. Half of a yard of black net.
7. Six inches of black Velcro®-type fastening material.

Procedure:
To construct vest:

1. Fold the yellow rectangle of cloth in half so the short sides of the rectangle come together.
2. Cut a half-moon shape in the center of the fold, large enough to slip easily over a child's head (about 9 inches long).
3. Sew binding tape around the neck opening, folding in the ends to prevent raveling.
4. Laying the rectangle flat, pin down and then sew on six black stripes of the trim, three on each side of the fold (the front and back).
5. If your fabric is one that ravels (unlike vinyl), hem the edges all the way around the rectangle.

6. Cut the fastening material in half. Sew "male" (spiky) sided strips to each end of center stripe on back, and "female" (fuzzy) sided strips to each end of center stripe on front, so that they extend, to be fastened under arms.

To construct wings:

7. Lay the net flat; fold in half the long way. Cut the ends to resemble a wing shape (note that you will be cutting through two thicknesses of net. This will result in a representation of a four-winged insect).
8. Gather the net from top to bottom, wrapping the fuzzy-sided strip of Velcro® around it. Sew in place.
9. Sew the spiky-sided strip of Velcro® to the middle of the center stripe on the back of the vest. Press the wings in place when desired. They can also be used alone, detached.

Social

1. *Making a Group Beehive.* Provide egg cartons, string, glue, thin wire, scissors, crayons, and markers. Explain to children that they will be working together to build a pretend beehive for the class. Help children plan how they will proceed and assist them in making the necessary compromises. The emphasis here is on joint, rather than individual, decision making.
2. *Ants Sharing Food*
   General Purpose: For children to practice cooperating with and helping one another.
   TFPs: 54–81.
   Materials: Wrapped drinking straws. Optional: pipe-cleaner antennae attached to headbands in ant colors: black, brown, rust, yellow, green, blue, purple, or red.
   Procedure:
   a. Introduce the activity through a discussion of ants, particularly their skillful mouths and habits of sharing food. Talk about the food-gathering worker ant who brings food home to the colony in her special stomach. A hungry ant strokes the food-gatherer's head to ask for a share. As they stand together, the gatherer passes food from her mouth into the mouth of her friend.
   b. Mention some foods that ants enjoy: dead insects, sap, berries, and fruit. Ask children which of these food preferences they share.
   c. Invite children to pretend to be ants helping their friends get food. Provide one wrapped straw for each pair of children. Tell them to imagine that the straws are ant food.
   d. Suggest that one child unwrap a straw and clench one end between her or his teeth, then crawl over to a partner.
   e. Direct the partner to stroke the first child's head gently, to let her or him know that he or she is hungry and would like a share of the food.
   f. Point out that the "food-gathering ant" should then stand and pass the straw to the "hungry ant," who should grasp the extended, not the mouthed, end in her or his teeth.

Hints for Success:
- For sanitary purposes, be sure that each new pair of children unwraps a clean straw and that they grasp opposite ends in their mouths.
- Children may enjoy wearing antennae and seeking a partner ant with antennae of a matching color. This indicates that both ants are from the same colony and so would be more likely to share food.

How to Simplify this Activity:
- Show children how to drop the food they are sharing at their partner's feet, rather than asking the second child to grab it in his or her teeth.

How to Extend this Activity:
- Children may take turns enacting the sharing episode while others watch, or several pairs may carry out the activity at once. Allow partners to trade roles if time allows.

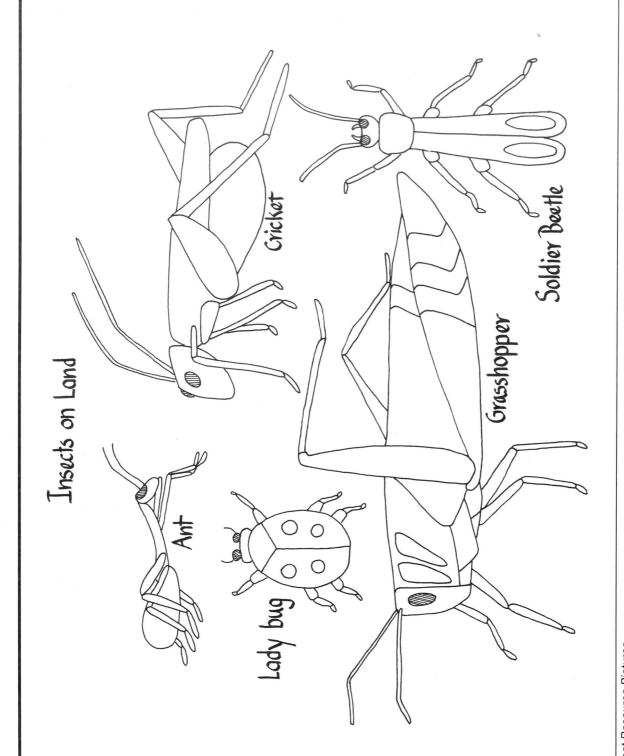

Insects on Land

Cricket

Soldier Beetle

Grasshopper

Ant

Lady bug

Figure 11.7a *Insect Resource Pictures*

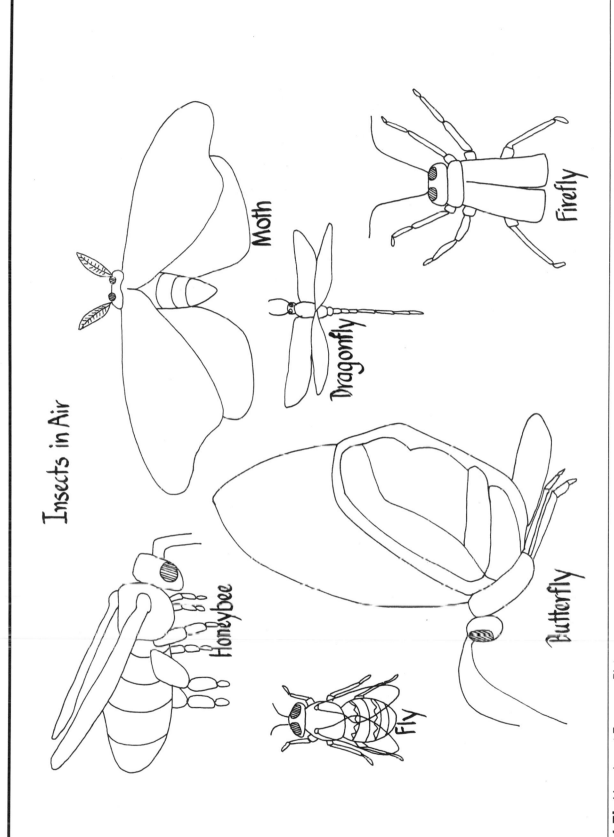

Figure 11.7b *More Insect Resource Pictures*

Insect Homes

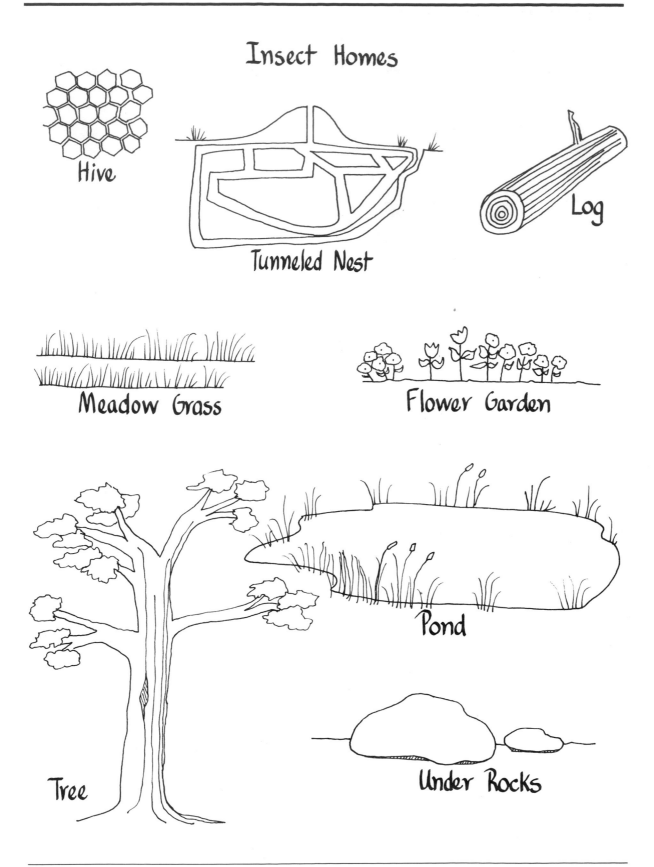

Hive

Tunneled Nest

Log

Meadow Grass

Flower Garden

Tree

Pond

Under Rocks

Figure 11.7c *What Kind of Insects Live in These Homes?*

TEACHER RESOURCES

Field Trip Ideas

1. Take a nature walk anywhere outside and look for various kinds of insects.
2. Visit an apiary. Observe how the beekeeper handles the bees and removes the honey.
3. Take a trip to a farm or an orchard. Draw children's attention to how people use insects or attempt to control them in relation to food production.
4. Visit a laboratory where scientists are studying insects.
5. Go to a museum to look at the insect collections.
6. Go to a pet store and observe crickets for sale. Purchase a few for the classroom.
7. Take a trip to a grocery or health food store. Examine all the different types of honey for sale. Arrange in advance for tasting or purchase several varieties and take them back to the classroom to try.

Classroom Visitors

1. Invite a beekeeper to visit and demonstrate equipment used in the profession. Ask if the beekeeper can bring a cross-section of a working beehive safely enclosed in glass (a terrarium).
2. Put a vase of fresh flowers on an open, sunlit windowsill. Watch for insect visitors.
3. Ask an entomologist to visit the class and explain why scientists study insects and how they go about it.
4. Invite a parent who gardens organically to talk to the children about helpful insects. Ask the parent to describe some nonchemical ways of controlling insect pests.

Children's Books

Allen, G. E. *Everyday Insects*. Boston: Houghton Mifflin, 1963.

Brinckloe, J. *Fireflies!* New York: Macmillan, 1985.

Carle, E. *The Honeybee and the Robber: A Moving Picture Book*. New York: Putnam Publishing Group, 1981.

———. *The Very Hungry Caterpillar*. Cleveland, OH: Collins and World Publishing, n.d.

Conklin, G. *I Like Butterflies*. New York: Holiday House, 1960.

———. *I Like Caterpillars*. New York: Holiday House, 1958.

Daly, K. N. *Ladybug, Ladybug*. New York: American Heritage, 1969.

Day, J. W. *What Is an Insect?* New York: Golden, 1976.

Dugan, W. *The Bug Book*. New York: Golden, 1965.

Freschet, B. *The Ants Go Marching*. New York: Scribner's, 1973.

Garelick, M. *Where Does the Butterfly Go When It Rains?* New York: Scholastic, 1961.

Harrington, H. E. *Let's Look at Insects*. Garden City, NY: Doubleday, 1969.

Heller, R. *How to Hide a Butterfly and Other Insects*. New York: Grosset and Dunlap, 1985.

Milne, A. A. *Winnie-the-Pooh*. New York: Dell, 1970.

Reidel, M. *From Egg to Butterfly*. Minneapolis: Carolrhoda, 1974.

Sabin, F. *Amazing World of Ants*. Mahwah, NJ: Troll, 1982.

Adult References

Callahan, P. S. *Insects and How They Function*. New York: Holiday House, 1971.

Fichter, G. S. *Insect Pests*. New York: Golden, 1966.

Milne, L., and M. Milne. *The Audubon Society Field Guide to North American Insects and Spiders*. New York: Knopf, 1980.

Suzuki, D. *Looking at Insects*. New York: Warner, 1986.

White, R. E. *A Field Guide to the Beetles of North America*. Boston: Houghton Mifflin, 1983.

Zim, H. S., and C. Cottam. *Insects*. New York: Golden, 1956.

Chapter 12

Wild Birds

•

Chirp, twitter, cheep, caw, honk, quack, squawk, trill, coo, flutter, tap tap, flap, chirrup cheerily. . . . Listen! Chances are that if you step outside and are very quiet, you will hear these sounds—bird sounds.

•

Birds are everywhere: city, country, town, forest, plains, desert, meadow, marsh, and seashore. The number and variety of birds in our environment is astonishing. Consequently, children have many opportunities to see and hear birds.

PURPOSE

This unit has been designed to highlight commonplace experiences for children and thereby increase their observational skills and enrich their understanding of bird life. Because of their great variety, birds provide an ideal panorama of interesting features to study in detail, not simply for their own sake, but to heighten children's appreciation of the natural world. The activities we present focus on both bird characteristics and bird behavior and give children opportunities to study birds and to act like birds. At all times, the emphasis is on giving children factual information that they can use to satisfy their own curiosity about the world around them.

IMPLEMENTATION

There is more than one way to approach the study of birds. Possible variations are described below.

Option One: Focus on local birds
Week One: Physical characteristics of birds.
Week Two: Bird behavior.

Option Two:
Week One: Backyard birds.
Week Two: Exotic birds.

Option Three:
Week One: General introduction to birds.
Week Two: Birds of the forest.
Week Three: Birds of the marsh and meadow.

Option Four: Implement the bird unit twice—once early in the year and once later in the year. Make particular note of current bird residents and the similarities and differences you observe during the different seasons.

The Birds unit is a natural follow-up to a unit on pets, the farm, or insects, which represent a second type of flying creature. This unit could easily precede one on bears, as another example of wildlife, or a unit on nonliving things that fly, such as kites, planes, and balloons.

TERMS, FACTS, AND PRINCIPLES

General Characteristics

1. Birds are feathered, warm-blooded animals that have:
   a. two wings
   b. two legs
   c. a bill or beak
   d. eyes that are flat, allowing them to see both near and far objects clearly at the same time.

2. There are many different types, or species, of birds.

3. Each species of bird is distinguished by particular characteristics: how it travels; how it communicates; the color and pattern of its feathers; the shape of its body, its bill or beak, its feet; what it eats; where it lives; the kind of nest it builds; the color, number, and size of the eggs it lays; and how it feeds and rears its young.

4. People tell birds apart by their characteristics.

How Birds Travel

5. Most birds fly.

6. All birds can walk.

7. Some birds swim.

8. Some birds cannot fly (ostriches, penguins, and peacocks, for example).

*9. Birds fly by leaping into the air and flapping their wings fast and powerfully enough to lift them from the ground.

*10. Birds have hollow bones.

*11. Birds' feathers, body shapes, and light, hollow bones aid them in their ability to fly.

12. Some birds soar, some swoop, some fly in a steady motion, some hover.

13. When flying, large birds flap their wings slowly and small birds flap their wings quickly.

14. To turn in the air, birds twist or bend their wings.

*15. Birds hold or use their bodies in a variety of ways during flight. Sometimes they stretch out their necks or hold them in an S-shaped curve; their feet might protrude or tuck in under their feathers.

16. Birds fly to find food, either in the air or on the ground.

17. Most birds fly or swim away when they sense danger.

*18. The feathers of swimming birds contain extra oil to protect the feathers against being soaked.

19. Some birds, such as ducks and geese, waddle.

20. Some birds, such as storks and peacocks, walk slowly.

21. Some birds, such as sparrows, walk quickly.

22. Some birds, such as ostriches, run.

Bird Feathers

23. All birds have feathers; all feathered animals are birds.

24. Birds vary in color and pattern. Differences in the color and location of feathers create colors and patterns on a bird's body.

*25. The colors of some birds help them blend with their surroundings and protect them from predators (their enemies).

*26. Birds that travel in groups, or flocks, are often brightly colored to attract the attention of other birds of the same species.

27. Male and female birds of the same species may not have feathers of the same color.

*28. The male uses the bright colors of his feathers to attract the female during courtship, or to draw attention or danger away from the female, whose colors blend better with the environment for her protection.

*29. Feathers are made up of tiny strands attached to a main shaft and each other.

*30. Each strand has tiny barbs something like a zipper's teeth.

*31. When a bird draws its beak over the feathers, the beak acts like the movable part of a zipper, causing the barbs to "zip" back together again. This process is called preening.

*32. Feathers trap air which keeps the bird warm in winter and cool in summer.

33. Individual birds have a variety of feathers including down (fine, soft feathers) for warmth, contour (curved) feathers to fit the shape of the body, and flight feathers for flying or gliding.

34. Some birds have special feathers that form head crests, dangle behind them in flight, or look like a cat's whiskers, growing from skin around the beak.

*35. Birds have an oil gland, which they use in caring for their feathers.

*36. Birds draw their beaks over their oil gland, pressing out oil that they smooth over their feathers.

*37. The oil on the feathers keeps rain and water from soaking them. It acts as a "raincoat" for land birds and helps swimming birds float more easily on water.

38. When birds molt, they lose all their feathers, a few at a time. They grow new ones to replace them.

39. Birds molt at regular intervals.

40. Some birds molt more frequently than others.

41. A bird's plumage may change color as the season changes to enable it to blend with the environment.

Body Shape

42. All birds have the same body parts.

43. The shape of each body part varies among different types of birds.

44. Bird silhouettes (the outline of the bird) vary from type to type.

45. Birds vary in size from a three-inch hummingbird that weighs about a third of an ounce to a three-hundred-pound ostrich.

Beaks and Bills

46. Birds have beaks that vary in many ways to help them catch and eat their food.
    a. Hooked beaks tear prey into pieces.
    b. Long, thin beaks spear fish.
    c. Short, stout, conelike beaks crack seeds and shells.
    d. Small beaks grab insects.
    e. Narrow, needlelike beaks extract nectar from flowers.
    f. Fringed beaks are used for straining food from mud or water.

47. Most birds drink by dipping their beaks in water and then throwing their heads back to get the liquid to their throats.

48. Some birds catch food while flying; others peck food from the ground; others suck it from flowers.

Feet

49. Birds have feet designed for special purposes.
    a. Some feet are for clasping or perching on branches.
    b. Some feet are shaped for running.
    c. Some feet are shaped to clasp vertical surfaces or even the underside of branches.
    d. Some feet have strong toes and sharp claws for catching and holding prey.
    e. Some feet have webbing between the toes for paddling or swimming.
    f. Some feet are shaped for walking or standing in mud without sinking.

Bird Communication

50. Each species of bird communicates with other birds by sound and movement unique to that species.

51. Birds make special sounds to warn of danger, to call their young, to protect feeding and nesting areas, and express well-being. These are called bird songs or calls.

52. Some birds can mimic (imitate) the sounds of other birds, animals, or even people (mockingbirds, catbirds, parrots).

53. Birds communicate in special ways during courtship through "bird conversation" or "bird dances" (called display) during which the male shows off his feathers to a female.

Food

54. Compared to their size, birds, both big and small, require a large amount of food to live because they use up a lot of energy very fast, especially in flight.

55. Birds spend much of their time looking for and eating food.

56. Birds eat a variety of foods such as fish, flying or crawling insects, worms, grubs, seeds, berries, small animals such as mice, and other smaller birds.

Living Space or Environment

57. Birds live in a variety of places, such as woods, meadows, plains, deserts, and cities, and near ponds, lakes, and oceans.

58. Birds live in a number of different climactic conditions.

59. At certain times during the year, some birds travel from one region or climate to another. This is called migration.

*60. Before winter comes in the United States, many birds in the north fly (migrate) south so they will have enough food to eat.

61. In the spring when food sources are available once again, birds who flew south return north and breed.

*62. Scientists are studying how birds know when to start their journey and how they are able to find their way during migration.

Nests

63. Each species of bird builds a nest peculiar to that species.

64. Birds build nests for the purpose of protecting their eggs, which contain their young.

*65. Nest building is an instinctive behavior. Birds do not decide to build nests, nor do they have to be taught to build nests.

*66. Birds build nests of varying complexity.

67. Different species of birds build their nests in different places.
    a. Some build their nests on the ground.
    b. Some build nests above the ground.
    c. Some species hide their nests.
    d. Some species build nests in the open.
68. Bird nests vary in size and shape.

Eggs

69. All birds lay eggs from which their young hatch.
70. Bird eggs vary in size, shape, and color from species to species.
*71. Most eggs that are laid in a hidden nest are plain and round.
*72. Most eggs that are laid in the open are oval and have colors that blend with the environment.
73. The number of eggs that a bird lays at one time varies from species to species. Some lay one egg at a time while others lay two or more.
74. Birds sit on their eggs to keep them warm and protected.
75. Baby birds are called chicks.
76. Some newly hatched chicks can see, walk, and feed themselves and are ready to leave the nest very soon after hatching.
*77. Some newly hatched chicks are blind and featherless, and they must remain in the nest dependent on parent birds for care and food for some time. Parent birds spend much time and energy caring for their babies.
78. When a bird is ready to hatch, it must peck its way out of the egg.

The Study and Protection of Birds

79. People study birds by watching them, keeping records of their appearance and behavior, and counting the kind and number of birds in particular areas.
80. Anyone can be a bird-watcher.
81. Some people use binoculars to watch birds. Binoculars are tools that make birds appear larger, allowing people to see them more clearly.
82. Scientists who study birds are called ornithologists.
83. Both men and women can be ornithologists.
*84. To study bird habits, scientists sometimes capture, band, and then release the birds. When the birds are recaptured, scientists can tell where they have been and how they have grown.
85. Many people work to protect birds by making sure that their living space is not disturbed, that their food is not contaminated, and that people do not kill them.
86. People have set aside areas as bird sanctuaries where birds are safe from hunters.
87. People visit bird sanctuaries to watch, study, and enjoy birds.

ACTIVITY IDEAS

Aesthetics

1. *Feather Dusters.* Collect an assortment of feathers from birds that are common to your area. If this is not possible, purchase feathers from a craft shop or ask children to bring in feathers they find on the ground. Tell children to examine the feathers, stroking them in every direction and feeling the shaft. Prepare several colors of paint in flat tins, varying the thickness of the mixtures. Demonstrate how to use the feather as a brush, using the point of the shaft or the feathers. Suggest that the children experiment with different strokes—broad, narrow, sweeping, and so on—to get a variety of effects.
2. *Fun with Feathers/Seeds.* Provide feathers or seeds in small containers for children to glue onto heavy construction paper or thin oak tag. (Seeds are heavy and require a firm backing.) Vary this project by drawing or cutting out a large outline of a bird and have children (individually or in small groups) glue the feathers inside the outline. This project can be carried out over a few days. If you use seeds, be sure that they vary in size, color, and texture.

3. **Bird Songs, Chants, and Fingerplays.**
   Teach children the following fingerplays, songs, and games emphasizing the enjoyment that comes from the rhythm of the words.

   Two Little Dickey-Birds
   Two Little dickey-birds
   Sitting on a hiil
   One named Jack
   One named Jill
   Fly away Jack
   Fly away Jill
   Come back Jack
   Come back Jill

   Bluebird, Bluebird
   This is an adaptation of a traditional singing game that can be chanted if you don't know the tune. Have children stand in a circle with their hands joined and raised to shoulder height. One child is designated as the "bluebird." As the children chant, the bluebird weaves in and out of the upraised hands (or "windows"). At the end of the song, the bluebird chooses another child to be his or her successor. Alternatively, the next child can simply follow the first "bird" through the "window."
   Song: Bluebird, bluebird through my window (3x)
   Buy molasses candy.

   Five Little Birds
   Five little birds without any home,
   Five little trees in a row.
   Come build your nests,
   In our branches tall,
   We'll rock you to and fro.

   Five Little Robins
   Five little robins lived in a tree.
   Father,
   Mother,
   And babies three.
   Father caught a worm.
   Mother caught a bug.
   The three little robins
   Began to tug.
   This one got a bug.
   This one got a worm.
   This one said, "Now it's my turn."

   If I Were a Bird
   If I were a bird, I'd sing a song,
   And fly about the whole day long.
   And when the night comes, go to rest,
   Way up high in my cozy nest.

4. **Beautiful Birds.** When you inform the children's parents about the Birds unit, ask them to send in items from home that depict birds in decorative ways. Examples might include china or pottery, woven articles, scarves, table runners, hangings, pictures, and tapestries. Find a corner of the room where these can be displayed. Prepare children to handle the items with supervision. Point out how the birds are shown on each article and how they enhance its beauty. If appropriate, show how the shape of the bird is used as an integral part of the design. For instance, a bird's head may be the handle for a teapot or casserole. To extend this activity, have children create their own bird decorations using clay, paper scrolls, or fabric.

5. **Chirps and Trills.** Over a period of several days, play records or tapes of bird calls. Help children become aware of similarities and differences in pitch, rhythm, quality of the songs (harsh, sweet), and melodies. Provide children with simple instruments. Include triangles, tambourines, sand blocks, sticks, maracas, and whistles. Invite the children to try to imitate a particular bird song. Help them to choose a song that matches the quality of their instrument (for instance, a crow's "caw" can be imitated using sand blocks or maracas, whereas a raven's song would be best imitated by a whistle). To extend this activity, have children create their own bird songs or calls using specific instruments. Encourage children to trade instruments so that they can explore different sounds.

Affective

1. **You Eat Like a Bird.** Have a variety of snacks available that represent the kinds of food that birds eat. Offer sunflower or other seeds and different nuts and fruits. Ask the children to decide which ones they

want to try and then, which one is their favorite. This activity will take on a cognitive focus if you extend it by asking children to determine which type of beak a bird must have to eat a particular food.

2. *Best Birds.* Prepare pictures of a variety of birds or arrange for children to see birds in nature or at a zoo or pet store. Make a list of the birds (with their pictures nearby) and ask each child to select his or her favorite bird. Write down their choices and the reasons for them.

3. *Sweet Tweet.* Purchase or make a bird feeder. Place it in a tree near the school or outside a classroom window. Have children take turns keeping the feeder supplied with seeds on a daily basis. If you have regular classroom "jobs," add this to the list. Prepare a roster of the children in the class with a place for them to check off the completed task. At the end of the day (or once a week), review the chart with the children.

4. *Big Bird.* Find out the height of several large birds, such as ostriches, flamingos, roadrunners, cranes, and storks. Make a chart depicting the height of each of these birds. If possible, draw a life-sized sketch of the birds right on the chart. Use a different color for each bird to help children differentiate them. Then, measure each child on the chart. Put a mark along with the child's name in the appropriate place. Give children an opportunity to figure out which birds they most nearly resemble in height. Older children can be encouraged to use comparative terms, such as "I am as tall as a _____; I am taller than a _____ ; I am shorter than a _____ ." Adapt this activity by making weight comparisons between children and a variety of birds. This activity may take place over several days. Leave the chart on the wall for the duration of the Bird unit, since children will want to refer to it several times. Remember that emphasizing the actual numbers involved is not necessary for this activity, since the focus is on increasing children's self-awareness. However, this plan could easily be adapted to the cognitive domain by emphasizing comparative sizes or by the inclusion of inches and pounds as the measuring units.

Cognition

1. *That's for the Birds.* Make bird feeders by spooning peanut butter on pine cones and rolling them in bird seed, or purchase a commercially made feeder. Have the children observe the birds that come to the feeder and tally how many birds they see each day. They can total their tally marks and find out how many they saw every day, throughout the week, or over a longer period of time. Keep a log book of the daily and weekly count. To extend this activity, count and record the number of each type of bird that visits the feeder. Information can be gathered about the different times of day that the birds feed by dividing the group into "early bird" counters and "late bird" counters.

   Alternatively, divide children into the "robin watchers," the "blue jay watchers," and so on. Graph the number of each different species that feeds at the feeder over time and compare. As a follow-up, repeat this activity during different seasons of the year and help children read their graphs to figure out bird feeding patterns over the course of a year. To make it easier for children to remember the different birds, hang pictures of the common ones on the window or wall near the feeder viewing area.

2. *Egg-zactly Correct.* Prepare a number of model nests of various sizes. Any shallow bowls filled with grass will work. Put a different number of model eggs in each nest, using either all of one size or a variety of sizes. Some ideas for eggs are: hosiery eggs, Ping-Pong balls, golf balls, tennis balls, marbles, and any other objects that resemble eggs. After preparing the nests, do the following activities with the children.

   • Give children time to explore the nests and eggs.

   • Ask them to count the eggs and tell you how many are in each nest.

- As the children count the eggs, put next to each nest a corresponding numeral card or one with egg shapes to equal the number of eggs in the nest.
- The next time children count the eggs, let them put the correct numeral or number cards next to each nest.

3. *Feathering Your Nest.* Bring several abandoned bird's nests to the classroom. Parents can help in the search, if you inform them long in advance that the group is going to be studying birds. Encourage children to examine the nests by looking at them, holding them, and feeling them inside and out. Introduce magnifying glasses only after children have explored the nests thoroughly. Ask children to describe what they are seeing and feeling. Using a sharp knife, cut one nest apart so children can examine its construction. Point out the kinds of materials the birds used in building the nest. Differentiate the materials that the birds had to collect (leaves, twigs, string, and so on) from those they produced with their own bodies (feathers, saliva). If possible, repeat this activity with nests of different species. Compare the materials used, as well as the shape and configuration of the nests.

4. *Feather Features.* Collect several feathers from the ground. Examine them closely with the children, by encouraging children to feel them, hold them, and manipulate them. Point out that each feather is made up of individual strands attached to a shaft. By brushing them in one direction, the feathers fluff and the strands separate. Show how the feathers can be "re-zipped" by brushing them in the other direction. Obtain books containing enlarged photos that show the feather barbs and point these out to children. Explain how birds use their feathers in flight and to help regulate body temperature. Be sure to try this activity yourself before introducing it to children, so that you know how to zip and unzip the feathers.

5. *Fields and Feathers.* Construct a set of flannel-board bird bodies and several sets of matching feathers. (Figure 12.1) To increase accuracy of representation, make pale brown bodies with colored heads and match the feathers to the head colors.

Set up a large flannel board. Place the bird bodies on the flannel board, but pile all the feathers together near the board.

Invite the children to assemble birds by selecting feathers and placing them on bodies as they wish. Allow several minutes for exploration and manipulation.

Increase the complexity of the task by providing three or more shapes and sizes of feathers in each of several colors, so that children can create bird combinations considering the attributes of size and shape as well as color.

As children assemble their birds, ask them to create "flocks of birds" that are alike and birds of different species that are not alike. Later, introduce additional flannel pieces representing varying habitats that match the colors of the birds you've constructed, such as a brown nest, a "meadow" or "field" of yellow straw, or bright jungle flowers. Tell children to create birds that match the environments depicted.

6. *Bird Habitats.* Laminate a collection of bird pictures and pictures of different bird habitats, such as fields, ponds, forests, and oceans. Tell children a story about some birds that flew far away from home and are looking for a new place to live. Explain that each bird must find a place where it can find food and make a nest. Examine the physical features of each bird, looking at its bill, feet, and body shape for clues to what it eats and where it might live most successfully, so that the children can help it find an ideal home. Once a decision has been made, match the bird to its habitat and repeat the activity with succeeding bird pictures. This activity is most appropriately carried out after children have learned something about birds since they will be looking at several attributes at one time and will be applying information they have learned to a new situation.

7. *The Shape of Things.* From existing pictures, draw or trace the outlines of a large variety of birds in different positions (flying, roosting, walking, nesting, feeding, and so on). Go over the outlines with black marker to create silhouettes. Glue these

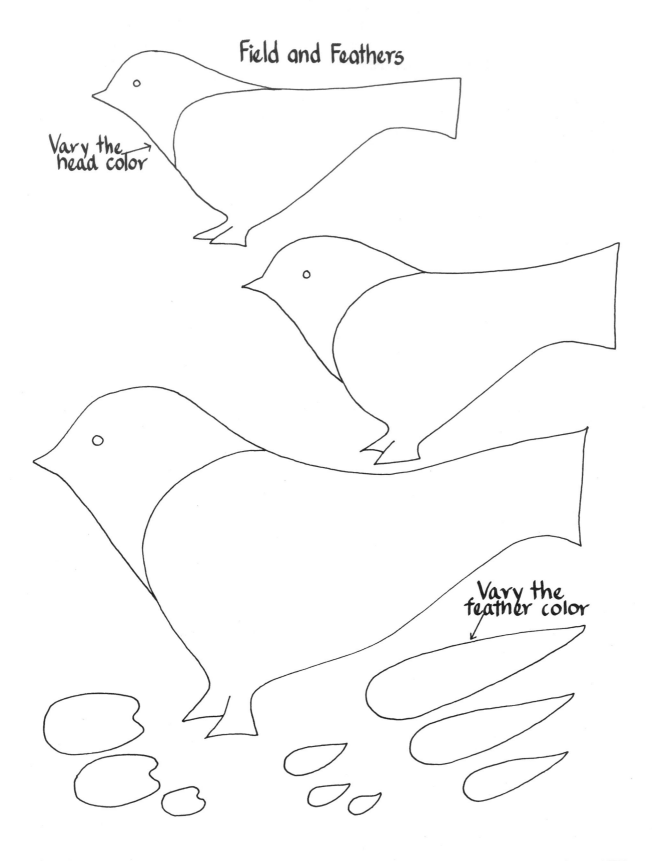

Field and Feathers

Vary the head color

Vary the feather color

Figure 12.1 *Flannelboard Birds and Feather Pattern*

on individual cards and laminate them or cover them with clear contact paper to preserve them. Back the pictures that you traced with oak tag or index cards. Cut out these birds and cover them with clear contact paper. Present the children with the two piles of pictures and tell them to match each bird with its silhouette. Begin with a few pairs and gradually increase the number as children gain experience. Be sure to choose pairs that differ in fine detail, as well as those whose distinctions are more obvious.

8. **Ruffled Feathers.** Introduce this activity with a discussion of the way the oil gland at the base of the bird's tail lubricates its feathers to make them more resistant to water. Explain why it is important that birds, like humans, keep dry. Coat one hand of each child with petroleum jelly, and leave the other uncoated. Tell children to dip their hands in a basin of water that you have provided. Have them describe what they feel and see. Be sure to provide paper towels for clean-up. Further demonstrate by cutting two identical bird shapes out of paper or cloth. Coat one with the jelly. Place both in the water. Allow children to handle the cutouts after they have been removed and to note the effect of the jelly on the bird. To ensure that children focus on the attribute of "coated" versus "noncoated" cutouts, make certain that the birds are the same in every other way (shape, size, color, material, and so on). This activity can also be carried out using real bird feathers.

9. **All Sorts of Birds.** Gather an assortment of reference books that specialize in birds. (See the list of adult reference books at the end of this unit for suggestions.) Then, cut out pictures of birds from magazines. Some of the pictures should be of birds alone for easy identification, and some should be of birds in groups, in trees, or with other creatures. Include birds as represented by artists of various cultures (Japanese ink drawings, Mexican wood cuts, European landscape painters, and so on). Present the books and a few pictures of birds to the children. For each cutout bird, ask them to find the corresponding picture in the reference book. At first, give children only one or two books to look through and realistic pictures of birds. Later on, show children more complex pictures and ask them to first pick out the bird and then find the same type of bird in the reference texts.

10. **Beaks and Bills.**

    General Purpose: For children to practice making discriminations by attributes and functions.

    TFPs: 1a, 46a–f, 54–56.

    Materials: A collection of pictures that depict birds with different beaks and bills.

    Procedure:

    a. Set up the area by placing a pile of bird pictures before each child seated at a table. Ask them to look at the birds' beaks and bills. Wait several minutes while they explore and examine the pictures.

    b. Introduce the activity by pointing out that there are many different kinds of beaks and bills pictured. Tell the children that different beaks and bills work best for picking up and eating different kinds of foods. Direct them to group their pictures according to characteristics that the beaks or bills share.

    c. Encourage the children to discuss their own ways of classifying, for example, "Manuel, tell me about a way that the bird beaks in this pile are alike. You noticed that they are all yellow." (The youngest or least experienced may focus on just one attribute at first, most likely color). "Sophie, you've put all the birds together. Tell me something about their beaks that made you decide they belong here." "They do all curve! You've noticed these beaks are hooked."

    d. It may be possible to encourage new strategies for classifying, by questioning or offering information: "These are small-beaked birds. Find another way to divide this pile up. Here are some hooked beaks; this other pile has curved beaks. Show me another way to put the birds together."

e. Direct children to line up their piles by beak type. Point out that long, thin beaks can be used like straws to suck nectar from flowers. Stronger-looking long beaks can be spears for fishing. "Which beaks look like they could be nutcrackers?"

Hints for Success:

- Provide enough variety of beaks in shape and color that the differences are easily seen.

- Expect that younger, less experienced children will group them by the most obvious physical differences, and that only later will they be able to group them by function or food type.

How to Simplify this Activity:

- Begin with large drawings or photographs of bird heads only, not whole birds.

- Introduce a few pictures at a time so children don't become confused by too much detail.

How to Extend this Activity:

- Introduce pictures of foods that birds eat. Tell children to match the beaks with the appropriate food.

Construction

1. *Build-a-Bird.* Over a period of several weeks collect chicken bones from the children's families. Be sure these are thoroughly cleaned, boiled, and dried to remove any bacteria. In addition, collect or purchase bird feathers. On oak tag or thin cardboard, draw an outline of a bird. (Use one large outline for several children to work on together, or provide individual outlines.) Older children may wish to draw their own. Place the outline on a flat surface and provide strong glue. Explain that the children are to create first a bird skeleton using the bones, and then a complete bird gluing on the feathers. If you wish to simulate skin covering the bones, use

pieces of cheesecloth. This project will likely take several days to complete—one for the bones, one for the skin, and the final day to put on the feathers. An alternative is to re-create the skeleton of a part of the bird, such as a wing.

2. *Clay Pigeons.* Let the children help measure and mix the salt clay.
   2 cups flour
   1 cup salt
   1 cup water
   1 tsp. oil
   When the dough is thoroughly mixed, encourage children to use the clay to construct a bird. Let the clay birds dry for a few days. Once they are thoroughly dry provide materials so children can paint them.

3. *The House I Live In.* Provide children with shoeboxes, straw, grasses, twigs, other natural materials, and wet clay. Encourage them to make a nest inside the box, where a bird would feel at home.

   Suggest that they use the clay as a mud binder for the other ingredients. Remind them to leave room for the birds and their eggs. If they wish, children can have the clay birds they made on a previous day live in the nests.

Language

1. *Bird Talk.* Play recordings of sounds that birds make. First, play the sounds for the children and just have them listen. Next, play the sounds again and show a picture of the bird at the same time. Discuss how people get enjoyment from listening to songbirds. As children gain familiarity with the songs, they can begin to match each type of bird with its unique song. To extend the activity, have children invent a bird language, assigning specific meanings to certain calls. Children can practice communicating with their fellow "birds" in the group.

2. *Bird Books.* Prepare blank books in the shapes of birds. These can be made by stapling two or three pieces of paper together with a construction paper cover and back. Cut the book into a shape of a

bird. Lead a discussion about bird characteristics and behaviors. Provide each child with a book and encourage him or her to create a book about birds. Children can make up a story about a bird, list facts about a bird, or fill their bird books in any way. They can dictate their information to an adult or write it themselves.

3. *Make Way for Ducklings.* Read the story *Make Way for Ducklings* by Robert McCloskey to the children. Lead an activity about the main idea of the story. Hold up a picture of a duck and a car. Ask the children which one the story is mostly about. Show the children a picture of a city and a picture of a rural place. Ask the children if the story is mostly about ducks in the city or in the country. Show the children a picture of ducks going for a walk and ducks looking for a place to live. Ask the children if the story is mostly about the ducks going for a walk or looking for a place to live. As children become more experienced in identifying the main point of a story, show them pictures that more closely resemble each other, so that they must differentiate finer details.

4. *Add-Along Story.* After a discussion about birds, start to tell a story about a bird. Ask the children to add to the story. Write down the children's ideas and give every child the opportunity to add to the story. Some suggestions for story starters are: "Once upon a time there was a goose named Tom. He had a broken wing and could not fly. It was getting cold and time for the birds to migrate. . . ." "Once there was a bird who was different from all of the rest of the birds. . . ."

5. *Story Sequence.* Prepare groups of cards depicting several steps in action sequences. For example, one set might include pictures of a bird taking off, of a bird flying in the air, and of a bird landing. Others might show an egg, then various stages of hatching. The activity will be more difficult with more cards. Have children work in pairs to put the cards in the correct order.

6. *Filling the Bill.* Prepare children for the story by first discussing the different kinds of bills that birds have. Also, talk about how bills help them to eat the kinds of foods that they like. Read the story. Prior to the children's arrival, prepare a set of flannel figures of birds and a separate set of matching bills as depicted in the story *Filling the Bill* by Aileen Fisher. Afterward, give the children time to explore the flannel pieces. Show the pictures from the story and ask the children to find the matching flannel-board birds and bills. Then have the children try to match them on their own.

7. *Flights of Fancy.* After discussions about how actual birds look and live, tell children that they will have an opportunity to create an imaginary bird. Individually or in small groups, have children dictate the name and description of their birds. Ask leading questions, such as, "Tell me what kind of nest your bird builds," or "What do the baby birds look like?" This activity can be carried out over a few days, so that children can add to their descriptions. Compile their invented birds into a classroom book entitled "Flights of Fancy." Make copies, if possible, and send one home to each child's family or pass the classroom book from family to family.

8. *The Green Grass Grew All Around.* This is a traditional cumulative song in which one adds a new element for each verse and then proceeds backward to the refrain. It can be chanted as well as sung. In addition, each line of the verse is repeated, so it can be sung/chanted in a call-response manner. Make a chart of the song, printing the words clearly and large enough for everyone in the group to see. (Figure 12.2a) For each of the objects (tree, bird, egg, and so on), cover the word with a drawing depicting the word on a separate strip of index card material. (Figure 12.2b) Back this with tape for easy removal. As children become more familiar with the song, remove the picture cards, revealing the words underneath. Place the cards next to, but not covering, the words. Children will learn the song through repetition and echoing the leader, and they will associate a word with a picture clue. Eventually, children can take turns leading the recitation, using the pictures or words to hint at what comes next.

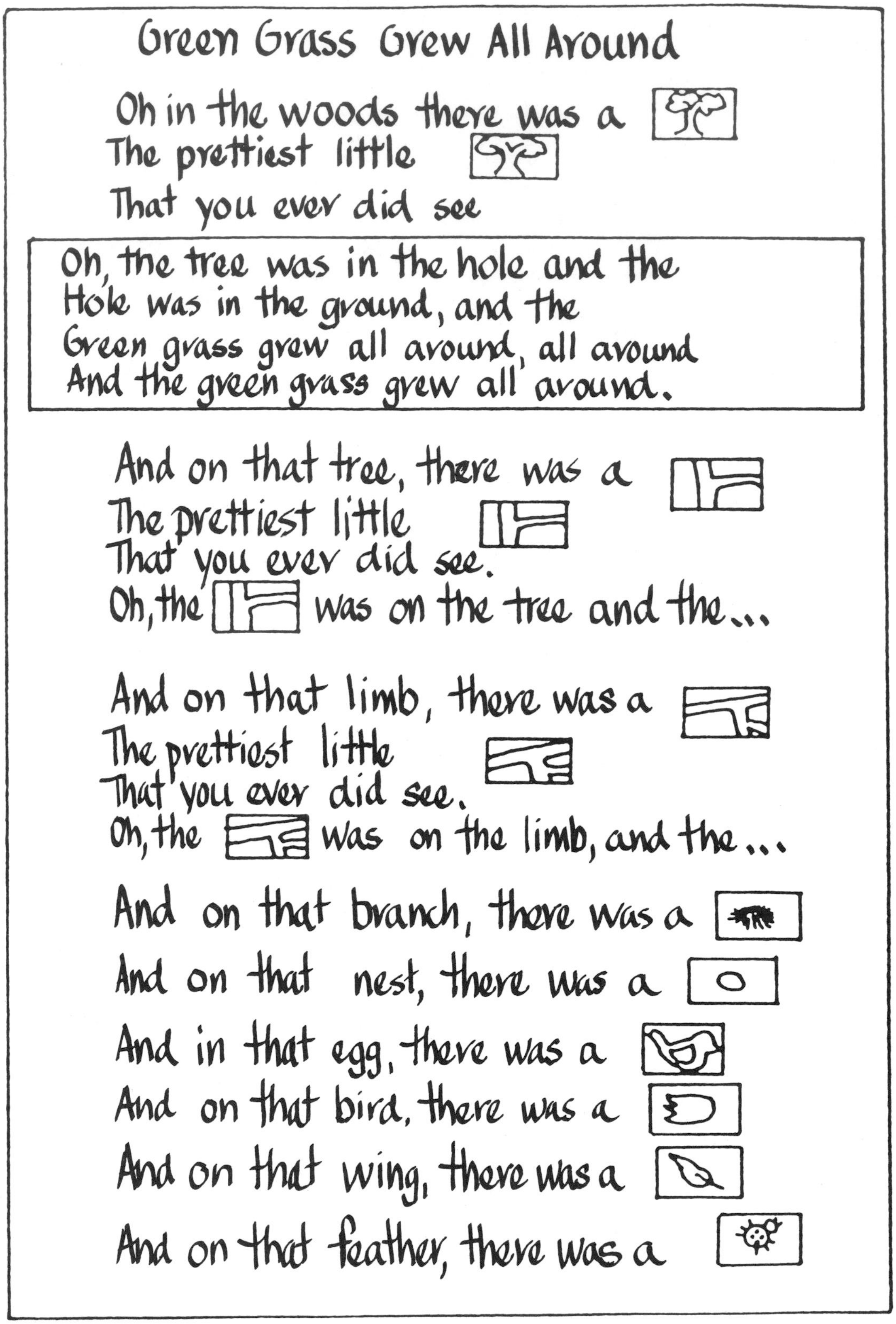

Green Grass Grew All Around

Oh in the woods there was a [tree]
The prettiest little [tree]
That you ever did see

Oh, the tree was in the hole and the
Hole was in the ground, and the
Green grass grew all around, all around
And the green grass grew all around.

And on that tree, there was a [limb]
The prettiest little [limb]
That you ever did see.
Oh, the [limb] was on the tree and the...

And on that limb, there was a [branch]
The prettiest little [branch]
That you ever did see.
Oh, the [branch] was on the limb, and the...

And on that branch, there was a [nest]

And on that nest, there was a [egg]

And in that egg, there was a [bird]

And on that bird, there was a [wing]

And on that wing, there was a [feather]

And on that feather, there was a [bug]

Figure 12.2a *A Song Chart Using Pictures for Key Words*

Green Grass Grew All Around

Figure 12.2b *Pictures for the Song "Green Grass Grew All Around"*

The words to the song are:

The Green Grass Grew All Around
(Traditional tune; Author unknown)

Verse 1:
Oh in the woods (Oh in the woods)
There was a tree (There was a tree)
The prettiest little tree (The prettiest little tree)
That you ever did see. (That you ever did see.)

Chorus:
Oh, the tree was in a hole and the hole was in the ground
And the green grass grew all around, all around
And the green grass grew all around.

Verse 2:
And on that tree (And on that tree)
There was limb (There was a limb)
The prettiest little limb (The prettiest little limb)
That you ever did see. (That you ever did see.)

Chorus:
The limb was on the tree and the tree was in the hole
And the hole was in the ground
And the green grass grew all around, all around
And the green grass grew all around.

Verse 3:
Branch on the limb

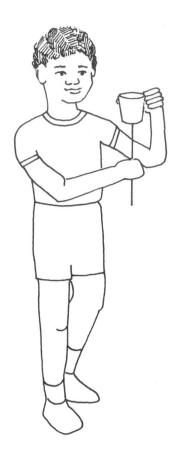
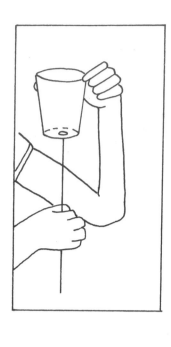

Figure 12.3 *Pull Down on the String to Make a Bird Sound*

Verse 4:
Nest on the branch

Verse 5:
Egg in the nest

Verse 6:
Bird in the egg

Verse 7:
Wing on the bird

Verse 8:
Feather on the wing

Some versions add a bug to the feather, an eye on the bug, an eyelash on the eye, and so on.

9. ***Find the Bird.*** Familiarize children with the story and recording of *Peter and the Wolf* by Peter Ilyich Tchaikovsky. Any currently available recording is appropriate. Explain to children that each character in the story is represented by a particular instrument. Tell children that there are two birds in the story—the duck and the flying bird. The next time you play the recording, ask children to listen closely and raise their hands each time a bird appears, as evidenced by the musical instrument. Add interest and challenge in subsequent repetitions of the activity by asking children to make one motion for the flying bird (flying motion with two hands) and a different one for the duck (quacking motion with one hand).

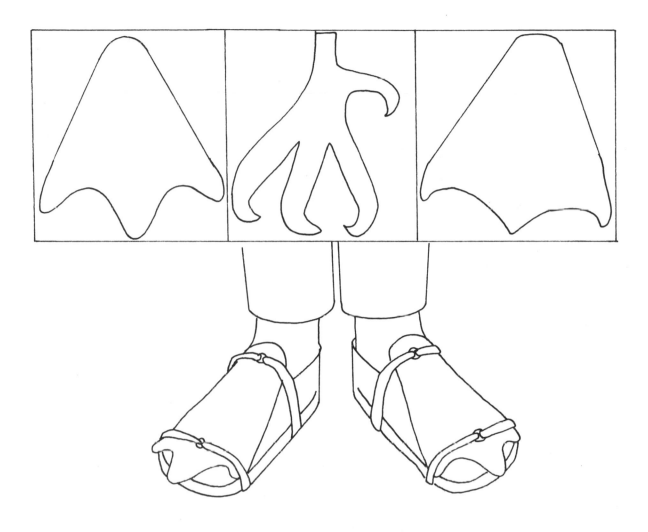

Figure 12.4 *Wearing Bird Feet*

Physical

1. *Calling All Birds.* Provide each child with a paper cup, string, and a paper clip. Instruct children to punch a small hole through the bottom of their paper cups. Have children put string through the hole and tie the paper clip on the end of the string so that it rests inside the cup. (Figure 12.3) Then moisten the string. Have children hold the cup with the opening up and the string hanging down. Tell them to hold the string between their thumbs and index fingers near the base of the cup and slide their fingers quickly down the string. The resulting sound simulates a bird call.

Encourage the children to use these in their pretend play

2. *Feet on the Floor.* Carry out this activity following a discussion of bird feet as described in TFP 49. Also, gather pictures showing different birds and their feet for children to refer to. In advance, prepare outlines of bird-feet shapes on twelve-inch squares of orange- or cream-colored poster board. (Figure 12.4) Give children a choice of foot shapes to cut out to make pairs. Next show them how to paper-punch two holes in each one as illustrated above. Using string or each child's own shoelaces, attach the bird feet to the top of

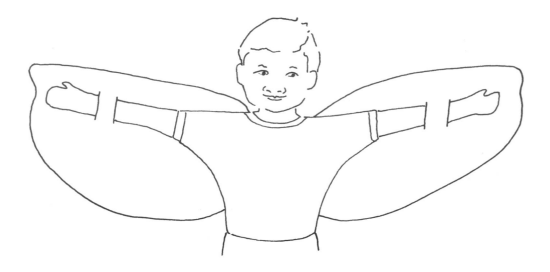

Figure 12.5 *Simple Bird Wings Stimulate Pretend Flying*

the children's shoes. Encourage the children to use the feet as they pretend to be birds.

3. ***Winged Victory.*** On paper bags, butcher paper, or oak tag, draw wing shapes as depicted in the diagram. (Figure 12.5) Each will yield two wings. Cut slots, as shown, for children to put their arms through. Children may wish to decorate their wings with crayons or glue and feathers. Encourage children to use the wings in their pretend play.

4. ***See the Birds.*** Provide children with toilet paper rolls, a paper punch, string, and rubber bands. Show them how to construct a pair of binoculars by tying two rolls together with string or rubber bands. Encourage the children to go "bird-watching."

5. ***Fly Away.*** Play this game as you would any follow-the-leader activity, but emphasize the movements of birds. Tell children that many birds fly in groups or flocks and that all the birds follow the leader bird exactly, both in their movements and direction. Explain further that the leadership changes over time. Talk about a variety of movements birds make as they fly, such as soaring, turning, landing, and so on. Determine with children how to rotate who will be the leader bird and when. Then send off the flock.

6. ***Bird Goodies.***

Birdseed Balls
Get some medium ground suet from a butcher. In a bowl, mix it with some birdseed until you can form it into a tight ball. Roll the ball in more birdseed until it is completely covered. Take a mesh bag (the kind that oranges come in) and place the suet ball inside. Hang this outside and watch the birds gather.

Pinecone Feeders
Provide children with pinecones, peanut butter, cornmeal, plastic knives, raisins, and yarn. Instruct the children to mix two tablespoons of the peanut butter with two tablespoons of cornmeal and spread the mixture on the pinecone. Then roll it in birdseed. Raisins can be placed in the open spaces on the pinecone. Help the children attach the yarn for hanging.

The feeders can be hung outside near the windows if possible so children can observe the birds. If you are sending the feeders home with the children, place each one in a sealable plastic bag.

Catbird Cake
Ingredients:

¾ cup raisins

1½ cups water

1 heaping T. shortening

1 T. baking soda

1 cup sugar

2 cups flour

Procedure:

1. Simmer the raisins in the water for 20 minutes. Drain and reserve 1 cup liquid.
2. To the liquid, add the shortening and the baking soda and let stand to cool.
3. Add 1 cup sugar, 2 cups floor, and stir in raisins.
4. Pour into an 8-by-8-inch cake pan and bake at 375° for 1 hour.
5. Cut into pieces to scatter on the ground.

Blackbird Biscuits
Ingredients:

2⅓ cups biscuit mix

½ cup white proso millet

⅔ cup cold water

Procedure:

1. Mix all ingredients till dough forms, then beat for 30 seconds.
2. Drop by spoonfuls onto an ungreased cookie sheet.
3. Bake at 450° for 8 to 10 minutes.
4. Scatter biscuits on the ground.

Caw, Caw Cornbread
Ingredients:

1 cup yellow or white cornmeal

½ cup cracked corn

1 eggshell, ground up

1 cup flour

4 tsp. baking powder

1 cup milk

1 egg, slightly beaten

¼ cup bacon drippings

Procedure:

1. Heat oven to 400°.
2. Combine dry ingredients. Add milk, egg, and bacon drippings.
3. Mix with spoon and pour into 8-by-8-inch pan.
4. Bake 20–25 minutes.
5. When cool, cut into cubes and serve on feeder tray or ground.

Grackle Grits
Ingredients:

1 cup mashed potatoes or cooked rice

½ cup cottage cheese

1 cup bakery scraps

Procedure:
Mix these three ingredients with a fork until you are able to shape into small balls. Toss on the ground.

These four recipes were adapted from the book *More of My Recipes for the Birds* written by Irene Cosgrove and published by Doubleday in 1989.

7. *Crack it Open.* Obtain a variety of seeds and nuts, some with hard shells, some with brittle shells. Provide tweezers, a small hammer, pliers, and nutcrackers. Allow children to figure out how to get the meat out of the shells using the implements as well as their fingers. Relate what they are doing to the ways in which birds use their beaks and feet to get at their food.
8. *Bird Jump.* Place four or five hoops on the floor or ground so that each is touching at least one other hoop. Designate each hoop as a particular kind of bird food (insects, worms, berries, and so on). Tell children that often birds have to find food on the ground. One at a time, have children jump from one hoop to another until they are "full" from eating all the food.

Pretend Play

1. *We are Your Babies.* Begin with a discussion about eggs, nests, and baby birds. Provide pictures of baby birds. Lead children in a movement activity pretending to

be baby birds. First demonstrate the movements while the children watch. Start by being very small and still, as if in an egg. Then demonstrate how a bird pecks its way out of the egg with its egg tooth. Next, demonstrate how a newborn bird might act. After demonstrating all actions, have the children join in and pretend to be baby birds by mimicking bird behavior.

2. *Feeding the Birdies.* Construct a cardboard box target that looks like a bird's nest. Draw a nest on the outside of a box at least two feet square. (The larger the box, the easier it will be for children to hit the target.) Cut an opening in or leave off the top of the box. Place stuffed birds, clear contact paper cutouts of birds, or wooden/plastic toy birds inside. You may wish to provide more than one "nest" so that several children can participate simultaneously. Set another box on a plastic tub in another part of the room or play yard (at least ten feet away; farther if possible). Fill the tub with Styrofoam "squiggles," rubber bands, or spirals of curled ribbon to represent worms.

Introduce the activity with a discussion of the large quantities of food that parent birds must provide for their young. Mention that many birds especially enjoy eating worms. Invite the children to become parent birds for the day. They will need to carry lots of food to their nests to feed their hungry children.

Place the "nests" on the floor, on a chair, or at eye level on a table or shelf. You may want to place more than one nest at more than one level, pointing out that some species of birds are ground-nesters while others construct above-the-ground nests.

Direct the children to begin carrying food to their young. Point out that birds can carry only a small quantity of food at a time and must make many trips to satisfy the baby birds' hunger. Remind them that they must move carefully, so they don't drop any precious "worms." Increase the dexterity required for this task by placing the nest at the top of a climber, by allowing the children to carry worms clenched in their teeth, or by making a claw "pincher" to grasp and carry food using kitchen tongs, tweezers, or folded squares of cardboard or plastic to hold in the palm.

Remind children that different species of birds communicate and travel in different ways. Suggest that they decide what kind of bird they are going to be and that they match their behavior to that of the chosen bird.

3. *Swallows.* Discuss ways that birds eat and drink. Have the children pretend to be birds while eating their snacks. Since birds do not have hands, invite children to eat the snacks without using their hands. Afterward, talk to the children about the experience. Ask them if it was difficult to do and how they adapted their bodies to complete the task.

4. *Bird Sanctuary/Aviary.*

General Purpose: For children to better understand bird behavior by enacting how they live.

TFPs: 5–7, 19–22, 46–50, 57, 63–69.

Materials: Refrigerator box, brown paint, green construction paper, portable wading pool, straw, plastic egg-shaped containers, toy or felt baby birds, construction paper wings with arm straps, large trays, rubber gloves, recordings of bird songs.

Procedure:

a. Cut a hole in one side of a refrigerator box large enough for a child to crawl through and for an adult to reach in for supervisory purposes. Cut the hole so the lowest edge is about one foot off the floor. Paint the box brown if you wish and cover the top with green construction paper leaves. This will serve as a "tree nest."

b. Nearby, set up a portable wading pool large enough for two to three children to sit in. This will represent a "ground nest."

c. Put straw in both the box and the dry, empty pool to serve as nesting material.

d. Provide egg-shaped containers and toy "baby birds" to fit inside the containers. Furnish construction paper wings with arm straps and large trays to represent a birdseed "feeder" and a birdbath. Have "wings" and "feet" that children have made available for use in the bird sanctuary. Instead of cardboard feet, you might use rubber gloves to represent the feet of wading or swimming birds.

e. Play recordings of bird songs during the play period to simulate the sounds of a bird sanctuary.

f. Invite children to take on the roles of "birds in the sanctuary."

Hints for Success:

• Children may benefit from seeing you take on the role of "bird" as a model to imitate. The more bird behaviors the adult demonstrates by pretending, the more roles children have to try and the more information they gain. Once familiar with the idea, children will be able to manage with considerable independence.

• Space the ground nest, the tree nest, and the feeder far enough apart so children will not get in each other's way.

How to Simplify this Activity:

• Begin with only one type of nest, either tree or ground. Introduce the feeding station after children have had opportunities to explore birdseed in other activities.

How to Extend this Activity:

• Invite the children to "furnish" the sanctuary themselves by making the nests and feeding stations.

• Concentrate on one type of bird at a time (ground-nesters or tree-nesters) so that children have a chance to delve more deeply into those life-styles and habits.

• Add binoculars, bird books, and note pads for children who wish to be bird-watchers rather than birds.

5. ***Three Blue Pigeons.***

General Purpose: For children to pretend together.

TFPs: 5, 9.

Materials: Optional: Three chairs, three pairs of large blue gloves.

Procedure:

a. Tell children that this is a pretending game about pigeons.

b. Arrange the three chairs in a line facing the group of children. Tell them, "This is the wall for the pigeons to sit upon."

c. Teach the following song (sung to the tune of the first two lines of "Three Blind Mice") or chant the words.

Three blue pigeons, sitting on a wall. (sung)
Three blue pigeons, sitting on a wall. (sung)
Then, they all flew away. (Said in a matter-of-fact voice.)
Aw . . . . (Said in a sad voice.)
No blue pigeons, sitting on a wall. (sung)
No blue pigeons, sitting on a wall. (sung)
Then, they all flew back. (Said in a matter-of-fact voice.)
Yeah!!!! (Said in an excited voice and accompanied by clapping.) (Repeat.)

d. Suggest a place in the room to which the pigeons could fly. Demonstrate how to fly away on the correct line of the chant and fly back on the corresponding lines of the song.

e. Choose three children to be the pigeons (sitting on the chairs and wearing the gloves if desired).

f. Encourage all the others to sing or chant the words as they watch.

g. Give everyone in the group a turn to be a pigeon.

Hints for Success:

• Assign an adult to be at the "fly away place" to help cue children when to fly back.

• As a variation, use a bigger or smaller number of pigeons to accommodate your group size and ensure the game doesn't take too long.

How to Simplify this Activity:

• Do one pigeon (child) at a time. "Fly" with the child, holding his or her hand.

How to Extend this Activity:

• Make this an addition and subtraction game by starting with a number of pigeons on the wall, singing about one or more flying away, and asking the children to tell you how many are left. Reverse the process as they fly back.

Social

1. *Fine Feathered Friends.* Familiarize children with a bird story such as *The Story About Ping* by Marjorie Flack. Copy each page of the text onto pieces of blank paper. After reading the story to the whole class, give a page to small groups of two or three children each. Help them "read" the words on their page. Then encourage the children to work together to illustrate the page. Emphasize the idea of working together to complete a task. When everyone is finished, have the children help put the story together. Post the story on the wall for the children to look at and read. Point out the value of everyone's contribution to the whole project.

2. *Bird Hunt.* Prepare puzzles of various kinds of birds by cutting apart pictures of birds that have been mounted on cardboard or oak tag.

   Give a puzzle to each group of two or three children. Help them work cooperatively to fit the puzzles together. At first, instruct them to take turns. After they gain experience, encourage them to ask for and offer help. Provide children with sample scripts, if necessary, such as, "I need help finding a piece" or "I can help you by passing the box of pieces." When everyone is finished, bring the children together and review the experience. Talk about how they worked together. Discuss the difficulties that often arise when people work together and talk about how to resolve them.

3. *Birdie in the Treetop.* This is a version of a group mural project. Make a tree wall decoration out of brown construction paper and hang it on a wall. (Add leaves if you wish to provide a seasonal touch.) Provide children with materials for making birds (paper, feathers, glue, yarn, scissors, and so on). Explain that everyone who wishes to can make a bird to add to the classroom flock. As children complete their birds, encourage them to find a place for it on the tree. Point out how each person's individual effort contributes to a complete picture that is pleasing for everyone.

4. *Birds of a Feather.* Mount pictures of birds on cardboard and then cut them in half. Pass out the cards making sure each person has a half that matches someone else's. If there is an uneven number of children, an adult can play. At the teacher's cue, children move around the room and try to find their partners, whoever has the other half of their bird. When they find their partners, they may sit down together on the floor until everyone has finished.

5. *Egg Foo Young.* Have one group of three or four children prepare this popular dish as a snack for the rest of the class.

Ingredients:

4 eggs

½ tsp. salt

⅓ cup carrots (cut into small pieces)

⅓ cup celery (cut into small pieces)

⅓ cup fresh garden peas

¼ cup scallions or green onions (dice)

Oil for cooking

Procedure:

1. Cook the carrots, celery, and peas in a small amount of water. Break the eggs into a bowl and beat with an eggbeater. Add scallions, salt, and the drained, cooked vegetables.

2. Pour enough cooking oil into an electric frying pan just to coat it. Turn the heat to medium.

3. Spoon the egg mixture into pan. Make small pancake-sized Egg Foo Young. Cook until the top of each pancake is nearly firm. Turn the pancakes with a spatula and cook on the other side for another minute or two. Serve.

4. This recipe makes sixteen small pancakes.

5. Encourage, but do not force, the children to taste the Egg Foo Young.

TEACHER RESOURCES

Field Trip Ideas

1. Take children to see real birds at a local bird sanctuary, zoo, nature center, or even a pet shop specializing in birds.
2. Visit a pond, stream, lakeshore, or seashore to watch wading and swimming birds.
3. Take children on a city neighborhood bird walk. Have them observe pigeons, sparrows, and other city dwellers, paying special attention to their habitats, movements, and songs.
4. If live bird-watching is not possible, make use of a local museum's collection of stuffed birds. Children can learn a great deal about how birds are "constructed" as they examine bird feathers, wings, heads, beaks, and eyes at close range.
5. Take a trip to an art museum or gallery to see how birds have been depicted by various artists.

Classroom Visitors

1. Contact a local nature center or pet store about the possibility of having live birds visit the classroom.
2. Some school families who own birds may be willing to bring their pets in for a day or two.

Children's Books

Alexander, M. *No Ducks in Our Bathtub.* New York: Dial, 1973.

Balian, L. *Sometimes It's Turkey—Sometimes It's Feathers.* Nashville: Abingdon Press, 1973.

Baskin, L. *Hosie's Aviary.* New York: Viking, 1979.

Brown, M. W. *The Dead Bird.* Reading, MA: Addison-Wesley, 1958.

Coleman, B. *Birds* (The Color Nature Library). New York: Crescent Books, 1978.

Dennis, W. *A Crow I Know.* New York: Viking, 1957.

Eastman, P. D. *Are You My Mother?* New York: Random House, 1960.

Fisher, A. *Filling the Bill.* Glendale, CA: Bowmar Publications, 1973.

Flack, M. *The Story About Ping.* New York: Viking, 1933.

Fujita, T. *The Boy and the Bird.* New York: John Day, 1970.

Garelick, M. *What Makes a Bird a Bird?* Chicago: Follett, 1969.

Goldin, A. *Ducks Don't Get Wet.* New York: Crowell, 1965.

Grabianski, J. *Birds.* New York: Franklin Watts, 1968.

Graham, M. B. *Benjy and the Barking Bird.* New York: Harper and Row, 1971.

Holman, F. *Elisabeth the Bird Watcher.* New York: Macmillan, 1963.

Krauss, R. *The Happy Egg.* New York: Scholastic, 1967.

Martin, B., and B. Martin. *The Merry Months of Birds.* Allen, TX: DLM Teaching Resources, 1989.

McCloskey, R. *Make Way for Ducklings.* New York: Viking, 1941.

Miller, E. *Duck, Duck.* Englewood Cliffs, NJ: Prentice-Hall, 1971.

Radlauer, E., and R. Radlauer. *Bird Mania.* Chicago: Childrens Press, 1981.

Schoenherr, J. *The Barn.* Boston: Little, Brown, 1968.

Tafuri, N. *Have You Seen My Duckling?* New York: Greenwillow, 1984.

Wildsmith, B. *Birds.* New York: Franklin Watts, 1967.

Williams, G. *The Chicken Book.* New York: Delacorte Press, 1970.

Adult References

Bull, J., and J. Farrand, Jr. *The Audubon Society Field Guide to North American Birds.* New York: Knopf, 1977.

Ham, J. *Kitchen Table Bird Book.* Lansing, MI: Two Peninsula Press, 1984.

Harrison, G. H. *The Backyard Birdwatcher.* New York: Simon and Schuster, 1979.

Peterson, R. T. *The Birds.* New York: Time-Life Books, 1968.

Zim, H. S., and I. N. Gabrielson. *Birds: A Guide to the Most Familiar American Birds.* New York: Golden, 1956.

Chapter 13

Bears

•

Once upon a time . . .
. . . there were three bears . . . a great big
Papa Bear, a middle-sized Mama Bear,
and a little wee Baby Bear . . . .

. . . a very long time ago now, about last
Friday, Winnie-the-Pooh lived in a forest
all by himself under the name of Sanders.

. . . the little animals held a sit-down
talk, and one by one and two by two
and all by all, they decided to go see
Bruh Bear and Bruh Rabbit. For they
know that Bruh Bear been around.

•

By age four or five, children are well acquainted with many make-believe bears. They are introduced to these fictional characters through oral storytelling, picture books, records, and film. During the early years, too, youngsters frequently play with stuffed toy bears, and likely as not, have one favorite who serves as a constant companion for them awake or asleep. It is also not unusual for children to see live bears on television, at the zoo, or in a circus. Moreover, bears often populate children's dreams (Ilg and Ames, 1967) and may alternately serve in the role of "friend" or "monster" depending on the situation. Thus, in one form or another, bears are familiar creatures to young children.

PURPOSE

In writing this unit on bears, we had two aims in mind. The first was to build on children's already developed interest in make-believe bears to further their observation and problem-solving skills. Toward this end we have included several activities that encourage children to explore the interesting features of toy bears and of bears in story and song. This involves children in the essential intellectual processes of analysis, inquiry, interpretation, and judgment making. Yet the avenues to explore and the problems to solve are not dictated by adults, but rather are generated through the children's own needs and interests. The unit becomes the vehicle through which children gain a deeper understanding of their own experiences and immediate environment.

Introducing children to the natural world of real bears, thereby enhancing their appreciation of these wild creatures, is the second goal we had in developing the Bears theme. This aim grew from our belief that human beings must develop a better understanding of animals in nature to maintain an ecological balance and preserve our earth for coming generations.

In determining how to address this issue in a manner relevant to young children, we considered bears to be an ideal subject for study. First, as fellow mammals, bears share many characteristics with humans, such as playfulness and caring for the young. These suggest interesting parallels that we have found children enjoy exploring. Second, children bring to this unit prior knowledge of bears, albeit pretend ones. This budding interest serves as a catalyst for children to learn more about the actual animals on which their imaginary bears are modeled. Third, most children experience live bears only in unnatural environments, such as zoos or circuses. These circumstances neither accurately portray how bears live, nor do they prompt an awareness of how bears fit into the natural order of things. Finally, black bears are common throughout the forested regions of North America from Florida to the tundra, from Maine to California. Thus, in reality many of us share a world in which bears live relatively close by.

With these thoughts in mind, we have designed an array of activities that highlight bear characteristics and bear behavior in the wild. We have purposely avoided featuring trained bears or those in captivity in our effort to emphasize natural habitats, bear life, and how humans can interface with bears without exploiting them.

IMPLEMENTATION

Option One: Focus primarily on fictional bears.
Week One: Conduct a general introduction to storytelling.
Week Two: Focus on plot and characters as essential elements of a story.
Week Three: Introduce one or more fictional bears as they appear in favorite children's storybooks. Highlight one story each day and create activities that revolve around such tales as *Goldilocks and the Three Bears, Blueberries for Sal,* or *Ask Mr. Bear.* Refer to the Storytelling unit in this book for activity ideas.

Option Two: Promote children's observation and investigative skills through a one- or two-week study of teddy bears.

Option Three: Concentrate on real bears as they exist in nature. Eventually contrast wild animals with those that have been domesticated.
Weeks One and Two: Implement the theme on pets.
Week Three: Introduce Bears theme.
Week Four: Compare bears with furbearing pets such as dogs and cats. Concentrate on people's relationships with both kinds of animals.

Option Four: Use the children's interest in bears to pique their curiosity about other wild animals.

Week One: Focus on characteristics and behaviors of real bears.

Week Two: Extend the topic of real bears to the people who study them.

Week Three: Concentrate on animals who share bear habitats. OR Study animals threatened with extinction, including the brown bear.

Option Five: Following a basic introduction to bears, draw children's attention to the facets of bear life that are similar to their own.

Option Six: Combine all three subheadings in this unit to facilitate a comprehensive study of bears.

Week One: Fictional bears
Week Two: Teddy bears
Week Three: Real bears

TERMS, FACTS, AND PRINCIPLES

Real Bears

1. Bears are large, heavyset mammals with shaggy fur and very short tails.

2. Bears have elongated heads, small eyes, and small rounded ears.

*3. Bears have five toes with nonretractable claws on each foot. When they stand, the entire sole of both feet touches the ground. (This means they are flatfooted.)

4. Bears vary in size and color.

*5. The largest of all bears (Kodiak brown bear) grows to over eleven feet tall and may weigh 1,500 pounds.

*6. Bears reach their maximum physical size by seven or eight years of age.

*7. Bears may live to be twenty to thirty years old in the wild. Twenty is considered old. In captivity bears may live as long as forty-five years.

8. Bears are very strong.

9. Bears have highly developed senses of smell and hearing.

10. All bears, except polar bears, have poor eyesight.

11. Male bears are called boars or he-bears.

12. Female bears are called sows or she-bears.

13. Baby bears are called cubs.

14. Bear homes are called dens.

15. Bears often group together in living units. A group of bears is called a pack or a sloth.

16. Bears are wild animals.

17. Wild animals live on their own in the natural world without help from humans.

18. To survive, bears need food, fresh water, and room to forage for food, play, rest, and establish territory.

Bear Behaviors

19. Bears usually walk on all four feet, moving both legs on one side of their body at the same time. This is called ambling.

20. Bears sometimes stand upright on the soles of their hind feet in order to see distant things better.

21. Bears make trails and follow them year after year.

22. Bears mark trees along their trails by rubbing against them with their bodies, scratching them with their claws, or marking them with their teeth.

*23. Bears have sharp, pointed teeth for gripping and tearing, as well as broad molars for grinding and cracking.

24. Bears are omnivores. That is, they eat animals as well as plants. Some of the natural foods they eat are berries, honey, fish, leaves, nuts, insects, rodents, and frogs.

25. The type of food bears eat is influenced by where they live and by the time of year.

26. Bears use their front paws/claws to dig for or gather food.

27. Some bears (brown, grizzly) scoop fish from water or catch them in their mouths for food.

28. Bears cover uneaten food with debris to save it for later.

29. Small and middle-sized bears are skillful tree climbers. They often climb trees to escape danger or obtain food.

30. Bears climb trees by hugging the trunk with their fore-limbs and holding on with the claws of all four feet.

31. Bears usually find a cave or open space between rocks or ice formations to use as a den.

32. If a bear cannot find a den it will make one by padding a space with moss, leaves, grass, and twigs.

33. Bears often live in the same den year after year.

34. To avoid the extreme cold of winter, bears accumulate considerable fat in late fall. This allows them to "den-up" and go into a deep sleep.

35. To sleep during the winter months, bears must eat a great deal in the spring, summer, and fall.

36. Bears sleep both day and night during cold weather, only occasionally waking up to look around inside or outside the den. (This is not true hibernation because bears remain fully conscious and lose little weight.)

37. In the early spring, bears become very active looking for food.

38. Bears establish territory to protect their living space and food supply.

39. Bears establish territory by marking trees with their claws and teeth.

40. Bears usually prefer to avoid trouble and will try to escape unless cornered, surprised, threatened, or hurt, or if their cubs seem to be in danger.

41. Bears are often unpredictable.

42. Bears make several sounds to communicate danger or other messages to each other. They may snuffle, growl, or grunt, or make sounds like "ruff, ruff."

43. Angry bears sit upright or stand on their hind feet and growl.

Bear Families

44. Bear cubs are usually born in the winter. Each litter contains from one to five young.

45. Cubs weigh less than a pound at birth, and they have no teeth, fur, or eyesight.

46. Cubs snuggle up to their furry mothers to stay warm and nurse.

47. Bear cubs stay with their mothers for one to three years.

48. Mother bears resemble human mothers in many ways: they feed, cuddle, teach, protect, and play with their cubs.

49. Mother bears are stern with their cubs when they disobey and will cuff or otherwise discipline them.

50. When walking in deep snow, mother bears break trails for their cubs by leaping and making holes so that the cubs can follow.

51. Mother bears eventually leave their cubs (after about two years), allowing them to live on their own.

52. Father bears leave their families shortly after mating; they are not involved in raising cubs.

Kinds of Bears

*53. There are several types of bears native to North America: black, brown, and polar bears.

*54. Bears found in other areas of the world include spectacled, sun, and honey bears.

*55. Giant pandas look like bears but *may not* be members of the bear family. Scientists are not sure to which animals the giant pandas are most closely related.

*56. Each type of bear is distinguishable by its size and the color of its fur. Fur color may be brown, black, white, cinnamon, yellow, or gray.

*57. The American black bear:
    a. is widely distributed in all the major forested areas of North America.
    b. grows to about six feet long and forty inches high and weighs from 200 to 400 pounds.
    c. eats grass, pine needles, leaves, fruits, nuts, insects, fish, frogs, snakes, small birds, and dead animals. They especially like honey.
    d. climbs trees in the fall to shake loose nuts that they later gather and eat.
    e. sometimes becomes a scavenger of human trash in populated areas.

*58. Brown bears live mostly in the Canadian Rockies, Alaska, and some small, isolated areas of the western United States.

*59. The grizzly bear, Alaskan brown bear, and Kodiak bear are subspecies of the brown bear.
   a. Grizzly bears grow to about seven feet long and forty-two inches high and weigh about 850 pounds.
   b. Alaskan brown bears grow to 8½ feet long and 42 inches tall and weigh as much as 1,700 pounds.
   c. Alaskan brown bears eat much the same things as black bears but are particularly known for catching and eating salmon.
   d. Brown bears all eat fresh meat, usually from dead deer, antelope, elk, and cows they find. They will seldom kill for food.
   e. Brown bears differ from black bears in color, size (much larger body, massive head), and shape (prominent hump at its shoulders).

*60. The brown bear's survival will depend on the maintenance of wilderness areas large enough to support its need for food and territory.

61. Polar bears:
   a. live in the polar regions of the Northern Hemisphere.
   b. grow to about 7¼ feet long and 48 inches tall and weigh from 650 to 1,700 pounds.
   c. eat fish, seal meat, grass, berries, and small rodents.
   d. can swim considerable distances.
   e. Females den-up in snowbanks; male polar bears are active all year.

People and Bears

62. A person who studies bears and other animals is called a zoologist.

63. Zoologists often tag and monitor the growth and movements of bears to better understand them.

64. Zoos and circuses are not natural environments for bears.

65. Bears that live in zoos or circuses are still wild animals who have come to depend on humans for their survival.

66. Sometimes people train bears to behave in certain ways.

Toy Bears

*67. Toy bears were first available when today's children's great-grandparents were young.

68. Children in many parts of the world play with toy bears.

69. Toy bears have some features similar to real bears: soft warm fur, short necks, small ears, short tails, four flat feet, and big heads.

70. Toy bears vary in how they look and in what they are made of.

71. Toy bears have some human attributes that real bears don't have. Some wear clothing, some make music or say words.

72. People create toy bears:
   a. People design toy bears.
   b. People sew and put together toy bears.
   c. People sell toy bears.

73. Both boys and girls play with toy bears.

74. Adults often like toy bears.

75. Some people collect toy bears.

76. Some people own one special toy bear.

77. People sometimes name their bears.

78. People keep toy bears for fun and for comfort.

Fictional Bears

79. People have depicted bears in stories and songs.

80. Fictional bears have some attributes that resemble real bears.

81. People often attribute human characteristics to fictional bears.

82. People have created bear characters to symbolize an idea or product.

83. Bears are often used to symbolize physical strength and strength of character and purpose.

84. Stories from many cultures include bears.

ACTIVITY IDEAS

Aesthetics

1. ***Textured Bears.*** Enlarge the bear outlines provided and use them to create bear-shaped papers on which children can paint. Include children in helping to make white, brown, and black paint using one or more of the following recipes:

For a textured paint, mix:
1 part powdered paint
2 parts powdered detergent
2 parts water

To make bumpy texture, add sawdust. For a gritty texture, add sand.

For a smooth paint, mix:
a 1-pound can of powdered paint
⅓ cup water
¼ cup liquid starch
1 T. soap powder

For a glittery, shiny texture, mix the following ingredients and apply this paint to a heavier surface, such as cardboard, with brushes or squeeze bottles.
1 part flour
1 part salt
1 part water
food coloring

In addition, using different applicators will give more textured effects. Dip into and apply paint with sponges, cotton balls, or pot scrubbers.

On a different day, make teddy-bear shapes for the easel and give children bright colors with which to experiment. (Figure 13.1)

2. ***Polar Portrait.*** Send a note to parents asking them to send small, white, fuzzy items they can no longer use to school with their child. Gather some additional items yourself (yarn, old socks, pieces of fake fur, cotton balls, etc.). Make a large outline of a polar bear on mural paper. Encourage children to find a place on the bear to paste or glue the items, or bits of the items, they brought in. Compare the textures, shapes, shades, and structures of the materials used.

Repeat this activity other days for both black and brown bears. Hang up the final results for all to see.

3. ***Picture Perfect.*** Collect realistic drawings or paintings of bears in their natural surroundings. Make these available for children to examine. Guide children's attention to the animals' activities and to the additional items the artists included in each work to make them look more realistic. On another day, invite children to compare the sketches with actual photographs of real bears. Encourage them to explore the similarities and differences between these two art forms.

4. ***Musical Bear Walk.*** Introduce the activity by talking about how bears move. Demonstrate ambling by placing your hands flat on the floor and bending at the waist with your knees relatively straight. (Figure 13.2) Move your right arm and right leg forward at the same time, then your left arm and left leg. Continue. Invite children to amble with you. Once they experience some success with ambling, ask children periodically to assume an upright posture to look about and sniff the air.

Later in the day, or on another occasion, add music to the activity. Ask children to listen carefully. As the music plays they are to amble; when it stops, they should assume an upright position; when the song continues, they can resume ambling. Play a musical selection, stopping it at random. Praise children for recognizing when the music stops and starts. Vary the activity by emphasizing the beat of the music. Explain that because bears have flat feet they tread heavily. Ask children to amble in time to the music as you clap or hit a drum to stress the beat.

Affective

1. ***Teddy-Bear Mine.*** Invite children to bring their favorite stuffed bears to school. Give each an opportunity to tell about his or her bear and why it is special. You might ask its name, how it was acquired, what it

Brown Bear

Teddy Bear

Black Bear

Polar Bear

Figure 13.1 *Make Large Bear Shapes for Children to Paste*

Walk Like A Bear

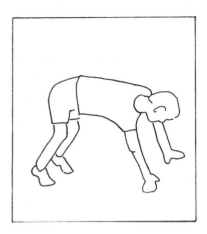
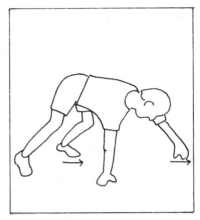

Figure 13.2 *Bears Have a Distinctive Way of Walking*

Figure 13.3 *Teddy Bear-Shaped Books*

looks like, what they do together, and how long he or she has had the bear.

Consider recording children's answers in individual "teddy-bear-shaped" booklets, assigning one comment per page (see Figure 13.3).

Cover Page: (child's name) *Teddy Bear*
Page one: My bear's name is _____.
Page two: My bear is or has _____.
Page three: etc.

2. ***Like a Bear.*** Introduce this activity after children have had numerous opportunities

to gather additional information about bears. Ask individual children to name *one* way in which they are like a bear. Identify their answers by name, writing them all on a large piece of easel paper. After several ideas have been offered, read the children's comments back to the group. Throughout the week, add ideas as children express them.

3. *Teddy-Bear Catalogue.* Have children tear or cut out pictures of toy bears from catalogues or magazines. Use these to create a teddy-bear catalogue. Each child selects a "favorite" bear to paste on an 8½-by-11-inch piece of paper. At the top of the page write the child's name, at the bottom write the child's exact words as to why he or she liked that bear best. Put all the pages together in a class book entitled "Bears We Like Best."

Cognition

1. *All "Sorts" of Bears.* Gather a wide array of bear pictures; include both real and toy bears. Place the pictures face down in a pile in the center of a table. Invite the children to look at the pictures one at a time. Ask them to sort the pictures into two groups—real bears and toy ones. Then ask them to explain their conclusions.

2. *Blueberries for Us!* Prepare the recipe chart as pictured. Make it large enough for children to see from a distance. Read the book *Blueberries for Sal* by Robert McCloskey to the children. Set out a bowl of blueberries for them to look at, smell, and taste. Later use blueberries to make blueberry muffins. As children work, draw their attention to the picture symbols and to the measuring process.

Blueberry Muffins
Ingredients:
2 cups flour
½ cup sugar
2 tsp. baking powder
½ tsp. salt
½ cup milk
½ cup melted margarine
1 egg
1 tsp. vanilla

Procedure:
Mix first four ingredients in a bowl and set aside.

1. Blend together last five ingredients.
2. Add liquid mixture to dry ingredients and stir just to combine.
3. Mash ¼ cup blueberries and stir into batter with a few quick strokes. Stir in remaining ¼–½ cup of whole berries.
4. Spoon batter into greased muffin pans or miniature muffin tins if available.
5. Bake 15 minutes at 400°.
6. Cool 5 minutes before removing from pans.

3. *Home for a Bear.* From magazines, cut out pictures of varying animal habitats: a forest, a cave, a desert, under water, the tundra, a meadow, the arctic, and so forth. Show the children the pictures one at a time, asking them to determine if each is a place where a bear might live. Encourage them to explain their reasoning. To make the activity more challenging, show a variety of forest, tundra, and arctic pictures, asking children to determine which type of bear might live in each locale.

4. *Measure the Bear.* Gather the following materials: teddy bears of varying sizes, several inch cubes, paper clips, plastic building bricks, small wooden blocks, a large sheet of paper, and a dark broad-tipped marker. Starting with one bear, ask the children to figure out a way to measure how tall it is, using the materials available. Encourage them to line up one type of material along the length of the bear and to count the items. Children can work cooperatively or each may choose a different item as a measuring tool. When the children have counted how many "blocks or paper clips tall" the bear is, make a chart by drawing a picture of each item and indicating how many equalled the height of the bear. Encourage the children to compare different results and to speculate as to the reasons for those differences. Repeat this process with the other bears.

Make the activity more challenging by asking children to estimate how many items "tall" the bear is prior to measuring it. Then have them compare their guess with the actual number needed.

Another alternative is to ask children to find out how much each bear weighs by collecting objects that may equal its weight. Use a balancing scale as an aid in determining equivalent weights.

5. **Bear Puzzles.** Mount pictures of real or pretend bears selected from magazines or calendars on firm, thin cardboard. In addition, make several small cards each marked with one of the following numbers: 2, 3, 4, or 5. Place the pictures and the number cards face down in the center of a small group of children. Ask the children to select one of each. The number drawn indicates the number of pieces in which each child should cut his or her picture to create a "bear" puzzle.

6. **Teddy-Bear Investigation.** Gather a large number of toy bears. (If you ask children to lend bears from home, make sure they will allow others in the group to handle their special treasures before including them in the activity.) Make the collection available to the children along with paper, writing tools, and measuring devices. Ask the children to examine the bears over a period of several days and describe their observations. As they explore and handle the bears, make note of the children's ideas in chart form or in writing. Review these observations periodically, adding or consolidating data as the children's interests dictate.

To get started, you might ask children to figure out how many different materials were used in making the various bears included in your array, or to determine whether each bear was patterned after a real species or a completely fantastical one. Once underway, this project could go in myriad directions. Encourage the children to determine what these will be. Record their ideas both individually and as a group. Review these ideas with them frequently to prompt other ideas. If possible, provide one or two bears that can be taken apart so that children can investigate the interior workings of the bears as well as outward characteristics.

7. **Bear Food Walk.** Following a discussion of bears' eating habits, ask children what things in their immediate vicinity bears might eat. Write down the children's ideas. Go for a walk outdoors, looking under

rocks, in rotting logs, under trees, and so forth for likely food items. Make a list of these as they are found. Return to the classroom and compare the children's anticipatory list with the things they actually saw.

8. **The "Bear" Facts.** This activity is best carried out toward the end of the Bear unit and following one in which children have explored some of the basics of pet care. *Annie and the Wild Animals* by Jan Brett is a good book to use as a lead-in. Prior to the children's participation, make a large chart, divided in half lengthwise down the paper. Mark one side "wild bear," accompanying the words with a picture of a real bear. Label the other side "furry pet," adding pictures of a dog and cat to illustrate what you mean. (Figure 13.4) On separate strips of paper, in writing large enough for children to see from a distance, draw the picture phrases listed at the end of this activity. Conceal these in a grocery bag. Explain to the children that individual youngsters will draw a paper strip from the bag and that as a group they will decide whether the description fits both wild animals and pets, or just one or the other. Proceed in this fashion using the strips to prompt discussion. Once a consensus has been reached for each phrase, tape it under one heading or the other. Those phrases that children believe to be true of both kinds of animals could straddle the middle.

Need room to exercise and play

Need food

Have fur

Need clean water

Have claws

Need a safe place to sleep

Need human beings to feed them

Find their own food

Some are sold in pet stores

Some live in the forest

Usually have an owner

No one owns them

Some can be touched

Should not be approached

Sleep in people's houses or yards

Sleep in dens

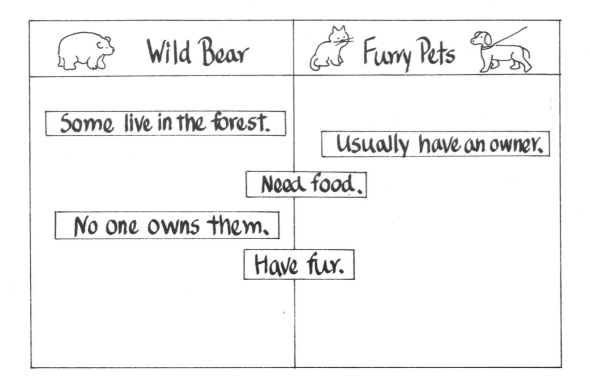

Figure 13.4 *Make a Chart to Compare Real Bears to Furry Pets*

9. ***Bear Buddies.*** Teach children the following chant:

Bear buddy, bear buddy,
Looking for a bear buddy.
Bear buddy, bear buddy,
Just like me.

Give each child seated in a circle a toy bear to hold. Select one child to be "it." While the others chant, "it" walks around the interior of the circle, stopping in front of a child holding a bear when the chant ends. Either the child who is "it" can name a similarity between his or her bear and the other child's, or the group can point it out. The seated child becomes "it" for the next time and must select a child not yet chosen. Continue this process until all have had a turn.

10. ***Sniff Out a Snack.***
    General Purpose: To increase children's awareness of the olfactory sense; to demonstrate strategies used by bears to find food.
    TFPs: 9, 10, 24–28.
    Materials: Canned salmon; honey (in honeycomb if possible); fresh mint or parsley leaves; strawberries, raspberries, or cherries; plastic or paper cups, bowls with tinfoil or plastic covers, or empty salt shakers; old towels or newspapers.

Procedure:
a. Set up the area prior to children's participation by placing a sample of each food in separate containers. Punch a small hole in the lids. Cover the containers with "debris" made by tearing towels or papers into strips. Display these on a table or in a large tub on the floor.
b. Invite children to join you by using the procedure bears follow to sniff out foods: "You can be a bear today. You're very hungry, but can't see very well. However, your nose is very curious about some smells. Bears can smell especially well and often know where to search for things to eat by following their noses."
c. Indicate the materials with glances and gestures as you encourage children to explore with their noses. Explain that there are special foods buried in the

debris and that bears save leftover food for another time by hiding it this way. Encourage children to act out similar behaviors.

d. As children begin sniffing the samples, mention some favorite foods of bears and challenge children to decide which food is in each container. Name a food and tell children to decide which container their noses tell them holds that food. Add information about particular bears when possible: "Grizzly bears love salmon! Tell me which food smells like the fish, salmon, to you."

e. Encourage children to decide which smells are tempting to them, and which are not.

Hints for Success:
- Allow children to unscrew the covers and look at the foods, to verify their identifications based on smell.

- Provide fresh samples of the foods at the snack table later for children to taste and/or see.

How to Simplify this Activity:
- Limit the containers to only a few.

How to Extend this Activity:
- Include some empty containers so children must differentiate between ones that contain food and ones that do not.

- Include some items bears wouldn't get in the wild such as popcorn or lemons. Ask children to find and identify these as nonbear foods.

11. ***Bear Necessities Collage.***
General Purpose: To give children practice drawing conclusions.

TFPs: 24, 25, 29, 31, 32, 50, 57a, 60, 61a.

Materials: Lots of magazines, especially nature-oriented ones; construction paper; glue and applicators; pictures of bears in the wild; scissors.

Procedure:
a. Introduce the activity after discussions of bears' habitats. Provide the supervising adult with a TFP list for reference.

b. Set up the area by stacking magazines on a table that can be reached from all chairs. Provide paper, glue, applicators, and scissors for each child. Explain that

the children can search the magazines for things they think bears might see if they peeked out of their dens or ambled through their territories. Remind children of bears' trailmaking behaviors and their ability to fish, hunt for food, and climb trees.

c. Have children cut out their pictures and paste them into a collage.

d. Encourage children to describe the pictures they choose, explaining why bears might see such sights.

e. Ask children to describe their collages. Write down some of the things children tell you at the bottom or on the back of their work.

Hint for Success:
- Read a story about bears before the activity and have children focus on what the bears' habitat looked like.

How to Simplify this Activity:
- Have pictures already cut out and available on the table.

How to Extend this Activity:
- Put out books about bears for children to look at to help them decide what images to choose.

- Provide markers so that children can make their own drawings of items or scenes not found in the magazines.

Construction

1. ***Build a Den.*** Provide children with cardboard boxes, brown grocery bags, newspapers, poster paint, brushes, construction paper, markers, and masking tape. Encourage them to create a bear's den from the materials at hand.

2. ***Teddy Bag Bears.*** Give children paper grocery and lunch bags, newspapers, glue, construction paper, markers, masking tape, buttons, ribbon, rubber bands, and scissors. Show children how to stuff the bags with newspaper to create a bear head (small bag) and a bear body (large bag). Have children attach the bags using tape or rubber bands. Tell children they can make ears, feet, and so forth out of paper and help them attach these to their bears. While some children do this, others can be

working on attaching buttons for eyes and a nose, placing ribbons around the bears' necks, and decorating their bodies with designs. This activity can be done by individual children or small groups. Encourage children to collaborate and problem solve while engaging in each of the steps.

3. *Bear Locator.*

General Purpose: For children to collaborate with classmates to construct a representative object.

TFPs: 62, 63.

Materials: An assortment of shoeboxes, paper towel rolls, aluminum foil, paper scraps, wooden knobs, wood glue, markers, cloth headbands, table, and chairs.

Procedure:

a. Set out all the materials prior to the children's participation.

b. Invite the children to create pretend radios that will be used to track bears. These will later serve as props in pretend play.

c. Explain that each device will have two parts: a transmitter and a receiver.

d. Boxes decorated with buttons and knobs will serve as the receivers.

e. Headbands colored with markers or otherwise decorated will serve as the transmitters.

f. Encourage children to help one another create both the receivers and the transmitters.

Hints for Success:

• If possible, display some pictures of animals wearing radio transmitters and scientists using the receiving equipment.

• Bring in samples of electronic equipment that have meters and dials for children to inspect.

How to Simplify this Activity:

• Offer precut paper dials and knobs for children to use.

How to Extend this Activity:

• Have children create pretend "insides" for the shoebox receivers as well as the outside knobs and dials.

Language

1. *Bear Stories.* Collect an array of pictures of real bears, nature objects, other animals, and people. Encourage the children to choose three or four pictures and make up stories about a real bear using the pictures selected. Write down the children's stories and read them back to the group. On another day, substitute toy bears for the real ones and household items for the nature objects. Repeat the same process.

2. *Three-Bears Scramble.* Create illustrations for the story of *Goldilocks and the Three Bears.* Tape them in random order on a wall or on a large easel pad. Read the story the way it is depicted. Ask the children to assist in unscrambling it.

3. *Bear Rhymes.* Discuss rhyming words. Give examples such as "bear-chair." Ask the children to tell you other words that rhyme with bear. Write down their ideas. Continue rhyming other bear-related words such as paw, honey, fur, den, and so forth.

4. *Characters Contrast.* Read aloud to the children the book *Blueberries for Sal* by Robert McCloskey. On a second day, prior to reading the story again, explain to the children that their job will be to listen carefully to the story and when it's over to tell you about Little Bear and Little Sal. Read the story. Afterward, at the top of a large piece of easel paper posted where the children can easily see it, write the words "Little Bear" and "Little Sal" as headings for two columns. Elicit descriptions from the group regarding each character and his or her actions, writing the children's exact words under the appropriate heading. After you have recorded several ideas, help the children compare the characters by figuring out how they were the same and how they differed.

5. *Teddy-Bear Descriptions.* Put two teddy bears in front of you so that children can easily see them. Explain that in this game, you will describe one of the bears and children will guess which one you are talking about.

Begin by giving broad clues that could apply to either bear. Gradually, make the hints more specific and applicable to only one of the pair. Be sure to include clues

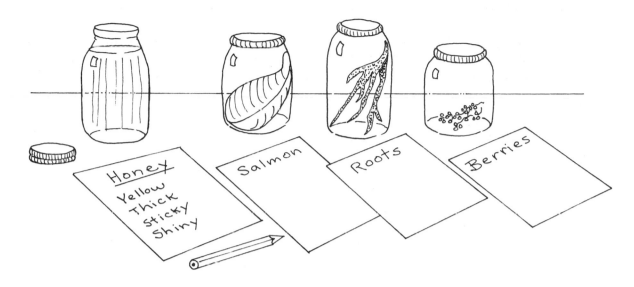

Figure 13.5 *Describe What Bears Eat*

that describe the absence of a particular characteristic ("this bear is not white"), as well as clues that describe the presence of certain attributes.

Gradually add challenge to the game by increasing the number of bears in the original group. Over time, have children take on the role of clue-givers.

6. ***Brown-Bear Variations.*** Read the storybook *Brown Bear, Brown Bear* by Bill Martin, Jr. Ask the children to help you write a new version using the same verbal pattern but substituting a polar bear, black bear, grizzly bear, or teddy bear for the Brown Bear. Help children figure out what objects would fit each bear's actual habitat.

7. ***Bear Adjectives.***

General Purpose: For children to expand their descriptive vocabulary.

TFPs: 24, 57c, 59c, 61c.

Materials: Smelling jars with bear foods inside, such as honey, salmon, roots, berries, and so on. If possible, make sure children can both see and smell the objects.

Procedure:

a. Put out jars on a table for the children to inspect. Tell them that each jar has something in it that a bear would like to eat. Discuss bears' use of smell to find

foods they like and to confirm what their poor sight tells them.

b. Give each child an opportunity to smell and look at the foods. Then ask them to describe what they smell and see.

c. On a large piece of paper write out the words children use to describe each jar's contents.

d. Review with them the words they chose.

Hint for Success:

• Work with a few children at a time so everyone has a jar to look at and smell.

How to Simplify this Activity:

• Instead of making a master list for the group, label the contents of each jar with words individual children generate, one at a time. As new children arrive, add their words to each list. Allow duplicate words to be used. (Figure 13.5)

How to Extend this Activity:

• Discourage duplication of words among the children.

• Ask children to use the words from their list to describe other objects or foods familiar to them.

9. ***Play-A-Story Center.*** Set aside a corner of your room as a place where children can reenact favorite bear stories. Focus on one

story at a time so that children do not become confused. Select *one* of the following stories:

Ask Mr. Bear by Marjorie Flack

The Three Bears (any author)

Brown Bear, Brown Bear by Bill Martin, Jr.

Blueberries for Sal by Robert McCloskey

Corduroy by Don Freeman

The Mitten by Jan Brett

Provide props to match. Useful supplies might include:

Two picture book versions of the story;

Recorded versions of the story (records or tapes);

Child-sized flannel board (made by gluing flannel to cookie tray or inside picture frame without the glass);

Larger flannel board for use by two or more children;

Child- and adult-sized gloves with story characters painted on the fingers;

Child- and adult-sized gloves with laminated story characters attached by Velcro® to the fingers;

Laminated pictures of bears with elastic finger-loops on the back;

Laminated pictures of bears with magnets glued to the back;

Puppet bears (tongue depressors, paper sacks, or socks);

Laminated circular brown frames and ears (for holding up to one's face);

Bear body costumes made from brown material (terry cloth towels, flannel, felt, or canvas);

Bear head coverings made from brown material with Velcro® or snap closing for easy on and off;

Bear ears made from sturdy cardboard and stapled onto a headband;

Bear feet and paws to tie to shoes and hands;

Brown sandpaper cutouts of bear characters;

Brown carpet sample cutouts of bear characters;

Photographs of children dressed up as bear characters

Keeping the props temporarily out of sight, begin by retelling the story using a book or flannel board. Next, ask the children to recall the story in their own words. Highlight story sequence and character attributes as children go along. Follow this by introducing the props and helping children to use them as you tell the story one more time. Finally, back out of the area and let children use the props to reenact their own version of the tale. Expect child-initiated innovations or deviations from the original plot or characters and do not require children to include any parts of the story they choose not to act out.

10. ***Ask Mr. Bear.*** Memorize the classic children's story *Ask Mr. Bear* by Marjorie Flack. If necessary, write the outline on cards as a reminder. Prepare puppets or rubber animals to represent the animals in the book and obtain actual items that the animals suggest for a present (wool, an egg, cheese, and so on). You may use pictures of these items, if you prefer. Explain to children that you will tell the story and that they should remember the animals and the corresponding presents. Tell the story using the props. With the whole group responding at once, ask children to name the animals and presents, holding up the appropriate figures as they answer. As a follow-up, place the figures of the characters and the presents on a table for children to match up, as they retell the story on their own.

Physical

1. ***The Bear Went Over the Mountain.*** Sing the first verse of the song "The Bear Went Over the Mountain" as children climb from the bottom to the top of a climber or flight of stairs. Ask each child what he or she can see from that higher vantage point. Insert relevant words into the second verse to describe the child's view. Sing this while the child climbs down.

The Bear Went Over the Mountain
(Traditional)
The bear went over the mountain
(Repeat three times.)

To see what s/he could see.
(Repeat three times.)

The bear went over the mountain
(Repeat three times.)

To see what s/he could see.
And all that s/he could see
(Repeat twice.)
Was (the other side of the mountain)
(Repeat three times using each child's words.)
Was all that s/he could see.

2. **Pokey Bear.** Introduce this chant to gather children into a circle or use it as an actual circle game.

Pokey Bear, Pokey Bear
Why are you so slow?
(Chanted at moderate speed. Children hold hands and circle to the right.)

I don't know, I don't know,
I like to be slow.
(Chanted at a very slow speed. Children slow down accordingly.)

Try to run, try to run
Running's lots of fun
(Words and children speed up. Change directions and circle to the right.)

Oh, no, no. Oh, no. no.
I like to be slow.
(Words and children slow down again.)

3. **Teddy Bear Turn Around.** Begin by teaching children the traditional jump-rope chant, "Teddy Bear Turn Around." Next, show children how to add the corresponding motions. Later, put several hula hoops on the ground across a large area. Invite each child to stand inside a hoop, one child per hoop. Show them how to jump on two feet in place while chanting the following traditional jump rope rhyme.

Teddy Bear, Teddy Bear, touch the ground. *(Child stoops to touch.)*
Teddy Bear, Teddy Bear, climb the stairs. *(Children make climbing motions.)*

Teddy Bear, Teddy Bear, say your prayers. *(Children make praying motion with hands.)*
Teddy Bear, Teddy Bear, turn off the light. *(Children make switching motion.)*
Teddy Bear, Teddy Bear, say good night. *(Children rest heads briefly on two hands held beneath their cheeks.)*

4. **Bear Poses.** Gather a large collection of realistic drawings and photographs depicting different types of bears in a variety of poses. Show these one at a time to the children. Ask them to strike a similar pose and to "freeze" until you say "relax."

5. **Trail Breaking.** Conduct this activity in the snow. Muddy ground or wet sand will also work if snow is unavailable. Select one child to be a "mother" bear. This child will make tracks in the snow that the other children, pretending to be cubs, will step into. Give the "mother" bear over-sized boots to make the trail easier for others to follow. Rotate roles periodically to give everyone a chance to be leader and cub.

6. **Lines and Squares.** In this activity, children can practice keeping their balance. Precede it with several readings (explaining unfamiliar words) of the poem "Lines and Squares" by A. A. Milne. Take one small group of children at a time to a sidewalk or a tile hallway. Point out the "lines and squares." Tell children that, just as in the poem, they will be moving from square to square without stepping on any lines. They can pretend that there are "bears waiting to eat the sillies that step on the lines in the street. . . ." Children who are waiting for a turn can pretend to be bears as they watch others moving from square to square. Mark a beginning and an ending place. Instruct children to move from square to square in the following sequence: walk forward, walk backward, tiptoe, jump, and hop on each foot. To maintain children's interest, tell them to practice "not being silly" by staying in the squares. To encourage them to walk backward, say, "Let's pretend a bear is in front of us, and we are so scared that we can't turn around. We'll have to walk backward to get away from it." To tiptoe, pretend that the bears are sleeping and that children should try not to wake them.

Pretend Play

1. ***Bear Care.*** Invite children to an area set up as a repair shop. Show them an assortment of stuffed teddy bears that need "repair." Encourage the children to identify problems and "fix" the bears as best they can. Provide props such as extra stuffing, tape, bandages, pretend needles made from cardboard, and so on.

2. ***Teddy-Bear Toy Shop.*** Create a toy shop specializing in teddy bears in an area of your room. Include a variety of toy bears, a cash register, and play money, as well as paper and markers for children to make signs for the store. Encourage children to take on the roles of clerk, cashier, and customer.

3. ***Bear Dens.*** Set up the area prior to children's participation by creating a "cave" using a large carton or card table covered with a blanket.

    Display a few foods and stuffed bears in the area. Put pictures of trees, forest animals, and bears on the walls. Make available additional blankets or towels.

    Invite children to join you as bears preparing for the winter. Encourage them to prepare a den. Prompt children to make bear grunts and growls and to communicate with gestures such as hugs and pointing. Children may wish to try these strategies with stuffed bears, each other, or you. Discuss ways bears collect food. Children can pretend to scoop "fish" with their "paws," shake "nuts" from "trees," and "sniff out" berries. Ask children to help you, the mother bear, take care of and teach the bear cubs.

    Eventually, retreat from the play as children begin assuming various bear roles. Be alert for signs of boredom or inappropriate uses of materials. If this happens, volunteer new information and/ or resume a bear's role yourself.

4. ***Scientist's Study Station.*** Invite children to an area set up as a research center where scientists can study the natural behavior of bears in the wild. Include tables, paper, markers, magnifying glasses, and binoculars; pretend walkie-talkies, radio trackers, and cameras; and cooking facilities (for the hungry scientists). Children could choose to be bears or people. The bears could leave trails, make dens, and teach their young. The scientists could track bears, count them, and record their behaviors. This activity works well when it is introduced following a few days of the *Bear Dens* activity.

Social

1. ***Follow My Trail.*** Introduce this activity with a group discussion of the trail-making behaviors of bears. Explain that bears leave signs all along their routes so they can find their way back to special places time after time. Ask the children to think of some things that bears might want to find over and over again (their dens, food, or water). Next, explain that bears often mark trees so they can see where they've been. While bears use their teeth or claws to make marks, the children will use chalk instead. Offer the children some pieces of chalk and invite them to join you on a trail-marking walk outdoors. Lead the children on a walk, encouraging them to leave chalk signs on trees, sidewalks, and buildings. Also, leave small piles of real nuts or paper fish at points along the trail. Either return to the start by retracing your steps, or have a second group of children follow, looking for the treasures left behind.

2. ***Ambling Partners.*** Pair each child with a partner. Have one child stand directly behind the other and hold the front child's waist. Designate a spot several yards away for the pair to reach by moving both right feet and then both left in unison. Once individual pairs of children are relatively successful in carrying out the motions, add another pair of children to the chain, asking them all to move together.

3. ***Bear Hugs.*** Prior to carrying out this activity, send home a note asking parents to help children choose a bear to bring to school for a day. Collect extras for children who cannot bring one or do not have one to bring. Begin by encouraging children to take turns showing and/or telling about their bears. Next, ask the children to circulate bears among the group, giving each a "bear hug" before passing it on. If some children hesitate to share their bears, explain that everyone is sharing today and taking good care of each other's bear buddies, but that they may keep their own bear

for hugging instead, if they wish. Let children volunteer at first, then involve others who may be more hesitant. End by offering "bear hugs" to children who would like to pretend to be cubs enjoying some cuddling with their parent bear. Talk about how good hugs feel!

4. *Bear Owners.* Take an instant picture of each child holding his or her toy bear (or one provided by the teacher). Invite individual children to name each child pictured. Older children may extend their awareness of classmates by matching first name labels to each photo.

5. *Whose Bear Is This?* Collect two sets of pictures, one depicting a variety of toy bears, another consisting of human beings. Make sure to include people of all ages and culture groups in the latter set. Ask children to match the people to "their" bears. Accept children's rationales for the pairings they create. Emphasize that all over the world, people of many different ages enjoy toy bears.

TEACHER RESOURCES

Field Trip Ideas

1. Visit a forest or natural wooded area to explore a bear habitat.
2. Visit a zoo to look at live bears.
3. Visit a natural history museum to see bear exhibits or a children's museum to view toy bears.

Classroom Visitors

1. Invite a zoologist to talk about bears, to show pictures of bears, and if possible, to demonstrate a tracking device.
2. Ask a seamstress to visit your class to demonstrate how to make a stuffed bear.
3. Ask a wildlife artist or photographer to show his or her work to the children.

Children's Books

Ballaty, S., and A. Lomeo. *The Baby Bears.* New York: Golden, 1975.

Bartoli, J. *Snow on Bear's Nose.* Niles, IL: Whitman, 1976.

Bonners, S. *Panda.* New York: Delacorte, 1978.

Bork, I. *Bru—The Brown Bear.* New York: Frederick Warne and Company, 1961.

Brett, J. *Annie and the Wild Animals.* Boston: Houghton Mifflin, 1985.

———. *The Mitten.* New York: Putnam's, 1989.

duBois, W. P. *Bear Circus.* New York: Viking, 1971.

Flack, M. *Ask Mr. Bear.* New York: Macmillan, 1958.

Freeman, D. *Corduroy.* New York: Viking-Penguin, 1968.

Freschet, B. *Grizzly Bear.* New York: Scribner's, 1975.

———. *Little Black Bear Goes for a Walk.* New York: Scribner's, 1977.

George, J. C. *The Grizzly Bear with the Golden Ears.* New York: Harper and Row, 1982.

Guilfoile, E. *Nobody Listens to Andrew.* Chicago: Follett, 1957.

Hall, D. *Polar Bear Leaps.* New York: Knopf, 1985

Hamilton, V. *The People Could Fly.* New York: Knopf, 1985.

Hoban, T. *Panda, Panda.* New York: Greenwillow, 1986.

Irvine, G. *Nanuck the Polar Bear.* Chicago: Childrens Press, 1982.

Lapp, E. *The Blueberry Bears.* Niles, IL: Whitman, 1983.

Martin, B., Jr. *Brown Bear, Brown Bear.* New York: Holt, Rinehart and Winston, 1983.

Milne, A. A. *When We Were Very Young.* New York: E. P. Dutton, 1952.

McCloskey, R. *Blueberries for Sal.* New York: Viking, 1948.

Pluckrose, H. *Bears.* New York: Gloucester, 1979.

Adult References

Craighead, F. C., Jr. *Track of the Grizzly.* San Francisco: Sierra Club, 1979.

East, B. *Bears.* New York: Crown, 1978.

McNamee, T. *The Grizzly Bear.* New York: Knopf, 1984.

Mills, W. *Bears and Men: A Gathering.* Chapel Hill, NC: Algonquin, 1986.

Sheldon, W. G. *The Wilderness Home of the Giant Panda.* Amherst, MA: University of Massachusetts Press, 1975.

VanWormer, J. *The World of the Black Bear.* Philadelphia: Lippincott, 1966.

Chapter 14

Water

•

For children, hardly a day goes by without a firsthand experience with water. Water is a medium for pleasure, a necessity for cleanliness, indeed, a must for life! We brush our teeth and splash our faces with it first thing in the morning, and we often end our days and begin our journey into night with one last drink. Water suggests an almost infinite variety of multisensory experiences. For example, walking through a puddle produces an array of delightful sounds: splish, splash, drip, woosh, and swoosh! The wet sidewalk, as well as one's boots, changes in color and becomes more or less shiny. Raindrops feel wet. Dissolving lemonade mix in a cup of water yields a new smell, a new taste, a new color. Water can be entered, drunk, thickened, boiled, frozen, and poured. From a baby's very first bath, water is a fascinating, functional part of life.

PURPOSE

There are many ways to take the study of water from familiar territory into the unknown. In spite of, or perhaps because of, children's familiarity with water, experimentation and scientific inquiry can be naturally introduced. Water can be studied for its own properties: solid to liquid to steam, absorption, and dissolution. Water can be introduced as a medium for life-forms: fish, turtles, and plants. Water can be examined for the part it plays in weather phenomena: rain, sleep, snow, fog, and clouds. The many forms that water takes can be the focus of study: puddles, ponds, lakes, streams, rivers, and oceans. Rather than narrowing our focus to only one of these possibilities, we chose a broad, panoramic approach instead. Consequently, we have included activities related to many facets of water study. They are designed to be representative of the kinds of things that children can do and should by no means be considered a comprehensive listing.

IMPLEMENTATION

Among the many adaptations you might consider for a Water theme are the following:

Option One: Plan a water unit to demonstrate change. Prepare ice in many shapes. Experiment with factors that cause the ice to melt.

Explore the questions, "Does it melt more quickly when immersed in water?" "What happens to ice placed outdoors on a cold winter day as compared with ice in a container on a sunny indoor windowsill on the same day?" Place a chunk of ice in an electric frying pan and watch how quickly it liquifies, boils, then produces steam on a mirror held overhead. Raise the mirror and watch the steam drip back into the pan as water.

Option Two: Plan a water unit based on the ways that people use water in their daily lives. Wash toys and dolls. Teach children the steps in hand washing and toothbrushing. Try these tasks without water! Plan a field trip to a beach or pond. Wade, swim, watch boaters enjoying their time afloat. Engage in a variety of cooking activities. Note how often water is used in food preparation and to clean up afterwards.

Option Three: Adopt a goldfish as a classroom pet. Investigate whether the fish drinks water and the reasons that it needs a watery home by consulting a variety of reference materials. Expand the study to other water creatures such as sharks, whales, turtles, frogs, seagulls, and bugs. How does their dependence on water compare, each with the other, and with humans and other kinds of animals?

Option Four:
Combine the above options into a three-week unit.
Week One: Focus on the properties of water.
Week Two: Concentrate on how people use water each day.
Week Three: Extend the theme to include how water is necessary for all living things including both animals and plants.

A unit on water could be followed by one on weather or the sky, by a more in-depth study of fish, or by units on land forms or pollution. A unit on food preparation would also be a logical follow-up.

TERMS, FACTS, AND PRINCIPLES

General Information

1. Water has various names depending on the form it takes: ice, snow, fog, mist, dew, steam, rain, hail, clouds, lakes, streams, seas, oceans, and so on.

2. Water in all its forms feels wet.

3. Water can be measured and weighed.

4. Water has no shape of its own.

5. As a liquid, water runs downhill unless something blocks its path.

6. As a liquid, water can be poured.

*7. The same water can take on different forms at different points in time.

8. Water takes the shape of the vessel into which it is poured or the area in which it is contained.

Water on the Earth

9. Water is a natural resource.

10. Water is everywhere. It is in the air, under the ground, and on the Earth's surface.

11. Water exists on the Earth's surface as lakes, oceans, rivers, ponds, and puddles.

12. Water covers much of the Earth's surface.

13. Water exists under the Earth's surface between layers of rocks.

14. Water exists in the air as water vapor.

15. All living things must continually have water to survive.

16. There is no substitute for water.

*17. Pure water is composed of two invisible gasses: hydrogen and oxygen.

18. Pure water has no color, no taste, and no odor.

19. When water has a color, taste, or odor it is because some other substance is in it.

20. The water found naturally on the Earth is either salty or fresh.

21. Saltwater contains a lot of salt.

22. Fresh water contains little or no salt.

23. Whales, porpoises, and some fish drink saltwater to live.

24. People and most other animals cannot drink saltwater to live.

*25. All living things have water as part of their basic structure.

26. People use water for many purposes: to drink, wash, cook, put out fires, play in, cool or warm the body, and for transportation.

*27. When the air is warm, water rises as vapor from the earth's surface and mixes with the air in a process called evaporation.

*28. When there is more water vapor in the air than the air can hold, the vapor turns into tiny droplets that form clouds.

*29. When the water droplets get big enough they fall down to the earth as rain, snow, sleet, or hail. This is called precipitation.

30. Precipitation occurs in the form of sleet, rain, hail, and snow.

31. When the temperature is warm enough, the precipitation falls as rain.

32. When the temperature is cool enough, the precipitation falls as sleet, snow, or hail.

33. Rain is liquid water.

34. Sleet is freezing water.

35. Snow is single drops of frozen water.

36. Hail is many drops of frozen water stuck together.

*37. Water is recycled naturally. Water that exists on the Earth as a liquid goes into the air as a vapor and returns to the Earth as precipitation. This cycle is repeated over and over again.

38. Precipitation is measured by its depth: in inches in some countries and in meters in others.

39. Some areas of North America get more precipitation than others.

40. When the temperature is lowered enough, water freezes into a solid called ice.

41. As a solid, water can retain the shape of the vessel in which it was frozen, even when the container is taken away.

42. As a solid, water can be broken.

43. When the temperature is raised enough, solid water melts into a liquid.

44. When the temperature is raised very high, liquid water becomes a gas called steam.

45. Some water vapor stays close to the Earth and appears as mist or fog when the temperature cools.

46. Some water vapor clings to plants and things outside. When the temperature cools, the vapor appears as dew or frost.

*47. Water vapor is always in the air even though its particles are too small to see.

*48. The amount of water vapor in the air is commonly described as the relative humidity.

*49. In condensation, tiny water particles which are invisible to the naked eye come together to form larger drops which can be seen.

50. Some substances dissolve or break apart in water while others retain their original form.

51. Some objects change when immersed in water while others remain the same.

Water Pollution

*52. Water can be harmful when dangerous substances get into it.

*53. Harmful water is said to be polluted.

*54. Polluted water can hurt everything in the environment.

*55. Some polluted water can be made clean again by filtering out the harmful substances.

*56. People do not yet know how to clean up all polluted water.

*57. Fish cannot live in polluted water.

*58. People cannot drink or swim in polluted water.

*59. Plants are destroyed by polluted rain.

*60. Buildings, roads, and machines are damaged by water and rain that is polluted.

*61. Fish and shellfish that live in polluted waters are unsafe to eat.

*62. Water never goes away completely. The water that is on the Earth and in its atmosphere today has been part of the Earth forever.

Erosion

63. Water can erode the land.

64. Erosion means that earth and rocks are broken down into smaller particles and washed away.

ACTIVITY IDEAS

Aesthetic

1. *Musical Water.* Collect enough rhythm sticks (in pairs), bells, and drums with drumsticks for each child to have an instrument. Discuss the sounds that water makes: rain drumming against a roof, water dripping from trees after a rain, a faucet running slow or fast. Invite the children to re-create some of these rhythms and tempos with their instruments. At first, you may want to describe a scenario. Tell the children that it is just beginning to sprinkle against the roof. Ask them to produce a sound that this brings to mind. Tell them that it's beginning to rain harder . . . and now it's pouring! At each step, invite musical interpretation. Turn on a nearby faucet, if possible. Invite children to listen to the sounds it makes. Turn it off. Invite experimentation with the instruments to approximate the sounds.

2. *Water in Your Ears.* Check your local library for recordings of music with a water theme that you can borrow. Some titles to look for are:

Classical Music
Water Music by George Frederic Handel
Daphnis et Chloé, an opera by Maurice Ravel (focus on the opening of Suite #2)
The Moldau (a Russian river) by Bedrich Smetena
Grand Canyon Suite ("Cloudburst" Movement) by Ferde Grafe

Concert Band Music
North Sea Overture by Ralph Herman
"Old Man River" by Jerome Kern
"Sea Songs" by Ralph Vaughn Williams
"The Savannah River Holiday" by Ron Nelson
"Flow Gently, Sweet Afton" by Robert Burns and James T. Spilman

Popular Tunes
"Raindrops Keep Falling on My Head"
"There's a Hole in the Bucket"
"Rain, Rain Go Away"
"Singin' in the Rain"
"Rainy Day Dances and Rainy Day Songs," a recording by Marcia Berman and Anne Barlin (Educational Activities, Inc.)

Tell the children that music will be playing in the background during the day's session, and that all of the music was written because it reminded the composers of water. Suggest that they think about what kind of water each song represents: stormy weather, oceans, lakes, and rivers. Invite children to move to the music or paint a picture that represents the music sometime during the day.

3. *Water Colors.* Set up an art table with watercolor paint pallets, water in small dishes, and fine paint brushes. Include two or three kinds of paper, such as construction paper, newsprint, and poster board. Direct children to experiment with the effects of a more or less wet brush applied to the paint and then to the various types of paper. Point out the different intensities of color and the different rates of absorption that result. Discuss what happens to the water as brushes that have been used in more than one color are remoistened. Provide fresh water to replenish the cups as necessary.

4. *Snow Paintings.* Obtain several types of bottles that dispense a small amount of liquid at a time, such as plant misters, contact-lens cleaning solution bottles, bulb-ended basters with small openings. Fill each bottle with a solution of paint and water. Food coloring can also be used in diluted form. On a day when snow covers the ground, invite children to create artwork on the snow with the bottled paint. Encourage sharing of colors and of types of dispensers. If snow seldom or never occurs in your area of the country or at the time of year when you wish to carry out this activity, substitute shaved ice in a water table, or spread long sheets of mural paper on the ground as a painting surface.

5. *Beautiful Bubbles.* Fill a water table with warm water to which bubble solution or dishwashing soap has been added. Add a light tint of color using food coloring if desired. Give each child a drinking straw. Before proceeding, you may want to make sure everyone knows how to blow. Provide each youngster with a small cup of water. Demonstrate blowing on your hand without the straw, then through it. Have each child practice this in clear water. Then, invite children to blow through their straws into the soapy water to produce

beautiful bubble formations. Add a new color for a change.

6. *Water Collage.* Initiate a discussion of collage as an art form. Tell children that collage artists produce their works by combining many pictures of flat objects together into one big picture that suggests some meaning or topic. Provide many magazines (nature magazines if possible), scissors, construction paper, and glue or paste. Tell the children to search through the magazines for pictures that include water and cut them out. Inexperienced children could be directed to tear out pictures, or you may want to complete this step yourself before proceeding. Encourage children to arrange a variety of pictures on a sheet of paper and secure them with glue (or paste). As children work, you may want to suggest that they represent a particular water theme: water sports, water in the home, water in nature, or creatures in the water, for instance. Encourage children to dictate a title or a sentence or two of description for you to write on their collages.

7. *Sprinkle Painting.* Carry out this activity on a day when it is sprinkling or raining lightly. You will need powdered tempera paint in shaker-top cans. Offer children two or three colors that will produce beautiful blends. Give each child a piece of white construction paper. Have them lay the papers on top of plastic trash bags spread on the ground in an outdoor yard. Choose a place that can be observed through classroom windows if possible. Direct children to sprinkle two or three colors of paint onto their papers. Wait for the raindrops to fall upon the paints, causing them to dilute and blend into colorful designs. Talk about how the water (in the form of rain) is causing changes in the paint. Hang the paintings in the classroom to dry, or wait for the sun to come out and bake them to perfection!

8. *Color-Soaked Circles.*
   General Purpose: To provide children with opportunities to increase their familiarity with various forms of art, and to reflect upon and talk about their observations and reactions to an aesthetic experience.

TFPs: 18, 19, 26, 50, 51.

Materials: Coffee filters shaped like fluted-edged baskets and flattened into circles (at least one per child); eyedroppers; food coloring or powdered paints; water; bowls or other small containers, trays or newspapers to place under the filters; a marking pen to label work with names.

Procedure:

a. Set out all materials on a table or work surface. Dilute the paint or food coloring with water, as children watch, to show the change that occurs in the water.

b. Give each child a filter. Direct them to write their names, or offer to do this for them. Arrange the containers of "paint" and the eyedroppers within easy reach of all children.

c. Mention that coffee filters are made of a type of paper that absorbs liquids. Tell the children that, when applied, one or more colors will "bleed" and blend into the special paper.

d. Demonstrate how to pick up a small amount of colored solution with an eyedropper. Distribute trays or cover a table with newspaper. Invite children to explore and experiment with applying the "paint" water to their own filters. Ask them to tell you about this special kind of painting as they work. Introduce the words "soak" and "absorb."

e. Encourage the use of more than one color. Ask children what is happening as the various colors are absorbed into one another and into the paper.

f. Praise children's attempts and results. Point out the many designs that different artists are creating using the same materials. As the paintings dry, ask about or discuss what is changing and what is staying the same.

Hints for Success:

• Food coloring is more difficult to remove from clothing and work surfaces than are most commercial children's paints.

• A "thin" solution of paint will be more easily applied with eyedroppers than a thicker one. Experiment with consistency before proceeding.

• Some children may find eyedroppers difficult to manipulate. Substitute basting bulbs or squirt bottles if necessary.

How to Simplify this Activity:

• Try painting on coffee filters with commercial watercolors and small brushes instead of more stain-producing paints and eyedroppers.

• Invite children to dip all or parts of their filters into large containers of colored water; observe as the colors blend and spread.

How to Extend this Activity:

• Experiment with wet versus dry filters for varying effects. Dip each filter in a tub of water; proceed as above. Repeat the procedure with dry filters.

• Provide construction paper and rubber cement or white school glue for children to mount their finished works with a framed effect.

• Introduce the concept of primary and secondary colors. Ask children to predict and test out what will happen to yellow areas when blue paint is applied over parts of them, or when blue is added to red, or red to yellow.

Affective

1. *"Water" You Feeling?* Initiate a discussion of the times that water makes us feel comfortable, secure, or happy. Mention that water can sometimes make people feel scared, uncomfortable, or unhappy, too. Ask children to think of a pleasant experience they've had with water. Describe a brief scenario yourself. Invite children to tell about wonderful water feelings. Next, ask children if they can think of a time when they wished water would go away. Talk about rainy days spent inside, flooded basements, or boat rides on rough seas.

2. *Clean Up, Clean Up, Clean Up the Room.* Initiate a discussion of clean-up jobs that require water. List children's ideas on a large sheet of paper. Prompt ideas with

questions, if necessary: "What is the best way to clean our paint table? What kinds of tools would we need?" "How do our snack dishes and juice pitchers get clean after we use them?" After a list has been generated, ask for volunteers to take on these jobs today. Add names beside each task. Help children to gather the necessary tools. Coach them through the clean-up jobs, pointing out that each of them is helping to keep the classroom clean. Continue to emphasize the importance of water in each of these tasks. Other possible jobs include cleaning windows; washing modeling dough cutters, toys, and dolls; providing water for classroom pets; changing the water in the fishbowl; or scrubbing out sinks.

3. *Who Likes This One?* Obtain several kinds of commercially bottled water. Include a carbonated water, an orange- or lemon-flavored water, seltzer water, and so on. Set up a tasting area with lots of small paper cups. Remember to have a bottle opener on hand if some bottles do not have twist-off caps. Invite children to look at the water first. Ask if they think all of them will taste the same. Ask children if the water at school tastes the same as that at home, at grandma's, or at restaurants. Is there one that they like the best? Distribute paper cups to each child. Ask children to indicate which water they'd like to try first. As you are pouring samples, you may want to tell children something about the source of his or her choice. Refer to the bottle label for this. As each child tries a second choice, inquire whether it tastes the same as the first. Encourage children to tell you whether they think one tastes better than the other. Continue with several kinds of water. Mention that although water itself has no taste, different minerals and flavorings make waters taste different.

4. *Hand Washing.*
   General Purpose: To encourage children to take responsibility for cleanliness and for effective grooming procedures.
   TFPs: 2, 26, 49, 50.
   Materials: Sinks, bars of soap or liquid soap in pump dispensers, paper or clean cloth towels.

Procedure:
a. Introduce the activity with a discussion of hand washing. Encourage children to give examples of when hands should be washed: before eating, after toileting, or when visibly dirty or covered with paint, glue, and so on. Point out that dirt is *not* always visible. Germs are invisible but can be unhealthy when transferred to the mouth while eating with one's hands or into the body through cuts and scrapes.

b. Explain that people must wash their hands even when they don't look dirty sometimes. Tell children that there are several steps to follow when doing a good job of hand washing, and that today they will learn these steps.

c. Demonstrate your hand-washing technique with "imaginary" equipment. Pretend to turn on a faucet with one hand. Hold the hand under an imaginary stream of water. Say, "First, I turn on the water and check the temperature—feel the water and decide if it's too hot or too cold." Adjust an imaginary faucet, saying "There it's just right—warm!"

d. Hold two cupped hands, palms up, under the "water." Explain that you are wetting your hands because soap does its work best when mixed with water. Pretend to pick up a bar of soap (or squirt some soap into one hand by depressing an imaginary soap pump with the other).

e. Begin rubbing your hands together, mentioning the lather that's being produced. Point out that the soap begins to dissolve in the water, producing cleansing bubbles. Replace the "soap." Carefully wash each finger, and the back of one hand and then the other. Rub vigorously over imaginary spots, explaining that you're scrubbing away a spot of paint or a bit of mud.

f. Again cup the hands under "running water," then rub them lightly together, saying "Now I'll rinse away the dirt and soap until my hands are no longer sudsy—there! My hands feel smooth and clean as can be!"

Figure 14.1 *Steps for Handwashing*

g. Remind the children to turn off the water.

h. Explain that it's important to dry your fingers and hands, too, while demonstrating related movements.

i. Take two children to each sink in a real washing area. Invite one to watch and one to wash. Praise as children practice. Point out initiative: "Walter, you've remembered to check the water's temperature! Good thinking! I like the way Nancy is washing each finger thoroughly. You must have really listened and watched!" Continue until each child has had an opportunity to carry out this hand-washing procedure.

Hints for Success:

• Gather the necessary tools for handwashing in a paper bag. Ask children to suggest what might be needed before carrying out the above demonstration.

Pull each item from the bag as it is named: a bar of soap, a towel, a washcloth. Add a nail brush.

• Repeat this demonstration another day. Make "mistakes," allowing children to correct you. Consider a third demonstration in which children "talk" you through the entire process.

• Make a hand-washing chart. Refer to it as you demonstrate. Hang it for future reference above the sink that children use. (Figure 14.1)

How to Simplify this Activity:

• Take two or three children to the bathroom with you at a time. Demonstrate hand washing as they watch. Invite each one to wash his or her hands as the other children remind him or her of the steps to follow. Make sure that each child has a chance to practice.

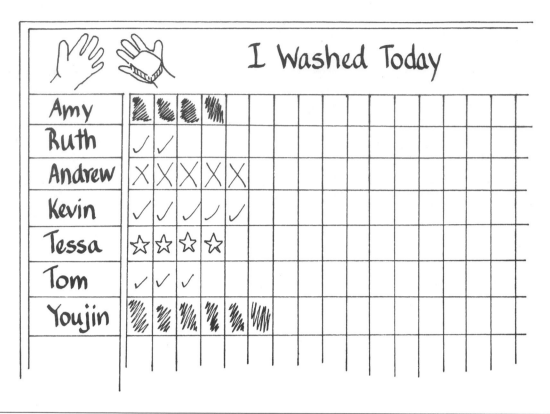

Figure 14.2 *Motivate Handwashing Often by Use of a Chart*

How to Extend this Activity:

• Make a chart with each child's name down the left-hand side with a line of graph squares beside each name. Hang a marking pen or a supply of star or dot stickers near the chart. Draw a picture that represents hand washing at the top. After introducing the chart's use at a circle time, hang it near the sink. Show children how to put a mark in the square beside their names after each episode of hand washing. You may want to color in the marked boxes at the end of each day to represent the total number of times hands were washed that day. (Figure 14.2)

Cognition

1. ***Erosion Experiments.*** Set up a sand table or sandbox environment prior to introducing this activity to the children. Make "mountains" of sand, clay, and rocks. Provide sprinkling cans or small measuring cup-sized pitchers of water. You could use a hose, if available. Initiate a discussion of erosion (see TFPs) before proceeding. Ask children to describe the size and shapes of the formations. Provide measuring instruments. Tell children to measure the height, width, and/or circumference of the mounds. Give two or three children at a time a hose or pitcher. Encourage predictions of what changes will occur as water is poured on each mound. Prompt close observation and description as children pour water on the different materials. Ask children, "Which mountain is affected by water? Why? How well did our predictions match what actually happened?"

2. ***Sink and Float.*** Collect a variety of objects, some that sink and others that float. Include one or more objects that float, but that will "carry" an object that sinks. Fill a water table. Provide two empty tubs, one labeled "things that sink" and the other, "things that float." If children have had few opportunities to explore a water table, allow several days of unstructured exploration before planning this experience.

When focusing on the phenomena of sinking and floating, begin by selecting an object yourself. Place it in the water. Ask children to tell you what happens. Choose another object and repeat this procedure. Introduce the words "sink" and "float" if children use other terms. Next, indicate the array of materials. Invite children to place them, one by one, in the water. Point out the tubs; explain what the labels say. Direct children to place each object in the appropriate tub as they determine whether it sinks or floats. Encourage children to make predictions about what will happen to objects before placing them in the water. Before they test out their prediction, ask children *why* they've decided an object will sink or float. Ponder what will happen to a "sinker" if it is placed on a "floater" and invite a child to test this out. Consider making a picture chart of children's predictions that they can use to confirm or reject them.

3. *All Mixed Up.* Gather several materials that will and won't dissolve in water, or ones that dissolve at varying rates: flour, salt, cornstarch, powdered paint, drink mix, dirt, dried pasta (macaroni), gravel, wood chips, and sand. Put each one in a separate bowl with a serving spoon. Provide each child with several see-through plastic drinking cups or paper cups. Add craft sticks to use as stirrers. Tell children that water causes different changes in different materials; invite them to choose a substance to try adding to water. Provide small pitchers of water; direct children to pour some water into a cup, then add a spoonful of one of the materials. Ask children with good verbal skills to predict what will happen before adding anything. After they've added the substance, children may want to try stirring to see if that action makes a difference. Provide a new cup and clean water for each solution to encourage comparisons, or provide a bucket in which to dump old solutions if the same cup is to be reused. Note that some materials (macaroni) will change only after some time underwater. Children may want to leave their concoctions for a time and check back occasionally to see if anything has changed.

4. *Pretty Flaky.* Catch some snowflakes on pieces of black construction paper. Provide children with small magnifiers. Invite them to look carefully at the flakes and decide if they are all alike or if they are noticeably different. Do this outdoors on a cold day so that the snowflakes hold their shapes longer.

5. *Is It Soup Yet?* Make vegetable soup with the children's help. Use water as the liquid base. Have the children work together to scrub and chop several vegetables; carrots, onions, potatoes, celery, broccoli, and cauliflower are good ones to try. Reserve small pieces of each ingredient, rather than adding them all to the soup. When the soup is ready, invite children to taste and compare the raw vegetables with the cooked ones. What has changed as they boiled in the water? While the soup is cooking, observe changes in the water from a safe distance. Point out the bubbles, the steam, and the changes in color that occur as the soup cooks.

6. *Exploring Water Displacement.* Introduce this activity by reading the book *Mr. Archimede's Bath* by Pamela Allen. After briefly discussing this story about a bathtub that overflows each time the characters climb in, even though the water level is low when they climb out, invite the children to experiment with water displacement. Fill a clear plastic tub or bucket about two thirds with water. Collect several objects of different sizes and substances: a chunk of wood, a few rocks, a cast-iron pan, a metal paperweight, and a sand-filled, nylon-covered bean bag. To illustrate the principle of displacement best, choose objects that will fit entirely into the water container and that will sink. Provide each participating child with a ruler or a stick. Have them measure the water level before placing any objects in the tub and put a mark on the ruler or stick to indicate it. Next, invite children to take turns choosing objects to put in the bucket. After each object is added, the children can once again measure the water level. Provide wax pencils or crayons to mark the water level on the stick or ruler or on the outside of the container as the activity proceeds. This will clearly illustrate what

is happening when objects are added or taken out. Encourage discussions about observed effects. Although it is not necessary for the children to learn the scientific principle, you may find that they are interested in the term "water displacement."

7. ***Measuring Precipitation.***

General Purpose: To encourage children's discrimination skills through experiences with measurement, observation, and/or recordkeeping.

TFPs: 1, 3, 7, 27, 33, 38, 48, (34–37, 39–44, and 47 can also be introduced).

Materials: Tall, thin plastic containers with mouths and bases that match, such as large test tubes, pint milk containers, or large, empty prescription bottles; fine-point permanent marker; small notebook or lined paper and pencil; sand or dirt; small shovels or large spoons. Optional: ruler or tape measure.

Procedure:

a. Introduce the activity with a discussion of rain and snow. Point out that some days bring lots of precipitation; the rain pours down or snow fills the air. Ask children to tell you whether they think people can tell just how much snow or rain has come down. Encourage them to speculate about methods of measuring precipitation. Introduce other facts as interest dictates (see TFP list).

b. Invite children to help you set up a small "weather station" in the school yard. (Results will be measurable and observable, and so the most interesting, when it *does* rain or snow, of course. You may wish to postpone this activity if the extended forecast predicts a dry spell.)

c. With the children's help, choose an open area in the yard that is not a high-traffic area, for accumulation of rain or snow. You may wish to secure the containers to poles or posts to insure that they are not tipped over easily.

d. Set up two or three "stations." Pile and firmly pack dirt or sand around the base of each cylinder to hold it upright if you have not chosen to secure the cylinders in place.

e. Point out that the cylinders (you may want to call them "precipitation collectors") are now empty. Ask children to tell you what they think might happen to them if it rains or snows.

f. Check the "weather stations" each day. If some water, snow, or ice has accumulated, mark its level on the side of each container. On paper, note the date and record children's observations. Ask them to tell you what they see in the precipitation collector. Measure the height of the precipitation if possible.

g. Ask children what the liquid (or solid, if ice or snow) really is: If necessary, explain that it's all water or demonstrate this by melting it. Point out changes in form as melting, freezing, and evaporating occur.

Hints for Success:

• Clear containers are best, since levels of accumulation can be easily observed through the sides.

• During dry spells, reverse the activity to focus on the observation of evaporation: Fill containers with water. Measure water *loss* each day. Secure containers above the ground to lessen chances of animals drinking from them.

How to Extend this Activity:

• Provide each child with a premarked science beaker. Label each with child's name and set them up as "weather stations."

• Have children compare results from one cylinder to the next. Encourage speculation about differences and about reduced levels as well as increased levels. Introduce the term "evaporation" when applicable.

Construction

1. ***Snip a Snowflake.*** See the cognitive activity for observing snowflakes, Pretty Flaky. Precede this activity with that experience, or with a discussion illustrated with photographs of snowflake formations. Cut tissue or tablet paper into eight-by-eight-

inch squares. Fold each square in half, then in quarters. Make at least one folded square for each child. Tell children that they can make snowflakes by cutting with scissors. Direct them to clip shapes along the four sides of their folded papers. After children finish cutting, have them unfold their flakes. These can be hung on strings, taped to windows, or mounted with glue or paste to black or blue construction paper.

2. *Block Harbor/Marina.* Add small wooden or plastic boats to your collection of unit blocks. Read a story about boats and harbors (for instance, *Harbor* by Donald Crews) early in the day. Invite children to re-create a harbor as they remember it from the story. As work proceeds, you may wish to make occasional suggestions or merely to acknowledge the children's efforts and to ask them to describe their constructions. Make the book you read as an introduction available as a reference. Suggest that children look back through the pictures for features that may be missing from their marina or harbor. Some children may enjoy constructing various kinds of boats, as well. Check into the possibility of visiting a boat show, marina, or boat sales showroom.

3. *"Water" Their Homes Like.* Collect the following materials: one large self-sealing plastic bag for each child, colorful aquarium gravel, construction paper in a variety of colors, scissors, and markers or crayons. Prepare a few heavy cardboard cut-outs of fish to be used as tracing frames. You may wish to include some table salt and fish-food flakes. Begin the activity with a brief discussion of the importance of water to fish: they live in it and drink it. It must be kept clean for them to live healthy lives. Some fish need saltwater, others need fresh water. Fish share their watery homes with other creatures, some who live solely in water, others who live on land some of the time and in water some of the time.

Invite the children to create aquariums with the available materials. Explain that aquariums are watery homes for fish and other creatures that are prepared and maintained by people. Suggest that children first create fish, then make their homes. Demonstrate direct tracing around the cardboard patterns, then cutting out the fish shapes that result. For some children, you may want to pretrace and/or precut some fish. Provide markers or crayons for children who want to decorate their creatures. Instruct them to write their names (or ask you for help) on their fish. (This will be visible through the plastic bag.) Discuss the items that fish might enjoy in an aquarium: colorful gravel, plants, toys, food. Encourage each child to place his or her fish in an aquarium/bag, then to add any of the other materials he or she wishes. Suggest that some people may want to cut out plants to add as well. Pinches of salt and/or fish-food flakes can be added as a final step.

Language

1. *Water Sounds.* Tape-record a variety of sounds associated with water in preparation for this activity. You might include the sounds of a toilet flushing, running tap water, a dishwasher, water running down the drain in a bathtub, a shower spraying, someone diving into a swimming pool, rain on the roof, and/or thunder. Leave about thirty to forty-five seconds of silence between each sound. Also, prepare a picture board with photographs of each sound source. Tell children that if they listen carefully to the sounds, they will hear water doing different things that they've heard before. Play the tape. Direct children to point at a picture that matches the first sound, or name its source. If this seems too difficult for your children, discuss all the sources of water that are represented *before* playing the tape, showing pictures if possible. To extend the activity, ask children to listen carefully for the *order* in which the sounds occur, then to remember what came first, second, and so on after the tape has been played. Begin with two or three sounds. If children can recall them in order, play a longer sequence next time.

2. ***Home in the Water.*** Invite children to think of animals they know that live in or near water. Hang a large sheet of paper on a wall or easel. Using a dark marker, write "Home in the Water" or "Animals that make their Home in Water" at the top of the paper. Ask children to take turns suggesting animal names. Write whole sentences if children share their ideas in that form, or simply make a list. Read back the statements, pointing to each word while doing so, after each two or three lines have been transcribed. Leave some space around the words for illustrations. After all children who wish to share animal names or statements have had a chance to do so, move the paper to a table. Provide crayons or markers. Invite interested children to draw pictures of the water-dwelling creatures near sentences that describe them. "This says turtles live in water. Who would like to draw a turtle near those words?" Hang up the illustrated paper as a classroom reference sheet.

3. ***A King-sized Dilemma.*** Review the storybook *King Bidgood's in the Bathtub* by Audrey Wood. Create a chart divided into two columns, one labeled "problem" and the other "solution." Make reproductions or drawings of the following characters: the page, the knight, the queen, the duke, and the court. Put these in a pile face down in order of their appearance. Keeping the chart and figures temporarily out of sight, gather the children in a circle. Tell them to listen carefully as you read about a king and his enormous bathtub. Explain that their job will be to listen carefully for the "problem" in the story and how people try to solve it. Read the story through using lots of expression. Emphasize the names of the characters as you read.

Afterwards bring out the chart. Ask the children to tell you what the original problem was. Tape or clip the picture of the page to the chart in the "problem" column as an additional cue. Prompt the group's thinking by saying, "First the page came out and said, 'We have a terrible problem!'" Children as young as three tend to know that the king would not get out of the tub. Once this has been established, show the children the knight and say, "The knight said, 'Time to battle.' What happened next?" Record the children's answers in the solution column and proceed with the rest of the characters by showing each one, describing what he or she said, and putting the picture under the "problem" heading on the chart. Then ask "What happened next?" and write down the "solution" that the children remember. Refer back to the text as necessary. Extend the story further by providing props and encouraging children to re-enact the main scenes later in the session. Use a plastic wading pool as the tub or create one with tape on the floor.

Physical

1. ***The Color of "Wet."*** Enlist the help of other teachers and parents to collect some paint rollers and house-painting-sized brushes, some flat paint pans and/or empty paint buckets. Invite the children to experiment with these tools by "painting" fences, trees, outdoor equipment, or the outside walls of the school with water. Teach children how to reach overhead with the rollers and apply water in a long sweep. Encourage lots of stretching and bending to reach as much surface as possible. Point out how water changes the looks of the "painted" surfaces. Ask children what happens after the sun or wind strikes them for a while. Later, you might invite children to stir some powdered paint into water and to paint at the indoor easel with the same tools.

2. ***Go with the Flow.*** Stock an indoor or outdoor water table with measuring cups, pitchers, funnels, and if possible, pumps and siphon hoses. Turkey basters and eyedroppers could be added another day. Encourage children to practice moving water from container to container by pouring, pumping, or siphoning. Encourage careful pouring and aim, as well as observations of which containers hold more than, less than, or the same amount as others. Invite children to work in pairs

at times. One partner can hold a container above the water, while the other person pours water into it from another container. Count the number of basters full of water it takes to fill a measuring cup.

3. ***Snatch It.*** Fill two dish tubs about half with water. Place several objects in one tub: some that sink; others that float; some that will absorb water and become "squishy," others that will remain firm. You might include pieces of sponge, small plastic cars or animals, corks, small rocks, feathers, or pinecones. Provide one child at a time with a pair of kitchen tongs. Challenge him or her to pick up each item in the first tub and transfer it to the second tub with the tongs. Talk about which objects are easier and which are harder to pick up.

4. ***Target Squirt.***

   General Purpose: To provide children with practice aiming at a target as well as the following motor experiences: squeezing, pumping, and coordinating eye-hand manipulation.

   TFPs: 1, 4, 7, 14, 26.

   Materials: Empty detergent bottles, spray bottles, and/or mechanical paint sprayers; three or four balloons; string. Optional: one or two turkey basters and/or eyedroppers; trees or outdoor play equipment (climber, swing set, etc.).

   Procedure:

   a. Prepare "targets" before children's arrival. Inflate balloons and tie string around the knotted neck of each. Hang these from a tree limb, swing-set top bar, or climber, so that each balloon is at children's eye level. Using other lengths of string, mark lines on the ground that children can stand behind (approximately three to six feet away; extend this distance as competency improves with practice). You may wish to hang balloons in a line, or distribute them around the yard so more children can participate. Consider available adult supervisors when setting up.

   b. Fill bottles with water. Invite children to play a new game with you. Provide each child with a "squirter." Encourage them to explore the method by which their "tools" dispense water. Direct them to squirt at the ground first.

   c. When children show some understanding of the operation of their tools, challenge them to squirt or spray their assigned balloon target. Point out the string marker on the ground. Direct children to stand just behind the string and aim their tools at their balloon targets.

   d. Reinforce children's efforts. When they miss, mention that they are trying hard; show enthusiasm for successful aim.

   e. Ask observers to think about which tools seem the most effective; does the eyedropper or turkey baster seem to work as well as the squirt bottles? Encourage "sprayers" to share turns with observers.

   f. Suggest alternative techniques as children experiment with the equipment. Paint sprayers work best when the pump handle is completely withdrawn and plunged. Aiming upward is more effective than letting the "squirter" droop. Keeping an eye on the target, rather than on hands or tools, increases accuracy.

   g. As children experiment, point out the different appearance of water as it is dispensed as a stream or spray. Introduce such terms as "vapor" or "mist" when possible.

How to Simplify this Activity:

• Use an outside wall of the school as a target. Direct children to hit any part of the wall with their squirting tool. Omit the eyedroppers and basters, as these are the most difficult to use.

How to Extend this Activity:

• Hang the balloons at increasing distances from the standing line, one at 2 feet, the next at 2½ feet, then at 3 feet, 3½ feet, 4 feet, and so on. Invite each participant to try to reach from one distance then the next with his or her squirter.

Pretend Play

1. *Fire Station.* Prepare an area as a pretend fire station. Gather some raincoats, rubber boots, and plastic fire hats. Cut an old garden hose into two- or three-foot lengths. Include toy fire trucks, telephones, and pads of writing paper and pencils. A child-sized bed or a couple of nap cots and a child-sized refrigerator and stove, along with foods and utensils could also be included. Badges could be made by covering cardboard cutouts with tinfoil. Write "Fire Chief" and "Firefighter" on them with permanent marker. Punch a hole; attach to clothing with a safety pin. Initiate a group discussion about the jobs that firefighters perform. They sometimes live at the firehouse for several days and nights at a time. People call firefighters on the telephone when their help is needed. They may drive to a house or building to put out a fire, or use their long ladders to help people or animals get down from high places. Sometimes they are sleeping when a call comes. They must jump out of bed, put on their special uniforms, and rush to the place where the call came from. Firefighters wear hard hats to protect their heads from things that fall. They wear rubber coats and boots to keep dry and warm. They use lots and lots of water to put out fires and cool off the hot surfaces left behind. They also use water to drink and cook their meals while living at the fire station.

   You may also want to consider arranging a field trip to a fire station, or a visit from a firefighter in uniform, before introducing the pretend play area. Invite children to explore the materials. Provide information about different roles they can play, as necessary. Someone can call in a fire and give an address to a firefighter who answers the phone at the fire station. Someone can bring the clothes and help everyone dress. Someone can be in charge of gathering hoses to bring along. Allow the play to expand into the block area, if possible. Some children could construct block buildings for the firefighters to save from fires. Encourage children to lead their own play as much as possible, joining in only occasionally to provide new information or suggest additional roles.

2. *What Needs Washing?* Move a water table to a place near your housekeeping area. Cover carpeted areas with plastic trash bags or tarps, if necessary. Add doll clothes, baby dolls, a clothesline (a paint drying rack could be called into service), and clothespins to your usual housekeeping setup. If available, provide a toy iron and ironing board. Partially fill the water table with warm, sudsy water. Invite the children to wash the doll clothes in the suds, then rinse them in a tub of clear water or in a nearby sink. Demonstrate how clothespins work to suspend the wet clothes from drying lines. As clothes dry, point out the functions of the iron and ironing board. On other days, use the water table to wash dishes and pans, or to give baths to baby dolls. Initiate occasional discussion about the ways that water is used in a home. Offer children waterproof smocks and start out with less water in the table. If this activity still proves too messy, set up a similar activity in a bathroom, using the sink as a washing station.

3. *Fishing Pond.* Prepare a dozen or more paper cutouts of fish covered with clear contact or laminated paper to extend their usefulness. Punch a hole in the nose end of each fish. Thread a paper clip through each hole. Prepare two or three fishing poles by attaching lengths of string to long, stout wooden pencils or pieces of dowling cut to twelve-inch lengths. (Longer poles can be difficult to supervise safely.) Tie a strong magnet to the end of each length of string. Set up a fishing pond area by spreading a four-foot-square vinyl tablecloth on the floor. (A large piece of paper could also be used.) Tape down the corners with masking tape. Set up a rocking boat, large cardboard carton, or double line of small chairs to serve as a boat. Invite children to catch fish with the magnets. You might also provide a small camping grill and a pan for other children to prepare a pretend fish dinner.

Social

1. *Bucket Brigade.* Gather four or five plastic pails. In an outdoor area, fill one large tub or water table with water. Gather a group of children. Briefly discuss present-day

firefighting techniques that use fancy trucks equipped with long hoses and sometimes their own water supply. Tell children that people didn't always have fire departments to call on for help with fires. One way that they helped each other to put out fires was by forming a bucket brigade. Show children the buckets. Point out the large tub of water. Tell them that everyone will work together as a bucket brigade. Mention that it's important to get the water to the "fire," spilling as little as possible. Choose a spot on the ground to represent a fire. Have the children form a long line stretching from the water supply to the "fire." Explain that the person nearest the water will be the bucket-filler, and the person nearest the "fire" will be the bucket-dumper. After it is dumped, the empty bucket must be returned to the water, and so the bucket-dumper will rush to the water source and become a filler. Everyone else's job will be to pass the water along, quickly and carefully, toward the fire. Tell the brigade to begin! Urge and praise children working together to keep the water moving. Cheer on the workers as they cooperate in a water-moving assembly line, until the tub is emptied of water.

2. **Boat Building.** Plan this activity for small groups of children. If the number of adult supervisors is limited, have five or six children work together each day to build a group boat, until everyone has had a turn. Gather a variety of materials such as Styrofoam packing chunks, lightweight wood, wood glue and/or woodworking tools, wooden dowels or pencils, pieces of cloth, and markers or crayons to decorate boat parts. Introduce the activity to each group. "Today, you will be all be working together to plan and build a boat. The main job of a boat is to float on water! When it is completed, you will have a chance to test out your boat design in the water table." Point out the array of materials. Tell children that any of these things could become parts of their group boat, but that the group will be making just one boat together. This will be a classroom boat; no one will take it home. Allow children to make their own decisions as much as possible. Bring along a picture book or maga-zine as a reference source, in case the children have a difficult time thinking of ideas. Supply terms for the parts of a boat as children work together: hull, mast, sail, and deck. Praise cooperative efforts! Make suggestions when necessary to help children proceed. "Someone might want to decorate the hull. Here are some markers. Another person could design a sail. Let's find some scissors to cut this cloth." When the boat is finished to everyone's satisfaction, lead the group to a filled water table. You might want to explain boat naming and launching ceremonies at this point. Urge children to make some predictions about what will happen when they launch the boat, and then to test their predictions. Did it float? What might be changed to improve its design? Display finished boats in a classroom window or on a table, or leave them available for water-table play.

3. **Pollution Problem Solving.** Fill a water table or wash tub approximately half with water. Gather some natural materials, such as leaves, sand, stones, grass. Also gather some paper scraps and some cooking oil. Make available strainers, sieves, and loosely woven fabric such as cheesecloth. Initiate a discussion of water pollution problems. Point out that some things that are dropped in water can be easily removed; other things are difficult or impossible to remove. Invite groups of five or six children at a time to work in teams. Tell them that each team will work together to experiment with ways of cleaning dirty water. Point out that the water in the table is clear and clean. Invite team one to decide together which of the substances they will dump in the water. Tell them that they will then have a chance to work together on the task of cleaning up the water. When the children have added as many things as they wish to the water, ask them to tell you about how the water looks and smells. What is different about it now? Provide one or two empty tubs, along with the strainers, sieves, and cheesecloth. Challenge children to work together to remove as many items and substances from the dirty water as possible. Encourage and praise cooperative efforts and group decision making. See the list of terms, facts, and principles at the begin-

ning of this chapter for discussion ideas. As the activity proceeds, encourage observations and descriptions of methods that work best and of substances that are the easiest and the most difficult to remove from water.

4. *Water "Pics."* Gather several photos of people engaged in water sports and activities. In addition to magazines, consider looking for a calendar with a water theme that can be cut apart as a source of photos. In a large- or small-group setting, hold up the photos, one at a time. Ask the children to describe what the person/people are doing. Discuss the reactions and emotions that the participants appear to be experiencing. Are they scared? Excited? Encourage discussions of what events may have contributed to the people's emotions, also ask children to identify how they would feel in similar situations.

5. *Siphoning Together.* Collect the following materials: four feet of half-inch clear plastic tubing, two buckets, a funnel that fits into one end of the tube and a cork that will plug the other end, and a small pitcher. Invite two or three children to work together as a siphoning team. First, direct them to fill one bucket about two thirds with water and carry it to a table top. Put the empty bucket on the ground nearby. Give one child the funnel and another the cork; have them place their objects into the two ends of the tube. While one child holds up the funnel end, have the other pour a pitcher of water into it. Direct the children to place the cork end of the tube in the empty bucket, and the open end (with the funnel removed) into the bucket of water. Next, ask the children what they think will happen to the water if the cork is removed from the tube. Now, remove the cork and see what happens! Encourage the team to experiment by lifting the tube as high as the table: does the water still flow? Provide different lengths and widths of tubing for further experimentation after the children have had plenty of time to explore siphoning together. This would be a fun way to recruit helpers to empty the water table in the classroom each day!

TEACHER RESOURCES

Field Trip Ideas

1. Plan a field trip to a pond, lake, or stream. Before setting out, discuss water safety, as well as creatures and features that children are likely to encounter.

2. Visit a water treatment plant with your class. Inquire whether a guide might be available who is willing to explain the processes and machines to the children. Prepare the children in advance for any unusual smells and sounds they are likely to encounter. Consider the pollution problem-solving activity as an introduction or follow-up to this experience.

3. Find out if a family in your school has a swimming pool that they would be willing to invite your children to visit. Discuss water safety ahead of time. Once there, ask the pool owners to demonstrate the steps they must follow to keep their pool clean. Also, ask about pool construction. Do they know how (or did they watch) workers put this pool in place?

4. Visit a marina, boat dock or harbor, or even a boat sales establishment to view the many kinds of boats that people build and purchase. Before the trip, discuss some new vocabulary that describes boats. Once there, ask children to find hulls, decks, sails, masts, centerboards, and so on. Follow up with a boat-making project back at school.

5. Visit a large water fountain somewhere in your town. Call the city parks department or an administrator in the building near the fountain ahead of time. Ask if it would be possible to view any behind-the-scenes machinery, or to watch as the fountain is turned off, then on again. Ask them to explain where the water for the fountain comes from. Is it recycled again and again? How is it kept clean? Share this information with the children.

Classroom Visitors

1. Invite a pool-installation and maintenance worker to visit your classroom. Ask him or her to bring pictures, pamphlets, and tools, if possible. Ask about the steps that

are followed in installing a pool. Why must it be cleaned regularly? How is this accomplished?

2. Invite a representative of the Coast Guard or of a sheriff's water patrol crew to visit your classroom and discuss water safety. You may be able to recruit a lifeguard as an alternative. Ask him or her to bring life vests or other equipment, if possible.

3. Ask a representative of a local fire station to visit your school. Arrange for him or her to arrive in an equipped truck, if possible. Request a discussion of tools, uniforms, and equipment, as well as of fire safety. Inform the visitor that you are learning about water; encourage an emphasis on the importance of water to his or her job.

4. Call a nature center, school, or university to find a visitor who will bring two or three water-dwelling animals to visit your school. He or she could bring and describe snakes, frogs, and turtles or perhaps a tankful of unusual fish. Ask the visitor to discuss the water needs of the creatures, as well as other aspects of their lives or features of their bodies. You may want to adopt one such animal and set up a home for it after this visit. Seek the visitor's advice about doing so.

5. Invite a plumber to visit the children. Ask him or her to bring along some pipes and tools. After the plumber discusses the job and the equipment, explore your classroom or school together, looking for signs of plumbing. Initiate a discussion of what happens to the water that is flushed down the toilet or that swirls down the drain after handwashing.

Children's Books

Allen, P. *Mr. Archimede's Bath*. New York: Lothrop, Lee and Shepard, 1980.

Bramwell, M. *Oceans*. New York: Franklin Watts, 1984.

Brandt, K. *What Makes It Rain?* Mahwah, NJ: Troll, 1982.

Crews, D. *Harbor*. New York: Greenwillow, 1982.

Davis, A. V. *Timothy Turtle*. New York: Harcourt, Brace and World, 1940.

Domanska, J. *If All the Seas Were One Sea*. New York: Macmillan, 1971.

Elkin, B. *Six Foolish Fishermen*. Chicago: Childrens Press, 1957.

Pallotta, J. *Ocean Alphabet Book*. Boston: Quinlan, 1989.

Spier, P. *Rain*. Garden City, NY: Doubleday, 1982.

Suess, Dr. *McElligot's Pool*. New York: Random House, 1947.

Tresselt, A. *Rain Drop Splash*. New York: Lothrop, Lee and Shepard, 1946.

Udry, J. M. *Mary Ann's Mud Day*. New York: Harper and Row, 1967.

Williams, V. B. *Three Days on a River in a Red Canoe*. New York: Greenwillow, 1981.

Wood, A. *King Bidgood's in the Bathtub*. New York: Harcourt Brace Jovanovich, 1985.

Yashima, T. *Umbrella*. New York: Viking, 1958.

———. *The Village Tree*. New York: Viking, 1953.

Zion, G. *Harry, The Dirty Dog*. New York: Harper Junior, 1956.

Adult References

Ashworth, W. *The Late, Great Lakes*. New York: Knopf, 1986.

Bradden, R., C. Dodwell, G. Greer, W. Shawcross, B. Thompson, and M. Wood. *River Journeys*. New York: Hippocrene Books, 1985

Couper, A., ed. *The Times Atlas of the Oceans*. New York: Van Nostrand Reinhold, 1983.

Thompson, P. D., and R. O'Brien. *Weather*. New York: Time-Life, 1973.

Chapter 15

The Sky

•

Good morning, merry sunshine,
How did you wake so soon?
You've swept the little stars away
And shined away the moon.
I saw you go to sleep last night
Before I ceased my playing;
How did you get 'way over there?
And where have you been staying?

•

The questions posed by this familiar verse have fascinated people throughout the ages. Today's children are no exception. One of the very first unceasing patterns of life that they come to recognize is that day follows night, night follows day, over and over again. The marked contrast between the daytime sky and the nighttime sky contributes to children's awareness of this pattern, as do their routines, which tend to revolve around things that are done when it's dark and things that are done when it's light. Thus, offering classroom experiences related to the sky enhances children's burgeoning interest in the celestial phenomena that affect their daily lives.

PURPOSE

The sky holds myriad seen and unseen wonders. This chapter focuses on phenomena visible with the naked eye from Earth. The unit on exploring space investigates planets and other distant objects.

One way to study the sky involves making obvious contrasts between day and night. Examining how the sky changes from the morning to the evening, as well as what activities and tasks people or animals pursue at what times, supports such a focus. On the other hand, some teachers favor using weather to draw children's attention to the sky. The sun, clouds, rainbows, and the earth's movement through space all relate to the experiences of snow, rain, warmth, and cold with which children are familiar. For this theme we have included TFPs and activities germaine to each of these approaches.

IMPLEMENTATION

Some ways to organize a unit about the sky follow.

Option One: Focus on the sun and its effects upon the Earth and its creatures. For some children, understanding the physical characteristics of warmth, brightness, and visible shading is sufficient. Others are ready to study such phenomena as what happens to plants in the sun versus those in the dark, or the differences in the evaporation rates of water placed in the bright sunshine and the shade.

Option Two: Extend sky gazing to a study of clouds. Children can observe the composition of clouds and their ever-changing shapes and colors. They can also learn what happens to stars, the moon, and the sun when clouds pass between them and the Earth. Introduce fantasy after facts have been established by having children write cloud stories.

Option Three: Follow a two-week unit on the sky with two weeks on Exploring Space. This helps children move beyond what they normally see in the sky to an investigation of the unknown.

Option Four: Explore the ways in which the sky appears similar and different to people in different parts of the world. This is the most abstract study of all and should be limited to the most experienced children.

Other units that would comfortably precede or follow The Sky include Seasons, Creatures That Fly, or Machines That Fly.

TERMS, FACTS, AND PRINCIPLES

General Information

1. The sky is the space seen above the horizon.
2. The horizon is the place off in the distance where the sky and ground seem to come together.
3. Many inanimate natural objects can be seen in the sky without the aid of special instruments.
4. Inanimate natural objects seen in the sky include the sun and other stars, the moon, clouds, and rainbows.
5. Some objects are visible in the sky during the day; others can only be seen at night.
*6. When a particular part of the earth is facing the sun, people on that part say it is daytime.
*7. People say it is nighttime when their part of the earth is not facing the sun.
8. The sky appears lighter when it is day than when it is night.
*9. The sun, moon, and stars appear to rise and set.

*10. When the sun, moon, and stars rise, they appear above the horizon.

*11. When the sun, moon, and stars set, they disappear below the horizon.

*12. The sun, moon, and stars appear to rise toward the east and set toward the west.

*13. The sun, moon, and stars appear to move across the sky in part because the Earth itself is moving.

14. The time when the light of the sun appears is called dawn.

15. The time when the sun disappears and the sky begins to darken is called dusk.

*16. The exact time of sunrise and sunset changes according to the time of year.

*17. The color of the sky varies with the time of day, weather conditions, and the angle of the sun's rays.

*18. During the day the sky usually looks bluish. Light is made up of many colors, and the blue light bounces off the particles in the air, more than the other colors do.

*19. At dawn or dusk the sun and clouds often look shades of red because the sun is low on the horizon and its light is passing through more air. The blue light has all gone away and red, orange, and yellow light remain.

20. Sometimes clouds come between the sun and the Earth and obstruct the view of the sun.

21. At night the sky looks black.

22. Sometimes lights from a town or city lighten the nighttime sky.

The Daytime Sky

23. Inanimate natural objects visible in the daytime sky are the sun, clouds, rainbows, and sometimes the moon.

24. Clouds and rainbows are part of the Earth; the sun and moon are far away from the Earth.

The Sun

*25. The sun is a star, that is, a sphere of hot, glowing gases.

*26. The sun is hot because there is a reaction like burning going on at its center.

27. The sun shines on the Earth giving off light and heat.

28. When people stand in the sunlight they can feel heat from the sun.

29. In the daytime, the sun so brightens the sky that people cannot see other stars.

30. The sun is far away from the Earth.

*31. The sun appears to move across the sky during the day from east to west.

*32. The sun appears to move because the Earth is turning like a top.

*33. The Earth makes one rotation each day.

Clouds and Rainbows

34. Of all the inanimate natural objects in the sky, clouds and rainbows are closest to the Earth.

35. Clouds are made of water in the sky.

36. Clouds look like white, gray, or black puffs, streaks, or blankets in the sky.

37. Sometimes clouds appear to cover the whole sky and sometimes only a part of it.

38. Clouds appear in different shapes.

39. Clouds are sometimes in the sky when it is sunny and the weather is dry.

40. Clouds are always in the sky when it is raining or snowing.

41. Clouds move across the sky pushed by winds.

*42. Cumulus clouds have flat bottoms and tops that rise and mound like hills.

*43. Stratus clouds are a uniform blanket of clouds.

*44. Cirrus clouds are thin, featherlike, wispy clouds.

*45. Clouds that produce rain are called nimbus clouds.

46. People can sometimes be in the middle of a cloud.

47. Clouds that form on the ground are called fog.

48. Rainbows sometimes can be seen in the sky after a rain.

*49. People are most likely to view a rainbow when standing with their backs toward the sun and gazing toward breaks in the clouds just after a rain.

50. A rainbow appears as an arch of colored light.

*51. A rainbow is produced when sunlight falls on tiny drops of water in the air.

*52. The colors of the rainbow always appear in the same order: red, orange, yellow, green, blue, indigo, violet.

*53. People can never actually touch a rainbow.

The Nighttime Sky

54. Stars, the moon, and clouds can be seen at night.

Stars

55. Stars are objects like the sun.

56. The sun is the closest star to us. That is why it looks biggest and brightest.

57. The other stars are much fainter and smaller than the sun because they are much farther away.

58. Stars, except the sun, appear to be points of twinkling light in the sky.

*59. Stars appear to twinkle because their light bounces off the air around the Earth.

60. Stars shine day and night but the brightness of the sun overpowers their light during the day.

*61. Stars vary in brightness, size, and distance from each other.

62. On clear nights, thousands of stars can be seen.

*63. The Milky Way is made up of millions of stars and looks like a bright band in the sky.

64. Some places in the sky seem to have fewer stars than others.

*65. Stars vary in age. Some stars are young and some are old.

*66. The sun is a middle-aged star, neither young nor old.

*67. Stars exist for a much longer time than people, but they do not exist forever.

*68. New stars are formed from the remains of old stars.

*69. People have given names to a few stars: the North Star, Sirius, and Vega, for instance.

70. A constellation is a group of stars that has been given a name.

*71. Some constellations seen in the sky above North America are the Big Dipper (or Big Bear), Orion the Hunter, the Seven Sisters, Cassiopeia, and Cygnus the Swan.

72. Sometimes clouds move between the Earth and the stars and block our view of the stars.

*73. Sometimes people see streaks of light in the sky that they call "falling" or "shooting" stars. These are not stars but are small chunks of rock and metal that go around the sun called meteors. When they come close to the Earth, they usually get hot and melt. When these objects hit the Earth, they are called meteorites.

The Moon

*74. Moons orbit planets.

75. People can see Earth's moon.

*76. The moon takes one month to orbit the Earth.

*77. The moon appears to move across the sky because the earth itself is turning.

78. The moon is almost round.

*79. The moon has no air.

80. Nothing lives on the moon, though people have visited it.

*81. The surface of the moon is dry and rocky.

*82. The moon gives off no light of its own.

*83. Moonlight is the reflected light of the sun.

*84. Sometimes the moon appears as a round ball, sometimes as a crescent shape, and sometimes it cannot be seen at all. These are called phases of the moon.

85. The moon is really the same size and shape all the time, but it looks different at different times of the month.

*86. The part of the moon illuminated by the sun is sometimes facing toward us and sometimes facing away from us. This is why we see different amounts of the lighted surface at different times.

87. Sometimes we can see the moon during the day. When this happens, the moon appears faint and pale.

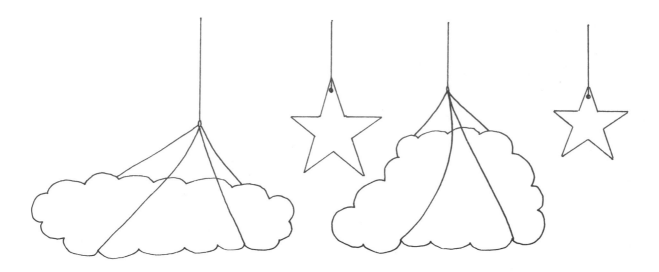

Figure 15.1 *Transform the Ceiling into a Wondrous Sky*

*88. While it is orbiting the sun, the Earth sometimes passes between the sun and the moon.

*89. While it is orbiting the Earth, the moon sometimes passes between the Earth and the sun.

*90. When the Earth, sun, and moon are in a line, the light of the sun is blocked. This is called an eclipse.

91. Sometimes clouds come between the moon and the Earth and block people's view of the moon.

ACTIVITY IDEAS

Aesthetics

1. *Sky Dances.* After some discussions of objects in the sky and some opportunities to observe them, have children choose places to stand where they can move freely. Remind them that clouds move across the sky, pushed by the wind. Invite them to float around like a cloud. Next, tell the children to change their "cloud shape," explaining that the wind is pushing you into constantly changing formations. If possible, provide soft music to encourage movement. Introduce a sunrise, sunset dance. Rise and fall, in place, to the music.

2. *Things Are Looking Up!* Decorate your classroom with fluffy clouds for children to enjoy gazing at overhead. Purchase packaged polyester quilt batting/pillow stuffing at a fabric store. One package will produce two or three clouds. Using thread or transparent fishing line, suspend torn-off bundles of batting from the ceiling of your room. Tie line loosely around the middle of the batting to keep the shapes cloudlike.

   Suspend tinfoil stars above the clouds. Make these from double sheets of heavy-duty foil. Cut with scissors through both layers at once; the pressure of the scissor blades will cause the edges to crimp together. Using a hole-punch, make a hole in one point of the star and attach a length of thread or fishing line. These decorations could be made by you alone or with help from the children. (Figure 15.1)

   Throughout the Sky unit, invite children to lie back and enjoy the view during quiet moments. You may also wish to tape small "clouds" of batting to the undersides of classroom tables. Children will delight in an opportunity to crawl beneath the furniture and lie "with their heads in the clouds"!

3. *Sky Etchings.* Offer children sheets of sky-blue construction paper, thick black paint, and paintbrushes. After they have painted

their papers black, allow the paint to partially dry. Offer children pencils or large toothpicks and show them how to etch some features of the sky through the black paint, revealing the blue paper beneath.

4. *"Cloud Song."* Teach children the following cloud song. Emphasize its beat by having children tap their thighs in time to the music.

Cloud Song
(Tune: "I am a Fine Musician";
Words: Kit Payne)

Verse 1:
We do our work with water.
We make the rain and snow.
You sometimes see us hurry by,
when winds begin to blow.

Chorus:
We're clouds,
We're clouds,
We are the fluffy clouds.

Verse 2:
We have a lot of different names,
like cumulus and cirrus,
and if you're riding in a plane
you may fly through or near us.

Chorus:
We're clouds,
We're clouds,
We are the fluffy clouds.

Use this song as a lead-in to the Cloudscapes activity that follows.

5. *Cloudscapes.* Give children sheets of pale blue or black construction paper, cotton balls, black paint, and glue. Encourage them to stretch, puff, poke, pull, and otherwise manipulate the cotton into cloud forms which they can then glue to a 'daytime' or 'nighttime' background. They can use the black paint to further enhance storm clouds.

Affective

1. *The Nighttime Is the Righttime.* Arrange a tape recorder and blank tape or paper and pen on a table. Invite children to join you, one or two at a time, to tell about things they enjoy at particular times. Begin by mentioning that some people think of themselves as nighttime or daytime people; offer examples of each. At first, ask children to complete a sentence that you begin: "I'm a daytime person because . . . ," or "I like the night because . . . ." Record each child's ideas on tape or paper. Encourage statements of preference by saying "Tell me another thing that you enjoy about the night (day)." "What is one thing you like to do at night (in the daytime)?" Introduce information about jobs that people traditionally perform at night. Encourage perspective-taking, as well: "Why do you suppose that some people prefer the night?" Read or play back what children have told you; then ask their permission to share their stories with the others.

2. *Weather or Not.* Begin this small-group activity with a discussion of weather, or by singing together the weather song. (See the language section of this unit.) Tell children that there are wonderful and not-so-wonderful things about all kinds of weather, and that one person may enjoy a kind of weather that another person doesn't like at all. Ask children to describe their preferences for rain, snow, sunshine, windy days, and so on, telling which weather they like and why. Encourage children to make comparisons among the members of the group or between themselves and one of their peers. "Both Wanda and Derek like to see clouds in the sky. Maureen likes it best when the sky is all clear and sunny!" Praise children for listening to each other's responses and for sharing their own ideas.

3. *Starry Names.* Using a broad-tipped marker, print each child's complete name, using capital and lowercase letters, on a four-by-ten-inch oak-tag strip. Spread out a few strips in the center of a table, inviting children to find their own names. Provide star stickers for children to use to outline the letters of their name in stars. Once the "starry names" are complete, put them back in the center for children to sort through a second time. Children could look for their own names again or look for the names of others in the group.

4. *Sun Tea.*
General Purpose: To encourage children to make choices and to follow a task through to completion.

TFPs: 26, 27.

Materials: Loose herbal (noncaffeinated) tea leaves; one glass jar per child with a lid that seals tightly (jelly jars, mayonnaise jars, etc.); commercial teaballs or squares of cheesecloth, approximately 5-by-5 inches, and rubber bands; teaspoons or tablespoons; a sunny windowsill or spot in the play yard; water; permanent marker to label jars with children's names; chart depicting the steps in the recipe.

Procedure:

a. Introduce the activity with a discussion of the heat that the sun provides to the Earth. Encourage children to share ideas about tasks that people accomplish with heat: warming themselves, drying clothes, cooking, and so on.

b. Tell children that they will have a chance to make sun tea. You may want to ask children to tell about other ways they have seen tea made. Explain that the sun can be used like a stove to heat foods and liquids, which sometimes causes them to change in size, color, or texture.

c. Show children the chart depicting the steps one should follow to make tea. Point out that each picture has a number and that the steps should be followed in order. Ask children to take turns telling the others about what they think the steps are, referring to the pictures for ideas.

d. Set out all the materials on a table. Display the chart on the table, or post it on a wall nearby. As children begin to prepare their jars of tea, prompt them to make predictions about what they think will happen to the water after the tea packets are immersed. What will change as the sun shines on the tea jars? Prompt children to refer to the sequence chart often as they proceed.

e. Encourage children to make personal choices about which tea leaves to use and about how much will fit in a cheesecloth bundle or a teaball. Invite them to choose a sunny spot for their jars, after they are sealed tightly. Inform them that it will be up to them to decide when their tea is ready, to choose whether to drink it at school or take it home to share, and to make a decision about whether they like it or not. You may choose to offer sugar, honey, or ground cinnamon in dispensers with which children can flavor their finished tea.

Hints for Success:

- Prepare your sequence chart on a long strip of poster board with one step following another in a single line, to help children determine the appropriate order of steps. Refer to the pictures and text at the end of this activity. Cut the text apart as indicated and mount the appropriate words below the corresponding picture.

- Demonstrate the steps yourself in a large-group setting first if children have had limited experience following a sequence chart.

- Write each child's name on a jar before work begins.

How to Simplify this Activity:

- Provide the children with commercially prepared teabags. Limit the steps to counting out three or four bags, placing them in a jar, filling the jar with water at a tap, and placing the jars in a sunny spot.

How to Extend this Activity:

- Choose tea leaves in many colors and flavors. Display each type in a separate bowl. Encourage children to smell, feel (with clean fingers), and look at the tea leaves as they make choices. Mention that children can mix several kinds of tea or use all the same kind.

- Invite children to plan a tea-tasting party. Each child can pour his or her tea into a small pitcher, then pour individual servings for friends who wish to try the special brews.

- After this activity, set up a pretend play area with tea party props. Allow older children to share real tea; remind younger children of their tea-making experiences as they pretend to share a cup with a neighbor.

Figure 15.2 *Use the Sun to Make Delicious Tea*

• Discuss the kinds of tea that have special meaning and are part of special ceremonies for people of different cultures.

Sample Sequence Chart: Sun Tea (Figure 15.2)

1. Write your name on a jar or ask someone to write it for you.

2. Put spoonfuls of tea in the middle of a cloth square.

3. Pull the corners together. Put on a rubber band tightly.

4. Drop the tea packet in a jar. Pour in some water, until your jar is almost full.

5. Screw the top on your jar very tightly.

6. Put the jar in a sunny spot. Be careful! It is made of glass! Wait for the sun to cook your tea. Decide when its color tells you it is ready.

Pour your tea in a cup. Drink your tea! Share it with your friends!

Cognition

1. *Creamy Clouds.* Introduce the names of several kinds of clouds throughout the week. As children gain familiarity with these terms, make shaving cream available on trays. Children will enjoy molding the cream into cloud shapes that you suggest and modeling or creating their interpretations of cloud formations pictured in photos and diagrams. Ask children to tell you about the clouds they are forming.

2. *Day Follows Night and Night Follows Day.* Prepare a set of cards by mounting photos or magazine clippings of the sky at dawn, high sun, low sun, sunrise and sunset, dusk, and dark. Discuss with children the time of day that each sky picture represents and the invariable sequence in which one follows another. Present a child or small group of children with the sequencing cards, suggesting that they be arranged in some order. Ask the child or children to choose one picture and then to place "the sky that goes next" beside it. Encourage participants to consult or take turns to continue the ordering. Prompt

rationales for placement: "Tell me why this one belongs here." Accept the children's reasoning without correcting them.

3. *Who Knows Weather?* Prepare or acquire a collection of pictures that show scenes, clothing, and items associated with sunny days and rainy days (raincoats, umbrellas and boots, beach toys and sunglasses, etc.). Ask children to choose pictures that "go with sunny days" and to place them in a pile. Suggest that pictures that "go with rainy days" be gathered in a separate pile. Ask children to describe each picture and the reasons they have placed it in a certain pile. Add pictures of other weather conditions and equipment, such as snowdrifts, shovels, and winter clothing, or fall leaves and rakes, as children gain experience and knowledge.

4. *Sky Riddles.* Transfer the following riddles to index cards for ease of reference. Conceal stick puppets produced for the Sky Is a Stage activity (described in the language section of this unit) in a small box or paper sack. Alternately, collect or create a picture of each of the objects mentioned below and conceal them likewise. Gather children into a small or large group. Tell them that you have some riddles to read to them about things they can see in the sky. Their job will be to guess what each riddle describes, so they must listen carefully. Indicate the "mystery bag or box" that holds final proof of the answer to each riddle. (If children are very young or not yet knowledgeable about sky objects, you may want to display each picture or object before concealing it.) Urge children to raise their hands silently if they think they know the answer, so that others will have a chance to think of an answer on their own. Read each riddle slowly and clearly, pause, and then invite children who think they can guess the answer to raise their hands. Read riddles a second time if necessary. Acknowledge all answers, inviting more than one child to tell their thoughts. After everyone who wishes to guess has had a turn, pull the correct object or picture from your bag so that all can see. Make the puppets or pictures available for children's use after the riddle game ends.

The Sun
I am a ball of fire;
my jobs are heat and light.
I'm bringing some folks daytime,
while others have their night.
By day you'll always find me
above you in the skies,
though clouds may come between us
and hide me from your eyes.

Stars
I twinkle in the dark of night;
I have a million friends like me.
The sun in day makes so much light,
we are impossible to see.
In groups, we're constellations,
and sometimes given names.
Alone, some people choose us
to play their wishing games.

The Moon
Sometimes a circle, sometimes a half,
sometimes a skinny crescent.
At night, a lot of people think
to gaze at me is pleasant.
I'm really round at anytime,
but circling the Earth,
I sometimes slip through shadows,
which hide part of my girth.

Rainbow
The sun comes out to warm a rainy day
and suddenly you see me in the sky!
My stripes of colors—seven every time—
begin and end down low, but curve up high.

5. *Day Watch/Night Watch.* Gather from magazines a collection of photographs showing people and/or animals involved in activities. Make sure that each includes at least a glimpse of the sky. Conceal the pictures in a bag or put them face down in the center of a small group of children. Ask children to select a picture, then look at it carefully to determine what part of the day it represents—daytime, nighttime, dawn, dusk, sunrise, or sunset. Talk with them about the inferences they made as well as the reasoning behind their decisions. Periodically change the format of the game by asking children what time of day is NOT depicted in the photograph they have chosen.

6. *Sky Experiments.* Set up one or more of the following experiments for children to observe and discuss:

- Making Clouds: Put a little water into a glass jar. Cover tightly. Place the jar in a sunny spot (on grass or in a sandbox to reduce the chances of breakage). Direct children to observe the jar now and then as "fog" begins to form on the inside.

- Condensation: Set up an electric frying pan in a large-group area, taking care that the cord is positioned safely behind the teacher. Direct the children to gather at a safe distance from the pan. Bring a quarter cup of water to boil. Hold a mirror with its glass side at an angle over the steam that begins to rise from the boiling water. Make sure that the angle allows the children to observe the "cloud" that begins to form on the mirror. Lift the mirror a little higher; the cloud will begin to rain in drops back into the pan.

- Shady Forms: Cover grassy patches of the play yard with a large piece of cardboard, a board, and/or a tire for a few days. Then move the objects aside. Ask children to describe what has happened to the grass that was hidden from the sun. Why do they think it has changed? What do they think will occur if the patches are again exposed to the sun? Check each of the areas over the next several days for signs of rejuvenation.

- Making a Rainbow: Spray water into the air on a sunny day, or provide children with prisms with which to create their own "rainbows."

7. *Clouds in the Wind.*
General Purpose: For children to become aware of effects of wind movement.
TFPs: 24, 34, 36, 38, 39, 41, 46.
Materials: Balloons (white, if possible) and/or bubble-blowing equipment; outdoor area. (This could also be demonstrated indoors with a fan, heating vent, or other moving air source.)
Procedure:
a. Introduce the activity with a discussion of some cloud TFPs, emphasizing that wind causes cloud movement. For in-

stance, the speed of the prevailing winds affects how quickly clouds move, and the wind direction at the altitude of a cloud affects the direction it is pushed.
b. In an outdoor area, blow up several balloons and/or set up bubble-blowing equipment. Invite children to note the breeze against their skin and hair. Ask children if they can feel which way the wind is blowing.
c. Hold a balloon high above your head. Ask children to predict in which direction the balloon will float when you release it. Release the balloon (or blow several bubbles) and watch its movement in the wind.
d. After you retrieve your balloons, invite children to evaluate their predictions. Point out that clouds are pushed along in a similar way. If there are clouds in the sky, invite children to watch them and see if they can detect movement.
e. Give interested children their own balloons to release, or blow bubbles for them to chase. Encourage them to try releasing them at different heights and in different parts of the yard to see if these changes affect the direction in which they float.

Hint for Success:
- If using balloons, begin with only one. Add more balloons as children grow interested in watching their movement and following their paths.

How to Simplify this Activity:
- Set up a floor or table fan in an indoor area. Gather the children in a group around the fan. Tie a string around the neck of an inflated balloon; secure the other end of the string to the fan. Point out that the balloon flies off in the direction in which the fan's "wind" blows.
- Dangle your balloon on a short string. Blow on the balloon to demonstrate the effect of wind on it. Invite children to take turns blowing it as you hold on.

How to Extend this Activity:
- Have children choose partners. Give each pair of children a balloon on a string. As one child holds the string, the other child can become the wind, blow-

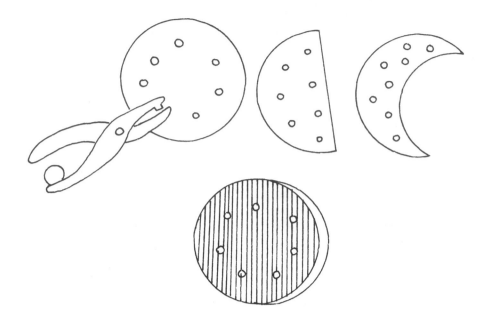

Figure 15.3 *Punching Holes Allows Light and Color to Show Through*

ing the balloon into the air. Invite "the wind" to walk around the string-holder, experimenting with the change in direction that the balloon makes as it is blown on from different angles. Encourage the partners to trade roles so that each child gets a turn as the wind.

• As children blow on partner-held balloons, encourage the holders to notice whether others' "winds" are pushing their balloons in the same or different directions. When do they float on a similar course? If your classroom has windows that can be opened, invite children to hold their balloons suspended near the windows and see if anything happens.

Construction

1. ***The Hole Picture.*** Prepare or collect the following materials: gluesticks, black construction paper or poster board cut in nine-by-twelve-inch rectangles, hole-punches, scissors, pencils or white chalk, and white or yellow sheets of construction paper or tinfoil. Using four-inch square pieces of cardboard, make cardboard tracing frames in the shapes of circles, half circles, and crescents. Invite children to create a pattern of night-sky holes in the black paper. They can trace around the frames with a pencil or piece of white chalk, then cut out the shapes. Demonstrate that a lighter backing can be glued in place so that it "shines" through the holes to create the effect of the moon and the stars. (Figure 15.3)

2. ***Sculpting the Sky.*** Provide children with white foam packing materials in a variety of shapes and sizes. Add thick blue paint and brushes, if desired, and set out glue. Direct children to think about or take a few moments to gaze out the window at a cloudy sky. Invite them to use the materials to represent a cloudy sky in the form of a sculpture. Ask children to tell you about their creations as they work. Wood glue dries particularly fast, and, although it is more difficult to clean up, it will lead to more immediate success as the children attempt to build sculptures. You can combine the blue paint and glue rather than using either substance on its own.

3. ***Sun Catchers.***
   General Purpose: To provide opportunities for children to experience effects of sunlight and heat while creating a tangible, representational product.
   TFPs: 26, 27, 28.
   Materials: Small, clear *plastic* (not paper or coated paper) drinking cups for each

child; permanent marking pens in a variety of colors; stout, strong needle or nail; thread or fishing line; oven or toaster oven; tinfoil. Optional: one or two decorative commercial suncatcher ornaments, suspended in a classroom window; cookie sheet.

Procedure:

a. Preheat oven to 350°.

b. Distribute a cup to each child. Arrange the marking pens in a central location. Tell children to write their names somewhere on their cups, or do this for them.

c. Discuss ways in which the sun is like an oven. Talk, also, about the bright light that the sun produces. Point out its effect on a suncatcher ornament if possible.

d. Invite children to use a variety of markers to decorate the insides, outsides, and/or bottoms of the cups.

e. Tell children to note the size and shape of their cups, the drawings, and where their names are located on the cups after they complete the decorating step.

f. Put several cups on a sheet of tinfoil. Place this on top of a cookie sheet for ease in handling, if you wish. Transfer the cups to the preheated oven. (Figure 15.4a)

g. If the oven has a glass viewing door, encourage children to watch what happens to their cups. Encourage predictions before baking.

h. Leave cups in the oven for four to five minutes, or until you observe that they have shrunk and flattened into disc shapes. Remove from oven, being careful to place the hot discs beyond children's reach. The plastic cools very rapidly; while it is still warm and softened, punch a hole near one edge of each disc with a needle or nail. Work quickly; cooled discs may crack when punctured. (Figure 15.4b)

i. Distribute lengths of thread or fishing line to the children. Tell them to thread a hanger through the holes in their discs. Knot these together for children. (Figure 15.4c)

j. Ask children to recall the previous shapes and sizes of the cups, their decorations, and names. How have they

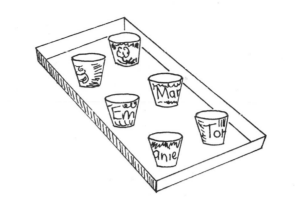

Figure 15.4a *Place Decorated Plastic Cups on a Cookie Sheet*

Figure 15.4b *Poke a Hole While the Sun Catcher is Still Warm*

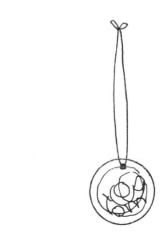

Figure 15.4c *Tie a String Through the Hole and Hang in a Sunny Window*

changed? What do they think caused these changes?

k. Children can hang their finished suncatchers in a window and watch the effects of sunlight shining through them, or they can wear them as necklaces.

Hints for Success:

- Only plastic (disposable) cups will melt and reharden as necessary for this activity.
- Ink from nonpermanent markers may "bead" and evaporate when heated.
- Distribute smocks to lessen chances of permanent marks staining clothing.

How to Simplify this Activity:

- Use larger cups for children with very small hands. Rather than having children use permanent markers with ink that is difficult to remove from clothing and hands, mark the names on each cup yourself, then invite children to predict and observe what will happen as the cups melt.

How to Extend this Activity:

- Make several cups for each child in this manner; invite children to string them into necklaces.

4. *Horizon Pictures.*

General Purpose: To increase children's awareness of the labels for and appearance of features of the sky.

TFPs: 1–8, 17, 18, 51. A complete list of Sky TFPs may help the supervising adult to introduce additional information and to answer questions as children's interests dictate.

Materials: Light blue construction paper; green or brown construction paper; glue and applicators; cotton balls; scissors; yellow paper *or* precut yellow circles; markers in rainbow shades. Optional: yarn, pipe cleaners, fabric scraps, etc.

Procedure:

a. Set out the materials on a table. Provide glue and scissors at each seat. Invite children to join you to make a horizon picture.

b. Mention that the horizon is the point in the distance where the sky and ground appear to meet.

c. Go outside or look out the window and help children observe the horizon. Ask them to tell you what color the sky looks. What about the ground?

d. Tell children that they can cut one blue sheet of paper in half, lengthwise, and glue it to a brown or green sheet. Ask children to tell you where on their papers the horizon appears.

e. Point out the other available materials. Invite children to think of ways to use them to produce pictures that include some features of the sky and some features of the ground.

f. Encourage children to think of, ask for, or find other materials they wish to add to their horizon pictures. Encourage description.

Hints for Success:

- Present this activity after a few days of discussion and activities that familiarize the children with sky phenomena.
- Expect and accept that some children will place collage materials anywhere they choose on their background sheets. Inquire into rationales for placement; accept "because I like it there" and other non-theme-related answers as appropriate for that child. Ask children to tell you about the world they've created and how it might be different from the one they've actually experienced.

How to Simplify this Activity:

- Glue blue-on-green backgrounds ahead of time or draw a line on blue paper for children to follow while cutting.
- Choose collage materials that represent features of the sky and ground more graphically: precut suns, twigs to represent tree trunks, small cupcake papers to use as flowers, and so on.

How to Extend this Activity:

- Provide night-sky horizon backgrounds, as well as daytime ones. Add star stickers and scraps of tinfoil to the array of collage materials. Direct children to choose ground and sky features to place on each of their background sheets. Encourage discussion of features that

Figure 15.5a *Stick Puppets of Things Children See in the Sky*

might occur in both the day and night as opposed to one or the other.

Language

1. *The Sky is a Stage.* Prepare in advance stick puppets of stars, clouds, a moon, a sun, and a rainbow. These could be cut out of heavy poster board in appropriate colors, then taped firmly to stout craft sticks. Or, cut pairs of each shape from felt. Sew each pair together, leaving a small opening through which to insert cotton batting.

(Figure 15.5a) Insert one end of a craft stick. Finish by hand, stitching the stick firmly in place.

Distribute one or two stick puppets to each of several children. Start by asking those children who think that their puppets represent objects seen in the night sky to hold them up, while others allow their day-sky objects to "set" below the horizon. Then say "Now day is breaking. Some objects are fading from sight, while others are becoming visible. Night-sky people, put down your puppets; day-sky people,

Figure 15.5b *A Sky Stage Ready for the Puppet Show*

let yours rise into sight!" Encourage children to think of other ways to combine their puppets in the same sky and to tell about their puppet manipulations. You might prepare a "horizon stage" by painting or drawing a scenario on a large cardboard box behind which children can stand or sit. Encourage nonpuppeteers to serve as audience. (Figure 15.5b)

2. *"Twinkle, Twinkle Little Star."* Prepare in advance a song chart that includes both written words and pictures illustrating the verses offered below. Using large pieces of easel paper or poster board, write each verse on a separate piece in letters big enough for children to see at a distance. Cover each page with clear contact paper, or laminate them. Begin by singing the traditional verse with your group as everyone creates hand and body movements to accompany the text. Next, introduce verses of the song that the children may not have heard before. Refer to the illustrated song chart to help them learn the unfamiliar words. Run your finger under the words as the group sings. After several sessions, if children seem ready and interested, introduce word cards representing the pictures on the charts. Pass these out to children in a group, one card for each child. As a picture-word is sung, the child who is holding that card can tape

it over the picture in the correct spot. Later, you may want to write some new verses that include references to other objects in the sky (the sun, the moon, clouds, or rainbows). (Figure 15.6)

Twinkle, Twinkle Little Star
(Traditional)

Verse 1:
Twinkle, twinkle little star,
how I wonder what you are.
Up above the world so high,
like a diamond in the sky.
Twinkle, twinkle little star,
how I wonder what you are.

Verse 2:
When the blazing sun is gone,
when it nothing shines upon,
then you show your little light,
twinkle, twinkle all the night.
Then the traveler in the dark
thanks you for your little spark.
How could he see where to go,
if you did not twinkle so?

Verse 3:
In the dark blue sky you keep,
often through my curtains peep.
For you never shut your eye
'til the sun is in the sky.
As your bright and tiny spark
lights the traveler in the dark
though I know not what you are
twinkle, twinkle, little star.

3. *Soaking Up the Sun.* Assemble a collection of heat-absorbent materials on a classroom windowsill that is exposed to the sun. These objects might include a rock, a piece of wood, a strip of metal, a sponge, and a paper or plastic cup of cool water. Invite children to touch each object and to think of words that describe what they feel. Encourage children to use comparative terms: "Is the rock *more* warm or *less* warm than the wood?" (warmer or cooler). "Tell me about the metal: How warm does it feel?" Encourage children to return to the objects now and then, and to come and tell you whether the temperatures of the objects have changed. Invite

Twinkle Twinkle Little Star

Twinkle twinkle little ☆
How I wonder what you are.
Up above the 🌎 so high,
Like a ◇ in the sky.
Twinkle twinkle little ☆
How I wonder what you are.

star
world
diamond
star

Figure 15.6 *Song Chart Using Pictures and Word Cards*

the children to add objects to the collection and to tell you about how the objects feel when they are first added, and how the objects feel after a time in the sunshine. Later, cover the collection with a dark cloth and ask children to feel under the cloth, describing objects as their hands encounter them.

4. ***Moonlight Memories.*** Select any *one* of the following books to read aloud: *Night in the Country* by Cynthia Rylant, *Midnight Farm* by Reeve Lindberg, or *Under the Moon* by Joanne Ryder. Read the story a second time later in the day. Precede this reading by asking children to listen carefully to find out who and what make nighttime sounds. Explain that when the story is over, they will generate a list of everything they remember about nighttime sounds. Read the book, then guide children in recalling relevant details. Write these down on a large sheet of easel paper so that children can see the list. Next, show children how to refer back to the book to check for accuracy. To vary this activity, focus on creating the sounds identified in the text. Invite children as a group, or one at a time in turn, to make an appropriate sound as you read about each one. Another variation is to ask children to recall the sequence of the story—what came first, next, and so on.

5. ***Guess What!*** Prepare flannel-board pieces illustrating the story *It Looked Like Spilt Milk* by Charles Shaw. Don't tell the children the subject of the book. Instead, ask them to listen carefully, explaining that you will be asking them to guess what the story is really about. Carry through on this plan. Afterward, take the group outside to see their own cloud images.

6. ***Sky Gazing.*** Request that parents send sunglasses with their children for the days or weeks of this unit. Take the class outside and point out clouds that you find beautiful or that remind you of other things. Have the children lie on their backs and observe the sky. Caution them against gazing directly at the sun. Ask children to take turns choosing clouds to describe. On cloudless days, direct children to close their eyes as they lie beneath the sun and to experience and/or describe the sensation of its warmth. Stand at their feet blocking the sun's rays and invite comparisons of how the shade feels.

7. ***Weather Song.***
   General Purpose: To increase children's descriptive vocabulary, especially of weather-related terms.

TFPs: 27, 36, 41, 50, 99. Additional TFPs could be introduced by creating new verses.

Materials: Optional: For teacher reference, an index card listing types of weather listed (rainy, snowy, sunny, cloudy, windy, breezy, etc.).

Procedure:

a. Tell children, in a large- or small-group setting, that you have a new song to teach them that is also a game. They can take turns thinking of words to add.

b. Explain that you will take the first turn. They can listen this time, then join in next time.

Weather Song
(Tune: "The Bear Went Over the Mountain"; Words: Kit Payne)
The rain falls on the rooftop,
the rooftop, the rooftop,
The rain falls on the rooftop,
when it's a rainy day.

c. Invite children to repeat this verse with you. Ask someone to substitute another word for rooftop. What else does the rain fall on?

d. Next, ask the children what the *sun* does when it's a sunny day. Does the sun *fall* like the rain? Encourage children to substitute another word, such as the sun *shines.* Sing a verse with these substitutions.

e. Continue with other weather conditions, such as the *wind blows,* the *clouds scoot* or *hang,* and so on. Encourage children to think of creative verbs; accept all ideas and try them in your song.

f. The song could also emphasize a variety of nouns upon which a weather condition acts. If it is a snowy day, for example, the children may enjoy thinking of as many objects as possible that the snow is drifting over or falling on.

Hints for Success:

• Introduce the song with an illustrated song chart (described in "Twinkle, Twinkle Little Star" activity earlier in this section) that includes the text for one simple verse, such as the one given above. Write the words to be substituted in subsequent verses in a different color, or underline them. Teach this verse and sing it several times before asking children to change it.

• Introduce rebus writing to more experienced children, providing stickers of stars, cotton balls for clouds, dot stickers for sun or moon, and so on. Suggest that children create sentences that include *both* words and pictures combined to tell a weather story. Write the words on the pages as they are dictated. Invite the children to insert symbols for star, cloud, sun, and moon in appropriate places, rather than using the words for these sky objects.

How to Simplify this Activity:

• Sing the song with a single weather condition (rain, for example), inviting children to substitute the surface on which it falls for several days or weeks before introducing a new condition that requires different actions and surfaces.

How to Extend this Activity:

• Invite children to create their own songbooks with a variety of verses and illustrations. Offer to write the verses that children dictate. As children become more familiar with the song and with writing and invented spelling, encourage them to copy words or whole verses from a classroom song chart, or to create their own sounded-out sentences. Encourage illustrations of a variety of weather and sky objects and conditions.

8. *Star Stories.*
General Purpose: To encourage children's creative language skills through personalized storytelling.

TFPs: 21, 54–56, 59, 63, 69–70.

Materials: Open art area (with paper, crayons, paste, scissors, etc.); pictures of the night sky with stars visible or an opportunity for children to view the night sky, which could be encouraged in a newsletter as a family activity or arranged as a special evening event at school.

Procedure:

a. Introduce the activity with a discussion about the permanence and quantity of stars. Show pictures of constellations if possible.

b. Point out that people have told stories and given names to stars for hundreds of years. Some stars are singly named, others are named in groups.

c. Invite children to "adopt" a star or group of stars (constellation). Children can choose stars as they discover them through viewing, or point out their own star(s) in a picture.

d. Discuss how some stars and constellations got their names. For example, someone might name a star after himself or herself, or a group of stars might look like the outline of an animal or object.

e. Invite children to name a star or constellation and to develop a book that introduces their star or constellation. Offer a variety of materials. Suggest that children cut out or draw pictures of their stars. Offer to write down the stories they tell about how their stars came to be, where their names came from, what life might be like there, and so forth.

Hint for Success:

• Use star stickers on black paper to outline a bear, a triangle, a person, or some other shape. Invite a child to tell you what he or she sees. Ask another child to name it. Give other children turns creating a story about the constellation. Tell children that this is their own constellation with its own special story.

How to Simplify this Activity:

• Invite each child to create a star-sticker picture on an individual sheet of black paper. Ask him or her to tell you something about the completed work. Write "Ben's Constellation" followed by all or part of his or her description on the picture. Use white chalk or crayon.

How to Extend this Activity:

• Encourage children to tell each other or the large group the story of their stars. Invite them to plan and dictate a description of a trip to their stars. What or who might they take along? How long might the journey be? What sort of vehicle would take them to their stars? How would they feel about such a journey?

Physical

1. *Shining in the Classroom Sky.* Arrange tinfoil, pizza cardboards, or poster-board circles and hole-punches and string on a table. Invite children to wrap the circles in foil, then to make a hole in the top of each to be threaded with string. Once this is accomplished, invite children to choose places in the room where they would like you to hang their moons or suns as room decorations.

   Add large star cutouts for more experienced children to wrap in foil and hang, or pretrace the shapes of stars, moons, and suns and invite children to cut them out before wrapping them. For children with limited fine-motor skills, provide precut lengths of foil and masking tape in place of hole-punches to attach the hangers.

2. *Pathway to the Stars.* Assemble sheets of star stickers, white or black construction paper, and pencils or white chalk at individual work places. Remind children of prior discussions about constellations. Provide a few star charts if possible. Invite children to peel stickers from the backing and to place them in some design on their papers. Distribute pencils for white paper or chalk for black paper. Show the children how to draw a line from star to star, creating an outline of a constellation. Ask children if their constellations have a name or a story they would like to tell you as you write it on the bottom or back of their work, or encourage them to add labels or descriptions themselves.

3. *Bob-bob-bobbing Along.* Purchase bubble solution. Outside, blow several bubbles. Invite children to become birds and chase the "clouds" across the sky. The children can try to catch a "cloud," or can follow its movement for a time, bobbing and darting on air currents as the bubble does.

4. *Sky Mobiles.*
   General Purpose: To provide an opportunity for children to increase their ma-

nipulative skills using common classroom tools.

TFPs: 4, 5, 20, 25, 36, 38, 57; others as interest dictates.

Materials: Star stickers; black, blue, white, and yellow construction paper; scissors; fine string; large needles; drinking straws; heavy cardboard tracing templates in the shapes of stars, crescent moons, circles, irregular cloud shapes, (each about 3 to 4 inches across); large pencils.

Procedure:

a. Set up the area prior to children's participation by arranging a variety of materials in the center of a large table. Place tracing patterns, pencils, and paper at each chair. For very young or inexperienced children, pretrace and/ or cut out some shapes ahead of time, encouraging them to manipulate the stickers, string, and straws on their own. Older children can participate in all the more difficult manipulative steps of the activity.

b. Invite children to join you. Explain that they can make a sky mobile by hanging several things they might see in the sky from strings. Encourage them to look over the available shapes, choosing ones they might want to include on their mobiles.

c. Direct or demonstrate template tracing: "Hold this shape down firmly with one hand. Hold a pencil in the other hand. Push the pencil's point against the edge of the shape. Now follow around the edge with your pencil." An adult can hold template in place if necessary.

d. Tell children that they can use scissors to cut out the shapes they have traced, or mention that they can ask you to cut out shapes if they wish. (Young children may be able to cut around a sun shape or a cloud shape, but would probably find the corners on a star very difficult to follow.)

e. Offer string to children that has been threaded through a large, blunt-ended needle. Demonstrate dropping the needle in one end of a straw then pulling the string through. Encourage them to try this with their own straws and strings.

f. Offer a sheet of star stickers to each child. Tell them that the stars can be used to stick the shapes to the strings. Some children may need to see this step demonstrated, then can be directed to repeat it on their own. (You can also attach shapes to the strings with tape.)

g. Encourage children to stick several shapes along both lengths of string that extend from each end of the straw. (Figure 15.7a)

h. Gently bend the straws in the middle. Help or direct children to tie a string at the bend to serve as a hanger.

Hint for Success:

• Distribute only a few of the materials at once, to help children concentrate on the procedure one step at a time. Provide children with tracing forms, paper, and pencils. When tracing is completed, pass out scissors. Clear away preceding mate-

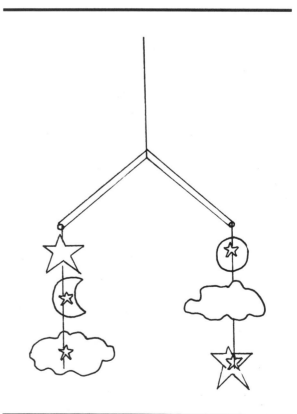

Figure 15.7a *Sky Mobile Made with a Bent Straw*

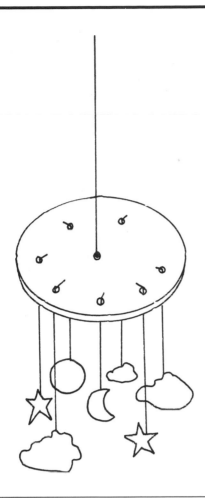

Figure 15.7b *Sky Mobile Made with a Round of Cardboard*

rials, then offer needles and string. Last, pass out straws.

How to Simplify this Activity:

• Pretrace larger shapes with fewer corners for beginning cutters. Suggest that only one shape be hung at each end of a string. Allow each child to drape his or her string over a prehung dowel to decorate the classroom. A curtain rod could also be used for this purpose.

How to Extend this Activity:

• Give each child a circle of heavy cardboard (such as a pizza is delivered on). Provide paper punches or prepunch several holes around the edge of each circle. Direct children to thread a string through

each hole, then to attach sky forms to the hanging ends of string.

If children have not mastered knot-tying, anchor strings to the board by twisting a pipe cleaner around them.

Finish by punching a hole in the center of the circle (or let children accomplish this by hammering a nail through it at a woodworking bench). Thread a final piece of line through the center hole to use as a mobile hanger. (Figure 15.7b)

• Add markers, crayons, or watercolors to the array of materials. Invite children to decorate their shapes before hanging them. Glitter and glue could also be provided.

Pretend Play

1. ***Head Through the Clouds.*** Acquire a few old white pillowcases. Cut a hole in the closed end through which children will put their heads. Cut armholes in each side as well. Bind all cut edges if possible to extend the life of your cloud costumes. (Figure 15.8a) Invite children to don the

Figure 15.8a *Wearing a Pillowcase Cloud Costume*

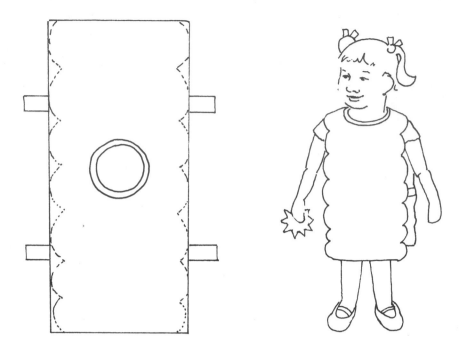

Figure 15.8b *A Simple Cloud Costume Design*

cases. Provide white foam packing squiggles for the cloud children to sprinkle as snow. Encourage children to float around as if on the wind, creating flurries in their wake. Cloud costumes could also be constructed of lengths of white felt or fabric folded in half. Cut a head-hole at the center fold. Attach Velcro® or make string side closures. Fluffy fake fur would make particularly beautiful clouds! (Figure 15.8b)

2. ***It's Raining, It's Pouring.*** Set up a sand table scene with plastic houses, trees, people, and/or vehicles. Twigs could be used to represent trees; rocks or seashells could also be added. Provide sprinkling cans or spray bottles. Invite children to assume the names of cloud types: cirrus, stratus, cumulus, nimbus. Encourage children to act as their cloud type might; some sprinkling water over the landscape, some pouring "rain," some hovering in beauty.

3. ***Bedroom: Slumber Party.***
   General Purpose: To encourage children's dramatization of and comfort with events that occur at night, both in the sky and in their lives and homes.

TFPs: 5–17, 21, 22; others as interest dictates.

Materials: Sleeping bags, cots, or small beds or mattresses; blankets; small dresser or table; lamp; alarm clock; stuffed animals; children's books; a window decorated with black construction paper and cutout stars, moon, planets; pajamas in sizes large enough to be worn over clothes. (Optional: Change the phase of the moon each day.)

Procedure:

a. Set up an area as a bedroom prior to children's participation. Make up one or two beds. Lay out pajamas. Place lamp and storybooks on bedside table or dresser. (Provide a battery-operated camper's lamp, if possible.) Position alarm clock near bed.

b. Invite children to join you; tell them it's almost bedtime! Point out the dark window. Ask children to tell you what time of day it looks like.

c. Encourage children to role-play "bedtime." (Point out that the pajamas can be put on right over their clothes). Discuss other purposes and functions of one's bedroom, as well.

d. Children may need encouragement in the form of adults taking roles: "I'm the little girl. You can read me a bedtime story, Mommy. Can I keep my light turned on tonight?" "Justin can be the daddy. Ask him to give you a goodnight hug." "I wonder what time we should set this alarm clock to wake us up in the morning," and so on.

e. Step back and allow children to guide the play as much as possible. If children appear uncertain about how to proceed, or they ask questions, introduce new ideas: "Let's be stargazers for awhile, before bed. Look at all the constellations! Find the moon for me."

f. Encourage children to discuss their dreams, their feelings about bedtime, and their nightly routines when preparing for bed. Talk about the return of daytime. When will it happen? Why does it happen? Introduce new vocabulary, such as dawn, dusk, sunrise, and sunset.

Hints for Success:

• Read a bedtime story to the group, before introducing the new area. A dream theme often leads to especially imaginative play.

• Limit the number of participants who can enter the area together, at first. Perhaps the availability of pajama sets could serve as a limiting factor.

How to Simplify this Activity:

• Substitute throw rugs for bed, if necessary.

• Invite parents to send a pair of pajamas to school with their child.

How to Extend this Activity:

• Organize a bedtime-routine-sharing day. Write a note to families, explaining that you are discussing the daytime and nighttime sky that week and that you will talk about bedtimes and bedrooms on a given day. Ask parents to help their child choose a special object from his or her sleeping area to bring to school. Suggest such items as a special stuffed toy or blanket, a favorite bedtime book, a pillow, or a pair of pajamas. Schedule a group time during which children can show and tell something special about what they've brought. Explain the option of adding some of the objects to your pretend bedroom area for a day or two, so that friends can enjoy sharing them. Respect the wishes of children who seem reluctant to share what they've brought; direct them to keep such objects in lockers and cubbies until it's time to take them home. Add masking tape name labels or request that parents label the objects with their children's names to make sure that precious bedtime treasures are returned to the right homes!

Social

1. **Our Sky Book.** Assemble the whole group of children for a discussion of sky phenomena. Initiate a discussion of the moon, sun, stars, clouds, and rainbows. Ask children which of these have been touched by people and which can only be seen. Ask children to tell you why they would or would not like to have an opportunity to visit each type of sky object. Divide the children into five smaller groups, assigning each group to create a story about one of the above phenomena. Stories could center around an imaginary visit to a cloud, a star, the moon or sun, or a rainbow. Groups could dictate their stories to an adult recorder, or produce an illustrated book of their own making. Later the same day, or the next day, call everyone together again to share their stories with each other. Consider assembling books into one larger volume about the sky. Attach a cover, entitled *Our Sky Book*.

2. **Solar-Powered Blimps.** Purchase a few lightweight black plastic trash bags. Assemble the children in an outdoor area on a warm, sunny day. Discuss the fact that

warm air rises in cooler air. Point out, also, that dark colors absorb more heat than do light colors. Divide children into groups of three or four. Give each group a trash bag. Challenge them to work together to figure out a way to inflate their trash bags with air, and then to keep the air contained within the bags. Offer tape, rubber bands, and/or wire twist ties as ways of sealing off the bags. If children have difficulty generating ideas, mention balloons; ask children to tell you one source of air that is sometimes used for inflating balloons. Praise children who realize that their own bodies (lungs) are a source of air. Demonstrate, if necessary, that one child can gather the open neck of the bag between his or her hands, then hold it to the mouth of another child while he or she blows in air. Encourage children to take turns as holders and blowers. When bags have been inflated as much as possible, help children to seal them tightly. You may want to tie string around the sealed neck at this point and attach an end to a fence, pole, or tree. Make sure that the bags remain in full sunshine. Invite children to feel the bags now and then as they heat up. Encourage conversations among children about what is happening. As the bags heat, they will begin to rise into the air. Read about or discuss hot-air balloons as an introduction or a follow-up to this activity; *Hot Air Henry* by Mary Calhoun is an appropriate story.

3. *Cooperative Rainbow.* Cut seven large crescents in graduated dimensions out of poster board or cardboard, in rainbow hues, if possible, to provide a visual cue to color order. Produce crescents that are as large as possible: perhaps seven feet wide by three feet across for the largest arch. (Figure 15.9) Assemble glue and tissue-paper squares or fabric scraps in red, orange, yellow, green, blue, indigo, and violet. Assign small groups of children to work on one or two of the crescents each. When the groups of children finish decorating their portions of the rainbow, call them all together again to assemble the full rainbow. Ask children to think of ways to attach the crescents together. Encourage an exchange of ideas and cooperative

efforts to carry them out. Hang the finished product on a classroom wall for all to enjoy.

4. *In the Night, Helping.* In a large- or small-group setting, read Maurice Sendak's *In the Night Kitchen*. Cue children to watch and listen for hints that tell them it is night in Mickey's tale. For example, "What is he doing at the beginning? What is shown in the pictures?" At story's end, discuss the people whom Mickey helped and the ways he helped them. Tell children to close their eyes and imagine falling away from their bed, into the night. Say, "Think of a place you could land, where someone will need your help." Suggest that children picture the tools that are there, or the furniture. What needs to be done? What are people working on? Encourage a child to describe the picture in his or her head, or to tell you her or his thoughts aloud. Make such comments as "Yes, I can see that, too!" "Why do you suppose the girl is stirring?" Comment with enthusiasm if a child concocts some means of completing a helpful task.

5. *Sky Mural.*

General Purpose: To provide children with an opportunity to plan and carry out a cooperative project.

TFPs: 3, 4, 5, 18, 19, 21, 23, 36–40, 42–45, 49–51, 53, 60, 69.

Materials: Roll of black or blue wrapping paper (paint white butcher paper if necessary); tinfoil; cotton balls; glue; markers; watercolors; variety of colors of yarn and paper scraps; writing tablet and pencil.

Procedure:

a. Introduce the activity in a large-group discussion. Tell the children that you would like them all to work together to produce a gigantic mural of the sky. This mural, or huge picture that tells a story, will decorate the classroom for many days. Explain that everyone will have some special jobs to do, and that the finished mural will belong to everybody.

b. Point out a table or set of shelves on which the materials are displayed. Tell the children that they will be the plan-

Cooperative Rainbow

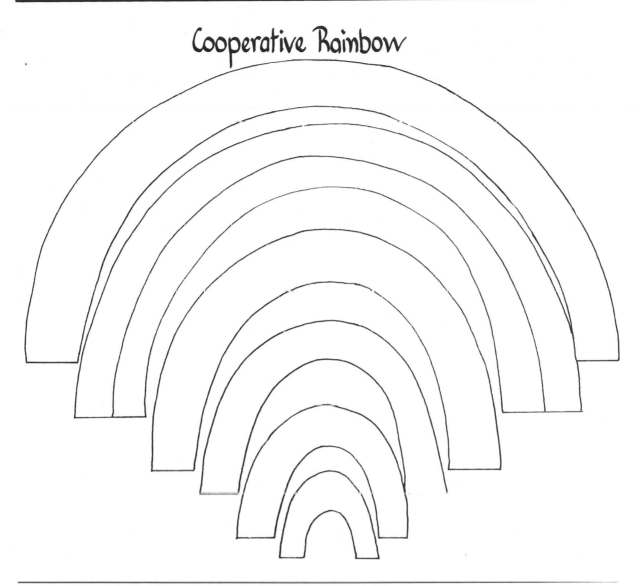

Figure 15.9 *Rainbow Pieces That Fit Together*

ners as well as the artists and should feel free to ask each other, you, or other adults for help when necessary.

c. Invite the children to think about all that they see in the sky. Tell them that the only "rules" about the mural are that it must include everyone's work, and it must tell a story about the sky.

d. Suggest that children choose special jobs, like making a rainbow, creating clouds, or cutting out a big yellow sun. They can work alone or in small groups on their special jobs. Offer to write down children's names beside the special jobs they choose, so everyone doesn't end up making the same thing. The sky is full of a great variety of objects, some that we see at night, some that only appear in the day. You would like to see many of those objects represented!

Hint for Success:

• Allow children freedom to create! Help by finding requested materials, answering questions, and offering suggestions to shy or disinterested children to get them involved. Freely praise efforts to keep pride-in-product high. Offer to label objects.

How to Simplify this Activity:

- Begin the activity by providing each child with an individual sheet of blue or black construction paper. Invite each of them to create a version of the sky. Decorate a classroom wall by hanging all the pictures together with slightly overlapping edges, to create a mural effect. Encourage the group to plan the placement of the pictures together, so that everyone's picture is included and appreciated.

How to Extend this Activity:

- Children may want to tell a progressive story, describing various parts of the finished mural as you record their words on tape or paper.

- Consider attaching the finished mural to the classroom ceiling instead of a wall. Invite children to recline on their backs later, gazing up at their "personal sky."

- Direct children to make a daytime sky mural one day, and a nighttime sky the next day.

TEACHER RESOURCES

Field Trip Ideas

1. Visit a planetarium. Call ahead to find out whether guided tours are offered, or any special events directed at children are planned.

2. Invite families to attend an evening sky-gazing event at school. Plan for some time outdoors "looking up." Lay out blankets for comfort. Conclude with a session indoors, at which you lead a discussion about what was observed. End by singing songs about the sky.

3. Visit an airport. Call small airstrips as well as public facilities. Ask for suggestions about pilots or airlines who would allow children to board a plane or view one up close. Or, simply enjoy watching take-offs and landings.

4. Check your yellow pages for hot-air balloon pilots. One may be willing to set up (inflate) his or her balloon, as children watch.

5. Visit a weather station. Many large airports have such facilities, as do some television stations. Ask a forecaster to demonstrate/explain some of the equipment.

Classroom Visitors

1. Check your yellow pages for a parachuting school or center. Ask someone who practices this sport to visit your classroom, bringing his or her gear. Encourage descriptions of how the sky looks and feels as one drifts through it under a parachute. The skydiver may be willing to open and inflate a parachute if it's a breezy day. Follow up with a parachute game. (Children can hold on around the edges and bounce balls within the chute, or watch it drift up and down "like a cloud.")

2. Invite a pilot to visit. Ask him or her to bring pictures of planes and to talk about the occupation and/or sport of flying a machine through the sky.

3. Ask a parent or sport shop employee to bring a kite to school. Have them discuss how it was constructed. Enjoy a demonstration of the kite's ability to soar in the sky. Invite children to design their own kites as a follow-up construction activity.

4. Check the field trip ideas for other possible visitors. If you cannot arrange to visit one of these places, perhaps a spokesperson would visit your school, bringing props and expertise.

Children's Books

Asch, F. *Moongame*. Englewood Cliffs, NJ: Prentice-Hall, 1984.

Belting, N. M. *The Sun Is a Golden Earring*. New York: Holt, Rinehart and Winston, 1962.

Berger, B. *Grandfather Twilight*. New York: Philomel Books, 1984.

Branley, F. M. *The Sky Is Full of Stars*. New York: Crowell, 1981.

Brown, M. W. *Goodnight Moon*. New York: Harper and Row, 1982.

Calhoun, M. *Hot Air Henry*. New York: William Morrow, 1981.

Carlstrom, N. W. *The Moon Came Too.* New York: Macmillan, 1987.

dePaola, T. *The Cloud Book.* New York: Holiday House, 1975.

Goudy, A. *The Day We Saw the Sun Come Up.* New York: Scribner's, 1961.

Lindbergh, R. *The Midnight Farm.* New York: Dial Books for Young Readers, 1987.

Myers, B. *Come Out Shadow, Wherever You Are.* New York: Scholastic, 1970.

Polgreen, J., and Polgreen, C. *Sunlight and Shadows.* Garden City, NY: Doubleday, 1967.

Rey, H. A. *Find the Constellations.* Boston: Houghton Mifflin, 1986.

Russo, S. *The Moon's the North Wind's Cooky.* New York: Lothrop, Lee and Shepard, 1979.

Ryder, J. *Under the Moon.* New York: Random House, 1989.

Rylant, C. *Night in the Country.* New York: Bradbury Press, 1986.

Santrey, L. *Discovering the Stars.* Mahwah, NJ: Troll, 1982.

Schneider, H., and Schneider, N. *Follow the Sunset.* Garden City, NY: Doubleday, 1952.

Sendak, M. *In the Night Kitchen.* Harper and Row, 1970.

Seymour, P. *Exploring the Solar System.* New York: Macmillan, 1986.

Shaw, C. G. *It Looked Like Spilt Milk.* New York: Harper and Row, 1947.

Simon, S. *Stars.* New York: William Morrow, 1986.

———. *The Sun.* New York: William Morrow, 1986.

Taylor, A. *Lights Off, Lights On.* Oxford, England: Oxford Press, 1989.

Tresselt, A. *Sun Up.* New York: Lothrop, Lee and Shepard, 1949.

Turkle, B. *The Sky Dog.* New York: Viking, 1969.

Wood. A. *The Napping House.* New York: Harcourt Brace Jovanovich, 1984.

Adult References

Jobb, J. *The Night Sky Book.* Boston: Little, Brown, 1977.

Mayall, R. N., M. Mayall, and J. Wyckoff. *The Sky Observer's Guide.* New York: Golden, 1985.

Ryan, M. *Weather.* New York: Franklin Watts, 1976.

Simon, S. *Look to the Night Sky.* New York: Viking, 1977.

Slote, A. *The Moon in Fact and Fancy.* Cleveland: World, 1967.

Zim, H. S., and R. H. Baker. *Stars.* New York: Golden, 1975.

Chapter 16

Rocks

•

Solid as a rock . . .
Stony silence . . .
Rock hard . . .
Stone face . . .
Carved in stone . . .
Stone cold . . .
Rock bottom . . .
Heart of stone . . .

•

Expressions such as these are common throughout our culture. They illustrate how easily human beings identify with rocks and how pervasive is our understanding of their characteristics. And it's no wonder! Rocks are everywhere.

Large or small, rough or smooth, shiny or dull, all one color or many different shades, each rock has a story to tell—where it came from, how it was formed, how it might be used. With their burgeoning curiosity in the natural world, children find rocks fascinating to explore. Some youngsters think about rocks in a purely aesthetic sense. They take great pleasure in gathering rocks, looking at them, feeling them. Rock features such as texture, color, pattern, size, and shape are all criteria these children use to make judgments about what is beautiful and appealing to them and what is not.

Other children find in rocks an intriguing entree to discovering more about the world in which they live. Examining rocks, collecting, organizing, and experimenting with rocks are some of the strategies they use to further their understanding.

In both cases, rocks provide a marvelous vehicle through which children can increase their capacity to perceive, respond, become sensitive to, and learn about the natural environment.

PURPOSE

The Rocks theme has been designed to accommodate both children's aesthetic and scientific interests. Most activities can enhance either perspective, depending on the inclinations of the children. However, regardless of which frame of mind children bring to these experiences, their attention will be drawn to the characteristics of rocks and the different ways rocks can be used or acted upon. In this way we hope to stimulate children's understanding and appreciation of nature.

IMPLEMENTATION

Only one prop is essential for the successful implementation of this unit—a large, varied array of rock specimens that children can handle easily. Although some store-bought samples may be necessary to round out your collection, many different kinds of rocks will be readily available in your locale if you make a concerted effort to look for them. Elicit temporary or permanent contributions from colleagues and parents as well. Once this has been accomplished, consider carrying out the theme in one of the following ways.

Option One: Focus on the aesthetic qualities of rocks. Encourage children to consider the emotions evoked by rocks and to express preferences for particular rock attributes.

Option Two: Approach rocks from a scientific standpoint. Select activities that highlight the different types of rocks and their varying origins.

Option Three: Teach rocks as a two-part unit. Spend the first segment exploring rocks in the natural world. During the second portion focus on how human beings use and study rocks. No matter which facet you choose, give children plenty of opportunities to examine, handle, organize, and experiment with rocks, both in and out of the classroom. Note too that rocks could easily precede a unit on dinosaurs or plants. It could also serve as a follow-up to a study of other natural phenomena such as water.

TERMS, FACTS, AND PRINCIPLES

Characteristics of Rocks

1. Rocks are hard pieces of stone found in nature.

*2. Rocks are made up of one or more minerals.

*3. Minerals are nonliving (inorganic) solids found in the natural world.

*4. Some rocks, such as quartzite or marble, consist of only one mineral.

*5. Most rocks consist of mineral combinations.

*6. Each mineral combination has been given its own name. Some rock names are obsidian, granite, cinnabar, limestone, gypsum, and coal.

7. Each kind of rock has particular characteristics by which it can be identified and classified.

8. Rocks vary in composition, shape, texture, color, weight, and hardness.

9. People sometimes use different words to describe the size of a rock.
   a. Particles of sand are really very tiny pieces of rock.
   b. Small (less than two inches), smooth rocks are called pebbles.
   c. Small (less than two inches), rough rocks are called gravel.
   d. Stones are 2½ to 10 inches in diameter.
   e. Boulders are very large rocks. They may be ten inches to fifty feet in diameter.

10. Rocks are everywhere (in mountains and hills and under seas, the soil of forests, the sands of deserts, and cities).

11. Rocks form part of the surface and interior of the earth.

12. Rocks have also been found on the moon.

13. Rocks are continually forming within the earth.

How Rocks Are Formed

*14. What a rock looks like depends upon how it was formed.

*15. Rocks are classified into three major groups based on how they were formed: sedimentary, igneous, and metamorphic.

*16. Sedimentary rocks form as small pieces of rock and animal remains are deposited on the floors of seas or rivers. Buried over many years, this material, called sediment, is compressed under the weight of the water and cemented together into rock.

*17. Igneous rocks are formed by heat. Some igneous rocks result from cooled volcanic lava.

*18. Metamorphic rocks are sedimentary rocks that have been changed by heat, pressure, or both.

19. All rocks eventually break down at the Earth's surface.

20. Wind, water, and the movement of the Earth or things on the Earth continually chip away at rocks making them smaller and smaller.

*21. Rocks erode when wind or water wear them away bit by bit.

*22. Weathering occurs when rocks expand and contract over and over again, eventually breaking down, due to changes in temperature.

*23. Some rocks take a long time to break down, while others break down more quickly.

*24. As rocks dwindle in size, they become the raw material for future sedimentary rocks.

People and Rocks

25. People use rocks in many ways.

26. Long ago, people used rocks as tools to scrape, grind, chop, pound, and roll. People also used rocks to cook or hold their food.

27. Today people use rock tools mostly for grinding and rolling, and sometimes rocks serve as bowls or trays. Other materials are more likely to be used to make pounders, scrapers, and choppers.

28. People build things from rock such as buildings, roads, sidewalks, and walls.

29. People who build with rocks are sometimes called builders or stonemasons.

30. People use a rock called coal for fuel.

31. People use rocks to make beautiful objects for people to wear, use, and look at.

32. People who create beautiful things out of rock are sometimes called sculptors, stone carvers, jewelers, artists, or craftspeople.

33. People study rocks to find out what they're made of and to learn more about the Earth.

34. The people who study rocks are called geologists.

35. People often have to dig rocks out of the ground to use them.

36. People who dig rocks out of the ground are called miners or quarry workers.

37. A mine or quarry is a large hole made in or under the ground where people go to dig out rocks.

38. All people who work with rocks use special tools to help them.

39. People sometimes collect rocks for pleasure and to learn more about them.

40. Some rock collections are small, others are large; some are designed for many people to see, some are for just a few people to enjoy.

41. In some places on the earth, rocks are easy to find; other places may have rocks that are not readily visible.

42. Rocks and rock formations prompt emotions in some people.

43. Reactions to a particular rock or rock formation vary from person to person.

44. Each person may have different ideas about what makes a rock beautiful, interesting, appealing, or unappealing.

Rocks and Other Living Things

45. Animals sometimes use rocks for shelter or protection.

46. Some plants, such as lichen, sedum, forget-me-nots, rhododendron, and cacti grow on or around rocks.

47. Fossils are rocks that contain the preserved remains of once-living animals or plants.

48. Fossils are found in sedimentary rocks.

49. Fossils help people to understand the earth of long, long ago.

ACTIVITY IDEAS

Aesthetics

1. *Sand Collage.* To prepare for this activity, mix about one tablespoon of dry tempera paint with a half cup of sand. (Salt could be substituted for sand.) Put this mixture into a plastic or metal saltshaker. (One with a handle works well.) Shake this over a pie tin to be sure the sand grains fit through the holes. Cover a table with newspaper, placing four empty pie tins on the table for collecting loose sand. Make glue available in squeeze bottles or in small containers with popsicle sticks as applicators. Give each child a piece of construction paper. Direct them to put glue on the paper first, in any design they wish. Then have the children shake the sand over the glue. Once the sand is on the paper, pour the excess off into the empty pie tins.

2. *Rock Printing.* Give the children several rocks that vary in size and shape. Also provide stamp pads or some liquid paint. Demonstrate how to put the rock in the ink or paint and then press the ink or paint side onto the paper. Encourage children to create prints with several different rocks.

3. *Rock Sculptures.* Prior to the children's participation, prepare a mixture of equal parts white glue and school paste. Combine and stir until smooth. Put rocks collected by the children in the center of a table along with the sticking mixture. Invite children to create a sculpture using these items. Provide a larger rock, a piece of wood, or a Styrofoam tray to function as the base for each sculpture.

4. *Finger Designs.* You will need large jelly roll pans or cafeteria trays and several kinds of small stones—common gravel, pebbles, course sand, fine sand, aquarium gravel. Fill each tray almost to the top with one type of stone. Invite children to make designs or draw pictures with their fingers in the different pans. Extend this activity outdoors by having children draw designs in the sandbox or a gravelly portion of the playground. To extend it further, talk with children about the rock gardens of Japan, large areas covered with gravel that are raked into abstract designs. It is said that people who contemplate these gardens gain insight into themselves and the natural world. Pictures of such gardens are available in travel magazines or other international publications such as *National Geographic*. If you choose this option, give each child his or her own tray of gravel as well as two or three larger rocks to place strategically within their designs.

5. *Sculpting with Rocks.* As children sculpt with modeling dough, give them smooth rocks to use for flattening it, contoured rocks for making prints, and various small rocks for decorating their creations.

6. *Drawing with Chalk.* Chalk is a limestone which was formed from the skeletons of tiny sea animals. Show children how to:
   a. Use the pointed end of the chalk for drawing thin lines or the entire side to produce wide ones. Use both thick and thin chalk, then compare the effects.

b. Brush buttermilk on paper, then apply the chalk over it to produce a slick, paintlike effect. This will also "set" the chalk so it won't rub off the paper.

c. Brush liquid starch on paper, then apply chalk to the wet surface. This will be similar to using the buttermilk, but will be more powdery when dry.

d. Brush water on paper and draw with the chalk on the wet surface to produce a smooth effect.

e. Use pale chalk on brown or black paper.

f. Use cotton balls to blend chalk lines and colors.

g. Rub chalk into the empty spaces of a simple stencil cut from cardboard. Lift the stencil to see the shape. A softer effect can be achieved by rubbing a cotton ball over the shape before lifting off the stencil.

h. Use chalk outside on the sidewalk or on large rocks.

i. Use chalk on slate as a way to use a rock on a rock.

7. *Rock Polishing.* Provide children with several grades of sandpaper from coarse to fine. Demonstrate how to rub a rock with the sandpaper to polish it. Allow children to choose which rocks they would like to polish and encourage them to try different types of sandpaper to create a pleasing effect.

8. *Rocky Landscapes.* Show children painted landscapes in which rock formations are prominently featured. Talk with them about their reactions to each and what mood the paintings may evoke. Encourage children to examine each work to discover artistic details that contribute to their impressions.

9. *Rock Band.* Carry out this activity to give children opportunities to experiment with rhythm and tempo. Prior to their participation, gather rocks (two for each pupil) that children can easily hold in their hands. Generate a list of familiar songs that have a strong, regular beat, such as "Twinkle, Twinkle, Little Star" or "Bingo." During a circle time, sing one or two songs while children clap their hands to the beat. Next, give each child two rocks and tell them to substitute tapping the rocks for clapping. Do this for awhile. Over time,

introduce variations by trying different tempos, volumes, and methods of making rock sounds. Encourage children to suggest ways to change the rhythm or tempo of each song.

10. *Sand Layering.*

General Purpose: For children to increase their familiarity with basic elements of art—color, texture, and design.

TFPs: 10.

Materials: Very fine sand; powdered tempera paint in at least three different colors; bowls to hold colored sand; scoops for each bowl of sand; one clear plastic container or baby-food jar per child; four or five toothpicks.

Procedure:

a. Mix the sand and powdered paint in bowls before the children begin this activity.

b. Explain to the children that they are going to use colored sand to make designs.

c. Instruct children to choose one color of sand and scoop some into their jars.

d. Direct them to pick a second color to make layer number two. Demonstrate how to pour the sand carefully on top of the first layer without shaking the jar. Then, have the children try it on their own.

e. Show the children how to make a design in the sand by using the toothpick to poke some of layer two into layer one.

f. Continue layering sand and poking until the jar is full. Place the top on securely.

Hint for Success:

• Make small lines on the outside of the jars with a grease pencil to show children how much sand to put in the jar for each layer.

How to Simplify this Activity:

• Use only two colors of sand.

How to Extend this Activity:

• Give children a choice of four or five sand colors.

• Provide them with larger containers.

• Encourage children to plan out their designs before trying to create them.

Affective

1. *Everybody Needs a Rock.* The book *Everybody Needs a Rock* by Byrd Baylor describes ten delightful principles and rules children can use to find their own special rocks. Become familiar with this book before reading it to the children so you can tell it in your own words. Write down and post the ten rules. As you talk about them to the group, hold your own special rock in your hand. When you are finished, invite the children to search for their own rocks outdoors or from a collection you have provided. Ask them to describe what makes their rocks special for them. Refer back to the principles you discussed earlier in the day.

2. *Brilliant Rocks.* Gather an array of tangerine-sized rocks near a water table half-filled with plain water. Encourage children to compare how the rocks look both dry and wet. Ask them to find a rock whose underwater appearance they particularly like and direct them to dry it off. When the rocks are no longer wet, provide the children with small containers of shellac, paintbrushes, and small squares of cardboard. Show the children how to brush the shellac onto their rocks. Place each shellacked rock on a piece of cardboard labeled with the owner's name, then move them to a safe place to dry. Ask each child to explain why his or her rock was a favorite. Write down the children's exact words and display their explanations near the corresponding rocks.

3. *Personal Rock Gardens.* Visit a local greenhouse; get suggestions from someone there about plants that thrive in a rocky terrain. Some examples are: varieties of cacti, sedum, creeping phlox, and heather. Select healthy bedding plants. Provide two or more varieties for children to select from. In addition, make available one cottage cheese or margarine tub for each child. Provide appropriate soil mix and pebbles. Help children plant and care for their rock gardens. Discuss with them the characteristics of rock garden plants: they tend to be low to the ground, are often succulents, and flower periodically. Label each garden with its maker's name and keep track on a chart of the changes observed in the plants each week.

4. *Using Rocks as Tools.*

   General Purpose: To give children an opportunity to master using age-appropriate tools.

   TFPs: 26, 27.

   Materials: Small plastic bags each filled with whole wheat flour, oat flour, cornmeal, or rice flour; several types of whole grains, such as oats, wheat, corn, rice; three smooth rocks about 3 or 4 inches in diameter; wooden chopping bowl, old wooden salad bowl, or sturdy plastic bowl.

   Procedure:
   a. Show the children the whole grains and the ground flours. Point out the correspondence between them. Explain that today people use machines to grind grain into flour, but there was a time when no such machines existed. While the children are examining the grains, ask them how they think flour could be made without machines. Discuss their ideas with them.
   b. Bring out the rocks, encouraging children to try grinding the different grains in a bowl with them.
   c. Encourage children to comment on the ease or difficulty of using rocks to grind grains, as well as on the features of the flour that results.

Hint for Success:
- Do this activity at a low table or on the floor so the children can achieve the best leverage for grinding.

How to Simplify this Activity:
- Provide softer grains for children to work with, such as oats or "puffed" grains.
- Give children graham crackers to grind into crumbs.

How to Extend this Activity:
- Have the children use the flour they ground in a baking project. Sample recipes follow. These were adapted from *Kids are Natural Cooks* by Lady McCrady (Boston: Houghton Mifflin, 1974).

Graham Cracker Cakes
Ingredients:

½ one-pound box of graham crackers (enough for 2 cups crushed)

½ cup butter, margarine, or shortening

½ cup honey

2 eggs

1½ tsps. baking powder

½ tsp. baking soda

¼ tsp. salt

½ cup milk

Procedure:

1. Have each child crush a portion of the crackers any way he or she wants—by pounding, squeezing, or rolling with the stone. The crackers should be well mashed, but a few lumps are acceptable.
2. Heat oven to 350°.
3. Melt butter in large pan over low heat.
4. Stir in honey and eggs.
5. Beat with a wire whisk or egg beater for a few minutes.
6. In another pan or bowl, mix the 2 cups of cracker crumbs together with baking powder, baking soda, and salt.
7. Pour half of the cracker mixture into the honey mixture, stir well, and add the milk.
8. Stir again and add the rest of the crumbs. Mix well.
9. Grease cupcake pans and fill them a little more than halfway.
10. Bake about 20 minutes.

Corn Pones
Corn cakes like this are most often made in the South, but the recipe is traditional among Native Americans. "Pone" comes from an Indian word for "bake."

Ingredients:

2 cups water

2½ cups stoneground cornmeal

1 tsp. salt

¼ cup corn oil

Procedure:

1. Reheat oven to 400°.
2. Boil 1¼ cups water and add to cornmeal and salt. Stir until well mixed.
3. Add corn oil and ¾ cup cold water to mixture and stir well.
4. Oil 2 cookie sheets. Flatten handfuls of batter on the sheets to make the cakes. You should have a dozen cakes each 3 inches around or so, more if you make them smaller.
5. Bake the pones 45 minutes or until they are brown around the edges.
6. Serve them hot with butter and jelly.

Cognition

1. *Metamorphic Rock Making.* Metamorphic rocks have been altered by heat and/or pressure. They include both minerals and other organic or inorganic matter. To demonstrate how rocks can be affected by high temperatures, have the children make the following baking dough mixture. Point out that the salt is a mineral, and the flour represents other matter that might eventually help form the rock. Engage the children in forming shapes from the salt dough. Bake some and leave some unbaked. Once cooled, ask the children to compare the baked sculpture with some of the unbaked mixture and describe the difference.

Baking Dough
Ingredients

4 cups flour

1 cup salt

½ (approx.) cup water

Procedure:

1. Mix to make pliable mixture that should not stick to hands. Knead for five minutes until smooth.
2. Make flat or standing forms and moisten slightly when sticking pieces together.
3. Bake on baking sheet for 1 hour at 350°. Cool.

2. ***Where Are the Rocks?*** To help children learn where rocks can be found, go for a rock hunt. Prepare the children for this activity by having them generate ideas about where they think they might be able to find rocks. Print their ideas on a large piece of paper in letters big enough for them to see from a distance. Read the list to the children when it has been completed. Inform them that they will have the opportunity to look for rocks in these places if the locations are near the school. After the hunt, ask the group to look at the list again and determine whether rocks were actually found in those spots.

3. ***Rock and Roll.*** Present a collection of five or ten rocks to the children. Include rocks that are round, bumpy, irregularly shaped, flat, small, large, and varied in color. Tell children to pick up the rocks and feel them. Set up a ramp, possibly a board about eighteen inches tall and five feet long with a support for the higher end that can be adjusted to change the degree of inclination. Once the children have had a chance to examine the rocks, show them the ramp. Direct them to put one rock at the top of the ramp and gently let go. Ask the children to describe what happened and explain why the rock moved or didn't move. Have them choose another rock and predict what will happen when it is placed at the top of the ramp. Encourage the children to test their predictions and then evaluate the results. Consider charting the results as a visual aid to help children evaluate what happened.

4. ***Sedimentary Rock Formation.*** This activity will demonstrate to children how sedimentary rocks are formed. At the beginning of the daily session, fill a clear gallon jar with water. Have available sand, gravel, and soil. Direct children to pour some of these materials into the water and stir it up with a long spoon. Place the jar on a shelf where it won't be disturbed. Have children check on the jar throughout this day and the next. Ask them to describe what they observe. Write down their observations. (Different textures of sediment should have settled in layers.) Show the children a sample of a sedimentary rock and explain that materials pile up on the bottoms of lakes, rivers and oceans. As many, many years go by, the materials get packed down until they harden into rock.

5. ***Rock Experiments.*** The first two experiments will demonstrate to children the effect of temperature and other elements on rocks.

Experiment One: Freezing rocks
When water freezes it expands. If the water has been absorbed within a porous rock and the rock freezes, it will most likely crack or break. Children can observe this phenomenon in the following experiment. Give children some pieces of sandstone to touch and look at closely. Put those pieces in a bucket of water. Wet one piece quickly and then take it out, let the other soak for one minute, and have a third piece sit in the water for an hour. Put the rocks in the freezer overnight in containers labeled with the amount of time they were in the water. Check on them the next day. Show them to the children and ask them to determine what, if any, change occurred. Write down the children's observations. Try the experiment again, possibly comparing a different rock with the sandstone or varying the amount of time the rocks are kept in the water and in the freezer. Encourage the children to generate ideas on how to change the variables and try out their ideas.

Experiment Two: Hot rocks
Find two rocks similar in size, shape, and composition. (Flagstones would suit the purpose.) Explain to the children that you would like them to try an experiment with rocks and heat. Show them the two rocks and have each child feel them. As children discuss how the rocks feel, ask them to notice that their temperature is the same.

Together, decide upon a sunny place in the classroom to put one rock, and a shady place for the other. Ask children to predict what they think will happen to the two rocks: will their temperatures remain the same, or will they change? If some think the temperatures will vary, ask them in what way. Record the children's ideas. Next, direct them to check on the rocks every few minutes to determine if there is any change in temperature. If there is a noticeable difference after a few hours, take the warmed rock out of the sunshine and place it next to the shaded one. In a discussion with the children, compare their predictions with the actual outcomes. Consider timing how long it takes for the warm rock to cool down.

Experiment Three: Rocky breakdown
This activity will show children some ways that rocks break down. Provide each child with a piece of sandstone at least the size of the palm of his or her hand. After discussing erosion and weathering, tell children they will have a chance to try to wear down their rocks in different ways:

- with water and a vegetable brush
- by rubbing two rocks together
- by grinding or mashing the sandstone with a pestle or mallet

Provide them with the necessary implements, encouraging them to try one or more methods. Ask children to describe the results they achieve. Write down their observations and review these with the group as a whole once everyone has had a chance to do the experiment. This activity works particularly well if staged in an empty water table where a pan of water has been provided. Safety goggles are recommended.

6. ***Between a Rock and a Hard Place.*** During an outdoor time, encourage children to make observations about what can be found under rocks. Have them look under rocks in different areas of the playground. Try spots that are shady, sunny, sandy, or grassy. Search with the children and write down the things they discover, making note of each location. Read the notes to everyone at the end of the outdoor time. Ask children to summarize their observations.

7. ***Shifting Stones.***
Day One: Show children one or more collections of items (rocks, shells, miniature cars, etc.). Explain what a collection is and ask the children why they think people might collect things. Make your collections available for children to examine throughout the day. End this portion of

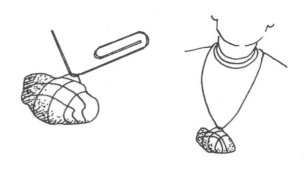

Figure 16.1 *Choose a Special Rock to Wear as a Necklace*

the activity by telling the children that they will take part in creating a collection of rocks for the classroom. Discuss with them what criteria they might use to select a rock for this project.

Children can gather rocks in two different ways. Either ask them to bring a rock from home, or take them on a "rock hunt" around the school grounds.

Day Two: Have children show their rocks to one another and give them an opportunity to examine the collection thoroughly.

Day Three: Explain to children that sometimes people organize their collections in a certain way: by size, by color, by shape, or by where each specimen was found. Tell children that the collection will be available for one or more days and that individuals or groups of children can organize it any way they like. Each idea will be recorded by the teacher or the children if they are able, and then the entire array of ideas will be reviewed by the group as a whole. Emphasize that the task is for the group to think of as many different ways to organize the rocks as it can.

Day Four or Five: Review with the children the organizational strategies generated earlier, having individual children demonstrate each one after it is described.

Construction

1. ***Create a Mountain.*** Give the children a twelve-inch square piece of Masonite or other sturdy material to use as a base. Making available stones and rocks the

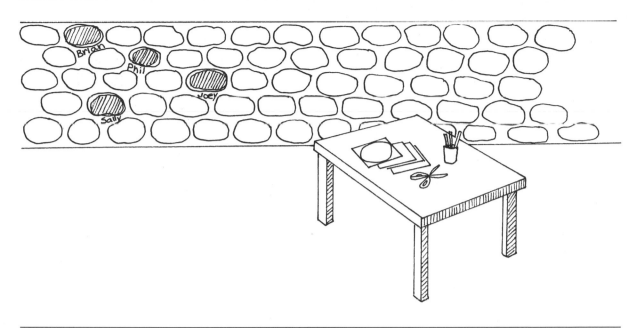

Figure 16.2 *The Children Can Help Construct a Paper Rock Wall*

children have gathered, challenge them to make a mountain by piling up and gluing the rocks. This activity would also work well carried out cooperatively among a small group of children.

2. ***Build a Rock House.*** Some homes are constructed with bricks or actual rocks. To enable children to build their own versions of a rock house, supply each child with a small box (such as a shoe box), a mixture of white glue and paste, and a large collection of pebbles from which to choose. Invite them to use the materials to create their own versions of a rock shelter. As children proceed, have them consider additional features, such as a roof, chimney, windows, and doors.

3. ***Make Rock Necklaces.*** To prompt children's interest in trying this activity, show them photographs of men, women, and children of various culture groups wearing stone jewelry. Ask each child to select one small rock that appeals to him or her. Explain that they will use these to make necklaces. Give each child a piece of thin wire to wrap around his or her special stone. Use the end of a paper clip to pull the wire away from the rock a tiny bit so that yarn can pass behind it. (Figure 16.1) Next, help the children string lengths of yarn through the wire. Make sure each is long enough to fit easily over the wearer's head. Tie the ends together to form a necklace. Note that some children may wish to string more than one rock on their yarn.

4. ***Rocky Walls.*** Before children participate, create, on mural paper, a stone wall by drawing the outline of individual rocks, each measuring approximately eight by eleven inches. Include at least one outline for each child in your class. Leave some space between the rocks to represent mortar. (Figure 16.2) Hang the mural so children can easily reach all of it. On a table, provide construction paper of various colors (tan, gray, white, black, brown, pink, salmon, and green) on which you have drawn "rock" shapes. It helps if these are approximately the same size and shape as those on the mural. Children will need scissors, markers, chalk, glitter, paper scraps, and glue. Reference books illustrating various kinds of rocks will also be useful. Tell children that each of them will have a chance to create his or her own rock from the materials provided. Prompt children's interest by asking open-ended questions, such as: What kind of rock would you like to try to draw? How might that rock look? How will you make your rock look like that? Once children have created rocks that suit them, they can find spots

for them on the "wall." Glue them in place and, in the mortar, identify the owners by name.

Language

1. *Shake, Rattle, and Roll!* With the children, make rock shakers using empty cardboard or plastic juice cans with lids. Set out bowls filled with fine sand, coarse sand, and pebbles. Label each bowl accordingly. Instruct the children to choose one kind of rock material to put in their containers. Let them decide whether to use a small or large amount. Once this is done, tape the lids on securely. Label the side of each can with the name of the material inside. Encourage the children to experiment with moving the cans in a variety of ways to produce sounds. They might shake them lightly, slowly, or quickly or roll the cans between their hands. Ask them to describe the sounds they make.

2. *Secret Stones.* Put a collection of rocks in a feely box. Invite the children to insert their hands into the box and feel the contents. As each child does this, describe one or two rock attributes, directing the child to search for one that fits your description. "Find a rock that is small and smooth." After the child has chosen a rock, allow him or her to take the rock out of the box and examine it.

3. *Standing Stones.* Present the children with a large and varied array of rocks. Have them carefully examine the rocks and ask each child to choose a favorite to contribute to a permanent classroom collection. For each specimen, write on a card the name of the "geologist" who found it and a dictated (or child-written) description including the characteristics of the rock and any special reason the child picked it. Work with the children to glue each rock and its accompanying information to a large piece of tagboard. Display this collection in a prominent classroom location.

4. *Stone Soup.*
   General Purpose: For children to practice listening for content, detail, sequence, and sounds in a story.

TFPs: 1, 8, 25.

Materials: Large, heavy cooking pot; hot plate or stove; five or six each of potatoes, carrots, and small cooking onions; salt; water; large spoon or ladle; source of water to wash hands and vegetables, and obtain water for soup-making; large stone; soupbone (any meat bone will do); adult-use-only paring knife and a few knives that are designed for safe use by children; bowls and spoons. Obtain a version of the story *Stone Soup.* A good one is available by Ann McGovern (Scholastic Press, 1968). Refer to it for other possible ingredients; stick as closely to the story as possible when gathering your materials.

Procedure:

a. Place the whole, raw vegetables and other ingredients in a paper bag. Bring the bag, along with the cooking pot and stone, to a large-group area.

b. Gather the children in a group. Show them the book *Stone Soup* and tell them that you have a wonderful story to read to them, and that the story will also teach them to make a wonderful food. Tell the children to watch and listen carefully to what happens in the story, and to remember what ingredients they will need to make stonesoup. Point out this word on the book's cover.

c. Read the story through, emphasizing the names of foods. Point out that all the women had to offer, at first, was water and a stone. After reading this story about a clever boy who finds a way to encourage others to share, tell the children that they will have a chance to make stonesoup today.

d. Hold up your big cooking pot. Tell the children that you will now pretend to be the boy in the story and that you will ask each of them to help make soup. First, pretend to ask for a stone, and, changing your voice to represent an old woman, offer one and drop it in the pot. If your version of the story has a repeating refrain throughout, say it: "Imagine that . . . soup from a stone."

e. Pass the bag of ingredients from child to child, inviting each person to take one. (If there are more children than ingredients, cut the items into pieces ahead of time.)

f. Ask children to remember what ingredient went into the soup, after the stone. If no one can recall it, refer back to the book. Move around the group with your pot, asking the children with that ingredient to drop it in. Repeat this step until all ingredients have been offered. Continue to repeat the refrain now and then, encouraging soup from a stone! When children recall ingredients in correct sequence, praise them. When no one recalls an ingredient, refer back to the book, pointing out that they can find the correct answer there.

g. End your group time by telling the children that the pot and ingredients will be moved to a table, and that anyone who wishes to can come over and continue to help with the soup. Invite some children to carry cups or pitchers of water to the pot. Others can scrub and/or cut up vegetables, or add seasonings. The soup must be cooked at a low boil for about forty-five minutes before the vegetables will soften. If your session is too short to allow eating it the same day, refrigerate and serve it the next.

How to Simplify this Activity:

• Make a pot of soup ahead of time, using the same ingredients. Carry out the activity as above, through step f. Tell the children that you have made the soup for them, because it takes so long, and that they have begun to make a pot for you. They can eat your soup today and you will eat their soup later.

• To make this an even shorter and easier activity, simply read the story, and then invite children to tell it back to you, in round-robin fashion, recalling the ingredients. Again, refer back to the book for help in recalling. Point out the pictures to prompt children's memories. Repeat the refrain together each time it appears.

How to Extend this Activity:

• Older children could use carrot peelers to remove skins from potatoes and carrots, as a fine-motor exercise. They could also use measuring spoons and cups to determine quantities of ingredients as they add them.

• Invite parents to join you at the end of your class session for a soup-tasting party! Encourage the children to tell their moms and dads the *Stonesoup* story and describe how they made their own stonesoup.

Physical

1. *Dig a Hole.* Preface this activity if possible by reading the Scottish tale *Deep Down Underground* by Olivier Dunrea. Point out all the creatures and objects found underground. Take the children outdoors and find a place where they can dig, such as in a sandbox or a nongrassy area. Give the children shovels. Tell them to dig a deep hole. As they dig, encourage them to look for rocks and underground treasures, then gather these to be studied indoors.

2. *Chalk Walk.* White chalk and dark, solid-colored socks are needed for this activity. Make several chalk marks on a cemented area. (Figure 16.3) Establish start and finish points. Instruct children to slip a pair of socks over their shoes and to walk, hop, jump, or run from one end of the "course" to the other without getting any chalk on their socks. When they reach the end, have the children sit down and look at the bottoms of their socks to determine whether they made it through the course without touching the chalky places.

3. *Cross the River.* Prior to the children's arrival, make a river out of two parallel strips of blue tape or two jump ropes placed about two feet apart on the floor. Or, draw two lines in a sandbox. Create "rocks" in the river bed from brown paper circles taped to the floor, or use flat stones in the sand outside. At first, encourage children to step from stone to stone to get from one side, or end, of the river to the other. Then have them try jumping with

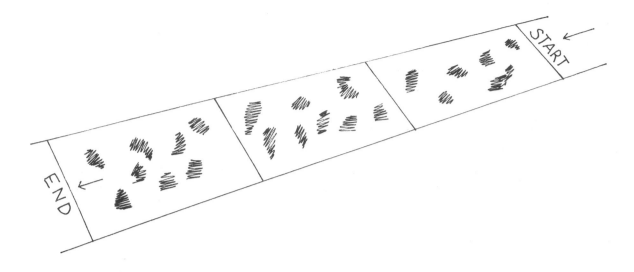

Figure 16.3 *Chalk on the Sidewalk Makes a Challenging Game*

both feet from stone to stone. Finally, introduce leaping (one foot lands at a time) as a way to cross the river. Gradually remove some of the rocks or widen the river to increase the physical challenge and maintain children's interest in the game. (Figure 16.4)

4. ***Stone Mosaics.***

General Purpose: For children to gain practice in coordinating finger, finger-thumb, and eye-hand movements.

TFPs: 8, 25, 31, 32.

Materials: Natural gravel or pebbles; white glue in small squeeze bottles; premade designs, such as a flower, house, or outdoor mountain scene, on poster board; newspaper to cover the table.

Procedure:

a. Ask children to sort the gravel by size and color before using it to create mosaics.

b. Cover a table with newspaper.

c. Give the children a selection of premade outlines from which to choose. Invite them to pick one with which to make a design.

d. Show children how to put dots of glue on the designs in the spots they would like to place pebbles.

e. Then encourage them to put pebbles on the glue.

f. Once children indicate that their mosaics are complete, find a flat place to put

them until the glue has dried. Then display the children's work prominently around the room.

Hint for Success:

• Use gravel or pebbles that vary widely in color to add interest to the activity.

How to Simplify this Activity:

• Provide larger pebbles and simpler designs, such as single circles, squares, or triangles.

How to Extend this Activity:

• Show children pictures of mosaics or visit a building where such works are displayed. Draw children's attention to the placement of the individual stones.

• Invite children to plan and draw their own designs prior to gluing the pebbles in the lines.

• Ask children to use tweezers to pick up and place their rocks.

Social

1. ***Your Weight in Stones.*** In some countries, a stone is a unit of measurement (one stone equals fourteen pounds). Allow the children to work cooperatively with this idea by setting up a simple scale. Securely attach a small wooden crate or sturdy plastic

Figure 16.4 *Cross the Rocky Riverbed*

basket to one end of a small seesaw. In a separate container, place several rocks about three inches each in diameter. Try to use rocks that are approximately the same size and weight. Show the children how to work together to weigh themselves. While one child sits on the open end of the seesaw, the other child places rocks in the crate. Once the crate of rocks balances with the child, have an adult hold onto the rock container while the child who was weighed gets down. Encourage both children to count the rocks, record the results, and then reverse roles. Verbally praise the children's cooperative efforts.

2. *Hot Lava.* This game is a rock rendition of Hot Potato. Following discussion of volcanoes and the formation of igneous rocks, use a small piece of real lava (or a beanbag to represent lava) as the prop for this game. Direct the children to sit in a circle. Tell them to pass the "hot lava" quickly from person to person, taking care not to get "burned" by the lava, or to let the lava drop on the floor. Play music with a relatively fast tempo while the lava is going around. Periodically clap your hands as a signal to reverse the direction in which the lava is passed.

This game is played most easily with about ten children so no one has to wait very long before getting a turn. If the group is larger, divide it in two and proceed with two circles passing lava simultaneously.

3. *Caring for Our Environment.* Read *The Mountain* by Robert Parnall to the children during the rock unit. After they are familiar with the story, gather a small group together. Explain that this book is about a problem; the children's job is to listen to the whole story, then figure out what the problem is. Read the book. Afterward, turn to the page that shows the characters who wanted to keep the mountain just as it was. Encourage the children to identify the problem by asking "What happened after the mountain was made into a park?" Summarize the children's comments and compare the first page of the story with the last. Ask the children to generate a solution. Invite them to rewrite the end of the story, considering ways people could visit the mountain without destroying it. Encourage the children to illustrate their own written or dictated stories. As a follow-up to this activity, accompany children outside on a "litter walk" during which they care for school grounds by picking up trash and disposing of it.

TEACHER RESOURCES

Field Trip Ideas

1. Take your class to visit a museum. Science museums or natural history museums often have rock or gem collections that your class could examine.

2. Visit an art museum or gallery. Visit a museum in which rocks have been used in artwork such as sculptures, mosaics, or landscape paintings.
3. Visit a rock store. Arrange in advance for the children to look at as well as touch rocks. Also ask that a store worker give a simple explanation of the rocks, including where they were found and possibly how they were formed.
4. In warmer weather, go to a local beach to observe and collect rocks and play in the sand.
5. Arrange to visit a stone quarry or gravel pit to observe people digging up stones.
6. Many building supply stores have large inventories of rocks. Take the children to look at the variety of rocks available for building and learn about how they are actually used.

Classroom Visitors

1. Invite a rock specialist from a museum to bring a collection of rocks to show to the children and discuss their particular characteristics.
2. Request that a jeweler demonstrate care of gemstones and possibly how to make simple jewelry from stones or pebbles.
3. Ask a stone polisher to show the children examples of unpolished and polished stones. In addition, ask the visitor to show children ways rocks are polished.
4. Invite a sculptor to display his or her work and to show children tools used and some fundamental sculpting techniques.

Children's Books

Aliki. *Fossils Tell of Long Ago*. New York: Harper and Row, 1972.

Arvetis, C. *What Is a Mountain?* New York: Checkerboard Press, 1987.

Bartlett, M. F. *The Clean Brook*. New York: Crowell, 1960.

Baylor, B. *Before You Came This Way*. New York: Dutton, 1969.

———. *Everybody Needs a Rock*. New York: Macmillan, 1985.

Baylor, B., and P. Parnall. *If You Are a Hunter of Fossils*. New York: Scribner's, 1980.

Branley, F. M. *Volcanoes*. New York: Harper and Row, 1985.

Carrick, C. *The Climb*. Boston: Houghton Mifflin, 1980.

Cole, S. *When the Tide is Low*. New York: Lothrop, Lee and Shepard, 1985.

Dunrea, O. *Deep Down Underground*. New York: Macmillan, 1989.

Fuchshuber, A. *From Dinosaurs to Fossils*. Minneapolis: Carolrhoda, 1981.

Gans, R. *Rock Collecting*. New York: Harper and Row, 1984.

Hendershot, J. *In Coal Country*. New York: Knopf, 1987.

McGovern, A. *Stone Soup*. New York: Scholastic, 1968.

Mitgutsch, A. *From Ore to Spoon*. Minneapolis: Carolrhoda, 1981.

Parnall, P. *The Mountain*. New York: Doubleday, 1971.

Roberts, A. *Fossils*, Chicago: Childrens Press, 1983.

Adult References

Bill, P., and D. Wright. *Rocks and Minerals*. New York: Macmillan, 1985.

Chesterman, C. W. *The Audubon Society Field Guide to North American Rocks and Minerals*. New York: Knopf, 1978.

Cipriani, C., and A. Borelli. *Simon and Schuster's Guide to Gems and Precious Stones*. New York: Simon and Schuster, 1986.

Rhodes, F. H. T. *Geology*. New York: Golden, 1972.

Ritter, R. *Rocks and Fossils*. New York: Franklin Watts, 1977.

Shuttlesworth, D. *The Story of Rocks*. New York: Doubleday, 1977.

Symes, R. F., and the staff of the Natural History Museum, London. *Rocks and Minerals*. New York: Knopf, 1988.

Chapter 17

Machines

Machines! Large or small, simple or complex, noisy or quiet, working or broken; there is no denying that we live in a world filled with machines. For good or ill, machines have always resulted from humankind's ingenuity and an increasing desire to exert greater control over the environment. Even in young children, exposure to machines stimulates a sense of wonder and feelings of mastery.

Children notice machines early in life and have strong emotional reactions to them. Infants are fascinated by the moving blades of an overhead fan, are soothed by the ticking of a clock, and may be startled by the unexpected whir of the vacuum cleaner. As youngsters mature, they are intrigued by how things work and want to know more about the mechanical objects they see day after day. Movement and sound still capture their attention, but their interest is sustained by curiosity about hidden parts and the prohibitions adults establish regarding appropriate use and safety. For all these reasons, most children ages three and beyond thoroughly enjoy the study of machines.

PURPOSE

For some early childhood professionals, the prospect of teaching about machines is an exciting one. They can envision numerous possibilities for classroom activities and anticipate intriguing discussions with children. However, other teachers find machines an intimidating topic—one they think is too dry or too difficult to explain. This negative reaction often comes about because they do not understand how machines work, or how to relate mechanical principles to children's experiences in everyday life.

This unit on machines has been designed with the latter concerns in mind. We have worked from the understanding that all complex machines are made up of combinations of the six simple ones (wheel and axle, wedge, lever, pulley, screw, inclined plane). It is our premise that lack of experience with and understanding of simple machines makes it impossible to accurately comprehend the more complex variety. Moreover, we have found that, generally, children can discover, create,

and control simple machines with minimal adult help or prohibitions. Consequently, the study of simple machines seems an excellent starting point for children and teachers alike.

The activities supporting the theme focus on identifying what the six simple machines look like, how they work on their own, and how they work together in complex machines. In addition, children will have many opportunities to experience how work can be done more easily with the aid of machines. At all times, the emphasis is on active child-exploration and self-discovery. Thus, most activities focus on the function of machines rather than on terminology.

IMPLEMENTATION

To facilitate the teacher's planning and children's understanding, we recommend that you incorporate the following instructional sequence into your approach to the unit.

Provide individual introductions to each simple machine by focusing on one machine a day.

1. Show the machine to the children. Label the machine and give information about its structure, function, and use. Demonstrate how the machine works.
2. Show the children other examples of the same simple machine. For instance, when discussing the wheel, present a wheel and axle, a doorknob, and a clock gear.
3. Have the children identify the machine in a collection of similar items, finding, for instance, the wheels and axles among objects such as a toy car or truck, a doorknob, a ball, and a paper circle.
4. Show the children a group of items, some that represent the machine under study, and some that do not. Ask the children to identify which items are *not* the machine.
5. Have the children find examples of the machine in the classroom, outside, or at home. On a subsequent day, show the children the original machine; ask them to label it and to tell how the machine is used.

Consider following this Machines unit with a theme that describes more fully the complex machines children see around them.

Such a unit could explore in greater detail the notion of parts and wholes, or human energy versus other forms of energy to power machines, or it could concentrate on additional safety issues. The unit on vehicles included in this book would offer another way to expand upon children's interest in machines.

TERMS, FACTS, AND PRINCIPLES

General Information

1. A machine is a nonliving thing that is used to do work.
2. Work is a force that causes change in the placement or form of an object.
3. There are many machines in the world.
4. Machines have different functions.
5. People cause machines to work.
6. People can stop or start the work of machines.
7. People invent machines to make work easier or faster.
8. The simple machines are the wheel, the pulley, the lever, the inclined plane, the wedge, and the screw.
9. One or more of the simple machines are combined to make other machines.
10. Machines cannot work by themselves; they need people or some kind of power (heat, air, water, wind, chemicals, electricity, or animals such as elephants, horses, dogs, bulls, or donkeys) to make them do their work.

The Wheel and Axle

11. The wheel is a round object on a flat rim on which it can balance, or against which it can engage another surface.
12. A wheel becomes a simple machine when it can turn around an axle inserted through its center.
13. A wheel makes it easier to move objects from place to place or to move parts of an object, one against another.
14. Some machines that use wheels to do their work are tricycles, wagons, roller skates, doorknobs, clock or watch gears, robots, cogs, automobiles, trucks, tractors, and vacuum machines.

The Pulley

15. A pulley consists of a wheel with a grooved rim in which a rope is fitted. As the rope is drawn (pulled), the wheel turns.
16. A pulley makes it easier to raise and lower objects.
17. Sometimes a pulley is used to pull an object sideways, from place to place (in mining for example).
18. Some machines that use pulleys to do their work are flagpoles, elevators, clotheslines, drapery rods, boat rigging, wells, and winches.

The Lever

19. A lever consists of a rigid length of some material that rests on a fulcrum.
20. A fulcrum is a support piece on which a lever tilts in raising or moving something.
21. Applying force at one end of the rigid length of a lever produces movement at the other end.
22. The rigid length of a lever must rest upon a fulcrum to work.
23. Changing the placement of the fulcrum changes the amount of work produced by its lever (its "leverage").
24. Some machines that use levers to do their work are seesaws, one-piece can openers, crowbars, balance scales, tire irons, hinged nutcrackers, and scissors.

The Inclined Plane

25. An inclined plane is any slanted surface.
26. Inclined planes make it easier to slide or roll an object from one level to another.
27. The degree of incline of a plane changes its effectiveness.
28. Some machines that use inclined planes to do their work are slides, ramps, stairways, and wedges.

Making An Inclined Plane

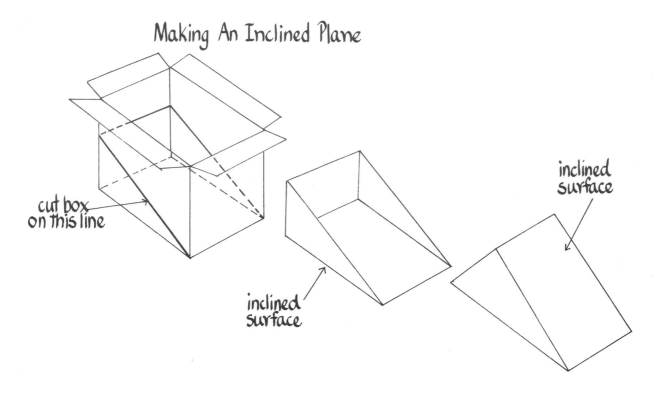

cut box
on this line

inclined
surface

inclined
surface

Figure 17.1 *Use a Box Bottom to Form an Inclined Plane*

The Wedge

29. A wedge consists of more than one inclined plane.

30. Wedges often take the shape of a triangle.

31. Wedges that taper sharply are used for cutting.

32. Wedges that taper less sharply are used for prying or holding edges apart.

33. Some machines that use wedges to do their work are axes, knives, screwdrivers, carpenter's planes, and needles.

The Screw

34. A screw is an inclined plane wrapped around a column.

35. A screw is used to fasten two things together, to gouge a hole, or to exert pressure on a surface.

36. The grooved edges of a screw increase its effectiveness.

37. Some machines that use screws to do their work are light bulbs, drills, pepper mills, food grinders, cranked nutcrackers, jars, and pencil sharpeners.

ACTIVITY IDEAS

Aesthetics

1. *Painting with Wheels and Gears.* Provide a variety of wheels, gears, and paint for making prints at the art table.

2. *Whirring Wonders.* Provide children with one or more of the following items: spinning tops or gyroscopes, music boxes in which the gears are visible, water wheels through which to pour sand or water, and eggbeaters. In each case, point out the movement of the gears, wheels, and axles as children enjoy trying and watching the objects. Emphasize children's pleasure in using such machines.

3. *Modeling Dough with Wedges.* Encourage the children to sculpt modeling dough

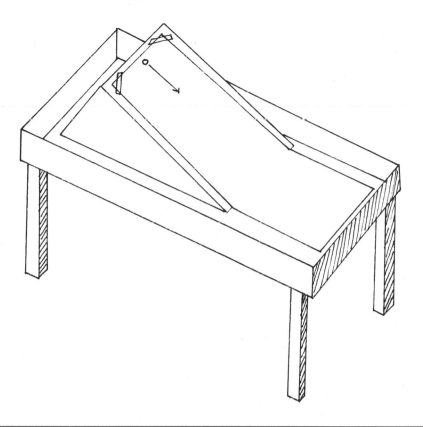

Figure 17.2 *A Water Table Makes a Good Place to Try Out the Incline*

using wedges. Provide plastic knives, tooth-picks, and scissors for them to use.

4. ***Marble Painting on an Inclined Plane.***

General Purpose: For children to derive pleasure from an art form using a simple machine.

TFPs: 25, 26.

Materials: An inclined plane (the bottom of a box about 8 inches wide, 15 inches long, 4 inches tall) (Figure 17.1); water table lined with newspaper; long precut strips of paper (8-by-24 inches) to cover and extend beyond the bottom of the inclined plane; tape; marbles; liquid tempera paint in three or four different colors; small pie tins to hold paint and four or five marbles per color; newspaper.

Procedure:

a. Line the water table with newspaper. If a water table is not available, cover a table or large area of floor with newspaper. Also cover a long rectangular unit block with newspaper and place it twelve inches beyond the base of the inclined plane to stop the marbles.

b. Place the inclined plane in the water table (or on the prepared surface) within the protected area.

c. Using the tape, attach a long piece of paper to the inclined plane extending it beyond the plane. If this is done on the table or floor, place the "blockade" at the end of the paper. (Figure 17.2)

d. Roll the marbles in the paint.

e. Invite the children to place a marble at the top of the inclined plane and let go. The marble will roll down the paper leaving a trail of paint. Ask the children to retrieve the marbles each time, placing them in the appropriate pie tin. Children may repeat this process several times with different colors of paint.

Hint for Success:

- Give children marbles to practice rolling down the inclined plane before starting to paint. Identify the inclined plane for the children.

How to Simplify this Activity:

- Use larger marbles or small balls. (Small, hard rubber balls or old tennis balls would be easier for the children to pick up.)
- Use one color of paint.

How to Extend this Activity:

- Increase and/or decrease the angle of inclination of the plane.
- Measure the distance the marble rolls as it goes down the plane inclined at various angles.

Affective

1. *Simple Machines from Home.* Ask each child to bring a simple machine from home to show the class. This activity would be appropriate to do after the children had already received information in school about simple machines. Provide some hints to parents about simple machines and the common objects that contain them.
2. *Working with Machines.*
   General Purpose: For children to master using machines.
   TFPs: 11–37.
   Materials:

   - Pulleys: several pulleys in various sizes; thin rope or heavy string to attach to pulleys; objects to attach to pulleys to lift (toy cars, small weights); structure to support pulleys. If pulleys are not available, use empty thread spools with small dowels as axles.
   - Levers: balance scale with weights; seesaw; baseball and bat; pliers; nutcracker with nuts; tongs with items to pick up; scissors with something to cut; claw hammer for removing nails from a board.
   - Wheel and Axle: doorknobs; toy vehicles; a pile of books and dowels to place

underneath to move it; roller skates; crank-type pencil sharpener with pencils to sharpen; waterwheels in the water table.
   - Inclined Plane: various lengths of flat boards with unit blocks; triangular-shaped unit blocks and triangular-shaped hollow blocks; playground slides; sleds on a hill in the snow.
   - Wedges: plastic needles with yarn and burlap; scissors with paper to cut; knives to cut modeling dough.
   - Screw: pepper mills with pepper to grind; food grinders with food (apples to make applesauce, for instance).

   Procedure:
   a. Provide the children with a choice of the above materials throughout their study of machines. Incorporate them in different activity areas indoors and outside. Allow the children time to explore, practice, and experiment with each machine.
   b. Encourage the children to talk about the simple machines when they use them and what they are doing to make them work.

Hint for Success:

- Introduce one set of simple machine tasks in a day. Focus on "The Simple Machine of the Day" by introducing the machine in a large-group time and giving the children a variety of ways they could use that type of machine throughout the day.

How to Simplify this Activity:

- Give a child a simple job to do with a specific machine. Describe how the use of the machine could help to get the task done.

How to Extend this Activity:

- Give the child an opportunity to do a task without a simple machine. After the child has attempted to do the task without the machine, have the child choose a machine that he or she thinks would be appropriate for the job. Have the child use the machine to attempt to do the task again and compare both attempts.

3. ***Machine Experts.*** Each day select one of the machines identified in the activity above. Teach one or more children how to use it by labeling the machine and its parts, demonstrating how it works, and allowing children to practice working with it. Designate the child(ren) as machine expert(s) for the day with a special name tag and by telling classmates that if they want to use the machine, they can ask the expert(s) for directions on how it works. Extend this activity by helping the expert(s) prepare a manual for the machine. Children can dictate directions and/or draw pictures to illustrate its use.

4. ***Using Simple Machines to Make a Salad.***
   General Purpose: For children to derive pleasure from doing work.

   TFP: 31.

   Materials: Wedges—plastic knives and vegetable peelers; vegetables such as lettuce, cucumbers, broccoli, carrots, cauliflower, tomatoes, green peppers, avocados; cutting boards; large salad bowl.

   Procedure:
   a. Place cutting boards on a table. Put a variety of vegetables on the table in the children's view. Keep knives and peelers out of the children's reach until they are ready to cut.
   b. Introduce the activity to the children by labeling the vegetables and asking each child to choose one he or she would like to prepare. After the children choose, say, "We can use simple machines to get the vegetables ready for the salad." Show the children the knife and a vegetable peeler and point out that both are wedges. Demonstrate each and ask children to select which wedge they want to use.
   c. Guide children as they cut or peel.
   d. After the vegetables are prepared, serve the salad for the next meal or snack.

Hints for Success:
- Ask children to bring in a favorite vegetable from home. Tell parents the vegetable should be one their child will be able to cut.
- Limit the number of children doing the activity to four or five.

- Parboil the hard vegetables, such as carrots, cauliflower, and broccoli, before the children begin the activity, so that the vegetables will cut more easily.
- Halve carrots lengthwise so that they won't roll as the children cut.

How to Simplify this Activity:
- Use plastic knives with "softer" vegetables that are easier to cut, such as cucumbers, lettuce, or green peppers.

How to Extend this Activity:
- Before bringing out the knives and vegetable peelers, have children try to prepare the vegetables without "simple machines."

Cognition
1. ***Rolling Objects on Inclined Planes.*** Roll toy cars and cylinders down ramps at varying angles of inclination. Compare the movement of the objects down the different ramps. Also, try rolling objects with no wheels, such as a block or a vehicle with no wheels. Discuss with children the differences between how wheeled and wheel-less objects move. Consider graphing the results to provide a visible comparison.
2. ***Moving Fulcrum.*** Experiment with moving the fulcrum point on a seesaw. Invite the children to predict how moving the fulcrum will affect the riders.
3. ***Comparing Nails and Screws.*** Attach two wooden objects with nails and then try to pull the objects apart. Repeat the procedure with screws. Have the children compare which were more difficult to take apart.
4. ***Machine Search.*** Find and count the simple machines in your room. (You could suggest that children also do this at home with their parents.)
5. ***Simple Machines within Complex Machines.*** Observe a complex machine such as a phonograph, steam shovel, vacuum cleaner, or fan. Identify and count the number of simple machines within the complex machine. For example, in a phonograph, the arm of the phonograph is a lever; the needle of the phonograph is a wedge; and the turntable operates as a wheel and axle.

6. *Sing a Song about Work with Simple Machines.* Sing this song that describes the functions of simple machines.

This is the Way We Work with Simple Machines
(Tune: "Here We Go Round the Mulberry Bush"; Words: Grace Spalding)
This is the way we split a log, split a log, split a log.
This is the way we split a log, with a wedge.

This is the way we open a can, open a can, open a can.
This is the way we open a can, with a lever.

This is the way we roll a wheelbarrow, roll a wheelbarrow, roll a wheelbarrow.
This is the way we roll a wheelbarrow, with a wheel and axle.

This is the way we pull out a nail, pull out a nail, pull out a nail.
This is the way we pull out a nail, with a lever.

This is the way we move furniture, move furniture, move furniture.
This is the way we move furniture, up an inclined plane.

This is the way we hold toys together, hold toys together, hold toys together.
This is the way we hold toys together, with a screw.

This is the way we lift heavy things, lift heavy things, lift heavy things.
This is the way we lift heavy things, with a pulley.

Have children think of additional jobs that can be done with the aid of simple machines and incorporate these into a song.

7. *Sliding on a Changing Surface.*
General Purpose: For children to practice problem-solving skills.
TFPs: 1–8, 25–28.
Materials: Slide (indoor or outdoor play equipment); scrap of soft fabric about 15 inches square (a diaper or baby blanket); scrap of rubberized material about 15 inches square (perhaps a piece of an air mattress); 15-inch-square scrap of vinyl tablecloth with flannel backing; waxed paper; tinfoil.
Procedure:
a. Invite children to join you in some experiences with inclined planes. Direct them toward the slide.
b. Ask the children to share some ideas about the way a slide works. Then say, "Tell me which simple machine is a slide."
c. Have the children examine the collection of materials you've brought to the slide. Allow them a few minutes of unstructured looking and touching.
d. Ask children to predict what might happen if they sit on a rubber surface as they attempt to slide.
e. Encourage someone to try; direct them to sit on the rubber square and push off gently.
f. Ask someone to explain what happened. Introduce the next surface and again ask for a prediction. Ask if the children think a soft fabric will cause them to slide more slowly or more quickly.
g. Try and discuss all the materials.

Hint for Success:
• Identify safety guidelines for going down the slide, such as going down frontward and waiting to go down until the person ahead is off the slide.

How to Simplify this Activity:
• Compare how children's clothing affects movement down the slide. For example, compare a snowsuit compared with cloth pants; a dark-colored snowsuit with a light-colored snowsuit; a wet bathing suit with a dry bathing suit.

How to Extend this Activity:
• Direct children to sit on the slide with knees bent and feet flat against the slide's surface. Compare sliding with rubber soles to sliding with soft socks. End the activity by ordering ease of sliding on various surfaces from easiest to hardest. Lay the materials in a row to show the order.

Construction

1. *Create Seesaws.* Provide children with triangular blocks and long planks so they can build their own seesaws (levers).
2. *Making Pulleys.* Provide children with short, thin dowels (about 5 by $\frac{3}{16}$ inches), empty thread spools and two- to three-inch lengths of thin rope or heavy string. Show them how to make a pulley by putting the dowel through the spool. Support the dowel ends with a block structure (of each child's design). Put the string over the spool and tie something to be lifted to one end of it. Pull the opposite end.

Language

1. *Wheel Experience Story.* Give the children opportunities to tell stories about experiences they have had with wheels on vehicles or on toys they have used.
2. *Picture Description.* Display pictures in the classroom of machines in factories or doing road construction. Have children identify the simple machines they recognize and describe how the machines work.
3. *Write Repair Tickets and Telephone Messages.* In the pretend play area, provide children with paper and pencils to use for pretend writing. Make repair tickets for the repair shop so the children will be able to fill them out. Have a pad of paper by the telephone for messages. Encourage children to create lists of items that are needed from the hardware store to replenish the repair shop's supplies.
4. *Message Machine.*

   General Purpose: To demonstrate to the children the use of machines in communicating ideas and messages to others.

   TFPs: 1–18.

   Materials: Open-weave plastic berry boxes *or* margarine tubs with holes punched in the sides; heavy string or lightweight rope; two blocks of wood; two pulleys (available in hardware stores); paper, pencils, and markers; tables; nails and hammer or screws and screwdriver.

   Procedure:

   a. Invite children to help you build a message center. First, find two vertical, flat surfaces in the room across from each other approximately eight feet apart. Attach one pulley (using nails, screws, or twine) to each surface about three feet above the floor. Direct the children to thread string or rope through the two pulleys, then through two holes in each side of a basket. Tie the two ends of the line together, positioning the knot *inside* the basket so that the rope can move easily through the pulleys.

   b. Place a small table and two or three chairs near each pulley. Provide paper, pencils, and markers at each table. (Figure 17.3)

   c. Invite children to experiment with the pulley, drawing on the rope in one direction and then the other. To be successful, the basket should move freely back and forth across the space.

   d. Inform the children that the machine they've helped to construct will be used to send messages. Children can write or draw a message on paper, fold it, and place it in the basket. They can then send it to a child at the other end of the line.

   e. Encourage the child on the receiving end to remove the first message and replace it with one of his or her own. Ask the children to tell you how the message is able to travel. Can the message machine work on its own?

Hint for Success:

- Place the message line close to a wall or in an area where no one will accidentally walk into it.

How to Simplify this Activity:

- Set up the message machine before the children arrive. Prepare a few messages for the children to send, such as Valentine's Day cards, birthday cards, or friendship cards.

How to Extend this Activity:

- Talk about other machines that are used for sending messages: telephones, facsimile machines, mail trucks, radios and televisions, and sometimes even robots.
- Talk about simple machines in use at your message center: wheels, pulleys,

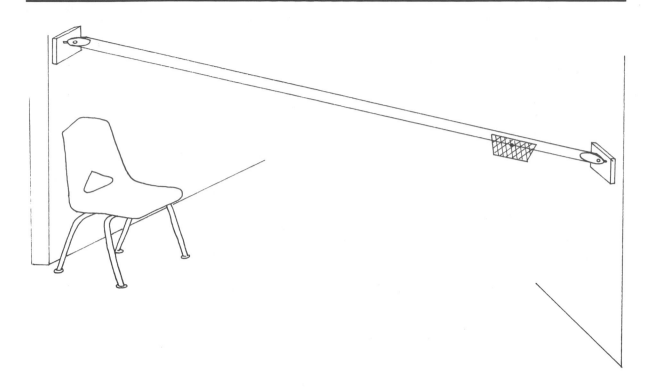

Figure 17.3 *Message Machine Using a Set of Pulleys*

perhaps screws. Look for the axle in the pulley's wheel.

Physical

1. *Painting with Brayers.* In printing, a brayer is a hard roller used to spread ink. It consists of a rubber roller (wheel) that spins on a metal rod (axle) that is connected to a handle. Give each child a brayer. Allow them ample time to experiment with the movement of the roller and the axle on a table. Discuss the action of the wheel and axle as the children roll the brayers. Next, show them how to dip and roll the brayer in a shallow pan of liquid tempera paint and then roll it on paper. Invite them to try.

2. *Wagon Pulling.* Give children wagons with wheels, and boxes or wagons without wheels to pull. Then fill each with unit blocks to emphasize how wheels and axles can make work easier.

3. *Woodworking with Simple Machines.* Point out simple machines at the workbench: nails (wedge), hammer (lever), hand

drill (screw, wheel and axle), C-clamp (screw), saw (wedge). Consult the following guidelines to promote children's appropriate use of each tool.

Wood:
- Choose soft wood for children to work with. Pine is an excellent choice. Avoid oak, birch, and most fruitwoods because they are too hard for children to hammer or saw successfully.
- Avoid all pressure-treated wood (commonly called "wolmanized" lumber) because toxic chemicals are used to treat it.
- Secure wood to the workbench in a vise, or clamp it to another larger object to make it stable as children attempt to drill, cut, or hammer.

Hammers and Nails:
Hammers come in a wide variety of types and weights. Typical household hammers weigh about sixteen ounces. Choose ones that weigh slightly less, but are not so light that children will have difficulty driving

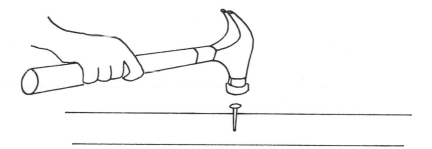

Figure 17.4 *After Setting a Nail, Pound Hard to Drive It into the Wood*

the nail. Use "common" nails. These come in a variety of lengths and diameters and have a large head that is easier for children to strike. Avoid using special-purpose nails such as roofing and finish nails. These have tiny heads, and they bend easily. Show children how to:

- Hold the hammer where it is most comfortable; slightly more of a weight should be at the front end. This allows maximum control. (Figure 17.4)

- Raise the hammer and strike the nail, driving it by the force of the hammer not the force of the arm movement. The object of hammering is not driving the nail fast, but rather striking the nail with the head of the hammer consistently.

- Hold the hammer in the dominant hand while holding the nail with the alternate hand.

- Hold the nail between the thumb and index finger, tapping it gently with small taps until it stands on its own without falling over.

- Continue striking the nail until the head is flush with the wood.

Saws:

Select a small cross-cut saw for children to use. These are saws designed to cut across the wood grain, making cutting easier. Show children how to:

- Make a mark or line on the wood to serve as a cutting guide.
- Rest the saw teeth on the line.

- Hold the saw in the dominant hand with the arm acting as an extension of the saw. (Figure 17.5)

- Place the alternate hand on the wood approximately nine inches away from the saw blade and the cutting line.

- Begin cutting by drawing or pulling the saw toward the body using minimal downward pressure. Next, lift the saw, place it on the line, and repeat the backward pulling motion. Continue this process until a groove has been established.

- Hold the saw with one hand, not two, and keep fingers away from the teeth. Once the initial groove is at the depth of

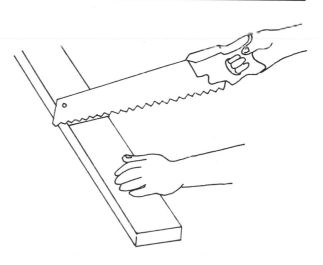

Figure 17.5 *Hold a Saw with One Hand and the Wood with the Other*

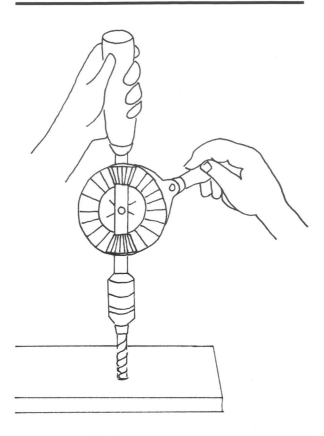

Figure 17.6 *This Hand Drill Requires Two Hands Working Together*

the saw's teeth, proceed with back-and-forth sawing motions.

* Maintain pressure through the backward and forward motion rather than by pushing down on the saw.

Hand drills:

Hand drills are used for making small holes to guide nails or screws. When selecting a hand drill, ask the salesperson to show you how to change the bits in your particular drill. Show children how to:

* Hold the drill with the dominant hand on the crank and the alternate hand on the handle to provide slight pressure. (Figure 17.6)

* Turn the crank in a clockwise direction.

* Keep the drill perpendicular to the drilling surface at all times. This will keep the bit from breaking.

* Exert even, moderate, direct pressure downward with the top hand.

* Turn the crank in a counterclockwise direction while pulling up lightly on the drill when finished.

Brace and Bit:

A brace is used with bits of varying sizes to make large holes in wood. Show children how to:

* Apply direct pressure from the top, down.

* Hold onto the middle handle and move it in a circular motion clockwise so that the blade of the bit cuts into the wood.

* Maintain even, moderate pressure, with the drill perpendicular to the surface on which it is being used. (Figure 17.7)

* Turn the handle counterclockwise and lift gently to remove the bit from the wood.

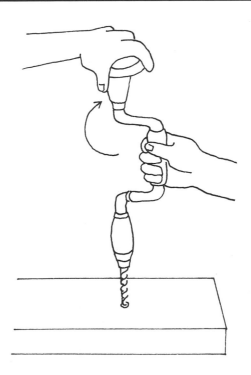

Figure 17.7 *A Brace and Bit Are Often Easier to Use than a Hand Drill*

4. *Cutting Tortillas into Wedge Shapes.* Introduce the activity by showing children an example of a wedge (such as a wedge used for splitting wood). Label the wedge for the children and explain how it is used. Tell the children that they will have the opportunity to cut food into wedgelike shapes. Demonstrate how to cut the tortilla into several wedge shapes. Provide the children with tortillas to cut. Give each child a small knife (plastic or paring knife) and allow them to cut the tortillas. Mention to the children as they are cutting that the knives are also examples of wedges. These tortillas can be eaten raw or can be lightly browned on both sides in a 350° greased skillet.

5. *Exploring Wheelchair Movement.* Obtain a wheelchair (child-sized, if possible) for children to use. Demonstrate how to operate it. Then, allow the children to try. Develop a path for the children to travel in the wheelchair. Include slightly inclined planes for them to go up and down. Talk with the children about which direction is easier or more difficult to navigate. Point out that the wheelchair is an example of a wheel and axle that helps people who cannot walk. Encourage the children to find the wheels and axles on the wheelchair.

6. *Demonstrating Features of the Screw.*
   General Purpose: To provide children with experience in scissor manipulation and pincer grip.

   TFPs: 8, 9, 25, 26, 28, 29, 33.

   Materials: One light-colored 4-by-6-inch rectangle of paper for each child; scissors; ruler; dark marker; thick pencils or broad crayons; large screws; unit block wedge; tape.

   Procedure:
   a. Holding the rectangle with the short side at the top, draw a thick diagonal line from the lower to the upper corner. Give one rectangle to each child to cut along the diagonal.
   b. This will result in two triangles for each child.
   c. Provide each child with a thick pencil or crayon. Demonstrate, direct, or assist children as necessary to wrap a paper "inclined plane" around their pencils. The dark outline will overlap in a spiral around the pencil, resembling the threads of a screw. Use tape to hold the wrapped inclined plane in place.

Hints for Success:
- Before the shape is wrapped, compare it to a unit block wedge. Point out that wedges often look like triangles.
- After wrapping, examine large screws and compare them with the paper and pencil version. Talk about the inclined planes in wedges and screws.

How to Simplify this Activity:
- Rather than having the children carry out the activity themselves, demonstrate it for them to more clearly point out the features of a screw.

How to Extend this Activity:
- Ask the children to draw their own diagonal lines.
- Repeat the activity using triangles of differing shapes and compare the results.

7. *Cutting with Scissors.*
   General Purpose: For children to coordinate finger, finger-thumb, and eye-hand movements.

   TFPs: 19, 20, 21, 24, 31.

   Materials: Left- and right-handed scissors; construction paper in 2-by-8-inch strips; construction paper with predrawn paths; pencils and markers.

   Procedure:
   a. Explain to the children that scissors are examples of wedges. Point out that each pair of scissors has two wedges, and the edges of each wedge are sharp for cutting.
   b. Show the children how to place their fingers in the handle of the scissors, thumb in one hole and middle finger or middle and index fingers in the other.
   c. Instruct the children to open and shut the scissors in the air to practice controlling their movements.

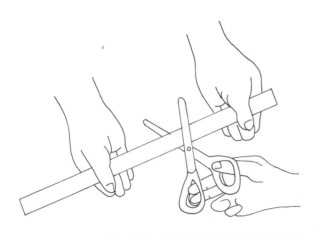

Figure 17.8 *Holding the Paper for the Child Simplifies the Task*

they are cutting along a curved line with an adult holding the paper only when needed.

j. Make available wide curved paths that go first in one direction, then the other.

k. Provide increasingly narrow double-curved paths until children are able to cut along a double-curved line.

l. Give children wide paths that include a corner.

m. Offer increasingly narrow paths with one corner until children are cutting along a line with one corner.

n. Give children wide paths with more than one corner. (Figure 17.10)

o. Next, provide increasingly narrow paths with more than one corner until children are able to cut along the line.

d. Give each child a strip of firm paper. Have them cut the paper into pieces, either with an adult holding the paper, or with the children holding the paper for each other. (Figure 17.8)

e. Provide children with a second strip of paper and show them how to make fringes along the edge, first with an adult holding the paper and then as they hold the paper on their own. Once children can handle both the scissors and the paper at the same time, proceed through the following steps, which are arranged in order from simple to complex.

f. Give children paper on which is drawn a path between two parallel lines approximately two inches apart. Direct each child to cut between the two lines. (Figure 17.9)

g. Provide increasingly narrow, straight paths until children are able to cut along a line with an adult holding the paper only when needed.

h. Offer a wide path with a single curve next, then provide a wide path with a single curve bending in the opposite direction.

i. Finally, give children increasingly narrow, curved paths to cut through until

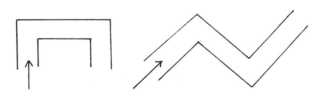

Figure 17.9 *Increasingly Narrower Paths for Cutting Practice*

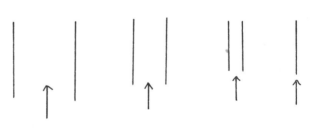

Figure 17.10 *Paths with Corners are More Difficult to Cut*

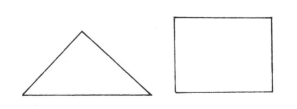

Figure 17.11 *Straight-Sided Enclosed Shapes*

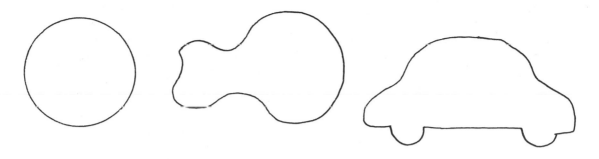

Figure 17.12 *Curve-Sided Enclosed Shapes*

p. Show how to cut along the edges of an enclosed figure. First, provide ones with straight sides and corners. (Figure 17.11)

q. Finally, introduce figures with a continuous curve. (Figure 17.12)

Hints for Success:

• Focus on the first few steps of the above procedure.

• Provide increasingly difficult paths for the children to try over time.

How to Simplify this Activity:

• Ask children to open and shut their hands with thumb and opposing fingers as a way to "quack." (This could be done while singing songs or doing finger plays about ducks.)

• Provide children with kitchen tongs to pick up small objects such as cotton balls or small blocks.

• Show children how to clip clothespins onto the cardboard edges of a box or sturdy plastic containers as a way for them to practice pincer motion.

How to Extend this Activity:

• Provide children with pencils, paper, scissors, stencils, and templates so that they can create their own shapes to cut out.

Pretend Play

1. ***Repair Shops.*** Many different kinds of repair shops can provide the basis for pretend play. The children can work on taking apart and putting together simple machines within complex ones. Possibilities for repair shops include record player and cassette player repair, wheelwright, or clock and watch repair.

2. ***Fruit Stand or Grocery Store.*** Use balance scales to weigh groceries, cash registers (with lever-type motion), grocery carts (wheels and axles), along with a variety of fruits or groceries. Label the machines being used so the children are aware of each one.

3. ***Bicycle Repair Shop.***

   General Purpose: to provide children with opportunities to manipulate and experiment with a variety of machines while engaged in make-believe play.

   TFPs: 1–10, 11–14, 25–28.

   Materials: Large wooden block platforms and ramps, tricycles, ball bearings, wrenches, loose spokes, cogs, and sprockets. (Notify a bicycle shop that you would appreciate a donation of discarded parts saved from repairs. About two weeks' notice should result in an interesting variety of materials.) Shop rags, aprons, telephones, "repair pads," pencils, tables, shelves.

   Procedure:

   a. Set up the area, indoors or out. Arrange large wooden blocks into a repair platform. Place ramps in two or three places. Arrange tools and a variety of bike parts on a table. Place a phone, repair pad, and pencil on another table. Display shop aprons and rags on shelves. Empty oil cans could also be provided.

b. Invite children to enter your bicycle repair shop. Tell them that you need some mechanics to work for you, to repair several broken tricycles. Tell them that someone must also answer the phone and greet other customers with repair needs. Point out the repair tickets (pad).

c. Ask a child to roll a tricycle up a ramp to the repair platform. Help children turn it upside down and rest it on its seat and handlebars. Encourage children to experiment with spinning wheels on axles. Help them examine the tricycle for other moving parts and simple machines. Repeat with other tricycles.

d. Some children may enjoy exploring other parts: cogs, gears, ball bearings, or spokes. Provide one of the above, then ask a child to find one like it on the tricycle. Explain that a trike mechanic first determines which parts are broken, then must find others like them in the shop to use as replacements.

Hints for Success:

• Discuss with children the potential danger of catching fingers in turning wheels and how to use tools in appropriate ways.

How to Simplify this Activity:

• Offer plastic tools rather than real ones for children to use. Omit the ramp and have trikes already upside down ready to be worked on. If possible, secure the trikes so that children will not turn them over and ride them.

How to Extend this Activity:

• Encourage classification and seriation of the materials. For example, ask children to arrange a variety of gears by size so shop employees can find the ones they need more easily, or ask the children to categorize tools by simple machine type as a way to take an inventory. In addition, gears could be placed side by side to see if their teeth will mesh.

Social

1. *Push a Tire with a Friend.* Provide old tires of varying sizes for the children to play with outside. Encourage them to work together to push the tires around the playground.

2. *Slide with a Friend.* Encourage children to hold hands with a friend and slide down a slide together, or to make a "train" and slide. As the children do this, mention that they are using an inclined plane.

3. *Making Applesauce.* To prepare for this activity, wash apples and cut them into quarters. Put them in a pan of water with cinnamon and cook until soft. Show the children a food mill before starting. Point out to the children the wheel and axle that are a part of the food mill. Give each child an opportunity to turn the food mill while it is empty. Have the children put a few apple sections into the top of the food mill. Let them take turns operating the crank. Discard the seeds from inside the mill as necessary. Eat the applesauce at mealtime, discussing the children's cooperative effort and how the applesauce was made.

4. *Let Me Take You Riding.*

   General Purpose: To encourage cooperative experimentation.

   TFPs: 1–14.

   Materials: Sturdy cardboard carton, 2½ feet of rope, scissors or box knife, wagon.

   Procedure:

   a. First create a cardboard box wagon. Prepare a carton by cutting a hole through which the rope can pass snugly. Then tie a large knot on the inside of the carton to secure the rope. Finally, tie another large knot at the end of the rope for a grip.

   b. Set the carton-wagon near a wheeled wagon. Invite a child to choose a partner to pull. Ask the pair which vehicle they think will move most easily: the wagon or the "boxcar." Encourage the children to explain their answers.

   c. Challenge the "puller" to take his or her partner for a ride in each vehicle.

d. Evaluate the earlier prediction. Involve both children (and any spectators, if possible) in a group discussion of the "machines" used. Which was actually easiest to move? Why? How could the boxcar be improved so that it would be more efficient?

Hint for Success:
• Do this activity on a smooth surface such as a sidewalk or linoleum floor.

How to Simplify this Activity:
• Invite a child to choose a friend with whom to ride in the wagon and then in the box. Pull the children yourself.

How to Extend this Activity:
• Talk about when a wagon might move without a person's help (on an inclined plane). If there is a hill available, ask children to compare pulling the wagon and boxcar up and then down the inclined plane. Next enlist children's help to figure out how many people must work to pull the wagon on a level surface. Then compare that number with how many children it takes to pull the wagon up a hill. Repeat this contrast using the "boxcar."

TEACHER RESOURCES

Field Trip Ideas
1. Visit a workplace where machines are being used, such as a hospital, construction site, farm, or restaurant. Go to the site before taking the children to make sure there is enough room for all of them to see from a safe vantage point. Prepare the children for the field trip by reading books about the machines that they will see, showing pictures of the machines and allowing the children to explore child-sized versions of the machines in the classroom. After the field trip, cooperatively write an account of the trip with the children to review what they saw and what each child enjoyed about the visit.

Classroom Visitors
1. Invite a carpenter to come to the classroom to make something with the children that involves the use of several machines. Be sure that the carpenter clearly describes the function of each machine to the children.
2. Have a furniture mover show the children how heavy objects can be moved more easily with the help of levers, wheels and axles, and inclined planes.
3. Have someone come to school during outdoor time to demonstrate how to use a wedge to split a log.
4. Invite the school's custodian or janitor to demonstrate simple machines used in the building, such as the industrial wash bucket on wheels with a lever-type handle for squeezing water out of mops or pulleys in the window shades. (If possible, have your visitor disassemble the window shade mechanism in front of the children to show the pulleys inside.)
5. Invite a person who depends on machines for his or her mobility. Have the person focus the discussion on how machines make his or her life easier and more independent.

Children's Books
Burton, V. L. *Mike Mulligan and his Steam Shovel*. Boston: Houghton Mifflin, 1939.

———. *Katie and the Big Snow*. Boston: Houghton Mifflin, 1943.

Crews, D. *Carousel*. New York: Greenwillow, 1982.

Gibbons, G. *New Road*. New York: Crowell, 1983.

Green Vale School. *Bulldozers, Loaders and Spreaders*. Garden City, NY: Doubleday, 1974.

Hoban, R. *What Does It Do and How Does It Work?* New York: Harper and Row, 1959.

Hoban, T. *Dig, Drill, Dump, Fill*. New York: Greenwillow, 1975.

Horwitz, E. L. *How to Wreck a Building*. New York: Pantheon, 1975.

Krahn, F. *Robot-Bot-Bot*. New York: Dutton, 1979.

Mathieu, J. *The Olden Days*. New York: Random House, 1979.

Peet, B. *Farewell to Shady Glade*. Boston: Houghton Mifflin, 1966.

Provensen, A., and M. Provensen. *Leonardo Da Vinci* . New York: Viking, 1984.

Relf, P. *Big Work Machines*. New York: Golden, 1984.

Rockwell, A., and H. Rockwell. *Machines*. New York: Macmillan, 1972.

Rudolph, M. *The Sneaky Machine*. New York: McGraw-Hill, 1974.

Wilkin, F. *Machines*. Chicago: Childrens Press, 1986.

Adult References

Clarke, D. *The Encyclopedia of How It's Built*. New York: A and W, 1979.

Keen, M. L. *How It Works*. New York: Grosset and Dunlap, 1972.

Macaulay, D. *The Way Things Work*. Boston: Houghton Mifflin, 1988.

Meyer, J. S. *Machines*. New York: World Publishing Company, 1958.

O'Brien, R. *Machines*. New York: Time-Life, 1968.

Schneider, H., and N. Schneider. *Now Try This to Move a Heavy Load: PUSH, PULL AND LIFT*. Boston: Young Scott Books, 1947.

Sharp, E. N. *Simple Machines and How They Work*. New York: Random House, 1959.

Skeen, P. *Woodworking for Young Children*. Washington, DC: National Association for the Education of Young Children, 1984.

Chapter 18

Dinosaurs

.

Teachers tell us that children enjoy the theme dinosaurs because, "Nobody can say 'No' to a dinosaur!" They note that youngsters experience a tremendous sense of power by transforming themselves into these huge creatures who, for a time, were absolute masters of their world. Another way children become empowered is by learning facts that they can use to dazzle adults who often know less than they do about dinosaurs. Children find in dinosaurs two attributes they desire in their own lives: power and prestige. Young children are intrigued by the idea of "monsters" that are real, and at the same time, are reassured that they are no longer a threat. Dinosaurs also offer children opportunities to explore both fact and fiction, to build their capacity for imaginative play and self-expression, and to expand their idea of time. Furthermore, dinosaurs appeal to children's emerging sense of humor as well as to their zest for collecting things. While toy cars, rocks, or stuffed animals are tangible objects that children collect, arrange, rearrange, and display, dinosaur facts, too, become a collection of sorts with which children similarly experiment.

PURPOSE

One fascinating aspect of this theme is that the body of knowledge about dinosaurs is constantly growing. While the terms, facts, and principles gathered for this unit represent the most accurate and up-to-date information available, they will be subject to change as new discoveries are made. There continues to be much controversy regarding dinosaurs. Scientists even disagree about the basic definitions of what dinosaurs were. Therefore, information that is presented in some reference materials is not the same as that contained in others. Consequently, we have made an effort to provide information that reflects scientific differences and to create activities that encourage children to arrive at some of their own conclusions. We hope to lay a foundation for children's continued interest in and curiosity about science-related knowledge and processes.

To support these aims, this unit has three carefully designed aspects that contribute to its child-centered approach. First, the unit includes an extensive collection of facts that are likely to appeal to young children. Second, the unit is designed to offer youngsters a variety of opportunities to use their imaginations, invent their own dinosaurs, and integrate facts into pretending. Finally, the unit provides activities and information describing human behaviors related to dinosaur investigation. Exploring the jobs of paleontologists, geologists, and museum personnel, children can assume roles that are cooperative and nonaggressive. Instead of encouraging children to take on the characteristics of fierce dinosaurs, the activities offer them opportunities to explore dinosaurs in other, socially acceptable ways.

IMPLEMENTATION

This unit may be implemented in several different ways.

Option One: Use a historical approach, selecting activities related to dinosaur life.

Option Two: Focus on present-day discoveries and the excavation of dig sites.

Option Three: Combine the two approaches above to create an extended unit. Designate the first week (or weeks) as "The Time of Dinosaurs." Teachers choosing this option should be careful to remove any human representations (dolls or human-made objects) from the dinosaur area of the classroom to reinforce the notion that there were no people alive when dinosaurs existed. Follow this introduction by another week or two designated as "Today," placing all dinosaur models into a museum setting or in a "dig" to reinforce the idea that there are no dinosaurs alive today. Instead of pretending with dinosaur models during these weeks, play in the classroom could revolve around discovery of fossils, preparation of dig sites, and exploration of dinosaur "remains."

How teachers treat a dinosaur unit depends on their group of children. Because of its abstract nature, this theme is inappropriate for two-year-olds. However, for groups of older children who show interest but have little experience with dinosaur information, the historical approach that centers on addressing simple dinosaur TFPs will be most successful. As children gain experience with the theme, the human aspects of the theme could be introduced. The combination approach will be most successful with groups who show high interest and are ready for the more complex facts about dinosaurs. Follow-ups to the dinosaur unit could be an exploration of rocks, life on earth today, or reptiles and amphibians.

TERMS, FACTS, AND PRINCIPLES

General Information

1. Dinosaurs are animals that lived on Earth a very long time (millions of years) ago.

2. Dinosaurs are the largest animals that ever lived on the land.

*3. The only animal larger than a dinosaur is the blue whale; blue whales still live on our earth.

4. No known dinosaurs live today. They are extinct, that is, they all died.

*5. The earth has changed in many ways since the dinosaurs lived. The shape, size, and location of land masses, the vegetation, and the terrain or land surface are all different than they were when dinosaurs lived.

6. Dinosaurs varied in size. Some were enormous—as tall as a three-story building (Ultrasaurus)—and some were as small as a chicken (Compsognathus).

7. Dinosaurs varied in the way they looked. Some had horns (Triceratops); some had long tails (Apatosaurus and Diplodocus), others had clublike tails (Ankylosaurus); some had rows of bony plates down their backs (Stegosaurus).

8. Some dinosaurs had one brain; others had two: one in the head and one in the base of the spine.

9. No one knows what color dinosaurs were.

10. No one knows what sounds dinosaurs made.

*11. Scientists study the hipbones of dinosaurs and use them to classify all dinosaurs into two main groups: the lizard-hipped dinosaurs (with hips spread apart) and the bird-hipped dinosaurs (with hips close together).

12. Dinosaurs have been given long names that can be fun to say, for example: Tyrannosaurus rex, Megalosaurus, Allosaurus, Apatosaurus, Trachodon, and Pachycephalosaurus.

*13. Many dinosaurs have been called by several different names because more than one scientist discovered the same dinosaur. For example, Apatosaurus and Brontosaurus are names given to the same dinosaur. Apatosaurus is now commonly used as the preferred name because it was discovered and named first.

*14. Dinosaurs lived during three different time periods in the history of our world: an early period (Triassic) about 225 million years ago, a middle period (Jurassic) about 180 million years ago, and a late period (Cretaceous) about 130 million years ago.

*15. Different dinosaurs lived in each time period.

*16. Some people once thought that dinosaurs were cold-blooded animals (that their bodies stayed as warm or cold as the air or water around them), but many scientists now believe that many dinosaurs were warm-blooded (that the heat of their bodies always stayed about the same temperature).

*17. Scientists once thought that all dinosaurs were in the lizard family. Many now believe that they are more closely related to birds.

Dinosaur Behaviors

All scientists do not agree about dinosaur behaviors; however, most scientists believe:

18. Some dinosaurs ate only meat, others ate only plants, and some ate both.

19. Dinosaurs did not eat people because there were no people on earth when the dinosaurs lived.

20. Dinosaurs lived in many different kinds of places on the earth, such as in the forests, on the plains, in the swamps, in the mountains, and in grassy lowlands.

21. Many dinosaurs laid eggs.

22. Some dinosaurs cared for their young after they were hatched.

23. Dinosaurs moved from place to place looking for food.

24. Dinosaurs moved in various ways. Some walked on four feet, some walked on two back legs, some swam in water, and others could fly. (Some scientists believe that true dinosaurs dwelt only on land.)

25. Dinosaurs used various body parts for different things, for example: some dinosaurs had horns (Triceratops) that may have been used for protection; some had long tails (Apatosaurus) that may have been used for balance; some had rows of bony plates down their backs (Stegosaurus) that may have been used for protection; some dinosaurs had large hollow head crests (Parasaurolophus) that may have been used for making sounds to communicate with other dinosaurs.

26. Some dinosaurs were aggressive and started fights with other dinosaurs (Tyrannosaurus rex); others were harmless and gentle (Trachodon).

27. Dinosaurs had various ways of protecting themselves against predators: some ran away, some hid, some fought.

*28. Some beliefs about dinosaurs, commonly held for many years, are now thought to be false. For example, most scientists thought Apatosaurus lived in swamps. Many now believe that it lived on dry land, eating leaves from tall trees.

*29. Because beliefs about dinosaurs are changing, some of the older books about and pictures of dinosaurs contain incorrect or misleading information.

30. Some people once thought that dinosaurs moved slowly, but now scientists believe many dinosaurs could move very fast.

Discovering Dinosaurs

31. Scientists who study dinosaurs are called paleontologists.

32. Paleontologists make guesses about how dinosaurs lived by studying their bones, tracks, and other fossil remains.

33. Fossils are hardened parts or imprints of plants or animals that are preserved in rocks found in the ground.

34. All of the bones inside a dinosaur are called its skeleton.

35. Many dinosaur skeletons, tracks, and other fossilized remains have been discovered around the world, even in the United States.

36. Fossil dinosaur eggs have been discovered in groups, or nests, covered with plants and leaves, leading scientists to believe that dinosaurs may have tried to protect their eggs from danger.

37. Inside the fossil dinosaur eggs, scientists have found fossilized remains of unborn baby dinosaurs.

38. Fossils must be handled with care because they are very fragile.

39. Paleontologists use special tools to dig and uncover fossils: shovels, trowels, soft brushes, sifters, and so on.

40. Scientists give each dinosaur they discover a name.

*41. Dinosaur names are chosen to describe something about the dinosaur: where it was discovered, how big it was, or something about how it looked. For example, "Ornitholestes" means "bird robber," "Brontosaurus" means "thunder lizard," and "Triceratops" means "three-horned face."

42. Scientists have discovered over three hundred different kinds of dinosaurs.

43. There may be many dinosaurs that have not been discovered yet.

44. Scientists who dig up the bones of dinosaurs often display them in museums so people can see what dinosaurs looked like and learn about them.

45. The place where scientists find and excavate dinosaur fossils is called a dig.

46. At the dig, scientists carefully number and photograph each bone. They use these pictures later to help put the bones in the correct places as they reconstruct the dinosaur skeleton.

*47. Sometimes fossils are found by accident; sometimes scientists look where they think they'll find fossils.

48. When a place is believed to contain fossils, the area is carefully divided into sections.

49. The sections of the dig are numbered and a map showing each part of the area is drawn.

50. As fossils are found in each section of the dig, they are drawn on the map to show the relationship of each bone to the others.

51. Sometimes scientists find many fossil bones; sometimes they find none, even after looking for a long time.

Extinction

52. Dinosaurs no longer exist (are extinct). Scientists are trying to discover why they died out long ago.

*53. There are several theories or guesses about the cause of dinosaur extinction.

*54. Some scientists believe that an enormous asteroid hit the Earth, raising dust that blocked the sunlight and killed all the plants. Since the dinosaurs had nothing to eat, they died.

*55. Some scientists believe that the Earth became too cold or too hot for the dinosaurs to live, killing them all.

*56. Some scientists believe that other prehistoric animals attacked and destroyed the dinosaurs' eggs, eventually wiping them out.

*57. Some scientists believe that the dinosaurs died of diseases.

ACTIVITY IDEAS

Aesthetic

1. **Bone Band.** Collect discarded chicken, turkey, or beef bones. Boil them until all the meat falls away, then bleach and dry them for a few days in the open air. Pass out larger bones to the children to strike with rhythm sticks or other bones to make a primitive musical sound.

   As an alternative, use rhythm sticks to simulate the sound of real bones. Ask children to tap in rhythm to music on records or to songs that the children sing.

2. **Dinosaur Colors.** On the painting easel or on a table, provide several colors of paints and large pieces of easel paper with dinosaur shapes traced on each. The dinosaur shapes in this chapter may be enlarged for this purpose. Remind children that since no one ever saw a living dinosaur, no one knows what colors they were. Encourage them to choose any color of paint to decorate their dinosaurs. Display the finished projects.

3. **Dinosaur Places Mural.** Arrange mural paper for the whole class to work on. On a large sheet of butcher paper, draw simple lines to indicate sky, land, and water areas. Provide children with materials to add dinosaur shapes, trees, fish, plants, and so on. Either have all the pieces precut, or provide shapes to trace and cut out. You might add dinosaur stickers or rubber stamps, as well. Older children will enjoy making their own dinosaurs using paper scraps, paste, and markers.

Affective

1. **My Favorite Dinosaur.** Display pictures or models of various dinosaurs and suggest children look them over and choose the one they like the best. Record their selections on a chart by writing their favorites next to their own names, or by allowing each child to place a star sticker under the picture of the one he or she likes the best. Provide a place for them to indicate "none of these," as some children won't like any dinosaurs. Later, read the chart to the group, pointing out how everyone has preferences.

2. **To Touch or Not to Touch.** Provide a display of sturdy dinosaur models. Tell the children that real museums have some things to touch and some things that people cannot be allowed to touch. Ask them to pretend that they are museum directors and can decide what is touchable. Make small signs (see Figure 18.1) that indicate hands-on or hands-off the models. Ask the children to take turns deciding which of the models should have TOUCH or DON'T TOUCH signs. Allow them to arrange the signs as they wish. Praise them for using their own ideas.

3. **Name-o-Saurus.** Make dinosaur-shaped name tags for the children and add "o-saurus" (meaning "lizard") to each of their

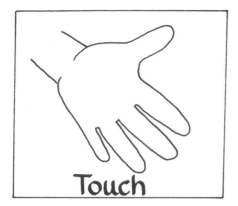

Figure 18.1 *Signs Show Children What's Expected of Them*

names. Examples would be Tommyosaurus, Lauraosaurus, Paulosaurus, and Katieosaurus. Variations might include Tommyodon or Katieodon.

Cognition

1. ***Measuring a Dinosaur.*** Choose a very long dinosaur. (Diplodocus was ninety feet long.) Cut a string or rope to the same length as the dinosaur. Teach the children some factual information about this dinosaur, showing a picture and asking them to imagine how much space it would take up if it were here. Take the class outdoors to an open space or use a long hallway floor. Then, suggesting children hold the ends, stretch the string out to demonstrate the true length of the creature. Have the children lie down, head to toe, to see how many children it takes to reach from the dinosaur's head to the tip of its tail. Repeat using meters as the unit of measurement. Measure other dinosaurs and compare them.

2. ***Dino-Lotto.*** Purchase or make a dinosaur lotto set according to the following directions. Invite up to five children to play at one time. Give a board to each player, suggesting the fifth child be the "caller." Put the playing pieces in a bag or dish so they can be pulled out one at a time by the caller. Provide a collection of "markers" for everyone to use (bingo chips, plastic coins, bits of paper, or flat Styrofoam bits) to cover the pictures on their boards as each dinosaur is called. Encourage children to notice the pictures on their boards and see how they match with the playing pieces before beginning the game. Begin the game with the caller showing one playing piece at a time and the players checking their boards to see if they have that picture. To avoid competition, clap for each person who covers his or her whole board, and continue to play until everyone's board is covered with markers. Trade boards and repeat.

Making a Lotto Game

To make a lotto game for four children you'll need: stiff poster board, scissors, a collection of eight small, different dinosaur pictures (photocopy them so you have four of each, or purchase several sets of matching dinosaur stickers), glue, and clear contact paper. (Figure 18.2)

To make the game pieces, cut out a set of eight two-inch squares of poster board. Attach one of each of the eight dinosaurs to each playing piece. Set these aside. To make the playing boards, cut poster board into four rectangles (about 8½-by-11 inches each). Then, draw lines on the playing boards to divide each into six equal sections. Next, lay out the four playing boards and attach one dinosaur picture to each section. Make sure none of the boards contain the same combination of pictures. Cover the boards and playing pieces with clear contact paper to protect them and make them last.

Dinosaur Lotto

Figure 18.2 *Making a Lotto Game*

3. ***Run, Dinosaur, Run!*** Have children play this game sitting on chairs in a circle. Give each child a picture of a dinosaur to wear or hold. One child stands in the middle of the circle as the "caller." When the caller calls out, "Run, meat-eaters, run," children must decide if their dinosaur is a meat-eater or not. If it is, they exchange chairs as quickly as they can with other meat-eaters. The caller also tries to locate an empty chair and claim it. The child who doesn't find a chair is the new caller. Callers may substitute other descriptors such as plant-eaters or thunder lizards; two-legged, four-legged, or horned dinosaurs; or they may use dinosaur names such as Stegosaurus, Ankylosaurus, and so on.

4. ***Dinosaur Match.*** Buy or make a set of matching pairs of dinosaur cards. Deal out five cards to each player and put the remainder in the center. Help children take turns asking each other for cards they need to match those in their hand. "Joe, do you have a dinosaur with wings?" or "Do you have a meat-eater?" If the child who is asked has one, he or she gives it to the person. If not, he or she says, "No, go to the fossil pile," and the asker takes one card from the center and lays down all of his or her pairs. Play then passes to the left. Avoid competition by continuing play until all of the pairs are made.

5. ***Dinosaur Memory Game.*** Using a set of commercially made or homemade dinosaur picture cards consisting of matching pairs, arrange the cards face down in several rows. Invite children to take turns turning two cards over to see if they match. Children keep turning cards in pairs until they don't find a match. For beginners, use only five or six sets of pairs. For experienced players, use more.

6. ***Scientific Guesses.*** Introduce children to three main theories of dinosaur extinction. (Refer to TFPs 53–58.) Show pictures and explain in simple terms how these are guesses: no one really knows why the dinosaurs died out. Make a chart with the children's names on one side and symbols or simple pictures representing the theories along the top. Let children vote for the theory they like the best and graph the results.

7. ***How Many Dinosaurs?*** Use a large die and a collection of small plastic dinosaurs. Ask children to take turns rolling the die and taking the number of dinosaurs they rolled. Assist them in counting slowly,

touching the dinosaurs as they say each number. Older children will enjoy accumulating and recounting as their piles get bigger.

8. ***Dinosaur Food.*** Demonstrate what dinosaurs ate by bringing in samples of plants (leaves, bark from trees, sticks, pinecones, weeds), meat (raw beef, chicken), fish, and water. Lead children in a discussion of where they think dinosaurs found their food and what might have happened when they couldn't find any food.

9. ***Guess What Happened?*** After children have been introduced to real theories of extinction, read *What Happened to Patrick's Dinosaurs?* by Carol Carrick. Explain that this is Patrick's funny made-up guess about the dinosaurs and why they're not on the Earth anymore. Tell children they can use their imaginations to make up their own guesses. Allow children to be as creative as they can be, and record their exact words. Suggest they make pictures to illustrate their ideas.

10. ***Dinosaur Teeth Game.*** Begin this game by passing a mirror around, encouraging children to examine their own teeth. Point out how they have both flat and pointed teeth for eating different foods. Explain that this was also true of dinosaurs. Make a chart with pictures of dinosaurs on one side. Give each child two cards, one with a picture of a flat tooth, one with a pointed tooth drawn on it. Suggest that they place the correct tooth shape next to the dinosaur who had that kind of teeth. Then, they could guess what kind of food that dinosaur ate. Help them check their answers by looking in a resource book.

11. ***Big and Little Footprints.*** Draw and cut out a huge dinosaur footprint. (The print of Tyrannosaurus rex was three feet long and three feet wide at its widest part.) Lay this out on the floor, showing children how a dinosaur footprint may have looked in the mud. Pass out paper in a contrasting color, pencils, and scissors. Have the children trace their own footprints, cut them out, and lay them on the dinosaur footprint. Ask them to count how many child footprints it takes to fill a Tyrannosaurus rex footprint.

12. ***Dinosaur Cousins.*** Read the book *Dinosaur Cousins* by Bernard Most to the

children. In a later discussion, highlight some of the dinosaurs and other animals from the book that are most familiar to them. Read the story another day. Before starting, tell the children to listen carefully. Their job will be to remember some of the dinosaur "cousins" described in the story. After you've read the book, ask children to recall the dinosaur cousins they heard about. As a follow-up activity, provide children with animal photos cut from magazines. In addition, give them several dinosaur reference books to look through. Invite the children to match the animal pictures to possible dinosaur "cousins" found in their dinosaur books.

13. ***What If? . . . Dinosaur Game.*** Make a collection of cards with facts about dinosaurs on one side and a "what if?" question on the other. Invite children to draw one from a basket and use it as a basis for individual discussion or a small-group talk. Tape-record their answers.
Examples:

- Dinosaurs are not alive any more; they are extinct. What if . . . they were alive and you had one for a pet?

- There were no people when dinosaurs were living. What if . . . there were people?

- Apatosaurus was seventy feet long and fourteen feet high. What if . . . one came to visit us at school?

- No one ever saw a dinosaur alive. What if . . . we saw one, what color would it be?

14. ***Footfalls.*** Obtain a set of dinosaur models with clearly defined feet. Be sure to include a variety of dinosaur types such as Tyrannosaurus, Stegosaurus, Triceratops, Iguanodon, Plesiosaurus, Pteranodon, Apatosaurus, and Ankylosaurus. Arrange the figures on a long sheet of paper (shelf paper) and trace carefully around the feet or the body/flippers (Pteranodon, Plesiosaurus) with a marker. Print the name of each dinosaur near its footprints. Remove the name of each dinosaur and cover the paper with clear vinyl or laminate it. Place the paper on a low shelf or table with each dinosaur figure placed on its prints. Tell the children that they may use the figures in their play and that when they are fin-

ished using a figure, they should return it to the appropriate place on the paper. Point out the differences in the placement of feet and the printed names as the children use and return the figures.

15. **Fossil Exploration.** After an initial introduction to fossils, provide a collection of real fossils for the children to examine. Show children how to look closely through magnifying glasses to see the details. Demonstrate your appreciation of the tiny impressions in the rocks and be sure to point out that the fossils are fragile.

*16. **Mixed-up Dinosaur Land.**

General Purpose: For children to generalize knowledge, applying what they have gained in previous experiences to new situations.

TFPs: 1, 5, 18, 19, 30.

Materials: Wet sand; small wooden or plastic buildings; miniature trees and shrubs; tiny cars; miniature people; miniature dinosaur figures; rocks; train and train track; small pie pan of water; books, pictures, or posters showing dinosaurs in their natural habitats.

Procedure:

a. Precede this activity with a discussion or presentation of factual information about the world as it was when dinosaurs were alive. Show the children pictures of artists' and scientists' ideas of dinosaurs in their natural environments.

b. Arrange all of the materials (except dinosaurs) into a miniature world in a large tray, sand table, or outdoor sandbox. Invite children to look at it carefully and tell what they see. Encourage them to explore visually without touching or moving anything in the display.

c. Add the dinosaurs to the display, saying, "Let's pretend this is the time of the dinosaurs, a long, long time ago. We'll call it Dinosaur Land. But there's something wrong with this world. Look carefully and think of one thing that's not right."

d. Encouraging children to take turns, call on each child to identify something that's not appropriate in the Dinosaur Land set-up. Ask them to tell why it doesn't belong and suggest that they

remove the object. Respond by acknowledging their correct ideas: "You know there were no houses when dinosaurs were alive."

Hint for Success:

- If someone wants to remove an object that should be left in Dinosaur Land (such as rocks or trees) acknowledge the idea, then suggest the child check the posters (or a book) to see if he or she is correct. Offer help by pointing out the natural surroundings depicted in resource pictures.

How to Simplify this Activity:

- Give children plenty of time to explore and play with the individual pieces before they see the display. Use only a few objects and limit the activity to one or two children at a time.

How to Extend this Activity:

- Include all of the objects, asking children to speculate on what would happen if dinosaurs had lived in this world. Follow up on this activity by encouraging children to collect natural objects and create their own dinosaur lands.

17. **Dinosaur Line-Up (Seriation).**

General Purpose: For children to recognize or construct relationships among objects and events through the process of seriation.

TFPs: 1. Seriation is the process of sequencing according to the magnitude of a particular characteristic.

2. Dinosaur pictures or models may be seriated according to many different characteristics: length, width, height, amount of something such as spikes, number of something such as spots, and so on.

3. Seriation can be based on a progression from most to least or from least to most of the characteristic.

Materials: A set of dinosaur pictures or models that vary in several different characteristics that can be seriated. (Figure 18.3)

Dinosaur Line-Up

Figure 18.3 *Dinosaurs That Can Be Seriated in Several Ways*

Procedure:

a. Encourage the children to explore the materials. Spread out the dinosaurs, inviting children to look at them, telling what they see and pointing out characteristics. Continue until the children appear familiar with the dinosaurs before moving on to the next step.

b. Compare and seriate two. Choose two dinosaurs that are obviously different in some way. Put all the other dinosaurs temporarily out of sight and place the two in front of the children saying, "Now we'll play a game. These dinosaurs have decided to make a parade down the mountain. They want to make a line so that the dinosaur with the most of something is in the front. These two are starting. Look at them and show me which one would be in the front of the line."

c. Clarify reasoning. After the children have made a selection, point to it and ask, "Why does this one go there?" or "What does this one have more of?" Listen and paraphrase, "You noticed this one is taller than that one. You wanted the tallest one in front."

d. Seriate more than two. Give the children another dinosaur saying, "Show me where this one goes in our line." Repeat steps c and d until all of the dinosaurs are seriated.

e. Reverse seriation of two. Mix all of the dinosaurs up again. Say, "Now all of the dinosaurs want to come back home in a different way, from the shortest to the tallest. Start with these two and put them into the line."

f. Reverse seriation of more than two. Repeat the process in steps c and d, encouraging the children to line up the dinosaurs in reverse order using the same characteristic as previously chosen.

g. Select a new attribute and compare. Collect all the dinosaurs again, telling the children a new story: "Now the dinosaurs are going to sleep. They want to sleep in a line from the most of something to the least of something, but they want to do it in a different way than how they went up and down the mountain." Choose two dinosaurs. Say, "Look at these two. What does one have more

of?" Listen to the children and paraphrase their ideas. Point out differences if children do not notice anything new.

h. Seriate according to a different characteristic. Say, "You noticed this one has more spikes than this one. Let's make a sleeping line from most spikes to least spikes." Repeat the process by adding more dinosaurs, helping the children maintain the new characteristic and praising their work.

Hint for Success:

• Begin by using only a few dinosaurs that exhibit major differences. Gradually add more dinosaurs with more subtle differences.

How to Simplify this Activity:

• Use dinosaurs that vary in only one characteristic. Many commercially produced seriation materials fall into this category. Use only a small number of objects (three or four) for the sequence.

• Work with only one or two children at a time.

How to Extend this Activity:

• Make your own materials more complex or look for objects that vary in several different aspects. It can be challenging for children to discover new ways to seriate the objects. Some children may enjoy making their own seriation objects. Help them figure out different ways to seriate the same set of objects and invite them to keep track of the variety of options they discover.

• Work with groups of three or four children and involve them in discussing and comparing their own reasoning and conclusions.

*18. *Erupting Volcano.*

General Purpose: For children to become aware of wonders in nature.

TFPs: 5, 19.

Materials: A pan or shallow box, wet sand or mud, a large empty orange juice can, baking soda, water, vinegar, dishwashing liquid, red food coloring. (Figure 18.4)

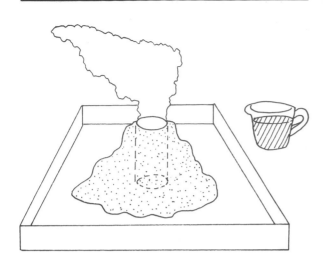

Figure 18.4 *Make Your Own Erupting Volcano*

Procedure:
a. Introduce the idea that dinosaurs lived at a time when the earth had many volcanoes. Explain what a volcano is and what happens when it erupts.
b. Make a volcano. Fill a pan or shallow box with wet sand or mud. Shape the mud into a mountain around a large, empty orange juice can. Place ¼ cup baking soda into the can. Mix up one cup water, ¾ cup vinegar, ½ cup dishwashing liquid, and 8 drops of red food coloring.
c. Pour the mixture into the can and watch the lava flow.

Hint for Success:
• Make the liquid mixture ahead or show ingredients as you mix them.

How to Simplify this Activity:
• Treat this experiment as a demonstration for children to watch.

How to Extend this Activity:
• Invite children to make their own volcanoes and do the experiment themselves.

Construction
1. *Clay Dinosaurs.* Give children experience playing with three-dimensional dinosaur models. Set those aside and invite the children to create dinosaurs of their own using multicolored plasticine clay or hardening clay. Children may display their models as is, or dry and paint them. Suggest that children make up names for their creations. Make a small sign that tells the name of each dinosaur and who made it.
2. *Dinosaur Skeletons.* Show children pictures of dinosaur skeletons or visit a museum where they can see skeletons of animals. Collect chicken, beef, or turkey bones. Boil them in a solution of vinegar and water. Allow them to dry completely for several days in the open air. Next, pass out bones, paper, pencils, and glue and suggest that the children create dinosaur skeletons of their own. These may be glued on paper or built in three dimensions.
3. *Pipe-Cleaner-o-Saurus.* After children have had some experience playing with three-dimensional dinosaur models, set those aside and introduce the idea of creating a model out of pipe cleaners. Allow children to experiment with bending, attaching pipe cleaners to each other and wrapping pipe cleaners around pencils or other objects, then sliding them off to produce three-dimensional shapes. Suggest that they could make their own strange dinosaurs using the pipe cleaners any way they want. Be available to children who need help getting started; suggest that they could begin with a body shape and then attach a head and neck, legs, and a tail. Other parts for children to consider adding could include horns, spikes, or wings.
4. *Dinosaurs That Never Were.* Ahead of time, cut a large selection of construction paper dinosaur parts (heads, tails, bodies, legs, horns, wings, etc.) in different colors. Provide glue or paste and large sheets of background paper. Remind children that many dinosaurs have been found, but that there may be many not yet discovered. Suggest that children construct dinosaurs that have not been discovered yet. Tell children that these imaginary dinosaurs could have more than one head, upside-down tails, and so on, and that they should give them invented names. Display the finished dinosaurs and accompany them with labels. (Figures 18.5a and 18.5b)

Heads for
Dinosaurs That Never Were

Figure 18.5a *Heads for Creating Dinosaurs That Never Were*

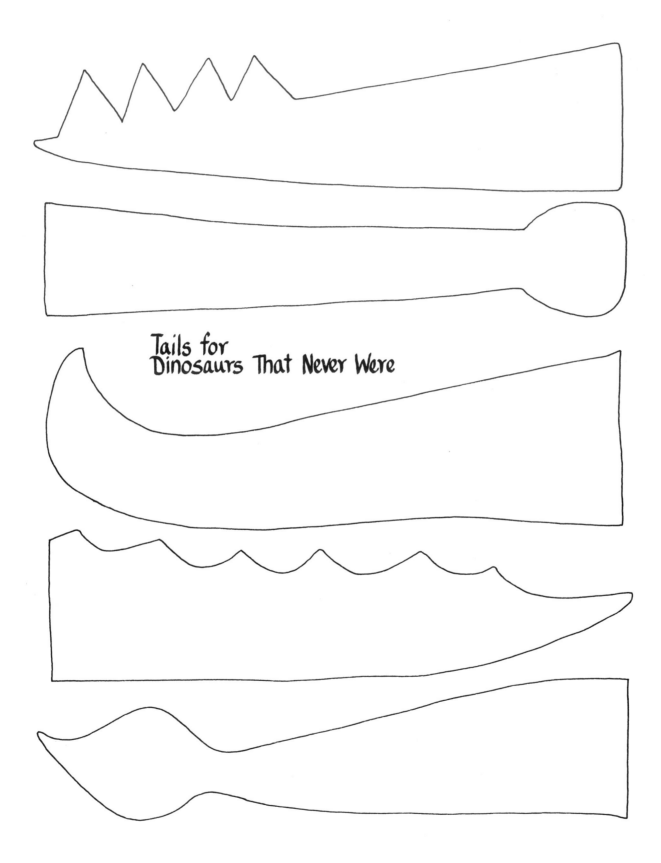

Tails for
Dinosaurs That Never Were

Figure 18.5b *Tails for Creating Dinosaurs That Never Were*

5. ***Catch a Dinosaur.*** Discuss how one might catch a dinosaur if it were loose in town. Suggest that children use large blocks or other materials to construct their dinosaur traps. Encourage many different solutions to the problem and avoid directing the construction. Once the traps are made, invite the children to explain how they would work.

6. ***Dinosaur Dioramas.***

General Purpose: For children to use their imaginations to represent an object or event utilizing various combinations of materials.

TFPs: 1, 5, 13, 19, 20, 21, 23, 30, 32.

Materials: Cardboard shoeboxes (for the floor and walls of the diorama); natural materials such as sand, dirt, small tree branches, pine needles, leaves, stones, mud, and so on; pictures of volcanoes, mountains, or swamps; collection of small dinosaur figures or pictures of dinosaurs; scissors; glue; crayons or markers.

Procedure:

a. Give children experiences with dinosaur displays in books or at a museum.

b. Discuss what they learned and tell children that they can make their own displays called "dioramas" based on their own ideas of a dinosaur's environment.

c. Provide everyone with a plastic dinosaur model, telling them to imagine where this dinosaur would have lived. Give children help in locating their particular dinosaurs in books, pointing out some of the things around them and how scientists think these dinosaurs lived.

d. Suggest that children collect materials for producing a diorama. Offer suggestions and allow children time to make their collections. Take the class outdoors to a natural area where they might find some things for their displays.

Hint for Success:

- Offer help while children are working on their dioramas. Avoid telling them how to make them; encourage individual differences. After the environments are constructed, use them as part of a pretend dinosaur museum in the classroom.

How to Simplify this Activity:

- Prepare some of the materials ahead of time (precut the shoe boxes or small tree branches) and demonstrate how to use clay or modeling dough to make things stand up.

How to Extend this Activity:

- Children could work on larger, more elaborate dioramas, or you might suggest that they work in pairs or small groups and produce whole scenes containing many dinosaurs. Use papier-mâché or salt and flour mixtures to create textured landscapes that harden and can be painted. (Figure 18.6)

Language

1. ***Dinosaur Ditties.*** Teach the following songs and fingerplays using fingers, pictures, or dinosaur models to count as you go through the words.

Ten Big Dinosaurs
(Tune: "Ten Little Indians";
Words: Donna Howe)
One big, two big, three big dinosaurs,
Four big, five big, six big dinosaurs,
Seven big, eight big, nine big dinosaurs,
Ten big dinosaurs!
They all lived a long, long time ago.
They all lived a long, long time ago.
They all lived a long, long time ago.
Now there are no more.

Figure 18.6 *A Shoe Box Diorama*

Ask children to think of other words to describe dinosaurs or invite them to substitute different descriptive words for the word "big," such as little, heavy, noisy, or hungry.

Allosaurus
(Tune: "Alouette"; Author unknown)
Allosaurus, Pachycephalosaurus,
Apatosaurus, Tyrannosaurus rex!
Stegosaurus, Trachodon, Triceratops,
Pteranodon.
Dinosaurs, Dinosaurs, Dinosaurs,
Dinosaurs,
Oh. . . .
Allosaurus, Pachycephalosaurus,
Apatosaurus, Tyrannosaurus rex!

Five Enormous Dinosaurs
(Author unknown)
Five enormous dinosaurs, letting out a roar,
One went away, and then there were . . . four.
Four enormous dinosaurs, munching on a tree,
One went away, and then there were . . . three.
Three enormous dinosaurs, didn't know what to do,
One went away, and then there were . . . two.
Two enormous dinosaurs, having lots of fun,
One went away, and then there was . . . one.
One enormous dinosaur, afraid to be a hero,
He went away, and then there were . . . zero.

2. *Fossil Directions.* Make a sequence of picture directions for children to follow in making their own fossils. Display the picture directions at a series of work stations, providing appropriate materials at each station. Encourage the children to "read" the directions as they go through the process of making fossil prints. (Figure 18.7)
3. *Dino-Names Are Fun.* Tape-record your voice saying the names of the dinosaurs pictured in a simple children's book. Insert pauses where children can say what they heard you say: "This is a Parasaurolophus. Now you say Parasaurolophus. (pause)" Be sure to include cues for turning the page, so children can go through the book independently. Set up a listening area with the tape recorder, the book, and the tape where children can hear the names and practice saying them.
4. *My Book of Dinosaurs.* Staple together several blank pages with a construction paper cover that says:

MY DINOSAUR BOOK
written by (child's name)

Encourage each child to dictate at least one thing every day that they have learned about dinosaurs; an adult could write it into their book, putting one statement on each page. Be sure to write the exact words the children say, even if their ideas are "incorrect" or "fantasy." Include a letter to parents in the back of each book, stating that the purpose of the book is to help children value and enjoy reading and writing, and that all ideas contained are the children's own interpretations, not necessarily accurate ones. Suggest that the children make pictures to go along with their "statements." Allow children to use their own version of writing instead of relying on dictation, if they would like.
5. *I Spy a Dinosaur.* Play a version of the traditional I Spy game, using dinosaur pictures instead. Display posters or other large pictures of dinosaurs near the children for this activity. Demonstrate the game and then ask children to take turns being the leader, saying, "I spy, with my little blue (or any color) eye, a dinosaur that _____ ." The child inserts a fact about the dinosaur they mean. For example, if the child is looking at the Stegosaurus, he or she might say, "I spy with my little blue eye, a dinosaur that has four sharp spikes on its tail." Challenge the other children to guess which dinosaur it is. To avoid competition, choose the next "leader" randomly by pulling a name from a hat.

Make Your Own Fossil

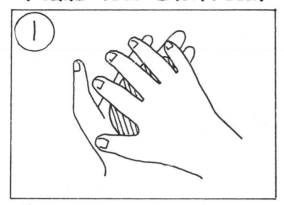

Flatten a ball of clay.

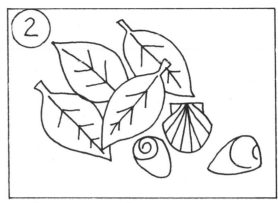

Choose a leaf or shell.

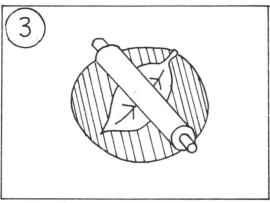

Roll or press it flat into the clay.

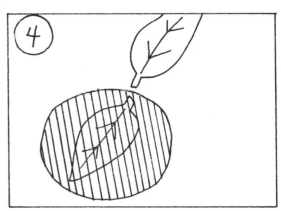

Peel it off and allow clay to harden.

Figure 18.7 *Display These Fossil Directions*

Physical

1. *Footprints, Footprints, Everywhere!* Cut household sponges into dinosaur footprint shapes. Demonstrate pressing these into different colors of paint and "printing" them using a down-up, down-up motion. (Figure 18.8)

   Have children practice this controlled movement to make simulated dinosaur footprints across long, narrow sheets of paper. When they've dried, attach the sheets end to end to form a continuous line of prints to hang on the wall or the ceiling for fun.

2. *Trace a Dino-Shape.* Make cardboard dinosaur shapes for children to trace. (Use the models provided at the end of this unit in Figures 18.12a, b, c, and d. Enlarge or use as they are.) Cover the finished shapes with clear contact paper or laminate them to keep them sturdy. Demonstrate tracing by holding the shape with one hand and drawing around it with the other. Provide large paper and assistance as children trace the dinosaurs they like.

3. *Dinosaur Dancing.* Discuss different ways dinosaurs moved. Show pictures of dinosaurs running, flying, swimming, walking,

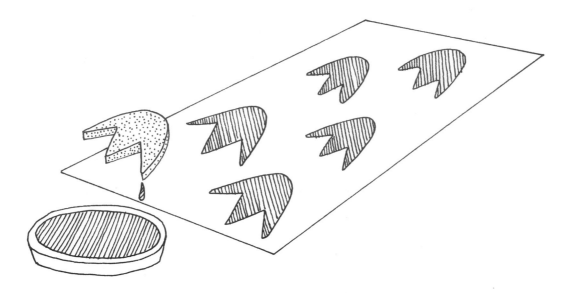

Figure 18.8 *Using a Sponge to Make Dinosaur Footprints*

eating, or fighting. Turn on some instrumental music and encourage children to move with you as a dinosaur may have moved. Allow free interpretation from the children, remarking to individuals about the way they thought to move. Avoid insisting that children follow the leader. Model various movements at high level (upright), middle level (crouching), and low level (on the floor).

4. ***Follow a Path to the Dinosaur.*** Create life-sized paths that children follow using their whole bodies, such as through an obstacle course. Make some paths (drawn on poster board in thirty-six-inch squares and covered with clear contact paper) that children can follow with model dinosaurs using large muscle control. Make some smaller but more complex paths on paper that the children can follow with a crayon using fine muscle control.

5. ***Dinosaur Hats.*** Give children the patterns for dinosaur-shaped hats in Figure 18.9 to trace and cut out. Children can wear these as hats or use them as part of dinosaur costumes for pretend play.

Enlarge the dinosaur-shaped hat shown in Figure 18.9 and cut it out of heavy cardboard. Encourage the children to trace it onto their own construction paper. Have them cut out two shapes and staple them together, leaving the bottom edge open.

6. ***Dinosaur Sandwiches.*** Provide dinosaur-shaped cookie cutters (available in many food preparation stores). Demonstrate how to press the cutters into bread to cut out dinosaur-shaped bread pieces. Have children make two or more pieces each and use them to make sandwiches, spreading the bread with soft cream cheese, creamy peanut butter, or jam.

7. ***Dinosaur Directions.***
General Purpose: For children to increase their physical flexibility.

TFPs: 22, 23, 24, 25, 26, 31.

Materials: None necessary, but pictures of dinosaurs help provide ideas.

Procedure:
a. Invite the children to join you in playing a game. "In this game, a leader will tell us what to do. We listen and then do what the leader says."
b. Help children spread out a bit so they don't bump into one another.
c. Take on the role of the first leader yourself. Model some different directions, encouraging children to imitate you. For instance:

"Walk slowly, Apatosaurus."
"Get stuck in the mud, Allosaurus."
"Swing your tail, Stegosaurus."
"Fly, Pteranodon."

Making a Dinosaur Hat

Trace a shape such as this onto a large piece of construction paper.

Hold two pieces of paper together, cutting two identical shapes.

Staple along the outside edge leaving the bottom open. Decorate with crayons or markers.

Open the bottom edge and wear as a hat.

Figure 18.9 *Children Can Make Their Own Dinosaur Hat*

Hint for Success:

- This game should be played in a large area where children can move around freely.

How to Simplify this Activity:

- Demonstrate each movement as you say it, pointing out what you are doing with your body, such as, "Look, my arms are way out and I am flapping them up and down as I move through the air."

How to Extend this Activity:

- Once the children are familiar with the game, invite them to become leaders, one at a time. Assist them by making suggestions as needed and doing the movements with the group.

Pretend Play

1. *Paleontologists' Headquarters.* Arrange an area of the room with hats, gloves, tables, and tools for children to use as they pretend to examine and clean fossils (rocks) and bones (chicken or soup bones). Provide information about things a paleontologist might look for in examining bones and fossils.

2. *Dinosaur Dig.* Provide a sand table or deep container of wet sand and bury clean bones and fossil-like rocks under the sand. Collect small tools (shovel, sticks, brushes, etc.) and a simple costume for a paleontologist (hat, gloves, work boots, scarf). Demonstrate to the children what scientists do when they work at a dig. Encourage a few children at a time to assume the role of scientists at a "dig." Found bones and fossils could be wrapped, recorded, and taken to the pretend paleontologists' headquarters or museum to be examined. To make this activity more authentic, use string to create a grid in the sand for children to explore.

   Invite the children to "search" one square of the grid at a time and record on a paper or a corresponding drawing the location of their finds. An easy way to

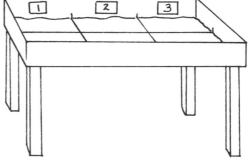

Figure 18.10 *In Which Section Were the Bones Found in the Dinosaur Dig?*

record this information is by taping a picture of a bone to a chart showing the sections. (Figure 18.10)

3. *Miniature Dinosaur Land.* Set up miniature dinosaurs and other props, such as rocks, small tree-shaped branches, nests, eggs, shells, and bones, for pretending on a surface that offers space for several players to re-create dinosaur life. Surfaces that would work well are:

- a section of the outdoors staked off on grass or sand:

- an indoor sand table;

- a floor area that is covered with a large dropcloth over pillows; or

- a large, flat box containing growing grasses and other plants. (Refer to the activity Making a Dino-Land Together.)

4. *Dinosaur Museum.*

General Purpose: For children to experiment with a variety of roles and characterizations.

TFPs: 33, 40, 42, 44, 46, 52.

Materials: Various dinosaur models, dioramas, pictures, books, (both commercial and child-constructed); a table and tools for cleaning and examining bones and fossils; magnifying glasses; posters, small TOUCH and DON'T TOUCH signs; tickets; phone; guide hats; dinosaur puzzles; games; a group-made Boxasaurus.

Procedure:

a. Arrange props, costumes, and furniture to suggest a museum.

b. Suggest roles for people in the museum such as scientist, director, visitor, ticket-seller, and guide.

c. Provide more information about museums if the children are unfamiliar with them.

d. Help children find ways to share materials, take on various roles, and experiment with the materials in appropriate ways.

Hint for Success:

• Include things to do as well as look at in the "museum." Children could match models to pictures, see a filmstrip, count dinosaurs, arrange fossil bones on a drawing of a dinosaur, color dinosaur pictures, buy tickets, and so on.

How to Simplify this Activity:

• Select a few things to go into the museum. Restrict the size of the space and the number of children who can be at the museum at any given time. Help children take turns by keeping a waiting list and establishing a time limit.

How to Extend this Activity:

• As children make things related to the theme throughout the weeks, suggest that they add them to the museum, determining where and how they should be displayed. Remind children to respect their classmates' creations and handle only those things that have TOUCH signs.

Social

1. *Allosaurus in the Swamp.* Play this singing game with a group of children using the traditional tune of "Farmer in the Dell." Have one child be the Allosaurus and stand in the middle of a circle of children who walk around holding hands and singing the song. Change the words to include names of dinosaurs instead of farm animals. Help children decide what dinosaur the Allosaurus will choose. For example, "Allosaurus picks Dimetrodon," and so on, until everyone is in the middle.

2. *Dinosaur Eggs and Nest.* Show pairs of children how to work together putting several layers of papier-mâché on a balloon to produce a "dinosaur egg." To make papier-mâché, mix enough flour and water together to make a *runny* paste in the quantity desired, or use wallpaper paste (available in hardware or paint stores) mixed according to directions on the box.

a. Place the mixture into a shallow bowl and soak strips of newspaper in it.

b. Demonstrate to children how to pick up a paper strip, using fingers to remove excess paste, and overlap the paper strips in layers all over the balloon to cover it completely.

c. Apply three or four layers until the balloon looks solidly covered.

d. Put the wet balloon in a bowl or balance it on a wide-mouthed glass to help keep it from rolling away until it dries.

e. When the "egg" is dry, suggest that children paint the egg and add it to a giant "nest" of dinosaur eggs that others in the class are constructing out of blocks, boxes, or pillows.

3. *Stegosaurus Parade.* From large paper grocery bags cut with armholes and eyeholes, fashion parts of a Stegosaurus body with a paper "spike" on top of each part. Have one child attach a long tail and one child make a head. When the children

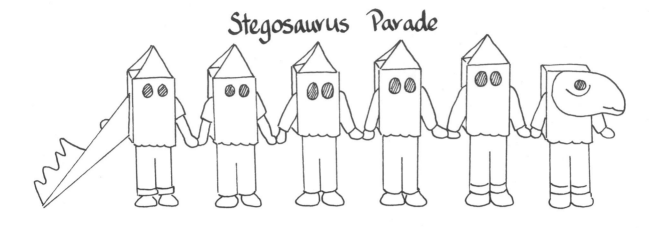

Figure 18.11a *Have a Stegosaurus Parade*

walk close together wearing their dinosaur parts, one large Stegosaurus (or Bagosaurus) takes shape. Take a picture so children can see the overall effect. (Figure 18.11a and b)

4. ***Paleontologist, Where's Your Fossil?*** Play this group game similar to the traditional Doggie, Doggie, Where's Your Bone?, but change the chant to: "Paleontologist, paleontologist, where's your fossil? Someone took it from your office." Have one child be the paleontologist, who sits in a chair facing away from the group. Tell the other children to sit on the floor behind him or her. The paleontologist "goes to sleep" with a "fossil" (a unit block) under the chair. Tap a child on the shoulder to signal that he or she should take the fossil and hide it behind his or her back. All of the children try to fool the paleontologist by holding their hands behind their backs, too. The paleontologist has three guesses to figure out who has the fossil. Whether the guesses are correct or not, whoever took the fossil becomes the paleontologist next.

5. ***Making a Dino-Land Together.***
   General Purpose: For children to learn ways to be cooperative.

TFPs: 1–27. Additional:
1. Cooperation means working together with others to accomplish a task.
2. When people work in groups, they often have to make decisions together.
3. Sometimes when people work together on a project, the work gets done faster and it's more fun.

Materials: A large low box (big enough for several children to play in at once); a large plastic lawn and leaf trash bag cut open and laid flat; strong masking tape; potting soil (large bag); grass seed; seed for other fast growing plants; spray bottle filled with water; small dinosaur figures. Optional: child-constructed volcanoes; rocks; small trees; pie pan pond.

Procedure:
a. Discuss the overall project with the whole class. Identify step-by-step each phase of production. Help children decide who will work on the various phases of the project. (Children may work on as many phases as they would like.)

Making a Stegosaurus Headpiece

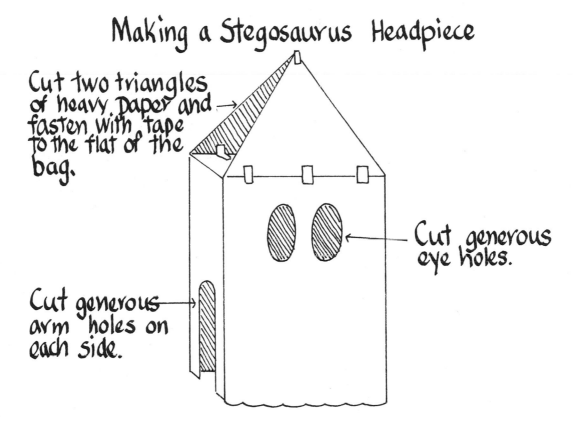

Cut two triangles of heavy paper and fasten with tape to the flat of the bag.

Cut generous eye holes.

Cut generous arm holes on each side.

Figure 18.11b *Headpiece for Part of the Stegosaurus*

b. Gather the materials into a sunny work area and begin work on the first phase. Continue through all of the steps, pointing out children's cooperative behavior and helping children find ways to work together.

- Secure a large plastic liner into a large flat box, attaching it with strong tape and/or staples.
- Fill the lined box with potting soil.
- Sprinkle grass seed and other seeds over the surface, covering them up with a thin layer of soil.
- Provide plenty of light and water the box daily; observe growth; and decide when it's ready to use with small dinosaur figures.

c. Make a list of who worked on each part of the project. Read the list to the children and praise their cooperation.

d. Evaluate the project with the children, asking them to tell what was easy, what was difficult, and how they liked working together.

Hint for Success:

- Plan and carry out this long-term project, beginning two to three weeks before you wish to use it for a miniature pretend area.

How to Simplify this Activity:

- Do some of the work for the children. Limit the size of Dino-Land, and have children work in pairs instead of groups.

How to Extend this Activity:

- Have one group of children make the box from wood, involving them in measuring, sawing, and nailing the sides together. Have another group plan a mountain for the center, making it out of hardening dough (see recipe) and painting it.

Hardening Modeling Dough

Mix 2 cups salt and ⅔ cup water. Cook over low heat until bubbly. Add food coloring if desired. Remove from heat. Mix 1 cup cornstarch with ½ cup cold water. Add to the salt and water mixture. Stir quickly. Keep in an airtight container. Hardens in 36 hours. Turn objects over to expose all surfaces to the air.

6. ***Boxosaurus Construction.***

General Purpose: For children to learn ways to be helpful.

TFPs: 1–27. Additional:
1. Being helpful means sharing information or materials, giving assistance, or offering emotional support to another person.
2. People who offer to be helpful are usually seen as friendly and are liked by others.

Materials: A large assortment of boxes, cardboard tubes, tape, paint, brushes, construction paper, glue, string, scissors, smocks.

Procedure:
a. Plan with the children how to make a large dinosaur out of boxes (a Boxosaurus). Ask for ideas from the group regarding parts of the dinosaur that should be made, tools or equipment that will be needed, and who will help on each stage of production: assembling, painting, and decorating. Write the plan on a large paper for all to see.
b. Gather materials and begin the assembly stage of production. Work with the children to decide how to put parts together so they will be secure. (Use strong masking tape or string on parts that appear loose.) Praise children for making suggestions, for sharing mate-

rials and information, or for offering assistance.
c. Introduce the painting phase of the project. Provide paint smocks, brushes, and plenty of paint. Once the structure is thoroughly dry, invite the children to decorate the Boxosaurus.
d. Have the children add eyes, nose, spots, stripes, scars, teeth, bow tie, or other details they want.
e. Evaluate the project with the whole group. Ask the children to consider such questions as: Could the job have been done as well by one person? How satisfied were the helpers with the results? How might the helpers change their plan in the future? What kinds of decisions were made by the helpers and how did they turn out? What kind of help did children give throughout the project?

Hints for Success:

- Ask parents to collect boxes well in advance of this project.
- Children should have had prior experiences with dinosaurs.
- Assume that this project will take at least three days to complete.
- Build the project on a dropcloth to protect the floor and make it easier to move the Boxosaurus to its display location.

How to Simplify this Activity:

- Have children work in pairs to produce small Boxosauruses.

How to Extend this Activity:

- After the project is complete, have children who want to continue being helpful paint a backdrop for the display or plan an unveiling ceremony for parents.

TEACHER RESOURCES

Field Trip Ideas

1. Locate a nearby museum that has dinosaur displays. Visit the site before you take the children so you are well prepared and can lead the group through the displays with some authority.

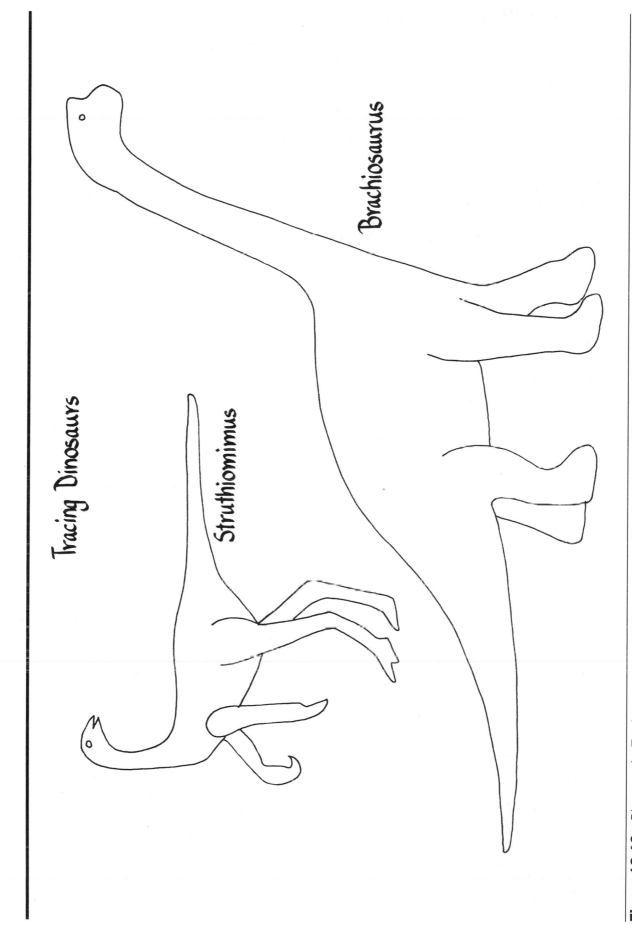

Tracing Dinosaurs

Brachiosaurus

Struthiomimus

Figure 18.12a *Dinosaurs for Tracing*

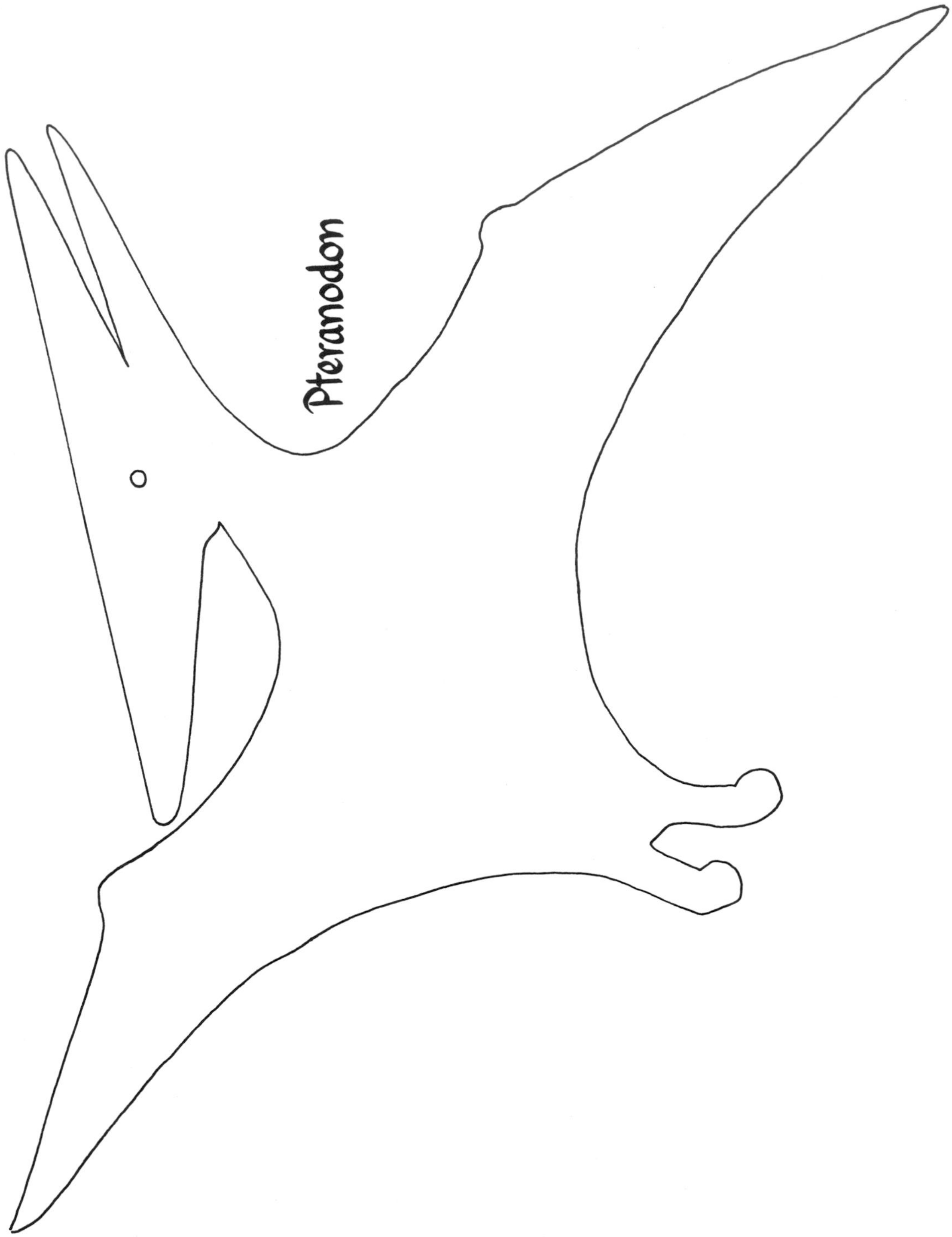

Pteranodon

Figure 18.12b *Tracing Pteranodon*

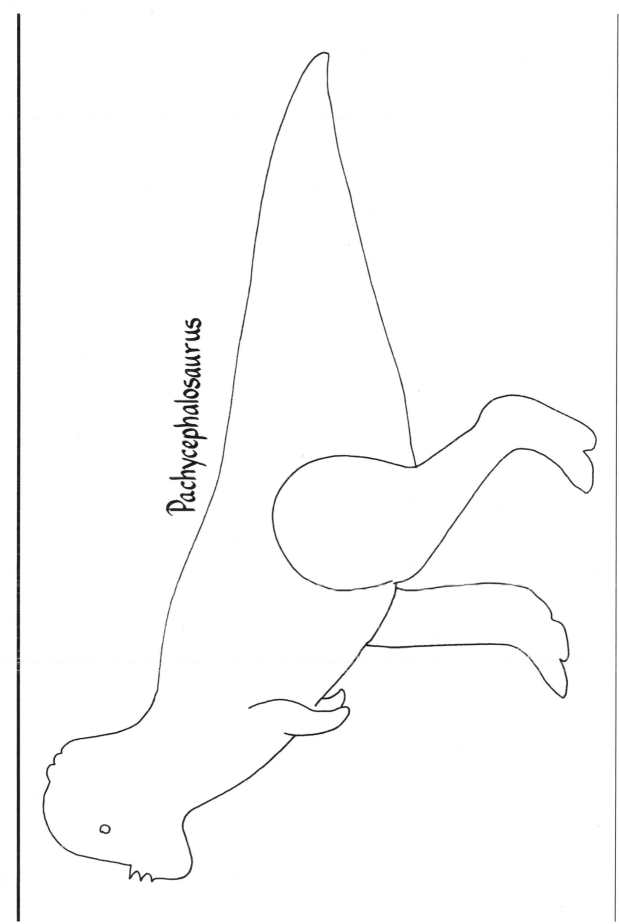

Pachycephalosaurus

Figure 18.12c *Tracing Pachycephalosaurus*

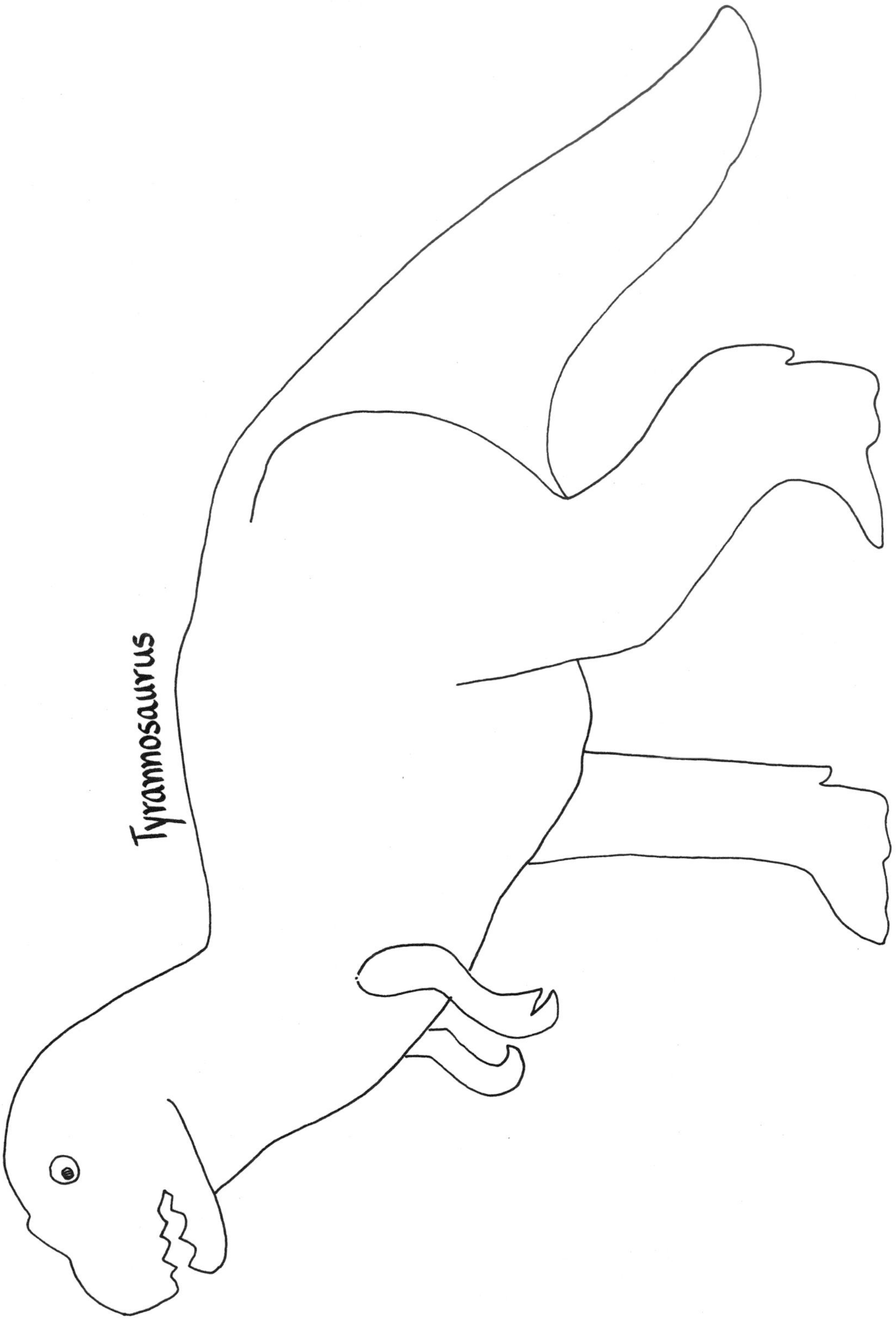

Tyrannosaurus

Figure 18.12d *Tracing Tyrannosaurus*

2. Call a local college or university to see if it has a department of geology or natural sciences. Find out if it has any rocks containing fossils that the children may find interesting.
3. Take your class to an outdoor area where the children might look for rocks that have been underground at some depth. Ravines, canyons, dry riverbeds, and other such places are likely spots. Provide pictures of things to look for and encourage children to bring strong bags to carry their finds back to school.

Classroom Visitors

1. Check area directories for colleges or fossil-hunting groups in your area. Call and inquire about an amateur or professional scientist who may be willing to show some paleontological tools, pictures of digs, fossils found, and so on.

Children's Books

Aliki. *Fossils Tell of Long Ago.* New York: Crowell, 1972.

———. *Digging Up Dinosaurs.* New York: Harper and Row, 1981.

———. *My Visit to the Dinosaurs.* New York: Crowell, 1985.

Carrick, C. *Patrick's Dinosaurs.* New York: Clarion, 1983.

———. *What Happened to Patrick's Dinosaurs?* New York: Clarion, 1986.

Daly, E. *Dinosaurs: Giants of the Past.* Racine, WI: Western, 1973.

Daly, K. N. *Dinosaurs.* New York: Golden, 1977.

Halstead, B. *Brontosaurus, The Thunder Lizard.* New York: Golden, 1982.

Jackson, K. *Dinosaurs.* Washington, DC: National Geographic Society, 1972.

Kauffman, J. *Little Dinosaurs and Early Birds.* New York: Crowell, 1977.

Milton, J. *Dinosaur Days.* New York: Random House, 1985.

Most, B. *Dinosaur Cousins.* New York: Harcourt Brace Jovanovich, 1987.

Parish, P. *Dinosaur Time.* New York: Harper and Row, 1974.

Prelutsky, J. *Tyrannosaurus Was a Beast.* New York: Greenwillow, 1988.

Radlauer, E. *Dinosaur Mania.* Chicago: Childrens Press, 1979.

Rowe, E. *Giant Dinosaurs.* Richmond Hill, Ontario: Scholastic-TAB, 1975.

Sattler, H. R. *Baby Dinosaurs.* New York: Lothrop Lee and Shepard, 1984.

Selsam, M. E. *A First Look at Dinosaurs.* New York: Walker, 1982.

Wilson, R. *Allosaurus.* Vero Beach, FL: Rourke, 1984.

Zallinger, P. *Dinosaurs.* New York: Random House, 1977.

———. *Prehistoric Animals.* New York: Random House, 1978.

Adult References

Asimov, I. *How Did We Find Out About Dinosaurs?* New York: Walker, 1973.

Bakker, R. T. *The Dinosaur Heresies.* New York: William Morrow, 1986.

Benton, M. *The Dinosaur Encyclopedia.* New York: Simon and Schuster, 1984.

———. *The Dinosaur Handbook.* New York: Simon and Schuster, 1984.

Cohen, D. *What Really Happened to the Dinosaurs?* New York: Dutton, 1977.

Colbert, E. H. *Dinosaurs: An Illustrated History.* Maplewood, NJ: Hammond, 1983.

Lambert, D. *A Field Guide to Dinosaurs.* New York: Avon, 1983.

Norman, D. *The Illustrated Encyclopedia of Dinosaurs.* New York: Crown, 1985.

Preston, D. J. *Dinosaurs in the Attic: The American Museum of Natural History.* New York: St. Martin's, 1986.

Part III

Language Arts Concepts

Chapter 19

Music Makers

•

Bingo

(Traditional)

There was a farmer had a dog

and Bingo was his name-o

B-I-N-G-O

B-I-N-G-O

B-I-N-G-O

and Bingo was his name-o.

•

Children all over the world clap, rock, and sway to traditional songs like "Bingo." Music is known in every culture and ethnic population worldwide and, as a result, most children hear and respond to music from birth. Even hearing-impaired children delight in rhythm and the beat of musical sounds. Children who don't speak the same language frequently find they can easily share the experience of making or responding to music. Music is truly the message!

Most teachers seek to encourage children's natural interest in music by integrating a variety of musical experiences into the classroom day. In many early childhood classrooms, music is used to reinforce new information, change the mood of the room, organize transitions, inspire feelings of group cohesiveness, and add enjoyment to the daily routine. Music can and should be utilized in these ways, for without music classrooms would be joyless places indeed. Thus, we assume that music already plays an important role in your early childhood setting.

PURPOSE

This unit is designed to highlight and enrich musical experiences for children. It is not intended to take the place of daily singing or enjoyment of music throughout the year. Rather, it presents music as a topic unto itself and helps teachers focus on music as both a receptive and an expressive art form. The receptive aspect encourages children to listen and receive messages from music. The expressive component invites children to respond to and make their own music.

To show children how music can be varied, to broaden their experience with instruments, and to appeal to children's interests in stories, the Music Makers unit is divided into three components. The first focuses on basic information about musical sounds (pitch, volume, tempo, and beat). The second deals with information about how musical sounds are produced (singing, using instruments, and combinations of these). The third provides an introduction to composing with an emphasis on how musical sounds and words combine to send a message or tell a story.

IMPLEMENTATION

This theme can be presented in various ways, depending on the needs of the children, how much time is available, and the depth of the children's interest in the topic.

Option One: Treat each of the three components as separate mini-units, or, in a more general approach, highlight a few TFPs from each.

Option Two: Focus on the area of most interest to the class (sounds, instruments, or composing), and then choose a culminating experience, such as producing a songbook of original songs for the rest of the school to enjoy. Other culminating experiences might include taking a field trip to hear an orchestra, or inviting a series of musicians to play for the children.

Having completed one or more aspects of this unit, teachers could extend the ideas presented in several different directions. The theme naturally leads to others dealing with dance or movement as means of self-expression. The aspect of music as a transmitter of messages could be extended into units on storytelling, creative drama, or television. In addition, by focusing on lyric-writing, children's writing interests could serve as the basis for units on books, writers, or newspapers.

TERMS, FACTS, AND PRINCIPLES

General Information

1. Music is a combination of agreeable sounds.

2. A musical tone is a single musical sound of a definite pitch.

3. Pitch is how high or low the sound is.

4. Volume is how loud or quiet the music is.

5. Tempo is how fast or slow the music is.

6. People discriminate between different musical tones by listening.

7. People match or reproduce musical tones using their voices or instruments.

8. A melody is a series of musical tones in a particular sequence.

9. The beat is the pulse of the music.

10. Rhythm is a regular occurrence of strong and weak beats.

11. People experience rhythm through their bodies.

12. Rhythms are fast or slow, regular or irregular.

13. A song is a particular combination of melody and rhythm.

14. Musical pieces have a beginning, middle, and end.

15. Some songs are comprised of melody and rhythm; some songs also have words.

Creating Musical Sounds

16. Music is made by a single voice or instrument, more than one voice or instrument, or a combination of voice(s) and instrument(s).

17. There are a variety of musical instruments.

18. Some instruments are played by touching strings to make the sound: guitar, violin, cello, harp, bass, piano, autoharp.

19. Some instruments are played by blowing air into them to make the sound: clarinet, trumpet, oboe, flute, trombone, saxophone.

20. Some instruments are played by striking or shaking them to make the sound: drum, maraca, triangle, clapper, xylophone, bells.

21. Each instrument has a distinctive sound.

22. Songs may sound different when played on different instruments.

23. There are special ways to care for instruments to keep them in good condition: cleaning, tuning, protecting them from heat and cold.

24. Each person has a distinctive singing voice.

25. People can create a variety of sounds using their bodies and voices.

Making, Writing, and Responding to Music

26. People all over the world play instruments and make music.

27. Instruments are made by people.

28. Everyone can make and/or respond to music.

29. There are many different kinds of music.

30. People have musical preferences.

31. People use music for many different purposes: for pleasure, for ceremonies or rituals, to convey messages, for relaxation, for self-expression, to tell a story.

32. People make and/or respond to music alone or with others.

33. People who create original music (music that has never been heard before) are called composers.

34. People play or sing their own music or music someone else has composed.

*35. People use special symbols to write down music.

*36. People learn to read musical symbols.

37. People who tell or signal other musicians when to start and stop singing or playing are called conductors.

38. People respond to music with their bodies and imaginations.

39. People who play, sing, compose, or conduct music are called musicians.

40. The words to songs are called lyrics.

41. Lyrics tell the message of the song.

42. Everyone can make up lyrics.

43. People often write down or record lyrics.

44. People write down lyrics using words.

*45. People sing original lyrics or lyrics made up by someone else.

46. People sing lyrics once or many times.

47. People learn and remember lyrics by listening to them, singing them, and thinking about them.

48. People who make up lyrics are called lyricists or songwriters.

49. The more often people sing the lyrics to a song, the greater their chances of remembering them.

50. People learn to read lyrics just as they read other words.

*51. People often learn lyrics from other people directly, through records and tapes, or from songbooks.

52. People write lyrics by themselves or with other people.

*53. Sometimes the lyrics and music to a song are composed by the same person, sometimes by different people.

54. People don't always know who composed the lyrics or music to a particular song.

55. A group of instrumentalists is called an orchestra or a band.

56. A group of singers is called a chorus.

*57. People sing or play music in different ways called interpretations.

*58. People vary their interpretations of music by changing its melody, rhythm, volume, and tempo.

*59. The same tones are rearranged to make different melodies.

*60. Different musical interpretations of the same song elicit different responses from people.

ACTIVITY IDEAS

Aesthetic

1. *Funny Fiddles and Daffy Drums.* Have children construct pictures of the funniest or silliest instruments they can imagine using a variety of materials, such as precut paper shapes, that can be put together in funny ways. Offer paste or glue, and once the instruments are made, encourage the children to paint or decorate them as they wish, offering glitter, polka dots, and silly stickers. Emphasize humor and experimentation in this enterprise.

2. *Look at Those Instruments!* Select and display picture books or posters of different instruments in one area of the classroom. Encourage children to look at them and ask questions.

3. *Musical Listening Center.* Arrange a tape recorder or record player and a collection of musical pieces in a quiet corner of the room. To focus attention on appreciation of music, select musical pieces that vary in style and format: instrumentals, familiar songs, catchy tunes from TV shows, commercials, marches, folk songs, and so on.

4. *I Like to Make Music.* Provide a variety of instruments—drums, triangles, maracas, tambourines, wrist bells, xylophones, and so on—in an area of the classroom or outdoors. Encourage children to make their own music alone or with friends.

5. *Notes Collage.* Provide opportunities for children to see written music. Show them sheet music and piano songbooks as examples of musical notation. Make a large chart of a song they know, writing the notes on a staff such as the one in Figure 19.1. Make large notes, time signatures, clef signs, sharps, and flats from various colors of paper. Provide children with predrawn staves and have them arrange the musical symbols any way they wish. (Figure 19.2)

6. *Music from Other Parts of the World.* Teach simple songs that originated in other countries or are sung in other languages.

Sarasponda
(A spinning song from Finland)

Part 1:
Bunda bunda bunda bunda
(sung in a chant as others sing Part 2)

Part 2:
Sarasponda, sarasponda,
Sarasponda ret-set-set.
Sarasponda, sarasponda,
Sarasponda ret-set-set.
A dore o, A dore bunde o,
A dore bunde, ret-set-set
Ah-se-pah-se-o, Heh!

Divide the class into two groups. One group should chant Part 1 while the other sings Part 2. Then have the groups switch parts.

Frère Jacques
(France)
Frère Jacques, Frère Jacques,
Dormez-vous? Dormez-vous?
Sonnez les matines, Sonnez les matines
Ding, dang, dong. Ding, dang, dong.

Are You Sleeping?
(English)
Are you sleeping, are you sleeping?
Brother John, Brother John?
Morning bells are ringing,
Morning bells are ringing.
Ding, ding, dong.
Ding, ding, dong.

Figure 19.1 *Simple Example of Typical Music Notation*

Are You Sleeping?
(Spanish)
Frey Felipe, Frey Felipe,
Duermes tu, duermes tu?

Tocan las campanas,
Tocan las campanas.
Tan, tan, tan.
Tan, tan tan.

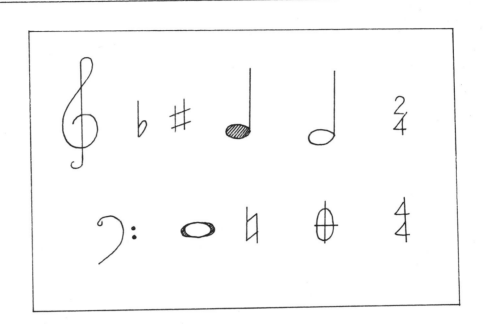

Figure 19.2 *Symbols to Enlarge and Offer for a Musical Collage*

Are You Sleeping?
(Yiddish)
Onkel Jakob, Onkel Jakob,
Schlafst du noch, schlafst du noch?
Ringe ander Glocke,
Ringe ander Glocke.
Bim, bam, bom. Bim, bam, bom.

Alouette
(French-Canadian singing game)
Alouette, gentille Alouette.
Alouette je te plumerai.
Je te plumerai la tête
Je te plumerai la tête
(or use *le nez*—the nose, *le cou*—the neck,
etc.)
Et la tête, Et la tête, Oh . . .
Alouette, gentille Alouette.
Alouette je te plumerai.

7. *Musical Creativity.*
General Purpose: For children to use their imaginations in relation to the arts.

TFPs: 1, 6, 11, 15–17, 28–32, 38, 58, 59, 60.

Materials: Recorded music in a wide variety of styles and from various cultures; finger paints, easel paints, or drawing materials, such as markers or chalk.

Procedure:
a. Introduce the activity by pointing out that music will be playing while children paint or draw.
b. Demonstrate different movements. "Let your fingers and hands move just the way the music tells you. Sometimes the music may make you feel like dancing— your hands and fingers or paintbrush can dance. Sometimes the music may

make you feel like swinging or swaying—your hands or brush can do that with the paints (markers)."

c. Provide the materials and encourage children to respond to the music.

Hint for Success:

• Introduce the activity to the whole group at one time. Record the musical selections you wish to use onto an audio cassette. This will allow the music to play continuously without having to turn records over. Arrange the tape player near the art area where it will be convenient but not in danger of being splashed with water or paints. As children finish in the area, tell them to invite others to take their place.

How to Simplify this Activity:

• Use familiar music so the children will not be distracted from the art materials.

• Select musical pieces with obvious differences of tone, tempo, and feeling (marches, lullabies).

How to Extend this Activity:

• Ask children to verbalize their responses to the music as well as to act them out through the art materials.

• Play some unfamiliar selections as part of the activity.

Affective

1. *Melody Mine.* Encourage children to select familiar tunes and sing their names over and over in place of the original words. Tape-record their efforts and play the tape back to them. Encourage older children to add personal descriptions to their songs for added variety (for example, to the tune "Are You Sleeping?"—I am Mary, I am Mary, I am tall, I am tall, I live in a red house with a cat named Henry, I am tall, I am tall).

2. *My Name in the Song.* Sing songs that provide opportunities for children to insert their names. Some examples are provided below.

Mary Wore a Red Dress
(Traditional)
Mary wore a red dress,
Red dress, red dress,
Mary wore a red dress,
All day long.
(Substitute children's names and one item of their clothing.)

I Wish I Had a Little Red Box
(Tune: Polly Wolly Doodle)
Oh, I wish I had a little (red) box,
To put that (Susannah) in.
I'd put him/her in and clap-clap-clap,
And take him/her out again.
(Substitute names and colors the children like.)

Everybody Do This
(Choose an action to demonstrate.)
Everybody do this, do this, do this.
Everybody do this, just like me.
(Have a child demonstrate an action and substitute his or her name in the song.)
Everybody do this, do this, do this.
Everybody do this, just like (Jimmy).

3. *My Hit Parade.* Allow one child at a time to select a favorite song to sing at particular times of the day. Structure the situation so children know in advance when they will have a chance to choose and where. Good times to sing may be at the beginning of large-group time, at clean-up time, or at dismissal. As you sing these songs, emphasize that each represents the choice of a particular child.

4. *Auditions.* Have the children listen to different interpretations of the same song on records or tapes. Ask them to vote for their favorites. Then graph the results, showing who chose which version of the song.

5. *What a Feeling!* Play a variety of musical selections and ask children to determine their own personal responses to them. Compare their feelings to others near them. Use music that represents different moods (scary, happy, sad, silly, and so on).

6. *Music I Like.*
General Purpose: For children to make choices and experience the natural consequences of personal decisions.

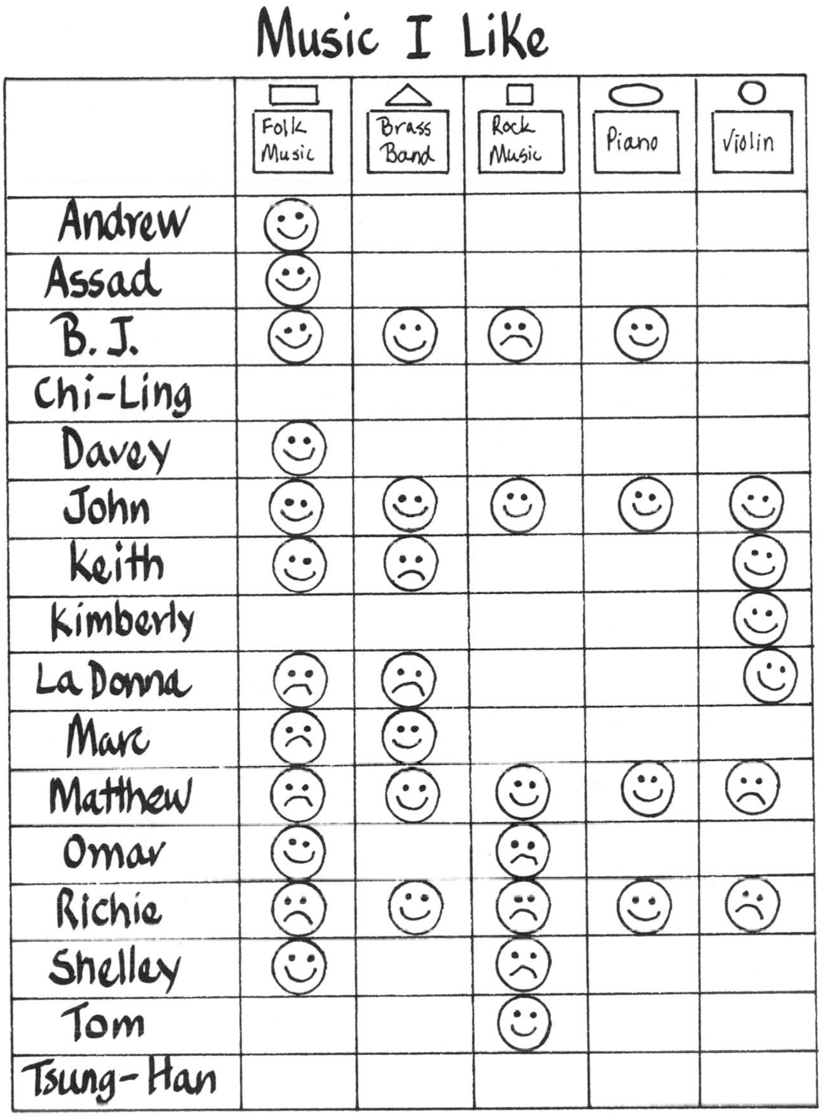

Music I Like

	Folk Music	Brass Band	Rock Music	Piano	Violin
Andrew	☺				
Assad	☺				
B. J.	☺	☺	☹	☺	
Chi-Ling					
Davey	☺				
John	☺	☺	☺	☺	☺
Keith	☺	☹			☺
Kimberly					☺
La Donna	☹	☹			☺
Marc	☹	☺			
Matthew	☹	☺	☺	☺	☹
Omar	☺		☹		
Richie	☹	☺	☹	☺	☹
Shelley	☺		☹		
Tom			☺		
Tsung-Han					

Figure 19.3 *A Musical Preference Chart for the Class*

TFPs: 1, 6, 15, 17, 29, 30, 59, 60.

Materials: A tape recorder or a simple record player; a collection of several different kinds of music (folk, rock, marching, jazz, lullaby, etc.) on tapes or records; preference chart made on 20-by-30-inch poster board (Figure 19.3); washable marker or removable stickers.

Procedure:

a. Arrange a listening center in a quiet area of the room to accommodate a few children at a time. Set up the record player or tape recorder with the musical selections (tapes or records) in a basket. Place the chart on the wall nearby with a marker for recording preferences.

b. Make the listening center as independent as possible. Demonstrate how to handle the tapes or records with care and how to start and stop the machine. Show children how to listen, determine their preferences, and indicate their preferences on the chart.

c. Keep the area open for several days until everyone has had a chance to listen and record their preferences.

Hints for Success:

- Place a shape (or sticker) on each recording to match the categories on the chart to help children differentiate the music independently. Be sure to point this out to the children.

- Make the chart reusable by covering it with clear contact paper, or by laminating it, before the exercise begins. Write on it with washable marker and when finished, wipe it clean.

How to Simplify this Activity:

- Provide fewer choices of music. If marking the chart is too difficult, provide removable stickers with smiles and frowns to indicate preferences.

How to Extend this Activity:

- Provide more choices or make an individual preference chart for each child to keep and place into a notebook that records the child's preferences regarding many things.

*7. **I Am a Conductor.**

General Purpose: For the children to evaluate themselves positively.

TFPs: 1, 14, 28, 32, 37, 39, 55.

Materials: A variety of rhythm instruments (either commercial or child-made), a conductor's stick or baton.

Procedure:

a. Introduce the activity. "Today, everyone who wishes to can take a turn being the leader of our orchestra (band). He or she will be called the conductor. The conductor is the person who decides when you should begin by giving this signal. (Demonstrate, for example, hands up.) When he or she decides you should stop, she or he will give this signal. (Demonstrate, hands down.) The conductor will also tell you which instruments to play at specific times. It is important to watch the conductor at all times and follow the signals. Let's practice these signals first. (Practice.) Now we're ready for our first conductor."

b. Select a child. Coach him or her on the signals, if necessary. Explain that he or she will decide when to begin conducting, decide how and when children are

to play, and then will choose when to signal the end.

c. Praise the child for doing a "splendid" job. Have him or her take a bow. Repeat with another child.

Hint for Success:

- This activity is most successful when children have had many experiences with the instruments and are able to refrain from playing whenever an instrument is in their hands.

How to Simplify this Activity:

- Give all of the children the same instrument.

How to Extend this Activity:

- Group similar instruments together. For example, put all the drums together on the floor, all the bells on one side, and all the triangles in the middle. Demonstrate how the conductor can point to a certain group to play at a certain time; show how different instruments can play separately or in overlapping intervals.

Cognition

1. **Follow the Picture Directions.** Choose the instrument illustrated here that could be made easily by the children in your group. Make large picture charts from the smaller ones that demonstrate the step-by-step procedure you want children to follow to make the instrument. Supply materials for several different instruments that could be made. Allow the children to decide which project to work on and encourage them to complete it through the last step. Some children may take more than one day to complete their projects. When children have finished making their instruments, ask them to summarize the steps they went through from start to finish. (Figures 19.4a, b, and c)

2. **Exploring Instruments.** Provide a collection of rhythm or melody instruments for children to look at, handle, and hear. Encourage comparisons, noting similarities and differences and investigating how each makes sound.

Making Simple Stringed Instruments

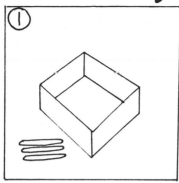

Take 1 box and 3 rubberbands.

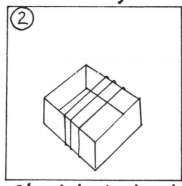

Stretch the bands around the box.

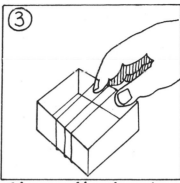

Strum the bands.

Figure 19.4a *Making the Simplest Stringed Instrument*

Making Tambourines

Take 1 plate, 6 bells and 6 pipe cleaners.

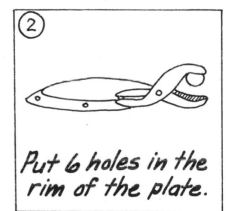

Put 6 holes in the rim of the plate.

Fasten the bells to the plate with pipe cleaners.

Hit the tambourine to make a sound.

Figure 19.4b *Follow the Picture Directions for a Tamborine*

Making a Kazoo

Figure 19.4c *How to Make a Kazoo*

3. ***Seriating Instruments.*** Give children opportunities to see and touch an assortment of real instruments, pictures of instruments, or paper drawings of real or imaginary instruments. Ask children to arrange the objects in order from those with the most of a particular feature to those with the least of that feature. Begin with only a few instruments and gradually add more.

4. ***I Am a Composer.*** Color code some of the keys on a piano, the bars on a xylophone, or a series of melody bells by attaching differently colored bits of paper to each key, bar, or bell. Make two-inch squares out of the same colors. Pile these in the center of a table, inviting children to select a few with which to create their own melodies. Ask the children to spread their squares in a line on the table from left to right or to paste them in a line on a piece of paper. Explain that each colored square represents one of the piano keys, xylophone bars, or melody bells. Invite the children to "play" their tunes by striking the corresponding keys or bars, or by ringing the corresponding bells. As children become more adept at matching the sounds and colors, increase the number of sounds they play, and the number of "lines" in their tunes, and help them pay attention to the spacing of their squares. Pieces close together might represent short sounds, blank spaces might mean silence, and so forth.

5. ***This Is the Way We Play the Horn.*** To the traditional tune "Here We Go 'Round the Mulberry Bush," sing a song about playing different instruments in a band. Use different words such as "This is the way we play the (horn, flute, guitar, banjo, etc.)." Use gestures and hand motions to "play" each instrument as you sing. Dis-

play pictures of the different instruments described in the song, or ask children to suggest ones they know.

6. ***Listen to Those Instruments!*** Provide individual pictures of instruments and a recorded example of what each sounds like. Show the picture and play the sound at the same time. (A good resource for instrumental sounds is *A Young Person's Guide to the Orchestra* by Benjamin Britten, available on audiotape.)

7. ***Count the Notes.*** Draw or paste quarter notes (in different colors) on cards and cover them with contact paper for durability. Each card should contain a different number of notes. On the back of each card, write a numeral to indicate the number of notes it illustrates. Play a game in which children count the notes on each card and then turn them over to see if they counted correctly. Make the game more interesting by having children count out the same number of buttons or small blocks as the number of notes on each card. In another variation, children use musical instruments to "sound out" the number of notes represented on each card.

8. ***Musical Glasses.*** Inside a water table or on a large tray, fill glasses of water to different levels. Tap each glass gently with a stick to produce different tones. Have children change the tones by adding water or pouring some out. Challenge children to match musical tones with the xylophone or tone bells. Add food coloring to the water to make it easier to see. After children have had time to play with these materials, involve them in predicting if a glass tone will be lower or higher than another; test out their guesses and ask them to evaluate why they were correct or not.

9. ***Instrument Lotto.*** Make a lotto game using pictures or stickers of familiar and unfamiliar instruments. Encourage children to match the pictures on the cards to the ones on their lotto boards.

10. ***Musical Symbol Match.*** Make matching pairs of cards with different musical symbols (whole notes, half notes, quarter notes, sixteenth notes, G clef, F clef, rests, sharps, flats, and so on). Play a game of concentration in which the object is to turn over matching pairs from a random array of cards placed face down on the table. For younger children, begin with four or five pairs only. Add more pairs as children seem ready. Note that it is not necessary for children to be able to name each symbol for this game.

11. ***Ordering Sounds.*** Demonstrate that sounds vary according to certain dimensions. Name dimensions and encourage children to practice making sounds that vary in those ways. Have children try to produce sounds with their voices or instruments that range from loud to quiet, quiet to loud, high to low, low to high, fast to slow, slow to fast, and so on.

12. ***Instrumental Silhouette Match.*** Make a game that requires children to match pictures of instruments to outlines of their shapes. A variation would be to match instruments to the shapes of their carrying cases. (Figure 19.5)

13. ***Sequencing Symbols into Songs.***

    General Purpose: For children to attach meaning to symbols in the environment.

    TFPs: 1, 16–21, 33–36.

    Materials: Five or six musical instruments, a set of ten to twelve card pairs depicting the instruments chosen.

    Procedure:

    a. Work with a small group of children. Distribute the instruments and encourage children to explore them for a few minutes.

    b. Introduce the activity by saying, "Today we are going to create some songs." Hold up each instrument and the corresponding card (showing the picture or symbol). Point out the relationship between them and tell children, "When I point to this card, you play the (pictured instrument) one time. But when I point to this other card, you play the (pictured instrument) one time."

    c. Allow children time to practice playing each instrument as you point to its symbol. Praise them for remembering what each means.

    d. Lay a simple series of cards out on the floor or table (drum, bell, triangle, mara-

Instrument Case Match

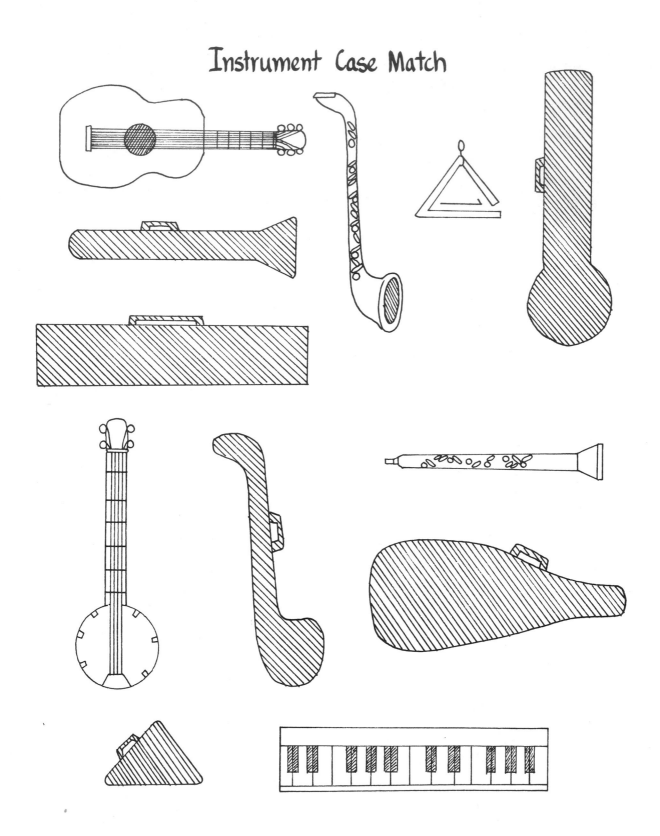

Figure 19.5 *Instrument Case Match-up*

ca). Say, "Now this is my 'song.' Let's take turns trying to play it. Dillon, you go first." Assist the child in striking the instruments in the order indicated.

e. Have the children take turns arranging and playing "songs" using the same symbols but changing the order.

f. As children become more skilled, introduce the use of repeated symbols (drum, drum, bell, bell or maraca, maraca, bell, drum, drum).

g. Finally, teach children a symbol for silence. Show them how this can be placed into a sequence (drum, drum, silence, bell, bell).

Hint for Success:

- Once children have the idea, they can work independently.

How to Simplify this Activity:

- Make symbols in the form of silhouette drawings or take photographs of the instruments you will use.

How to Extend this Activity:

- Use more abstract symbols (shapes or colors) for older children. For children who read, use the words for the instruments on the cards. To produce more permanent "songs," photocopy the symbols, cut them apart, and allow children to make up long songs, pasting their symbols onto long strips of paper. Display the songs and suggest that they play their songs for others. (Figure 19.6)

14. *Matching Sound Patterns.*

General Purpose: For children to recognize or construct relationships among objects and events through the process of patterning.

TFPs: 6, 7, 16–22.

Materials: Two matching sets of four or five rhythm instruments, a screen or low wall.

Procedure:

a. Show children the sets of instruments, pointing out that each set includes the same instruments. Allow children to try them out and explore the sounds of each.

b. Place one set of instruments and a child on either side of the screen so players cannot see each other, but can hear each other.

c. Explain the game by demonstrating how one person plays a short sequence of sounds (bell, drum, triangle) and the other tries to match the pattern by playing the exact same pattern on his or her instruments, using the sense of hearing only.

d. Help children reverse roles and take turns being the leader and follower.

Hint for Success:

- Keep patterns short. Patterns of two or three sounds should be used until the children appear ready for more complex sequences.

How to Simplify this Activity:

- Give each child two instruments and ask the leader to select one for the other player to match.

- Use only one instrument on each side of the screen and focus on matching the rhythm instead of the different sounds.

- Remove the screen so one child can watch as the other plays the pattern.

How to Extend this Activity:

- Encourage children to vary both the kind of sound (instrument) and the rhythm played (bell, bell, pause, drum, drum, drum).

15. *Different Instruments Sound Different.*

General Purpose: For children to recognize or construct relationships among objects and events through the process of matching.

TFPs: 2, 4–8, 30, 31.

Materials: A set of six instruments, pictures of each instrument in the set, a small portable screen or short wall.

Procedure:

a. Lay the instruments out and encourage children to play them. Then show the

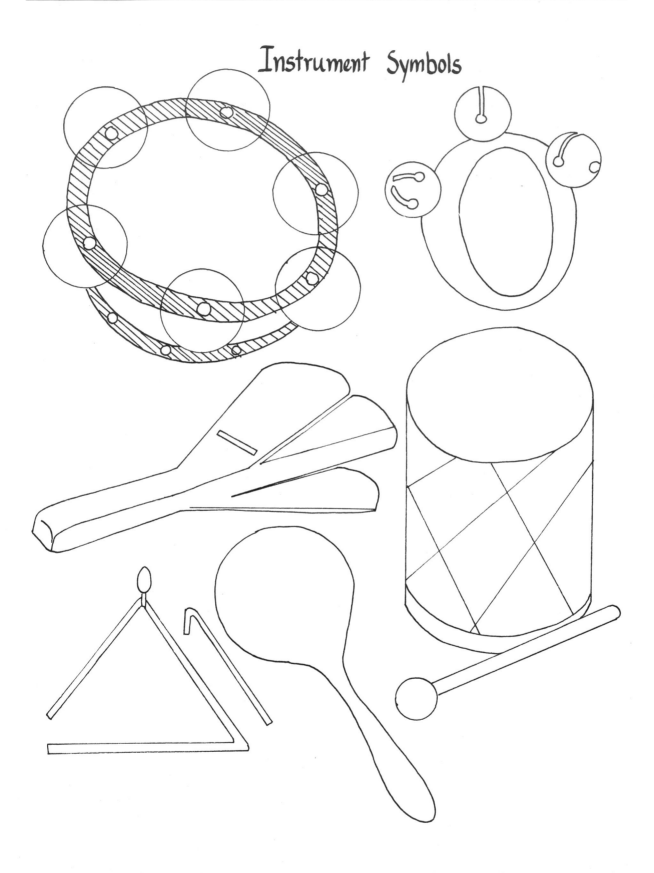

Instrument Symbols

Figure 19.6 *Simple Rhythm Instruments*

pictures of the instruments and tell children their names.

b. Demonstrate the sound of each instrument as you hold up its picture to establish the relationship for the children.

c. Invite children to match pictures and instruments on their own.

d. Set up the screen between yourself and a child. Arrange the instruments on your side and their pictures on the child's side. Say, "I'll play an instrument on this side of the screen where you can't see it. You listen and hold up the picture of the one you think I played."

e. Play one, wait for the child to respond. Praise correct responses. When a child responds incorrectly, show the instrument you played. Repeat with a different instrument.

Hints for Success:

• This game works well with one child or a pair of children who learn the game at the same time and take turns guessing.

• The screen can be any opaque wall or even a cafeteria tray or piece of cardboard.

• Have one child teach another how to play the game and encourage them to continue independently.

How to Simplify this Activity:

• Ask children to distinguish between only two instruments. Allow lots of practice in relating the sound to the picture before using the screen.

How to Extend this Activity:

• Use unusual instruments that children may have not heard before; or play two instruments at a time, asking the child to identify them both. Later, play more than two and ask the child to discriminate among them with help from a friend.

16. ***Who Is Playing?***
    General Purpose: For children to develop finer degrees of sensory acuity.
    TFPs: 16, 22, 28, 31.
    Materials: A variety of musical or rhythm instruments. Optional: a blindfold.

Procedure:

a. Seat a small number of children in a circle. Give each child an instrument. Allow time for children to investigate and play their instruments, then signal for quiet.

b. Introduce the game: "This is a guessing game. Each of you will have a chance to be 'the guesser.' One child sits in the middle of the circle and covers his or her eyes or wears the blindfold. I will tap another child, and he or she will make a sound on his or her instrument. The person in the middle will then open his or her eyes and point to the one who played the instrument."

c. Carry out the game, having children periodically trade instruments or change their places in the circle.

How to Simplify this Activity:

• Do this as a small-group activity, limiting the number of "players" to three or four, with one "guesser" in the middle. Place the instrument players on carpet squares at four opposite sides: to the right, to the left, in front of, and behind the guesser.

How to Extend this Activity:

• This game can be adapted to give children practice in discriminating among the sounds of different instruments by having the guesser point and tell what instrument was played before looking.

• Decrease the volume of the sounds.

• In another extension of this game, the adult will tap two or three children in sequence while the guesser has his or her eyes closed. The guesser must then determine who played when.

Construction

1. ***Musical Fantasy.*** After the class experiences a band, chorus, or group of musicians (on film, in a book, or in person), supply pictures of instruments, players, and singers for children to glue onto paper to create their own imaginary musical groups.

Making Maracas

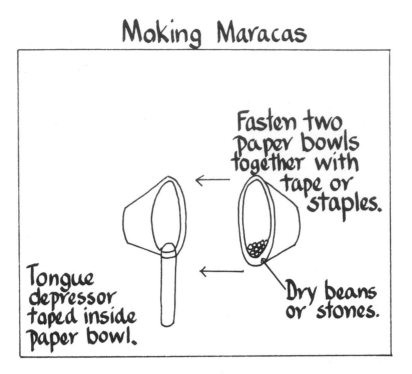

Fasten two paper bowls together with tape or staples.

Tongue depressor taped inside paper bowl.

Dry beans or stones.

Figure 19.7 *An Easy Way to Make Maracas*

2. ***Creating My Own Drum.*** After giving children experiences with several kinds of real drums, encourage them to make their own. Provide construction materials such as round oatmeal boxes or large coffee cans, paper, cloth (for drum heads), rubber bands, markers, paste, and sticks. Avoid making a model for them to follow. Encourage children to discover ways to put the materials together in their own fashion.

3. ***Let's Make Maracas.*** Following experiences with real maracas, suggest that children make some of their own and decorate them as they like. Provide small paper bowls, beans or small stones, a stapler, flat tongue depressor sticks, tape, and markers. Assist in fastening the bowls together as necessary. Encourage creative use of color and design. Avoid making a model so children are free to construct their instruments as they wish. (Figure 19.7)

4. ***Building a Musical Place.*** Give children experiences with a real stage, where musical productions, concerts, and perfor-

mances are held. Show them where the audience sits, where the performers stand or sit, where the orchestra plays, and so on. Then, provide large blocks and a large open space for children to create their own interpretation of a stage. If large blocks are not available, provide boxes or crates for them to build a child-sized version. Other materials for miniature constructions would be small blocks, lock-together plastic blocks, or wood scraps and glue.

5. ***My Imaginary Flute.*** After children have experienced wind instruments (flute, oboe, clarinet, recorder, saxophone, etc.) by trying them or seeing them played by other people, make a collection of materials available for them to construct imaginary versions of their own. Provide paper tubes, hole-punches, round-hole reinforcement stickers, paper circles, paste, and crayons or markers. Avoid making a model. Instead, encourage children to put the materials together many different ways. Ask children to tell you about their finished instruments.

6. ***Making My Own Stringed Instrument.***
General Purpose: For children to have an opportunity to represent a single object using various combinations of materials and techniques.

TFPs: 16, 19, 22–24, 27.

Materials: Pieces of soft wood of varying lengths and widths; several kinds of nails; two hammers; two safety goggles; rubber bands; 1-by-3-inch pieces of stiff cardboard; markers or paints.

Procedure:

a. Introduce children to several different kinds of stringed instruments, such as violin, cello, bass, autoharp, guitar, piano, and so on. Demonstrate the actual instruments, listen to recordings of different stringed instruments, and/or show pictures of the instruments. Discuss differences and similarities. Point out how the strings are attached to the instruments and how they make sounds when plucked, bowed, or strummed.

b. Suggest that children make their own stringed instruments. Display the materials for construction, showing the children how to hold and pound the nails while attaching "strings."

c. Allow two children to work at a time; give each a pair of safety goggles to wear and supervise them closely for safe use of the tools.

d. Encourage children to make their stringed instruments according to their own designs. Praise them as they think of their own ideas.

e. Remind children of the various kinds of instruments that use strings and of their different names. Display pictures of stringed instruments on the wall nearby. Ask the children to tell you what they want to call their instruments.

Hint for Success:

• Check to see that the nails are pounded far enough into the wood so they won't fall out.

How to Simplify this Activity:

• Give assistance with the hammer and nails, or provide softer materials such as Styrofoam with golf tees.

• Dip the tees into glue before hammering them into the Styrofoam to make them more permanent.

How to Extend this Activity:

• Suggest ways for children to individualize their finished instruments. Painting and decorating them, shellacking the wood, or shaping the wood with files and sandpaper are some possibilities. Find a special place for their names, as violin makers do. Encourage children to think about ways they'll take care of their instruments, how they will carry them, where they will put them, and so on.

• Children could make carrying cases for their instruments out of cardboard boxes.

Language

1. ***Imitating Clapping Patterns.*** Clap a pattern (clap, pause, clap, pause) and ask children to repeat it. Begin with very simple patterns, move on to more complex and longer ones as the children gain experience. Eventually have the children clap each other's patterns.

2. ***Song Charts.*** Select a few familiar songs. Write the lyrics large enough for children to see them easily. Keep these posted in the classroom. As you sing the songs, run your hand under the lyrics. Repeat these songs frequently.

3. ***Writing Familiar Song Lyrics.*** Make pencils and paper available to children. After children have been exposed to song charts for a long time, explain that they can write the lyrics to a favorite song in the best way they know. Since this is not an exercise in copying, do not make children copy actual lyrics. This exercise will likely encourage children to write using scribbles or some partial letter forms. These manifestations of writing development are typical for young children and developmentally appropriate. Avoid insisting on correct spellings or correctly formed letters. Children will work on this activity at many different

levels. Avoid comparing this work. Keep folders of their writings to monitor the progress of individuals over time.

4. *My Songbook.* As a follow-up activity to song charts and writing familiar lyrics, choose a very familiar song and make a simple songbook with one line or phrase of the song on each page, leaving empty spaces for illustrations (either made by you or the children). Give each child a copy of the book. (Figures 19.8a and b) Demonstrate how (and when) to turn the pages while singing the song. Tell children that they are "reading the song." Allow plenty of opportunities for children to use the songbooks over and over. Soon they will be recognizing words and will begin to understand the act of reading.

To make a songbook using the sample pages:

Copy the two sheets back to back with the cover (find the star) and page 1 as a back-to-back guide. Cut pages apart on the horizontal line and fold on the vertical. Slide the pages inside and staple them together on the folded edge.

---

5. *Describing Instruments.* Display a picture of an instrument and a picture of a real instrument or an instrument that children have made. Ask children to describe it in words. Focus on the verbal descriptions. Use leading responses such as, "Tell me more about the . . ." or "What else do you see?" Write down what each child says in a story form, using the exact words.

6. *I Can Make Up Parts of Songs.* Sing songs for which children supply a key element (an article of clothing, a name of a person or animal, a food, etc.). "Mary Wore a Red Dress," "Aiken Drum," "Rig-a-Jig-Jig," and "Come On and Join Into the Game" all encourage these kinds of contribution.

Aiken Drum
(Traditional tune or chant)
There was a man lived in the moon,
Lived in the moon, lived in the moon.
There was a man lived in the moon,
And his name was Aiken Drum.

Verse 1:
And he played upon a ladle,
a ladle, a ladle,
And he played upon a ladle,
And his name was Aiken Drum.

Children can make up their own additional verses such as:
And his coat was made of roast beef, etc.
And his buttons were made of strawberries, etc.
And his hair was made of spaghetti, etc.

Come Join Into Our Game
(Traditional tune or chant)
Let everyone clap hands like me.
(clap, clap)
Let everyone clap hands like me.
(clap, clap)
Come join into our game.
You'll find that it's always the same.
(clap, clap)

Repeat using other actions such as: everyone sneeze, everyone laugh, everyone jump up, everyone sit down, etc.

Rig-a-Jig-Jig
(Tune: "Let's All Sing Like the Birdies Sing")
As I was walkin' down the street,
down the street, down the street,
A (color)/(animal),
I happened to meet,
Hi ho, hi ho, hi ho.
Rig-a-jig-jig and away we go,
Away we go, away we go,
Rig-a-jig-jig and away we go,
Hi ho, hi ho, hi ho.
(Repeat with new color and animal.)

7. *Musical Conversations.* Using a simple two-note phrase, sing simple sentences to children and encourage them to answer you using a singing voice, matching the tones you used. Begin with: "Hel-lo" (do-la). Allow time for children to respond. Other sentences could be: "How are you?" (do - do - la) and "I am fine" (do - do - la). Use this activity during a large-group or small-group activity time, or with individuals as they play during free choice time. It is most successful with children who have had many singing experiences.

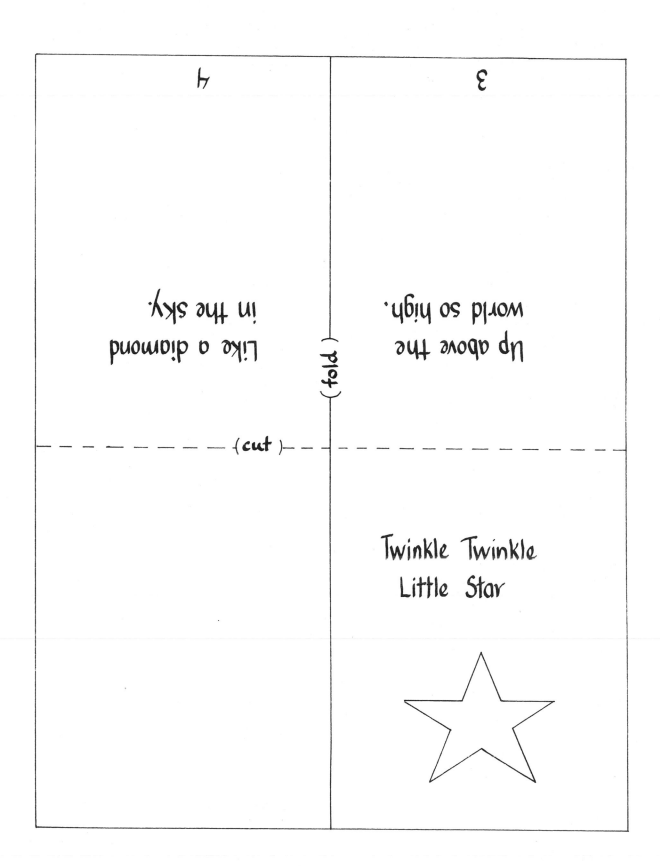

Figure 19.8a *Making Your Own Song Books*

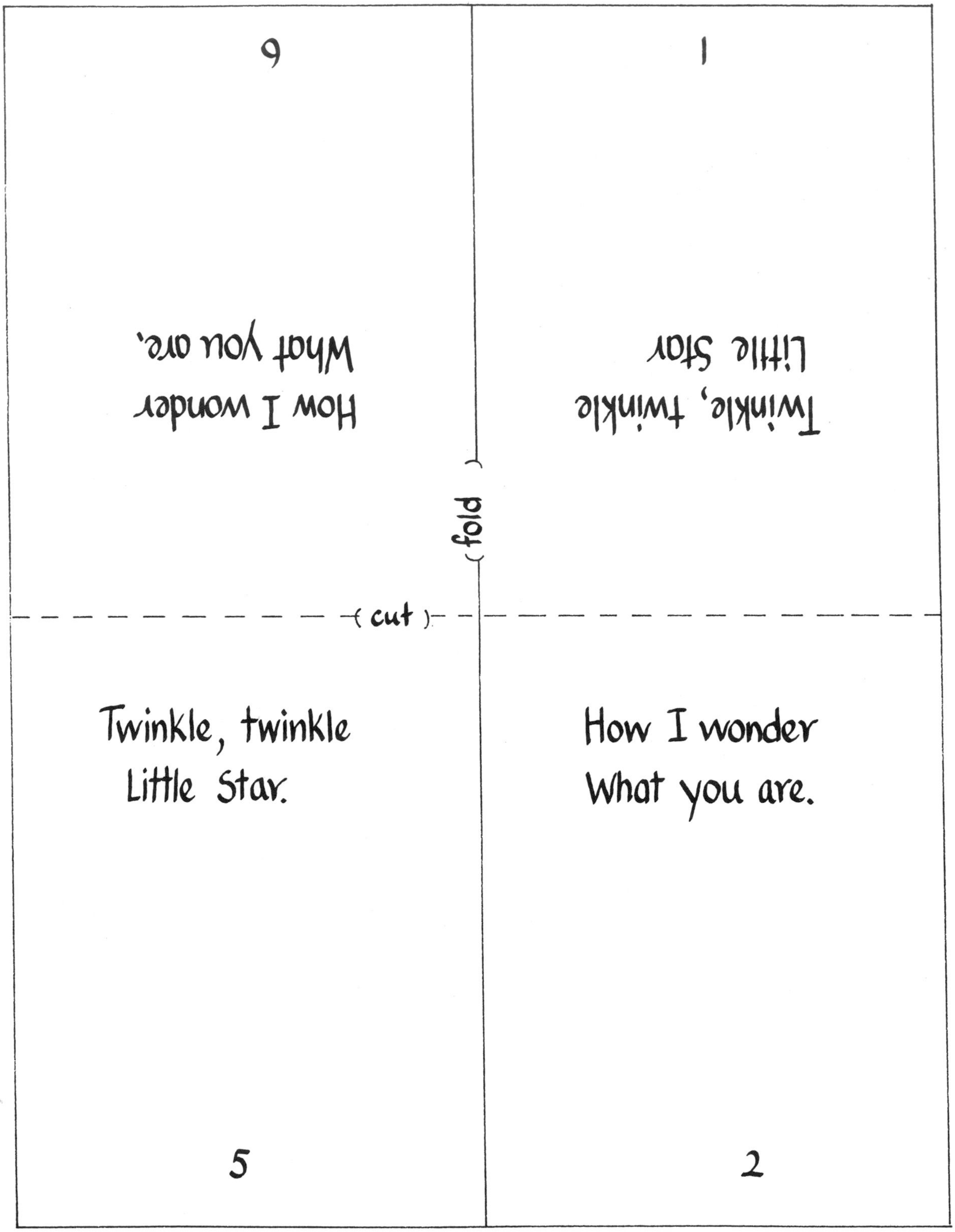

9

1

How I wonder
What you are.

Twinkle, twinkle
Little Star

(fold)

- - - - - - (cut) - - - - - -

Twinkle, twinkle
Little Star.

How I wonder
What you are.

5

2

Figure 19.8b *Making Your Own Song Books (continued)*

8. ***Story Songs.*** After reading one of the following storybooks to the children, introduce the tune that the story suggests. Invite children to sing along as you go through the book again. Extend the activity by having children create their own illustrations for the words or by making up a tune for a simple storybook they like.

Aliki. *Go Tell Aunt Rhody*. New York: Macmillan, 1974.

Aliki. *Hush Little Baby: A Folk Lullaby*. Englewood Cliffs, NJ: Prentice-Hall, 1968.

Bonne, R. *I Know an Old Lady*. New York: Scholastic, 1961.

Child, L. M. *Over the River and Through the Woods*. New York: Coward, McCann and Geoghegan, 1974.

Conover, C. *Six Little Ducks*. New York: Crowell, 1976.

Eberly, B. *One Wide River to Cross*. New York: Scholastic, 1966.

Graboff, A. *Old MacDonald had a Farm*. New York: Scholastic, 1969.

Kellogg, S. *Steven Kellogg's Yankee Doodle*. New York: Parents Press, 1976.

Nichol, B. P. *Once: A Lullaby*. New York: Greenwillow, 1983.

Paterson, A. B. *Waltzing Matilda*. New York: Holt, Rinehart and Winston, 1970.

Pearson, T. C. *Sing a Song of Sixpence*. New York: Dutton, 1985.

Spier, P. *The Erie Canal*. Garden City, NY: Doubleday, 1970.

————. *Fox Went Out on a Chilly Night*. Garden City, NY: Doubleday, 1961.

————. *London Bridge Is Falling Down*. Garden City, NY: Doubleday, 1985.

Wadsworth, O. A. *Over in the Meadow*. New York: Puffin Press, 1985.

9. ***Sing Us Your Name.***
   General Purpose: For children to experiment with language sounds and pitch.
   TFPs: 1–3, 7, 16, 28.
   Materials: None.
   Procedure:
   a. Gather the children together and introduce this new singing game. With the help of an adult aide or a child who has been prepared for the game ahead of time, demonstrate how to play before asking the children to try.
   b. Say, "Today we're going to sing a different kind of song. In this song, I sing a line, then you sing a line, then we all sing a line. We'll start by using Martha's (the name of your adult or child assistant) name in the song. Listen to us."
   You sing: "Sing us your name."
       (do do la do)
   Answer: "My name is Martha."
       (do do la do do)
   All sing: "Her name is Martha."
       (do do la do do)
   Try to match the pitch of each tone.
   c. Invite children who want to have their names in the song to raise their hands. Repeat the song, directing the first phrase to the child. Help children who hesitate by singing the response with them. All sing the final phrase together.
   d. Encourage any response. Participation may be difficult for inexperienced children. As they become more confident, their responses will likely follow this sequence: silence, whispered name, spoken name, spoken phrase, sung phrase, sung phrase matching the tones.

Hint for Success:
- Repeat this activity frequently over several weeks. More children will participate and their responses will become more confident.

How to Simplify this Activity:
- Use the syllable "la" as a substitute for all the other words of the song. Say, "Listen to this: la-la-la-la," using the correct sequence (do-do-la-do) of pitches.
- Use your hand to indicate the levels of the pitch (high, high, low, high) and when it changes.
- Have children practice echoing your voice exactly.

How to Extend this Activity:
- Once children can easily match these two pitches, expand to add a third pitch, lengthening the phrase slightly ("Sing us your name please") using do-do-la-so-so as the sequence of pitches, and indicating with your hand high, high, low, mid-

dle, middle. The response should echo the pitches you establish.

10. *I Am a Songwriter.*

General Purpose: For the children to expand their abilities to use words to represent knowledge, events, ideas, imaginings, and perceptions.

TFPs: 15, 40, 41, 43, 44, 48, 52.

Material: Tape recorder and tape, stuffed toy and/or pictures of people and animals.

Procedure:

a. Introduce the activity by discussing the role of song lyrics (see TFPs).

b. Choose a simple song with a familiar melody such as "The Farmer in the Dell" or "Mary Had a Little Lamb."

c. Tell each child to select a toy (or picture) to sing about. Talk about the item with the child; help him or her to think of a brief story. "Tell me one thing that will happen in your song." Encourage the child to try telling a simple story without music.

d. Ask the child to put his or her words into the melody. Assist the child who hesitates. Sing with him or her.

e. Record the child's song, showing the child how to operate the recorder so that he or she can play it back.

f. Repeat this with other children.

Hint for Success:

• Some children may sing songs that go on forever! Limit them to a few lines; they will have an easier time remembering what they have said. Stuffed animals can be used to motivate and inspire ideas. However, any prop may be used for this purpose.

How to Simplify this Activity:

• Model the activity first. Sing a familiar melody with your own words. Leave blanks that the child can fill in, such as "Three *little cats,* see how they *sleep,*" sung to the tune of "Three Blind Mice."

Physical

1. *Movement to Music.* Play recorded or taped music for children. Suggest that they respond to it by moving their bodies the way the music makes them feel. Encourage variety by making your own tape of short segments of music with brief pauses between the different musical styles. Use selections that have a variety of styles and moods, such as country, jazz, lullabies, bouncy polkas, and so on. Structure the space so children have room to move without bumping into each other. Stimulate movement by providing scarves or crepe-paper streamers.

2. *Step to the Beat.* Identify the steady, regular beats of familiar tunes. Begin by humming each tune and clapping its beats for the children; then have them clap it with you. Later, sing the song and clap the beat as children join in the singing. Finally, have them try walking by stepping forward on every beat.

3. *Jim-Along Josie.* Sing the traditional song, "Jim-Along Josie," having children do the body motions as you change the active words. Repeat for walk-along, hop-along, and so on. End with sleep-along.

Jim-Along Josie
(Traditional)
Jim, Jim, Jim-along Josie
Jim, Jim, Jim-along Jo.

(Change to action *words.)*
Walk, walk, walk-along Josie
Walk, walk, walk-along Jo.

Jump, jump, jump-along Josie
Jump, jump, jump-along Jo.

Clap, clap, clap-along Josie
Clap, clap, clap-along Jo.

4. *Tracing Instruments.* Cut simple outline shapes of familiar instruments from cardboard. Encourage children to trace around them onto paper.

5. *Hi/Low, Here We Go.* Use a piano, recorder, guitar, or xylophone to produce musical sounds. After demonstrating high- and low-pitched sounds to the children, explain that they will have to listen for differences in pitch to play this game. Ask the children to spread out into a circle and begin walking to the right. When they hear a high pitch, they will walk on tiptoe with their arms extended over their heads. When the pitch is low, the children will

crouch down low and continue moving until the sound changes again. Begin by using extreme differences in pitch; gradually make the differences more subtle.

6. *Stop/Go—Fast/Slow.*

General Purpose: For children to engage in a variety of motor activities designed to enhance flexibility.

TFPs: 5, 11, 12, 32, 38.

Materials: Hand drum or tambourine.

Procedure:

a. Introduce the activity by telling children: "I'm going to play some rhythms on this drum."(Demonstrate by playing a moderate, steady beat.) "Sometimes I will play fast, sometimes slow. Move around this circle at the speed (tempo) the drum tells you. When the drumbeat stops, freeze. Move only when the drum is sounding."

b. Play a moderate beat on the drum and watch children as they move. When you stop, praise children for remembering to freeze.

c. Continue the activity, varying the tempo each time you begin again. Continue to praise children as they become better able to stop and go on the appropriate signals.

Hints for Success:

- Once you have begun a beat, maintain a steady tempo until you stop. The object is for children to establish a regular rhythmic pattern before they freeze.

- Vary the tempo from episode to episode.

How to Simplify this Activity:

- Move with the children, holding someone's hand if necessary.

How to Extend this Activity:

- Vary the tempo more for each episode and suggest other ways of moving, such as skipping, galloping, running, hopping, moving very high in space, or moving low in space.

Pretend Play

1. *Instrument Maker's Repair Shop.* Provide materials and tools for making and repairing instruments. (Supply a variety or a different collection of materials each day.) Arrange tables and chairs for the "instrument makers," an area for repairs, and a display area for the finished instruments. Put out a cash register and receipts for selling instruments and encourage children to take on roles that interest them (instrument maker, salesperson, repair person, or customer).

2. *Music Store.* Supply an area of the room with shelves, real or pretend instruments, music books, pretend records, pretend money, cash register, and so on. Discuss the different roles that could be played in this store (owner, salesclerk, customer, helper). Demonstrate to children ways to start playing if they are inexperienced or appear confused by the props.

3. *Recording Studio.* After discussing the place where records, tapes, and CDs are made and recorded, equip an area with pretend microphones, tape recorders, control panels, instruments, or other props for recording.

4. *Musical Theater.*

General Purpose: For children to experiment with a variety of objects, roles, and characterizations.

TFPs: 14, 15, 25–34.

Materials: A pretend stage, a set of instruments, costumes, telephones, hats, glasses, an audience setup, cash register, tickets, chairs, pretend microphone, cameras.

Procedure:

a. Invite children to explore the materials and the arrangement of the theater. Define theater (a place where people go to be in a show or to see a show). Answer questions about the props and limitations of the area.

b. Describe what people do in a musical theater. Ask if any children have seen a musical show on a stage or on television.

c. Encourage children to assume roles: announcer, actor, player, ticket seller, audience member, and so on.

d. Inspire thinking by asking open-ended questions such as: "What kind of show could you make?" "What else could you do?" "How can you use the drum in your show?"

e. Praise children for creative thinking and for using their own ideas.

Hints for Success:

- Do not insist on a "story" or a "play" on the stage. Children will want to perform in many different ways.

- Limit the number of children on the stage at a time, suggesting that they need an audience as a way to occupy other players for a short while.

How to Simplify this Activity:

- Expect younger, less experienced children to focus on trying on costumes and performing all at the same time, not paying much attention to each other. Limit the props.

How to Extend this Activity:

- More experienced players can work together to share the stage, take turns, or even stage a "show" together that would be performed at a specific time for a specific audience.

5. *Pretend a Story Song.*

   General Purpose: For children to explore dramatizing a familiar song.

   TFPs: 31, 40, 41.

   Materials: None.

   Procedure:

   a. Prepare the children by teaching a song that tells a story well in advance of carrying out this activity. (See suggestions provided at the end of this exercise.) Practice it until they know it well.

   b. Review the song, going over the story line. Have children identify the characters and discuss what happens. Suggest that they practice being one or more of the characters. ("Let's all be Humpty Dumpty sitting on the wall. Now let's all fall off the wall. Now let's all be the king's horses and king's men, trying to put Humpty Dumpty together.") Encourage children by praising their ideas, use of their bodies, gestures, and movements to portray the characters.

   c. Tell them they'll all have a chance to act out the story song together. Suggest that they can choose to be one or several characters in the song. Say, "I will sing the song and when your character does something, you can act it out. Listen for my voice and we'll begin."

   d. Start the song, moving from event to event and allowing time for the children to portray the characters or depict the actions. Allow children to take on as many or as few roles as they wish. Allow them to change roles as the story changes, even in the middle of the song.

   e. At the conclusion of the song, say "the end" and tell everyone to sit down. Praise children for their participation.

   f. Repeat the story song immediately if time permits and then, many times over the next few days to allow children to take on different parts and expand their portrayals.

Hint for Success:

- This method of dramatization allows all of the children to be active and involved simultaneously. Some children may choose to watch; encourage but do not insist on their active involvement. Children learn by watching and some are more likely to participate once they've seen others do it.

How to Simplify this Activity:

- Use short folk songs and nursery rhymes, such as "Old Mister Rabbit," "Hickory Dickory Dock," "Jimmy Crack Corn," "The Old Gray Cat," and "Mary Had a Little Lamb."

How to Extend this Activity:

- Use songs with more complicated stories and more characters, such as: "Frog Went a Courtin'" and "Animal Fair."

Old Mister Rabbit
(Traditional)
Old Mr. Rabbit
You have a mighty habit,
Of jumping in my garden,
And eating all my carrots.

Hickory Dickory Dock
(Mother Goose, traditional)
Hickory dickory dock,
the mouse ran up the clock.
The clock struck one,
the mouse ran down.
Hickory dickory dock.

The Old Gray Cat
(Traditional)

Verse 1:
The old gray cat is sleeping,
sleeping, sleeping.
The old gray cat is sleeping in the house.

Verse 2:
The little mice are nibbling,
nibbling, nibbling.
The little mice are nibbling in the house.

Verse 3:
The old gray cat comes creeping,
creeping, creeping.
The old gray cat comes creeping
through the house.

Verse 4:
The little mice all scamper, scamper,
scamper.
The little mice all scamper back to
their nest.

Social

1. *Group Singing Games.* In a large or small group, lead children in games that involve singing or rhythm. Teach the song first, then show how it fits into the game. The words and game rules may vary from region to region since many of these games have been passed down orally from one generation to the next. Two examples of singing games that could be adapted for many different age groups are provided here. Others may be found in the adult reference books cited at the end of this chapter.

Making a Purple Stew
How to Play: Children walk around in a circle holding hands, singing this song. Anyone wearing that color steps into the center and becomes part of the stew. Repeat the song with another color, until everyone is in the stew.
The Song (tune of "Animal Fair"): We're making a purple stew. We're making a purple stew, with purple potatoes, and purple tomatoes, and how about some of *you*!"

A Tisket A Tasket
How to Play: The group sits in a circle on the floor. One child carries a basket around the outside of the circle. The basket contains paper "letters" (or hearts, or any other shape). Child (A) drops a "letter" behind another child (B) and gallops or skips around the circle fast. Child (B) picks the "letter" up and chases after child (A). Child (A) sits down in the empty spot and gives the basket to the standing child. The game repeats until everyone has a letter.
The Song: "A tisket, a tasket, a green and yellow basket, I wrote a letter to my friend and on the way I dropped it. I dropped it, I dropped it, and on the way I dropped it."

Other tuneful social games are:
"The Farmer in the Dell"
"London Bridge Is Falling Down"
"I'm a Little Teapot"
"Hokey Pokey"
"Ring Around the Rosey"

2. *Cooperative Music.* Have each child sit with a partner. Explain that they will be cooperating to make music. Pass out one rhythm instrument to each pair of children. Encourage them to find ways to share and cooperate to make music. They might take turns, play together simultaneously, trade roles (holder and striker), and so on. Praise any successes at cooperation. Point out to the group some ways people found to cooperate.

3. *Making a Real Purple Stew.* Teach the children the singing game "Making a Purple Stew." (See the Group Singing Game activity.) Then, tell them they could all contribute to making a real "purple stew" by bringing in vegetables the following day. Be sure to have children wash their hands before participating in any part of the activity. Provide a food preparation area where, with adult supervision, children could wash, peel, and cut up their vegetables. The cooking area might be a kitchen, a hot plate and pot, or an electric frying pan. After vegetables have been washed and prepared, place them in a large cooking pot with hot water and dissolved beef bouillon or a can of chopped

tomatoes for a base. Any vegetables may be used, but cook the harder vegetables longer. (Carrots and potatoes will take fifteen to twenty minutes, depending on the size of the pieces.) As vegetables are added to the stew pot, sing the song along with the children, deciding what color stew they are making. Serve the "purple stew" for snack or lunch.

4. *Sociable Sounds.* Gather the children in a group, then pass out objects that make distinct sounds, such as bells, shakers, or cans partially filled with pebbles or dried beans. Ask the children to spread out in a large area. When you give the signal, they will begin to make sounds with their objects. Then their tasks will be to find the others in the group who are making similar sounds. Use sound makers that look alike but make noticeably different sounds so children rely on auditory rather than visual cues to find a "match."

*5. *Waiting My Turn to Play.*

General Purpose: For children to practice delaying gratification.

TFPs: 18–23, 28, 32, 38.

Materials: Instruments children have made or other rhythm instruments.

Procedure:

a. Gather the children into a circle. Introduce the activity by saying, "Each of you has an instrument. We are going to hear how every instrument sounds, one at a time. That means, when it is someone else's turn to play, you hold your instrument quietly in your lap. When it is your turn to play, everyone else will hold their instruments quietly in their laps. You will know it's your turn when I hold my hand on your shoulder. When I take my hand away, your turn is over." Demonstrate, using either another adult or a child.

b. Begin the game. Praise children throughout the activity for waiting their turns. "I really like the way you are waiting and keeping your instruments quiet." Remind each child as he or she begins, that this is his or her special time. "Now Jeffrey gets his turn." "And now it's Larry's turn."

c. As the game proceeds, give children hints or ask them for ideas about how to

make the "wait" easier. (Sing in your head to the sound that someone else is playing; tap your foot lightly in rhythm to the instrument being played, etc.)

Hint for Success:

• Remember that the focus is on turn-taking and delay of gratification. Therefore, keep the turns short at first.

How to Simplify this Activity:

• Do this in small groups so waiting time is shorter.

How to Extend this Activity:

• With older or experienced children, extend each turn. Eventually, allow the children to take over the leadership role.

TEACHER RESOURCES

Field Trip Ideas

1. Locate a music store in your community. Take the class to visit it, pointing out the instruments, records, tapes, and so on. Ask a salesperson to play some of the instruments for the group if possible. Plan to purchase something at the store for your classroom such as sheet music, a new record, or a guitar pick.

2. Find out who repairs broken instruments in your community. Take the children to visit this shop, pointing out the various tools that are used for such work. Ask one of the repair people to demonstrate what he or she is working on, showing a technique being used.

3. Check into the possibility of walking your class through some of the music rooms at your local high school. Ask if the children might visit while the band or orchestra is rehearsing. Point out the different instruments, the conductor, and the music everyone is using.

Classroom Visitors

1. Locate and invite a musician from the area to your classroom. A parent, community bands, local orchestras, and high schools can often suggest possible visitors. Ask the visitor to demonstrate his or her instrument, show its parts, and tell how they

learned to play it. Ask your guest to play a favorite tune and explain something about the piece to the children.

Children's Books

Brenner, C. *Cunningham's Rooster*. New York: Parent's Magazine Press, 1975.

Brown, M. W. *The Little Brass Band*. New York: Harper and Row, 1955.

Bunting, E. *The Traveling Men of Ballycou*. New York: Harcourt Brace Jovanovich, 1983.

Ciardi, J. *John, J. Plenty and Fiddler Dan*. New York: Lippincott, 1963.

DePaola, T. *Sing, Pierrot, Sing*. New York: Harcourt Brace Jovanovich, 1983.

Duff, M. *Johnny and His Drum*. New York: Henry A. Walck, 1972.

Duvoisin, R. *Petunia and the Song*. New York: Knopf, 1951.

Freeman, D., and L. Freeman. *Pet of the Met*. New York: Viking, 1968.

Grifalconi, A. *The Toy Trumpet*. New York: Dodds-Merrill, 1968.

Gustafson, S. *Animal Orchestra: A Counting Book*. Chicago: Calico Books, 1988.

Hoban, L. *Harry's Song*. New York: Greenwillow, 1980.

Howath, B. *Jasper Makes Music*. New York: Franklin Watts, 1967.

Isadora, R. *Ben's Trumpet*. New York: Greenwillow, 1979.

Keats, E. J. *Apt. 3*. New York: Macmillan, 1971.

Maiorano, R. *A Little Interlude*. New York: Coward, McCann and Geoghegan, 1980.

McCloskey, R. *Lentil*. New York: Viking, 1940.

McMillan, B. *The Alphabet Symphony*. New York: Greenwillow, 1977.

Williams, I. *Music, Music for Everyone*. New York: Greenwillow, 1984.

Adult References

Ardley, N. *Music*. New York: Knopf, 1989.

Baines, A. *European and American Musical Instruments*. London: Chancellor Press, 1966.

Barnes, C. A. *Harper's Dictionary of Music*. New York: Noble, 1972.

Berger, M. *The Photo Dictionary of the Orchestra*. New York: Methuen, 1980.

*Challis, E. *Jumping, Laughing and Resting, Songs for a New Generation*. New York: Oak Publications, 1974.

Crawford, R. *American Folksongs for Children*. New York: Oak Publications, 1948.

*Fowke, E. *Sally Go Round the Sun*. London: McClelland and Stewart, 1981.

*Glazer, T. *Eyewinker, Tom Tinker, Chin Chopper*. Garden City, NY: Doubleday, 1973.

Luttrell, G. *The Instruments of Music*. New York: Nelson, 1977.

Nelson, E. L. *The Funny Song Book*. New York: Sterling, 1984.

Rubin, R., and J. Wathen. *The All-year Long Songbook*. New York: Scholastic Book Services, 1980.

Siegmeister, E. *The New Music Lover's Handbook*. Irvington-on-Hudson, NY: Harvey House, 1973.

Smith, R., and C. Leonhard. *Discovering Music Together*. Chicago: Follett, 1968.

*Winn, M., and A. Miller. *The Fireside Book of Fun Games and Songs*. New York: Simon and Schuster, 1974.

*Raffi. *The Raffi Everything Grows Songbook* (and tape). New York: Crown, 1989.

Raffi. *The Raffi Singable Songbook* (and tape). New York: Crown, 1980.

Adult Audio References

Britten, B., conductor. *A Young Person's Guide to the Orchestra*. Performed by the London Symphony Orchestra. London Records #425659-2

*Songbooks that include musical fingerplays.

Chapter 20

Storytelling

.

"Once upon a time . . ."

Few people can resist the enjoyment promised by those words. Everybody likes a good story! Hence storytelling is a time-honored custom among all cultures. It is a traditional way to transmit ideas, beliefs, and history from one person to another and from one generation to the next.

Stories come in many varieties—short, long, made-up, true, humorous, sad, and frightening. Some stories are known worldwide, some are particular to a given culture, and some are unique to individual families. Certain stories are designed to convey specific information, while others have no greater aim than to entertain. Yet whatever their style or substance, stories are such a common aspect of daily living that it is the rare child who has never heard one told, or begged to hear a favorite tale "one more time."

For children, storytelling represents a natural, comfortable mode of communication. Through it, fantasies can be expressed, ideas explored, and language manipulated and created. Storytelling is a means of expression at which all people can succeed. Just as everyone enjoys listening to stories, so too does everyone have a story to tell.

PURPOSE

The Storytelling theme affords children the pleasure of hearing many different stories, as well as the opportunity to tell all kinds of stories themselves. In creating this unit, we have chosen to emphasize the latter function. We reasoned that while most youngsters have heard stories told or read to them, they less often find themselves in the more active position of storyteller. This is a role that offers many rewards: self-satisfaction, opportunities for creative language development, and numerous experiences with modes of representational thought. Consequently, while we have incorporated several "listening" activities into the suggestions provided, we have usually extended those plans to involve children in recreating some or all of the story, or in developing stories of their own.

Moreover, we have made certain to develop activities through which children can represent the world and the events in it on at least three different levels: enactive, iconic, and symbolic.

Children who represent the world enactively use their bodies to reconstruct or act out events and roles using objects, gestures, sounds, and words. This is a very tangible, concrete way to "think through" an experience and is the most basic form of representation (Lawton, 1987).

A somewhat more abstract mode of representation involves children making pictures or constructing three-dimensional images of what they see and think about. These are iconic representations. Youngsters who reproduce or create their own interpretations of objects and events using art or construction materials, such as blocks, are demonstrating iconic representation.

The ultimate and most abstract means of representation is symbolic. In this mode, children manipulate words and symbols, such as letters or numerals, to interpret and represent particular phenomena. We have included many activities using words and written language so that children have numerous opportunities to represent the world symbolically.

IMPLEMENTATION

You may choose to implement a unit on storytelling in any one of several ways.

Option One: Develop single-week units that concentrate on a particular genre of story, such as folktales or myths. For younger, less experienced children, we recommend focusing on nursery rhymes, folktales, or animal stories. Older youngsters, or those more familiar with storytelling, enjoy myths and legends, tall tales, and biographies. Create multiweek units by highlighting a different story type each week for a two- or three-week period.

Option Two: Select a particular story around which to build classroom activities. For instance, activity plans designed around *The Three Bears* might include a house with three bowls, chairs, and beds in pretend play, porridge for a snack, telling the story using flannelboard pictures, and counting using miniature bears. Toddlers and younger preschoolers benefit when such an emphasis is carried over at least two days. Four- or five-year-olds as well as first-graders appreciate a different story each day.

Option Three: In week one, focus on fictional stories. In week two, present nonfiction stories. In week three, include both fiction and nonfiction, comparing and contrasting the two.

Option Four: In week one, present a general overview of storytelling, concentrating on the TFPs related to story structure (plot sequence of events and characters). In week two, focus on a different mode of storytelling each day, such as pantomime, puppetry, storybooks or story songs.

TERMS, FACTS, AND PRINCIPLES

General Information

1. A story is an account of an event or a series of events that happens to real or imaginary people, animals, or things.

2. Stories are created by people.

Story Types

3. People sometimes create stories on their own and sometimes in cooperation with other people.

*4. People create stories for amusement, to teach a lesson, or describe or explain certain phenomena or events.

5. Stories may be about real or imaginary places, people, animals, objects, or happenings.

*6. There are many kinds of make-believe stories including myths, legends, tall tales, folktales, fables, fairy tales, animal stories, and fictional accounts of lifelike happenings.

*7. Myths and legends are created by people as a way to explain things that happen in their world.

*8. A tall tale is an exaggeration of life that involves a character and a deed she or he supposedly did.

*9. Folktales are simple stories that have been handed down from generation to generation either in writing or by word of mouth.

*10. Fables are stories that teach a lesson.

*11. Fairy tales are stories involving magic and enchantment.

12. Many make-believe stories about animals give them human characteristics such as the ability to talk, wear clothes, or engage in human pastimes.

*13. Fictional stories are about imaginary people or events that seem like they could be real.

*14. Sometimes people tell real stories about their own lives. These are called autobiographies.

*15. Sometimes people tell real stories about people, places, or events they have seen or heard about.

*16. Some stories take place in the past, some in the present, and some in the future.

*17. Some stories are based on factual events but have been embellished to include more than facts.

Story Characters

18. The people and/or animals portrayed in a story are called the story characters.

*19. Each character in a story has a particular function within that story.

*20. Each character in a story has specific attributes that distinguish him or her from other characters.

*21. In specific cultures, the same story characters sometimes appear over and over again.

*22. Different cultures assign to certain animals specific human personality traits, such as cleverness, stupidity, wisdom, fearfulness, timidity, wiliness, courage, patience, honesty, and deceitfulness.

Telling Stories

23. All stories have a beginning, a middle, and an end.

*24. The sequence of events in a story is important to the story's meaning.

*25. Changing the sequence of events in a story or adding or dropping parts of the story may change the story's meaning.

*26. Stories vary in length, number of characters, setting, and plot.

27. Relating a story to others is called storytelling.

28. Storytellers are people who retell/recite stories.

29. Stories and storytelling are common to all cultures.

30. Everybody has stories to tell.

31. Anyone can create a story.

*32. Sometimes storytellers recite stories another person has created, and sometimes they make up their own stories to tell.

*33. Sometimes the origin of a story is known; sometimes it is unknown.

*34. Some stories have been passed down through many generations, others have been recently created.

*35. Some stories are told in poetry, others are told in prose.

*36. Poetry is the rhythmical arrangement of verses sometimes having words that rhyme.

*37. Prose is the ordinary form of written or spoken language without rhyme.

38. Storytellers combine words, voice tones, facial expressions, gestures, and other body movements to communicate their stories.

*39. How storytellers use their voices, gestures, and words influences people's understanding of and reactions to the story.

40. Storytellers often use traditional phrases to signal the beginning or end of their tales.

41. Some storytellers use props to enhance their telling of a story.

*42. Stories are sometimes told by one person; sometimes by groups of people.

*43. When groups of people tell stories, sometimes each person tells a different part, sometimes everyone tells the same part at the same time.

44. Besides being "told," stories can be conveyed in many forms.

*45. Some storytellers use no words at all and rely on facial expressions, gestures, and other body motions to communicate their stories.

*46. Sometimes groups of people act out a story by pretending to be the characters in it.

47. Some stories are presented in books.

*48. Some books relate the story in pictures, some in words alone, and some in a combination of pictures and words.

49. Some stories are conveyed through music or song.

50. Some dances depict a story.

51. Some works of art represent a story.

52. The same story can be conveyed in many different forms.

53. Stories are told and retold many times.

54. There may be more than one version of the same story. That is, major events or characters may be the same from version to version, but the details of the story may differ from one storyteller to another.

Story Preferences

*55. People often have emotional reactions to the stories they hear.

*56. The same story may prompt different reactions in different people.

57. People have favorite stories.

58. People like a story "best" for many different reasons.

59. Sometimes different people have the same favorite stories.

60. Sometimes people's favorite stories are unique to them.

The Audience

61. One way to share a favorite story is to tell it to someone else.

62. Storytellers need someone to pay attention to their stories.

63. How the audience acts during the storytelling affects the storyteller.

64. People who talk, make noise, interrupt, and move around a lot while a story is being told make it harder for the storyteller to perform and/or make it harder for other people to enjoy the story.

65. People who listen quietly and look carefully while the story is being conveyed

make it easier for the storyteller to tell the story and for other people to enjoy it.

66. People show the storyteller they enjoyed the story when they smile, clap, or ask to hear or see it again.

ACTIVITY IDEAS

Aesthetics

1. *Stories in Art.* Show children different illustrators' versions of the same story. Talk with them about the variations and similarities among the pictures. Ask children which they like best and why. Make these illustrations available for children's continued enjoyment throughout the unit.

2. *Musical Stories.* Choose a brief instrumental selection that tells a story or part of one. Possibilities include:

   - *Night on Bald Mountain* by Modest Moussorgsky

   - "In the Hall of the Mountain King" (from the *Peer Gynt* Suite) by Edvard Grieg

   - "The Sleeping Beauty Waltz" by Peter Ilich Tchaikovsky

   - "The March of the Wooden Soldiers" from *The Nutcracker Suite* by Peter Ilich Tchaikovsky

   - "The Waltz of the Flowers" (from *The Nutcracker Suite*) by Peter Ilich Tchaikovsky

   - "The Sorcerer's Apprentice" by Paul Dukas

   - *Peter and the Wolf* by Sergei Prokofiev

   - *The Carnival of the Animals* by Camille Saint-Saens

   - *Pictures from an Exhibition* by Modest Moussorgsky

Briefly tell children the story, then play the music or part of it. Ask children to describe their reactions to what they have heard. Expand this activity by inviting children to move to the music as you play it a second time.

3. *Tell Me a Tale*

   General Purpose: For children to gain pleasure from literary experiences.

TFPs: 1–40, 47, 48, 55–66.

Materials: A variety of narrative picture books.

Procedure:

a. Invite children to a quiet area saying, "Come sit with me and I will read you a story," or "Here is a book about . . . ."

b. Introduce the book by holding it up so all the children can see and say, "The title of this story is _____. It was written by _____, and the pictures were made by _____."

c. Open the book to the first page with text *or* illustrations and hold it so the children can see it. Illustrations on the first pages before the text begins often give information important to the story.

d. Read the story, continuing to hold the book so the children can see the pictures at all times.

e. Change the speed, pitch, volume, and rhythm of your voice to correspond to and enhance the meaning of the text.

f. Articulate each word and use punctuation cues to help provide meaning to the text.

g. Change your voice for each character in the story, varying pitch, rhythm, accent, or dialect.

h. Provide an opportunity for children to participate in the story by joining in repetitive phrases, providing appropriate sound effects, or responding to questions or clues contained in the text or illustrations.

Hints for Success:

- Establish a reading area where children can listen to stories and look at books comfortably. A large area rug, carpet squares, or several large floor pillows will help make the area inviting.

- Choose books according to group size. When reading to a large group, select a large book that has big, clear illustrations. Read smaller books with more detailed illustrations to fewer children at a time.

- Arrange the children so that all of them will be able to see clearly. With a small group, have a few children sit on either side of the reader so that all are facing in the same direction. In a large group, arrange the children in a semicircle. Grasp the book at the base of the spine and hold it to one side so that both the reader and the audience can see. Turn the pages from the bottom to avoid interrupting the children's observation of the pictures. With a large group of children, sit on a low chair to make it easier for children to see.

- Become familiar with the book before reading it. This will allow you to read fluently while still maintaining periodic eye contact with the children.

- Select stories that portray particularly beautiful, intriguing, or funny illustrations, characters, plots, or word usage. Focus primarily on the enjoyment of the storytelling experience rather than on facts presented in the story.

How to Simplify this Activity:

- Choose short stories with few words and many pictures.

- Choose books with simple rhymes, repeated phrases, or other patterns in the text.

- Read stories that are old favorites. Introduce new stories occasionally and reread them often so that they will become familiar.

- Read to a few (no more than four) children at a time so that they can gather close enough to see and touch the book very easily.

How to Extend this Activity:

- Choose longer, more detailed books with fewer illustrations and more words.

- Choose stories with more complicated plots, more characters, and more advanced vocabulary.

- Choose stories that introduce children to new ideas, people, or places.

4. *Mixed Media*
   General Purpose: For children to become aware of varying forms of storytelling.

TFPs: 1, 27, 38, 41, 44, 47, 48–53, 58, 61, 66.

Materials: Children's picture book; a flannel board and flannel pieces depicting the book you have chosen; simple stick or hand puppets that can be used to tell the same story. Optional: hats, or props with which the adult could retell the story; a filmstrip of the story; a story record.

Procedure:

a. Choose a short, simple book.

b. Make or gather two or three additional sets of props that could be used to retell the same story in different ways.

c. Invite children to join you for a storytelling session. Mention that the same story is often told in various forms.

d. Read the book you have chosen, allowing plenty of time for children to enjoy the illustrations and the rhythm of the text.

e. Announce that you will retell the story in another form. Using puppets, objects, or flannel pieces, tell the same story again. For children who are enjoying the experience, continue retelling the story, varying the method of presentation each time.

Hints for Success:

- Keep props that are not in use out of sight.

- Let children choose which storytelling option you will use next. For example, offer children a choice between puppets and a record.

How to Simplify this Activity:

- Compare only two methods of storytelling at a time.

How to Extend this Activity:

- Initiate a discussion about how the various storytelling methods were similar and different.

- Ask children to identify the one they liked best.

- Invite children to take turns as the storyteller. Allow each to choose which storytelling method to use.

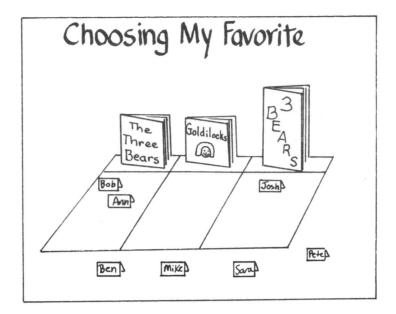

Figure 20.1 *Use the Actual Objects Whenever Possible*

Affective

1. *A Story About Me!* Provide opportunities for children to tell stories about their own lives. Record these on tape or in writing for children to hear again. Treat this as an ongoing project to which children could add new chapters over the year.

2. *Choosing Favorites.* Obtain more than one storyteller's version of the same tale. Present all of these to the children on the same day or on different days. When you have presented all versions, ask each child to select a favorite and explain his or her choice to the group. Extend this activity by making a three-dimensional graph depicting the children's choice. (Figure 20.1)

3. *Create a Character.*

   General Purpose: For children to practice making choices.

   TFPs: 12, 18, 20, 22.

   Materials: Mouse, frog, and rabbit character books (Figures 20.2a and b); paste; paste brushes or craft sticks; crayons or markers; paper word labels.

   Procedure:

   a. Prepare materials in advance. Make a character book for each child by cutting 8½-by-11-inch paper in half horizontally. Then staple the half sheets together down the side to make booklets of six to eight pages each. Print the following information on each page.

   Title Page: My Character
   By
   (write child's name here)
   Page 2: My character is a (girl or boy) frog, mouse, or rabbit named

   _____

   Page 3: My character lives _____
   Page 4: My character wears _____
   Page 5: My character owns a _____
   Page 6: My character likes to eat _____
   Page 7: My character likes to play ___
   On the last page either draw or provide a cutout of the type of animal the child chose.

   b. Introduce the activity by saying, "Today we're going to tell animal stories. First, each of you will have to decide if you want your story to be about a mouse, a frog, or a rabbit."

   c. Give each child a character book matching his or her preference, after all have selected their animals. Show the children that there are pages inside the books and explain that on every page they will be asked to make a decision about some facet of their characters.

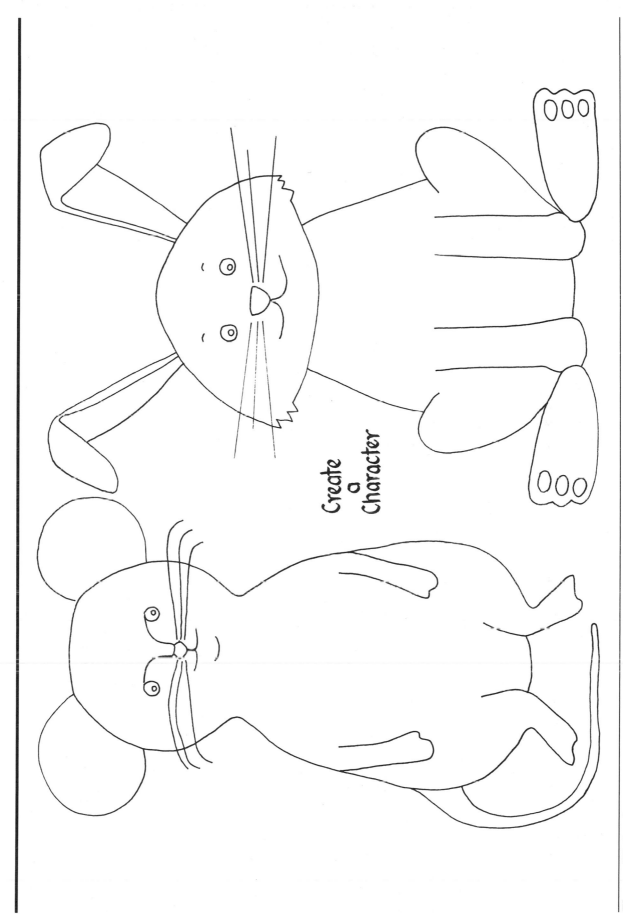

Create
a
Character

Figure 20.2a *Create a Character Choosing a Mouse or a Rabbit*

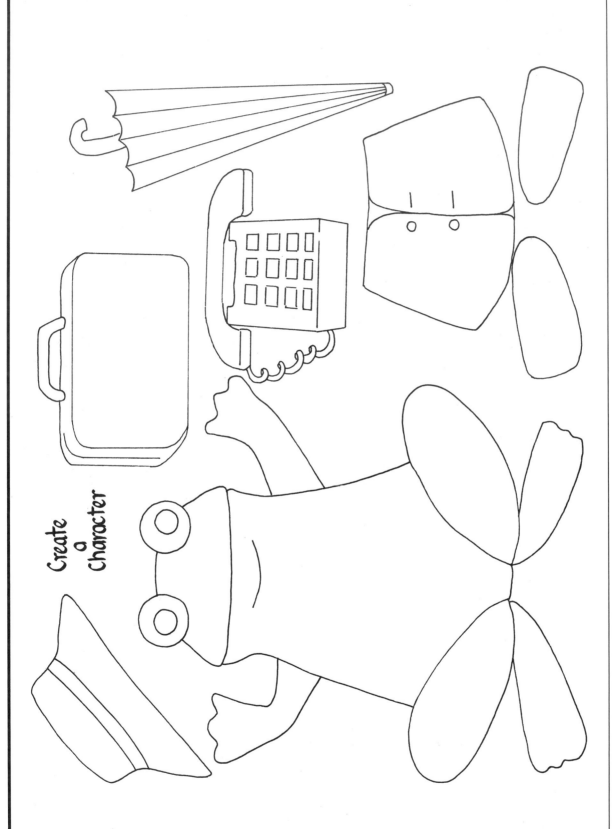

Create a Character

Figure 20.2b *More Create a Character Choices*

d. Go through the pages one at a time, offering children appropriate choices such as those listed below. Write down or ask children to record their choices at the bottom of each page, and/or give them the corresponding words or pictures to glue into place.

Sample Choices

Animal—mouse, frog, or rabbit

Gender—boy or girl

Name—as child desires

Home—in a tree, under a bridge, on a boat

Clothing—shoes, hat, vest

Possessions—umbrella, suitcase, telephone

Food—popcorn, ice cream, macaroni, pizza

Play—golf, work with blocks, pretend, Ping-Pong

Offer these choices verbally only, or illustrate or write them on paper labels as well for children to glue in place.

e. Reinforce children's decision-making skills throughout the activity by saying something like, "You chose the _____," or "You had to decide between _____ and _____ , and you picked _____ ."

f. After children have formulated decisions about all the attributes included in their books, review individual children's characters. Point out similarities and differences among the decisions made.

g. Offer children paste and crayons or markers to decorate their character books.

h. If children remain interested in the activity, invite them to tell a story about the characters they created.

Hints for Success:

• Allow children to change their minds as they attempt to make decisions.

• Always name the character on the second page of each book. Identifying names gives children a foundation upon which to build the rest of their characters.

• If a child finds none of the choices regarding a particular attribute acceptable, allow him or her to make a "no" choice, such as deciding that the character owns no objects.

• If a child wants to choose something not offered, such as a purse instead of a telephone, umbrella, or suitcase, accept this decision.

How to Simplify this Activity:

• It is easiest for children to think about physical attributes and tangible objects.

• Offer only two choices about any attribute.

• Limit the character books to three or four pages.

• Make up a story about the children's characters yourself rather than asking them to do so.

How to Extend this Activity:

• Include activities and personality traits as choices among which children must decide.

• Increase the number of choices children must make by increasing the length of the character books.

• Increase the number of alternatives children must consider by offering four or five choices for each attribute.

• Make all of the choices on each page completely open ended.

• Invite a child to tell a story that includes both his or her own character and the character created by another child.

• Follow up on this activity by having children make puppets that represent the characters they created. Refer to the puppet-making activity plan in this unit for further directions.

Cognition

1. *Endings.* Read a simple story to children from beginning to end. On the same or the following day, reread or retell the story almost to the end. Ask children to decide on a new way to finish the tale. Write down the children's exact words. This could be a group decision or could involve having each child think of his or her own ending. If you choose the latter approach, be sure

to take time to read the different endings to the class. Point out similarities and differences among the endings that individual children developed.

2. *Who Might You Meet on the Street?* Describe or show a story character to children. Ask them to decide whether the character seems real or imaginary. Talk with children about the criteria they used in making their decisions.

3. *Who Uses What?* Select story characters with whom children are familar. Reproduce them in some way. (Draw, copy, or create them with flannel or interfacing materials.) Gather an array of "props," using either real objects or props you create in the same way as the characters. Ask children to match the characters with the appropriate props and explain the reasoning behind their choices. Simplify the activity by using only a few characters from a single story and props that are actually mentioned in the story. Extend it by increasing the number of stories represented, the number of characters portrayed, and by adding props that are not specifically referred to in the stories. Keep the actual books at hand so children can refer to them.

How to Make Flannel-Board Figures from Interfacing Material

Materials: Interfacing material, pencil, indelible ink pen, crayons or waterproof markers, hairspray.

Traditionally, flannel-board figures are made from colorful pieces of flannel or from cardboard or paper with a strip of flannel across the back to help them stay on the board. Another alternative is to make figures from interfacing material. Interfacing material is relatively inexpensive, sold by the yard in most fabric stores, and comes in varying weights. Figures made from this material stick well to the board and need no further adhesive.

Procedure:

a. Buy two or three yards of medium weight, white interfacing material. (Pellon is one nationally available brand of such material.)

b. Place a single layer of material over an illustration in a book and trace it in pencil.

c. Once you have traced all the illustrations you want, go over the pencil outlines with indelible ink.

d. Color in the illustrations with crayons or waterproof markers.

e. Spray the final product with hairspray to make the colors set and to keep them from coming off onto your hands.

Additional sources of figures to trace include coloring books, as well as *Storytelling with the Flannel Board*, Volumes One and Two, by Paul S. Anderson, (Minneapolis, MN: T. S. Denison Co., Inc., 1963, 1970.).

---

4. *Let's Write a Sequel.* Gather large sheets of easel paper, a dark-colored marker, and tape or tacks for posting the "sequel" where children can see it. Select a story character with which the children are already familiar. Characters that appear in a series of books are a good choice. (We have provided suggestions in the Teacher Resource section of this unit.)

Talk with the children about the attributes of the character that stood out to them. Once they have mentioned several attributes, review the list briefly and tell the children that today they will create their own story about the character.

Prompt the children to begin by saying, "Once upon a time (character name) was . . . ." Select a child to complete the phrase. Accept whatever idea the child expresses and write it down. Invite a second child to continue the story by saying, "Then . . . ." continue this process until all of the children who want a turn have had one.

Record the children's story and conclude by reading it back to the group. Point out the consistent attributes of the character within their tale.

5. *"What If?" Stories.*

General Purpose: For children to apply rules of cause and effect they have learned in previous experiences to new situations.

TFPs: 1, 4, 5, 45, 55, 56.

Materials: None.

Procedure:

a. Implement this activity with the class as a whole or with small groups of children.

b. Tell the children that you will start a story and they will have to provide the ending. Rather than telling their ending in words, each child will *act out* his or her idea.

c. Begin with a simple situation. "What if the floor was covered with deep snow?" Ask the children to act out their responses.

d. Give them verbal hints to guide their reactions. "How might you walk? What about your face? Would you be happy or sad? How would your body feel—warm or shivery? What might you say?"

e. Point out that not all children will react the same way; each will act out the story of a snowy day in his or her own way.

f. Suggest a change in conditions. "Now the floor has turned to ice! How will you get across it? I wonder how skating might look?" Or, "The sun is shining down and warming your head, and the ice is turning to a pool of water! Now what will you do?"

g. Describe the reactions you observe.

h. Point out ways that children's behaviors differ from person to person within the same situation. Also mention similarities in children's reactions.

i. Praise children's efforts throughout the activity.

j. Repeat this activity using some of the following "What if?" scenarios.

What if you were a lizard looking for flying insects for lunch?
What if you were a dancer and there was music playing now?
What if you were on a flying carpet flying high above the ground?
What if you had a house that needed to be painted?
What if you were a monkey in the zoo?
What if you were the strongest person that ever lived and a huge tree fell on the school?

What if you were at a beach and it was very hot?

Hints for Success

• Demonstrate as necessary to help children get involved.

• Provide children with scarves, crêpe-paper streamers, pompons, or paper towel rolls to encourage dramatization.

• If children have difficulty reacting spontaneously, ask them just to listen to your beginning, then verbally generate a response, and finally act it out.

How to Simplify this Activity:

• Create "what if?" statements that more closely parallel real life. For instance:

What if you wanted to show someone that you liked them?
What if you had to hurry and put your clothes on?
What if you had to eat something you didn't like?

How to Extend this Activity:

• After the children have acted out a scenario, ask them to use words to describe the endings they created. Initiate a discussion in which children explain why they reacted as they did.

• Invite one child to act out a situation while the others attempt to interpret his or her solutions to the "What if?" questions.

• Vary the activity by asking children to describe their reactions rather than acting them out.

Construction

1. *Stagehands.* Visit backstage at a community theater or school auditorium. Provide materials (boxes, crayons, blocks, cardboard, paints, and so forth) so children can build and/or decorate their own interpretations of a stage.

2. *Costume Shop.* Implement this activity after children have had an opportunity to hear and become familiar with several

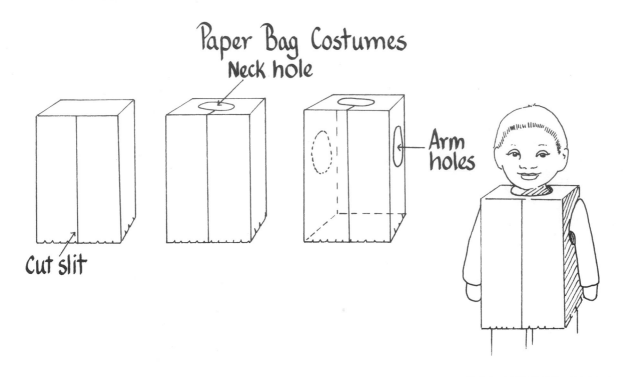

Figure 20.3 *Making a Paper Bag Costume*

stories. Make available paper-bag or cardboard-box costumes for children to decorate. (Figure 20.3)

Procedure:

a. Starting from the top edge, cut a slit up the back of each grocery bag.

b. Cut a round or oval neck hole in the bottom of the bag using approximately ⅙ of the total surface. Start cutting at the place where the back slit ends. Leave a wide margin of paper around the front and sides of the hole.

c. Cut arm holes in the sides of the bag.

d. Reinforce all edges with tape.

e. Carry out the same process using cardboard boxes, cutting the neck holes in the bottoms.

Provide a variety of decorating materials, such as stickers, crayons, markers, glitter, glue, rickrack, cotton balls, and paint. Use the stories you have read to help children generate ideas for the kinds of costumes they would like to make. Be sure to encourage the children's interpretations of what the costumes should look like rather than demanding exact replications of those shown in illustrations.

3. ***Puppet Making.***

General Purpose: For children to create their own characters in the form of a puppet.

TFPs: 12, 18, 20, 22.

Materials:

General: Glue or paste, markers or crayons, a variety of construction paper scraps, scissors, pipe cleaners, fabric scraps, fur scraps, buttons, yarn pieces, tiny pom poms, egg carton pieces, cardboard, foil, string, spools.

Styrofoam/Stick Puppets: Small Styrofoam ovals or balls, wide tongue depressors. Optional: three-ounce paper cups. (Figure 20.4)

Sock Puppets: A collection of clean tube socks, felt pieces. (Figure 20.5)

Paper Bag Puppets: Brown and white lunch bags. (Figure 20.6)

Procedure:

a. Gather all materials in advance.

b. Introduce this activity after children have had a chance to complete the Create a Character activity described in this unit.

Figure 20.4 *Use a Foam Ball and Tongue Depressors to Make a Puppet*

c. Remind children of the characters they created. Use each child's character's name. Say, "You created (character name) on paper and in your imagination. Now you can make a puppet of (character name)." Help children recall their characters. For example, say, "John, tell us some things you'll want on your puppet. Good, you remembered that your character is a mouse and he has a tail and small ears."

d. Display the materials for one kind of puppet making. Say, "Today we're making _____ puppets." Demonstrate manipulation of the basic materials (the paper bag, the sock, or the Styrofoam and stick). "This is how you'll use your hand and fingers to make the puppet move." Avoid showing a finished model.

e. Encourage children to investigate the materials they'll use for their puppets. "Look at all the things we have to use." Hold up the various pieces saying, "What can we use for a nose, ears, and tail?"

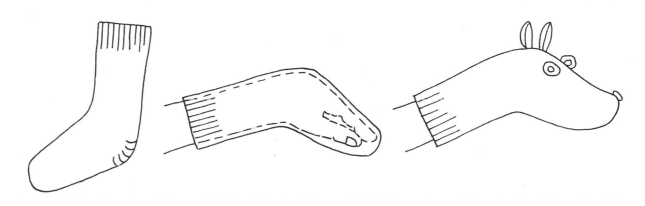

Figure 20.5 *A Clean Sock Makes a Fine Puppet*

Figure 20.6 *Small Paper Lunch Sacks Transformed into Puppets*

f. Help children choose materials to make their own characters. Offer assistance or clues for attaching parts. Encourage children to make their own interpretations of their characters so that each is unique.

g. Praise children for using their own ideas and representing some aspect of their original characters.

Hints for Success:

• Mix equal parts of paste and white glue together. Whip it with an electric beater. (This makes a stronger adhesive and is easier to apply with paste brushes.)

• When making a Styrofoam/stick puppet, dip the tongue depressor into the paste or glue mixture before inserting it into the Styrofoam ball.

How to Simplify this Activity:

• Use the directions for the paper-bag puppets.

• Provide a small collection of materials.

• Praise any attempt to reconstruct any aspect of the original character.

How to Extend this Activity:

• After children have constructed their characters using one set of materials, provide a different set and suggest that they make their characters with those materials.

Language

1. *Story Chorus.* Read aloud stories that contain repetitious phrases such as those used in *The Three Little Pigs, The Three Bears, The Gingerbread Man, The Little Red Hen, Caps for Sale,* or *The Billy Goats Gruff.* Encourage children to act as a chorus, joining in each time the phrase occurs.

2. *Picture This.* Gather a wide array of animal, object, and people pictures. Mount each picture on a separate piece of construction paper. Place the pictures face down in front of a small group of children. Ask them, one at a time, to select two pictures and tell a story linking the pictures they have chosen. Increase the number of pictures as children become more experienced.

3. *Authors.* Help children create books in which they develop a collection of real or make-believe stories. Each day for a week, select a category of story for children to tell. For instance:

Day One: a story about themselves
Day Two: a story about someone in their family
Day Three: a story that describes something that happened at school
Day Four: a silly story
Day Five: an animal story

Use at least one 8½-by-11-inch sheet of paper for each story and one for a cover. Staple them all together along the left side.

Tell each child to dictate or write a story that fits the topic of the day. Give children plenty of time to illustrate their stories using their own drawings or pictures from magazines.

4. ***Sing Me a Story.*** Ask children to listen as you sing a song relating a simple event. "Mary Had a Little Lamb" or "Five Little Ducks" are examples. Before you sing, tell the children to listen for the story in your song. Using the TFPs as a reference, give them hints about what to listen for and how to do so. When you are through, ask children to retell (not sing) the story in their own words. As children become more adept, increase the length and complexity of the songs you choose.

5. ***Mixed-up Stories.*** Select a story with which children are familiar. Provide four pictures of key scenes in the tale. Putting the pictures in correct sequence, tell the story or have the children tell it. Next, ask the children to close their eyes. Switch two of the scenes. Ask youngsters to try to tell the story according to this new sequence. Repeat this process more than once. Invite children to switch the scenes themselves.

6. ***Pantomime Tales.*** Explain to the children that you will tell a story without using words. Instruct them to watch closely to figure out the story. Act out a simple scene consisting of a simple action—waking up, brushing your teeth, or jumping rope. Ask children to retell your story in their own words. As children gain experience, increase the number of events in the story.

7. ***Rhyme Time.*** Help children make up nonsense rhymes. Give them a line to start. "There was a pink pig who liked mud." Ask children to supply a rhyming line. Begin with two-line rhymes. As children become more experienced, add additional lines to form short verses.

8. ***Dance a Story.*** Using traditional or made-up tunes, sing a simple plot such as, "The sun is hot—the flowers droop—the rain begins to fall—the flowers are refreshed." Ask children to dance their own interpretation of the story. You may choose to sing the whole story at once and then have the children perform, or to sing the story line by line as children dance in response to your words.

9. ***Paper-Bag Stories.***
   General Purpose: For children to practice communicating with others and participate in creative language experiences.

   TFPs: 1, 2, 3, 5, 27, 28, 30, 31, 32, 40, 41, 62–66.

   Materials: Large grocery bags, assorted objects with which children are familiar.

   Procedure:
   a. Prepare the materials by placing objects with a similar function in a bag together. For example, one bag contains household utensils; one bag, small articles of clothing; one bag, small toys.
   b. Introduce the activity by saying, "Today, we are going to tell stories. One at a time, you will reach into the bag, pull out an object, and tell a story about it. Each of you will have a turn."
   c. Allow the children, one at a time, to select objects from a bag. It doesn't matter whether or not they look.
   d. Signal the beginning by saying, "Once upon a time . . ."
   e. Listen while each child tells a story. Encourage the other children to listen to the storyteller.
   f. Prompt children to continue by using such phrases as, "And then what happened?" or "Tell us more about . . ."
   g. Avoid rushing children, cutting them off, or interrupting.
   h. If a child continues for so long that other children become restless, bring the story to a close by saying, "And finally . . ."
   i. Indicate the end of a story by saying, "The End." Clap.

Hints for Success:
- Periodically paraphrase children's words as a way to help them remember what they have said so far and reach a graceful conclusion.

- The first time you try this activity, expect stories that are only one or two phrases long. Repeat the experience on subsequent occasions and help the children increase the length of their tales.

How to Simplify this Activity:
- For inexperienced children, place only one or two objects in each bag. As children gain experience, add more objects.
- Limit this activity to a few children at a time. As children gain experience, form larger groups.

How to Extend this Activity:
- Vary the activity by inviting each child to select three items from one bag or one from each of the three bags. Ask him or her to use all three items to tell a story.
- Write down the exact words children use and read their stories back to them at the conclusion of the activity.

Physical

1. *Follow the Leader.* Read the book *Make Way for Ducklings* by Robert McCloskey. Use this as an introduction to Follow the Leader. Ask a child to be a mother or father duck and to lead the "ducklings" through the room or play yard. Periodically change leaders. At first, ask children simply to follow the leader's path. Once children can do this with ease, ask the leader to initiate an action such as hopping, twirling, or walking heel to toe and invite the other children to mimic this action as they follow in a line.

2. *Jack-Be-Nimble.* Recite "Jack-Be-Nimble," substituting each child's name as individual children take turns jumping over objects. Vary the height and the width of the object(s) as children gain experience and skill. Extend children's skills by having them jump down from a step or up to a step over an object.

3. *The Billy Goats' Bridge.*
   General Purpose: To help children develop good balance.
   TFPs: 1, 4, 9.
   Materials: walking board or balance beam measuring 2 by 4 by 10 inches. Optional: one 11-by-14-inch sheet of brown construction paper and one 11-by-14-inch sheet of green construction paper.
   Procedure:
   a. Sometime prior to implementing this activity, tell children the story of the *Three Billy Goats Gruff.*

b. Put the brown paper at one end of the beam to represent the barren field and the green paper at the other end to symbolize the grassy meadow.
c. Show children the balance beam and ask them to pretend that it is the bridge in the story. Explain that they will cross the beam from the barren field to the grassy meadow.
d. Ask children to take off their shoes. Invite them to try crossing the beam in any way they wish.
e. Once children have experimented with crossing the beam in their own ways, introduce the following variations. The sequence outlined below progresses from easy to more difficult movements.
   - Walk forward on the beam, one foot in front of the other, using arms for balance.
   - Walk backward on the beam, using arms for balance.
   - Sidestep along the beam. First, lead with the right side of the body, then with the left.
   - Walk forward, keeping one foot always in front. Alternate feet.
   - Walk backward, keeping the same foot always in back. Alternate feet.
   - Walk forward, heel to toe.
   - Walk forward, then backward, then sideways, hands clasped behind back.
   - Walk forward, then backward, then sideways, arms at sides, elbows bent, forearms parallel to ground.
   - Walk forward, then backward, then sideways, arms at sides, elbows bent, back of palms near shoulders.
   - Walk forward, then backward, then sideways, arms held straight overhead.
   - Walk forward, then backward, then sideways, arms held straight out from sides of body.
   - Walk forward, then backward, then sideways, arms held straight out in front.
   - Walk forward to the middle of the beam, turn around, walk the rest of the way backward or sideways.

- Walk forward, backward, and sideways on tiptoe.
- Move forward, backward, and sideways on hands and knees.

f. Remind children to look straight in front of them when crossing the beam.

g. As you provide the directions, phrase them in terms of the *Three Billy Goats Gruff*. For example, "Pretend you're the biggest billy goat. You decide to cross the bridge very quietly, one foot in front of the other."

Hints for Success:

- Introduce only a few of the variations described in step e at any one time.
- Give children several opportunities to practice each variation before introducing a new one.
- If children have difficulty keeping their eyes straight ahead, give them a target to focus on. Hang a whiffle ball from the ceiling at children's eye level at the "green field" end of the beam. Tell them to look at it while crossing the beam.

How to Simplify this Activity:

- Use a walking beam that is wider than four inches.
- Proceed through the proposed variations by having children walk a line made of masking tape stretched on the floor.

How to Extend this Activity:

- Ask children to try the variations in step e with small beanbags balanced on their heads or on their outstretched palms.
- Swing the whiffle ball so children must keep their eyes on a moving target.

Pretend Play

1. *Storytelling Theater.* Make a stage. Use duct tape to hold a single layer of large wooden hollow blocks together to form a platform, or simply mark an area on the floor with tape boundaries. Create seats for onlookers with additional blocks or chairs. Put a few dolls or stuffed animals in these seats to serve as an audience. For older children, consider including a space for a cashier and some pretend tickets. Provide children with information about how to be "storytellers" and "listeners." Make available hats and dress-up clothes or costumes. Display murals or posters depicting familiar stories. Hang a different one each day or several at once.

2. *Familiar Facades.* On large sheets of mural paper, create one or more backdrops related to a familiar story. Hang these in sequence on the walls around a section of the room. Provide children with a few additional key props to help them get into character. Explain to children that they can "act out" the story using the backdrops as scenery by moving from one station to the next in order. To vary this activity, make cardboard scenery for children to stand *behind* that includes cutout spaces for their heads and hands. Children then recite familiar lines while posing behind each facade. (Figure 20.7)

3. *Show Me a Story.*

General Purpose: For children to practice pretending.

TFPs: 1, 2, 3, 4, 5, 19, 20, 23, 24, 45.

Materials: Optional props, especially for younger children, might include a telephone, plastic fruit or flowers, and a spoon.

Procedure:

a. Introduce the activity by saying, "People tell stories in many different ways. Sometimes they use words and sometimes they just use their bodies. The stories you tell with your body can be very short."

b. Demonstrate. "Watch me, I'm going to show you a short story using my body. When I finish, tell me the story you saw." Act out a simple action like eating or sleeping, without using a prop.

c. Ask children to interpret your action.

d. Instruct the group to imitate your story. "Now it is time for you to tell the same story."

e. Repeat this activity, either at the same time or later. Add imaginary props (like balls) as children become more skilled. When children seem comfortable repeating your story, introduce the next step.

Facade for "Caps for Sale" by Esphyr Slobodkina

Cut out for children's heads.

Figure 20.7 *A Large Cardboard with Holes for Heads*

f. "You've had lots of chances to show my stories. Now you will have a chance to show your own."

g. Have one child at a time select a simple action. Make suggestions if children cannot think of actions for themselves: pick a flower, feed a baby, wake up in the morning, go to sleep, catch or throw a ball. Have the child whisper the idea to you. Tell the child to "show" his or her story.

h. "Max showed you a story. Now everyone tell us the story."

i. Repeat this using more complex "story" lines over time.

j. As children gain experience, introduce yourself as a character, "I am a little girl" or "I am a hungry bear."

k. Introduce a story in which you and a child pretend the same action. Throw and catch an imaginary ball for instance. Add a second child.

Hints for Success:

• Select an activity area where children have plenty of space to move about.

• When modeling, exaggerate and simplify your actions as a way to highlight them.

• If children have difficulty mimicking your actions, reenact the scene while describing out loud what you are doing.

How to Simplify this Activity:

• Use realistic props (see materials list). Gradually, over time, introduce less realistic representation; for instance, a block could be used as a truck.

How to Extend this Activity:

• Introduce two or more actions in a sequence for children to imitate (going for a walk, seeing a flower, picking the flower, and smelling the flower or stretching a balloon, blowing it up bigger and bigger, and pretending it pops). Later, have children make up their own sequences.

4. **Basic Puppetry Skills.**
   General Purpose: For children to assign symbolic meaning to objects using language and gestures.

   TFPs: 12, 18, 20, 22, 38, 41.

   Materials: Animal and people hand puppets made from cloth. Optional: large 2-by-6-inch "dress-up" mirror positioned horizontally in the activity area.

Procedure:

a. Begin by explaining to the children that today you will show them how to create a story character using a puppet. Emphasize that it will be important for them to listen to your directions throughout the activity.

b. In front of the children, spread out an array of as many puppets as there are children plus two.

c. Invite each child to choose a puppet. Give them several minutes to examine and handle the puppets prior to making a final choice. Select a puppet to use yourself.

d. Ask the children to put their puppets on their hands and try moving their fingers around in a variety of ways. Demonstrate as you talk. Tell them, "Make your puppet move toward you, away from you." Offer the mirror so children can see what their puppets look like when they move them.

e. Once the children have experimented with a variety of methods of manuevering their puppets, ask them to give their puppets names. Invite each to announce the name to you and to the other children.

f. Build on the preceding steps by giving the following directions:

- "Give your puppet a voice."
- "Have your puppet tell its name to the group using the voice you have given it."
- "Show the group how your puppet walks, sits, runs, sleeps, and so on."
- "Show the group how your puppet would express feelings such as happiness, sadness, fear or excitement."
- "Tell the group if your puppet is friendly, shy, bouncy, lazy, and so on."
- "Show how your puppet demonstrates the characteristic you have chosen."
- "Tell the group one way your puppet is like (not like) the puppets you have met here today."

g. Show children how to use their puppets to act out a simple sequence of actions such as, "The boy walks down the street, sees a flower, then smells it," or

"The cat is sleeping, hears a loud crash, and scampers away." Demonstrate first and have the children mimic your actions. Eventually, describe a short vignette for them to enact without a demonstration. Continue to use the mirror to help children see their puppets' actions from another perspective.

h. Praise children throughout the activity for listening to your directions. Point out to them that they are creating characters for their puppets.

Hints for Success:

- Introduce puppetry to children only after they have seen you use puppets several times as a means of telling a story.

- Do not simply make the puppets available and expect children to know how to use them.

- Give children puppets that fit one hand well. Avoid oversized puppets or puppets that require two hands to operate.

- Introduce this activity using puppets in which children use their fingers to make the hands and heads move, rather than the mouths. The latter is likely to elicit more aggressive behavior from inexperienced children than is the former.

- Make available cloth puppets that can be manipulated easily and that look like actual animals or people before you introduce more abstract renditions, such as paper-bag puppets, or less malleable ones, such as hard plastic hand puppets or stick puppets.

- Consider implementing this activity after children have had experience using character books in the Create a Character activity earlier in this unit.

How to Simplify this Activity:

- Conduct this activity with only a few children at a time.

- Limit the activity to steps a through the third instruction in f.

How to Extend this Activity:

- Introduce the final parts of step f through step h.

- Proceed as you did in step f to teach children how to use their puppets to act out simple conversations or interactions. In this way, children begin to learn how to use their puppets in conjunction with one another.

• Introduce simple props as another way to extend children's puppetry skills.

• Invite children to reenact familiar folk tales such as *The Three Little Pigs* or *The Tortoise and the Hare* using puppets. Introduce this phase of puppetry *only after* children have been through all the preceding steps.

• Give children opportunities to go through the process outlined here using various kinds of puppets such as finger, stick, paper-bag, or sock puppets.

5. ***Whole Group Dramatizations.***
   General Purpose: For children to become involved in role-playing.

   TFPs: 38, 39, 42, 43, 45, 46.

   Materials: Storybook of a familiar tale (*Caps for Sale, The Three Little Pigs, The Three Bears,* etc.).

   Procedure:
   a. Select a story that has a fairly simple plot, some action, and several characters.
   b. Familiarize the children with the story over time through filmstrips, readings, tellings, or using the flannel board.
   c. Confer with other staff members (if available). Explain how the story is to be dramatized and assign adults specific roles within the reenactment.
   d. Explain the activity to the entire group. "You all know the story of _____. Today I am going to tell you the story and then you will have a chance to act it out. You can pretend to be several characters."
   e. Explain that role-playing is a particular way of pretending. Describe roles as parts children play in a scene. Tell youngsters that they may act out how they would feel in a given situation or how they think another person or character might feel under those circumstances.
   f. "Now I will tell the story of _____." Tell (do not read) the story, using

appropriate dramatic techniques: eye contact; variation of tone, pitch, and volume of voice; changes in body position.
   g. "Now you've heard the story of _____. Tell me something about the story. What happened first? What happened next?"
   h. "Tell me something about the characters." Encourage children to identify the characters and things that they said and did.
   i. "Now you really know all about the story." Set the scene. Tell children that this time you will tell the story and they will have a chance to act it out. Explain that each child can be any character he or she wishes and can decide to be several characters in turn (first the peddler, then a monkey). Explain that you will be the storyteller and perhaps take on the role of one or two characters as well (the peddler in *Caps for Sale,* the mother and the wolf in *The Three Pigs,* etc.).
   j. Help the role-players get into character. Allow youngsters to select props or costume items to further establish their roles.
   k. "Listen to my voice and I will tell the story again." Begin the story.
   l. Continue the story moving from event to event until the conclusion, following appropriate language and action cues.
   m. Extend each episode of the story, making sure you actively include all the children. Model words and actions. For example, if you were acting out *The Three Little Pigs,* you would say things like:
   "Now it's time for the three pigs to go out into the world and build their houses. Come on little pigs let's look for some material to use. Oh, I see *Neil* found some straw. We can all help build *his* house." (Pantomime building a house.) "Uh, oh that wolf is really hungry. I'm going to hide in my house and maybe he won't know I'm there. Come in little pigs, let's be really quiet." (Pantomime hiding in a corner.)

When you assume a role be sure to take on all the attributes of the character, such as voice, body posture, and movement, and any words or phrases associated with the character. ("Little pig, little pig, let me come in.") Watch the role-players attentively and applaud their efforts.

n. In a follow-up, reinforce the children's participation by saying, "That was fun. You all pretended so well. Some children pretended to be the _____, some the _____, and so on. We will play that story again some time. You can even play that story yourselves."

o. Ask children to develop alternate scenarios. "What could the peddler do if the monkeys decided to keep the caps?" Have youngsters act these out, then discuss the varying outcomes.

p. Summarize the key points of the children's discussion. Identify similarities in their thinking as well as differences. Highlight the one or two major points that seemed most important to the group.

q. Repeat the procedure another time, fading out the narrator's role as children take upon themselves more of the responsibility for keeping the story moving.

r. Suggest that children "play" the story outdoors or at another time of day.

Hints for Success:

• Precede this activity with the Show Me a Story activity.

• Carry out the activity only after children are thoroughly familiar with the story.

• Choose a place for the dramatization that has clear boundaries and enough room for children to move around. Use screens, tables, or chairs to define the boundaries, if necessary.

• At the beginning, keep the story moving along so it is relatively short (five to seven minutes). As children become more experienced, extend the time.

• Nursery rhymes make ideal "first" stories.

How to Simplify this Activity:

• Younger children will benefit from realistic props. This step is critical for children younger than seven years of age who otherwise might have difficulty enacting and sustaining a role. Young children may need to hang a picture or symbol around their necks if their roles are abstract or good props are not available.

• Model simple actions associated with particular characters.

• Have children focus on one character only, while you act out the roles of the other characters.

• Choose a phrase that re-occurs for children to repeat at the appropriate times.

How to Extend this Activity:

• Choose more complex stories to act out.

• Allow children to select a story.

• Invite a child to be the "storyteller."

• Have a small group of children choose, practice, and present their story to the rest of the group.

Social

1. *What Could We Do?* Read or tell part of a story that describes a problem or conflict among characters. Ask the children to identify the problem and talk with them about ways they might resolve the dilemma. Read the ending and help the group compare their ideas with the author's. Possible selections might include *The Terrible Thing That Happened at Our House* by Marge Blaine, *Sam* by Ann Herbert Scott, *Alfie Gives a Hand* by Shirley Hughes, and *William's Doll* by Charlotte Zolotow.

2. *Adventure Add-on.*
Conduct this activity with children in a group. Begin an adventure story by supplying the first line. Invite each child to add to the story. Write down the children's words exactly. Read the entire story aloud before asking the next child to contribute an idea. When all children have had a turn, indicate that the story is over by writing "the end" for all of the children to see.

3. ***Pasta in a Pot.***

Day One: Read the story *Strega Nona* by Tomie dePaola. Discuss Strega Nona's magic pasta pot. Explain to the children that tomorrow they will make their own pasta in a pot. Send a note home to parents requesting that each child bring a handful of any kind of uncooked pasta (one to two ounces) to school the next day.

Day Two: First, invite children to examine the different varieties of pasta they brought in. Then ask them to help you prepare the following recipe.

Ingredients:

1–2 oz. raw pasta per child (up to 10–14 children)

2 medium onions, chopped

1 mashed garlic clove

¼ cup snipped parsley

½ cup fresh sliced mushrooms

1½ lbs. provolone cheese

½ lb. mozzarella cheese

¼ cup parmesan cheese

1 16 oz. can stewed tomatoes

1 14 oz. jar spaghetti sauce

Procedure:

1. Cook pasta *al dente* in boiling water, then drain.
2. Chop onion, mash garlic, slice mushrooms, snip parsley.
3. Cube provolone cheese.
4. Slice mozzarella cheese.
5. Pour half of the pasta into a deep casserole.
6. Cover with half the sauce and half the cheese.
7. Repeat steps e and f.
8. Cover and bake at 350° for 40 minutes.
9. Uncover, sprinkle parmesan cheese over the top, bake until golden.

   Makes 10 to 14 child-sized servings.

Other story-inspired cooking experiences might be vegetable soup (*Stonesoup*), blueberry muffins (*Blueberries*

for Sal by Robert McCloskey), or hot cereal (*The Three Bears*).

4. ***A Colorful Story.***

General Purpose: To give children practice in working together toward a common goal.

Materials: A 24-by-36-inch sheet of paper; black, blue, red, purple, yellow, and green markers; blue, red, purple, yellow, and green objects or cardboard shapes.

Procedure:

a. Print the following story on the paper, making the words large enough for children to see when sitting in a group. Print the color names in the corresponding color and the rest of the words in black.

A Colorful Story

Once upon a time there were some *red* cherries hanging in a *green* tree. Above, there was a *yellow* sun in the *blue* sky. Now along came a *purple* bird, who ate the *red* cherries and flew off into the *blue* sky, right up to the *yellow* sun. Below, the *green* grass grew and little flowers also grew with *purple* and *red* and *yellow* blossoms and *green* leaves. One day the *blue* sky got dark. The wind blew and the rain came down hard so the *purple* flowers grew even taller and everyone was happy.

THE END

b. Post the story where children can see it. Read the story once through. Then tell children, "Today we will all work together to tell this story. My part will be to read the words. Your part will be to make special sounds for each color."

c. Give each child one object, such as an inch cube or a plastic block, in a color mentioned in the story.

d. Explain to the children that when they hear the name of their color they will make a special sound to help tell the story.

Red—Yeh!
Blue—Ahhh!
Yellow—Oooo!
Purple—Mmmm!
Green—Da-da!

e. Have each color group practice its sound.

f. Tell the story, pointing to the words as you say them. As you say each color name, cue children to make the appropriate sound.

g. Repeat the story after children have traded colors.

Hints for Success:

• At first, hold up a colored object to match the color mentioned. This will be an additional cue to the children as to whose turn it is.

• At the end of each rendition of the story, point out to the children that they are telling it as a group and that they are working well together.

How to Simplify this Activity:

• Rather than dividing the group by colors, ask all the children to make all the sounds.

• Reduce the number of colors mentioned in the story.

How to Extend this Activity:

• Assign or allow children to choose a color without providing the additional cue of a colored object or shape.

• Invite children to write their own colorful stories than read them aloud with the appropriate sound effects.

• Ask children to make up new sound effects to illustrate the story.

TEACHER RESOURCES

Field Trip Ideas

1. Visit your local or school library. Ask the children's librarian to tell a story. Follow up by retelling the story back in the classroom or by having children pantomime or make puppets of a character from that story.

2. Visit your local or school library. Arrange in advance for the librarian to display a variety of storybooks suitable for your age group. Prior to the trip, talk with children about what they look for in a favorite story. Explain that each child will be able to select a storybook to borrow from the library. Make the trip. Allow each child to choose one story. During the weeks that follow, make sure to read each child's story, allowing the youngster to explain why he or she picked it.

3. Go to a bookstore. Find the children's section. Purchase a book for the class. Or, arrange for someone at the store to explain why they have stocked particular storybooks.

4. Make a trip to a puppet or live theater for a performance.

Classroom Visitors

1. Invite a storyteller to demonstrate his or her skills.

2. Contact a local theater group to visit. Consider an amateur community group, high-school drama club, or Boy Scout or Girl Scout troop. Ask them to come to school and act out a simple story for the children in your group.

3. Ask parents to visit and share their children's favorite stories with the class.

4. Arrange for a singer to visit the class and perform a story song.

Children's Books

General Fiction

Aardema, V. *Bringing the Rain to Kapiti Plain*. New York: Dial, 1981.

———. *Why Mosquitoes Buzz in People's Ears*. New York: Dial, 1975.

Allard, H., and J. Marsh. *Miss Nelson Is Missing*. Boston: Houghton Mifflin, 1977.

Barrett, J. *Cloudy with a Chance of Meatballs*. New York: Atheneum, 1978.

Berridge, C. *Grandmother's Tales*. New York: Andre Deutsch, 1981.

Blaine, M. *The Terrible Thing That Happened at Our House*. New York: Parents, 1975.

Erickson, K., and M. Roffey. *I Can Settle Down*. New York: Scholastic, 1985.

Hughes, S. *Alfie Gets in First*. New York: Lothrop, Lee and Shepard, 1981.

———. *Alfie Gives a Hand*. New York: Lothrop, Lee and Shepard, 1983.

Hutchins, P. *Rosie's Walk*. New York: Macmillan, 1968.

Leonard, M. *Little Owl Leaves the Nest: A Choose Your Own Adventure Book*. New York: Bantam Press, 1984.

Lingren, A. *The Tomten*. New York: Coward, McCann and Geoghegan, 1961.

Pomerantz, C. *Whiff, Sniff, Nibble and Chew: The Gingerbread Boys Retold*. New York: Greenwillow, 1984.

Roth, H. *Autumn Days*. New York: Grosset and Dunlap, 1986.

Scott, A. H. *Sam*. New York: McGraw-Hill, 1967.

Sendak, M. *Where the Wild Things Are*. New York: Harper and Row, 1963.

Slobodkina, E. *Caps for Sale*. Reading, MA: Addison-Wesley, 1968.

Stanek, M. *All Alone After School*. Niles, IL: Whitman, 1985.

Wittman, S. *A Special Tirade*. New York: Harper and Row, 1978.

Ziefert, H. *Bear's Busy Morning*. New York: Harper and Row, 1986.

Zolotow, C. *William's Doll*. New York: Harper and Row, 1972.

Poetry

Ebsensen, B. J. *Cold Stars and Fireflies: Poems of the Four Seasons*. New York: Harper and Row, 1985.

Jones, H. *The Trees Stand Shining: Poetry of the North American Indians*. New York: Dial Press, 1971.

Larche, D. W. *Father Gander Nursery Rhymes*. Santa Barbara, CA: Advocacy Press, 1985.

Milne, A. A. *Now We Are Six*. New York: Dutton, 1980.

———. *When We Were Very Young*. New York: Dutton, 1980.

Silverstein, S. *Where the Sidewalk Ends*. New York: Harper and Row, 1974.

Stories in Series

Bemelmans, L. *Madeline*. New York: Viking, 1939.

———. *Madeline and the Bad Hat*. New York: Viking, 1956.

———. *Madeline and the Gypsies*. New York: Viking, 1959.

———. *Madeline in London*. New York: Viking, 1961.

———. *Madeline's Rescue*. New York: Viking, 1953.

Bridwell, N. *Clifford the Big Red Dog*. New York: Scholastic, 1972.

———. *Clifford's Family*. New York: Scholastic, 1984.

Bright, R. *Georgie and the Noisy Ghost*. New York: Scholastic, 1971.

———. *Georgie and the Robbers*. New York: Scholastic, 1963.

De Brunhoff, J. *The Story of Babar*. New York: Random House, 1933.

De Brunhoff, L. *Babar's Castle*. New York: Random House, 1962.

DePaola, T. *Strega Nona*. New York: Simon and Schuster, 1975.

———. *Strega Nona's Magic Lessons*. New York: Harcourt Brace Jovanovich, 1982.

Freeman, D. *A Pocket for Corduroy*. New York: Scholastic, 1978.

———. *Corduroy*. New York: Viking, 1968.

Hill, E. *Spot's First Picnic*. New York: Scholastic, 1987.

———. *Spot Visits the Hospital*. New York: Scholastic, 1987.

Hoban, R. *A Baby Sister for Frances*. New York: Harper and Row, 1964.

———. *Best Friends for Frances*. New York: Harper and Row, 1969.

———. *Bread and Jam for Frances*. New York: Harper and Row, 1964.

Johnson, C. *Harold and the Purple Crayon*. New York: Harper and Row, 1955.

———. *Harold's Circus*. New York: Harper and Row, 1959.

———. *Harold's Trip to the Sky*. New York: Harper and Row, 1957.

Keats, E. *Pet Show*. New York: Macmillan, 1972.

———. *Peter's Chair*. New York: Harper and Row, 1967.

———. *The Snowy Day*. New York: Viking, 1962.

———. *Whistle for Willie*. New York: Scholastic, 1964.

Lobel, A. *Days with Frog and Toad*. New York: Scholastic, 1979.

———. *Frog and Toad All Year*. New York: Scholastic, 1976.

———. *Frog and Toad Are Friends*. New York: Harper and Row, 1970.

———. *Frog and Toad Together*. New York: Harper and Row, 1972.

McCloskey, R. *Blueberries for Sal*. New York: Viking, 1948.

———. *Make Way for Ducklings*. New York: Viking, 1969.

———. *One Morning in Maine*. New York: Viking, 1952.

Minarik, E. *Father Bear Comes Home*. New York: Harper and Row, 1959.

———. *Little Bear's Friend*. New York: Harper and Row, 1960.

Rey, H. *Curious George*. Boston: Houghton Mifflin, 1941.

———. *Curious George Gets a Medal*. Boston: Houghton Mifflin, 1957.

———. *Curious George Rides a Bike*. Boston: Houghton Mifflin, 1952.

Turkle, B. *Obadiah the Bold*. New York: Viking, 1965.

———. *Rachel and Obadiah*. New York: Dutton, 1978.

———. *Thy Friend, Obadiah*. New York: Viking, 1969.

Waber, B. *Lovable Lyle*. Boston: Houghton Mifflin, 1969.

———. *Lyle, Lyle, Crocodile*. Boston: Houghton Mifflin, 1965.

Zion, G. *Harry the Dirty Dog*. New York: Harper Junior, 1956.

———. *No Roses for Harry*. New York: Harper Junior, 1958.

———. *Harry and the Lady Next Door*. New York: Harper Junior, 1958.

———. *Harry by the Sea*. New York: Harper Junior, 1965.

Adult References

Abrahams, R. D. *Afro-American Folk Tales*. New York: Pantheon, 1985.

Alderson, B. *The Brothers Grimm, Popular Folk Tales*. Garden City, NY: Doubleday, 1978.

Bauer, C. *Handbook for Storytellers*. Chicago: American Library Association, 1977.

Baylor, B. *Sometimes I Dance Mountains*. Scribner's, 1973.

Carlson, B. W. *Listen! And Help Tell the Story*. Nashville, TN: Abingdon Press, 1965.

Carr, R. *Be a Frog, a Bird, or a Tree*. Garden City, NY: Doubleday, 1973.

Castle, S. *Face Talk, Hand Talk, Body Talk*. Garden City, NY: Doubleday, 1977.

Cole, J. *Best Loved Folk-Tales of the World*. Garden City, NY: Doubleday, 1962.

D'Aulaire, I., and E. Parin. *D'Aulaire's Book of Greek Myths*. Garden City, NY: Doubleday, 1962.

Lawton, J. T. "The Ausubelian Preschool Classroom." In J. L. Roopnarine and J. E. Johnson (eds.), *Approaches to Early Childhood Education*. Columbus, OH: Merrill, 1987.

Mendeza, G. *The Marcel Marceau Alphabet Book*. Garden City, NY: Doubleday, 1970.

Trelease, J. *The Read Aloud Handbook*. New York: Penguin Books, 1983.

Chapter 21

Writers

Children are surrounded by writers: their parents, their grandparents, their older siblings, people in stores, people in doctors' offices, teachers, and other children—they all write! Young children imitate this writing behavior, as they do so many behaviors they observe in adults and older children. In other words, *they* write! Not everyone can read children's first writing efforts; sometimes not even they can read it. However, if you look carefully at the scribbling of very young children, you will note that it does resemble the writing that youngsters see modeled by older persons in their society. Studies have shown cultural differences among these early scribbles and that it is possible to determine with fair accuracy the written language that a child has seen demonstrated most frequently by examining his or her own attempts at creating print (Schickedanz, 1982).

While these first scribbles are not readable, they are often meaningful to the writer, who happily interprets them to anyone interested. Eventually, these interpretations become stable over time, and the young writer is able to consistently read what she or he writes, even after some days or weeks have passed. With continuous practice and encouragement, this early writing evolves into a more standardized writing that can be read by the writer as well as by others.

PURPOSE

It is our contention that by taking advantage of this early tendency to imitate writing, we can encourage young children to BE writers! One important goal of teachers is to convince the young child that she or he *can* do things. Writing is one of those important tasks. We designed this unit to assist you in fostering the development of early writing skills.

IMPLEMENTATION

We believe that writing activities and materials should be available in the classroom on a daily basis. Establish a Writing Center with paper, pencils, chalkboard or dry-erase board, child name cards or a printed class list, individual writing folders, and writing samples as a permanent part of your classroom. Children should be encouraged to use this area frequently for self-initiated writing experiences and, also, to use the materials for activities suggested by the teacher. Set aside some of your classroom display space to exhibit the children's writings so that their efforts are recognized and parents will see that you value these early efforts.

Support fledgling spelling attempts and refrain from correcting or always providing accurate spellings, even when asked. Note that we have suggested providing a list of child names or individual name cards so that the recipients of messages will be happy to receive them rather than being critical or disappointed because their name is "wrong." For all other words, encourage the children to "write it so you can read it to me" and assure them that learning to write takes practice just as do all of the other skills that they have mastered. If a child is particularly interested in writing it "the right way," help her or him to identify the words that are most important and include some word cards in the child's writing folder with these special words correctly spelled so that they may be read, copied, and learned. Start with only a few words and add to them as the child's skills increase.

Use the activities in this unit in any of the following ways.

Option One: Incorporate some writing activities from this unit into your daily classroom procedures. In addition to the Writing Center, ongoing experiences might include waiting lists for popular centers or areas (Next, Please activity); providing continuous access to the written names of classmates (Name Cards activity); offering opportunities for classroom writers to be recognized (Writer's Showcase activity); and providing a special place for the delivery and acceptance of messages from you or other class members (For Your Eyes Only activity).

Option Two: In addition to ongoing support of writing activities, plan and carry out a one- or two-week teaching unit that focuses specifically on children's roles as writers. Continue throughout the year to support the message-sending and story-writing activities that begin during these weeks.

Option Three: For older children who have mastered the basic mechanics of writing, select one of the pretend play ideas and use it as the basis for a week's activities. If possible, visit one of these places or invite a worker to visit and share information about her or his job. Follow up by turning the entire classroom into a newspaper office or bookstore for the week and allow the children to act out their interpretations of the setting while writing news articles or books. Introduce the idea of editing and rewriting. Follow up by duplicating and distributing copies of children's final works.

TERMS, FACTS, AND PRINCIPLES

1. People create written language as a way to reveal, communicate, and store their thoughts, knowledge, and ideas.

2. People who write are called writers.

3. Writers write many different things: notes, lists, letters, books, poems, plays, songs, stories, jokes, and journals.

4. Anyone can be a writer.

5. Writers write *with* many things: pencils, computers, typewriters, pens, brushes.

6. Writers write *on* many things: paper, computers, chalkboards, sidewalks, billboards.

7. Writers write about things that are funny, sad, frightening, exciting, mysterious, true, or make-believe.

8. Writers write about what they see, hear, smell, taste, touch, learn, experience, imagine, feel, anticipate, and think about.

9. Writers write for different purposes such as helping them plan, remembering things, figuring something out, communicating with others, demonstrating, explaining, teaching, persuading, and for self-satisfaction and enjoyment.

10. Sometimes writers write for themselves, sometimes for other people.

11. Sometimes writers copy what others have written.

12. Sometimes writers record what others say (to take dictation).

13. Beginning writers are often the only ones who can decipher what they have written.

14. In many cultures, the written symbols people use to represent what they say are referred to as letters.

15. There is more than one way to write each letter.

16. Writers combine and recombine letters to form words.

17. Writers combine letters in a particular order to form particular words.

18. Writers combine and recombine words in phrases and sentences to create messages.

19. In some cultures, people use written symbols other than letters to represent what they say.

*20. To increase mutual understanding, over time people have agreed on the positions of letters and the spellings of words.

*21. Using standard letter positions and spellings is one way writers make their messages easier to understand.

*22. One way writers show where one word ends and another begins is by leaving a space between words.

*23. Writers use marks called punctuation marks to make their written communications more clear.

*24. Writers sometimes change what they have written after they write it and read it. This is called editing.

*25. Two writers writing about the same idea may choose different words or details upon which to focus.

ACTIVITY IDEAS

Aesthetics

1. *Beautiful Print.* Make an assortment of books that feature a variety of print styles available for the children to examine and enjoy on a regular basis. If it is possible to obtain some books that feature reproductions of illuminated manuscripts with highly decorative initial letters, include these in your collection of beautiful print materials, as well as some examples of cal-

ligraphy. Some children's books that have interesting and varied type styles are:

Millions of Cats by Wanda Gág (interesting type style)
On Mother's Lap by Ann Herbert (interesting type style)
How Do I Put It On? by Shigeo Watanabe (large print)
Bringing the Rain to Kapiti Plain by Verna Aardema (unusual title print)
Dinosaur Cousins by Bernard Most (interesting type style)
Feelings Alphabet by Judy Lalli (distinct print)
Color Dance by Ann Jonas (colored print)

2. ***Explore Writing Tools and Surfaces.*** Set up a large table with an assortment of writing tools and/or surfaces for children to use. Include pencils of varied widths, lengths, and colors; pens with fine, medium, and broad tips; watercolor markers with fine and broad points; and a variety of crayons and chalks. Surfaces can include smooth (mimeo paper or stationery) and rough (construction or manila paper) in a wide array of colors and sizes; and sandpaper, chalkboards, cardboard, flat wood pieces, and Styrofoam trays. Encourage the children to try various tools on different surfaces.

3. ***Give Me an "A"!*** Cut simple letter shapes from large plain newsprint and encourage children to use these when painting at the easel. If desired, feature a particular letter each day, or make available letters that correspond to the initials of the children in the class.

4. ***Lovely Letters.*** Cut block letters three or four inches high from pastel construction paper. Provide glue and beautiful decorating materials such as glitter, sequins, feathers, doilies, and buttons. Tell children to select letters and decorate them as they choose.

5. ***Wonderful Writers.*** Gather a collection of well-written and beautifully illustrated children's books and encourage the children to read them often. Discuss frequently how much pleasure well-written books give to many people.

Affective

1. ***All the Ways to Write My Name.*** Prepare a name card for each child in the class that contains the child's entire name: first, middle, and last. On heavy paper or tagboard, print with manuscript printing, using upper- and/or lower-case letters as appropriate. Protect the cards with clear vinyl self-stick paper if you wish. Provide the name cards, paper, and writing tools and ask children to write their names in as many different ways as they can. Some suggestions include first name only; first and last names; first name and last initial; first name, middle initial, and last name; first initial, middle name, and last name; or first initial and last name. Encourage children to continue this activity during the year, not only on paper, but also on a chalkboard or dry-erase board if these are available in your classroom, in the sand, on the sidewalk with chalk, and so on.

2. ***I.D. Cards.*** Prepare an identification card form for each child. These should include a space for the child's name and some identifying information. The form will vary depending upon the age and abilities of the children in the class, but may include any or all of the following: address, phone number, age, birthday, eye and hair colors, height, weight, favorite color, nickname. Direct the children to fill out the forms with information about themselves. If possible, attach a snapshot or instant photo of each child. The I.D. cards may be placed in a class book or displayed in a prominent place in the classroom.

3. ***Initially Yours.*** Prepare a name tag for each child in the class by cutting a three- to four-inch block letter of the child's first initial out of tagboard or poster board. Print the child's entire first name on the initial, cover it with clear self-adhesive vinyl, and punch a hole for a pin or ribbon. Have children wear these throughout the day. Use the initials to give directions to the class; for example, "If your first initial is J you may pass out the papers," or "All of the people whose initials are A, B, or C may get in line."

4. ***Monograms.*** Show the children some examples of monograms on towels, cloth-

ing or stationery. Explain that a monogram is an arrangement of a person's initials with the last initial in the middle, and that a monogram can be very plain or fancy. Provide letter stencils or templates, paper, and writing tools such as pencils and markers. The paper may be cut in squares, ovals, or circular shapes for added beauty and interest. Tell the children to use these materials to create their own monograms. Small flower or animal stickers may be added if desired. The finished monograms could be used to decorate the children's cubbies or other personal spaces or belongings.

5. *Name Collage.* Provide an assortment of magazines, scissors, paper, and glue or paste. Tell the children to look for words in the magazines that contain letters that are in their names, cut out these letters, and glue them onto paper. Encourage them to place the letters randomly on the paper and to overlap them as they arrange their collages; it is not necessary to arrange them in order. Direct them to find as many letters as possible. The children may enjoy keeping track to see which of the letters appear most frequently in their names.

6. *Next, Please!* Use sign-up sheets near popular materials or activities in the classroom. Place numerals from 1 to 10 down the side of a piece of paper and direct children who wish to have a turn to write their names in the first empty space. A heading stating "Waiting List for _____" can be added. Be sure to mount a pencil with the list. The list can be posted on the wall or kept on a clipboard. When a child finishes using the material, she or he notifies the next person on the list.

7. *This Is Mine!* Provide self-adhesive removable labels or paper and masking tape and pencils. Tell children that they may make name labels for their belongings by writing their names on the labels and placing them on the items. Suggest that they mark their personal spaces such as lockers or cubbies, chairs or desks, and belongings such as books, rulers, crayon boxes, snack cups, art works, or block structures.

8. *Writer's Showcase.* In order to encourage and support children as they begin writing, it is important to recognize their efforts. There are many ways in which this may be accomplished. Set aside a prominent area in the classroom for the display of written work. Direct children to post their work in this area. Encourage the writers to read their efforts to a friend.

Start and maintain a "Writer's File" for each child. Keep written work in a folder to retrieve easily for comparisons or additions. Provide a date stamp for children to record the date on each paper.

Institute the Author's Chair as described in the activity of that name.

9. *Activity Diaries.* Prepare a booklet for each child in the group consisting of several pages with space for a date and a short listing of classroom activities on each. Direct the children to place their names on the covers of these booklets. Provide a brief time at the end of each day for the children to record their day's activities at school, using one page each day.

Initially, make available a listing of school activities for the children to copy when recounting their days. Another idea is to print up booklet pages with a listing of general categories of activities that the children may check off. As children become more familiar with the process, invite them to write comments about their days as well.

Eventually, provide time at the beginning of the session for children to indicate their plans for the day and time at the end of class to evaluate how they carried out these plans. Also, encourage the children to read over past entries to review how they are spending their time at school.

Cognition

1. *Battered Books.* Collect several old books that are in poor condition with tears, scribbles, and bent or missing pages. Tell the children that you have some works by writers to show them and display these "battered books." Ask the children to tell you what they notice about the books. Invite them to describe what they think happened to these books. Continue with a discussion of how books should be treated and how writers feel when their works are mistreated. Provide materials such as tape and erasers that children can use to repair the books as best they can.

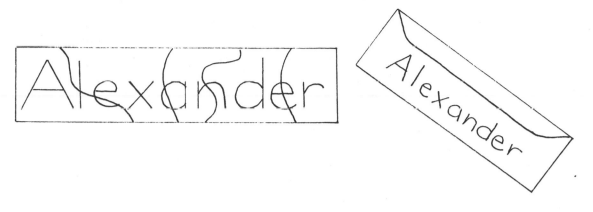

Figure 21.1 *Name Puzzle*

2. ***Name Puzzles.*** Prepare a name puzzle for each child by printing his or her name on a piece of three-by-eight-inch tagboard with a broad-tip marker. Cut these into four or five pieces. (Figure 21.1) Place the pieces in an envelope with the child's name printed on it. Tell the children that you have a different way for them to write their names—with a puzzle! Distribute the puzzle envelopes and tell them to remove the pieces from the envelopes and put their special puzzles together. Remind children to keep the puzzles in the envelopes when not using them.

3. ***Writers Write in Many Languages.*** Obtain copies of books printed in several languages and have these available for the children to investigate. Be sure to include some that use an unfamiliar alphabet. If possible, invite some visitors to the classroom who speak and read in other languages. Have the visitors read and interpret some of the books for the children. In addition, obtain letters from people who write in different languages and place these on display in the classroom after reading them to the group. It is most desirable to have all of the letters contain a similar message.

Sample:
"This letter is written in (*name of language*) which is written and spoken in (*name of country*). I hope that you are enjoying your day at school."

(signature)

4. ***Cook It Up!*** Show the children some cookbooks that contain recipes of dishes that they have made in the classroom. Point out that each recipe contains the name of the item to be prepared, a list of ingredients, and directions. Have the children dictate or write their own versions of their favorite recipes. Collect these and place them in a class cookbook or duplicate and send home to parents.

5. ***Alphabet Bingo.*** Prepare a set of bingo game cards (enough for all of the players, either the entire class or a small group of children) with alphabet letters in place of the usual numerals. Also obtain, or make, a set of alphabet cards to use in calling during the game. Distribute a game board to each of the players; give each child markers (such as buttons or inch-cubes) to cover the letters called. Tell children to look at the cards and listen carefully as the letters are called. "When you see a letter on your card that I have called, place a marker on it. When your card is filled, say 'Bingo'." Select one card at a time and say its letter clearly. Wait to see if children are able to recognize the letter correctly from its name; if they have difficulty, show them the card so that they may match it visually with those on their game boards. Continue until all players are winners. If you make the game boards, include one or two identical letters on every card and call one of those last—everyone wins! If you do not make the boards, refer to the first winner, second winner, and so on as children fill

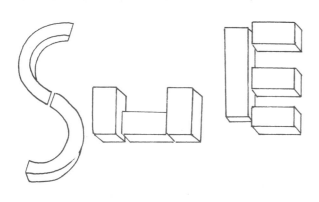

Figure 21.2 *Unit Blocks Used to Make Names*

their cards. When first introducing this activity, use game boards with a limited number of letters, perhaps five or six. Show the letters as they are drawn. As children become more adept at the game, use game boards with lower-case letters and "calling" cards with upper-case letters. Also consider assigning a child as the caller.

Toward the end of the year, instead of saying the letter names, say the sounds those letters make.

Construction

1. *Alphabet Blocks.* Provide alphabet blocks in the block building area of the classroom and encourage the children to "read" what they "write" as they build with them.
2. *Block Names.* Demonstrate how unit blocks can be used to form letters when laid flat on the floor in particular arrangements. (Figure 21.2) Encourage the children to use the blocks to write their names and other simple one- or two-word messages. If possible, take instant pictures of these efforts to preserve them. Display them in the writing area of the classroom.
3. *Book Cover-Ups.* Provide nine-by-twelve-inch pieces of cardboard with holes punched along one side, fabric pieces cut to fit the cardboard, glue, wide plastic tape in a variety of colors, felt pieces, yarn, scissors, markers, and notebook rings (optional) or yarn needles. Prepare a plain book cover as an example. (Glue fabric to both sides of two cardboard pieces;

tape the edges to cover fabric and provide a finished look; connect the front and back covers with notebook rings or yarn through the prepunched holes in the cardboard.) Tell children that they may use these materials to construct book covers for their favorite pieces of writing. Show them your undecorated sample cover. Encourage children to use the felt and yarn pieces to add interest to their covers. Assist children in preparing and mounting their writing choices in the completed "books."

4. *For Your Eyes Only.* Before carrying out this activity, collect one shoe box with lid for each child in the class. Ask the children's parents to help with this effort; ask your friends; clean out your closet; talk with the manager of a nearby shoe store. Prepare the boxes by cutting a slit large enough to accommodate an envelope or note in one end. (Figure 21.3)

You will also need enough counter or shelf space to hold the boxes when they are finished, for the children will be converting them into individual private mailboxes. Along with the boxes, provide wallpaper pieces or self-adhesive vinyl, glue, markers, construction paper, scissors, paper fasteners, and tagboard triangles.

Tell the children that they may each use a box and the other materials to construct their very own mailboxes. Demonstrate how to make a "flag" to signal a message in the box by using the paper fastener to attach a triangle of construction paper or tag board to the edge of the lid. Remind them that they will want to keep the mail

Figure 21.3 *A Shoe Box Mailbox for Each Child*

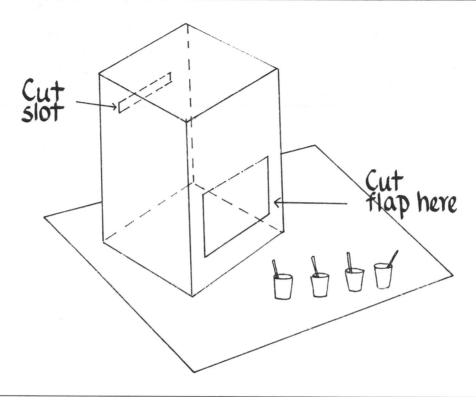

Figure 21.4 *A Large Cardboard Carton Makes a Class Mailbox*

slot clear and that the lid must be removable in order to retrieve the mail. Direct them to put their names under the mail slots to ensure accurate delivery of messages. Put the boxes into place and await delivery of private messages from classmates. If you are able to do so, write a brief note to each child to initiate the process.

5. *Mailbox.* Obtain a large, sturdy cardboard box and cut a "mail slot" near the top of the front and an opening flap for removal of mail on the back. Provide containers of red, blue, and white easel paint; newspaper for the floor; brushes; smocks; and plenty of water in buckets for clean-up. (Figure 21.4) If possible, also obtain a photograph of a genuine U.S. mailbox for the children to use as a model. Tell the children that they will use this mailbox to send messages to friends in the classroom, but that it does not look like a mailbox yet. They can paint it to look more authentic. Have the children roll up their sleeves and get to work. After drying, use this mailbox in your pretend-play post office or place it

near your classroom writing center. Add to children's cultural awareness by showing them pictures of typical mailboxes from other countries and inviting them to create an international array of letter boxes.

Language

1. *Classroom Labels.* Prepare and mount some identifying labels on items in the classroom. Use sturdy paper such as tag board and write the letters 1½ to 2 inches high. Place labels on six or seven items such as the chalkboard, light switch, easel, art shelf, desk, wall, and so on. Leave several obvious items without labels. Point out the labels to the children. Ask if they can think of other items that could be labelled. When children think of other items, ask them to make the labels. Provide paper and markers. When labels are finished, provide masking tape and guidance while the children put them into position. As the year progresses, ask children to dictate sentences to describe each item

Letter Lotto				
S	C	R	U	B
Q	B	L	O	W
B	L	A	C	K
O	M	A	N	Y
S	U	P	E	R

Letter Lotto				
H	E	A	T	P
Z	O	P	E	N
B	O	O	K	C
U	F	C	A	R
M	O	S	T	M

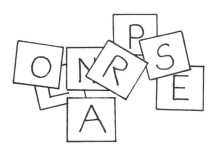

Figure 21.5 *Letter Lotto is Easy to Make*

or the way children in the class use it. Gradually have children write these descriptions themselves.

2. ***Dictionary.*** Make available some children's picture dictionaries for your class to examine for a few days. After they are familiar with the commercially prepared versions, tell children that they may each write a dictionary of their own. Prepare paper booklets and provide magazines or catalogues with pictures for cutting, paste, scissors, pencils, and crayons. Direct children to select items that they would like to include in their dictionaries and to cut out and paste or draw these items in their booklets. Then ask children to write their definitions or dictate them to the teacher. Encourage them to label or describe and define the items rather than tell stories about them. The completed dictionaries can be used at school or taken home.

3. ***Letter Lotto.*** Prepare some lotto boards that contain simple words and miscella-

neous letters. Also make alphabet cards, each containing one letter (you will need lots of these). Distribute one game board to each child and have them all look at and identify the letters on their boards. Select one of the alphabet cards and show it to the group. If a child has a matching letter on his or her board and identifies it, he or she may have the letter card to place on the corresponding letter. Tell the children to watch their boards carefully and to call out, "I'm a writer!" when a word has been formed from the alphabet cards on their board. The first child to correctly form and read a word is the first writer. Continue the game until all players are writers. (Figure 21.5)

4. ***Write a Picture Story.*** Cut out several pictures of common objects from magazines or catalogues. Gather pictures, paper, paste, and pencils. Place the pictures face down on a table. Tell a child to pick three pictures, place them in a row on the table,

and make up a sentence using the objects in all three pictures. If the child is able to make up a sentence, write it on a piece of paper and give the child paste to mount the pictures, in the order used, above the sentence. If the child is unable to make up a sentence, have him or her return the pictures and select three others.

If this activity seems too difficult, have the child select only one or two pictures to start.

Eventually, have the child write the sentence as best as he or she can.

5. *Author's Chair.* Once the children in the class have begun writing, encourage them to share their efforts with their classmates by providing a special time and place. Designate an Author's Chair and put it in a prominent spot in the classroom. Place a sign on or near it and decorate it in any way that suits you and that makes it appear very special to the children. You may select a particular time of the day for children to sit here and read their writing aloud to the entire class, or you may wish to allow each child to decide when he or she is ready to invite a few friends to listen to his or her writing. If you designate a particular time, it may be daily or twice weekly. Provide an "announcement board" where the children may write their names to have a turn in the Author's Chair.

6. *The Super, Terrific, Very Good Day!* Gather the following materials: At least one copy of Judith Viorst's *Alexander and the Horrible, Terrible, No-Good, Very Bad Day,* pencils, crayons, or markers, and paper booklets made from white or light-colored paper. Each should have six 5½-by-8½-inch pages. Print the following copy at the bottom of the pages, leaving room for illustrations.

Cover:
(space for child's name)
and the Super, Terrific, Very Good Day!

Page 1:
This morning I had _____ for breakfast and I got to wear my _____.
I could tell that this was going to be a super, terrific, very good day!

Page 2:
When I went outside, I saw a _____ .
This was a super, terrific, very good day!

Page 3:
After lunch, I went to _____ with _____ . It was a super, terrific, very good day!

Page 4:
My friend, _____ , and I played _____ . It was a super, terrific, very good day!

Page 5:
We had _____ for supper, and I love _____ . For dessert, we had _____ , my favorite. It was a super terrific very good day!

Page 6:
At bedtime, we read _____ and I played with _____ in the tub. It was a super, terrific, very good day!

Prior to introducing this activity, read Judith Viorst's book to the class, discuss it, and make it available for independent exploration. Tell children that they will have a chance to write (or dictate) a *different* kind of book about a super, terrific, *very good* day. Display and read the prepared booklet, pointing out the blank spaces as you read. Give a booklet and pencil to each child and direct them to fill in the blanks with a story about a wonderful day that they have had or would like to have. Tell children that they may use the crayons or markers to illustrate their books if they wish. After a child completes a booklet, have her or him read it to the class.

7. *Funny Fortunes.*
General Purpose: For children to recognize and use humor as a means of communication.

TFPs: 2, 3, 4, 6, 7, 10.

Materials: Recipe ingredients and chart, measuring spoons and cups, mixing bowls and spoons, nonstick skillet, egg-beater or mixer, empty egg carton, paper strips and pen, oven.

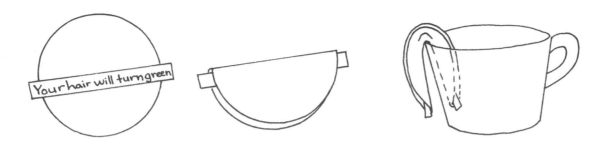

Figure 21.6 *Make Your Own Funny Fortunes*

Fortune Cookies

Ingredients:

⅓ cup flour

1½ T. cornstarch

4 T. brown sugar

dash of salt

2 T. oil

1 stiffly beaten egg white

4 T. water

¼ tsp. vanilla

Procedure:

1. Combine dry ingredients.
2. Mix oil and egg white; add to flour mixture.
3. Add the water and vanilla and mix well.
4. Pour 1 heaping T. batter into skillet over medium heat. Spread into 3-inch circle.
5. Cook 4 minutes until brown.
6. Turn and cook 2 minutes on other side.
7. Remove from pan. Place fortune strip on circle. Use oven mitt to fold circle in half, pressing firmly. (Figure 21.6)
8. Cool in an empty egg carton.
9. Crisp cookies in a 350° oven for 10 minutes. Makes 8 cookies.

Procedure:

a. Prior to making the cookies, provide paper strips and pens and tell the children to write jokes and riddles for the fortune cookies. Remind them that the space is small so the jokes will have to be short.
b. Set up a cooking station with the recipe chart posted and the needed materials available. Direct children who are helping to wash their hands before cooking.
c. Assign each child a specific preparation task such as measuring an ingredient, beating the egg white, mixing, inserting fortunes, and so on.
d. Prepare the batter with children's help.
e. Cook the batter and proceed as the recipe directs.
f. Serve the fortune cookies as a special treat and have the children read their fortunes to the class. Enjoy the humor that the young "fortune writers" have provided.

Hints for Success:

• Prepare a picture recipe chart for the children to follow while cooking.

• Carefully supervise the skillet cooking and work with only one child at a time to reduce burn hazards.

• Children who have difficulty waiting for turns or who are very anxious to get involved sometimes do better if they are given something important to hold onto while they wait. "Here, Craig, please hold the potholder for me so that I will know where it is when I need it."

How to Simplify this Activity:

• Suggest that the children write one word "fortunes" such as pretty, great, fun, and so on.

How to Extend this Activity:

• After a child reads a fortune aloud, direct the class members to try and guess who wrote that fortune.

Physical

1. ***Body Letters.*** This activity will require a large amount of space so that all of the children can move freely without colliding. Tell the children to stand in a circle with enough room to move their arms and legs without bumping a neighbor. Stand very straight and tall with your arms at your sides and tell the children that you are making a letter with your body. Ask if they can name the letter *(I)*. Tell them to copy your letter I with their bodies. Encourage the children to take turns naming and forming letters; have all of the children imitate each "Body Letter." Suggest that more than one body may be required to make the shape of some letters. Also, tell the children that they may find it easier to do some letters if they lie on the floor.

2. ***Fit the Space.*** Provide grid paper with one-inch squares, alphabet rubber stamps, and stamp pads. Direct children to use the rubber stamps to form words by stamping each letter in one square of the paper. Challenge them to place the stamps so that the letters are not touching the lines of the boxes. Tell them to leave an empty box between words.

   Simplify this activity by providing word cards with three-letter words for children to copy; cross out the extra boxes on each line so children are not confused. (Figure 21.7) To make this activity more challenging, provide stencils for children to use in forming the letters inside the boxes instead of rubber stamps.

3. ***Spot to Spot.*** Give each child a colored marker and a sheet (or half sheet) of printed newspaper with writing (no pictures or advertisements) on it. Direct the children to look for a frequently used letter, such as "e" or "t" or "s," and to place a marker dot on each of these letters on the page. When they dot all of the letters, tell children to connect the dots to create surprise pictures.

   Make this activity easier by using printed matter with less writing than a newspaper, such as a large-print magazine.

   Once children are adept at finding one letter, direct them to find several letters and to dot each with a different color.

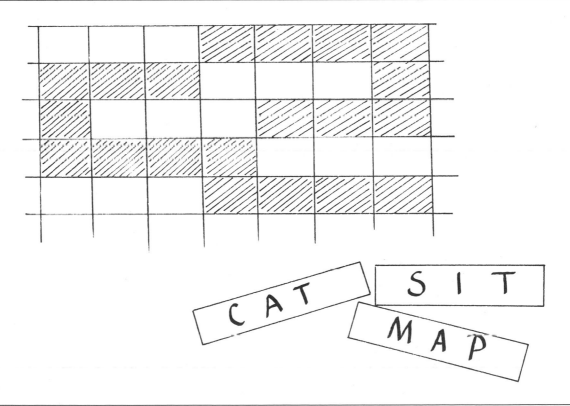

Figure 21.7 *Pieces for the "Fit the Space" Game*

4. **Squirt Bottle Writing**. This is an enjoyable outdoor activity for a warm day. Fill squirt bottles, such as those that contained liquid dish detergent, with water. Demonstrate writing your name with water from the bottle on the sidewalk. Distribute the bottles to the children and tell them to use these to write their names or other short messages.

5. **Write On!** Post large, clearly formed single-letter models in the classroom for children to see as they practice forming letters in various ways. These should include dots or arrows that indicate where to begin and the direction of the strokes used to form each letter. Encourage the children to refer to these as they practice writing with a variety of media.

Provide large cafeteria trays that contain a layer of sand or salt. Direct children to "write" in the sand using fingers or sticks.

Children also enjoy writing in the sand outdoors. Provide small hand-held hoes or rakes to prepare the surface and to use as "erasers."

Provide a large tray or a low, flat plastic container, cornstarch, and water for each child. Direct the children to add a little water to their cornstarch and mix it with their fingers. When it is blended, tell the children to spread it out and write in it with fingers or sticks.

Model writing in the air and direct the children to imitate. Be sure to stand with your back partially turned so that the children see exactly how to form each letter as you "write" and describe your actions.

Suggest that the children work in pairs and take turns writing letters on each other's backs with their fingers.

Pretend Play

1. **Bookstore**. Set up a store area with cash register, bags, purses, pads, pencils, and telephone. Also arrange an assortment of books on shelves in the area to serve as merchandise. Be sure to display a variety of books including picture books, easy readers, cookbooks, dictionaries, atlases, and other reference books. Tell children that they may be clerks or customers at the Bookstore. Encourage the clerks to become familiar with the variety of their merchandise so that they can help the customers to make choices and find what they wish to buy. Model some customer behavior for the children by asking for assistance in finding "a book that my nephew would enjoy" or a "book about elephants" or a "cookbook." Invite one child to be a "visiting author" and to read or discuss a recent work.

2. **Stationery Store/Card Shop**. Set up a pretend play store setting with a display area, sales counter, cash register, money, telephone, merchandise bags, and purses. The merchandise will be greeting cards, either real cards that have been collected and saved or cards made by the children; stationery, real or child-made; writing implements such as a variety of pens, colored pencils, and markers. Encourage the children to assume roles of storekeeper, clerks, and customers.

To extend this activity, encourage the children to use their purchases to write messages to classmates or family.

To simplify this activity, limit the amount of merchandise available at any one time. Keep an extra supply put aside to add as items are purchased, or close the shop and collect the already bought items to return to the store before reopening for business.

Also set up a work room where children produce cards and stationery. Provide four-by-eight-inch construction paper, markers, stickers, and pencils. Direct the children to fold the paper in half to form cards, decorate the fronts, and write verses or messages for the inside pages. Provide plain white or pastel paper for the children to decorate with small rubber stamps or sticker or stencil designs to make stationery. If envelopes are available, they will greatly enhance the play. Substitute lightweight paper folded in half and fastened with tape if envelopes are not available.

3. **Library**. Set up a library area with checkout counter, telephone, stamp pad and

rubber date stamps, pencils, calendar, checkout sheets, and library cards (if these are used in your community). Also provide an assortment of books to be checked out. If possible, place some library card-holders in these for the date slips to reduce the possibility of the children stamping dates on the pages of the books. Tell children that they may be librarians or patrons at the library. Encourage children who have written books to place their books in the library for others to enjoy.

4. *Newspaper Office.* Set up an office area with desks, telephones, typewriter, paper, pencils, newspapers, and maps. Also place some signs by each work space designating which section of the paper is written in each area (sports, fashion, school news, local news, etc.). Show the children some actual newspapers and the sections that they feature. Tell children to choose a working area and to write an article related to that topic. If the children get really involved in this project, you may be able to produce an issue for distribution to the parents.

5. *Post Office.*

General Purpose: For children to practice role-playing.

TFPs: 2, 4, 9, 10.

Materials: Paper, pencils, envelopes, stamps (save magazine stamps or seals that you receive in the mail), child name cards with names of each child in the class, mailbox, mail bags, mail sorting area, counter, cash box and pretend money, letter carrier hats.

Procedure:

a. Set up the post office area and provide a mailbox for each child if the classroom does not already have such an arrangement. Include a counter for the postal workers and lots of table space for the letter writers.

b. Invite the children to take on the roles of postal workers, who sell stamps and sort and deliver mail; or writers, who write and send the mail.

c. Model some writer behaviors by writing a message to a friend (the classroom pet), placing it in an envelope, buying and affixing a stamp, and dropping it in the mailbox.

d. Encourage children to write and send mail to their friends. Respond with genuine enthusiasm to any mail that you personally receive!

e. Tell letter carriers to deliver mail to the appropriate "mailboxes."

Hints for Success:

• Be sure to use nonsexist role titles such as letter carrier and postal clerk when discussing roles and tasks in the post office.

• Provide name cards or a list of the children in the class to help children write each other's names accurately. Those who receive mail will be happy to see their names written correctly by a friend. Add teacher names to this list.

How to Simplify this Activity:

• Provide envelopes with children's names on them.

• Provide simple, preprinted letter forms with blanks to be filled in with words from a suggested list.

Sample Form:
Dear _____ ,
I am having a ___1___ day at school. I hope that you are feeling ___2___ . I am ___3___ that we are friends.

(signature)

Sample Lists:

1	2	3
fine	well	glad
fun	good	happy
great	happy	pleased

How to Extend this Activity:

• Maintain a message-writing station and mailbox area in the classroom for the children to use after this unit is completed.

Figure 21.8 *Two-Sided Name Cards*

• Occasionally write messages to each of the children and place them in the appropriate mailboxes. Encourage the children to answer your notes. Be sure to identify a place where they can deliver messages to the teacher!

Social

1. ***Bookmark for a Friend.*** Provide two-by-eight-inch strips of construction paper in a variety of colors, small stickers, markers, and a list of the children in the class. Also obtain some commercially made bookmarks to show the children; use them to reserve your place when reading books to the group. Tell the children that they each can make a bookmark for a friend. Direct them to select paper strips and write their friends' names on them using the class list if needed to assure accurate spellings. Add stickers and deliver!

2. ***Come to a Party!*** Provide paper, pencils, and crayons. Encourage children to use these materials to design and write invitations to friends for a "party" at the snack table or a "tea party" in the pretend play area.

3. ***Name Cards.*** Prepare a name card for each child in the classroom. Use sturdy paper such as tagboard or poster board, cut into three-by-eight-inch rectangles. Carefully print each child's name on both sides of a card and cover with clear adhesive vinyl. Use either all upper-case or do one side in upper-case and the other side in lower-case letters. (Figure 21.8) These should be available in the writing center at all times for children to refer to when they write messages to their classmates or practice writing their own names.

4. ***Class ABC Book.***

   General Purpose: For children to learn to work with others toward a common goal.

   TFPs: 14, 15.

   Materials: Published ABC books, twenty-six sheets of paper, markers, pencils, crayons, list of children in the class, book cover up made by teacher or a child, small pieces of construction paper, magazines, scissors, glue.

   Procedure:

   a. Prior to carrying out this activity, have available several beautifully illustrated, professionally published ABC books for children to examine.

b. Tell the children in the group that they are going to make a class ABC book.

c. Show the children where the materials for this project will be kept and where they will be working.

d. Instruct each child to tell you which letter he or she will be working on *before* beginning a page, or assign a particular letter to each child.

e. Encourage each child to draw or cut and paste a picture of something that begins with his or her letter and to write the word on the page.

f. Once all of the pages are completed, have some children assist you in arranging them in alphabetical order and mounting them in the book cover.

g. Keep this book available in the classroom for all to enjoy.

Hint for Success:

• Have each child tell you the plan for the page to assure that the word selected fits his or her letter.

How to Simplify this Activity:

• Provide each child with a page with a letter already written on it. Tell the child the letter and say some sample words that begin with that letter. Direct the child to draw or cut and paste a picture of an object that also begins with that letter.

• Provide suggestions to help fit the letters on the pages that the children are working on.

How to Extend this Activity:

• Provide many small pages and direct each child to make an individual ABC book.

*5. *Pen Pal Notes.*

General Purpose: For children to develop friendship skills.

TFPs: 2, 3, 4, 9, 10, 16, 17, 18.

Materials: Paper, pencils, envelopes, photographs of children with names attached.

Procedure:

a. This project will involve participation with another classroom. If you teach two half-day sessions, you can do it yourself. If you teach a full-day session, seek a partner who will conduct this activity in his/her classroom at the same time.

b. Show the children the photographs of the children in the other classroom. Tell them that they may choose one of those children as a pen pal. Tell them, "A pen pal is a person to whom you write letters even though you may not ever see them in person."

c. Provide the writing materials and post the photographs near the writing center of your classroom.

d. Tell the children to write a message to the person they have chosen as a pen pal and indicate a designated place where these messages may be left for delivery.

e. Collect the messages and see that they are delivered. Encourage the recipients to respond.

Hints for Success:

• Help the child to select a child who will be receptive and who is most likely to respond.

• Keep track of the children who participate and to whom they send their messages. After the initial phase of this activity, if it seems appropriate, assign the children a specific person to whom to write so that all of the children are involved in receiving and sending letters.

How to Simplify this Activity:

• Write a group message to the other class. Introduce this during a group experience and give each child an opportunity to add to the message later in the day, either by writing or dictating. Encourage each child to sign his or her name to the letter before sending it.

• Provide simple form letters with blanks that the children may fill in.

• Continue the pen-pal relationships over time. Provide a folder or box in which notes may be saved and reread. After several weeks, plan a special get-together so that the pen pals may meet each other in person.

TEACHER RESOURCES

Field Trip Ideas

1. Take the children to visit a bookstore, library, newspaper office, magazine stand, or post office. Look for writing in each location, and arrange for someone there to talk about or demonstrate how writing influences his or her job.

Classroom Visitors

1. Invite to your classroom an author, calligrapher, librarian, poet, printer, or reporter. Ask guests to demonstrate how they use writing in their work. Focus, too, on how the budding writers in your group could imitate or duplicate the visitors' activities in the classroom.

Children's Books

Ahlberg, J., and A. Ahlberg. *The Jolly Postman or Other People's Letters.* Boston: Little, Brown, 1986.

Alexander, S. *Dear Phoebe.* Boston: Little, Brown, 1984.

Aronsky, J. *Mouse Writing.* New York: Harcourt Brace Jovanovich, 1983.

Bang, M. G. *Tye May and the Magic Brush.* New York: Greenwillow, 1981.

Boynton, S. *Chloe and Maude.* Boston: Little, Brown, 1985.

Davis, M. *Grandma's Secret Letter.* New York: Holiday House, 1982.

Gibbons, G. *Deadline! From News to Newspaper.* New York: Crowell, 1987.

Hamsa, B. *Fast Draw Freddie.* Chicago: Childrens Press, 1984.

Hoban, L. *Arthur's Pen Pal.* New York: Harper and Row, 1976.

Johnson, C. *Harold and the Purple Crayon.* New York: Harper and Row, 1955.

———. *Harold's Circus.* New York: Harper and Row, 1959.

———. *Harold's Trip to the Sky.* New York: Harper and Row, 1957.

———. *A Picture for Harold's Room.* New York: Harper and Row, 1960.

Keats, E. J. *A Letter to Amy.* New York: Harper Junior, 1968.

Kellogg, S. *The Mystery of the Stolen Blue Paint.* New York: Dial, 1982.

Lisowski, G. *The Invitation.* New York: Holt, Rinehart and Winston, 1980.

Lund, D. H. *The Paint-Box Sea.* New York: McGraw-Hill, 1973.

Schick, E. *My Album.* New York: Greenwillow, 1984.

Schwartz, A. *Begin at the Beginning.* New York: Harper and Row, 1983.

Additional References for Writers

Aardema, V. *Bringing the Rain to Kapiti Plain.* New York: Dial, 1981.

Gàg, W. *Millions of Cats.* New York: Coward-McCann, 1928.

Jonas, A. *Color Dance.* New York: Greenwillow, 1989.

Most, B. *Dinosaur Cousins.* San Diego: Harcourt Brace Jovanovich, 1987.

Scott, A. H. *On Mother's Lap.* N.Y.: McGraw-Hill, 1972.

Viorst, J. *Alexander and the Horrible, Terrible, No-Good, Very Bad Day.* New York: Atheneum, 1979.

Watanabe, S. *How Do I Put It On?* New York: Philomel, 1979.

ABC Books for Writers

Downie, J. *Alphabet Puzzle.* New York: Lothrop, Lee & Shepard, 1988.

Ehlert, L. *Eating the Alphabet.* San Diego: Harcourt Brace Jovanovich, Pub., 1989.

Feeney, S. *A is for Aloha.* Honolulu: University of Hawaii Press, 1980.

Hague, K. *Alphabears.* New York: Holt, Rinehart and Winston, 1984.

Lalli, J. *Feelings Alphabet: An Album of Emotions A to Z.* Rolling Hills Estates, CA.: B. L. Winch & Associates, 1984.

Lobel, A. *Alison's Zinnia.* New York: Greenwillow, 1990.

Martin, B., Jr. *Chicka Chicka Boom Boom.* New York: Simon and Schuster Books for Young Readers, 1989.

Mayers, F. C. *ABC: Museum of Fine Arts, Boston.* New York: Harry N. Abrams, 1988.

Mayers, F. C. *ABC: Musical Instruments from the Metropolitan Museum of Art.* New York: Harry N. Abrams, 1988.

Merriam, E. *Where Is Everybody?* New York: Simon and Schuster Books for Young Readers, 1989.

Owens, M.B. *A Caribou Alphabet.* Brunswick, ME: The Dog Ear Press, 1988.

Small, T. *Tails, Claws, Fangs & Paws.* New York: A Bantam Little Rooster Book, 1990.

Adult References

Calkins, L. *Lessons from a Child.* Portsmouth, NH: Heinemann, 1983.

Hennings, D. G. *Communication in Action: Teaching the Language Arts.* 3rd ed. Boston: Houghton Mifflin, 1986.

McCrum, R., W. Cran, and R. MacNeil. *The Story of English.* New York: Viking, 1986.

Newman, J. *The Craft of Children's Writing.* Portsmouth, NH: Heinemann, 1984.

Turbill, J. *Now We Want to Write!* Portsmouth, NH: Heinemann, 1983.

Part IV

Mathematical Concepts

Chapter 22

Number and Numerals

Every day, children explore, invent, and construct relationships among objects as a way to make sense of the world in which they live. Frequently, these relationships focus on how much or how many of something exists.

Thus, children count—one cookie . . . two shoes . . . three candles on the birthday cake . . . four children at the sand table. Children compare—Which has more? . . . Which has fewer? . . . Will there be enough? . . . Who has extra? . . . Who still needs some? . . . Children calculate—How many will fit? . . . Now, I have five. . . . I need one more. . . . Children create—That makes enough. . . . Now they're the same. . . . One cup for me . . . one cup for you. . . . One spoon for me . . . one spoon for you.

In all of these instances children are developing a notion of quantity through active manipulation of the objects in their environment. Experiences such as figuring out how many crackers to take at snack time, lining up boots in front of cubbies to see if everyone's are there, or sorting the shells into piles are typical of how children use their own activities to reveal and investigate mathematical concepts.

However, while children can learn the label "spoon" through social transmission, or discover that spoons can be shiny, hard, and bendable through sensory perception, they will comprehend the "fourness" of four spoons only by constructing that concept from within. "Fourness," in this case, is not a physical property of the spoons themselves. Rather, it represents a construct that exists in the child's own mind when relating the spoons to one another or to other spoons and objects in the world. Such abstractions come about gradually through children's experience and experimentation in day-to-day circumstances and are results of their own mental activity. Consequently, due to its intuitive nature, number concept cannot be taught to children directly. Simply telling them that there "are" four spoons does not insure that children recognize the "fourness" of the situation. Neither do paper-pencil exercises or verbal recitations of number combinations get to the fundamental concepts needed for understanding. Yet, this lack of responsiveness to direct instruction does not mean that the early childhood teacher should ignore mathematics or assume that it requires no special planning. On the contrary,

children's intellectual growth and development are influenced by the quality and variety of their experiences as well as by the availability of an understanding adult with whom to talk and the quality of the language that teachers use to describe mathematical concepts as they occur. Moreover, how children feel about their experiences with math and about themselves as learners greatly affects their ultimate success with mathematical concepts (Balogh, 1989; Leeper, Witherspoon, and Day, 1979). Hence, in supporting children's mathematics-related curiosity and abilities, the early childhood teacher should strive to:

1. Stimulate and support children's interest in mathematics.
2. Structure a "mathematics-rich" classroom environment.
3. Offer planned and incidental activities that promote the development of mathematical thinking and concepts.

PURPOSE

We have a fourfold purpose in developing a theme entitled Number and Numerals. The first is to demonstrate to teachers how to integrate mathematics-related experiences into all areas of the early childhood curriculum. In this way we hope to familiarize teachers with how to teach mathematics within the context of the total curriculum, rather than reserving such experiences for "math time" or the "math table" only.

Second, we want to give teachers ideas for foundational activities to introduce early in the school year, then return to and build on within other themes. Such activities could be adopted for virtually every other unit in this volume.

Our third purpose in developing this theme is to consciously draw children's attention to number concepts so that "number" will be viewed as an exciting, enjoyable concept to investigate. Our field studies indicate that older preschoolers and kindergartners were particularly enthusiastic about the activities.

Finally, mathematical concepts encompass a wide range of experiences: matching, sorting and classifying, ordering, number concepts, graphing, and measuring. However, for the purpose of illustration, we have chosen to focus on numerals and number concepts only. We did this as a way to help adults distinguish between these elements and to make it clear that the two are not the same.

IMPLEMENTATION

Option One: This unit could serve as a concentrated introduction to numbers and numerals early in the year for a wide range of ages. The attention devoted to this material provides an opportunity for the teacher to assess the skills of the children through observations and interactions with them. Such information could then be used to plan further experiences. In addition, many of the activities described are intended to become part of the daily routine in the classroom for they provide the repetition and familiarity that young children require to really learn. We suggest that some of these be incorporated into the daily classroom routine from the beginning of the school year even though the actual unit may not be taught until several weeks have elapsed.

Option Two: For older children, present an entire week of number and numeral experiences two or three times during the year. You may also wish to follow up with a unit on measuring and another on a related topic such as stores. This approach provides opportunities for continuous assessment and adjustment of expectations and experiences to suit the development of the children.

No matter which option you choose, we assume you will incorporate number and numeral activities into your program on a daily basis to provide the youngsters that you teach with a firm foundation in these essential mathematical concepts.

TERMS, FACTS, AND PRINCIPLES

1. Number refers to how many of something there are.
2. People count to find out how many things there are.
3. When counting, each thing is counted only once.
4. The number of objects is determined by how many objects there are, not by what they are, how they are arranged, or the order in which they are counted.
5. Numbers occur in an order (sequence) that is always the same.
6. Adding one to each number equals the next number in the sequence.
7. A particular quantity is always the same number.
8. People use many different words to describe quantity.
9. Exact amounts are described using number names.
10. A particular number name such as two or six is always associated with the same quantity.
11. People have created special words to describe certain quantities, such as couple or pair meaning two and dozen meaning twelve.
12. Approximate amounts are described using words such as few, many, lots, several, some, or not many.
13. A group of objects is called a set.
14. A set may contain any quantity of objects.
15. Sets are sometimes compared.
16. When compared to one another, sets may contain the same quantity of objects, or one set may be more or less than the other.
17. Some words used to describe comparisons of quantity are more than, less than, and the same as.
18. If the number of objects in two sets is the same, the sets are said to be equal.
19. If the number of objects in two sets is not the same, one set has more objects or is greater than, and one set contains fewer objects or is less than.
20. Zero means there are no objects to be counted.
21. The number of objects in a set changes when objects are added or subtracted.
22. People use words, marks, pictures, or numerals to describe and record number.
23. When marks or pictures are used to represent number, find out the number by counting each one.

24. A numeral is a special type of symbol that represents a number.

25. The words number and numeral have different meanings.

26. People around the world have agreed that particular numerals represent particular numbers.

27. A person must learn what number each numeral represents in order to use numerals accurately in daily life.

28. People use numerals to indicate how many of something there are or how much of something is needed.

29. While the same numerals are used the world over, different cultures use different words to name them.

*30. People the world over have agreed that certain written signs represent particular mathematical operations.

*31. The plus sign tells people to add.

*32. The minus sign tells people to subtract.

*33. The equals sign tells people the sum, or that sets contain the same number.

ACTIVITY IDEAS

Aesthetics

1. *Art Treasure Hunt.* Select and display a print or a painting that contains enough of a particular item to count. Count these items with the children.

2. *Beautiful Numerals.* Provide an assortment of numerals cut out of construction paper or tagboard at the art table. (The numerals may be of any size, from three inches high to nine inches high.) Also make available glue and decorating items such as glitter, ribbon pieces, yarn strips, or stickers. Invite children to select and decorate the numeral(s) of their choice. Be sure that children orient their numerals right-side-up while decorating.

   To simplify this activity, draw block numerals with a thick marker and invite the children to decorate inside the figures. To extend it, invite children to trace and/or cut their own numerals, or direct them to place on each beautiful numeral the number of stickers that corresponds to that numeral. Then they can add glitter or sequins to enhance their creations.

3. *Number Songs.* Choose from the wide array of number songs popular in preschools and early elementary grades the ones that you like best to sing with your children. Sing them often. However, be aware of the inappropriate connotations in some of these old favorites and avoid them by altering the lyrics when possible. For example, *Ten Little Indians* can be reworded to be about ten little or ten big anything else (such as dinosaurs, pumpkins, and so forth) to eliminate the inaccurate labeling that is offensive to many Native Americans. In *Five Little Ducks*, have Grandma Duck, Sister Duck, or even Mama Duck recall the little ducks to eliminate the sexist implications of Daddy Duck being the only power to whom the little ducks respond. The revised version goes as follows:

Five Little Ducks
(Traditional)
Five little ducks went out to play.
(Use fingers of one hand to represent ducks.)
Over the hill and far away.
(Move the "ducks" up over "hill" and then behind back.)
Mama Duck called "Quack—quack—quack."
(Other hand opens/closes.)
Four little ducks came waddling back.
(Show hand with four fingers.)
(Repeat this with one less duck each time until:)
No little ducks went out to play.
(Show hand with fingers tucked in.)
Over the hill and far away.
Grandma Duck called "Quack—quack—quack!"
(Very loud voice.)
Five little ducks came waddling back!
(Five fingers return.)

Children also enjoy naming different family members to try calling the ducks each time. Another wonderful number song, especially for helping children to learn

Making Puzzles

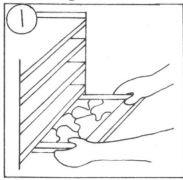

Choose a puzzle.

Look at the picture.

Take the pieces out one at a time.

Fit the pieces back into the puzzle.

Complete the puzzle.

Put the puzzle away.

Figure 22.1 *Complete the Puzzle Sequence*

counting to twenty, is *The Number Rock.* In this rhythmic singing of the numbers, children seem to enjoy the beat and the repetition. It is on an album called *We All Live Together,* Volume 2, by Steve Millang and Greg Scelsa on Youngheart Records.

Affective

1. *Clean Up—Count Up.* Place number/numeral labels on toy storage containers and shelf spaces to correspond to the number of items stored there. Encourage the children to count these items as they help with clean-up.

2. *Countdown to Completion.* Post simple numbered picture directions for children to follow as they perform school routines and engage in activities. Introduce these to the children as a group and refer to "step 1," "step 2," and so on as you explain each step. Post picture directions for routines such as handwashing, toothbrushing, snack time or dressing for outdoors, easel painting, woodworking, or puzzle assembling. (Figure 22.1)

3. *Help Yourself!* Incorporate numbers into snack time or mealtime by labeling serving containers to indicate portion amounts. Younger children can practice one-to-one correspondence as they match the crackers

they take to the indicators (clothespins clipped to side of a bowl or pictures on a card with a symbol representing each piece). Add numerals to these visual cues, or the numeral plus the printed word ("2, two"). Always let children know that the number tells them the maximum allowed, and that they may choose to take fewer items if they wish. (Figure 22.2)

4. *Sharing Five.* Request the cooperation of the children's parents for this activity. Ask each child to find five of something to bring to school from home. (Some suggestions to parents could include pebbles, straws, pennies, small twigs, bottle caps, pencils, small boxes, buttons. Stress that you desire nonedible items!) Gather a group of four or five children and their collections and allow each child to display and discuss "five" in turn. After all have had an opportunity to share their fives, try some or all of the following. Invite children to:

- temporarily trade items and count someone else's five;
- divide their fives into two groups and tell you how many are in each;
- combine his or her fives with a group belonging to another child;
- give you one or two of their fives and tell you how many are remaining;
- combine all the groups and count the result.

Repeat this activity on other days for different numbers.

Figure 22.2 *Help Yourself at the Snack Table*

5. *Supply Clerk.* Designate one child as supply clerk in an area for the day, in the block area or at the art or snack tables, for instance. The supply clerk will "take orders" for materials from other children and count out the needed items. Older children could also keep a written record of orders requested and filled.

6. *Fruit Kabobs.* Prepare an assortment of fruit pieces (pineapple chunks, apple chunks dipped in orange juice, grapes, berries, banana slices) and place in small bowls with numerals on each indicating amounts to be used. Provide some wooden skewers or straws. Tell the children that they may prepare their own snacks by counting out the number of fruit pieces posted on the bowls and placing them on the skewers to make fruit kabobs.

Cognition

1. *Counting Boards.* Make some counting boards and keep them available in the classroom near a supply of small objects to be counted. Change the supply of objects to be counted occasionally to maintain interest and encourage children to use them frequently. To make counting boards:

   a. Use a piece of poster board, cardboard, or other fairly sturdy material. The size will depend upon the number to be counted.

   b. Divide into equal-sized sections and number from zero to _____ .

   c. Indicate zero in a special way (Give it a different color or set it apart.) (Figure 22.3)

   d. Cover the entire board with laminating material to protect the surface and extend its life.

   e. Another method is to print numerals on circular self-adhesive file folder labels to stick on the board.

   f. If making a board with a hundred spaces, the tens spaces may be made larger or of a different color to facilitate counting by tens.

   g. Show children how to use the board by placing one object on each space in

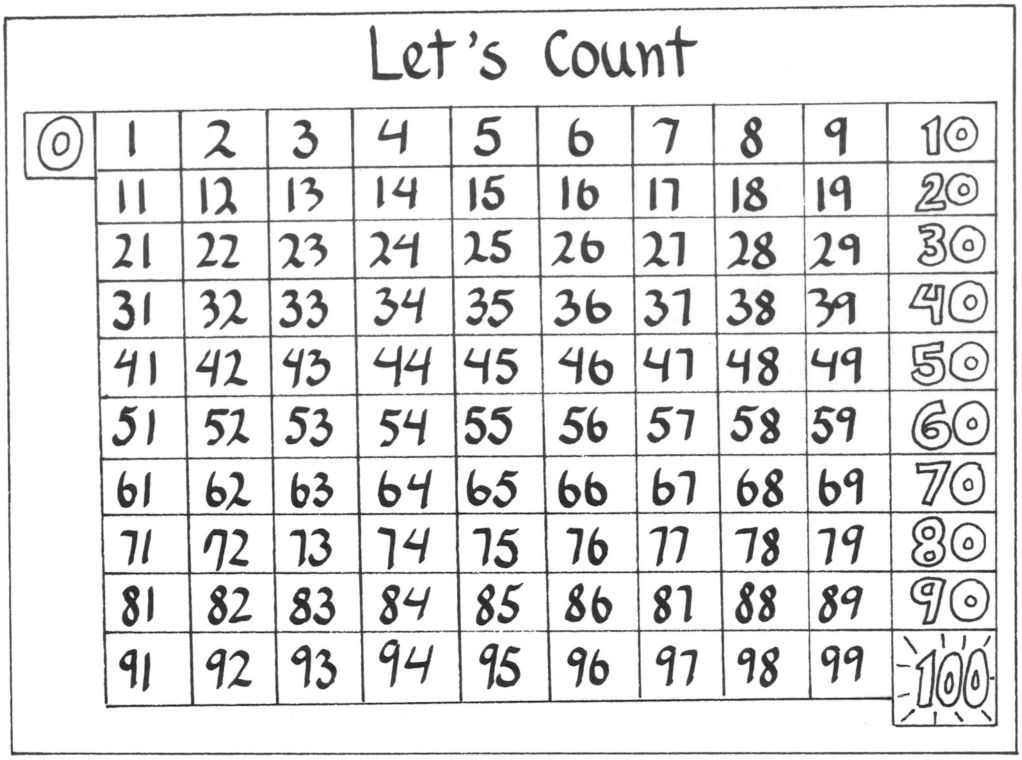

Let's Count

0	1	2	3	4	5	6	7	8	9	10
	11	12	13	14	15	16	17	18	19	20
	21	22	23	24	25	26	27	28	29	30
	31	32	33	34	35	36	37	38	39	40
	41	42	43	44	45	46	47	48	49	50
	51	52	53	54	55	56	57	58	59	60
	61	62	63	64	65	66	67	68	69	70
	71	72	73	74	75	76	77	78	79	80
	81	82	83	84	85	86	87	88	89	90
	91	92	93	94	95	96	97	98	99	100

Figure 22.3 *Counting Boards Used to Count Different Objects*

order and then saying the corresponding numeral.

h. When they are finished, children also enjoy "clearing" the board with a magnetic "wand" if the counters used contain some iron.

2. *Number Detectives.* Prepare a set of poster boards with a large numeral on each one. Use 2, 3, 4, and 5. Gather the children in a group and show them the "2" board. Tell them to be Number Detectives and look for twos in the classroom while you record the things that they find on the board. Point out two of something as an example, saying "I see two books on the table. I will write 'two books'." Record their discoveries with the name of the "detective" who reported each throughout the day and read them to the class at the end of the day. Post the reporting board in the classroom. The next day, repeat the activity using the "3" board. Continue with a different number to be detected each day. At the end of the week, count the discoveries of each number with the children and write the total on each board. In an alternate approach, assign pairs or small groups of children different numbers and send them off to search the room or playground for sets of those numbers. Children could also leave numeral labels with each set, or maintain a record of the sets detected. This could become a long-term activity if each number group has a large recording sheet to which it adds sets of the number as they are discovered over time.

Some sample numbers that the children may see include two shoes, four children at the snack table, three pencils on a table, five blocks in a stack, three teachers, four paint colors at the easel, four brushes at the easel, or two guinea pigs.

3. *Earth Survey.* Prepare a loop of string for each child. (All should be about the same size; size will be determined by the number of children and the available space.) Invite each child to select and mark off, with the loop, a section of ground and to count the number of particular items found there—

stones, twigs, dandelions, or seeds. Record the results, or have each child record his or her results. Each child could make an individual graph of items found or a class graph of items could be developed.

4. ***Puzzle Ponder.***

General Purpose: To provide opportunities for children to develop problem-solving skills.

TFPs: 2, 3, 4, 17, 22, 24.

Materials: An assortment of puzzles containing different numbers of pieces, paper to write on, pencils.

Procedure:

a. Introduce the activity to a large or small group of children by demonstrating the following process. Select and display two puzzles. Tell the children that you are going to do both puzzles, but first you are going to try to predict or guess which puzzle will be easier to put together. Ask children to suggest how to do this. Acknowledge and accept their ideas.

   Introduce the idea of counting the pieces as one way to determine simplicity. Count and record on paper the number of pieces in each puzzle. Determine which has more or less. Predict which will be easier and record the children's choice. Assemble each puzzle and evaluate the children's prediction.

b. Invite a child to choose two puzzles.

c. "Tell me which of these puzzles will be the easier." (Record the child's choice.)

d. "Count the number of pieces in this puzzle." (Point/record.)

e. "Count the number of pieces in this other puzzle." (Point/record.)

f. "You thought that the _____ puzzle would be the easiest to do. Do you still think so?" (Record.)

g. Direct child to assemble both puzzles.

h. "Which puzzle was the easiest?"

i. "You thought that the _____ would be easier and it was"; or "You discovered that the _____ was easier than the _____ ."

Hint for Success:

• Select relatively simple puzzles of similar complexity, differing only in number of pieces.

How to Simplify this Activity:

• Provide only two puzzles from which to choose.

• Vary the numbers of pieces greatly. Provide, for example, a three-piece puzzle and a seven-piece puzzle.

How to Extend this Activity:

• Provide several puzzles that vary only slightly in the numbers of pieces.

5. ***Rational Counting.***

General Purpose: To provide opportunities for children to construct a concept of quantity.

TFPs: 2, 3, 4, 5, 6, 20.

Materials: Anything that occurs in a quantity, such as children, chairs, cups, blocks, beads, dolls, rocks, leaves, flowers, books.

Procedure:

a. Decide what is to be counted and make sure that the objects are within visual range of all of the children.

b. Point out the objects to the children. "Look at the birds on the wire."

c. Invite children to count with you.

d. Say each number slowly and clearly as you point to or touch the objects you are counting.

Hint for Success:

• Repeat this process frequently, more than once a day if possible.

How to Simplify this Activity:

• Count objects that are few in number.

How to Extend this Activity:

• Once children are accustomed to this process, encourage them to count objects independently during the day.

• Count objects that are great in number.

6. ***Visual Patterning.***

General Purpose: To provide opportunities for children to recognize or construct relationships among objects through the process of patterning (repeating a particular configuration).

TFPs: 18, 22.

Materials: A set of patterns and the corresponding materials, such as:

Set 1: Colored inch cubes, pattern cards for colored inch cubes;

Set 2: Colored beads, pattern cards that match beads;

Set 3: Large or small parquetry, matching pattern cards.

Procedure:

a. Introduce the materials (without patterns) and encourage children to explore them.

b. Join the children working with the materials or invite a few children to join you. Arrange a few pieces of the material in a simple design and direct children to "make one just like mine."

c. Refer to this design as a pattern and repeat this step several times, increasing the number of pieces and the complexity of the design.

d. Invite children to create simple designs for you and others to duplicate.

e. Introduce pattern cards and demonstrate how to use them by placing corresponding pieces on the card.

f. Give children simple pattern cards and ask them to place matching pieces directly on them. (Figure 22.4a)

g. Repeat steps e and f, asking the children to place their pieces in the corresponding pattern next to their cards.

h. Show children a simple pattern card briefly; then remove the card and have them duplicate it from memory.

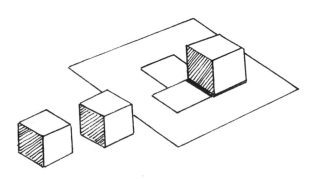

Figure 22.4a *Building a Simple Pattern on the Card*

Hints for Success:

• Patterning experiences should always be available in the classroom.

• Initial exploration may take several days or weeks.

How to Simplify this Activity:

• Materials can be changed frequently to maintain interest.

• Carry out the steps described above over time (several days or even weeks).

How to Extend this Activity:

• Gradually increase the complexity of the patterns provided and change the method of patterning from a direct match on the card, to re-creating the pattern beside the card, to re-creating the pattern from memory.

• In an optional experience, have the child create a simple pattern with objects and then extend the pattern several times. (Figure 22.4b)

Construction

1. *Five Books.*

General Purpose: To provide opportunities for children to represent "five" in a variety of presentations.

TFPs: 3, 7, 10, 18.

Materials: A premade booklet for each child containing several pages with the numeral 5 and space for the child's name on the cover; enough stickers, toothpicks, straw pieces, or construction paper pieces for each child to have five for each page; glue; pencils.

Procedure:

a. Distribute the booklets and ask the children to write their name on the covers, or do this for them.

b. Distribute five of the items to each child and direct them to arrange them on the first page in any manner that they choose.

c. Provide glue and ask the children to glue the objects in place.

d. Distribute five more items and tell children to arrange them on the second page in a different design.

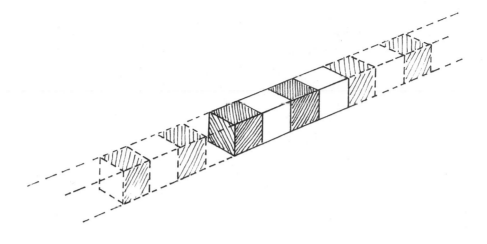

Figure 22.4b *Continuing a Simple Pattern in Two Directions*

e. Continue the above process until all pages are complete.

f. Point out that although all pages contain five identical objects, the sets look different because of the arrangement of the objects.

Hints for Success:

- Count frequently as this is carried out. Point out that a page has two here and three here and that makes five.

- Be sure that each page contains five items and help each child to observe and make corrections as needed.

How to Simplify this Activity:

- Include only a few pages in each child's booklet.

- Do a booklet using only two or three objects per page.

How to Extend this Activity:

- Provide directions and allow older children to help themselves to materials once they understand the purpose of the activity.

- Have children make books of other numbers in the same way, utilizing a variety of materials.

2. ***10-20-30 Structures.*** Provide an assortment of different types of blocks in the block area. For example, you could use one-inch cubes, small colored building blocks, or unit blocks. Tell children that they are going to build structures using a particular number of blocks and designate how many of each type should be used by placing labels on the shelves or containers. Help children to count out the appropriate number of blocks before they start their structures. After children complete their structures, point out that although children used the same number of blocks, different arrangements make the structures look unique. You may wish to do this designated number building for several days, changing the numbers and block types. If possible, take pictures of the structures to record and compare. Be sure to include number labels on the pictures!

3. ***3-5-7 Collage.*** Provide an assortment of three different collage materials. Some suggestions include cotton balls, toothpicks, paper strips, ribbon pieces, straw pieces, and buttons. Tell children that they may choose three of one item, five of another item, and seven of another to create their pictures. Help children to count out the items, or assign a "supply clerk" to perform this task. Provide construction paper, glue, and pencils. Direct children to arrange their chosen 3-5-7 items on the paper in any design that they desire and to glue them in place. Re-count the items after each picture is completed.

Count the total numbers of items as well. Try this activity another day using a different combination of numbers.

4. *Number Book.* Make a booklet for each child by assembling pages of construction paper approximately four inches square. Each cover should say "My Number Book" and have a space for the child's name. Each page should have a number on it and be arranged in correct numerical order. Provide glue and items to place on the pages. The items may be identical for each page or children may select items to represent each number. Direct children to place the number of items on each page that corresponds to the numeral on that page.

Begin with only a few pages, then gradually increase their number as children become more proficient.

Language

1. *Add a Character/Subtract a Character.* Select a story that has multiple characters appearing in a given sequence and prepare a set of corresponding flannel-board figures. Appropriate stories include *The Big, Big Turnip; The Gingerbread Man; Chicken Little.* Tell the story to a group of children using the figures. After the story is complete, review the characters and discuss them one at a time, mentioning the sequence in which each appears in the story. Count the figures as you add them. Discuss how the story would change if a character was subtracted or taken away or if additional characters were added. Make the figures available to children for independent use later in the day. Encourage children to count the characters, add characters, and subtract characters.

2. *Number Riddles.* Tell the children some number riddles and encourage them to tell their friends. Older children may enjoy creating their own versions. While these may get rather silly, they are fun and enjoyed by all. They also reinforce number concepts! These examples will get you started.

   Q. What is a bird after it is four days old?
   A. Five days old.

   Q. How many lions can you put in an empty cage?
   A. One, because then it is no longer empty.
   Q. What birds have four feet and yellow feathers?
   A. Two canaries.

3. *Old Favorites with Numbers.* Select some favorite old stories with number associations to tell, retell, and act out frequently in your classroom. Tell them with books or flannel-board figures, have the children act them out, tell them with props or puppets, or just TELL the stories. Some suggestions include *Goldilocks and the Three Bears, The Three Little Pigs,* or *The Three Billy Goats Gruff.*

4. *Can This Be True?* Prior to conducting this activity, read and enjoy *How Much is a Million?* by David M. Schwartz to provide opportunities for the children to form beginning concepts of the vast quantities represented by numbers like million, billion, and trillion. After they have been exposed to these ideas, read *Millions of Cats* by Wanda Gàg. Before reading, tell the children to listen carefully so that they can tell you some of the things that could really happen and some of the things that could not really happen. After reading, lead a discussion of possible and impossible events in the story. Write these, as the children mention them, on two separate poster boards. As you write, slowly say each word. Repeat the entire phrase when it is completed, pointing to each word as you read. Review the completed lists, again pointing to each word as it is read. Post these at child eye level in the classroom so that the children can see and read them independently during the week. At a later time, read the story again and ask the children to substitute other statements for those that they identified as impossible after the initial reading. These new statements could be either possible or impossible.

5. *Peek-A-Boo Number Books.*
   General Purpose: To provide children with opportunities to increase their receptive vocabulary.

Figure 22.5a *This Number Book Has Peeking Slots*

TFPs: 8, 10, 12.

Materials: Prepare booklets for each child of five-inch-square construction paper, each inside page cut with a ½-by-1½-inch flap. (Figure 22.5a) Print a set of words describing quantities for each child: couple, few, some, many, lots, not many, pair, and so on. (Words should fit behind the flaps cut into the pages.) Small paper bits, scissors, glue.

Procedure:

a. Prepare a demonstration booklet with a few words illustrated to show to the children.

b. Invite the children to choose booklets, write their names on the covers, and select or cut out one of their quantity words. This should be glued to the back of the first page so that the word is visible when the flap is lifted. (Figure 22.5b)

c. Once a word is in place, ask the child to choose a quantity of paper pieces to represent the word and glue them into place on the page.

d. Continue until all the pages are complete.

e. Have children "read" their books to you, and then to each other.

Hint for Success:

• Keep the selection of items to be glued simple to focus attention on the words.

How to Simplify this Activity:

• Use fewer pages.

How to Extend this Activity:

• Invite children to write their own words. Note that this takes a lot of control to make the words fit the flap space.

Physical

1. *Choose a Target.* Provide children with some possible targets to be reached with a physical movement. These may be simple things such as the chair in the corner or actual targets such as signs or plastic cones. Invite each child to select a physical movement (step, roll, hop, jump, etc.) to use to reach the target of choice and count the number of actions required to reach it.

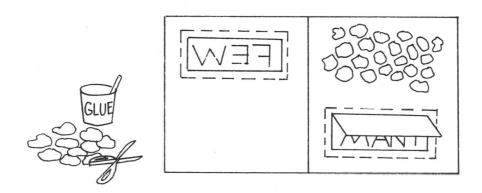

Figure 22.5b *Putting Together a "Peek-a-Boo" Number Book*

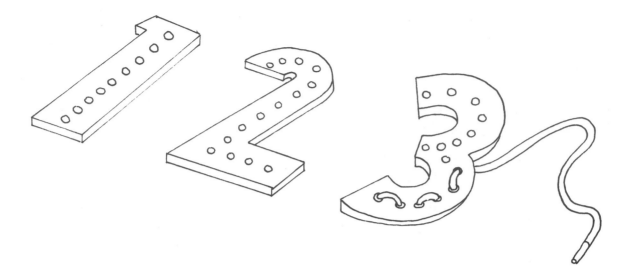

Figure 22.6 *Numeral Shapes for Lacing*

Vary the activity by selecting different movements, by trying to reduce or expand the movements needed, or by choosing a new target.

2. *Hopscotch.* Prepare a hopscotch pattern on the floor with tape or on an outdoor sidewalk with chalk and show children how to hop (on one foot) and jump (on two feet) from one numeral to the next in order. Encourage children to try to move in the same pattern, calling out the numerals as they proceed.

3. *Lacing Numerals.* Provide children with a set of numeral cards to lace with shoelaces or yarn threaded on large plastic needles. These cards can be made easily by using heavy cardboard. Draw the numeral on the cardboard and cut out the shape to correspond with the shape of the numeral. Punch holes in it with a nail at one- or two-inch spaces. (Figure 22.6) Punch with large holes in some numerals for inexperienced children and punch smaller holes in others to create a challenge for youngsters with more advanced skills. Print the number name on one side of each numeral.

4. *Moving a Pile.* Provide children with a pile of something to be moved. This may be a pile of blocks indoors or a pile of sand, leaves, or snow outdoors. The children will probably enjoy creating the piles as well. Provide tools to use to move the contents of the pile. These might be shovels, scoops, buckets, wagons, paper cups, spoons, or sacks depending upon contents, size, and location of the pile. Tell children that they are to move the contents of the pile from one place to another and count the number of loads needed to move the entire pile. The pile could be moved back and forth or relocated if interest is high.

5. *Stand and Be Counted.* Prepare a set of numeral cards (1–10) large enough to be seen by the entire class when held up by the teacher. Tell the children that they will be playing a balancing and counting game. Direct the children to stand so that each has enough space to move without bumping into a neighbor and so that they can see you. Hold up one of the numeral cards and ask children to identify the numeral. Tell them to stand on one foot while slowly counting to the number shown on the card. Provide a counting beat and count with the children. Provide many encouraging phrases as children succeed in balancing for the entire count. Continue this game by providing different balancing challenges for the children to try while counting: stand on tiptoes; balance on the toes of one foot; balance on one foot with arms up in the air, extended, at sides; balance on one knee, on stomachs, on bottoms with arms and legs in air; and so on.

The children may enjoy thinking of other ways to balance.

To simplify this activity, include symbols to count on the cards, as well as numerals. To expand it, use two cards to form double digit numerals such as 14, 23, and so on. Or, show two cards simultaneously and have the children add them together to determine the counting and balancing number.

Pretend Play

1. *Bank*. Older children may enjoy setting up and operating their own bank. Provide pretend money, cash drawers, deposit slips, and "bank books." Add rubber stamps, telephones, a vault (large box with a "door" that opens and closes), purses, and dress-up clothes. First, mention that banks keep our money safe and return it to us when we want it. Discuss with the children the various jobs that people in a bank perform. Tellers take the deposits and pay out the money at the customer's request; loan officers discuss borrowing money with people; someone operates the safe-deposit vault where people can store special, valuable items; executives run things; and security officers help to keep the bank and the customers safe. Encourage "bank personnel" and "customers" to count the money as it goes in and out of the bank.

2. *Post Office.*

   General Purpose: For children to take on a role and act out their interpretation of that role.

   TFPs: 24, 25.

   Materials: Hats, bags, "mail," paper, envelopes, stamps, rubber stamps, cash register, store front, mail slots with numerals on them to match the prepared "mail," a scale, mailbox. Write the numerals on the mail slots and on the mail to be delivered so that all of the children are more likely to be successful in matching identical numerals.

   Procedure:
   a. Set up the area to resemble a post office with a space for sorting mail, accepting packages and selling stamps, and writing letters.

   b. Invite children to take on the roles of letter carriers, postal clerks, and customers.
   c. Encourage the letter carriers and clerks to match mail to the numerals on the slots.
   d. Encourage older children to establish their own individual "addresses" and to place these on a mail delivery location, such as the child's cubby, so that children may communicate with their special friends.

Hints for Success:
- Keep numerals in the addresses simple and large enough to be easily seen and matched.
- Post a sample numeral sheet where children may see and copy the numerals when they are writing the addresses on their mail.

How to Simplify this Activity:
- Use fewer materials and single-digit "addresses."

How to Extend this Activity:
- Ask children to assist in preparing the materials. Invite them to paint a large box to serve as a mailbox or to wrap small boxes and containers in brown paper to serve as packages. Cut large paper sacks into letter carrier sacks.

3. *Spaghetti and Pizza Parlor.*
   General Purpose: To provide opportunities for children to interact with other children in make-believe situations.

   TFPs: 2, 3, 4, 5, 6, 7, 10, 17.

   Materials: Dishes, pots and pans, tablecloth, aprons, chef's hats, order pads, cash register, menus, spaghetti (white or ivory yarn cut into 8- or 10-inch pieces), meatballs, (brown yarn pom poms), pizza bases (heavy cardboard circles covered with felt), pizza "fixings" (felt bits of orange "cheese," tan "mushrooms," green "pepper," magenta circles for "pepperoni," add olives, sausage, onions if desired), salad (paper bowls with tissue paper or construction paper salad ingredients).

Figure 22.7 *Numerals Used on a Bingo Game*

Procedure:

a. Set up the area to resemble a restaurant with table(s) for customers, a counter for taking orders and collecting money, and a kitchen area with working space to create pizzas.

b. Invite children to take on the roles of customers, serving persons, cooks, or cashiers.

c. Encourage children to order pizza with specific amounts of ingredients. Chef then fills the order by counting out each ingredient.

d. During end-of-day clean-up, encourage children to count dishes, meatballs, menus, and other items as they put them away.

Hint for Success:

• Provide small containers for each pizza ingredient and encourage the children to keep them sorted into the appropriate containers during play to maintain order in the kitchen.

How to Simplify this Activity:

• Limit the choice of ingredients to only a few.

How to Extend this Activity:

• Plan a salad-making activity at the art table to provide salads for the restaurant. Use small paper plates, glue, green tissue and green construction paper, and construction paper vegetables (orange carrots, red tomatoes, etc.). Cover with plastic wrap to preserve.

Social

1. **Bingo.** Obtain or make a set of bingo game cards. Distribute the cards to the children and explain that you will be playing a game called bingo. The object of the game is to cover all of the numerals on each card with a marker or disk. Players should cover each numeral as the caller draws a card and reads that numeral out loud. The teacher should probably be the caller for the first several times that the game is played. Once the children understand how to play and are fairly proficient at recognizing the numerals, they could have turns being the callers.

If you make your own bingo cards, vary the number of boxes to cover and make some very simple cards with all numerals under 10 for the first games or for younger players. Consider making cards that all contain one identical numeral so the teacher can call that numeral last and assure that all children will win simultaneously. (Figure 22.7)

2. *Can I Play?* Post number symbols in activity areas to indicate the maximum number of children who may participate. After an initial explanation, encourage children to count to see if there is room for another player. Keep some extra symbol cards available so that they may be changed as appropriate. (Figure 22.8)

3. *Numbers-in-a-Row.*

   General Purpose: For children to practice being cooperative.

   TFPs: 9, 10, 20, 21, 22, 23, 24.

   Materials: A long (100 inches) strip of paper (shelf paper may be used) divided into eleven equal sections and numbered with numerals from 0 to 10; an assortment of items to depict the numbers associated with each numeral (stickers, rubber stamps, self-sticking dots, small pictures, etc.).

   Procedure:

   a. Explain that the children will be working together to create a number chart to help them with counting.

   b. Assign each child or small group of children a different numeral to illustrate.

   c. Explain that each group will be responsible for counting out and placing the correct number of items on its section.

   d. Explain that each section should eventually contain the number of objects its numeral represents.

   e. Encourage the children to count out the objects carefully so that the number chart is accurate. (Figure 22.9)

Hint for Success:

- Ask children to work on only one or two numerals at a given time so that the work can be observed and corrected if needed.

How to Simplify this Activity:

- Make a number line that stops at five.
- Give each group a separate piece of paper with a numeral on it. Assemble when each is complete.

How to Extend this Activity:

- Make a number line that goes up to twenty. Ask children to make smaller, individual versions for their personal use.

4. *Hide and Peek.* Play this game with small groups of four to six children. Provide each child with an identical set of five to twenty objects and a container (such as a shoe box) under which to "hide" items. Designate one child at a time as game leader. Direct all children to choose some of their objects and hide them under their boxes. After all the children are ready, the leader reveals his or her hidden set of objects and announces "I have a set of (number)." Other children each have a turn to uncover and announce, "My set of (number) is (more, less, or the same as) Margaret's set of (number)." Less experienced children may simply reveal their objects and announce the number to see if anyone matches the leader. As children become adept at this game, ask them to adjust their number of hidden objects to match the leader's. Encourage them to tell how they changed their number.

5. *Voting.*

   General Purpose: For children to explore that number is dependent on amount, rather than other natural cues.

   TFPs: 2, 3, 4, 5, 6, 24, 28.

   Procedure:

   a. Introduce the activity in the following way. "Today, we're going to decide (a

Figure 22.8 *A Sign Shows How Many Can Play in the Area*

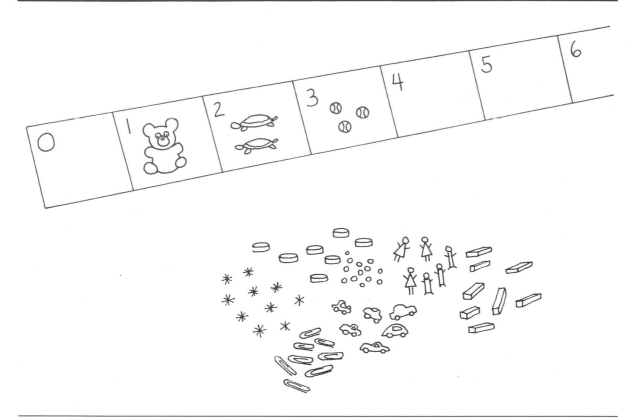

Figure 22.9 *Use Actual Objects on This Large Counting Board*

name for our pet, which color is our favorite, etc.). We are going to vote. That means each person will have a chance to pick his or her favorite (name, color). Then we will count all the people who chose each one and find out which was the most popular. Popular means the one most people liked. We will find out the most popular choice by counting the number of people in each group. The group that has the most people will also have the highest number."

b. Begin the process of choosing the alternatives. Limit the number of possibilities to three to five, enough that children can have a real option, but not so many that the clusters of children for each group are too small. Explain the limit to the children. Solicit suggestions and write down the first three to five ideas on a chalkboard or large piece of paper. Read each suggestion as you write it down. When the list is complete, read each entry, running your hand under the word as you say it.

c. Write each option on a piece of oak tag. Designate a part of the group area and, if possible, a particular adult to represent each option. Place each name card (and adult) at the appropriate station.

d. Then tell the children they are going to vote. Ask each child in turn to select a favorite from the list. You should reread the list before each child picks if it seems necessary. As soon as a child has chosen, send him or her to the spot that represents the selection. Repeat for every child in the group. Children may choose to abstain from voting. They should be directed to remain in their places. Give them another chance when everyone else has finished.

e. Once the group has divided into areas, instruct children to look at the small groups and estimate which has the most people (which choice is the most popular). Paraphrase their ideas ("Tony thinks that Rainbow is the most popular name for our pet. Tell me what you think, Jenna.")

f. Tell children that there are several ways to find out which is most popular. Line up two groups and ask the children which line is longer.

g. Paraphrase children's responses. Compare another group line with the longer line. Continue comparing until the longest line is determined. Then ask children which line has the most people.

h. With the children assisting, count the members of each group and record the number on the board or chart. Ask children which number is largest.

i. Explain again that the group having the largest number of members represents the most popular choice. Ask children to tell which entry "won the voting." Announce the result and mark it on the chart or board.

Hints for Success:

• A child may insist that the name he or she has chosen is most popular (even if this is not the case). Differentiate what the child "wants" to be true from what he or she "thinks" is true. Carefully review the evidence (counting again if necessary) until the child can accept the answer. Be patient. This is evidence of egocentric thinking, not stubbornness.

• Children may wish to change their minds as they see friends choosing other options. Explain that this time they must stay with their choices. On another occasion they will have a chance to pick another favorite.

How to Simplify this Activity:

• Younger children may tire of the process before the final decision. If you detect signs of restlessness, move to the final step quickly (you may have to skip a few steps) so the children experience closure to the activity.

• Limit the children's choices to two or three.

How to Extend this Activity:

• Experiment with the small groups once they have been formed. Change their shape. Have children cluster, stand in a circle, sit down, kneel, and so on. Ask if those changes make any difference in how many members are in the group. Change the same conditions relative to another group and ask the same question.

• At a later time, ask children to recap the decision-making procedure that occurred and discuss the results.

• Re-vote after a period and compare the results with the original outcome.

TEACHER RESOURCES

Field Trip Ideas

1. Visit locations where many numerals are used, such as a gasoline service station; grocery store or supermarket or any other store where prices are posted; post office; or a restaurant.

2. Take a walk around the neighborhood and look for numerals on houses, traffic signs, billboards, license plates, and so forth.

Classroom Visitors

1. Invite to your classroom a collector of almost anything in quantity who is willing to bring items to show and count.

2. Ask a community worker to visit your class. He or she could describe how number and numerals are used in his or her job. Select some professions in which the use of number and numerals is obvious (banker, teller, or grocery checkout person), as well as some for which the use of number and numerals is not so readily clear (hairdresser, pet store worker, etc.).

Children's Books

Anno, M. *Anno's Counting House.* New York: Philomel, 1982.

Asimov, I. *How Did We Find Out About Numbers?* New York: Walker, 1973.

Bang, M. *Ten, Nine, Eight.* New York: Greenwillow, 1983.

Bendick, J. *Names, Sets and Numbers.* New York: Franklin Watts, 1971.

Bruna, D. *I Can Count.* New York: Children's Books, Ltd., Methuen, Inc., 1968.

Carona, P. *A New True Book—Numbers*. Chicago: Childrens Press, 1982.

———. *The True Book of Numbers*. Chicago: Childrens Press, 1964.

Charles, D. *Count on Calico Cat*. Chicago: Childrens Press, 1974.

Froman, R. *Less Than Nothing Is Really Something*. New York: Crowell, 1975.

Gàg, W. *Millions of Cats*. New York: Putnam, 1977.

Hoban, R., and S. Selig. *Ten What? A Mystery Counting Book*. New York: Scribner's, 1974.

Hoban, T. *Count and See*. New York: Macmillan 1972.

Hutchins, P. *1 Hunter*. New York: Greenwillow, 1982.

———. *The Doorbell Rang*. New York: Greenwillow, 1986.

Kredenser, G., and S. Mack. *One Dancing Drum*. New York: Phillips, 1971.

Maestro, G. *One More and One Less*. New York: Crown, 1974.

Matthews, L. *Bunches and Bunches of Bunnies*. New York: Dodd, Mead, 1978.

Mayer, M. *Little Monster's Counting Book,* New York: Golden, 1978.

Nolan, D. *Monster Bubbles*. Englewood Cliffs, NJ: Prentice-Hall, 1976.

Pape, D. *Count and Leo Lion*. Champaign, IL: Garrard, 1973.

Scarey, R. *Learn to Count*. New York: Western Pub. Co., Golden, 1976.

Schwartz, D. M. *How Much Is A Million?* New York: Scholastic, 1987.

Sendak, M. *One Was Johnny: A Counting Book*. New York: Harper and Row, 1962.

Seuss, Dr. *One Fish, Two Fish, Red Fish, Blue Fish*. New York: Random House, Beginner Books, 1960.

Wildsmith, B. *Brian Wildsmith's 1, 2, 3's*. New York: Franklin Watts, 1965.

Zaslavsky, C. *Count on Your Fingers African Style*. New York: Thomas Y. Crowell, 1980.

Ziner, F., and P. Galdone. *Counting Carnival*. New York: Coward-McCann, 1962.

Adult References

Balogh, C. L. "Mathematical Concepts." In J. S. McKee (ed.), *The Developing Kindergarten: Programs, Children, and Teachers*. East Lansing, MI: Michigan Association for the Education of Young Children, 1989.

Baratta-Lorton, M. *Mathematics Their Way*. Menlo Park, CA: Addison-Wesley, 1977.

———. *Work Jobs I* and *Work Jobs II*. Menlo Park, CA: Addison-Wesley, 1973.

Daves, C. *Early Maths*. New York: Longman, 1977.

Kamii, C. *Number in Preschool and Kindergarten,* Washington, DC: National Association for the Education of Young Children, 1982.

Leeper, S. H., R. L. Witherspoon, B. Day. *Good Schools for Young Children*. New York: Macmillan, 1984.

Tarron, N. B., and S. W. Lundsteen. *Activities and Resources for Guiding Young Children's Learning*. New York: McGraw-Hill, 1981.

Warren, J. *Learning Games*. Palo Alto, CA: Monday Morning Broods, 1983.

Chapter 23

Measuring

•

Fill it half full.

You're forty inches tall.

This weighs ten pounds.

I'm looking for the widest one.

Which of these is the longest?

•

Children hear and make statements such as these each day. All have their basis in the mathematical concept of measurement.

From infancy, children explore the physical properties of objects. Through hundreds of naturally occurring, everyday experiences, they become aware that objects have size, weight, and volume and that these attributes vary in magnitude from item to item. Consequently, young children become intensely interested in finding out "How big am I?", "Which has more?", "How high is my tower?", "How far can I run?", or "How much will this hold?"

Initially, their answers come from concrete, self-discovered comparisons: "I'm bigger than the cat"; "My Dad's bigger than me"; "My tower is shorter than his"; "If I add a block, the two towers will be the same." Through this type of playful observation and experimentation, children form the notion that size, weight, and volume are relative concepts involving the relationships between objects. At about this same time, children also begin to refer to units of measure, most of which they create themselves. "My tower is as high as my shoulder," or, "This tower is as tall as two teddy bears." Gradually, youngsters become aware of other ways of measuring as they observe adults and older siblings use rulers, cup measures, and scales to determine, "How much?"

PURPOSE

The aim of this unit is to build on children's naturally developing concept of measurement and its relationship to the world in which they live. Our intent is not to hurry children into the use of standardized measuring units, but rather to provide them with numerous hands-on experiences involving measurement. Activities have been designed to give children opportunities to manipulate real-life objects in a variety of circumstances and to provide time for youngsters to reflect on their emerging ideas. Additionally, we have designed this theme to be taught in the context of the total curriculum, not limited to "math time" or the "math center" only.

IMPLEMENTATION

The theme Measuring has been successfully field-tested with toddlers as well as children in elementary school. The following developmental sequence is offered as a guide for deciding how to adapt it for use with a particular age group (Balogh, 1989).

Phase One: Provide numerous opportunities for children to make direct and indirect comparisons without measurement tools.

Phase Two: Offer children many experiences to measure using nonstandard units.

Phase Three: Give children frequent chances to participate in measurement activities using a variety of materials of different sizes and shapes. Encourage them to estimate before measuring.

Possible options for carrying out the measuring theme are as follows:

Option One: Teach a one-week unit that introduces the broad nature of measuring. Use TFPs 1–9 as well as a few simple ones from the weight, dimensions, and volume subsections of the unit.

Option Two: Develop a one-week unit concentrating on only one aspect of measuring, such as weight.

Option Three: Create a multiweek approach in which you address one subsection of the unit (general overview, weight, dimensions, and volume) each week.

Option Four: When working with older children, formally present the Measuring theme three times during the year. In the fall, focus on experiences related to phase one of the developmental sequence described above. Move to phase two in the winter and phase three in the spring.

TERMS, FACTS, AND PRINCIPLES

General Information

1. Measuring means finding out how much of something there is.
2. People measure objects and space.

3. Two of the things people measure are weight and size.

*4. There are units by which people measure objects and space.

*5. The measuring units people choose depend on what they are measuring.

*6. There are standard units of measure upon which people in the world have agreed.

*7. Groups of people sometimes develop their own units of measure.

8. People use tools to measure weight, dimensions of objects, and volume.

*9. There are many reasons why people measure things.

Measuring Weight

10. All objects have weight.

11. Weight is measured in ounces, pounds, and tons, or in grams.

12. People have invented scales to weigh things.

13. A scale is a mechanical device for weighing.

14. Terms used to describe weight are heavy and light.

15. Terms used to compare weights are heavy, heavier, heaviest; light, lighter, lightest; heavier than; lighter than; and the same weight as.

*16. A thing that is lighter than one object may be heavier than another or equal to it.

17. Different objects may have the same weight.

18. Similar objects may have different weights.

19. People cannot determine how much something weighs simply by looking at its size, shape, or how much of it there is, or by knowing how old it is.

20. People weigh things to find out how heavy they are, how much weight is enough, how much weight is too little, and how much weight is too much.

21. Weight can change. Things can be changed to weigh more, and things can be changed to weigh less.

*22. Changes in weight can cause an object to look different.

*23. Weight only changes when something is added or taken away, not when the form of the object is changed.

Measuring Dimensions

24. A dimension is the measurement of how far it is from point a to point b.

25. All objects have the dimensions of height, width, and length; containers have depth.

26. Dimensions are measured in inches, feet, yards, and miles, or in centimeters and meters.

27. People have invented tools to measure dimensions. Some of these include rulers, yardsticks, and tape measures.

28. Some terms used to describe dimensions are long and short, wide and narrow, fat and thin, tall and short, big and small, deep and shallow, and high and low.

29. Terms used to compare dimensions are long, longer, longest; short, shorter, shortest; wide, wider, widest; narrow, narrower, narrowest; fat, fatter, fattest; thin, thinner, thinnest; tall, taller, tallest; big, bigger, biggest; small, smaller, smallest; deep, deeper, deepest; shallow, shallower, shallowest; high, higher, highest; low, lower, lowest; longer than; shorter than; the same length as; wider than; narrower than; the same width as; fatter than; thinner than; the same width as; taller than; shorter than; the same height as; bigger than; smaller than; the same size as; deeper than; shallower than; and the same depth as.

*30. An object that is longer than one object may be shorter than another or equal to it.

*31. An object that is wider than one object may be narrower than another or equal to it.

*32. An object that is taller than one object may be shorter than another or equal to it.

*33. An object that is bigger than one object may be smaller than another or equal to it.

*34. An object that is deeper than one object may be shallower than another or equal to it.

35. Different objects may have the same dimensions.

36. Similar objects may have different dimensions.

37. People measure the dimensions of objects to find out how much space they take up; how long, wide, fat, tall, big, deep, or high is too much; how short, narrow, thin, small, or low is too little; and how much is enough.

*38. Changes in dimension can cause an object to look different.

*39. Dimensions change when something is added or taken away, or when the form is changed.

Measuring Volume

40. Some materials, such as liquid, flour, salt, sand, and dirt, do not have a rigid shape.

41. Materials that do not have a rigid shape are measured by putting them in a container.

42. Volume is the measurement of how much of a given material fits into a container.

43. The amount of a substance that a container holds is called the capacity of the container.

44. Volume is measured in ounces, cups, pints, quarts, gallons, or liters.

45. People have invented containers to measure volume, including measuring spoons, measuring cups, and gallon containers.

46. Terms used to describe volume are more, less, and the same as.

47. Terms used to describe how much of a container is filled with a substance are full, empty, almost full, almost empty; *half full, half empty; and **a quarter full, a third full, a quarter empty, a third empty.

48. Terms used to compare volume are *more, most, the same as, less, least; and **half as much as, twice as much as.

*49. Containers that look different may have the same volume.

*50. Substances of the same volume may have different weights.

51. People measure the volume of a substance to find out how much of something they have, how much of something is needed, how much of something is enough, how much of something is too much, and how much of something is too little.

*52. The capacity of containers remains stable, regardless of what is put in them.

*53. The volume of a substance can change when more of the substance is added or some is taken away.

*54. The volume an object or substance occupies is independent of the shape of the container.

*55. The capacity of containers remains stable, regardless of what is put in them.

*56. The volume of a substance can change when more of the substance is added or some is taken away.

ACTIVITY IDEAS

Aesthetics

1. *Dancing in Full Measure.* Invite the children to help you measure spaces on the floor in various sizes. Mark out, for example, a one-foot square, a circle one-yard wide, or an equilateral triangle with sides one meter long. Outline the dimensions of each space with cloth tape, making them different colors. Put on a record that has short melodies differing in tempo and mood. Ask children to choose spaces in which to dance. As the melodies change, have the children try out different-sized spaces.

2. *Inch Square Mosaics.* Give children whole sheets of construction paper, paste, and a large supply of one-inch squares of colored paper. Ask them to make a design, pasting the squares on the larger paper.

Affective

1. *Body Tracings.* Make a life-sized body tracing of each child. Then help children measure and record various body measurements on the tracing itself.

2. *Measuring What I Can Do.* Create a chart or booklet for each child on which are recorded the measurements of their activities, such as "How far I can stretch," "How far I can reach," "How much I can lift," "How heavy I can be," "How low I can bend," and "How wide I can stand."

3. *Smaller than an Elephant.* Invite children to describe things they are taller than, heavier than, wider than, narrower than,

and so forth. Record their words on paper or audiotape, then read or play their stories back to them.

Cognition

1. ***Tutti Fruity.*** Weigh whole pieces of fruit. Invite the children to predict whether the fruit weighs more, less, or the same when it is whole than it does after it is cut up. Then cut up each piece and weigh the fruit again. Ask children to evaluate their predictions.

2. ***Creative Measuring.*** Measure the same dimension, such as the width of the room or the height of a chair, using different nonstandard units of measure (inch cubes, hand lengths, shoe lengths, etc.). Make a chart showing how the different measurements compare.

3. ***Comparing Capacity.*** Implement this activity in a sand table filled with wet sand. Give children pairs of measuring cups that have the same capacity but are different shapes. Ask them to fill one of their cups with the wet sand, then predict whether their empty cups will hold more, less, or the same amount as the ones they have filled. Direct children to test out their predictions by dumping the contents of their filled cups into the empty ones. Repeat this process with additional cups of the same size or with a new array of cups a different size.

4. ***Class Graph.*** Involve the children in making two graphs, one depicting the heights of all the children in the class, another their weights. Consider graphing some of the other attributes addressed in the children's body tracings, or the "measuring what I can do" charts, which are described in the Affective section of this unit.

5. ***Weight Change.*** Encourage children to experiment with various ways to make an object weigh more or less, using objects such as a sponge, an empty pail, an empty bicycle tube, an air-filled playground ball, or a child. Provide appropriate scales children can use to test out their ideas.

6. ***Weighing Modeling Dough.*** This activity is best conducted after children have had previous experience using a scale. It requires a large batch of modeling dough. Introduce the activity to the children by showing them the ball of dough and helping them weigh it. Record the weight in a place where all the children can see it. Invite the children, one at a time, to change the shape of the dough. Youngsters may make any changes they want, but they must use all the dough. Weigh the dough each time its shape changes and record the results. Talk with children about their observations throughout this process.

Modeling Dough Recipes

Uncooked Modeling Dough
Ingredients:
4 cups flour
2 cups salt
Food coloring
Water

Procedure:
Add enough water slowly to the flour and salt to make a soft, workable dough. Stop when the dough is still a little dry. Add food coloring. Work by hand for 10 minutes.

Stove-top Modeling Dough
Ingredients:
1 cup flour
½ cup salt
2 T. cooking oil
2 tsps. cream of tartar
1 cup water
Food coloring

Procedure:
Stir mixture over low heat until it begins to pull away from the sides of the pan. Remove from pan and knead until smooth. Keep refrigerated in an airtight container.

Microwave Modeling Dough
Ingredients:
2 cups flour
2 cups water
1 cup salt
2 tsps. cream of tartar
2 T. cooking oil
Food coloring

Procedure:

Mix in a large microwave-proof bowl. Microwave on high for 5 minutes. Stop every minute to stir until thick. Cool and knead with hands until smooth. Store in a cool, dry place.

7. *As Tall As Me.* Provide building blocks and encourage children to make things that are as tall as they are. Take time to note and compare heights before they take them down. Preserve a record of each child's construction by taking a photograph of it and later displaying it in the block area.

8. *Mixed-up Muffins.*

General Purpose: For children to explore principles of cause and effect.

TFPs: 1–6, 8, 51–54.

Materials: One large, see-through mixing bowl; forks for mixing; one set of measuring cups; gempans (miniature muffin tins) to make 48 tiny muffins or regular muffin tins to make 24 medium muffins; 5-pound bag of flour (regular, not self-rising); 3 cups sugar; 1 cup salt; 1-pound can vegetable shortening; at least 2 eggs; 1 pint milk; masking tape; sponge and water for clean-up; a large piece of easel paper on which the following recipe is written in pictograph form; individual paper strips on which are drawn one each of the measurement pictographs, large enough to cover each of the measurement pictographs on the easel paper. (Figure 23.1)

Muffins

Ingredients:

2 cups flour

¼ cup sugar

3 tsps. baking powder

½ tsp. salt

¼ cup shortening

1 egg

1 cup milk

Procedure:

1. Stir together dry ingredients.

2. Add shortening, egg, milk.

3. Mix ingredients with fork just until blended.

4. Grease muffin tins. Fill ⅔ full. Bake 20 minutes at 400° until golden. Makes 12 medium muffins or 24 mini-muffins.

Procedure:

a. Gather all props and ingredients in advance. Keep the paper strips out of sight until it is time to use them (step i of this procedure).

b. Ask children to wash their hands before beginning the activity.

c. Introduce the activity by explaining, "Today, we will make muffins. We will use a recipe to tell us how much of each ingredient to put into them."

d. Put the recipe where children easily can see it. Read each step of the recipe aloud. Draw your finger under the corresponding words and hold up the appropriate measuring tool after you announce each item. Talk about the importance of using the right amount of each item.

e. Make a single recipe with the children. Follow one direction at a time through the step of putting the batter in the tins. Allow children to do the measuring and stirring themselves. Depending on their abilities, either you describe how much of each item is going into the bowl or ask children to do this. Focus most of your comments on the actual measuring that is taking place and how the mixture looks.

f. Put the filled tins aside.

g. Explain to the children, "Now we will make some mixed-up muffins."

h. Review the recipe. Emphasize the amounts of each ingredient used in the first batch of muffins.

i. Pull out the paper strips you have held in reserve. Show them to the children and demonstrate how each strip corresponds to one measurement in the recipe.

j. Announce, "We're going to mix up these measurements. Then we'll see what happens when we make muffins with the amounts the mixed-up measurements tell us to use."

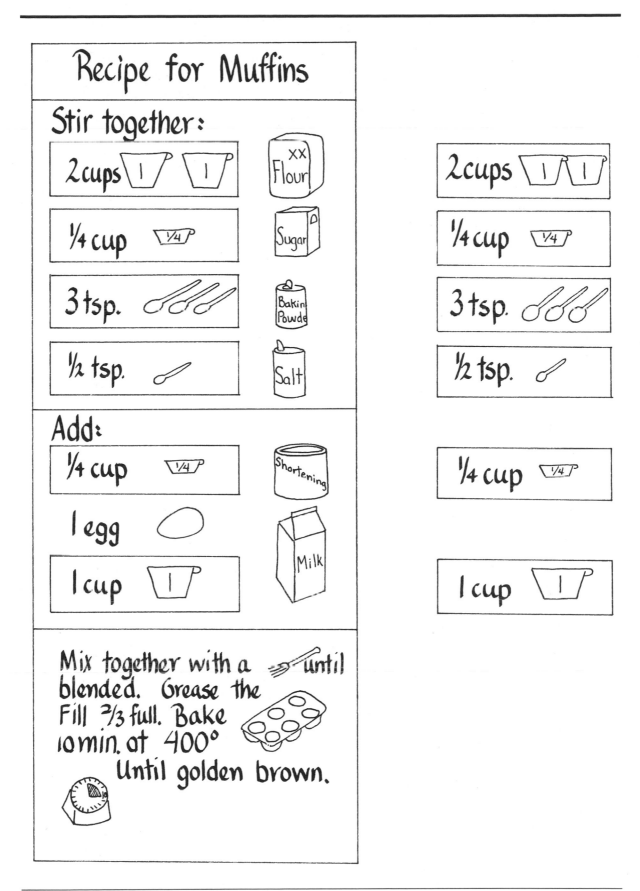

Figure 23.1 *Recipe Sheet for "Mixed-Up Muffins"*

k. Begin with the "cup" measurement pictograph strips. Put all four of the 'cup' strips face down and invite a child to select one as the first measurement in the recipe. Tape the child's selection over the original measurement for the flour. Continue this process for the sugar, shortening, and milk. Repeat the same procedure for both teaspoon measurements. The need for a single egg remains the same.

l. Carry out the mixed-up recipe with the children through the step of putting the muffins in the tins. Talk with children about the measuring that is going on and how the mixture compares to the first mixture.

m. Mark the two sets of muffin tins so you can tell them apart.

n. Bake the muffins at 400° for 20 minutes.

o. While the muffins are baking, ask children to predict how the two sets of muffins will turn out.

p. Give each child a sample of the two types of muffins.

q. Talk with them about how the muffins are alike and how they are different. Ask children to describe how they think measuring related to the results.

Hints for Success:

• Make pictographs on the recipe card and the individual paper strips by tracing the outlines of the actual measuring cups and spoons you will use with the children.

• This activity is most successful if introduced after children have had other cooking experiences using measuring cups, measuring spoons, and a recipe.

• To save time, follow steps a through e of the procedure with a larger group of children, then divide the group in half. Have one group make the correct recipe while the second group makes the mixed-up recipe. Bring the youngsters back together to compare the results.

How to Simplify this Activity:

• Skip steps g through m and steps o and g.

How to Extend this Activity:

• Repeat this activity using other recipes, such as the ones for modeling dough described earlier in this unit.

• Invite the children to record the measurements as you carry them out.

9. *What Fits in the Box?*
   General Purpose: For children to practice problem-solving skills.

   TFPs: 1, 2, 3, 4, 7, 45, 46, 47, 48, 51, 53, 55.

   Materials: At least three empty boxes with separate lids: one smaller than a shoebox, one shoebox size, one larger than a shoebox; a small array of objects, some that will fit into each box and some that won't.

   Procedure:

   a. Place the smallest box in the center of the table or on the floor where you will be working. Keep the other two boxes in reserve, out of sight.

   b. Begin by directing the children to sit in a circle around the box. Then say, "Look carefully at this box. It's empty." Show children the box from all angles. Pass the box around for them to see and touch. Say, "We could put lots of different things in it. Stay seated while you look around this room for something you think would fit inside this box. It has to fit all the way inside so I can close the top of the box." Demonstrate that some objects fit in the box so the lid is snug and other objects do not.

   c. Give children a moment to survey their surroundings.

   d. Invite children to predict what objects will fit inside the box by saying, "Someone tell me what they chose. Beth Anne tell me an object you think will fit."

   e. Invite the child to test out his or her prediction with these words, "You chose the _____. Go get it and let's see if it fits."

   f. Have the child put the object in the box and put the lid on the box. Then say, "Tell me if your prediction was correct."

   g. Paraphrase the child's response. "Your prediction was correct. The _____ fit inside the box and the lid closes," or

"You discovered that the _____ did not fit into the box. Tell me why. Find something else that might fit."

h. Repeat steps b through g with different children and objects.
i. Repeat steps b through g with boxes of different sizes.

Hints for Success:
- Set up the activity in a place where children will have access to a wide variety of objects.
- Direct each child to return the item to its original spot when his or her turn is over.

How to Simplify this Activity:
- Rather than having children choose objects from around the room, collect an array of objects from which they can choose.
- Prior to having children predict which objects will fit into the box, give them an opportunity to experiment with placing the various objects into the box and putting the lid on.

How to Extend this Activity:
- Ask one child at a time to choose three items, all of which will fit into the box simultaneously.
- Ask children to identify items that will *not* fit into the box.
- Ask each child, one at a time to select an object to place into the box. Explain that the goal is for all the objects to fit inside at the same time. Encourage them to keep looking into the box to gauge how much room is left.

10. *Shadow Hunt.*
    General Purpose: To help children explore nature through direct experience.
    TFPs: 2, 3, 24–27, 31, 38, 41, 51.
    Materials: measuring tapes, paper, rulers, writing tools, yardsticks.
    Procedure:
    a. Conduct this activity outside on a sunny day during the mid-morning or mid-afternoon hours.
    b. Gather the children in a group, explaining that today they will hunt for shadows outside. Point out some shadows in

the immediate vicinity so they will know what to look for.
c. Ask children, individually or in small groups, to find shadows to measure within a designated area such as the confines of the playground.
d. As each child or group finds a shadow, talk about its interesting shape and how the shadow looks in comparison to the real object.
e. Ask children to determine which part of the shadows they would like to measure. Help them to do so, allowing children to do as much for themselves as they can. Write these measurements down. Then talk with the group about the measurements they made.

Hints for Success:
- Select an area for children to explore where some trees, bushes, or flowers stand alone and their shadows are distinct.
- If you are in an area of heavy shade, invite children to measure splashes of sunlight instead.
- In a variation of this activity, select two shadows, then outline them on paper. Measure the outlines and compare them by cutting out both silhouettes and superimposing one over the other.

How to Simplify this Activity:
- Follow steps a through d. Rather than having children measure the shadows, invite each to stand next to the shadow or within it to see if his or her own shadow is wider, thinner, or longer.
- Conduct step e as a demonstration. Once children have selected a shadow, measure it yourself, calling out the numbers. Get children to help with the measurement process as much as possible by having them hold the end of the measuring tape or mark off lengths of the ruler.

How to Extend this Activity:
- Measure parts of a shadow using different measurement tools to see if the dimensions remain the same.
- Put a stick in the ground at the top of a shadow. An hour later return and see

how the shadow has shifted. Measure it again and compare these measurements with those taken earlier.

- Measure some dimension of a real object and compare it with the same dimension of its shadow.

- Invite the children to move from shadow to shadow, guessing which one is shortest, longest, widest, and so forth. Refer to the recorded measurements to assist them in deciding which guesses were most accurate.

11. *Measure Hunt.*

General Purpose: For children to develop problem-solving skills.

Materials: A treasure for children to find (envelope containing a sticker for each child); one-foot ruler for each child; masking, colored, or plastic tape; indelible marker; direction sheet; 8-foot measuring tape for teacher-supervised use.

Preparation:

1. Read all of the following preparation steps before trying this activity.

2. Make tape clues. Cut several strips of tape three inches long, cut one strip five inches long. Draw arrows on all but one tape strip to indicate in which direction children are to measure the next clue.

3. Put the tape strips in different places on the floor and walls of the room where children will hunt. Reserve the blank strip as the final clue.

4. Hide the treasure when children are not present by taping the envelope securely to the underside of a table or chair above the final clue.

5. Measure the space between the tape strips and prepare a direction sheet of measurements to correspond to them. (You needn't use all strips.) Sample instructions might read: "Find the piece of tape that is five inches long. When you find it, call out but leave it in place. For step two, measure three feet in the direction of the arrow. In step three, measure five teacher feet in the direction of the arrow." The directions for the final clue should tell children to measure in all directions to find the treasure.

Procedure:

a. Invite children to join you on a Measure Hunt. Explain that they will be using rulers to help find the hidden treasure.

b. Distribute one ruler to each child. Look at and discuss the tools.

c. Give children the first clue. "There are many pieces of tape around here. Find one that is exactly five inches long. When you find it, leave it in place and call us."

d. When the first tape is found, gather the group and give each child an opportunity to verify by measuring with his or her ruler.

e. Continue the "hunt" with the adult reading each measurement from the direction sheet and the children figuring out how to measure. (Each clue arrow indicates direction of next measurement.)

f. Continue to final clue with *no* arrow. Tell children to measure in *all* directions until they locate treasure. (They must measure *up* to find treasure.)

Hint for Success:

- The following sequence of clues is suggested to encourage problem solving and cooperation:
  four-inch piece of tape
  four feet (Encourage children to use rulers end to end if they don't think of it.)
  eight teacher feet (Walk off heel to toe. Let children figure out what it means!)

How to Simplify this Activity:

- Use unit blocks as measuring tools and state directions as follows:
  measure a three-block length
  measure a one-block length, and so on.

How to Extend this Activity:

- Introduce large measurements that require children to add inches using several one-foot rulers.

- Introduce other measuring tools such as yardsticks or a measuring tape.

Construction

1. *Making Crowns.* Provide children with tape measures, heavy construction paper, masking tape, and decorative art materials such as markers, stickers, and glitter. Use

the measuring tape to measure each child's head. Then, help children measure the correct lengths of paper for their crowns. (Older children may be capable of helping one another do both these steps.) Encourage children to decorate their crowns once they have finished measuring.

2. *Same Size.* Place a ball of modeling dough under a piece of fabric so children will not be able to see it. Ask children to feel the modeling dough through the cloth. Give each child some modeling dough and tell them to make balls the same size. Then lift the cloth to compare the balls. Repeat, varying the size and shape of the modeling dough.

3. *Made to Order.* Make available to children unit blocks from the block shelf, measuring tools as available, a wipe-off board, and markers. Direct them to find specific sizes of blocks to use in their buildings. "I would like a building that uses two long blocks; please build it for me." Write the "order" on the board to use while working and to check the final product. Encourage children to compare lengths of various blocks and help them to discover the relationships among the different sizes. Suggest that they measure the blocks with the available tools before and after building. Use open-ended statements to elicit information about the structures that children create.

4. *The Long and Short of It.*

General Purpose: For children to construct sample lengths using a variety of materials.

TFPs: 24, 27, 29, 30, 41, 44.

Materials: Measuring tape; yardstick; ruler; unit blocks or table top blocks; large sheets of newsprint; markers, crayons, or chalk; modeling dough; pieces of string cut in 6-foot lengths; large pop beads; an 8-by-11-inch piece of paper or a 4-by-5½-inch paper booklet for each child marked with the child's name and the words "long" and "short" in two columns or on separate pages.

Procedure:

a. Introduce the activity with a discussion of "long" and "short." Demonstrate these terms with real objects by comparing a short sock with a long one, a short carrot with a long carrot, a short rod with one that is longer. Measure each object. Explain that by measuring you learn how short is short and how long is long.

b. Tell the children they will have a chance to create their own examples of long and short. Also, they will measure what they create and record these measurements on paper or in booklets.

c. Select a material and give each child his or her own supply with which to work. Ask the children to create something long and something short.

d. Allow children to combine their materials to make something "even longer" if they choose.

e. Help the children measure long and short. Write down the results or help the children record the results themselves.

f. Repeat steps c, d, and e with different materials.

Hints for Success

- Introduce one material at a time; keep the others out of sight until they are needed.

- An alternate method of introducing this activity is to present it to the class as a whole at the beginning of the day. Then make the different materials available in various locations throughout the room for children to use during the session.

How to Simplify this Activity:

- Give children fairly rigid materials such as pop beads or unit blocks with which to work.

- Show children an example of a "long" construction and a "short" one. Ask children to copy your example using a like material.

How to Extend this Activity:

- Give children flexible items such as string or clay with which to work.

- Take the activity outside where there may be larger spaces within which the children can work.

- Focus on other dimensions such as height, depth, or width.

- Repeat the activity using weight or volume as the measurement focus.

Language

1. ***Dig Down.*** Conduct this activity outside in a sandbox. Invite children to dig holes in the sand using hands or shovels. As they dig, periodically make nonjudgmental comments describing and comparing the width and depth of their holes. "Lisa, you made a long, narrow channel." "John, your hole is deeper than mine." "Karen, your hole is as wide as Matt's." Eventually, ask individual children to describe the holes they are making in general and in comparison to yours or another child's. Offer rulers and tape measures if children would like to use them to confirm their observations.

2. ***Cup Talk.*** Gather four to six children in a circle. Have ready an array of clear plastic tumblers, containing varying amounts of modeling dough. (Make sure the tumblers are sealed with foil or plastic wrap.) Put the cups where the children can see them. Ask them to describe the contents using the words full, almost full, empty, almost empty, more, most, the same as, less than, or least as appropriate. Extend the activity by putting all the cups in a bag, inviting the children to select one cup each, then asking them to describe the volume of modeling dough they each have, both in general terms and in comparison to one another. Repeat this step until children lose interest. Conclude the activity by inviting the children to play with the dough.

3. ***Creating a City.*** On three-by-twelve-inch oak tag strips, print directions (one sentence per strip) similar to the following: "Build *a wide* road" or "Build a *narrow* bridge." Make available to children some type of construction materials. Explain that the city planners have left directions for how the city is to be built. Read or help each child read one direction he or she is to follow. Give children plenty of time to build. Then ask them to point out short, wide, and narrow structures. Add complexity by having children identify struc- tures that can be described in multiple terms such as, "This road is long and wide."

4. ***"Measuring" Chant.***

   Sometimes I Am Tall
   Sometimes I am tall.
   (Stretch on tiptoe, arms held up, bent at elbow.)
   Sometimes I am small.
   (Crouch down low.)
   Sometimes I am very, very tall.
   (Stretch on tiptoe, arms completely extended.)
   Sometimes I am very, very small.
   (Crouch down very low.)
   Sometimes tall, sometimes small.
   (Stretch then crouch.)
   See how I am now.
   (Stand upright or children may choose to stretch or crouch.)

5. ***Measuring Millions.*** Read children the story *How Much Is a Million?* by David Schwartz. Prior to a second reading, tell children to listen for words and phrases that refer to measuring (taller, as high as, etc.). Afterward, print on a large piece of paper in letters big enough for children to see at a distance all the "measuring" words they remember from the story. Show children how to refer back to the book to determine the accuracy of their recollections. Read the book one more time, either later or on another day, asking children to clap once each time they hear a word that refers to measurement.

6. ***Table Top Town.***
   General Purpose: For children to practice using adjectives to describe height, length, and width.

   TFPs: 25–27, 31, 38, 41, 44, 45, 46.

   Materials: Fifteen sandwich-sized, plastic bags with locking strip, 150 colored inch cubes, paper and markers to record children's descriptions, ruler. Optional: trays or placemats.

   Procedure:
   a. Prepare three sets of materials in advance.

Set One: Five plastic bags—five cubes per bag

Set Two: Five plastic bags—ten cubes per bag

Set Three: Five plastic bags—fifteen cubes per bag

Vary the color combinations of the cubes from bag to bag in each set.

b. Invite three to four children to make table top buildings with you. Give each child a bag from Set One and offer trays or placemats to create individual work spaces if you wish.

c. Tell the children to use their own sets of blocks to make a building. Encourage them to stack one on top of the other or line them edge to edge in any arrangement they like.

d. As children explore the materials, periodically make nonjudgmental comments comparing height, length, and width of the buildings. "Your building is taller than mine. My building is shorter than yours. Your building is wider than Tom's. Tom's building is the same width as John's."

e. Help children count the cubes in their buildings to determine differences and similarities in height, length, and width. Have them measure the buildings with a ruler.

f. Vary the activity by asking each child to point to a building that is taller, shorter, longer, narrower, or as wide as what he or she built.

g. Ask children to describe their own buildings in comparison to other children's. Write down what the children say and read it back to them. Emphasize the measurement terms each child uses. Also, point out the many different words that can be used to describe the same building.

h. Praise children's use of descriptive vocabulary.

Hints for Success:

- Concentrate on Set One of the materials with two- and three-year-olds. With older children, move beyond Set One as soon as they demonstrate a basic understanding of the terms under discussion.

- Introduce small figures or tiny cars to keep children interested in the activity. Use masking tape for roads. Tell children the game is to build a town.

- Repeat this activity providing unit blocks with which children can build on the floor.

How to Simplify this Activity:

- Focus only on steps a through d.

- Add steps e through g, one at a time, on subsequent days.

How to Extend this Activity:

- Ask children to rearrange their cubes or to add or take away cubes to make their buildings longer, wider, higher, or as tall as a model in the center of the table.

- Give children signs to add to their buildings that describe the dimensions in comparison to other children's structures. A child's building might have a sign that reads "taller than John's," "wider than Amy's," or "as short as Sam's."

7. *Large Words.*

General Purpose: For children to attach meaning to print.

Materials: *Large* pieces of paper (a roll of shelf paper or extra large easel paper), marker, tape.

Procedure:

a. Tell children that you are talking about measuring this week and that people use lots of interesting words to describe the size of things they measure.

b. Use the marker to write "LARGE" in large letters on one of the large pieces of paper. Explain to children that you are writing the word "large" with large letters to show that it means large.

c. Invite children to think of other words that also mean large.

d. Write out the words children suggest. Make the look of the printed words match their meanings. (Figure 23.2)

Hint for Success:

- Make sure children can see as you say each letter.

Figure 23.2 *These Words Show What They Mean*

How to Simplify this Activity:

• Use this activity to increase vocabulary with words supplied by the teacher. You may wish to include big, huge, enormous, gigantic, colossal, immense, massive, spacious, bulky, vast.

How to Extend this Activity:

• Help spell or sound out the words.

Physical

1. ***Jump the Creek.*** Place two ropes, sticks, or marks parallel to one another a foot apart on the floor. First, have the children measure the distance between the sticks. Then, encourage them to jump, hop, or leap over the "creek." After each child experiences success, move the lines farther apart to make the task more challenging. Emphasize each child's increased skill in comparison to his or her own past performance rather than comparing the distances jumped between one child and another.

2. ***Throwing for Distance.*** Provide children with objects small enough for them to grip easily with one hand, such as tennis balls, beanbags, or yarn balls. To promote appropriate skill development, show children how to throw overhand rather than underhand and encourage them to throw hard instead of focusing on accuracy.

Make a tape line on the floor. Invite children to take turns stepping up to the tape and throwing. With additional tape, mark where each ball or beanbag lands. Ask children to measure how far they've thrown. Repeat this procedure, inviting them to compare one trial versus another. Vary this activity by draping an old bed sheet over any tall object, such as a piano, for children to throw over, or by asking children to sit on benches and throw from there.

3. ***Stretch Long—Stretch Short.*** Provide children with rubber bands of various lengths and colors, as well as commercially available or homemade geoboards. Also offer rulers and measuring tapes for children to use.

Keeping the geoboards out of sight, direct the children to measure the length of a rubber band as it lies on the table. Then ask one child to stretch the rubber band, while another child measures its expanded length. Compare the lengths. After a few repetitions, introduce the geoboards. Show children how to stretch a rubber band over the nails on the board. Invite them to measure the length. Compare lengths as children add more rubber bands.

As children work, use words such as long, short, longer, or shorter to describe the relative length of one rubber band to

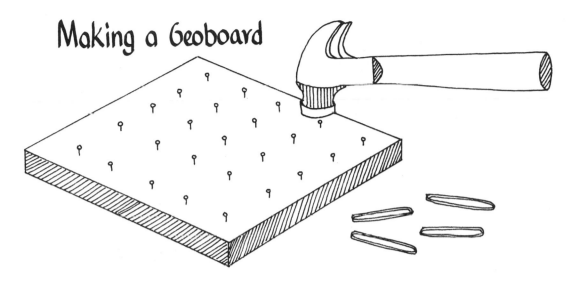

Figure 23.3 *How to Make a Geoboard*

another, or ask them to use these words themselves in describing their projects.

How to Make a Geoboard

Materials:

25–50 1½-inch round-head nails per board.

10-by-10-inch square piece of soft wood, 1 inch thick.

Directions:

1. Drive the nails ½ to ¾ inch into the wood.

2. Space them apart in a uniform pattern of columns and rows. (Figure 23.3)

Pretend Play

1. *Shoe Store.* Provide children with rulers or a brannock device to measure foot size as well as an assortment of shoes. Encourage them to help others find shoes that approximate their actual shoe sizes. Children may take on the roles of both customers and salespeople. Carry out a similar plan in a pretend clothing shop where the children first measure then match customers to certain items of apparel.

2. *City Planner.* Encourage the children to plan, construct, and play with a city made of blocks. Prompt discussions about and measurements of building sizes, widths of streets, and distances of homes from stores, parks, or schools.

3. *Grocery Store.* Give children the opportunity to measure amounts of foods such as fruits and vegetables or others commonly sold in bulk. Practice more measuring by seeing how much will fit into a grocery bag and how much each bag weighs. This play also could be carried out in a pretend hardware store.

4. *Merry Measurement Parcel Service.*

   General Purpose: For children to create play themes that involve measuring.

   TFPs: 1–13, 12–29, 46–52.

   Materials: Yardstick, rulers; measuring tape; masking tape; scales; writing paper; pens, cashbox or cash register and counters; coins or substitutes, a variety of wrapped boxes filled with materials of varying weights small enough to weigh with the available scales, tables. Optional: wagon or riding toy to be used to make deliveries (a cardboard carton with attached rope handle could be used if wheeled toys are unavailable).

   Procedure:

   a. Set up the area prior to children's participation. Make a measuring table by taping a yardstick to a table top and arranging the scales, rulers, and measuring tape on or near it. Create an "order table" with cash register, counters, paper, and pens. Pile all the boxes nearby.

b. Invite children to operate a delivery service. Suggest some jobs that could be filled: "This business needs some clerks. They are the people who help customers weigh and measure their packages. We will also need a cashier, the person who lets the customer know how much money—how many coins—to pay."

c. Take on the role of a customer yourself to get things started and demonstrate the tasks involved. Say something like, "I would like to have this package delivered. Who can help me measure it? You will have to decide how long it is, how wide it is, and how much it weighs. Tell me how much it will cost to have this package delivered."

d. Help or suggest that a child write down numbers that represent the measured dimensions. Encourage children to cooperate on tasks: one can hold a package while another passes a tape measure along its edges and a third records the numbers. Another child could load packages on "delivery vehicles."

e. Recruit a delivery truck driver. This child might also enjoy collecting money from children to whom packages are delivered. (Explain COD if you wish.)

f. Periodically make observations or ask open-ended questions to keep the play going or extend children's understanding of the TFPs. "These two packages look alike. I wonder if they weigh the same, too." "This is an oddly shaped package. How do you think we could figure out what size it is?"

g. As children become involved in the roles, back out of the play, allowing them to take over.

Hint for Success:
• Add interest to the activity by making sure that some of the wrapped packages are identical in size and dimension, but different in weight. Make available other packages of differing dimensions that weigh the same.

How to Simplify this Activity:
• Very young or inexperienced children will enjoy simply trying the measuring tools and taking deliveries.

How to Extend this Activity:
• Provide wrapping paper or give the children materials to make their own (plain brown paper, crayons, markers, and stickers). Show the children how to measure the paper as a way of deciding how much they will need to wrap a particular package. Invite the children to wrap some of the packages using the paper, tape, and string.

Social

1. *Measure a Friend.* Ask the children to choose friends to measure. Record measurements of each child's various body parts in his or her own booklet. Include obvious measures such as overall height and weight, as well as length of arms, legs, hands, or feet. Add interest by measuring other less common body parts such as hair length, circumference of waist, width of ear, or span of palm.

2. *In Double Measure.* Have children work in pairs to measure a variety of objects. Provide a way for each pair to record its results. Direct partners to take turns both measuring and recording.

3. *Group Sculpture.*
General Purpose: To help children develop interpersonal skills (how to initiate, maintain, and end interactions, as well as how to negotiate).

TFPs: 1–8, 21–48.

Materials: A variety of boxes and lightweight containers; fast drying, strong glue (wood glue works well); glue applicators; masking tape; string; stapler and staples (for children four years and older): yardstick; ruler; measuring tape; markers, poster paints, or crayons for decorating; paper and pencils for charting measurements.

Procedure:
a. Schedule this activity to take place over two or more days. Choose either a

structured small-group or a free-choice format. The structured small-group approach involves dividing children into "teams," each to work on its own project. In the free-choice format, the entire group will work on one sculpture, and the participants may enter and exit the activity at will.

b. *Day One:* Explain to the children that they will work together to construct box sculptures. Tell them their products can be anything they choose and have any shape, size, or configuration.

c. Ask the children to select the boxes they wish to include in their construction(s).

d. Advise children to work together to figure out where different boxes should go and how to fasten them together. Acknowledge and praise collaborative problem solving. Provide assistance and direction when necessary to encourage appropriate use of materials, attention to task, and cooperation. Allow children to decorate the sculpture(s) using markers, poster paint, or crayons.

e. *Day Two:* Tell the children that today they will measure their structure(s). Provide rulers, yardsticks, and tape measures to the group(s).

f. Help children measure each portion of the box sculpture(s). Record the measurements on the structure(s).

g. Bring the group(s) together. Conduct a discussion in which children describe and compare the measurements of the sculpture(s). Praise use of descriptive measurement terms like longer, shorter, higher, lower, or taller.

h. Keep the sculpture(s) available for another day or two so children can look back on their work and remeasure if they so desire.

Hints for Success:

• One or two weeks prior to implementing this activity, ask parents to send in empty boxes and containers of all shapes and sizes.

• Allow plenty of time the first day for children to build together (no less than thirty minutes).

• If this is presented as a free-choice activity, encourage each child to contribute something to the building phase. However, do not require them to stay from beginning to end if they don't want to.

How to Simplify this Activity:

• Provide a large box as the base and make available only a few medium-sized items to attach.

How to Extend this Activity:

• Help the children create a chart on which to record the overall dimensions of each portion of each sculpture. Encourage the children to make comparisons among the parts.

• Ask children to create their own standard of measure such as "finger-lengths" or "spoon-lengths" or "teddy bear-lengths." Use these to measure the sculpture again. Record the results and discuss them.

• Measure the sculpture in feet and inches as well.

• Work with children to figure out a method of weighing the sculpture.

• Ask the children to describe how they decided what pieces went where and how they were fastened together.

TEACHER RESOURCES

Field Trip Ideas

1. Visit a dry goods store where products are weighed and measured.
2. Visit a fabric store where cloth and ribbon are measured and cut.
3. Visit a parcel service. Watch the packages being weighed and stamped.
4. Visit a commercial bakery. Watch as various ingredients are measured.

Classroom Visitors

1. Invite a parent or local carpenter to demonstrate measuring while constructing something out of wood such as a shelf or birdhouse.

2. Ask a parent or a local seamstress or tailor to demonstrate measuring while cutting and sewing a simple garment.
3. Invite an assayer to demonstrate the special measuring tools of his or her profession.
4. Stage a cooking demonstration, in which a visiting parent or other cook emphasizes dry and liquid measures while putting together a recipe.

Children's Books

Branley, F. M. *How Little and How Much*. New York: Crowell, 1976.

Carroll, S. *How Big Is a Brachiosaurus?* New York: Putnam, 1986.

Eastman, P. D. *Big Dog . . . Little Dog*. New York: Random House, 1973.

Friskey, M. E. *About Measurement*. Chicago: Melmont, 1965.

Kellogg, S. *Much Bigger than Martin*. New York: Dial, 1976.

Krasilovsky, P. *The Very Little Girl*. Garden City, NY: Doubleday, 1953.

Kraus, R. *The Littlest Rabbit*. New York: Scholastic, 1961.

Krauss, R. *The Growing Story*. New York: Harper and Row, 1947.

Leaf, M. *Metric Can Be Fun*. New York: Scholastic, 1976.

Lionni, L. *Inch by Inch*. New York: Astor-Honor, 1960.

Myller, R. *How Big Is a Foot?* New York: Atheneum, 1972.

Pienkowski, J. *Sizes*. New York: Holiday House, 1975.

Rowe, E. *Giant Dinosaurs*. New York: Scholastic, 1973.

Russo, M. *The Line Up Book*. New York: Greenwillow, 1986.

Schneider, H. *How Big Is Big?* New York: Scholastic, 1946.

Schwartz, D. M. *How Much Is a Million?* New York: Scholastic, 1985.

Srivastava, J. J. *Weighing and Balancing*. New York: Crowell, 1970.

Tresselt, A. *How Far Is Far?* New York: Parents, 1964.

Adult References

Balogh, C. L. "Mathematical Concepts." In J. S. McKee (ed.), *The Developing Kindergarten: Programs, Children, and Teachers*. East Lansing, MI: Michigan Association for the Education of Young Children, 1989.

Bendick, J. *Measuring*. New York: Franklin Watts, 1971.

Epstein, S., and B. Epstein. *The First Book of Measurement*. New York: Franklin Watts, 1960.

Moore, W. *How Fast, How Far, How Much?* New York: Putnam, 1966.

Pine, T. S., and Levin, J. *Measurements and How We Use Them*. New York: McGraw-Hill, 1974.

Chapter 24

Stores

•

"This little piggie went to market . . ."

"Simple Simon met a pieman . . ."

"To market, to market, to buy a fat pig . . ."

•

People, including young children, have been involved with some form of commerce for as long as humans have lived in social groups. From early trading of furs, blankets, and beads to today's high-tech home video buying shows, shopping has been, and remains, an integral part of American society.

Learning about the marketplace is a lifetime endeavor. At every age, there are different consumer choices to be made and different economic concepts to be learned. Gaining monetary knowledge and skills cannot be put off until adulthood, nor are these automatically acquired at that time. Instead, financial understandings evolve gradually from the early childhood years through maturity. Children become consumers at an early age and make spending decisions with their own or their parents' money. They also influence their parents' spending decisions (Schram, 1984).

Some of the basic elements of commerce that later preschool- and early elementary-aged children begin to encounter in their day-to-day activities are money, stores, needs, wants, decisions, private property, prices, ownership, purchases, products, advertising, and salesclerks. Furthermore, children frequently experience marketplace demands such as choosing among many alternatives and coping with the undeniable truth that wants often exceed resources (Stampfle, Moschis, and Lawton, 1978). In fact, the store is probably the first and most familiar out-of-home environment that many young children encounter. Infants and toddlers regularly accompany their parents on visits to supermarkets and malls. Preschoolers can often describe "their" store very well, including the extra added attractions like riding horses and candy machines that reinforce their desire to visit. By the elementary years, children can easily match items they want to the various stores that sell them.

PURPOSE

Children learn much about the world of commerce through vicarious experiences such as parental modeling and watching television. In addition, there is evidence that they benefit when marketplace concepts are more directly and systematically addressed both at home and at school (Stampfle et al., 1978). Indeed, purposeful education about and experience with money, stores, and consumerism at an early age can help people develop more positive and satisfying money management skills over their lifetimes (Schram, 1984).

With these ideas in mind, we selected stores as the vehicle for a unit dealing with consumerism, choices, and money. It is not our intention to have children memorize isolated facts such as the names of the coins or how many of one equals another. Rather, we designed an integrated array of activities that translate basic marketplace concepts into appropriate vocabulary and relevant, age-appropriate experiences for children. Ultimately, we hope that as children gain an understanding of the world of commerce and of the consequences of the choices that they make as consumers, they will be better equipped to respond to the commercial world now and in the future.

IMPLEMENTATION

Because we believe that an understanding of the concepts included in the Stores unit is very important to the development of adults who can function successfully in our society, we urge you to present this material in a variety of ways throughout the school year. Provide multiple opportunities for children to make choices and evaluate their satisfaction with the consequences of those choices. Help them to reflect upon the factors that influenced those choices and recognize that their choices are often affected by the ideas and actions of others. Children have opportunities to experience scarcity and supply and demand when they must wait for a turn with a coveted toy, or when the supply of scissors is not large enough to satisfy the needs of the total group. Take advantage of these "teachable moments" to help children deal with emotions and discover alternative solutions to problems.

Implementation of the Stores theme will require you to become more aware of the resources available in your community. Store personnel are often very willing to support your teaching efforts by contributing materials that can be used by children in art and construction projects and as props for pretend play situations. Parents, too, are frequently willing to cooperate in teacher efforts to acquire the desired materials. Plan ahead and let people know the kinds of things that you will be using. In addition to helping you gather desired materials, visits to local merchants can also assist you in identifying possible field trip sites. Store managers are usually very willing to accommodate a group of young visitors, to assign a store employee to show the children around, and, perhaps, to offer a snack during your visit.

Option One: Having presented the activities of the Stores theme in an integrated fashion early in the year, repeat them in conjunction with other themes. Since store pretend play situations are so popular with children and are frequently available in early childhood classrooms, there should be many opportunities to introduce and reinforce the ideas related to choices and commerce.

Option Two: Present the Stores unit midway through the year as a follow-up to the Number and Numerals unit and the Measuring unit. Activities from both of those can be easily repeated in connection with a theme on stores.

Option Three: Present a Stores unit several times during the year. Select different types of stores upon which to focus each time, and repeat some of the activities to provide multiple opportunities for children to begin to grasp these complex ideas.

TERMS, FACTS, AND PRINCIPLES

General Information

1. A store is a place where people buy things that are needed or wanted such as food, clothing, furniture, toys, tools, and appliances.
2. Most people cannot make or grow everything they need to live so they rely on various kinds of stores to sell the merchandise they want to buy.
3. Some stores have only one kind of product for sale such as food, clothing, shoes, or automobiles.
4. Some stores sell many kinds of products. A department store, for instance, may sell clothing, cosmetics, lawn mowers, appliances, and toys.
5. Stores vary in size.
6. A group of stores may be clustered together in a downtown shopping area, in a shopping center, or at a shopping mall.
7. Some stores sell things all year long.
8. Some stores feature seasonal merchandise such as fruits, vegetables, or Halloween pumpkins and sell things only during a portion of the year.
9. Stores are owned by people.

People in a Store

10. A person who goes into a store to look for or buy something is called a customer, shopper, or consumer.
11. A person who works in a store and helps a customer may be called a clerk, salesperson, checker, cashier, or bagger.
12. Some stores are organized so that a customer can find most of the things she or he wants without help.
13. Some stores have sample merchandise on view, and a store worker must get the items that a customer wishes to purchase from a stock or storage room.
14. An owner is someone to whom all or part of a store belongs.
15. Some stores have managers who help the owner run the store.
16. Some stores have stock people whose job is to keep the shelves supplied with merchandise and to keep track of the number of items in the store, the number of items that have been sold, and the number of items that should be ordered.
17. Some stores have buyers whose job is to choose the things that the store will offer for sale to customers.
18. Department and gift stores often have a special place in the store where a customer may take a purchase and have it gift wrapped.
19. At some stores the customer can take a defective product to a special place or person and get his or her money back or exchange the product for a different one.
20. Some stores have people who repair items that have become worn or broken during use.
21. In a small store, the owner may do all of the jobs.

Products and Merchandise

22. The amount of money that a person must pay to buy an item is called the price.

23. Usually, each product has a price stamped on it, on a tag attached to it, or on a display sign nearby.

24. Some stores, such as a roadside vegetable stand or craft store, sell products that the owner has made or grown.

*25. Most stores buy what they sell from other sources or suppliers and sell it to the customers at a higher price so that the operating expenses (workers' salaries, rent, heat, phone, etc.) can be paid and the owner may make a profit.

*26. Owners use their profits to buy new things for themselves or for their businesses.

27. Sometimes, stores place advertisements in newspapers or catalogues, or use commercials on radio or television to tell customers that the store has certain items available.

28. Some manufacturers also advertise their products to encourage people to look for them when shopping.

*29. Manufacturers sometimes provide coupons that enable consumers to try products at reduced costs.

30. Advertisements and commercials are designed to convince a customer or consumer that a product is desirable, needed, useful, and worth buying.

*31. Sometimes, advertisers exaggerate or tell only part of the truth about their products.

32. Consumers must make choices among items because they usually do not have enough money to buy everything they want.

*33. Sometimes a store sells products at a lower price than usual; lower prices often are called sale prices.

*34. Generally, a consumer wants to buy an item or service for the lowest possible price.

*35. Sometimes a shopper goes to more than one store looking for the lowest price on the item he or she would like to buy.

36. Sometimes a shopper goes to a store to enjoy looking at the various products available (to browse).

*37. Sometimes a consumer goes to a store to ask questions about how a product is made or about its durability.

*38. A consumer may be willing to pay a higher price for something if it is of better quality or more attractive than similar products.

*39. Items bought in a store are usually wrapped, bagged, or boxed to protect them as they are transported and so it is easy to tell that the customer has paid for them.

40. Frequently, a store will deliver large items, such as furniture or appliances, to a customer's home.

Using Money in the Store

41. Money is a thing that people have agreed to exchange for objects.

42. In order to buy things from a store, a person must spend money or exchange something of equal value.

43. In a store, the customer gives the cashier or clerk the money to pay for the items purchased.

*44. People sometimes write checks or use credit cards to avoid carrying large amounts of cash.

*45. A check may only be used if the person writing it has enough money in the bank to pay it.

*46. When people use credit cards, they must pay for the items purchased at a later time when they receive their bills.

47. In the United States, money is made by the government in the form of paper bills or metal coins.

48. In our country, we use coins called the penny (one cent), nickel (five cents), dime (ten cents), quarter (twenty-five cents), half-dollar (fifty cents), and silver dollar (one hundred cents).

49. The size of a coin is not related to its value.

*50. Pennies can be combined to equal the value of any other coin or bill.

*51. People use bills and coins of different values to avoid carrying lots of pennies.

*52. People earn money to buy things by working.

ACTIVITY IDEAS

Aesthetic

1. *Bag Art.* Provide an assortment of paper bags from various stores and art materials such as markers, paper scraps and glue, stickers, glitter, and paint. Direct the children to select and decorate bags in a manner that is pleasing to them. If desired, these may be stuffed with wadded newspaper and tied tightly to give the artwork an interesting shape.

2. *Box Art.* Provide an assortment of boxes, cartons, tubes from store-bought items, and plenty of glue. Direct children to create box sculptures by gluing the boxes and tubes into horizontal and vertical structures. These box sculptures may be enhanced by the addition of paper scraps, ribbon or yarn pieces, and paint.

3. *Can Do.* Before beginning this unit, ask parents and friends to save big tin cans so that you will have one for each child. Large coffee cans work best with the plastic lid placed on the bottom end for protection and cushioning.

   Punch two holes near the top of each can, on opposite sides, and insert and secure a rope handle. (Figure 24.1)

   Provide cans, decorating materials such as small, assorted pieces of self-adhesive vinyl (contact paper), colored tape, fabric scraps, and craft glue. Ask children to select pieces and cover their cans in a manner pleasing to them, overlapping the pieces to cover the entire outer surface. Permanent markers may be used to write children's names on the finished carriers. Use cans to carry artwork, messages, or snacks to and from school.

Affective

1. *Bakery Shop Game.* Before playing this game, prepare a set of construction paper "donuts" in a variety of colors, about four inches in diameter. Make dots on the top

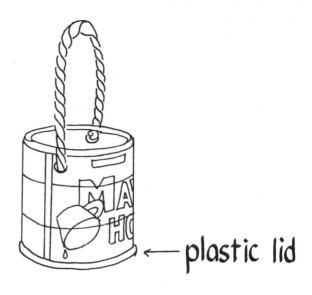

Figure 24.1 *Make a Coffee Can Carrier*

surface to represent nuts, raisins, and so on. Gather the group of children in a circle on the floor and tell them that you are going to play a game. Explain that each child will have a chance to be the shopper at the bakery shop and that she or he will be able to choose a donut color and topping in turn. Place the donuts on the floor in the middle of the group of children, one at a time, counting as you place each donut. You should have enough donuts for each child, with a few extras to assure choices for the last children to play. Select a child to be the first shopper and direct her or him to move to the center of the circle and choose a donut as you chant. After choosing a donut, the child should return to her or his place in the circle. Before beginning to chant, ask the child if she or he wants nuts, raisins, or frosting on the donut.

The Chant:
Down at the corner, at the bakery shop, sat (insert number) donuts with (insert topping child has selected) on top. Along came (insert child's name) all alone, and (s/he) took a (insert color) one home!

After all children have had an opportunity to choose a donut, collect the paper pieces for the next time that you play.

Collecting the donuts is a fine way to dismiss children from the circle time to another activity period. Collect one color at a time and after children have turned in their donuts, tell them to proceed to the next situation.

2. ***Dollar Portraits.*** Cut large pieces of easel paper into rectangular shapes and put dollar signs in each corner. (Figure 24.2)

Gather markers, crayons, or bits of paper, yarn, paste, and scissors. Provide one or more mirrors for children to use. Introduce the activity by showing children real "bills" in varying amounts. Point out that human portraits are often included in the design as a way to "honor" important people. Since all the children in the class are important people, they too, will get to have their pictures on pretend money. Put out the paper and other materials; encourage the children to make pictures of themselves on their own "bills." Elicit self-descriptions from the children as they work. Concentrate on physical attributes, offering the mirrors for children to refer to as needed.

3. ***It's Not What I Wanted!*** Before carrying out this activity, write a note home to the parents of the children in your group and ask for their assistance. Request that they help their child identify a product recently purchased in a store that was disappointing for the child in some way. Suggest that it may be a toy that was not quite as wonderful as the child thought it would be after seeing it in the store or in commercials, or perhaps it is a food item that did not live up to the child's expectations. Ask the parent to discuss the reasons for the disappointment with the child so that he or she can share these perceptions with the class. Invite the children to bring these disappointing items to school and provide an opportunity for them to display the items and tell the class about them. Encourage the children to share other consumer disappointments with each other. Discuss the reasons for the choices and why the items were not as satisfactory as anticipated.

4. ***Pick a Snack.*** Purchase an assortment of unusual crackers in boxes; include both plain and fancy boxes in your selection.

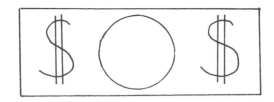

Figure 24.2 *Dollar Portraits of Our Own*

Display the boxes during a group time and have the children indicate the one that they would most like to try. Record these choices on a chart or graph. For snacktime, display the crackers on plates with the corresponding boxes placed behind the plates. Invite children to select their own snacks from the choices offered after looking at the boxes and the actual crackers. Compare these choices with the ones they made earlier based only on the boxes. As children are eating the crackers, lead them in a discussion of how the actual crackers compare to the pictures on the boxes.

5. ***Art Supply Store.***

General Purpose: To provide opportunities for children to make choices and experience the consequences of personal decisions.

TFPs: 10, 16, 19, 32.

Materials: Table, chairs, counter or table with an assortment of art materials arranged in a buffet or display fashion (include a variety of paper, markers, glue, scissors, tracing templates, pencils, crayons, etc.); baskets to hold merchandise selected by "shoppers."

Procedure:

a. Welcome children to the Art Supply Store. Tell them that they should think about something they want to make using the materials available. Explain that they may make only one trip to the store to select the materials with which they will work.

b. After children have made their initial selections, encourage them to put their materials to use at the art table.

c. After they have selected materials and begun to work, they must obtain any additional materials by trading with a friend or by exchanging something at the store.

Hints for Success:

- If limiting the number of items that may be selected, package a few crayons or markers in baggies so that the package counts as one choice.
- Discuss each child's intended project as items are chosen and encourage the child to think carefully about what will be needed to complete it.

How to Simplify this Activity:

- Present only paper and tools in the "store." Have other materials available on the art table for use by all children participating.

How to Extend this Activity:

- Limit the number of items each child may choose.

6. *Commercial Consideration.*

General Purpose: To provide opportunities for children to make choices and experience the consequences of personal decisions.

TFPs: 28, 30, 31, 32.

Materials: "Super Wonder Product"—a large, beautifully wrapped, colorful box containing enough single sheets of folded newspaper for each child in the class; "Plain Product"—a small, brown-paper wrapped box containing enough treats (stickers or sugarless gum) for each child in the class; a fancy hat for the teacher; a noisemaker or a whistle.

Procedure:

a. Gather the children into a group and briefly discuss commercials. Ask if they have seen any commercials on television, why they think there are commercials, and who they think pays for the television shows that they watch on commercial television.

b. Following this discussion, or on the next day, tell children that you are going to do two commercials. Tell them to listen *very carefully* to what you say during the commercials and that they will get to choose one of the products after they have listened to both commercials.

c. "Listen to the first commercial." Put on the hat, make some noise (or put on a catchy record or tape) and get the attention of the group with a very enthusiastic, loud, happy voice and a smiling laughing face. Move quickly about as you extol the virtues of "Super Wonder Product" in the big, attractive box. Wave the box around as you speak. Say things such as "Super Wonder Product can be used for many different things." "Every home needs Super Wonder Product." "Super Wonder Product is terrific. It can help with your pets. It can be used for art projects." Be enthusiastic, be loud, *do* be truthful, but exaggerate and really "sell" Super Wonder Product. Then put down the big box.

d. Move very slowly and quietly to the smaller, plain brown box and sit down. "Now, please listen to the second commercial." Sit very quietly, and gently and softly present a commercial for "Plain Product." Mention that it is something that you know each child will enjoy; refer to it often as Plain Product. Use a very quiet and subdued manner throughout this presentation. Tell the truth without revealing the contents.

e. "Now, you have heard the commercials for both products. It is time for you to decide which product you would like to have. Raise your hand if you would like what is in the Plain Product box." (Hold box up.) If many hands are raised, record the choices. Discuss briefly with the children why they chose Plain Product.

f. "Raise your hand if you would like what is in the Super Wonder Product box." Lead the children in a discussion of why they chose Super Wonder Product.

g. Open the Plain Product box and distribute the treats to those who chose Plain Product.

h. Open the Super Wonder Product and distribute the newspaper sheets to those who chose Super Wonder Product.

i. Discuss with the children the reasons for their choices and their feelings about their choices. Remind them that you told the truth about each product. Encourage them to analyze why the Super Wonder Product commercial appealed to them. Ask if they ever see commercials on television that use the same techniques to attract buyers.

Hints for Success:

- If any consumers are not satisfied with their choices, you may allow exchanges after a brief discussion of their disappointment.

- It is imperative that all information you give during the commercials be truthful.

- Encourage continued discussion of television advertising over the next several days.

How to Simplify this Activity:

- Keep the presentations very brief; discuss the claims made during the commercial with the children immediately after making each statement.

How to Extend this Activity:

- Present the commercials early in the day. Delay opening the boxes until later; use some of the time in-between to encourage children to discuss and/or record their ideas about the contents.

Cognition

1. *Balancing Act.* Set up a balance scale for children to use and explore. Provide an assortment of coins to use with the scales. Direct children to compare the weights of identical coins and then try weighing coins of equal value to see if they have the same weight. For instance, do five pennies weigh the same, more, or less than a nickel? Which is heavier—a half-dollar or fifty pennies? Encourage the children to predict what will happen with certain combinations on the scale and then test out their theories. To provide further experiences with the balance scale, add some coins from other countries and some other types of metal disks.

2. *Cash Sales Only.* Repeat the Art Supply Store activity from the Affective section of this unit, but place prices on the items and give each shopper a certain amount of "Classroom Cash" to use while making purchases. Limit children's selections of materials to what each can afford with his or her amount of "cash." Encourage the children to plan their projects and purchases carefully so that they will be able to afford all of the materials needed.

3. *Classification.* A unit on Stores provides many opportunities for classification experiences.

   Request that each child bring from home an empty package or container from a store-bought item. Place these on a table and direct children to group items that share some attribute in common.

   Provide an assortment of coins from around the world for children to explore, manipulate, and classify.

   Suggest that children sort the merchandise in classroom pretend play stores. Store personnel can do this daily as the stores are restocked and organized.

4. *Coin Match.* Provide pairs of all U.S. coins. Allow children several opportunities to explore and manipulate the coins. After children are familiar with them, play a matching game by asking children to put identical coins together, first looking at "heads," then at "tails," and finally matching heads and tails of corresponding coins. Prepare a set of game cards for this activity by taping coins to cards, if you wish.

5. *Comparison Shopping.* Gather several pairs of identical objects. Put one to five colored dots on each item, making the number of dots on members of each pair unequal. (Figure 24.3)

   Use a masking tape line to divide a table in half. Put one item from each object pair on either side of the tape. Describe the table as representing two stores. Show children how each item is marked with a "price" in dots. Ask them to figure out which item in each pair costs less.

   As a variation, put the paired items side by side on shelves. Give the children shopping bags or toy carts into which to put the cheapest object from each pair.

6. *Department Store Set-Up.* Prior to the children's participation, draw six or seven squares or rectangles to represent the different floors and rooms in a department

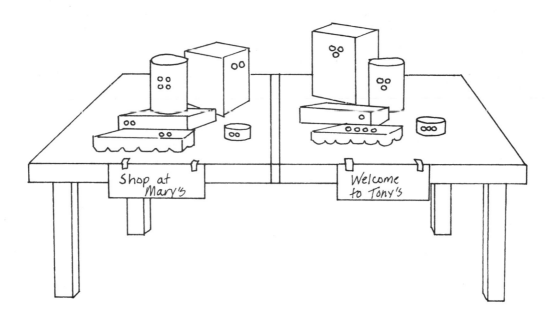

Figure 24.3 *Comparison Shopping*

store on a large piece of mural paper. In each space paste a magazine picture of an object. Make each a different type of item: an appliance, a child's pair of shoes, a toy, a book, and so on. After children arrive, read the story *Department Store* by Gail Gibbons to remind them of the various items sold in such places. Next, explain that your Department Store needs merchandise to sell. Each child can take on the role of buyer and select items to be sold in the store. Giving the children magazines and catalogues, direct them to cut out or tear out pictures of items they would like to include. Once several objects have been identified, encourage the youngsters to look at the ones already in each department, and to paste the new things where they best fit. As children find spots for their selections, ask them why they grouped them as they did. Later, to extend children's interest after all their items have been used, introduce a few objects they hadn't seen. Either direct the children to categorize these or put them in various departments yourself, inviting children to decide whether each is appropriately placed or not. Encourage children to verbalize the reasoning behind their decisions. Accept all answers as given.

7. ***May I Fill Your Order, Please?*** Set up an area of the room where several items are displayed on shelves. Provide cardboard boxes in which more than one of the objects might fit at a time. Using magazine pictures or simple line drawings, create several sample orders based on the available merchandise. Cover these with clear contact paper. If children use water-soluble markers, the forms can be wiped clean to be used again. (Figure 24.4)

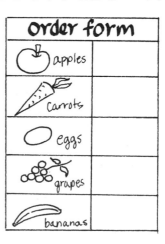

Figure 24.4 *Order Form for Fruits*

Explain that the area is a store and that the "stock people" will receive orders to fill for customers. Demonstrate how to do this by putting the items that correspond to one of the orders into a box. Have children continue this process, periodically restocking the shelves so new orders can be filled.

8. *Money Memory.* Prepare a set of eight to ten pairs of game cards by gluing play coins on them. Print the value of the coins on each card. Place the cards coin down on a table and direct the children to take turns revealing two cards to see if they match. When a child gets a match, she or he keeps the cards in a pile on the table. At the end of the game, see who has gathered the greatest number of pairs. To reduce competition, limit each player to two cards per turn, whether a match is made or not. Initially, prepare simple card amounts for the children, such as two pennies, one nickel, and one dime.

After children are familiar with the game, require the child who has made a successful match to name the amount pictured on one card, or the total on both, before adding the cards to the matching pile. As an alternative, use identical amounts, but different coins, for some of the pairs. For example, pair five pennies with one nickel; two nickels with one dime, and so on.

9. *Price Bingo.* Make some bingo cards that have prices—with dollar signs and cent symbols—instead of the usual numbers on them. Also make a set of individual cards with corresponding prices for the caller to draw and read. Provide a game card and a set of markers (pennies are good for this game) for each child. Choose cards one at a time, from the caller's pile and read each price to the children. Direct children to cover that price on their cards with markers. Instruct children to call out "sold!" when all of the prices on their cards are covered.

To reduce competition, make sure that one price is the same on every game card. When playing the game, always choose that price last, so that all of the children "win" at the same time.

10. *Take Stock.* Prepare some simple inventory sheets for use in the classroom. These may be used in connection with a pretend store or may be used to take stock of materials in the classroom. Include space for the item name (or a picture) and the child's name and a tallying space large enough to make marks to represent each item found. Also include a space for recording the total number of items with a numeral. Provide one of these sheets and a pencil or crayon to the "stock taker" and direct the child to count or tally the assigned item by filling in the sheet.

Another method of taking stock is to assign several children to the task of inventorying a particular material. Provide a large, poster-sized, tallying sheet with pictures representing items to be counted and columns for the tally marks or numerals. The unit block shelf is an excellent resource for this purpose. Trace the shape of the blocks to be inventoried on the record-keeping sheet. Then, direct children to remove all of the identical blocks from the shelf and tally (make a mark on the paper for each block) each one as it is returned to the shelf. Post the tallying sheet on a wall in the block area and continue with the inventory until all of the blocks have been included.

Construction

1. *Classroom Cash.* Provide gray, brown and green paper; scissors; sturdy circle shapes of varied sizes to trace; rulers; and markers, pencils, or crayons. If possible, also provide some pictures of actual money to serve as models and inspiration. Direct children to use the materials to create "Classroom Cash" for use in the pretend play stores in the classroom. The gray and brown paper may be used to create coins; the green to make bills.

Demonstrate how to trace a circle, write in a numeral to show the coin's value, and cut out a coin. Also demonstrate how to use the ruler to draw straight lines before cutting to create bills. Numeral rubber stamps and an ink pad are helpful materials to add to this activity.

2. *Choose and Carry.* Collect several large, sturdy boxes and create carrying handles by fastening lengths of rope through holes near the top of each box and knotting the

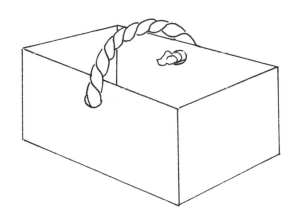

Figure 24.5 *Make a Carry-all*

ends securely. (Figure 24.5) Provide these boxes and decorating materials such as fabric or paper scraps, glue, markers, stickers, and paint. Direct children to decorate boxes as shopping baskets to be used in the pretend play stores.

3. ***Recycled Towers.*** Collect a large assortment of sturdy packing boxes and make them available in your block corner or outdoors for children to use in imaginative construction projects. These can be lined up to create houses, garages, fire stations, or stores, or stacked to construct towers.

4. ***Shopping Mall.*** Provide unit blocks, cars, delivery trucks, small boxes of merchandise, traffic signs, and small dolls in a large floor area. Direct children to use the materials to construct a shopping mall. Remind them that stores, parking lots, delivery areas, and walkways for customers are all found at a mall.

5. ***Store Merchandise.*** Children can construct the merchandise for some of the pretend play stores that you may wish to feature in your classroom. Provide the materials and allow the children to construct their own versions of the following suggested merchandise with limited assistance and/or direction from adults. This merchandise can be constructed before the pretend play setting is arranged or to keep a store stocked after it has opened for business.

For a Card Shop, the children can construct greeting cards using paper and markers or watercolor paints. Using paper, pencils, rubber stamps, and stickers, children can also create calendars or stationery.

For a Hat Shop, provide paper plates, tissue paper, ribbon, yarn, scissors, holepunches, and glue or tape to be fashioned into hats for display and sale.

For an Ice Cream Store, older children can create the ice cream by making yarn pompoms using small pompom makers or cardboard circles. To make pompoms using cardboard circles, cut two four-inch circles with a one-inch circular hole in the center of each from cardboard. Hold the circles together and wrap a length of yarn around the entire surface, from center to edge. (Figure 24.6a)

The cardboard should not be visible when wrapping is completed. Hold firmly and cut the yarn with a very sharp knife or razor blade, slitting it between the two cardboard circles. For safety reasons, an adult should do the cutting. While still holding firmly, slip a piece of yarn between the two circles and knot securely. Remove

 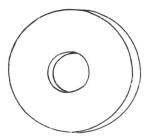 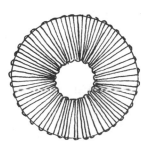

Figure 24.6a *Starting a Puff Ball*

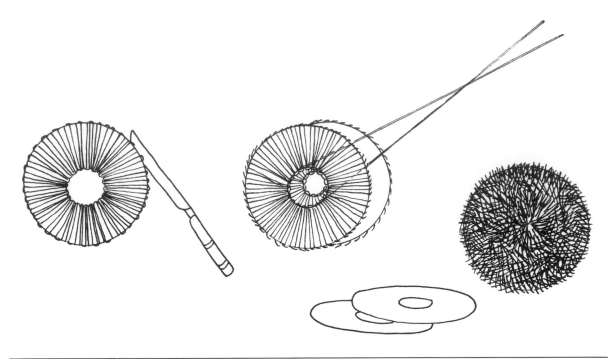

Figure 24.6b *Finishing the Puff Ball*

the form and fluff up the resulting ball with your fingers. (Figure 24.6b)

Language

1. *A Word from Our Sponsor.* Set up a pretend microphone and/or TV camera, or use a tape recorder, and encourage children to take turns presenting commercials for items of their choice. Provide a few "products" from which they may choose. Some ideas might be a favored classroom toy, a cereal or cracker box, or a familiar book.

   Direct the "advertiser" to describe the product, tell why she or he likes it, and try to convince others that it is a worthwhile product. Encourage children to listen to the commercials of others and make suggestions regarding other information that might be useful.

2. *Blue-Light Special.* On paper, prepare a large outline of a store and depict numerous items for sale, or use the one children made for the Department Store Set-up activity in this unit. Gather several blue poker chips or other type of blue marker. Explain that shoppers in the store often hear announcements regarding special sale items. These are sometimes designated by a flashing blue light nearby, hence the name "blue-light special." Give each child a few of the blue chips. Tell them that you will describe a sale item without telling them exactly what it is. They are to guess which one(s) you're talking about and place a blue chip on one of the objects that matches your description.

   Proceed in this way, emphasizing different object attributes such as size, shape, color, or function. Begin with features shared by numerous items, then narrow it down to only a few possible choices. After children make a selection, ask them to explain their reasoning. Once children figure out how the game works, have them take over the job of announcer. Children in this role may do better describing an object depicted on a separate card that corresponds to one in the store. The cards could be concealed in some fashion, with children drawing one from among several and then using that as a basis for description. Other children may benefit from being asked specific questions such as: "What color is the object?" "How big is it?" "What do people use this object for?"

3. *Catalogue Cut-ups.* Gather an assortment of store fliers, magazine advertisements, and old catalogues. Provide these along with blank booklets made of construction paper (two or three sheets of paper folded in half and stapled along the fold), paste, scissors, and pencils or markers. Direct children to construct a catalogue featuring items of their choice that might be found in a store. Assist the children by writing in item names or encouraging them to write their own. Remind children to include prices for the merchandise displayed in their catalogues. If the catalogues fit in with a pretend play situation in the classroom, use them to extend play in that area.

4. *Forgetful Frodo.* First, obtain a hand puppet, which you will call Frodo. Next, gather pictures of items commonly sold in stores. Make sure to include several compound word items (ice cream, shoelaces, raincoat, sewing machine, lawn mower, potato chips), as well as single syllable (lace, plate, hoe, ball) and multisyllable (umbrella, clippers, shovel) objects.

Explain to children that the "storekeeper" wants Frodo to help with an inventory of everything in the store. Frodo wants to help, but sometimes forgets things. The children's job is to "listen" very carefully as the storekeeper calls out an item and Frodo repeats it to put on the inventory. If Frodo "forgets" part of the word, the children are to supply the missing portion. Show the children a picture (raincoat). Say the whole word and have Frodo repeat only part (_____coat or rain_____). Ask the children whether Frodo was "right," and if not, what part of the word was missing. Repeat this process several times. As children become more adept at figuring out the missing parts, move to multisyllable words, leaving out a syllable (_____brella). Eventually, move to single syllable words and leave out certain sounds (plate = ___late). Extend the activity with more experienced children by including word labels and pointing out or having

them point out the missing words, syllables, or letter sounds. In another variation, print out the words as Frodo repeats them and then add the missing parts that children identify.

5. *Fun with Rhymes.* Read aloud the story *Don't Forget the Bacon* by Pat Hutchins. Prior to reading it another time, print on a large piece of mural paper a list of the correct items the child is supposed to get at the store. Leave plenty of space for additional words to be added later. (Figure 24.7)

Preface a second reading by reminding children of the story and by going over the list. Explain that their job is to listen for all the "mixed-up" ideas the boy thinks of as he goes to the store. Read the book all the way through. Ask children to recall what they heard and then write down their ideas near a rhyming item on the original list. After several words and phrases have been suggested, refer back to the story to check for accuracy of memory.

6. *Peddler Tales.* Esphyr Slobodkina's classic tale *Caps for Sale* and *The Ox Cart Man* by Donald Hall provide glimpses

Don't Forget The...

Six farm eggs

A cake for tea

A pound of pears

Bacon

Figure 24.7 *A Simple Rhyming Board*

into a past era of shopping, when stores were not as commonplace as they are today. Read one or both of these stories to your group for enjoyment the first time through. Repeat the story and follow the reading by discussing with the children the sequence of events, how the peddler felt, how the peddler made his living, and how this method of shopping varies from the way we do our shopping today.

7. *Store Scavenger Hunt. Corduroy* is another classic children's tale by Don Freeman that has to do with commerce. It features a large department store and can serve as the basis for a visit to a local store, where children can search for things that are mentioned in the book. Read the book to the class several times so that the children are familiar with the story and the sequence of events. Have them contribute ideas to a list of "Things in Corduroy's Store That We May See." Follow up with a visit to a store and take the list with you. Refer to it during the trip and check things off as the children see them. Add other things to the list that they spot during the visit that were not mentioned in the book. Repeat the reading when you return to school and compare your list with the things you actually saw during the visit.

8. *Store Signs and Posters.* Provide large sheets of paper, poster board or cardboard, pencils, and markers. Encourage children to create signs to be used in the pretend play stores in the classroom. In addition to signs related to specific merchandise and prices, some other signs might be OPEN, CLOSED, ENTER, EXIT, CASHIER, SALES DESK, CUSTOMER SERVICE, TELEPHONE, GIFT WRAPPING, RETURNS, SALE, and REDUCED IN PRICE.

Physical

1. *Merchandise Move.* Prepare some large, heavy packages and leave them in obvious view on the playground or in the classroom. Challenge children to move them from one location to another without lifting them from the ground or floor. Suggest pushing or pulling with various body parts. "Try to move the box using your elbows." "Move the package using only the tips of your fingers."

2. *Roll-a-Can.* Provide several empty or sand-filled cans (like those you'd find in a grocery store) and pushing or steering poles. (Empty gift-wrap tubes are long and safe). Prepare a pathway using chalk or masking tape. Direct children to move the cans from one end of the pathway to the other using only the pole. Remind them that it is important to remain inside the pathway and that gentle pushes are more easily controlled.

3. *Streamer Fun.* Obtain some rolls of cash register tape. Invite the children to examine the paper closely. Next, cut the paper into eighteen-inch lengths, or ask the children to do this. Provide each child with a strip or two, scissors, tape, and a toilet tissue tube. Also have available markers, glitter, sequins, and glue. Direct children to cut the strip(s) in half, lengthwise, and decorate the thinner strips as desired. Demonstrate how to fasten the tube to the strips with the tape to form a handle for the streamers. Use the streamers outside or during a creative movement experience indoors.

4. *Wrap It Up.* Set up a package wrapping station. This may be connected to a pretend play setting or may be treated as a separate activity. Provide boxes of various sizes and wrapping paper; plain brown or gift wrapping paper will both work. Add scissors, tape, rulers, string, yarn or ribbon, and pencils. Demonstrate how to measure a box to determine the size of paper needed and how to fold and secure the paper around the box. Direct children to wrap the packages using the materials available.

Pretend Play

1. *Furniture and Appliance Store.* Direct children to use blocks to create stores and houses. Provide dollhouse furniture and appliances to display and sell. Add doll figure "customers," small signs listing items and cost, and trucks for delivery.

2. *Grocery Store.* Set up an area in the room to resemble a grocery store. Provide a

large assortment of "groceries" (empty boxes, cartons, and cans; plastic fruits and vegetables; other play food that you may have available), grocery sacks, shopping carts (doll strollers or wagons may be used, or try large baskets), cash register, bills and coins, coupons, purses, dress-up clothes (including aprons for the stockers and clerks), scales, and signs. Arrange the groceries so that similar items are stocked together just as in a real store. You may wish to include sections for canned goods, dairy products, produce, meat, baked goods, cereals. Prior to play, discuss the roles that children may assume: customer, cashier, stocker, clerk, or manager. During play, close the store to restock the shelves when needed and encourage the children to keep items in their designated categories as they help with this chore. Since your busy shoppers will probably want to take their groceries home, set up a separate home area nearby with a cupboard and refrigerator.

To extend the play, label each grocery item with a price (either an actual cash amount or color symbols to match your coins) and direct the cashier to collect the marked price for each item. Remind children that they may only purchase those items for which they have sufficient funds.

To simplify the play, use only a few grocery items; limit roles to customers and cashiers.

3. *Lemonade Stand.* This is an enjoyable activity for outdoor pretend play on a warm day. Provide a store (table or storefront), cash (pretend coins, plastic disks, or child-made paper coins), plenty of paper cups, and a large jug of cold water with a dispensing spout. Add a sign that children have prepared to announce that the "Lemonade Stand" is open for business and a trash bag to collect the used cups. Recruit a few child volunteers to operate the store and serve the thirsty customers. Change the curricular focus of this activity by altering the set-up. To support physical development, add small pouring pitchers for small motor practice, or designate a particular price and encourage children to count coins and/or make change to promote cognitive skills.

4. *Lumberyard.* Wrapping paper and paper towel tubes can be used as "lumber" for this outdoor or indoor pretend play activity. Set up a storage area, sales counter, and a delivery system using wagons or carts. Direct children to sort, stack, sell, and deliver the lumber to interested customers.

5. *Variety Stores.*

General Purpose: To give children role-playing opportunities.

TFPs: All.

Materials: All of the following store set-ups will be enhanced by the addition of a cash register and something that may be used for money; dress-up clothes for customers and store workers to wear; purses, wallets, bags; and materials for making signs.

Procedure:

a. Set up one of the following types of stores or invite children to help you create one using the props suggested below.

Hat Shop

Hats, hat boxes, mirror, hair accessories, ribbons, scarves, Styrofoam head shapes.

Clothing Store

Blouses, shirts, dresses, skirts, gloves, scarves, ties, pants, shorts, jackets, measuring tape, boxes or bags from a clothing store.

Ice Cream Store

Yarn ball "ice cream" in store tubs, ice cream scoopers, dishes, napkins, spoons, glasses, ice cream store posters, pint or quart ice cream containers, plastic fruit.

Hardware Store

Tools, nails and screws, nuts and bolts, keys, paint cans, brushes, ruler mounted on a piece of wood.

Shoe Store

Shoes, shoe boxes, chairs, footstools, shoehorns

b. Encourage the children to act out the roles of customers and store workers.

Hint for Success:

• Set up all store areas with a sales counter and a merchandise display area. Encourage children to assume appropriate roles and assist in keeping the stores in order.

How to Simplify this Activity:

• Use limited amounts of merchandise for all store settings. Set up only familiar stores.

How to Extend this Activity:

• Prepare some inventory sheets and have children count and record stock, sales, customers, and so on.

• Set up more than one type of store at a time to create a "mini" mall in which customers and workers can interact.

6. *Bakery.*

   General Purpose: To provide opportunities for children to integrate construction into pretend play episodes.

   TFPs: 3, 10, 11, 22, 43.

   Materials: Play oven, tables, sink, shelves for display, baking pans, rolling pins, cookie cutters, hot pads, bakery boxes, bags, empty spice containers, measuring cups and spoons, bowls, spoons, brown and white modeling dough (use recipes from the Measuring unit in this volume) *or* ingredients and recipe chart, photos of bakery goods, brooms, and dustpan.

   Procedure:

   a. Set up the area to resemble a bakery with work and display areas and a sales counter. Explain to the children that the bakery will need bakers as well as salespeople and customers.

   b. Provide baking equipment for the bakers and have the children help you to make an uncooked dough by combining 2 cups of flour, 1 cup of salt, and 1–1½ cups of colored water. Mix well and knead; store in refrigerator until needed. Or, provide modeling dough. Direct the bakers to create good things (cookies, donuts, breads, cakes, and pies) for the salespeople to sell. (If appropriate, make a list of bakers who are awaiting a turn.)

   c. At the end of the classtime (close of the business day), direct the children to clean up the bakery and store the dough in airtight containers for use the following day.

Hints for Success:

• Set up the bakery display area with baked goods arranged neatly and attractively on trays and plates. Similar items should be displayed together.

• Point out the order that exists in the bakery and encourage the children to maintain this display area throughout the classtime.

• Provide tongs, waxed paper, small paper sacks, and bakery boxes for the clerks to use in filling orders. The papier-mâché baked goods can be stored and reused for many years if they are handled with care.

How to Simplify this Activity:

• Prepare the papier-mâché baked goods yourself well ahead of time and provide them as props for the children in a bakery shop setting.

How to Extend this Activity:

• Plan on carrying out the bakery theme for two weeks. During the first week, have the children make papier-mâché baked goods using the directions that follow this activity.

Papier-mâché Baked Goods

Day One: Tear newspaper into very small (½-inch) pieces. You will need lots of it, a large bucketful. Cover with water and soak overnight.

Day Two: Squeeze out as much of the water as possible and mix the wet paper with wallpaper paste prepared according to the package directions. Use enough to work into all of the paper. Knead this *very thoroughly* until it is the consistency of clay. This will take a long time and is best done in small batches so many children can participate. If time does not permit you to move to step 3, store overnight in an airtight plastic bag in the refrigerator.

Day Three: Remove the mixture from the refrigerator and allow to warm to room temperature. Direct the children to form it into baked goods such as cookie shapes, bread in small loaf pans, donuts, and cupcakes in paper-lined muffin pans. Allow to air dry in a warm, dry area for a few days. This process may be hastened by placing the items in a very low-temperature oven for several hours to remove much of the moisture.

Day Four: Assist the children in mixing tempera paint colors to resemble baked goods. Browns of varying hues, white, yellow, and pink are good choices.

Day Five: Paint the finished baked goods with the tempera paints when they are thoroughly dry. To extend the life of these items, coat them with a clear protective covering if desired. (This should be done by adults.) Use these baked goods as the products in the classroom bakery.

Social

1. *Can Collection Cash-In.* Before beginning this activity, ask the parents of the children to support the unit by saving soda pop cans to donate to the classroom. Discuss with the children how customers sometimes pay an extra charge for each can that they purchase and that this fee is returned when the cans are returned to the store. Tell children that you are going to see if lots of people working together can collect enough cans to earn enough money to do something that all of the class will enjoy. Discuss with the children possible uses for any money raised: a special snack treat, a new toy or other classroom materials, supplies for a special project, or a contribution to a local charity. Direct children to ask if they may have some cans to bring to school. Provide a special collection container, perhaps something decorated by the children, and collect cans for a specified period of time. After the collection period is over, count the cans, arrange a field trip to a nearby store to turn them in, collect your refund, and spend it as decided by the group. Throughout the duration of this activity, point out that it is the combined effort of all of the children in the class that is making this a successful project! If your community does not participate in bottle and can deposits and refunds, perhaps a local recycling center pays for empty aluminum cans.

2. *Community Cook.* This activity should be conducted as a follow-up to a field trip to a grocery store or supermarket where the children buy the ingredients. During a group time, show the collected foods and allow children to name and handle them. Discuss the store(s) and departments where they were obtained. Tell children that they will be working together to prepare a snack for everyone in the class to enjoy. Set up a cooking area where the children can wash and cut the vegetables, make the dumplings or meatballs, and prepare them for eating.

    Both of the following recipes require items from different departments at the grocery store.

*Double Dumpling Soup

This soup has little meatballs and cheese balls floating in it. The first thing you need is about half a cup of broth for each person you want to serve. Ingredients for broth:

Some bones with meat (beef and/or chicken)

Some vegetables: one or two each of a few different kinds, such as onions, celery, carrots, tomatoes, turnips

Some seasonings: parsley, bay leaf, thyme, marjoram, peppercorns, etc.

Procedure:

1. Combine ingredients in large pot.
2. Put in enough water to cover the mixture.
3. Bring it to a boil.
4. Turn down the heat and cook it over low heat for at least two hours.
5. Pour the broth through a strainer into another pot. Taste it and add as much salt as you think it needs.

---

*This recipe was adapted from *Kids Are Natural Cooks* by Lady McCrady, Houghton Mifflin, 1974.

Make the dumplings next. For the meat dumplings, use raw ground beef. If you have made your own broth, you can separate the cooked meat from the bones and add it to the soup.

Ingredients for meat dumplings:

About 1 pound ground meat

1 egg

½ tsp. salt

Bread crumbs, enough to make a stiff mixture

Procedure:

1. Mix together the ingredients.
2. Shape the meat mixture into little balls (20 or so).

Now make the cheese dumplings. (These amounts will make about 13 medium-sized dumplings.)

Ingredients for cheese dumplings:

2 T. soft butter or margarine

2 eggs

6 T. flour (whole wheat or unbleached)

½ tsp. salt

½ cup grated cheese

Procedure:

1. Beat butter and eggs in a bowl.
2. Stir in flour, salt, and cheese.
3. Heat the broth until it is boiling.
4. Put in the meatballs and drop in little spoonfuls of the cheese batter.
5. Watch the pot, and you will see the dumplings start to float to the top as they finish cooking. They should be ready to eat in about 10 minutes.

Mrs. Tedesco's Minestrone

This recipe makes enough soup for at least 24 children. Cut all amounts in half for a smaller group, or make it all and freeze half for another day.

Ingredients:

3 to 4 cloves garlic

1 large onion, chopped

5 T. olive oil

3 large potatoes

2 carrots

5 to 6 medium zucchini

1 to 1½ cups string beans

2 large cans whole tomatoes

1½ cups cooked kidney beans

½ head cabbage

6 cups beef or chicken broth or vegetable juice

3 to 4 medium leeks, sliced (about ½ cup)

Salt and pepper to taste

Fresh parsley, chopped

Large pinch of celery seeds

1 tsp. dried basil

1 tsp. oregano

1 cup macaroni or broken spaghetti

1 cup grated parmesan cheese

Procedure:

1. Chop the fresh vegetables without peeling them.
2. Mince the garlic and onions and snip the parsley.
3. Heat the olive oil in a large kettle and add the onion, garlic, potatoes, and carrots. Sauté these vegetables for a few minutes, until the onion is soft, then add the broth and herbs.
4. Bring to a boil, lower heat, and gently simmer for 15 minutes.
5. Add the zucchini, half of the tomatoes, the cabbage and the beans. Simmer another 15 minutes.
6. Add the pasta, the rest of the tomatoes, and the leeks.
7. Season with salt and pepper and cook only until the pasta is al dente, another 12 to 15 minutes.
8. Serve hot and pass grated parmesan cheese to sprinkle on top.

TEACHER RESOURCES

Field Trip Ideas

1. Take your class to visit a bakery. The children will be able to see products made, packaged, displayed, and sold. They will also see workers performing a variety of store-related tasks. Conclude the visit by making a purchase for a snack.
2. Visit a grocery store. Help the children notice the various sections into which the store is organized. Divide the class into groups and direct each group to find a particular item to purchase for a class cooking project. If you arrange the visit in advance with the store manager, you may be given a tour behind the scenes where the children will be able to see how various items are received and prepared for sale.
3. Visit a shopping mall. Take along paper and pencils to record the number and types of stores there. Point out window displays and signs to give the children ideas for things that can be constructed when they return to school.
4. Visit a hardware store. Arrange ahead of time with the manager to show the children a variety of tools and hardware. Be sure to purchase some nails, screws, and washers for use at the woodworking bench.

Classroom Visitors

1. Invite a grandparent or other older person to visit the class and share remembrances of shopping when he or she was young.
2. Ask a bank teller to describe what his or her job entails.
3. Get a cashier, salesclerk, or store manager to talk about the variety of tasks involved in those jobs.

Children's Books

Baker, E. *I Want to Be a Sales Clerk*. Chicago: Childrens Press, 1969.

Berson, H. *The Rats Who Lived in the Delicatessen*. New York: Crown, 1976.

Burningham, J. *The Shopping Basket*. New York: Crowell, 1980.

Chalmers, M. *A Hat for Amy Jean*. New York: Harper and Row, 1956.

Davidson, A. *Teddy Goes Shopping*. New York: Holt, Rinehart and Winston, 1985.

Freeman, D. *Corduroy*. New York: Viking, 1968.

Gibbons, G. *Department Store*. New York: Harper and Row, 1984.

Gordon, M. *The Supermarket Mice*. New York: Dutton, 1984.

Hall, D. *Ox Cart Man*. New York: Viking, 1979.

Hutchins, P. *Don't Forget the Bacon*. New York: Greenwillow, 1976.

Lobel, A. *On Market Street*. New York: Greenwillow, 1981.

Patz, N. *Pumpernickel Tickle and Mean Green Cheese*. New York: Franklin Watts, 1978.

Phillips, M. *The Sign in Mendel's Window*. New York: Macmillan, 1985.

Rayner, M. *Mrs. Pig's Bulk Buy*. New York: Atheneum, 1981.

Rice, E. *New Blue Shoes*. New York: Macmillan, 1975.

Schwartz, A. *Stores*. New York: Macmillan, 1977.

Slobodkina, E. *Cups for Sale*. Reading, MA: Addison-Wesley, 1968.

Sobol, H. L. *Cosmo's Restaurant*. New York: Macmillan, 1978.

Williams, V. B. *Something Special For Me*. New York: Greenwillow, 1983.

Ziefert, H. *Bear Goes Shopping*. New York: Harper and Row, 1986.

Zimelman, N. *Positively No Pets Allowed*. New York: Dutton, 1980.

Zinnemann-Hope, P. *Let's Go Shopping*. New York: Margaret K. McElderry Books, 1986.

Adult References

Burstiner, I. *Basic Retailing*. Homewood, IL: Irwin, 1986.

Consumers Union of United States, Inc. *Penny Power*. Published bimonthly for children aged 8–13.

Davis, K., and J. T. Taylor. *Kids and Cash*. New York: Bantam Books, 1981.

De Camp, C., and the editors of the U.S. News and World Report Books. *Teach Your Child to Manage Money.* Washington, DC: U.S. News and World Report Books, various dates.

Hendrickson, R. *The Grand Emporiums: The Illustrated History of America's Great Department Stores.* New York: Stein and Day, 1979.

The Home and School Institute. *Families Learning Together.* New York: Simon and Schuster, 1981.

"Kids and Money: What They Need to Know, When They Need to Know It." *Changing Times,* June 1981, pp. 17–20.

Scharlatt, E. *Kids Day In and Day Out.* New York: Simon and Schuster, 1979.

Schram, V. R. "Children and Money: Learning to Take Responsibility." *Two to Twelve,* Vol. 2, no. 3 (1984), pp. 7–9.

Stampfle, R. W., G. Moschis, and J. T. Lawton. "Consumer Education and the Preschool Child." *Journal of Consumer Affairs,* Vol. 11 (1978), pp. 12–29.

Stevens, M. *Like No Other Store in the World: The Inside Story of Bloomingdale's.* New York: Crowell, 1979.

Curricular Domains

AESTHETICS

Developmental Focus
Enjoyment
Stimulation
Insight
Satisfaction

Ultimate Goal
For children to integrate feeling, thought, and action within art, music, and other sensory experiences to achieve pleasurable, personally meaningful ends.

Intermediate Objectives
The following objectives lead to the ultimate goal.

Children have opportunities to:
1. increase their familiarity with varying forms of art and music;
2. develop familiarity with the basic elements of art (line, form, color, texture, space, and composition);
3. develop familiarity with the basic elements of music (musical sounds, melody, volume, rhythm, pitch, tempo, beat, and harmony);
4. use tools and techniques related to art and music to achieve a desired aesthetic effect;
5. reflect upon and talk about their observations and reactions related to their aesthetic experiences;
6. contribute to the aesthetic environment of the school;
7. demonstrate appropriate behaviors related to aesthetic appreciation;
8. recognize their own strengths as artists and musicians;
9. gain pleasure from a variety of sensory experiences with no other goal in mind.

AFFECTIVE DEVELOPMENT

Developmental Focus
Trust
Autonomy
Initiative
Industry
Self-concept
Self-esteem

Ultimate Goal
For children to feel lovable, valuable, and competent.

Intermediate Objectives
The following objectives lead to the ultimate goal.

Children have opportunities to:
1. learn that school is safe, predictable, interesting, and enjoyable;
2. engage in affectionate relationships beyond the family;
3. identify the characteristics and qualities that make each of them unique;
4. explore similarities and differences among people to gain personal insight;
5. practice self-help skills (such as dressing and pouring);
6. independently begin and pursue a task;
7. make choices and experience the consequences of personal decisions;
8. develop mastery in using age-appropriate materials and tools (pounding tools, writing implements, cutting tools, computers, tape recorders, record players, typewriters, etc.);
9. complete a task they have begun;
10. gain awareness of personal emotions;
11. learn to accept both positive and negative emotions as a natural part of living;
12. become familiar with the situational circumstances that influence personal emotions;
13. learn how to act deliberately to affect their own emotions;
14. understand the concept of possession and ownership;
15. value their own gender, culture, and race;
16. increase their knowledge, understanding, and appreciation of their own cultural heritage;
17. develop cross-gender competencies of various kinds;
18. experience the pleasure of work;
19. keep trying in situations that are difficult for them;
20. learn how to recover from setbacks;
21. evaluate themselves positively.

COGNITION

Developmental Focus
Perception
Physical knowledge
Logical mathematical knowledge
Representational knowledge
Critical thinking skills
Conventional social knowledge

Ultimate Goal
For children to integrate knowledge and experiences as they construct new or expanded concepts.

Intermediate Objectives
The following objectives lead to the ultimate goal.

Children have opportunities to:

1. attend to particular sensory stimuli while ignoring extraneous stimuli;
2. develop finer degrees of sensory acuity;
3. coordinate their use of the senses;
4. learn about the attributes of objects;
5. develop concepts related to objects and events;
6. recognize or construct relationships among objects and events through the process of comparing (perceiving likenesses and differences and discovering incongruities in a systematic manner);
7. recognize or construct relationships among objects and events through the process of classification (grouping according to perceived similarities and differences);
8. recognize or construct relationships among objects and events through the process of seriation (sequencing according to the magnitude of a particular characteristic);
9. recognize or construct relationships among objects and events through the process of patterning (repeating a particular configuration and discovering inconsistencies);
10. construct a concept of number invariance (conservation and one-to-one correspondence);
11. construct a concept of quantity (counting, working with equal and unequal sets, associating a number of objects with a numeral, measurement);
12. develop a concept of time;
13. develop a concept of space;
14. attach meaning to symbols in the environment;
15. learn how to define problems and set their own goals;
16. learn information-gathering techniques (questioning, experimenting, observing, consulting);
17. develop and practice a repertoire of strategies for remembering;
18. develop strategies for analyzing objects and events;
19. apply current knowledge to make inferences or predictions;
20. learn how to review and summarize what they have experienced;
21. learn how to evaluate their experiences (monitor, establish standards, verify);
22. develop perspective-taking skills (determining how objects or events are perceived from more than one point of view);
23. use the scientific method (observe, hypothesize, predict, test out, evaluate);
24. integrate decision-making skills (observe, infer, define, generate alternatives, analyze, select a solution, implement, evaluate);
25. become aware of their own thought processes;
26. learn about the natural world;
27. learn about the interdependence of all things in the world;
28. learn about history, folklore, and traditions relevant to them;
29. acquire factual information that is interesting and useful to them;
30. recognize and use diverse sources of information.

LANGUAGE

Developmental Focus
Listening skills
Receptive language
Expressive language
Writing
Reading

Ultimate Goal

For children to interpret accurately the communications of others as well as communicate more effectively themselves.

Intermediate Objectives

The following objectives lead to the ultimate goal.

Children have opportunities to:
1. learn how to use and interpret nonverbal messages accurately;
2. learn appropriate attending behaviors (looking at speaker, waiting for own conversation turn, responding meaningfully to oral and visual cues);
3. learn how to interpret interpersonal verbal messages accurately;
4. improve memory skills related to nonverbal, oral, and written messages;
5. practice listening for content, details, sequence, and sound;
6. extract and interpret relevant content from auditory information presented to them;
7. increase their receptive vocabulary;
8. experiment with language sounds, rhythm, volume, pitch, and words;
9. expand their ability to use words to represent knowledge, events, ideas, imaginings, and perceptions;
10. increase their repertoire of verbal strategies;
11. recognize and use humor as a means of communication;
12. expand their ability to present ideas to others coherently;
13. seek out book experiences for pleasure and information;
14. use their prior knowledge to make sense of literary experiences;
15. become familiar with the elements of the story in order to gain increased pleasure and meaning from literary experiences (setting, characters, detail, plot, main idea, sequence, mood, etc.);
16. attach meaning to print;
17. explore the mechanics and conventions of reading and writing;
18. express themselves in their own form of writing.

PHYSICAL

Developmental Focus

Physical development:
—Body awareness
—Gross-motor development
—Fine-motor development
Physical health

Ultimate Goal

For children to achieve mastery of the environment through improved body control and to develop attitudes, knowledge, skills, and behaviors related to maintaining, respecting, and protecting their bodies.

Intermediate Objectives

The following objectives lead to the ultimate goals.

Children have opportunities to:
1. gain confidence in using their bodies;
2. develop awareness of the location of their own body parts;
3. develop spatial awareness (understanding of personal and general space and direction);
4. engage in a variety of activities that require balance;
5. engage in activities that require coordinated movements;
6. sustain a vigorous motor activity over time in order to develop endurance;
7. engage in a variety of activities that require flexibility;
8. engage in motor activities that require agility;
9. use their whole bodies in appropriate activities to strengthen muscles and muscle groups;
10. develop fundamental motor skills such as jumping, hopping, throwing, kicking, striking, running, or catching;
11. coordinate finger, finger-thumb, and eye-hand movement;
12. control the movement of their bodies in relation to objects;
13. use their bodies to move or change objects;
14. develop a positive attitude about their bodies;
15. learn how to keep their bodies clean;

16. learn how to keep their bodies fit;
17. learn and practice good nutritional habits;
18. learn appropriate safety procedures for school, home, and neighborhood;
19. discriminate good and poor health and safety practices;
20. learn how to apply health and safety knowledge in making choices in daily life.

SOCIAL DEVELOPMENT

Developmental Focus
Social skills
Socialization

Ultimate Goal
For children to develop successful patterns of interaction as well as internal controls and pro-social values.

Intermediate Objectives
The following objectives lead to the ultimate goal.

Children have opportunities to:
1. develop play skills (how to join a group at play, how to make suggestions, how to take suggestions, how to deal with unpleasant social situations and the emotions associated with them, how to play productively alone);
2. develop friendship skills (how to constructively initiate, maintain, and terminate interactions and relationships);
3. learn how to negotiate conflicts in democratic ways (compromising, voting, bargaining);
4. develop empathy for others (recognize others' emotions, respect others' emotional responses);
5. become aware of similarities and differences in opinions, points of view, and attitudes;
6. perceive adults as sources of gratification, approval, and modeling;
7. learn how to control antisocial impulses;
8. learn how to delay gratification;
9. learn how to conform to reasonable limits set upon behavior, play space, use of materials, or the types of activities in which they are involved;
10. identify the reasons for classroom rules;
11. learn how to be cooperative (work with others toward a common goal);
12. learn how to be helpful (share information or materials, give physical assistance, offer emotional support);
13. distinguish acceptable classroom behavior from unacceptable classroom behavior;
14. use their knowledge of appropriate behavior in one circumstance to determine appropriate conduct in another circumstance;
15. develop awareness and concern for the rights and well-being of others;
16. learn approved behaviors related to social customs;
17. develop an appreciation of the family compositions, traditions, values, ethnic backgrounds, and cultures of others;
18. develop a sense of responsibility for the environment.

CONSTRUCTION

Developmental Focus
Iconic representation

Ultimate Goal
For children to translate mental images into tangible products that represent their own interpretation of an object or event.

Intermediate Objectives
The following objectives lead to the ultimate goal.

Children have opportunities to:
1. engage in a wide range of experiences from which to draw their interpretations;
2. interpret events and reconstruct them in tangible ways;
3. use diverse approaches to represent objects or events:
   a) represent a single object or event using different materials or techniques
   b) represent different objects and events using one material or technique;
4. interact with classmates to collaboratively construct a representative object.

PRETEND PLAY

Developmental Focus
Imitation
Role-playing
Symbolic play
Dramatization

Ultimate Goal
For children to integrate meaning derived from their experience with knowledge and skills from all developmental domains as they create roles or scenarios.

Intermediate Objectives
The following objectives lead to the ultimate goal.

Children have opportunities to:
1. mimic in their play behaviors they have seen or experienced;
2. use their bodies to represent real or imaginary objects or events;
3. assign symbolic meaning to real or imaginary objects using language or gestures;
4. take on the role attributes of beings or objects and act out interpretations of those roles;
5. create play themes;
6. experiment with a variety of objects, roles (leader, follower, mediator), and characterizations (animal, mother, astronaut, etc.);
7. react to and interact with other children in make-believe situations;
8. dramatize familiar stories, songs, poems, and past events;
9. integrate construction into pretend play episodes.

Participation Chart

CLASSROOM PARTICIPATION CHART OF CHILDREN'S INVOLVEMENT IN FREE CHOICE ACTIVITY CENTERS

CLASSROOM __M. Sanchez__   A.M./P.M.   Date: __1-20-91__   M. W. (T.) TH. F.

CHILD'S NAME	9:30	9:40	9:50	10:00	10:10	10:20	10:30
Anna	A	A	H	D	D	D	D
Brycen	C	C	C	H	D	D	E
Emily P.	C	C	Bath Room	H	C	C	E
Emily M.	F	F	locker	H	D	D	D
Jung-Hyun	G	A	B	B	Bath Room	B	G
Katie	G	G	G	E	G	E	E
Meera	A	A	D	D	F	H	G
Nathan	F	F	F	H	F	F	G
Omar	D	D	D	A	A	A	G
Paul	E	E	E	H	C	C	Cubbie
Reid	G	A	A	A	A	D	E
Sarah	G	C	C	C	C	E	Wander
Trevor	—	—	—	—	—	—	Absent
Vanessa	G	G	G	A	A	A	B
Young-Jin	D	D	D	H	H	H	D

TIME

A = Language Arts
B = Math/Science
C = Table Toys
D = Art Table
E = Pretend Play
F = Blocks
G = Large Motor
H = Snack Table

CLASSROOM PARTICIPATION CHART OF CHILDREN'S INVOLVEMENT IN FREE CHOICE ACTIVITY CENTERS

CLASSROOM _____   A.M./P.M. _____   M.   T.   W.   TH.   F.   Date: _____

CHILD'S NAME

TIME

CHILD'S NAME														

A = Language Arts   C = Table Toys   E = Pretend Play   G = Large Motor
B = Math/Science   D = Art Table   F = Blocks   H = Snack Table

Theme Planning Worksheet

Activity Types

1. Firsthand experiences
2. Simulations
3. Demonstrations
4. Discussions
5. Projects
6. Indirect teaching through theme-related props
7. Thematic atmosphere
8. Spontaneous events

Content Areas

1. Aesthetics — focus on stimulating children's appreciation of the arts.

2. Affective — focus on promoting self-awareness and positive self-esteem.

3. Cognition — focus on expanding children's perceptual, conceptual, and problem-solving skills.

4. Construction — focus on enabling children to create tangible products that represent their own interpretations of objects or events.

5. Language — focus on increasing children's abilities to represent thoughts, ideas, feelings, and perceptions through language.

6. Physical — focus on improving children's gross-motor and fine-motor skills as well as contributing to a positive body image.

7. Pretend Play — focus on providing opportunities for children to engage in role-playing, make-believe, and dramatization.

8. Social — focus on teaching children to develop more successful patterns of interaction and to gain greater self-understanding.

INDEX

Cognition

Construction

Language

Physical

Pretend Play

Social

RECIPES

Animal Food

Arts and Crafts

People Food